KU-296-277

European Community Economies

A Comparative Study

SECOND EDITION

Edited by Drs Frans Somers
International Business School
Hanzehogeschool, Groningen

Contributors
Ian Stone
Richard Bailey
Marisol Esteban
Andrea Fineschi
William Glynn
Milagros García Crespo
Arantza Mendizábal
Rudi Kurz
Kirk Thomson

PITMAN
PUBLISHING

PITMAN PUBLISHING
128 Long Acre, London WC2E 9AN

A Division of Longman Group UK Limited

First published in Great Britain as *European Economies* 1991
Second edition 1994

© Milagros García Crespo, Andrea Fineschi, Rudi Kurz, Frans Somers,
Ian Stone, Kirk Thomson 1991
© Milagros García Crespo, Andrea Fineschi, Rudi Kurz, Frans Somers,
Ian Stone, Kirk Thomson, William Glynn, Richard Bailey 1994

British Library Cataloguing-in-Publication Data
A CIP catalogue record for this book is available from the British Library.

ISBN 0–273–60347–7

All rights reserved; no part of this publication may be reproduced, stored
in a retrieval system, or transmitted in any form or by any means, electronic,
mechanical, photocopying, recording, or otherwise without either the prior
written permission of the Publishers or a licence permitting restricted copying
in the United Kingdom issued by the Copyright Licensing Agency Ltd,
90 Tottenham Court Road, London W1P 9HE. This book may not be lent,
resold, hired out or otherwise disposed of by way of trade in any form of
binding or cover other than that in which it is published without the prior
consent of the Publishers.

Typeset by PanTek Arts, Maidstone, Kent.
Printed and bound in Great Britain by Page Bros.

The publisher's policy is to use paper manufactured from sustainable forests.

HERTFORDSHIRE
LIBRARY SERVICE

No.

Class

Supplier	Price	Date
JMLS	£21 95	3/95

CONTENTS

PREFACE TO THE SECOND EDITION

For the second edition, this book has been considerably expanded. First, in contrast to the first edition, surveys of the economies of the seven smaller Ec countries (the Netherlands, Belgium, Denmark, Portugal, Greece, Ireland and Luxembourg) are included as well. This has been done in order to give a complete overview of all national economies of the European Community. As with the major economies, the analyses of the smaller countries, although less detailed, focus mainly on long-term trends and developments and have the same structure. Naturally, the smaller countries are also incorporated in the part on international comparisons.

Second, the introductory chapter, dealing with the development of the European Community, has also been extended. More attention, not only here but throughout the book, is paid to the discussion of common EC policies and regulations, since their impact on the economies of the individual countries is of growing importance. The common monetary policy, which is aiming at the introduction of one common European currency before the end of the millennium, and the completion of the internal market by the end of 1992, for instance, has far-reaching consequences for the national economies and national economic policies of the Member States. At this moment it is far from certain, that the European Economic and Monetary Union (EMU) will be introduced on schedule as agreed upon in the *Maastricht Treaty on European Union* of 1991. The problems on the currency markets in 1992 and 1993 and the near breakdown of the Exchange Rate Mechanism of the EMS in August 1993, do not feed optimism in this respect. Nevertheless, the Maastricht Treaty, and European integration in general, will be of major importance for economic policy and practice of the EC Member States in the coming years. That is why they have been given more stress in this new edition.

Because of the addition of the smaller countries, the structure of the book has been slightly altered. Part A deals with the development of the European Community; Part B discusses the five major EC countries (Germany, France, Italy, the UK and Spain) and Part C the seven smaller ones. Part D is concerned with international comparisons and Part E provides statistical information (in time series) on all twelve economies and in many cases on the US and Japan.

In addition to these extensions, the book has been completely updated. Developments up until July 1993 are included. The events on the currency markets and the changes of the ERM in August 1993 are discussed in a special postscript to Chapter 1 (Part A).

The chapters on the smaller countries are partly written by new contributors: Dr Richard Bailey (Portugal and Denmark) and William Glynn (Ireland). Dr Ian Stone, author of the UK section, prepared the chapters on Greece and Belgium/Luxembourg, and the undersigned the chapter on the Netherlands. From a practical point of view it was not possible to invite a resident from each country involved this time. I would like to express my gratitude to all the old and new contributors, especially for the enthusiasm they showed in the preparation of this book. In particular I would like to thank Dr Ian Stone, who not only wrote three chapters, but also gave invaluable language support in this complicated international project.

Frans Somers
Groningen, The Netherlands
November 1993

PREFACE TO THE FIRST EDITION

This book is concerned with the individual economies of the five major countries of the European Community (EC): Germany, France, the United Kingdom, Italy and Spain. These countries are by far the largest in terms of Gross Domestic Product, area and population in the EC.

Since the war Western Europe has experienced a strong trend towards economic and political integration. The European Community, founded in 1957 by six countries, nowadays comprises twelve members. Within the EC the progress towards integration has been accelerated by the adoption of Single European Act at the end of 1985, which sets the route for the achievement of a European Single Market before the end of 1992. The final goal of the Act is the foundation of a European Economic and Political Union, mainly based on the principles of a free market economy (*see* part A in this book).

Although Western Europe is moving towards being an economic entity, many differences will remain between individual countries in the Community in terms of economic structure, national policies, labour market, industry, trade patterns, etc.; not to mention distinctions in mentalities, tastes and cultures.

This book is intended to provide a basic understanding, within a limited space, of the economies of the major countries of the Community. It focuses on long-term developments and underlying trends rather than on short-term economic surveys. In this respect it differs greatly from the existing publications from international organisations like the OECD. Special attention is paid to the strengths and weaknesses of each economy, its dominant industries, trade patterns and future perspectives within the emerging common market (part B).

In section C comparisons are made between the countries involved. Differences and similarities in the fields of government involvement, output and growth, productivity and competitiveness and the financial system are mentioned and possible fields of specialisation are identified.

The book concludes with a uniform Statistical Annexe with harmonised data, mainly based on Eurostat and OECD sources (part D). In other parts of this book, referrals to tables in this Annexe are frequently made (prefixed with a D).

At the end of the country chapters in part B the reader will find lists of information sources where additional information on the country concerned can be found (other publications, statistical institutions, government and private agencies).

The book thus serves as an accessible introductory text, giving the reader a basic grasp of the economic structure of the major European countries, as well as a source of information for further investigations. In this sense, it can be used to 'guide' study of the economies of the main EC countries.

The book is aimed at students in business schools, polytechnics and universities. It can be used for business environment studies, EC courses, course offerings focusing on economic policies, preparation for studies abroad.

This publication is the result of a considerable exercise in international co-operation. The chapters on the individual countries are exclusively prepared by contributors living in that particular country: Professor Rudi Kurz from Germany, Professor Andrea Fineschi from Italy, Dr Ian Stone from the UK, Kirk Thomson and Rachel Condon from France and Professor Milagros García Crespo, Dr Marisol Esteban and Professor Arantza Mendizábal from Spain.

The editing, introductory chapter and chapter on international comparisons was done by someone from a 'neutral' country: the Netherlands.

Most of the participants in this project are working for institutions co-operating in international programmes with Hanse Polytechnic Groningen, having its seat in that country.

In total citizens from six EC member states were involved in this project. It did not turn out to be a barrier to a very fruitful co-operation and intensive and interesting discussions.

Frans Somers
Groningen, The Netherlands
January 1991

CONTRIBUTORS

Frans Somers *(Editor)* is Lecturer in Economics at the International Business School, Hanzehogeschool, Groningen, The Netherlands, and is also manager of International Projects and International Liaison Officer at that institution. Since graduating in 1973, he has worked mainly in the field of higher education and has published several books; one on political economy (1980), two on macroeconomics (1988 and 1990) and two on government policy (1990 and 1993). From 1988 to 1990 he was Editor-in-Chief of an economics magazine intended for business students and lecturers.

Dr Ian Stone is a Principal Lecturer in Economics and Head of the Newcastle Economic Research Unit at the University of Northumbria, Newcastle upon Tyne. He has previously held lecturing posts at Victoria University in Wellington (New Zealand) and the University of Newcastle upon Tyne. His research interests are in the areas of regional and industrial development in the UK and European context. Recent work includes a study of inward investment and its impact on local labour markets (for the Employment Department) and restructuring of defence industries (jointly funded by the European Parliament and Rowntree Foundation).

Richard Bailey was educated at the London School of Economics and Warwick University. He is currently Principal Lecturer in the Department of Economics and Government at the University of Northumbria. Research interests and publications in the areas of Comparative Economics and International Political Economy.

Marisol Esteban studied at the University of the Basque Country, the London School of Economics and the University of California at Berkeley. She is a Senior Lecturer in Urban and Regional Economics at the Faculty of Economics and Business Administration of the University of the Basque Country in Bilbao, where she has also lectured on Contemporary Spanish Economy. Her special fields of interest include land and housing markets and policies, labour markets and regional economic development. She has published several books and articles on these topics and has done consultancy work for the public administration.

Andrea Fineschi is 'professore straordinario' of political economy at the University of Messina after previously teaching in the universities of Siena and Florence. His special fields of interest include aspects of economic theory of the classical economists and problems of the Italian economy.

William Glynn is a lecturer in Marketing at University College Dublin. In industry he has previously worked for Swedish Match, Abbott Laboratories and Guinness. Before joining University College Dublin he was employed by Dublin City University in Ireland and EPSCI – Groupe ESSEC in France. He was appointed Director of the B. Comm. (International) Degree programme at University College Dublin in 1993.

Milagros García Crespo is Professor of Applied Economics at the University of the Basque Country. She was Head of the Faculty of Economics in Bilbao from 1982 to 1987. Her interests in European issues led her to set up in 1983 a European Documentation Centre at the same University. She established and maintained links with European academic institutions (Kingston Polytechnic in London, Université de Grenoble). From 1987 to 1989 she was Councillor of Economy to the Basque Government. In 1989 she was appointed First

President of the Public Accounts Court of the Basque Country, a post that she currently holds. She is the authour of many books and articles on economic policy, the Spanish economy and European issues.

Arantza Mendizábal is Professor in Economics in the Faculty of Economics and Business Administration of the University of the Basque Country in Bilbao where she has been Rector of the University. She has considerable experience on economic policy issues and has written widely on the economy of the Basque Country. Since February 1991 she has been a member of the Central Parliament in Madrid where she belongs to the Commissions on Economic and European Issues.

Dr Rudi Kurz worked for ten years as a research fellow and as Deputy Managing Director at the Institute for Applied Economic Research Tübingen (IAW). He prepared studies and specialist reports for the German Federal Ministry of Commerce and for the Commission of the European Community during that time. He has undertaken research in the United States and was guest scholar at the Brookings Institution, Washington DC. He is a Professor of Economics at the Pforzheim Business School and consultant to the IAW since 1988. He published books and articles on technology policy, competition policy and environmental issues.

Kirk Thomson studied at the London School of Economics, the Free University of Berlin and at the Sorbonne. He is now Director of Studies at the Ecole des Practiciens du Commerce International in Paris, where he also lectures in Economics and on aspects of the European Community.

PART A

Introduction

CHAPTER 1

The European Community

Frans Somers

1.1 INTRODUCTION

Since the signing of the *Treaty of Rome* in 1957 European integration has made significant progress. An internal market is in place and there are serious plans for achieving economic and monetary union before the end of the millennium. Does this mean that it is no longer necessary to study the existing national economies? Certainly not.

In the first place there are still substantial differences between these countries both in terms of economic performance and in government policies. Possibly these will narrow in the future; economic convergence and policy harmonisation are prerequisites for further integration.

In addition, there are considerable distinctions in economic structure among the Member States. Every country has its own industrial structure and business traditions, reflecting historical circumstances, comparative advantages, government decisions, geographical conditions and chance. These differences will not necessarily disappear. Indeed, with further integration some features will even be reinforced. Integration can lead to more specialisation, because it is to be hoped that full exposure to international competition will lead to a better allocation of factors of production. This reallocation may be realised on the basis of existing trade patterns, comparative advantage, development of new trade relations, etc.

In this book we will examine the economies of the twelve countries which form the European Community at present: Belgium, Denmark, France, Germany, Greece, Ireland, Italy, Luxembourg, the Netherlands, Portugal, Spain and the United Kingdom. In 1992 their combined Gross Domestic Product (GDP) amounted to 5,422 billion ECUs[1], roughly 1.2 times that of the USA and 1.9 times that of Japan, the other two large economic blocs in the world. With a total population of 347 million, as against 257 million for the USA and 124 million for Japan, the EC is the largest economic entity in the world[2], even without enlargement through the admittance of adjacent countries.

Within the EC there are substantial differences in size between countries in terms of GDP and population (see Figure 1.1). Germany is by far the largest country, in 1992 accounting for 27.4% of total Community GDP and some 23% of population. France (19.1% of Community GDP), Italy (17.5%) and UK (14.8%) form a

[1] ECU stands for *European Currency Unit*, a basket containing fixed amounts of all EC currencies (for further explanation, see section 1.3.2).

[2] If the North American Free Trade Agreement (NAFTA) is ratified, an economic bloc which is even slightly bigger in terms of GDP and population will come into being.

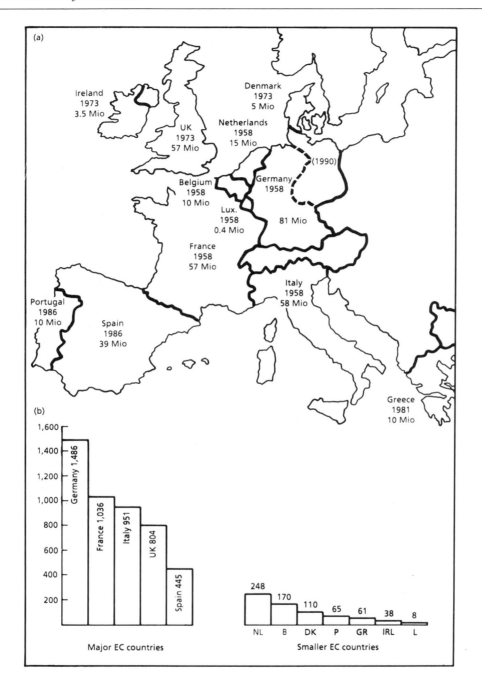

Figure 1.1 The Community in 1992. (a) Population in millions (indicated on map). Total EC population 347 million. (b) GDP at current prices in billions of ECU (European Commission estimates); Total EC GDP = 5,422 billion ECU.

Source: European Commission, *European Economy*, 1993, no. 54.

second group. Spain is a medium-sized country, with a GDP 8.2% of the combined Community GDP, while the other seven countries are considerably smaller with a GDP ranging from 4.6% of Community GDP (The Netherlands) to only 0.16% (Luxembourg).

This introductory chapter will start with a discussion of the European integration process: its origins, aims, progress and policies. This will be followed by an assessment of the size, relative strength and importance of the European Community. The chapter will end with a brief survey of the main economic indicators of the twelve member economies.

This provides the framework within which the national economies will be studied in more detail in the following chapters of the book. Special attention will be paid in each of the country studies to their institutional and historical background, industrial structure, trade patterns, strengths and weaknesses and problems and prospects within the Europe of the future.

1.2 EUROPEAN INTEGRATION

1.2.1 The origins of the European integration process

The aftermath of the Second World War was marked by a very strong impetus in Europe towards international co-operation. Several factors contributed to this attitude. First of all there were economic considerations. The war left Europe with immense physical destruction, loss of capital goods and an impoverished population. In order to revitalise the European economy, the United States introduced the Marshall Plan in 1948 (by means of the *Foreign Assistance Act*). The initiative was intended to provide Europe with sufficient funds and goods to carry out the necessary recovery programmes. The US aid was granted on a *European* rather than on a *national* basis. A special international institution, the Organisation for European Economic Co-operation (OEEC), was created to distribute the aid among the member countries and to co-

ordinate the assistance programmes. Within the framework of the plan, separate measures were taken to intensify intra-European trade.

The OEEC, however, was not abolished after the termination of the Marshall Plan in 1950. It continued to promote the liberalisation of international trade and economic co-operation. In 1961 it transformed itself into the Organisation for Economic Co-operation and Development (OECD), an organisation at the service of all developed industrial countries in the Western world.

A second driving force behind European integration was the Soviet threat and the beginning of the Cold War. By the end of the 1940s the division of Europe into a Western sector and a Soviet-dominated sphere became apparent, after Soviet-inspired Communist take-overs in Rumania (1945), Bulgaria (1946), Hungary (1946), Poland (1947) and Czechoslovakia (1948). In response to this development a range of organisations was established, including the West European Union (WEU), NATO (North Atlantic Treaty Organisation) (both in 1948) and the Council of Europe in 1949. The objectives of these organisations were not merely defence against the Soviet threat, but also the protection of values such as freedom, democracy and human rights.

Finally, an important incentive for West European integration was the 'German question'. After two world wars, a completely independent Germany was considered as a potential threat to peace. A solution to this problem would be to link the newly established Federal Republic of Germany as firmly as possible to the other European countries.

This question became urgent in the light of what was seen as the increasing Soviet threat to Europe. A strong Europe, both in the military and the economic sense, was thought to be absolutely essential. The German contribution to the strengthening of Western Europe was of great importance, though care had to be taken to avoid allowing Germany the opportunity once more to dominate its neighbours militarily and politically.

For these reasons the French Minister of Foreign Affairs, Jean Monnet, came up with his plan in 1950 to place the European coal and steel industries under one single supranational authority and to establish a common market in this field. This plan would enable a rapid expansion of these industries, which are of vital importance to the defence industry and overall economic development, without allowing the new West German state full control over them. In addition to France and Germany, other European countries were also invited to participate in this arrangement.

As a result, the European Coal and Steel Community (ECSC) was established (*Treaty of Paris*) in the spring of 1951 by France, the Federal Republic of Germany, Italy, Belgium, the Netherlands and Luxembourg. The foundation for the construction of a much more extensive European Community was laid. For a variety of reasons major countries like the UK remained outside the Community for the time being.

Attempts by the same six countries to create a common army (the European Defence Community (EDC)) in the early 1950s failed, however. It would have required a supranational political power, which was too advanced a notion at that time. Co-operation was first sought, then, in the economic field on a more modest basis. The Six founded the European Economic Community (EEC) and the European Atomic Energy Commission (Euratom) in 1957 by the *Treaty of Rome*. Euratom was designed for the peaceful development of atomic energy. The treaties came into effect on 1 January 1958.

1.2.2 Towards an economic and political union

A major difference between the ECSC and the EEC at that time was that the EEC was only minimally equipped with supranational powers; the main decision-making body within the EEC was the Council of Ministers (of Foreign Affairs), leaving considerable powers to the national authorities. Important decisions could only be taken by unanimity.

Despite this, the Treaty of Rome envisaged progress towards a kind of economic union. Article 2 of the Treaty of Rome states that:

> The Community shall have as its task, by *establishing a common market* and *progressively approximating the economic policies of the Member States* (author's italics), to promote throughout the Community a harmonious development of economic activities, a continuous and balanced expansion, an increase in stability, an accelerated rise of the standard of living and closer relations between the States belonging to it.

The three Communities (ECSC, Euratom and EEC) duly amalgamated in 1965 to form the European Community (EC).

According to Article 8 of the Treaty of Rome the common market was to be reached within 12 years (from 1958). A *common market* can be defined as an association of nations with free trade among its members, a common external tariff and free mobility of factors of production. If, in addition, economic policies are harmonised then the association is called an *economic union*.

The six members failed to meet their original target. By 1970 only the first two of the common market criteria had been met: the removal of all internal tariffs and quota restrictions and the erecting of a common external tariff. Free mobility of factors of production and the substantial harmonisation of economic policies were far from being realised by 1970. In fact, it took another twenty years before these goals were met to any extent. A number of factors can be held responsible for the slow progress of the integration process.

First, there is the question of national interests. A real economic union means that the bulk of national power is transferred to supranational authorities. This implies a substantial loss of national sovereignty for the Member States. From the very beginning of the EEC in 1958, however, individual Member States have been reluctant to accept this idea. The Treaty of Rome envisaged that the replacement of decision making by unanimous agreement by decision making by a qualified majority vote for a wide range of issues would be achieved by 1966. Because of the French opposition, however, Member States kept a right of veto in situations where vital national interests are involved (the Luxembourg compromise of 1966). Subsequently, since its entrance in 1973, it has been mainly the UK which has tried to slow down the integration process for nationalistic reasons.

A second impediment to rapid progress towards an economic union was the successive enlargements of the Community. The UK, Ireland and Denmark joined the EC in 1973, Greece in 1981 and Spain and Portugal in 1986. These enlargements shifted political attention to other questions and made negotiations on common policies even more complicated.

Finally, the economic crises of the 1970s and the early 1980s created an unfavourable climate for free trade. National governments were inclined to return to protectionist policies and to support national industries in order to counter the effects of the international crises upon the domestic economy.

In the early 1980s, however, the drive towards European integration received new impetus. During the economic crisis of these years it became clear that the problems in Europe were intensified because producers in the Community were losing ground to their main competitors in Japan and the USA. The fragmented home market of the Community was seen as a major reason for this development, and a call for the speeding up of the integration process was made. A single European market, it was argued, would stimulate economies of scale in production, marketing, research and development and also strengthen competition, enhancing the efficiency and competitiveness of European industry.

A necessary condition for accelerating the creation of the internal market was a change in the Community decision-making procedures, which until then required unanimity in many cases. This condition was met by the adoption of the *Single European Act* in 1985, whereby in matters concerning the internal market the condition of unanimity was replaced by a qualified majority. The Act, which after ratification by all 12 members came into force in 1987, also contained the provision that the internal market should be completed before the end of 1992. In addition to setting a timetable for the creation of an 'internal market without frontiers' the Single Act also amended the original Treaty of Rome by adopting policies in the fields of economic and social cohesion, the environment, monetary and political co-operation, etc. The Single Act can be seen as a major, but not as the final step towards the ultimate goal of an economically united Europe.

Achievement of this goal involves the establishment of an Economic and Monetary Union (EMU), which requires the far-reaching co-ordination of monetary and economic policies of the Member States. Monetary policy, for instance, would be largely transferred from national authorities to an independent European System of Central Banks (a kind of European Fed), led by a European Central Bank (ECB), and national currencies would be replaced by a common currency, managed by the ECB. In the field of fiscal policy, national governments would retain much of their autonomy, but their control would be limited considerably by common policies and restrictions.

At the EC summit meeting of October 1990 broad outlines of a treaty on EMU were set. According to a plan, developed by the EC Commission, chaired by the Frenchman, M. Jacques Delors, EMU should be reached in three stages; the final one to be completed towards the end of the decade. As control has to be substantially surrendered to supranational powers, EMU can only be realised if it is accompanied by a significant degree of *political* integration.

Maastricht and beyond

A final decision was taken at the Maastricht meeting of the European Council of Heads of State (or Government) in December 1991 (the *Maastricht Treaty*). A *Treaty on European Union* was concluded in February 1992, amending the Treaty of Rome substantially. The Maastricht Treaty contains an agreement on an irreversible movement towards EMU as well as an agreement on a number of political issues.

According to the Treaty, the Economic and Monetary Union is to be established not later than 1999. By then, the currencies of the individual Member States eligible to join EMU will be replaced by a single currency, the ECU, managed and controlled by an independent European Central Bank. However, without economic convergence, including a certain degree of economic and social cohesion, the introduction of a common currency will not be possible. That is why convergence programmes are to be adopted to prepare the individual Member States for eligibility.

The term *economic convergence* has two distinct meanings. The first refers to the convergence (i.e. gradual decrease in initial differences or disparities over time) of macroeconomic variables, which directly influence exchange-rate variables, like inflation, budget deficits and interest rates. This is usually called *nominal convergence*. *Real convergence,* on the other hand, is the approximation of economic and social conditions (e.g. standards of living, rates of unemployment) throughout the Community; it is commonly measured in terms of the reduction of existing disparities in GDP per capita. Nominal and real convergence are interrelated; in addition nominal convergence is assumed to create the proper conditions for sounder economic growth for the Community as a whole. To be admitted to EMU the Member States should satisfy certain nominal convergence criteria (considered below).

It is envisaged that the Economic and Monetary Union should be reached in three stages:

- *Stage I* (July 1990–31 December 1994): Completion of the internal market, including totally free movement of goods, persons and capital (before 31 December 1992), start of economic convergence programmes of the Member States. All countries are expected to enter the narrow band of the Exchange Rate Mechanism of the EMS.
- *Stage II* (1 January 1994–between 1997 and 1999): Adoption of multi-annual convergence programmes; establishing a European Monet-

ary Institute which will co-ordinate (but not control) monetary policies and prepare the setting up of the ECB in Stage III. Member States must start procedures leading to independence for their central banks.
- *Stage III* (starts between 1997 and 1999): Founding of the European System of Central Banks (ECSB) and the European Central Bank (ECB); replacement of national currencies of Member States admitted to EMU by the ECU. The ECSB will be made up of the ECB and the national central banks, where the latter will be responsible for the implementation of monetary policies set by the (independent) ECB.

The Maastricht Treaty, implies an *irrevocable* commitment by the Member States to move to Stage III, provided *they satisfy the necessary conditions*. These conditions consist of the following five nominal convergence criteria.

1 *Price stability*. The inflation rate should not exceed the average inflation rate of the three countries with the lowest price increases by more than 1.5 percentage points.
2 *Currency stability*. The exchange rate should not have been subject to devaluation within the narrow band of the Exchange Rate Mechanism of the European Monetary System during the last two years before the date of entry to EMU (see also section 1.3.2).
3 *Public deficit*. The budget deficit must not exceed 3% of GDP.
4 *National Debt*. The public debt must be lower than 60% of GDP.
5 *Interest rates*. The nominal long-term capital interest rates should not deviate by more than two percentage points from the average of the long-term interest rates of the three countries with the lowest inflation rates.

According to the Maastricht Treaty, the Heads of Government will decide before the end of 1996 whether the majority of Member States do satisfy the nominal convergence criteria and at what date EMU can be launched. If no other date has been set, EMU will be instituted on 1 January 1999, but it will be confined to those Member States which fulfil the necessary conditions. The UK and Denmark obtained an 'opting-out' clause, meaning that each of these countries was allowed to reserve its decision, although in both cases the issue has been resolved subsequently at national level in favour of participation.

The principle of economic and social cohesion has been stressed in the Treaty. A special Cohesion Fund will be set up to give financial support for environmental and transport projects in Member States with a per capita income of less than 90% of the Community budget (Greece, Ireland, Portugal and Spain) over the years 1993–9. Other resources allocated to these countries will be increased as well. These measures are intended to speed up *real* convergence and to ease these countries in meeting the *nominal* convergence criteria by the end of the century.

In addition to EMU the Maastricht Treaty on European Union contained an agreement on *political and social issues*, such as the introduction of a union citizenship, including freedom of movement, the right of free residence and the right to vote and to be eligible for elections at the municipal and European level. The Treaty also includes provisions on a common foreign and security policy which will lead in time to the framing of a common defence policy. In the social field the Treaty, in an annexed protocol, provides for the consolidation of workers' basic rights, along the path set by the *Social Charter* of 1989 (a non-binding declaration of principles). The UK, however, opted not to sign this part of the agreement.

The Treaty contains a special provision aimed at ensuring that decisions are taken at the level closest to the ordinary citizen: the so-called *subsidiarity principle* (Article 3b). According to this article, the Community should act only if an objective can be better achieved at Community rather than at national level and furthermore the means employed must be proportional to the aimed objectives. The inclusion of this article mainly serves to prevent too great a concentration of political power in 'Brussels'; its object can be seen as the ruling out of an over-centralised federalist approach. In addition, its aim is to reduce the 'democratic deficit' of the Community, i.e. the limited input of Euro-level elected representatives in the decision-making process. The position of the European Parliament, the role of which is mostly advisory, has in fact been strengthened further by granting it the power to veto the adoption of a large range of EC rules and regulations. Though the Treaty is a new milestone in the European unification process, it cannot be considered as an unambiguous step towards a federal Europe. The British especially were very keen on dropping the so-called 'F-word'. The EC remains primarily a 'Community of Nations' for the time being.

It was intended that all twelve EC countries would ratify the Maastricht Treaty on European Union in the course of 1992. The Danes, however, rejected the Treaty in a referendum in June 1992. Although the French accepted the terms of the Treaty in their September 1992 referendum, they did so with the smallest possible majority. The British decided to postpone ratification of the Treaty until after a new Danish referendum. After guaranteeing the Danish a number of additional opting-out clauses, the latter referendum resulted in a clear 'yes' vote. With British ratification following in 1993, all Members have now approved the Treaty.

Ratification problems apart, it is unlikely that a sufficient number of countries will meet the EMU convergence criteria by the end of 1996. In 1992, only Luxembourg and France managed to do so (see Table 1.1); but even Germany would not have qualified in that year (mainly because of unification problems).

The movement towards a monetary union was subsequently frustrated by turbulent developments on the currency markets in 1992. Rather than moving to more stable exchange-rate relationships within the framework of the European Monetary System, the system came under severe strain. Several realignments took place, including the devaluation of the Italian lira, the Spanish peseta and the Portuguese escudo. Sustained pressure made the British government decide to suspend its participation in the Exchange Rate Mechanism; the Italian government took a similar decision. In early 1993 the Irish pound and again the Spanish peseta and

Portuguese escudo were devalued within the ERM. These events prompted discussion as to whether the movement towards EMU will result in a *two-speed Europe*, consisting of a group of economically strong countries (such as Germany, France, Belgium, The Netherlands and Luxembourg) moving quickly to EMU and another group made up of economically weaker ones, lagging behind. The big issue here is whether a two-speed Europe will reinforce unequal development or, on the other hand, constitute a convenient solution for countries who want to stay out for the time being because they need a longer period of preparation or even want to opt out. In the latter case, a mandatory standard menu would be replaced by a kind of Europe-à-la-carte, leaving Member States to choose the degree to which they would like to participate in common arrangements. This outcome might be especially attractive for countries (e.g. the UK and Denmark) reluctant to move to unification in all its dimensions.

Political complications aside, it seems that support for international integration mostly flourishes in times of economic prosperity; during recessions the enthusiasm for such notions sharply diminishes. In contrast with the second half of the 1980s, the early 1990s did not really constitute a favourable climate for sustaining the spirit of international integration. In economically hard times short-term self-interest, protectionism and nationalism are inclined to rise. It is thus perhaps not surprising that progress in relation to 'Maastricht' has been slow compared to the Single Act of 1985. Implementation of the latter has turned out to be rather successful. By the end of 1992 almost all (nearly 95%) of the scheduled proposals were adopted by the European Council. Frontier checks on goods have been abolished by the adoption of new VAT and excise arrangements and most non-tariff barriers have been removed.

Table 1.1 Nominal convergence criteria for EMU. Deviation from norm in 1992. EC Commission estimates

	Convergence criteria					
	Inflation rate[1] (%)	Long-term int. rate (%)	Budget deficit (% of GDP)	Public debt (% of GDP)	Currency score	Number of criteria satisfied
Norm	2.5 ± 1.5%	8.7 ± 2%	< 3%	< 60%	+ / −	
Luxembourg	**2.2**	**7.9**	**0.4**	**6.8**	+	5
France	**2.9**	**8.6**	**2.8**	**50.1**	+	5
Denmark	**2.5**	10.1	**2.3**	74.0	+	4
Germany	5.3	**8.0**	3.2	**45.9**	+	3
Netherlands	**2.7**	**8.1**	3.5	79.8	+	3
Ireland	**2.9**	**8.7**	**2.7**	99.0	−	3
Belgium	**3.6**	9.1	6.9	132.2	+	3
United Kingdom	4.6	**9.1**	6.2	**45.9**	−	2
Spain	6.3	12.2	4.6	**47.4**	−	1
Italy	5.2	13.7	10.5	106.8	−	0
Portugal	13.1	15.0	5.6	66.2	−	0
Greece	15.6	21.0[2]	13.4	105.6	−	0

[1] Deflator GDP
[2] Rough estimate

(Bold figures indicate that the criterion concerned has been met.)

Source: European Economy, Annual Economic Report, 1993, No. 54.

Enlargement of the Community

In addition to the debate on *deepening* there is also intense discussion going on with respect to widening the European Community. While some of the present Member States are hesitant in relation to (further) European integration, there are many other countries striving towards membership. First, there is the group of countries belonging to the European Free Trade Organisation (EFTA): Sweden, Norway, Finland, Iceland, Austria, Switzerland and Liechtenstein. Second, most ex-Communist countries in Central and Eastern Europe are very eager to join the Community as soon as possible. The third group consists of countries on the periphery of Europe, like Turkey, Malta, Cyprus.

The EC is not against the admission of new members. However, in 1992 it was decided, that enlargement of the Community could only take place on the basis of the Treaty of European Union, meaning that the Maastricht Treaty should be ratified first by all members before negotiations on new memberships can be concluded. Apart from this, candidates should in general fulfil the following conditions:

- They should have a European identity, a democratic status and respect for human rights.
- They should not only accept Community laws and regulations (subject to temporary transitional arrangements) but also be able to implement them. This condition presumes that an applicant has a well functioning market economy backed by an adequate legal and administrative framework.

On the basis of these criteria the EFTA countries could join the EC in a relatively short term, while even for the most advanced countries in Eastern Europe (Hungary, the Czech Republic and Poland) a period of preparation of approximately ten years will be required. Cyprus, Malta and Turkey are not eligible as yet because, regardless of the fulfilment of the second condition, they do not yet (completely) satisfy even the first condition.

The integration of the EFTA and East European countries into the European Community will proceed gradually. Two important steps have been taken since the end of 1991. In 1992 the EC and EFTA countries signed the *European Economic Area (EEA) Agreement,* which is intended to extend the internal EC market to the EFTA countries, guaranteeing free movement of goods, services, people and capital across countries of both blocs. The ultimate aim is the integration of the economies of all the countries involved. The agreement has not been ratified as yet, and was even rejected in a referendum by the Swiss people. A modified treaty will be submitted in the course of 1993. In the meantime, Sweden, Finland and Austria have applied for full membership. Negotiations on the accession of these countries will start soon after the ratification of the Maastricht Treaty. In general no fundamental economic problems are foreseen with respect to enlargement of the EC with EFTA states. The economies of these generally rich countries are similar to the existing EC countries, both in structure and stage of development. Both parties will probably benefit from the entry of (former) EFTA members. Problems are more likely to emerge in the political field: most of the EFTA states are concerned about losing a considerable part of their independence, especially as they would have to give up their neutrality.

The other important step made since the end of 1991 was the signing of the so-called '*Europe Agreements*' with a number of former Communist countries in Central and Eastern Europe: Poland, Hungary, Czech and Slovak Federal Republic, Rumania and Bulgaria. The Agreements, which include commercial as well as political and cultural elements, are intended to pave the way for the full integration of these countries into the Community. There are a number of necessary conditions which have to be met, however, before integration can take place. First, political and economic reform should continue until a full-scale market economy is accomplished. Second, the economies of the countries concerned need to reach a level of development which enables them to cope when they are fully exposed to international competition. At present, the EC considers these economies too weak to withstand such competition. The Agreements provide for a gradual opening of EC markets for all products in a few years' time, except for agricultural produce. For their part Poland, Hungary and the Czech and Slovak Republics have to introduce reciprocal arrangements, though they are granted a longer period of time to do so. With Albania and the Baltic States, a less extensive trade and economic co-operation Agreement has been concluded as well.

For both sides immediate membership for the former Communist countries does not make sense. The latter countries would face severe problems in coping with the suddenly increased competition from Western Europe, while the EC, on the other hand, would face heavy claims on its budget for regional and cohesion funds and would see its monetary policy undermined by weak currencies. The East German experience so far does not advocate such an approach. It will probably take almost a decade (from 1992) before the most advanced countries in the region are prepared for full membership.

Nevertheless, serious questions can be raised concerning the way the Europe Agreements have been implemented so far. The EC may maintain its tariffs and/or quotas for at least five years (from 1992) on 'sensitive' goods like steel, textiles and meat; for most other agricultural produce they will not be lifted at all. These products, however, just happen to be those on which the East Europeans are assumed to have a competitive advantage. In addition to tariffs and quotas, there are specific clauses enabling the EC to restrict imports from the East, like anti-dumping clauses, animal-disease regulations and rules on state subsidies. Nevertheless, although the EC appears reluctant to liberalise its trade with Eastern Europe, trade with Poland, Hungary and the Czech and Slovak Republics, in particular, increased sharply at the beginning of the 1990s. It will be to the general benefit of both parties if this development continues, including an increase in trade in farm products.

1.3 MAIN OBJECTIVES AND POLICIES OF THE EUROPEAN COMMUNITY

1.3.1 A free and single market

The overall objective of the European Community is, according to Article 2 of the Treaty of Rome, the promotion of the harmonious development of economic growth and the accelerated increase of welfare and the standard of living in its Member States. Such an objective could be reached in different ways. It is clear, however, that the Community opted for *the free market* as its main instrument to achieve its goals in preference to planning or other state interventionist strategies. A large, free and competitive market is expected to create improved efficiency of production, more economies of scale, an optimal allocation of factors of production and to stimulate research and development. This would, in turn, result in lower unit costs and increased competitiveness of European industry.

Government involvement, on the other hand, is generally considered as detrimental to competition and the optimal allocation of the factors of production. For this reason Article 2 focuses on the establishment of a Common Market as the main tool for the achievement of a higher level of welfare. The necessity of approximation of economic policies (also in Article 2) is based on the idea that harmonisation of national policies is required to ensure fair competition and to avoid uncertainty in international trade relations. For instance, different tax systems create unequal production costs and profit opportunities and hence discriminate between the producers of different Member States. The same applies to subsidies, environmental policies, social security policies, health and safety standards and quality controls.

The importance of the free market as a method of gaining a higher level of productivity, income and employment and of reducing costs and prices is also embodied in the European Single Act of 1985. According to the so-called Cecchini Report, prepared on behalf of the European Commission, the benefits of the internal market will be derived in a large part from *enhanced competition* within a deregulated internal market. A second factor is the *increased scale of production*. Competition and scale are mutually reinforced by each other. In the medium term, it was estimated that real Community GDP would go up by an extra 5 to 7% and additional employment of 2 to 5 million jobs would be created.

Competition in the internal market will be encouraged by:

- the removal of entrance barriers erected by national frontiers;
- the opening up of (national) public procurement markets;
- elimination or reduction of (national) monopolies;
- market deregulation and liberalisation, for instance in the area of financial markets.

This enhanced competition is expected to lead to a fall in production costs, gains in efficiency and price reductions.

In addition to the static effects, there are also dynamic effects to be expected from the completion of the internal market.

A more competitive environment is an essential element determining the pace of technological innovation, according to the Cecchini Commission. Pursuit of economies of scale and competition will together encourage the emergence of large, truly European companies, better equipped to compete with their US and Far Eastern counterparts and to command strong market positions. Hence the internal market will eventually affect economic structures which, in turn, will produce an accelerated rate of growth.

Although great emphasis is given to developing market forces, this is not to say there is no role for government in a united Europe. The Treaty of Rome already explicitly identifies a number of common policies to be adopted, e.g. in the fields of competition, agriculture, transport, monetary relations, external trade, taxation and social security. Implicitly it also deals with regional policies. In addition, the European Single Act mentions common policies in the area

of the environment, scientific and technological development. The Maastricht Treaty on European Union stresses a common monetary and social policy, and makes extra provisions for a (regional) cohesion fund.

Most of these policies are intended to:

- ensure free competition on fair terms
- guarantee stability, and
- provide (quasi) public goods.

Thus, although the Community relies heavily on free market ideas, common policies are not excluded. They are mainly (but not only) meant to compensate for 'market failure' at the Community level.

1.3.2 Common policies

Competition policy

In order to create a more competitive environment, the Community has adopted, for instance, a rather strict system of competition rules. These rules forbid:

- restrictive agreements and practices of firms
- the abuse of a dominant position by firms
- national government aid to businesses

but only in so far as they affect the trade between Member States. Cartels, operating only at a national level, for instance, are not prohibited by Community laws (although they may be banned by national law). Most of the competition laws are governed by the Treaty of Rome.

Article 85 outlaws *restrictive agreements* and practices between companies affecting trade or leading to distortion of competition within the Community. Examples of such agreements are price fixing, market sharing, production restrictions and exclusive purchase and distribution agreements. However, part 3 of the same article grants individual or block exemptions in cases where the reduction in competition will be offset by the likely benefits to the public interest. Examples are joint research and development, patent licensing and motor vehicle dealerships. Research and development, for instance, may have positive external effects or may be too costly to be undertaken by a single firm.

Article 86 prohibits *abuse of a dominant position* within the common market by firms. A dominant position is identified as the ability of a firm to affect the outcome of the market by exercising monopoly power. It is not the dominant position as such which is prohibited, but merely the abuse. That is also why this article can seldom be used to prevent mergers or acquisitions. Special regulations dealing with these matters did not come into force until 1990 (see below). It is left to the Commission and eventually to the (European) Court of Justice to define the terms 'abuse' and 'dominant position' (measured in terms of market shares) in individual cases. Their assessment will depend on the product, type of market, market structure and so on.

Articles 92–4 ban national government aid to domestic industries which distorts or threatens to distort competition between firms within the Community. Only some exceptions are made, notably development subsidies or regional industry aid.

Articles 87–91 specify the implementation procedures relating to EC competition law. The principal body dealing with this is the *European Commission*, which is delegated by the Council of Ministers to investigate restrictive behaviour and to take appropriate actions. This may range from imposing fines or penalty payments to issuing an order to the firm or firms to stop the behaviour. The Commission can start investigations on its own initiative or at the request of injured parties. Those concerned may appeal against Commission decisions to the Court of Justice.

In addition to the Treaty of Rome, regulations with respect to mergers and acquisitions have been developed separately. The need for this kind of regulation became apparent in the run-up to the single market, when many companies were looking for merger or acquisition partners in order to prepare for the enlarged market. Under the *Merger Control Regulation*, which came into force in 1990, mergers or take-overs involving firms with a combined annual turnover of 5 billion ECUs need prior authorisation from the European Commission. Smaller inter-Community mergers are subject to national mergers and acquisitions regulations, but the Commission may intervene at the request of national governments.

EC competition law has precedence over national legislation, but it does not replace it. It is mainly intended to secure free competition in an international (inter-Community) context. National regulations are generally much more tolerant, with the clear exceptions of Germany and the UK.

Monetary policy

The Community's monetary policy has been introduced primarily to eliminate uncertainty in international economic relations. Wildly fluctuating currencies have a negative impact on international trade, because they make international transactions more risky. The call for a European stabilisation policy arose after the collapse of the Bretton Woods fixed exchange rate system in 1971. After some earlier attempts to reach a common arrangement, the *European Monetary System (EMS)* came into force in 1979. All Community countries became members, though the UK did not participate in the *Exchange Rate Mechanism (ERM)* until October 1990. Of the later entrants (Greece, Portugal and Spain), only Greece has thus far not joined the ERM; Spain entered in 1989 and Portugal at the beginning of 1992.

Within the Exchange Rate Mechanism of the EMS, currencies are only allowed to fluctuate within narrow ranges of ± 2.25% ('narrow band') or ± 6% ('wide band') around a central rate. The central rates are calculated on the basis of the *ECU (European Currency Unit)*, a basket consisting of fixed quantities of all EC currencies. The quantity of each specific currency in the basket depends on the economic weight of the country concerned in terms of (among others) GDP and intra-Community trade. The quantity is re-assessed every five years or on request. Table 1.2 gives an overview of the composition of the ECU as of September 1989 and the central rates on 1 February 1993.

Table 1.2 The European Currency Unit (ECU): composition and central rates within the ERM

Currency	Units in ECU[1]	Central ECU rate[2]
Belgian franc	3.3010	40.28
Danish krone	0.1976	7.45
German mark	0.6242	1.95
Greek drachma[3]	1.440	(259.3)
Spanish peseta	6.885	142.15
French franc	1.332	6.55
Irish pound	0.0086	0.81
Italian lira[4]	151.8	(1796)
Dutch guilder	0.2198	2.20
Portuguese escudo	1.393	180.62
UK pound sterling[5]	0.08784	(0.81)

[1] Composition as of September 1989
[2] Central rates as of 1 February 1993
[3] Notional central rate
[4] Temporary notational central rate as from 17 September 1992
[5] Notional central rate as from 17 September 1992 (suspension of sterling participation in ERM)

Source: European Economy, No. 54, table 51

The ERM forms a *parity grid* of bilateral exchange rates, in which the individual currencies are pegged to each other by means of a fixed relation (within margins) to their ECU central rates. The system is adjustable, however. In case of a persistent upwards or downwards pressure on a currency, caused by economic fundamentals, it may be decided collectively to devalue or revalue a currency by changing the ECU central rate. Such *realignments* have taken place quite frequently, especially in the early 1980s. So in fact, the ERM is not a system of totally fixed exchange rates; some flexibility is built in by the margins and more substantial adjustments are also possible. Even so, its intention at least is to provide short-term exchange rate stability. Until 1992 it did so quite successfully.

Fixed exchange rates have wide-ranging implications for other economic policies. With the exchange rates more or less pegged, it becomes very difficult for Member States to conduct independent economic policies. Exchange rate management and the use of tariffs are not available any more as means of adjusting balance-of-payments imbalances. This means that inflation, wages and productivity rates, taxes and other

factors that determine international competitiveness must be brought into line with each other. Since (within the framework of the internal market) currency controls have been abolished, interest rates cannot diverge significantly either.

The conclusion is that monetary integration can hardly be realised without both economic convergence and harmonisation of economic policies and even political integration. That is also the reason why the Community is attempting to establish an Economic and Monetary Union (EMU) into which the EMS is incorporated. EMU would create an optimal macroeconomic framework for intensified competition. The option to protect domestic industries against competition from other EC countries by means of devaluing would no longer exist.

The experience with the ERM up until 1992 was quite positive. Though frequent realignments took place, the system nonetheless succeeded in stabilising exchange rate fluctuations, at least in the short term. Moreover it is assumed that the EMS contributed substantially to bringing down inflation in the Member States participating in the ERM. A major explanation for this achievement is that – by pegging them to the ECU – the EC currencies were more or less linked to the German mark. The size of the German economy and the strong commitment of the German monetary authorities to price stability guaranteed a relatively low inflation level, not only in Germany but also in other countries participating in the ERM. The solid German mark acted, in fact, as a monetary anchor in Europe.

So far, so good. The problems in the monetary field started, however, when in the early 1990s the economies of the Member States started to diverge, instead of converging as was intended. The UK economy is a clear example in this respect. It probably entered the ERM in 1990 at too high a central rate for the pound in relation to British competitiveness. The UK position was further undermined as the UK went into recession well ahead of its EC partners. Germany, on the other hand, found itself still in the unification boom, which clearly fuelled inflation. The independent German Central Bank (Bundesbank) responded by adopting tight monetary policies, resulting in relatively high interest rates, in order to bring inflation down. In contrast to this policy, the UK Government was inclined to reduce interest rates to boost the weak British economy. These events put heavy strains on the ERM, culminating in the suspension of the UK's ERM membership in September 1992. The example serves to show that a fixed exchange rate without economic policy co-ordination is an illusion. The UK government reproached the German authorities on the ground that they allowed their national objectives to prevail over Community interests, i.e. currency stability in Europe.

In the same period in 1992 the Spanish peseta and the Italian lira were similarly forced into devaluations. These realignments were a clear illustration of convergence problems. The Spanish and especially the Italian economies were hit by severe imbalances, resulting in significant losses in competitiveness.

Both the British example and the Spanish and Italian cases demonstrate that fixed exchange rates are unrealistic and may not even be advisable if they are not backed up by co-ordinated economic policies and if the economies concerned diverge too much. Convergence is a prerequisite for monetary integration, though it can also be argued the other way around: convergence may be encouraged by co-operation in the monetary field.

Since the disappointing developments in 1992, a debate has started on the implementation of the ERM rules in that year. Instead of treating the ERM as a fixed-rate system, it was argued, the authorities should have regarded it as a fixed-but-adjustable system. Timely and more frequent realignments could have prevented the strains on the system which almost led to its total destruction. Undoubtedly, it did not make sense to act as if Stage III of EMU had already been reached. As long as the basic conditions have not been met, the system should be operated much more flexibly. Strictly fixed exchange rates presume much more convergence than has been realised as yet.

Taxation, social and environmental policies

As has been said before (common) taxation, social and environmental policies are adopted principally to guarantee fair competition, because taxes, social security contributions and pollution norms, for instance, affect costs of production. Harmonisation and standardisation of tax burdens, pollution norms, working conditions and so forth are the primary objectives of these policies.

It would have been possible, of course, to leave all these issues to national governments. Every country can set its own political priorities and economic objectives, for instance, on matters affecting the size of the public sector, government spending and environmental protection. The problem is, however, that distinctive national policies in a single market will distort international competition by creating unfair advantages for companies operating in countries with lower taxes and less strict norms in the areas of pollution and worker protection. Not all regulations do affect international trade, however.

Taxation

In the field of tax harmonisation, two approaches are possible: an absolute equalisation with respect to tax bases (the measure of value upon which a tax is levied) and related tax rates and an approach which tries to minimise the externalities of each state's tax systems, especially in the field of competition. The latter approach, which still allows for substantial differentials, has been adopted by the EC. It is based on the principle that differences in the individual tax systems of the member states should not influence the international 'free movement of goods, persons, services and capital' in a single market. Clearly, this requires a certain degree of co-ordination of tax policies.

Taxes can be of two types: *direct* taxes (taxes on wealth and income) and *indirect* taxes (surcharges on prices, which are paid eventually by consumers, e.g. VAT and excise taxes). Since *indirect* taxes immediately reflect on prices, they should be aligned to a certain degree. Evidence from the United States of America indicates that

– in the absence of frontier obstacles – indirect tax differentials between Member States of an economic union should not exceed five percentage points in order to avoid tax-induced border trade. There is no case for a complete equalisation, however. That is why the EC decided not to aim at a *harmonisation* of indirect taxes but only at an *approximation*. Value Added Tax (VAT) will be the common sales tax throughout the Community. In October 1992 the Council adopted a directive requiring the approximation of VAT rates, setting the standard rate of VAT at not less than 15% and the optional reduced rates at not less than 5% for 'necessities'. Zero rates may be maintained for a transitional period for a very limited number of products. VAT controls at the internal Community frontiers have disappeared since the establishment of the internal market (as of 1 January 1993). The tax will be collected by the country of final consumption (the so-called *destination principle*), which means zero rating for exports. A common VAT system (with equal structure and rates) is not foreseen in the near future. The present system will be in force till at least the end of 1996.

Plans to harmonise or even to approximate excise duties (levied on fuel, spirits and tobacco) in the foreseeable future have been abandoned, however. Only some rules with respect to inter-country trade have been relaxed. As of 1 January 1993 individuals are allowed to purchase in other Member States dutiable products for their personal use at the rates operating there.

Direct taxes are supposed to affect international competitiveness as well. Personal income taxes and social security contributions increase the costs of production. Corporate taxes and taxes on wealth may influence the movement of factors of production from higher to lower taxed places. The revenues from taxes, on the other hand, will enable governments to supply a range of public goods and services (e.g. education, infrastructure, health services), which will be beneficial both for the inhabitants and for the business of a country. It can be questioned whether a substantial convergence is needed in the field of fiscal policies. The disadvantage of a high level of taxes can – at least to a certain extent – be compensated for by a high level of public provisions. Nevertheless, some policy competition may occur with respect to some taxes (e.g. corporate taxes) and with respect to the efficiency of the public sector in terms of costs and benefits (see also section 13.2.4).

Apart from these considerations, fiscal policy is pre-eminently accepted as a matter of *national sovereignty*. The provision of social services, health services and education are left to national governments. Decision making with respect to taxation requires unanimity of the Council of Ministers, even after the adoption of the European Single Act. The Member States have been very reluctant to harmonise direct taxes. So far, there has been hardly any progress in this field.

Environmental policy
Environmental protection has received greater priority in the last decade, especially since the adoption of the Single Act. There are mainly two reasons for this. First, the increasing pollution does not stop at frontiers and is therefore automatically a matter of common concern. A clean environment can also be considered as a public good, which probably can be secured most appropriately through the intervention of a supranational authority. Second, different standards and norms in Member States can distort competition. Polluting activities may be relocated in the Member States with less strict norms, which will benefit from increased production and employment, while other States generally will be confronted with the resulting pollution as well. This clearly offers an unfair advantage.

Environmental policy was not mentioned in the Treaty of Rome. It was only launched in 1972, when the Heads of State decided to develop a Community policy in this respect. Since then a large number of directives, regulations and decisions have been adopted. A milestone, however, was the explicit inclusion of environmental policy in the Single European Act (SEA) of 1987, giving it a legal basis. It was agreed that the most important principles for the common environmental policy from then on should be *prevention* and the *'polluter pays principle (PPP)'*. The latter means that external costs (costs not accounted for in the market price) should be 'internalised' (included in the price). The PPP relies on the use of market forces to implement environmental policies. In the 1990s even greater emphasis will be put on this kind of approach. Economic instruments like taxes and tradeable permits will become of increasing importance to achieve the goals set by the policy makers. An example is the introduction of a combined CO_2/energy tax, proposed by the EC Commission in 1992.

Guidelines and objectives for environmental policies are outlined in the so-called *Community Action Programmes* on the environment. The fifth, called *'Towards Sustainability'* was adopted in 1992 by the European Commission and Parliament. It stresses the concept of sustainable growth which will not compromise the abilities of future generations to meet their own needs. There remains a lot of work to be done, however. Compared to other economic blocs, the standards set by the Community are mostly only minimal.

Social policy

The Treaty of Rome explicitly mentions the promotion of the improvement of living and working conditions and close co-operation between Member States in the social field. The latter should be pursued in order to set the same (basic) standards throughout the Community and to avoid 'social dumping'. Nevertheless, social policy got minimal attention in the first decades of the Community. Marked progress was made only in such areas as the freedom of movement of workers, equal treatment of men and women and health and safety protection.

The neglect of social policy in the early years of the Community has been severely criticised. The call for a more comprehensive policy resulted in the adoption of a *Social Action Programme (SAP)* in 1974. The main objectives of this programme were the attainment of full and better employment and the harmonisation of working and living conditions. Social policy gathered momentum, however, with the adop-

tion of the *Social Charter* in 1989 by the Heads of State. There were major concerns at that time that the aimed internal market, as proposed by the SEA, would lead to a downward pressure on social standards induced by increased competition. The Social Charter is a declaration of principles, which should be transformed into rules and regulations by means of a Social Action Programme. It covers, for instance, the following subjects: improvement of living and working conditions (e.g. maximum working week), right of freedom of movement, social protection (e.g. establishment of a national minimum wage and the guarantee of social assistance for people without jobs), health protection and safety at the workplace, worker consultations and equal treatment of men and women.

The Social Charter was not signed by the UK. For this reason the UK was also against the proposal to include a Social Chapter in the Maastricht Treaty on European Union. The British opposition resulted in a separate protocol, attached to the treaty, offering the eleven other Members the opportunity to make laws in the social field, based on the Social Charter, without UK involvement. This problem apart, it is not very likely that an approximation of social policies will take place very rapidly within the EC. Different social standards do not only reflect differences in attitudes and political priorities but are also caused by economic disparities. Without real convergence it will remain very difficult to bring social policies in line with each other.

Transport policy

For international trade, *transport costs* are of vital importance; in fact they form a substantial part of production costs. In many countries elements of the transport sector are heavily subsidised. This is because transport generates considerable external benefits, e.g. in environmental protection, energy conservation, infrastructure, industrial development and employment. Transport can, in fact, be considered as a quasi public good, although the criteria of non-rivalry in consumption and the equal distribution of benefits are not applicable in this area, it is nevertheless at least partly provided by government. In most countries transport markets are highly regulated and protected. Without a common policy in this respect, the industry's production costs will be substantially distorted by national policies. Such a common policy should aim basically at the removal of discriminating regulations with respect to market entry and use of national infrastructure, the harmonisation of fiscal, social and technical conditions of operation and the co-ordination of the development of an European transport infrastructure.

Until recently progress in this field has been rather limited. The completion of the internal market in 1992 has resulted, however, in a number of new directives which should eventually lead to the opening up of national transport markets to non-residents. Transport quotas will be gradually abolished. According to a White Paper, adopted by the Commission in 1992, the freedom to provide services everywhere in the Community will be the ultimate goal. Many conditions still have to be fulfilled, especially in the field of harmonisation, before this goal will be achieved.

The conclusion so far is that most of the common policies support the working of the free market rather than hinder it. They create in fact the necessary conditions for the operation of the market or are intended to offset market imperfections. There are some major exceptions, however, such as the agricultural policy and the regional and industrial policies.

Common Agricultural Policy (CAP)

The Common Agricultural Policy (CAP) is very important in the Community. Although expenses under the CAP have been sharply reduced in the last decades, in 1992 they were still responsible for about 55% of the total expenses of the Community Budget (which is, apart from the CAP, fairly small). In the early 1970s they amounted to even more than 80% of the Budget.

Agriculture is heavily subsidised and protected within the Community; it is certainly not left to the forces of the market. The main reason for this policy is that the Community wants to remain to a substantial degree self-sufficient in food production, which is of vital interest for any society. As a consequence of this principle, producers are guaranteed a fair standard of living, mainly by setting minimum prices and levying tariffs for food imports. Other goals of the CAP are the stabilisation of markets, regular supplies and reasonable prices for consumers. Prices would be much lower in many cases, however, if there were no CAP at all. The CAP is heavily criticised, because of its interventionist approach, which creates high costs and excess production (because of the guaranteed prices) and discriminates against non-EC suppliers; but there is also a strong political lobby in its favour.

Nevertheless, the CAP has come under severe pressure in the last decade. The emphasis has shifted from protection and guaranteed prices to restructuring and output restriction. Quotas have been set (e.g. in the case of milk); guaranteed farm prices have been reduced and price support for most products has been limited to maximum quantities. A set-aside scheme was introduced to compensate farmers prepared to take their land (or parts of it) out of production. In the early 1990s the need to reform the CAP became more urgent by pressure from the EC's trading partners (especially the USA) within the framework of the GATT talks. The high level of protection for agriculture is clearly a major obstacle for further trade liberalisation.

Regional policy

Like agricultural policy, regional policy is not in line with the general market orientation approach of the Community. It is adopted mainly to support weak regions within the Community. These regions consist of

- regions lagging behind in development,
- declining industrial areas and
- underdeveloped rural areas.

They are generally characterised by low incomes and high unemployment rates. As can be seen in Figure 1.2, there are large regional differences in wealth within the Community.

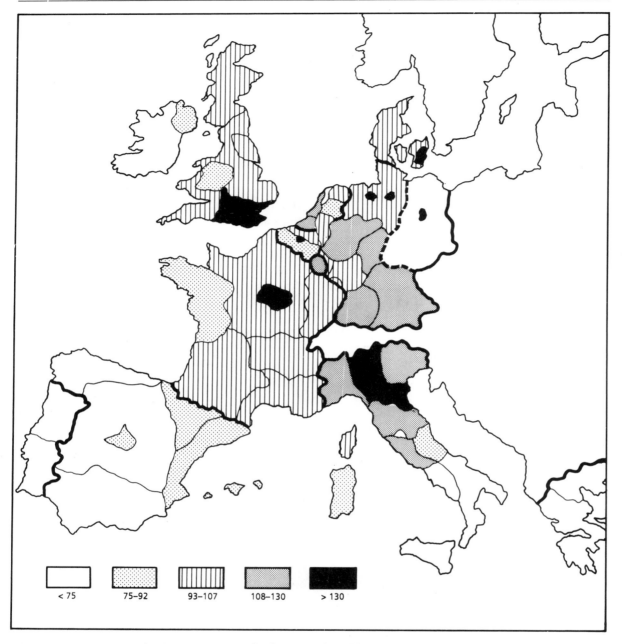

Figure 1.2 GDP in purchasing power standards per region, 1989, EUR 12 = 100

Source: Eurostat, European Commission

Portugal, Greece, Spain and Ireland have per capita incomes far below the EC average for all regions. The poorest region is situated in North Portugal, with a per capita income of about 45% of the EC average (in 1989).

Among the more wealthy countries considerable regional disparities can be found. The peripheral regions of the UK (including the North of England, Northern Ireland and Wales) and the South and Islands of Italy are notable for their low levels of income, emigration and poor job opportunities compared to the national average. Per capita income in Italy's Mezzogiorno is only two-thirds of the EC average. In most cases lower income regions are less developed rural areas (Portugal, Greece, Spain). Other regions have problems due to the decline of staple industries, such as coal and steel, textiles, shipyards (North of England, Wales, parts of Belgium and North of Spain), or because of an unfavourable geographical position (e.g. too far away from the centres of economic activity).

Wealth is generally concentrated in large urban areas, like the Paris region (Île de France) with a per capita income of 162% of the EC average (in 1988), the region around Milan (Lombardia, 139%), Hamburg (174%) and Bremen (142%), London (the South East of England, 131%), Brussels (157%) and Copenhagen (136%).

The disparities between the different regions, therefore, are very substantial. The problem is that in practice they have a natural tendency to intensify. The prosperous centres are generally characterised by considerable *external economies of scale*, because of the availability of a developed infrastructure, skilled labour, suppliers, output markets and usually also because of their accessibility. This produces very unbalanced development.

Free movement of labour and capital within the EC can worsen this situation, because these factors of production are seeking the highest yields. The conclusion is that economic integration can further accentuate regional imbalances; but these imbalances in turn can be a (political) threat to further integration. Convergence in economic performance (real convergence) is of great importance for integration. That is why the EC is involved in regional policy making and why this matter is not left entirely to national governments. Another reason is that frequently there is a need to co-ordinate investments in basic infrastructure, especially if these invest-

ments are beneficial for more Member States (e.g. border-crossing transport networks). The policies are intended to counterbalance unequal development and to support weaker regions. They are additional to national policies and consist of public aid to local industries, investment in infrastructure, loans for restructuring industries, etc.

The regional policies are mainly financed by the EC Structural Funds, which include (among others) the European Regional Development Fund (ERDF) and the European Social Fund (ESF). Funds are also distributed by the European Investment Bank and the Social Cohesion Fund. By far the largest part of the aid of the Structural Funds (around three-quarters) goes to the regions whose development is lagging behind. To qualify for this aid a region must have a per capita income of less than 75% of the EC average income. That is why Portugal, Greece, Ireland, Spain and the South of Italy (see Figure 1.2) receive by far the bulk of the money (more than 70%). For a country like Greece EC regional aid is equivalent to about 3% of its GDP. For countries like France and the Netherlands this percentage is generally less than 0.3%. In addition, countries with a per capita income of less than 90% of the EC average (Greece, Ireland, Portugal and Spain) will receive additional aid between 1993 and 1998 from the Cohesion Fund. The setting up of this Fund was provided for in an annexed protocol on economic and social cohesion of the Maastricht Treaty. Such cohesion, it was argued, is a necessary condition for successful integration. The additional aid package should help the poorer Member States to prepare for the EMU and was an important reason for these states accepting the Maastricht deal.

The effects of EC regional policies should not be overestimated. Although the amounts of money which are allocated to these policies have been increased substantially, they are still fairly limited, and generally also smaller than the national funds. For some of the peripheral countries the help is of considerable importance, however.

Industrial policy

Industrial policy (apart from to competition policy) can be defined as government actions to influence industry and thus can be considered as a state interventionist policy. It is a highly debated issue within the Community. On the one hand, it was warmly supported by countries with a rich national tradition in this respect like France and Italy, while countries like Germany, the Netherlands and the UK were generally more in favour of liberal economic policies.

Industrial policy was not explicitly included in the Treaty of Rome. In the first decades of the Community it was mainly used to restructure declining industries like coal, steel, shipyards, textiles and clothing. In terms of money, Community involvement with industry was of limited significance in this period though.

In the 1980s attention shifted to the more advanced industries such as information technology, telecommunications, nuclear energy, aerospace and bio-technology. Several programmes were adopted to promote research and development (R&D) for high-technology industries. The ESPRIT (European Programme for Research and Development in Information Technology) was launched in 1983 to support joint private research and development in the information industry. It was followed by further programmes such as ESPRIT II, RACE and BRITE, supporting private joint R&D in the field of advanced technology.

Since 1984, co-operation between companies in the area of R&D has been granted a 'block exemption' from competition rules. In the Single European Act, the Treaty of Rome was changed in order to give this technology support a legal basis. In so-called 'Framework Programmes' with a duration of four years, goals are defined and budgets assigned. The third Framework Programme of 1990–4 is provided with a budget of 6.6 billion ECU.

The main reason for this heavy emphasis on technology support is that the Community fears it will lose the technology race to Japan and the USA.

Advocates of this policy argue that there are substantial external benefits and economies of scale related to R&D. These market imperfections can be offset by government support to industry in this respect. Opponents stress that state intervention constitutes a potential danger to free international trade, because subsidies distort prices and provoke similar reactions by the governments of trading partners.

Apart from financial aid to specific industries, the EC industry policy in the last decade focused very strongly on improving the general business environment of EC industry. The creation of the internal market is supposed to be an incentive for industrial concentration (by means of mergers, take-overs and expansion) and thus for economies of scale. Technical harmonisation and standardisation (part of the 1992 project) should also contribute to the creation of the right conditions for mass-production. This, in turn, should be a stimulus for innovation, because R&D expenses can be spread across more units of production in that case.

The improvement in the operation of markets is the basic pre-condition for increased industrial competitiveness, according to the EC Commission in the communication in 1992. This should be the cornerstone of industrial policy.

Conclusion

The European integration process is based on a market-oriented approach. With a few clear exceptions, most of its policies are designed to realise a large, free, internal market characterised by strong and fair competition.

This approach is not very remarkable when we put it in its historical context. The integration process began right after the war, with the adoption of the Marshall Plan, which strongly reflected American free market ideas. During the era of the Cold War, attempts were made to build up a strong counter-force to the Communist threat in Europe and to defend freedom and democracy. In the beginning the general idea was that this should be a military and political power, as was reflected by the proposals for the European Defence Community and the

ECSC during the early 1950s. But at a later stage emphasis shifted to economic power. The large and free market was to play an important role in the development of such a power as can be observed in the Treaty of Rome, for instance. The adoption of the European Single Act can be considered as a European attempt to keep up with the USA and Japan; countries with very large, competitive home markets. The Act was written in a period in which free market ideologies were generally very dominant. The (Maastricht) Treaty on European Union was to be the final step towards an economically united Europe, based on free market principles.

The bringing into line of national and EC interests and policies constitutes a major challenge over the coming years. A common currency and common monetary policy, for instance, require a far more nominal and real convergence than has been realised so far. The lack of nominal convergence (inflation, interest and exchange rates, budget deficits), in turn, partly reflects differing views on fiscal and monetary policy, e.g. with respect to recessions. Real convergence (GDP per head) will probably not be realised, although three of the four less developed economies (Portugal, Spain and Ireland) have made remarkable progress in recent years. Another problem undermining the market-based integration may be the strong views of Member States on the (remaining) role of the national states and the public sector in the economy. Last but not least, nationalism and the fear of loss of independence constitute major obstacles for further integration. There remains a great deal to be done before Europe will be truly united economically.

1.4 THE EC: ITS SIZE AND RELATIVE IMPORTANCE

As a single identity, the European Community is one of the three dominant economic blocs in the world. With a GDP of 5,422 billion ECU the EC surpassed, in 1992, the USA, which had a GDP of 4,523 billion ECU in that year. Japan followed, at some distance with 2,852 billion ECU (see Table 1.3).

Table 1.3 Main economic indicators, EC, USA, Japan, 1992

	EC	USA	Japan
Population (millions)	347	257	124
Gross Domestic Product (GDP) current market prices (billion ECU)	5,422	4,523	2,852
per head[1], PPS, EC = 100	100	135	117
Unemployment rate[2]	9.5	7.3	2.1
average 1983–92	9.0	6.8	2.5
Inflation[1] (average GDP deflator 1983–92)	5.6	3.7	1.5
Gross fixed capital formation[1] (average % of GDP 1983–92 at current market prices)	19.8	17.8	29.5
Private consumption[1] (average % of GDP 1983–92 at current market prices)	61.7	65.7	58.3
Nominal unit labour costs[1] (relative to 19 industrial countries double export weights, 1980 = 100)	88.0	98.9	127.8
Exports of goods and services[3] (% of GDP at current market prices)	8.1	10.7	10.3
Imports of goods and services[3] (% of GDP at current market prices)	9.2	11.3	7.6
Balance on current account (% of GDP), average 1983–92[1]	0.2	−1.8	2.8
1992	−0.6	−1.0	3.2

[1] EC excluding East Germany.
[2] Percentage of civilian labour force: EC excluding East Germany; USA and Japan percentage of total labour force.
[3] EC External exports/imports: goods only.

Source: European Economy, No. 54, 1993
Figures based on European Commission estimates.

These figures, however, are strongly dependent on exchange rates (the dollar depreciated considerably against the ECU in 1992).

In terms of population, the EC also leads with 347 million inhabitants compared to 257 million in the USA and 124 million in Japan. United States citizens still are on average the richest of the three blocs. Measured in purchasing power index figures, their average income was 135 in 1992, Japan being second with 117 and the EEC third with 100. The EC and, in particular, Japan are catching up (the latter very rapidly); in 1960 the USA was leading with 182 against 100 for the EC and only 54 for Japan.

The relative strength of the Japanese economy can also be seen from the very favourable unemployment and inflation figures and the large current account surplus. The negative trend of the double-weighted unit labour costs are not caused by internal factors but largely by the strong appreciation of the yen since the middle of the 1980s.

Worthy of note is also the large proportion spent on investment in Japan and the relative low level of spending on consumption. Gross fixed capital formation amounted to 31.1% in 1992; the estimated figure for the whole of the last decade is about 30%. This indicates that Japan puts heavy stress on technical innovation and the growth of its production capacity. The Japanese stance is in strong contrast to that of the USA, where gross investment is relatively low and consumption high. The EC occupies a position in between, but it is closer to that of the USA.

A break-down at industry level shows that the Community, compared with Japan and the USA, has the largest market share (in terms of value added) in industrial activities with a moderate or even weak growth in demand. Examples of these industries are: food products, tobacco, beverages, textiles, leather, clothing and metal products. In strong demand sectors like office and data processing machines, electrical and electronic goods and chemical products, the Community is clearly surpassed by the United States and, despite its bigger size (in terms of GDP and population), its market share does not deviate very much from that of Japan. The conclusion is that the proportion of Community industry in the strong demand sector in relation to the whole of Community industry is obviously smaller than that of the two other blocs. Products of industries in strong demand sectors generally have a high technological content and require huge R&D investment. They are normally only produced on a very large scale to cover development costs. A large home market is a prerequisite for these products.

The awareness of a growing gap between the Community and its two rivals in the field of fast growing high-tech industries became a major driving force behind the speeding up of the integration process within the Community at the end of the 1980s. The Community's industries can only keep up if they operate within a large unfragmented internal market, as exists today on completion of the 1992 project. Relative backwardness in the technological field also explains the present emphasis on joint R&D research in the Community's industrial policy.

The current account of the EC is normally in balance; in contrast with that of Japan which over many years has shown a large surplus and that of the USA which mainly has a large deficit (see Figure 1.3). Exports and imports of goods and services generally constitute about 10% of GDP in the three blocs.

Developing countries and other European OECD (non-EC) countries are by far the most important trading partners for the Community, accounting for, in 1991, 33% and 30% of extra-Community exports respectively and for 30% and 25% of its imports respectively. Exports to the USA and Japan accounted only for 22% of total EC exports and for 29% of imports. The trade deficit with Japan reached 28.5 billion ECU in 1991.

The Japanese trade pattern is completely different. About 51% of the total exports of Japan went to the EC and the USA and 37% of its imports originated from these areas (1990).

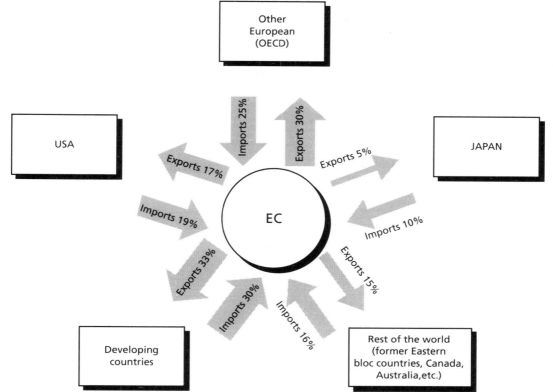

Figure 1.3 Extra-Community trade (excl. East Germany) in percentages of total in 1991. Total exports: 416 billion ECU. Total imports: 487 billion ECU.

The trade between the three dominating blocs is clearly out of balance; a problem which has provoked many disputes. The USA reproach the EC for using unfair trade practices like subvention and protection, especially in the field of agriculture. Americans fear that despite its free market rhetoric, the EC will build up a 'Fortress Europe', with little access for foreign imports.

The EC, for its part, complains about limited access to the Japanese market due to non-tariff barriers and feels itself flooded with Japanese high-tech products (electronics, cameras, cars, computers and so on). But the EC's main orientation towards less developed countries and neighbouring countries obviously shows a lack of competitiveness in the advanced strong demand sectors – a structural weakness which among others may be overcome by a more integrated large single market within an integrated European economy.

1.5 THE TWELVE EC COUNTRIES

Germany

Of the twelve EC countries *Germany* is the largest. With a population of 80.7 million people (including East Germany) it outnumbers by far the next countries in rank in this field: France, Italy and the UK, all having a population between 57 and 58 million (1992, see Table 1.4.(a)). Its GDP of 1,487 billion ECU exceeded France, the second country, by 44%. The Western part of Germany is – after Luxembourg – also leading with respect to GDP per head; it had until recently (also after Luxembourg) the lowest inflation and unemployment rates and its competitiveness and export performance are impressive.

Its real GDP growth rate in the last decade was only moderate, but until recently it was a very stable and balanced economy. The integration of the East German economy (after the unification in 1990), however, involves high costs for restructuring, cleaning up the environment, infrastructure, education and measures in the social field (unemployment, retraining and retirement). As a result, Germany – after an initial expenditure boom – is confronted with serious imbalances in the field of inflation and public deficit and with a stagnation in growth. Long-term prospects are uncertain; eventually unification may turn out to be an advantage for the combined German economy in terms of market enlargement, investment opportunities

and catching-up opportunities, but in the mid-term it obviously has significant drawbacks.

France

While most of the other European countries adopted policies of strict austerity and supply-side policies in response to the crises of the early 1980s, France experimented with Keynesian-inspired reflation policies and state intervention strategies. Whatever may be said about the current relevance of Keynesian demand management, it certainly does not work if it is only carried out by one country, which has a rather open economy and is not big enough to dominate its international economic relations. The result was

Table 1.4 Main economic indicators, 1992

(a) The five major EC countries

	Germany	France	Italy	UK	Spain
Population (millions)	80.7	57.4	57.9	57.7	39.1
Gross domestic product (GDP)					
current market prices (billion ECU)	1487	1036	951	804	444
average real growth in % 1983–92	2.7[1]	2.1	2.4	2.2	3.2
GDP per head, PPS, EC = 100%	118.7[1]	111.5	103.5	95.3	76.7
Unemployment rate average 1983–92	6.0[1]	10.1	10.2	10.8	18.0
Inflation (GDP deflator) average 1983–92	2.9[1]	5.7	8.1	5.5	8.0
Gross Fixed capital formation average 1983–92 (% of GDP at market prices)	20.2[1]	20.1	20.2	17.5	21.7
Private consumption average 1983–92 (% of GDP at market prices)	61.9[1]	60.4	61.7	63.0	63.4
Real unit labour costs (1980 = 100)	92.4[1]	89.8	96.3	101.2	84.5
Exports of goods and services (% of GDP at market prices)	33.6[1]	22.6	19.5	23.7	17.5
Imports of goods and services (% of GDP at market prices)	26.5[1]	21.3	19.3	25.3	20.5
Current balance (% of GDP at market prices)	0.9[1]	0.1	−2.4	−2.7	−3.7

[1] Excluding East Germany

(b) Smaller EC countries

	Nether-lands	Belgium	Denmark	Portugal	Greece	Ireland	Luxem-bourg
Population (millions)	15.2	10.0	5.2	9.4	10.4	3.6	0.4
Gross domestic product (GDP)							
current market prices (billion ECU)	248	169	110	65	61	38	8
average real growth in % 1983–92	2.4	2.2	2.1	2.7	1.8	3.7	4.1
GDP per head, PPS, EC = 100%	102.9	106.1	106.0	57.5	47.4	70.7	129.1
Unemployment rate average 1983–92	6.7	8.2	9.5	4.8	7.7	17.8	1.9
Inflation (GDP deflator) average 1983–92	1.6	4.1	4.2	16.8	17.2	4.0	3.5
Gross Fixed capital formation (% of GDP at market prices) average 1983–92	20.4	17.6	17.9	25.1	18.5	18.4	24.6
Private consumption average 1983–92 (% of GDP at market prices)	59.3	63.8	53.6	65.5	68.5	58.1	57.6
Real unit labour costs (1980 = 100)	89.0	91.6	89.2	84.5	93.9	84.6	98.3
Exports of goods and services (% of GDP at market prices)	53.0	69.5	36.6	28.9	23.7	63.0	90.8
Imports of goods and services (% of GDP at market prices)	47.7	66.4	29.1	37.9	32.5	51.5	98.7
Current balance (% of GDP at market prices)	3.6	1.8	3.0	–2.1	–3.3	0.1	19.9

Source: European Economy, 1993, No. 54.

a large trade deficit, inflation and rising unemployment. Since 1982, France has undergone a major shift in its economic policies towards more liberal and free-market approaches. Together with the improving world economy this caused a sound recovery of the French economy in the second half of the 1980s. The country succeeded with this policy of 'competitive disinflation' in reducing inflation and the budget deficit to very acceptable levels, in improving the competitiveness of its export industry and in realising a balanced current account. Nevertheless, France has been severely hit by the depression of the early 1990s and is confronted with high and very persistent unemployment. It is expected, however, that growth rates will pick up soon if the international situation improves.

Italy

Italy, on average, has shown moderate growth rates in the last decade. A remarkable feature of the Italian economy is the large presence of small and medium-sized companies, which have turned out to be one of the major driving forces behind Italian success. The growth is lacking in terms of balance, however. While the economy of Milan and other northern regions was booming in the late 1980s, the economy of the South was rather stagnant. The gap between the two parts of the country is widening even further. Full exposure to international competition within a united Europe may even fuel this development. Other significant problems are the inefficient public sector, the large budget deficit, the high inflation rates and – last but not least – political uncertainty. All these problems have to be addressed if Italy wants to maintain confidence in its economy.

United Kingdom

The UK has succeeded in the last decade in bringing to an end a long period of poor performance. In the 1960s and 1970s the average UK growth rate was only a meagre 2.6% against an average of 4.0% for the present 12 EC members. But in the upturn of 1983–90 the 3.1% was slightly above the average EC rate of 2.9%; and although the UK was first and most severely affected by the recession in the early 1990s, it appears to be on its way back. The financial service sector, in patricular, is very strong; the UK has become the financial sector of Europe. Nevertheless, the UK economy still exhibits important structural weaknesses, such as regional disparities, low investment levels, an underdeveloped infrastructure, and a large current account deficit. The latter can be considered as a structural weakness in competitiveness; an aspect which possibly partly explains the UK's hesitation to ratify the Maastricht Treaty and to support other steps leading in the direction of the economic unification of Europe.

Spain

The Spanish GDP per head is still far below the EC average; but, since 1986, it has been catching up rather rapidly. The Spanish economy has shown a large number of imbalances in the last decade, e.g. high unemployment, interest and inflation rates. Due to the policies of the Franco era it was a rather closed, protected, regulated and monopolised economy. Recent Spanish governments, however, have implemented quite successfully policies to prepare Spain for full integration into the Community after 1993. The Spanish economy is much more competitive now and possesses great growth potential. For instance, a much greater part of the female population could be integrated into the labour force. Investment in the 1980s was very high,

much of it financed by foreign capital. Although the recession in the early 1990s resulted in a marked worsening of most economic indicators, Spanish economic growth has remained above the EC average so far. If Spain succeeds in getting its imbalances under control, the economy could continue to grow at a quite fast rate.

The Netherlands

The Netherlands suffered most of all EC countries from the crisis in the early 1980s, chiefly due to the effect of rising labour costs caused by increased social security expenditure. In the last decade rather successful policies were implemented aimed at reducing labour costs, the size of the public sector and the budget deficit and increasing the profitability of the private sector. These resulted in a recovery in economic growth. Strong points of the Dutch economy are the low inflation level, the international competitiveness, stable currency and central location. The low labour participation and high social expenditure level remain matters of concern.

Belgium

Belgium has realised only moderate growth in recent decades. It is an extremely open economy, characterised by low inflation rates and a high degree of competitiveness. Major problems, on the other hand, are the excessive national debt, high public deficits, high labour costs and regional disputes and disparities. The central location and international orientation put the country in a favourable position with respect to European integration.

Denmark

Danish growth has been lagging behind the average EC growth rate over the last three decades. Explanations for this underperformance are the high starting level in the 1950s and the slow growth of productivity. The latter is mainly due to the high levels of public expenditure and high levels of non-market services employment. Rigidities in the labour market are a further constraint. Recent Danish governments have tried to decrease public intervention in the economy with modest success. The cost competitiveness and international orientation of the Danish economy are its strong points.

Portugal

Portugal has shown very high growth rates in the last three decades. Its entry into the EC appears to have been beneficial for the country. It is in the process of restructuring, aiming to convert the formerly highly regulated, state-dominated economy into a market-oriented one. Unemployment and investment are very high, but extreme inflation rates and weak competitiveness remain matters of concern. Supply-side improvements are of vital importance to withstand increased competition in the open internal market after 1992 and to maintain its favourable long-term growth rates.

Greece

Greek economic performance in the last decade has been relatively poor, in spite of substantial aid from the EC structural funds. The most important problems for Greece are fiscal imbalances, public sector inefficiency, lack of competitiveness, underdeveloped infrastructure and low investment. Part of the difficulties arise from the high degree of state intervention during the 1980s; since 1991 the Greek government has been trying to address the problems.

Ireland

Ireland has managed to realise impressive growth rates in both the long and the short term. It succeeded in redressing a number of imbalances in the 1980s, like high inflation rates, the budget and the current account deficit. It has been quite successful in attracting foreign investors, mainly multinationals, by offering favourable investment conditions. The rather advanced foreign sector is not very well integrated with the more traditional indigenous sector, however. The main problem remains job

creation; together with Spain, Ireland has the worst unemployment rate in the EC.

Luxembourg

Luxembourg has shown an outstanding performance in terms of growth and virtually all other macroeconomic indicators in the last decade. It is the smallest, but also by far the richest country in Europe. It has become a major international financial centre and is also heavily engaged in other international services. The outlook is also favourable.

1.6 POSTSCRIPT

In the last week of July 1993 the Exchange Rate Mechanism (ERM) of the European Monetary System (EMS) went into crisis again. The direct cause was a massive attack by speculators on the French franc, the Danish krone and the Belgian franc. Although France did not have balance-of-payments problems at all at that time, speculators expected the franc to be devalued, because the French government was inclined to reduce interest rates. Lower interest rates would boost the French economy, which was sliding into recession and was confronted with very high and increasing unemployment rates. The French government, however, was very strongly committed to the *'franc fort'* policy: moreover, a devaluation of the franc would strike at the heart of European monetary co-operation. A way out would be a reduction in German interest rates, which would remove the strains on the ERM to a great extent.

On Thursday, 29 July, however, the independent Bundesbank did *not* reduce the discount rate. The main reason was that Germany was still confronted with excessively high inflation rates (triggered by excess spending due to the German unification process). The statutory obligation of the Bundesbank is to avoid inflation not to guarantee international currency stability. In order to come up with a solution, EC finance ministers decided over the weekend (before the foreign exchange markets opened again) to widen the fluctuation margins of the ERM from 2.25% to 15% on either side of the currency's central rates, resulting in total band widths of 30% (except for the D-mark/guilder exchange rate). This way, formal devaluations could be avoided while the relatively high nominal German interest rates could be maintained.

One of the Maastricht convergence criteria, however, requires currencies to stay within narrow 2.25% bands for two years before moving to monetary union. Does this mean that the plans for reaching an EMU and a single currency in Europe have been given up and that even an effective ERM has been abandoned? Not necessarily. The ERM still exists: a 30% spread is much less than the wild swings of the dollar *vis-à-vis* the mark in the last decade. Moreover, in the period immediately after the Brussels meeting it turned out that most governments were quite determined to defend their currencies, even if they had to maintain high interest rates. The ERM system is still in place; the narrow bands could be restored overnight. According to the agreement of the EC finance ministers the measure is of limited duration; the ERM will possibly return to its narrow bands by early 1994.

Nevertheless, it is very unlikely that the Maastricht timetable for EMU will be realised. Even a narrow-band ERM turned out to be too much of a straitjacket for the EC currencies in the early 1990s. There are two basic reasons for this. First, the European economies still exhibit a high degree of divergence. Persistent inflation differentials, resulting in changes in competitiveness, put strong pressure on the exchange rates of the weaker countries. Second, and maybe even more important, is that a rigid system with narrow bands cannot cope with strongly divergent economic policies, caused by economic shocks (German unification) or diverging phases of the business cycle (the UK in 1992 and France *v* Germany in 1993).

Most Community politicians, however, are still committed to the idea of moving towards a single European currency in the near future. The case for monetary union is still very strong: exchange risks and costs will disappear, competitive devaluations will be avoided, competition

enhanced and inflation reduced. The question is how it should be reached, keeping the 1992/1993 events in mind. Three options should be mentioned.

1 *The reintroduction of the recently dismantled controls on international capital movements*. Capital controls could be used, for instance, to prevent speculation against currencies, particularly in cases in which such speculation would not (or would hardly) be justified on purely economic grounds, as in the case of the French franc in 1993. Currency controls, however, would jeopardise the benefits of financial integration. In addition, it could be questioned whether such controls could be implemented in practice, given the state of modern financial technology and the opportunities to do business under less regulated conditions.

2 *The relaxation of the convergence criteria*, including the requirement for currencies to stay within the narrow band of the ERM for two years. This would allow more countries to qualify for EMU, increasing the chance that EMU will be launched before 1999. The price stability of the common European currency, however, will be less certain in this case. Countries with a strong anti-inflationary reputation, like Germany, will probably not be very happy with this solution. They may not be prepared to sacrifice their own stable currency for a possibly weaker ECU.

3 *Full preservation of the original convergence criteria set by the Treaty of Maastricht*. Only a limited number of Member States will be able to join EMU in this case, which will consequently only start in 1999, unless (contrary to th Maastricht Agreement, see section 1.2.2) it is decided that a minority of Member States may institute EMU as well. Other countries would follow later. This option resembles the 'two-speed Europe' case, discussed in section 1.2.2. It is uncertain whether the economically weaker countries would agree to this idea.

If the Community decides to hold on to its aim of establishing EMU, it will probably have to choose between options 2 and 3, the first not being very realistic. That would result in a trade-off between a potentially strong currency with a limited number of participants (option 3) and a potentially weaker currency adopted by the majority of Member States (option 2). The decision is up to the politicians.

1.7 BIBLIOGRAPHY

Commission of the European Communities: *General Reports on the Activities of the European Communities* (annually)

Griffiths, A. (1992): *European Community Survey*, Longman, Harlow

Hitiris, T. (1991): *European Community Economics*, second edition, Harvester Wheatsheaf

El-Algraa, A. (1990): *The Economics of the European Community*, third edition, Philip Allan

McDonald, F, Dearden, S. (eds) (1992): *European Economic Integration*, Longman

The five major EC countries

CHAPTER 2

Federal Republic of Germany

Rudi Kurz

2.1 INSTITUTIONAL AND HISTORICAL CONTEXT

2.1.1 Historical overview

Rising from the ruins after World War II, the German economic model has been a success story of full employment, stable prices, the peaceful resolution of social conflicts, a strong currency and international competitiveness. These have been the characteristics of German economic performance throughout most of the post-war years. The German economy is now entering a period of major challenges which will test its inherent stability and capabilities to the full.

Germany's economic success has been attributed to a large extent to the particular economic system that was established after World War II – the *Soziale Marktwirtschaft* (social market economy). It is essential for anyone who wishes to understand the German economic miracle to become acquainted with the major features of this system. Anyone planning to do business in Germany should understand how it works, because not only does it grant basic economic freedoms but also it defines the conditions that apply to the use of private resources in business and the obligations that have to be met. The *Soziale Marktwirtschaft* is intended to be both efficient and humane (W. Eucken). It is an attempt to achieve a balance between market efficiency and social interests (A. Müller-Armack). To adapt this system to changing conditions in the process of economic development is a constant challenge.

The post-war economic development of West Germany may be subdivided into the following three periods:

- *1948–65* A reconstruction period characterised by high growth rates, price stability, the return of full employment and the establishment of a strong position in international trade. Distribution and environmental issues caused little concern.
- *1966–79* A state interventionist period characterised by the Keynesian principle of state-guaranteed full employment and an extension of the welfare state. Deficiencies inherent in the basic ideas and two oil price crises brought this period to an end.
- *1980–90* A period of liberalisation characterised by the withdrawal of the state on all fronts: the policy of full employment was replaced by a policy of long-term growth, government intervention in the market was replaced by deregulation and privatisation and the levelling off of increased expenditure on social security and subsidies.

In the 1990s a new period is beginning which is

characterised by new challenges and which will demand unconventional approaches without ideological restraints. Liberalisation will no longer be adequate as a label for this period – rather it is going to be *perestroika (Umbau)* without the sacrifice of liberal principles. Among the challenges are environmental protection, disarmament and conversion of the defence industry, and aid to East European states and to the Third World. However, in the near future, these international challenges will be subordinated to coping with the problems of German unification.

Unification makes it difficult for anyone to describe the condition and the prospects of the German economy at this moment. While reliable data is available for the former West German states (*Bundesländer*), it will be a considerable time before reliable and comparable data becomes available for the five new (east) German states. For years to come significant differences between East and West Germany are going to prevail. Given these circumstances, it is not yet possible to describe Germany as an integrated entity. Therefore the following text still refers in large parts to the old Federal Republic of Germany (FRG) only – which represents about 90% of the German gross domestic product (GDP). Remarks on the special problems of the new states are to be found throughout the text and in a more general perspective at the end of the chapter (see section 2.6.1).

2.1.2 Major characteristics of the economic system

Constitutional principles

The German constitution – the *Grundgesetz (GG)* of 1949 – does not codify the *Soziale Marktwirtschaft*. It leaves open the possibility of changes in the economic system. However, there are narrow limits to such changes because any economic system has to be compatible with inalienable human rights and the decentralised political structure, i.e. the strong position of states (*Bundesländer*) and the local communities. Private property is guaranteed. Its use has to serve the general welfare of the community. Expropriation and adaptation for social use are possible (Article 15 GG) if this benefits the community and if financial compensation is paid. In Article 20 of the *Grundgesetz* the Federal Republic of Germany is defined as a democratic and social federal state ('*demokratischer und sozialer Bundesstaat*'). This is to emphasise the significance of social justice for the long-term existence of a market economy and to protect the federal structure of the state. The latter is defined by attributing specific functions and sources of revenue to every level of state activity. With regard to the division of labour within the government sector, the principle of subsidiarity (*Subsidiaritätsprinzip*) applies: state and federal involvement occur only when local authorities (*Gemeinden*) are unable to cope. Decentralisation creates co-ordination problems, but experience shows that the advantages of flexibility and autonomy are dominant factors.

Law relating to competition

Competition is based on the freedom to make agreements and to form enterprises. However, both may be restricted to protect consumers or competition itself as an institution. The most important law in this field is the *Gesetz gegen Wettbewerbsbeschränkungen (GWB)*. Its major contents are as follows.

- Cartels and concerted actions by groups of companies are in principle forbidden, with some exemptions defined by the law.
- The conduct of monopolies (*marktbeherrschende Unternehmen*) is controlled in order to prevent them from abusing their market power.
- Large firms are subject to provisions governing mergers. If the cartel authority (*Bundeskartellamt*) rejects a merger, the Minister of Commerce may grant permission if the economic advantages outweigh the disadvantages of restricted competition (e.g. Daimler-Benz/ MBB in 1989). Mergers of European dimension are subject to the EC Merger Guideline of 1990.

In additon to the general laws governing competition, a large number of specific rules (market regulations) for entry into or competition in various markets exist. To mention only a few examples:

- Some industries such as transportation, postal services and telecommunications, public utilities (electricity, gas, water), banking, insurance, and agriculture are partly exempt from the GWB and subject to the control of specific regulatory authorities. Market entry and pricing in these industries are not free from regulation. However, these regulations are changing significantly now as a consequence of the EC single market programme.
- Shops are allowed to open Monday to Friday from 7 a.m. to 6.30 p.m. and on Saturday from 7 a.m. to 2 p.m. (first Saturday of each month until 4 p.m.). After lengthy debate this has been liberalised and shops may now open until 8.30 p.m. every Thursday. A more comprehensive liberalisation is unlikely to take place because unions and small and medium-sized enterprises (SMEs) are opposed to it.
- Craft codes (*Handwerksordnungen*): craftsmen have to have special training and a formal qualification (*Meisterprüfung*).

The numerous codes of practice (partly in guild tradition) are an example of how the German inclination for order can go wrong. Many of these regulations will have to be adapted in order to allow for more (international) competition and to improve the German economic system (regulatory reform).

Financial system

The *Gesetz über die Deutsche Bundesbank* of 1957 rules that the Deutsche Bundesbank is autonomous, i.e. independent from the Federal Government. The Bundesbank is obliged to support the economic policy of the Federal Government only to the extent that it is compatible with the Bundesbank's sole goal: the stabilisation of the price level. By defining minimum reserve standards, changing conditions of refinancing (discount rate) and open-market intervention, the Bundesbank controls the liquidity of banks and the supply of money in circulation. The Bundesbank may provide credit for public budgets only within well defined, narrow limits (to bridge liquidity gaps). Because of the great importance of the banking system, this industry is subject to specific control by a regulatory authority (*Bundesaufsichtsamt für das Kreditwesen*). The FRG is a member of the European Monetary System and hence the Bundesbank is obliged to intervene in order to stabilise exchange rates (within margins of fluctuation of $\pm 2.25\%$). For all other currencies flexible exchange rates apply.

Legal foundations of labour markets

1 The freedom to design individual labour contracts is restricted by labour laws and by the existence of collective agreements between unions and employers (*Tarifverträge*) from which individual labour contracts may deviate only if such deviation is to the advantage of the employee (*Günstigkeitsprinzip*). Laws on labour conflicts (strikes and lock-outs) do not exist and so courts have to participate in resolving such conflicts.

2 No employee who has worked more than six months in a firm may be laid off without good reason. To prevent the circumvention of this rule, labour contracts for a limited period of time may last no longer than 18 months. Temporary workers may not be employed in the same firm for more than six months. In cases of mass lay-offs (more than 10% of a firm's employees), a social plan (*Sozialplan*) has to be negotiated between management and employees. The equivalent of several months' pay has to be awarded to those laid off.

3 The working time of employees is restricted by various legal rules: Sundays and public holidays are in principle free and only work which is in the public interest may be performed (e.g. in hospitals) and, in rare special cases, also for economic reasons (e.g. maintaining continuous production). For juveniles specific restrictions apply (e.g. piecework is not allowed). Women are granted paid holiday of six weeks before and eight weeks after

the birth of a child. Normal working hours may not exceed eight per day. The number of days paid holidays per year must be a minimum of 18. Many of these provisions are of little practical relevance because collective agreements in most cases go far beyond these minimum standards (e.g. as regards working hours per week and paid holidays).

4 Employees are granted extensive rights of co-operation and co-determination. For all enterprises with more than five employees the *Betriebsverfassungsgesetz* of 1972 applies. This law grants employees and their elected representatives *(Betriebsräte)* comprehensive rights of information and consultation (working hours, breaks, workplace design, etc). For large corporations (*AG, GmbH* with more than 2,000 employees) – of which there are about 500 – the *Mitbestimmungsgesetz* of 1976 goes far beyond that. It stipulates that half of the members of the board (*Aufsichtsrat*) shall be elected by the employees. In stalemate situations the vote of the chairman (who is a representative of the capital-owning side) counts twice. This means that we do not have full parity in employees' co-determination.

Social security system

The FRG has built up one of the world's most advanced (and most expensive) social security systems, which has contributed significantly to the avoidance of social conflicts. Its main elements are as follows.

- *Pension fund:* for all employees with an income of less than 4,450 ECU per month membership of the scheme is mandatory. Contributions amount to 17.5% (19.5% in 1994) of gross income and are paid half by employers and half by employees. Individual pensions depend on the amount of contributions made and the general increase in incomes of the active workforce (*Generationenvertrag*). Pensions are index-linked, i.e. they increase according to the level of average net incomes. The average pension of a married couple is about 1,600 ECU per month.

- *Health insurance:* all employees with less than 2,700 ECU monthly income must have health insurance. Contributions are paid half by employers and half by employees and amount to about 13% of gross income. Major efforts have been made by the Federal Government to contain the cost explosion in the health care system (*Gesundheitsstrukturgesetz* of 1992).

- *Unemployment insurance*: all employees have to contribute to the scheme regardless of the level of their income. Contributions amount to 6.5% of gross income (to a maximum of 3,600 ECU per month) and are paid half by employers and half by employees. Based on his or her contributions an employee who becomes unemployed receives up to 68% of his or her last net income (but not more than 1,200 ECU) and contributions for pension fund and health insurance are paid. After one year of unemployment, payments are reduced to a maximum of 58%.

- *Social aid:* this aims at enabling all people to live with dignity even if they are without income. It is paid only if no other source of income is available (e.g. from property or family members). Social aid is paid by the local authorities.

- *Insurance against accidents in the workplace*: employers are obliged to pay for rehabilitation and damages in case of accidents in the workplace. To cover this risk, employers pay contributions to an insurance scheme (*Berufsgenossenschaften*). The rates of contributions depend on the risks in the firms and the employees' incomes.

A controversial debate has arisen over adding a public insurance for the nursing of the old (*Pflegeversicherung*) to the system. In total the firms' additional social costs of labour already amount to more than 80% of wages, i.e. they are the highest in the world. In order to avoid a further increase in this burden, no additional elements are going to be introduced into the social security system without compensating exemptions (e.g. less paid holidays or first days of illness no longer paid).

2.1.3 Participants in policy formation

Parties and their political power

Political development in the FRG has been dominated by three political parties: the *Christlich Demokratische Union (CDU)* and its affiliated party in Bavaria (*Christlich Soziale Union, CSU*), the *Sozialdemokratische Partei Deutschlands (SPD)* and the *Freie Demokratische Partei (FDP)*. CDU/CSU and SPD are *Volksparteien*, trying to address all groups in the electorate and currently both have a potential share of the votes of about 40%. The FDP's following is the upper middle class; as a consequence this party now and again has difficulty in obtaining the minimum 5% of the votes necessary for representation in federal and state parliaments. However, this small party has played an important role because none of the major parties has had an absolute majority and hence they have depended on coalitions with the FDP. In recent years only one party has successfully challenged this structure: the Green Party, which is focusing on environmental problems and peace. It has a potential electorate about the size of the FDP's. Extreme right-wing parties (*NPD, Republikaner*) have had only short-term successes in the past, but have taken advantage of high immigration rates and unemployment for an unexpected revival. The *PDS*, the successor to the communist *SED* which governed the German Democratic Republic (GDR) for forty years, is struggling to become an additional left-wing player in the party system – with little success so far.

The economic policy of the post-war period has been characterised by stability and continuity. Most of the time Conservatives and Liberals set the course. When Social Democrats participated in the Federal Government from 1966 to 1982 there were no radical changes, partly because they had to compromise with their coalition partners (CDU or FDP). This political continuity has greatly benefited the FRG economy. In the Social Democrat–Liberal era, the welfare state was expanded and Keynesian strategies of full employment were applied – with the consequence of an increasing public deficit. Since 1982

when the FDP formed a new coalition with the CDU/CSU ('*Wende*') emphasis has been given to eliminating deficits and to improving conditions for long-term economic growth (supply-oriented economic policy). The government also applies that concept as a guide for the 1990s. However, in the recent economic crisis, Keynesian strategies have been revived.

Major lobby groups and business associations

A large variety of organised groups participate in formulating economic policy employing formal (e.g. hearings) and informal (e.g. financial support and lobbying) methods. Most important are the unions with about nine million members organised in various industries and 7.8 million of them united in the *Deutsche Gewerkschaftsbund (DGB)*. Traditionally, unions have a close relationship to the SPD, however this affinity is declining. Employers organise themselves in industry-specific associations where membership is voluntary. The most important umbrella organisations are the *Bundesverband der Deutschen Industrie (BDI)* and the *Bundesvereinigung der Deutschen Arbeitgeberverbände (BDA)*.

All enterprises are mandatory members of regional chambers of commerce (*Industrie und Handelskammer, Handwerkskammer*). These serve as bodies of self-administration, organise examinations on completion of apprenticeships and for qualification as foremen, give consultation to and educate young entrepreneurs, settle internal industry disputes and undertake public relations work. The umbrella organisations are the *Deutsche Industrie- und Handelstag (DIHT, Bonn)* and the *Deutsche Handwerkskammertag*.

2.2 MAIN ECONOMIC CHARACTERISTICS

2.2.1 Population, labour force, employment

Even before unification the FRG had the largest population of all EC countries (see Table E14).

The new states added about 16 million to the population, so that the total population of Germany is about 81 million. Population density is high but has declined somewhat owing to unification (from 247 inhabitants per square kilometre to about 225). In West Germany the population decreased from 1975 to 1985 by one million and then increased steadily to the level of 64 million. The increase is due mainly to a wave of emigrants with German ancestors from East Europe. Almost 6 million of the (West) German population are foreigners, of whom 1.9 million are in employment.

The age structure of the population is changing significantly. The proportion of older people in relation to the active population (i.e. people 65 and older/people 15–64) in the FRG – as in other European countries – will increase dramatically, from the current 25% level to more than 45% in 2040, and this will cause serious economic and social problems during the coming decades.

The participation rate of the labour force declined from the mid-1950s to the late 1970s by five percentage points. It then started to increase and is now 47.6% (see Table E15). The West German labour force is 29.8 million. About three million of them are self-employed or work in family businesses. The new states added about 8 million people, making a total German labour force of about 38 million. However, too many of these people are currently unemployed.

Labour market problems in (West) Germany began in the mid-1970s after years of full employment (unemployment rate about 1%). They culminated in 1985 with an unemployment rate of 7.1% (see Table E4). Economic growth then made the unemployment rate decrease to less than 5% in the early 1990s. At the end of a decade of economic expansion two million new jobs had been created and yet the number of unemployed people was still almost two million – a much too high level at the beginning of the recession. Added to the West German problems were the mass unemployment in the new states after exposure to competition (see section 2.6.1). Altogether, Germany currently faces a deficit in jobs of about 6 million, i.e. the unemployment rate is actually about 15%.

The resolution of the unemployment problem has been rendered more and more difficult because it is the result of a number of very different factors and deficiencies. Part of the problem is cyclical and will disappear with the next boom. A factor more difficult to quantify is the relative decline in competitiveness of German products in the world market. This may increase further if we find no innovative answers. Job creation in the service sector is difficult because of high labour costs. An increasing proportion of the unemployed are older people who have health problems or people who are without adequate qualifications. As a consequence long-term unemployment has increased, i.e. the number of people who have only little chance of being reintegrated into a normal working life. This in turn is one of the factors which make the social security system more and more costly. Furthermore, there are large regional differences in unemployment rates (from 4% in the south west to about 20% in the east) and these are not disappearing because mobility of labour is limited.

Unemployment is costly. The cost per unemployed person is calculated at 15,000 ECU in total (expenditure plus revenue losses). Multiplied by the official number of 3.5 million unemployed, this is a total economic loss of about 50 billion ECU. Greater emphasis on existing programmes of active labour market policy, including retraining, job creation schemes and wage cost subsidies, could contribute towards reducing these costs. However, in an effort to save money, the federal government is restricting subsidies to the labour market authorities (*Bundesanstalt für Arbeit, Nürnberg*). The combination of unemployment, immigration and the large number of people seeking asylum has contributed to political radicalisation and hostility against foreigners. This is a high price which we have to attribute to our inability to create more jobs.

A sectoral break-down (see Table E16) reveals that the percentage of the West German labour force employed in industry is still very high at about 40%, i.e. the highest proportion among all EC nations. There has been a long-term decline from 44% in 1980 and 49% in 1970. Also declining is the proportion employed in agriculture (now 3.4%). Government employment has expanded significantly but has recently begun to level out at about 15%. An increasing number of people (40% of the labour force) work in the service sector (including trade and transportation). There are hopes that this sector could absorb even more people and thus make a greater contribution to easing unemployment. Within the industry sector, small and medium-sized enterprises (SMEs) with less than 1,000 employees provide 60% of all jobs, large firms (2% of all firms) 40%.

2.2.2 Growth and business cycles

The FRG's gross domestic product (GDP) at current prices is 1,400 billion ECU (1992), excluding the new east German states (see Table E18). The new states add to that an estimated GDP of about 100 billion ECU – half of it originating from transfer payments by the old states. In sum, Germany's GDP accounts for roughly 27% of the EC's GDP. As a consequence of this high proportion, the German business cycle has a crucial impact on other EC economies. Within the EC, the West German per capita GDP is surpassed only by Luxembourg; it is twice as high as Greece or Portugal. However, the per capita GDP of the USA is still considerably higher (see Table E20). As a consequence of unification, per capita GDP in Germany declined significantly. It is now lower than that of Italy, for example.

During the post-war period West Germany faced only three major recessions: a mild one in 1966/67 and two more serious recessions in 1974/75 and 1981/82. The typical pattern of business cycles were growth cycles, i.e. cycles without a decline in real GDP. The 1980s brought continuous expansion at an average annual rate of 2.1% (see Table E19). A fourth recession hit the united Germany in mid-1992. Real GDP growth rates have shown a declining trend over the last 30 years. Declining growth rates do not imply economic decline: in 1989, for example, real GDP increased by 30 billion ECU, i.e. by 3.4%; in the early 1960s this would have been an 8% growth rate. Compared with

the EC average, the German growth performance is about the same; Germany has not been an engine of growth in the recent past but neither has it been retarding economic growth in Europe. Continuous expansion with only minor changes in the growth rates of real GDP (*Wellblechkonjunktur*) during the 1980s does not conform with traditional theories of business cycles. The difference in pattern is related to the change in the principles guiding economic policy. Since the early 1980s the emphasis has been on stimulating long-term growth (supply-oriented policy) rather than on trying to reduce unemployment by means of Keynesian deficit spending. As a consequence there was no spectacular boom and no significant reduction in unemployment. However, the economy had become more robust and was able to absorb shocks such as the stock market crash of 1987.

The period of steady growth came to a sudden end in the early 1990s. First, German unification caused an extraordinary boom in 1990/91 with a real GDP growth rate of 5.1% (1990) – the highest in 20 years. The unification boom was also to the advantage of Germany's European neighbours (especially France) because their exports to Germany increased significantly. This boom ended abruptly in 1992 when the demand-side fireworks were over and old structural problems (international competitiveness) as well as new ones (German unification) became dominant. GDP grew by only 1% in 1992 and is expected to decline by more than 2% in 1993. Germany currently is in the worst recession of the post-war period and negative spill-over effects are visible throughout the EC.

A demand-side analysis of recent years reveals some details of the sudden turnaround in West Germany's economy.

1 Private consumption, which amounts to about 60% of aggregate demand (see Table E21) increased by 75 billion ECU to approximately 640 billion ECU (in real terms) within the five-year period from 1988 to 1992. This stimulus was most favourable for the automobile industry, furniture, tourism and food industries. The increase in consumer expenditure was based on the steady increase in dispos-

able incomes – with an extraordinary increase of 9.9% in 1990. Higher real wages, over-time working and tax reduction contributed to that. The personal savings rate (personal savings divided by disposable income) recovered from its minimum of 12.2% in 1983 to 14.7% in 1990 and has declined since then to 13.8%. In 1992 disposable income grew only 4.2% – which was about the inflation rate – i.e. it stagnated in real terms. As a consequence real consumer demand increased only by 1%. The share of government consumption in aggregate demand peaked in 1981 (20.7%) and then declined continuously by three percentage points within a decade.

2 Gross fixed capital formation (relative to GDP) in West Germany was significantly above the EC average in the 1960s but has only been about level with the average since the early 1970s (see Table E25). In the first half of the 1980s the investment share stagnated. From 1986 on, capital formation, especially investment in equipment provided dynamics for growth (see Table E26). Within six years (1986–92) annual investment in equipment grew by almost 50% in real terms. The major reasons for the investment boom were a high rate of capacity utilisation (up from 88% in 1982 to 99% in 1991) and a significant increase in profits after 1983. In 1992 there was a sharp change in equipment investment which decreased by 2% (in real terms). This reduction is at the core of the current recession – together with the stagnation of consumer demand. Investment in construction is still growing at a rate of 5% as it did in the preceding years. With a decline in long-term interest rates, a pressing housing shortage in the West German states and low housing quality in the new states, this is likely to continue and to stabilise demand.

3 The traditional surplus in the German balance of exports and imports of goods and services was extremely high throughout the 1980s. It peaked in 1989 at 6.4% of GDP (70 billion ECU). Exports grew by almost 30% from 1987 to 1990 (i.e. by 80 billion ECU in real terms). This increase was due mainly to the strong growth of world trade and the competitive prices of German products due to relatively low inflation rates. In the 1990s imports started to soar while exports grew only slightly, i.e. no expansive impetus came from abroad while the demand pull of German unification spread to other countries (see section 2.5.1).

Income distribution: The share of gross labour income in national income is 71.9% (1992). This share has been declining since 1982 – when it was 72.4% – to a low of 70% in 1990. The decline in the labour share resulted from the improving of incomes from profits and assets which more than doubled from 1982 to 1992. In 1991 and 1992 the increase of labour income was higher than that of profits and hence reversed the income distribution slightly. Actually real profits declined in 1991/92 and this was one of the reasons for the end of the investment boom.

Inflation: The German inflation rate has always been much lower than in the other EC states. In fact, until recently, it was only about half the EC average (see Table E27). For a while it even seemed as if inflation had been completely defeated in the FRG. From 1985 to 1988 the consumer price index increased only 1.2%. However, since the end of 1988 the risk of inflation has been revived as a consequence of higher import prices (oil, raw materials), the depreciation of the DM (against the US dollar and the Yen), increases in indirect taxes, fees for government services, sectoral bottlenecks (e.g. in house construction), higher wage increases. These factors together with the demand pull from the new states generated a wave of price 'hikes'. The inflation rate was 3.5% in 1991 and 4% in 1992 for West Germany. If the new states are included, the German inflation rate is about 5% – higher than the EC average and more than 1.5 percentage points above the average of the three most stable EC-countries (violating one of the Maastricht Treaty convergence criteria). The Bundesbank sought to prevent a new price–wage spiral and responded with monetary restraints and higher interest rates – with negative effects on domestic demand and international economic activity.

Prospects for economic growth in Germany over the next few years are gloomy. German economic policy has to deal with an accumulation of different problems:

- the cyclical problem of a recession in the West German economy;

- the structural problem of German unification which will cost billions for many more years, and has to be paid for by consumers and industry in West Germany;
- the long-term problem of a relative decline in international competitiveness of German industry (see section 2.6.3).

Economic growth (real GDP, %)

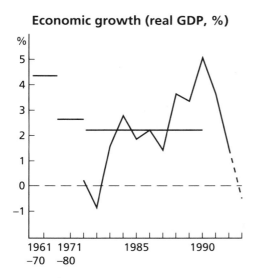

Inflation rate (%)

Unemployment rate (%)

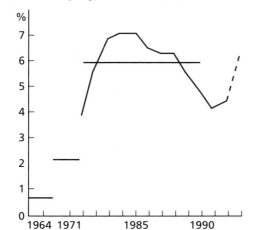

Balance of current accounts (% of GDP)

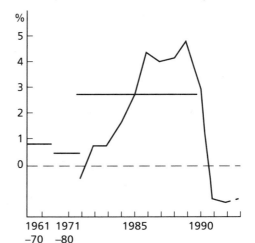

Figure 2.1 Major indicators of German economic performance, 1960–92. Horizontal lines on the graphs show the averages for the periods indicated.

Source: European Economy, Statistical Annexe, Tables E17, E19, E27; *Sachverständigenrat* (1992, Tables 26*, 64*) and author's calculations.

The resolution of these interrelated problems requires both solidarity from all groups of society and political leadership. Currently there is a lack of both and therefore the next couple of years will be hard and crucial ones for Germany. To overcome the recession in the West German economy, demand should increase. However, public budgets are highly indebted and hence government expenditure cannot be boosted. For the same reason there is little room to cut taxes in order to stimulate investment and consumer demand. A significant stimulus from the new states is unlikely for various reasons (see section 2.6.1) although rebuilding infrastructure and industry provides ample opportunities for business activity. All hopes currently focus on lower interest rates, stable construction investment and stimuli from abroad, e.g. from the success of the GATT negotiations or expansion in the USA.

2.2.3 Cost of production and productivity growth

The FRG has the highest labour costs in the world. The total cost of about 20 ECU per hour (1991) splits up into two components: wages are about 11 ECU per hour and additional labour costs such as (half of the) social security contributions, paid holidays, bonuses, etc, which are more than 9 ECU per hour, i.e. roughly 85% of wages. In some sectors, e.g. in banking, it is even 100%. The additional labour costs are much higher than in any other nation. They result from a most elaborate set of social security and fringe benefits. Total labour costs in the UK are a little more than half of those in Germany, in Portugal they are only 20%. Japan has lost its status as a cheap labour economy; its labour costs have climbed to about 75% of those in Germany. As economic crisis persists, firms are now beginning to cut those parts of additional labour costs which are internal to the firm and optional.

The increasing labour costs are in part compensated for by productivity growth, which has been 1.6% per annum over the last decade. Combined with the moderate wage policy of the unions this growth has led to a decline in real unit labour costs (see Table E23). In this respect

German competitiveness has actually improved over recent years – within the EC as well as compared with the USA – and has maintained its position with respect to Japan. The question is whether German productivity, reliability and quality can maintain a competitive advantage large enough to pay for the high additional labour costs in global markets. At least more flexibility in terms of working hours may be necessary. The effective number of working hours (taking into account holidays, illness days and overtime) in the FRG is the lowest in the world: 1,500, i.e. less than 30 hours per week. In the USA it is 1,850, in Japan 2,100. However, the FRG is also among the nations with the fewest number of working hours lost through strikes. Efforts to reverse the trend to shorter weekly working hours are popular now. However, the real challenge is to find innovative solutions for more flexible working hours which allow for a higher utilisation rate of fixed investment.

The acquisition of financial resources, especially venture capital, in the FRG has been burdened with high capital costs caused by various taxes on capital transactions. These taxes were eliminated in 1990/91 (*Finanzmarktförderungsgesetz*). This represents part of the effort to make the FRG a more attractive international financial marketplace and to reduce the discrimination between equity and debt financing. Efforts to implement a more comprehensive taxation of capital incomes caused a massive flight of capital in 1989 (*Quellensteuer*) and again since mid-1991 (*Zinsabschlagsteuer*). This is taking place although the new tax scheme (30% of interest collected by the banks) grants high allowances so that 80% of all savers are not affected. Some estimates say that more than 50 billion ECU, almost half of private households' annual savings, go abroad. Most of the money goes to institutions, affiliated to German banks, operating in Luxembourg which in turn invest in German bonds. European harmonisation of capital income taxation could help to reduce this problem.

Although the cost of electrical power represents only a small fraction of industry's expenditure, a great deal of attention is given to it in political discussion. Commercial users of electrical power in the FRG pay the highest prices in Europe. In France prices are only about two-thirds of those in Germany, and in Denmark they are even lower. Compared with France the disadvantage for German industry is estimated at 8 billion ECU annually. During the last four years the average electricity price for industrial customers in Germany decreased by 3% while it increased in the other EC countries by almost 10%. In some countries industry prices are cross-subsidised and hence private households pay more than in Germany. During the coming years some of the older nuclear power plants will have to go out of service and no consensus has yet been agreed on how to replace them. Prospects for lower energy prices in Germany are not good: environmental considerations (especially the greenhouse effect) demand energy saving and require higher energy prices in order to stimulate saving efforts and investment in energy efficiency. More competitive European energy markets could contribute to mitigate energy price increases.

Other costs of production, e.g. for communication, state bureaucracy, environmental protection are also higher than in competing nations and hence are now subject to reform efforts. However, some costs may increase further, e.g. for transportation (fuel tax, Autobahn duties, road pricing) and for education of the labour force (more private enterprise initiatives requested).

2.2.4 Economic structure

Sectoral structure

The analysis of economic activity by major sectors reveals that manufacturing – most importantly automobiles, chemicals, machine tools and electrical engineering – still has a dominant position. Its share in gross value added is only a little higher than 30% (down from 40% in the 1960s). Construction, mining, energy and water supply have a combined share of less than 8.5% now (13% in the 1960s). Agriculture's share is only 1.5% (5.5% in the 1960s). The share of trade and transportation has been declining slightly (to

15%). The government's share increased until the early 1980s, has declined since then and approaches 10%. The only sector which has expanded its share markedly is the service sector, including banks, insurance and other services. Within 30 years its share has doubled and is now more than 30%. Private households account for 2.5%. In a reduced three-sector perspective we have: agriculture 2%, industry 39%, services 59%. Industry share is the highest in the EC but is lower than the Japanese (see Table E22).

Industry structure, concentration and firm size

The investigations of the *Monopolkommission* (1992) reveal no clear trend towards concentration in German industry. While concentration ratios have increased in some branches, they have either remained unchanged or have declined in others. The most concentrated industries are (market share of the ten largest firms): tobacco (98%), air and space (95%), oil (94%), mining (92%), computers (88%), automobiles (74%), iron and steel (74%), shipbuilding (71%), rubber (62%), and pulp and paper (56%). The number of mergers and acquisitions has increased significantly since 1983 (when the *Bundeskartellamt* registered 586). This is in part interpreted as a reaction to the challenge of the European single market. Small and medium-sized firms (SMEs) still play an important role in the FRG economy and are crucial to its strength and flexibility. Their position is not endangered, although the interdependence between large enterprises and SMEs is increasing, for example as a consequence of lean production and just-in-time policies. In the current economic crisis large firms try to negotiate new agreements with their SME suppliers. SMEs, especially automobile suppliers and machine tools manufacturers, respond with co-operative solutions, e.g. by sharing R&D expenditure.

Regional structure

Based on indicators such as the unemployment rate and GDP growth, there seems to be a north–south divide in the FRG with prosperous regions concentrated in the south (the states of Baden-Württemberg and Bavaria). More recently the debate has ceased, primarily because it has become clear that the south is still in the process of catching up, in terms of per capita income, and some inherent limitations to development for the booming regions in the south have become apparent, such as rocketing real estate prices and rents, traffic congestion, problems with waste disposal, etc. While the regional disparities within the old FRG were small compared with European standards, this changed significantly with the incorporation of the new states. Average income in the new states is only a third of that in West Germany. Environmental damage, unemployment, quality of jobs, etc., all combine to widen an already huge gap in the quality of life between the two regions. In order to avoid large migration to the West, major regional development and restructuring efforts are urgently needed.

2.3 GOVERNMENT INVOLVEMENT IN THE ECONOMY

2.3.1 Government expenditure, taxes and deficits

Government expenditures

Government expenditure, including social security as a share of GDP reached its peak in 1982 (49.7%), then steadily declined to 45.5% in 1989. During the 1980s it was lower than the EC average, although it was higher during the two preceding decades (see Table E28). The decline in government's share is a consequence of the change in political attitudes and of improved economic performance (higher employment) which relieved the social security system. Further reductions in government expenditure can be achieved by means of the reduction in subsidies, e.g. for declining industries (steel, shipbuilding), reduction in military expenditure (still about 25 billion ECU), privatisation and trimming of the social security system. Action in

these fields is even more urgent today because German unification led to an explosion in government expenditure. In 1992 the government share in GDP was more than 50% – higher than it has ever been.

Total government expenditure is 650 billion ECU which includes more than 250 billion ECU of expenditure on the social security system. The federal budget amounts to more than 200 billion ECU. The major items of expenditure are social security (one-third), defence (one-fifth) and interest payments on federal debt (one-tenth). Government subsidies for business activity, according to the official report (*Subventionsbericht*), amount to 50 billion ECU. The most subsidised sectors are agriculture, energy and transportation. Financing the social security system incurs total public expenditure of 350 billion ECU per annum (5,600 ECU per capita); related to GDP (*Sozialleistungsquote*) this is 30% (up from 25% in 1965, peaking at 34% in 1975). Despite this high expenditure, there is poverty in the midst of wealth. In 1990 3.3 million people received social aid (50% more than in 1980) resulting in costs of 17 billion ECU. If all the people receiving less than half the average income are defined as poor, the poverty rate in the (old) FRG is 10% and is even higher for Germany as a whole. In comparison, the official poverty rate in the USA is 13%. The social security system is now widely perceived to be too expensive and there is an intense debate going on regarding how to reduce and reform it.

Taxes

The sum of taxes and compulsory contributions to social security insurances relative to GDP increased significantly during the 1970s and early 1980s. The trend was then reversed and the gap between the FRG and the EC average was becoming smaller. The proportion was 43.7% (taxes only 25.1%) in 1992, much higher than in the UK (33%) but still lower than in Denmark (49%). The most important government sources of revenue are income taxes (about 50% of all tax revenues) and value added taxes (almost 30%). All tax revenues are distributed to federal, state or local level in a complicated scheme for revenue sharing formulated in the constitution and there are additional compensation payments between the public budgets (*Finanzausgleich*).

It has often been stated that taxation of profits in Germany is 70% of pre-tax profit and hence higher than in all competing nations. This rate is calculated from high (personal or corporate) income tax rates (up to 53% until recently) combined with taxes which are not profit-related, such as local trade tax on business capital (*Gewerbekapitalsteuer*) and property tax (*Vermögensteuer*). The figure of 70% is misleading, however, because the calculation starts only with taxable profits and does not account for tax allowances which enable firms in Germany to reduce significantly the amount of 'profit' on which they are finally taxed. Moreover, the level of subsidies and the infrastructure provided by government should be included in any international comparison to arrive at a balanced judgement.

A major tax reform which was implemented in three phases from 1986 to 1990 resulted in net tax relief of almost 25 billion ECU. The most important part of this reform was a flattening in the curve of income tax progression. This progression had arisen, because, as a consequence of inflation, medium-level incomes had been growing and entering the higher tax brackets over the years. This 'hidden progression' had reduced incentives to work (especially for qualified persons) and encouraged the 'black economy'. The tax reform reduced the top marginal rate from 56% to 53% for annual taxable income of 60,000 ECU (120,000 ECU for married couples) and over. The corporate income tax rate on retained profits was lowered from 56% to 50% (the rate for distributed profits remained 36%). The tax allowances reduced or abolished to compensate in part for the cost of the tax reforms included provision for R&D, investment in energy saving and residential building.

In an effort to make investment in Germany more attractive, part of a more comprehensive programme for the reform of corporate taxation was passed in mid-1993 (*Standortsicherungsgesetz*). The top marginal rate for income from business activity will be reduced to 47% (from 53%), the corporate income tax rate for retained profits is going to be 45% (instead of 50%), and the burden on distributed profits is reduced to 30% (36%). However, this reform is to be roughly revenue-neutral and hence depreciation provisions will be less favourable in the future to compensate.

In order to finance German unification, taxes (e.g. personal income tax, mineral oil tax, value-added tax, insurance tax) and contributions to social insurances have been increased. Income taxation has been increased temporarily in 1991/92 by a 7.5% surtax (*Solidaritätszuschlag*). As of 1995 the *Solidaritätszuschlag* will be reintroduced – for an indefinite period. Value-added tax was increased to 15% (reduced rate 7%) as of 1 January 1993.

Public debt

Public debt – federal, state and local – amounted to 580 billion ECU at the end of 1991 (45% of GDP). This includes off-budget institutions like the German Unity Fund (*Fonds Deutsche Einheit*) but not public enterprises like *Treuhand-anstalt*, *Bundesbahn* and *Bundespost* (an additional debt of 100 billion ECU). In 1994 total public debt will surpass 1,000 billion ECU, i.e. 12,500 ECU per capita and 70% of GDP – well above the 60% level formulated in the Maastricht Treaty. The federal government is responsible for half of the public-sector debt; the rest has been incurred at state and local levels and by public off-budget institutions. A significant part of the public debt (110 billion ECU) is foreign debt and hence directs interest payments of about 8 billion ECU abroad annually. Total interest payments on government debt are 35 billion ECU per annum. Public net borrowing (including social security insurances) as a proportion of GDP has declined from a maximum of 5.6% in 1975 to zero in 1989 (see Table E29). The efforts at budget consolidation had succeeded but German unity brought a new wave of public deficits. The deficit in all public budgets has been more than 50 billion ECU each year from 1990 to 1992. It will be significantly higher in 1993 and in 1994 will absorb almost all domestic saving. Net borrowing relative to GDP surpassed the critical 3% level – another Maastricht convergence criterion. As a consequence of mounting debt, interest payments take up an increasing part of the public budget (see Figure 2.2) and will increase further to about 15%.

In the face of mounting economic troubles over the last few years, fiscal policy has undergone several changes in emphasis. In a first phase (1989/90) federal government failed totally to recognise the problems. Then an increase in public debt – mainly by off-budget institutions – was tolerated in order to defend the 'no problem' – philosophy. When increasing public debt finally became an obstacle to lower interest rates and a threat to international confidence in the German mark, federal government

had to admit that sacrifices were neccessary and steps were taken to increase revenues. Now that we are approaching the limits of taxation, another shift in emphasis is taking place. A radical reduction in government activity and expenditure – primarily in social security – is now at the top of the agenda .

2.3.2 Industrial and technology policy

Total R&D spending in West Germany is about 36 billion ECU (1991), i.e. 2.6% of GDP, down from 2.9% in 1989. The rate is now significantly lower than in Japan (3.0%) and the USA (2.8%). The relative decline is primarily due to a stagnation in private R&D spending. About 60% of total R&D spending is privately financed (up from 55.4% in 1981). The public share is divided between federal government (21%) and the eleven states (14%). The federal government share is not concentrated in one department but is at the disposal of various departments: the Federal Ministry of Research and Technology (BMFT) accounts for more than half of federal government R&D spending, followed by the Ministries of Defence (about one-fifth), Education and Commerce with less than 10% each. In real terms the BMFT budget has shown no significant increase in the last eight years.

A large part (about 20%) of the federal government's R&D spending goes into basic research (for example to the *Max-Planck-Gesellschaft, Fraunhofer-Gesellschaft, Deutsche Forschungsgemeinschaft*). Another 20% is devoted to military research. The rest is spread widely over a variety of areas summarised under the headings 'preventive research' and 'key technologies': air and space technologies, energy research and technology (primarily nuclear power), information technology (including production engineering), environmental and safety research, research on new materials and biotechnology. Only weak elements of industrial policy, i.e. targeting of specific technologies or industries, can be identified based on these figures (for example, air and space and nuclear technologies).

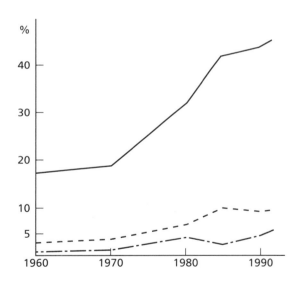

—— Government debt (federal,state,local) as proportion of GDP

----- Government budget deficits as proportion of GDP

—·— Government interest expenditure as share of revenues

Figure 2.2 Public debt, interest payments and budget deficits.

Source: Sachverständigenrat (1992, Tables 41*, 44*) and author's calculations.

To support and stimulate innovation in small and medium-sized enterprises the Federal Department of Commerce (*BMWi*) provided 1.6 billion ECU between 1979 and 1987 to subsidise employment of R&D personnel (*Personalkostenzuschuß-Programm*). Owing to a shift in emphasis, that programme has not been retained. Instead the federal government is relying primarily on more favourable general conditions for innovation in SMEs. Among these are:

- The income tax reform, in three phases 1986/1988/1990, brought significant tax reductions for nine out of ten SMEs (which are unincorporated).
- Universities and colleges are given more freedom and incentives to co-operate with SMEs.
- SMEs benefit from the reduction of regulations (market entry) and bureaucracy costs.
- In public procurement there will be a greater insistence on SME-subcontractors, for example, in the Airbus programme or in space projects.
- Assistance by consultants and access to technological information for SMEs has been improved and subsidised.

The federal government emphasises that SMEs receive a greater share of public funds (28%) in comparison with their share of total private enterprise R&D expenditure (15–20%).

Competition policy has been adapted in various ways to prevent it from becoming an obstacle to innovation. Joint R&D ventures will only in rare cases result in anti-trust problems. The Daimler-Benz/MBB deal was strongly opposed by the *Bundeskartellamt*, but was approved by the Minister of Commerce who has the final decision. Recently, large West German corporations have been taking over former state-guaranteed monopolies in East Germany, thus protecting their position against new competitors.

The expansion of industries is hampered by numerous regulations. Progress in deregulation or regulatory reform is slow in Germany. Much of the deregulation which has been and will be enacted is due to the EC 1992 internal market programme. Rate-setting in surface transportation was abandoned (in 1989) and was replaced by reference rates. But control of market entry (concessions) still exists. As a precondition for deregulation in the haulage industry the German government requests the harmonisation of taxes, safety and social standards in order to provide a level playing field for competition with the Netherlands, Italy and other EC countries. The state-owned railways (*Deutsche Bundesbahn, Deutsche Reichsbahn*) are going to be re-organised into three sectors (passenger transportation, freight transportation, network) and will be privatised step by step. Their debt of about 25 billion ECU will be taken over by the federal government. In telecommunications a major step has been taken in opening up markets for private investors. The *Deutsche Bundespost* has been divided into three public enterprises (telecommunication, postal services, banking services) and will be privatised. A holding company dominated by the federal government is going to control the three enterprises. Market entry has been liberalised in telecommunication equipment, value-added services (e.g. data transmission), satellite networks and mobile radio transmission. More liberal regulations for field experiments in biotechnology have been passed in order to prevent this key industry being driven abroad.

In general there is still a decisive rejection of industrial policy approaches in official government and lobby statements. However, as economic crises endanger even industries like automobiles and machine tools, government becomes more inclined 'to help'. The idea of state intervention to save 'industrial cores' in the new states is now widely accepted.

2.4 FINANCIAL SYSTEM

2.4.1 Structure of financial institutions

The banking system

A characteristic of the German banking and financial systems is the dominating role of commercial banks which, unlike the specialised banks in other countries, engage in all kinds of bank business: short-term and long-term deposits, short-term and long-term credits, issue of and trade in bonds and stocks. In addition most banks engage in insurance, building-society and real estate activities. This system has advantages for the customer: many firms rely on only one bank (*Hausbank*). However, it also causes problems because of the concentration of information and economic power. Once again there is a revival of the debate on restricting the banks' share of stocks of industrial firms and their participation on the boards of competing firms. The close interrelationship between banks and industry also has some drawbacks regarding the development of financial markets, e.g. a very narrow stock market, and little information for the public on firms' activities.

The German banking system, with a total business volume of about 3 trillion ECU (sum of balance sheet), consists of different bank groups focusing on different kinds of business and customers. The three large banks (*Deutsche Bank, Dresdner Bank, Commerzbank*) have a share of 9%, subsidiaries of foreign banks a share of less than 2%; regional savings banks and savings and loan associations and their institutions (*Girozentralen, DG-Bank*) have a dominant position with about half of the business volume and a large network of branch offices.

Money and capital markets

About 2,100 stock corporations exist but only 500 of them are quoted on the stock market. In addition, about 500 foreign stocks are traded in German stock markets. There are eight exchange centres, the main one being Frankfurt/Main. The role of stock markets in business financing has traditionally been relatively minor, but the volume of new issues has steadily increased over the last few years. The exchange turnover in the FRG is the second highest in Europe, next to the UK. The major issuers of bonds are (large) banks and the government, primarily the federal government. This is the most common method by which banks refinance the credits they grant to business and the public sector.

The structure of corporate financing

On average firms finance about 20% of their activities from their own capital resources, 60% by credits and 20% through reserves, especially for firms' pension funds. Credits are primarily short term with a large share of credits granted by suppliers. Capital market credits play only a minor role. In the early 1980s there was an intensive debate about the declining capital resources of firms relative to the sum of the balance sheet. As a consequence, it was asserted that firms would be unable to invest in new ventures which typically involve high risks and for which banks were reluctant to provide financing. Hence, the low capital endowment of enterprises was identified as a major obstacle to innovation and growth. Since the mid-1980s, with profits higher, the capital resources of firms have improved and the debate has lost its momentum. The average share of capital resources, relative to the sum of the balance sheet, is about 20%; in large stock companies the share is above average and there is a great variation between industries. Above average are chemicals, automobiles, electrical engineering; below average textiles, steel, retail trade.

Trends and perspectives

The universal bank concept has been extended to create 'Allfinanz', the merging of banking and insurance activities. New financial superpowers are emerging but there is also fresh competition between giants like Deutsche Bank and Allianz which have up till now operated in separate markets. Control of these superpowers will also come from foreign competitors who may extend their activity into the FRG when banking and insurance markets are liberalised within the EC. In 1994 a new law against insider trading (*2. Finanzmarktförderungsgesetz*) is due to be passed creating a new institution for controlling capital market transactions and imposing high fines on misuse of insider information.

2.4.2 Money supply, interest rates, exchange rates

In the 1970s the Bundesbank's monetary policy moved towards monetarism, although this position never became totally dominant as it did at times in the USA and the UK. From 1974 on, the Bundesbank formulated a target for the expansion of the quantity of money (M3). This intermediate goal is now announced every year in December for the following year. In 1986 and in the subsequent two years, the Bundesbank did not meet its monetary target. M3 growth overshot the target. After the crash of 1987, the Bundesbank, like most other central banks, provided additional liquidity to the banking system and low interest rates in order to avoid a spill-over of the crisis. Then, in mid-1988, the Bundesbank changed its course and returned to a more restrictive policy by significantly increasing central bank interest rates (e.g. discount rate from 3% to 6%). As a consequence the level of interest rates rose generally: consumer credits were charged almost 13%, housing loans were up to almost 10%. Higher interest rates in the FRG were also a necessary reaction to high interest rates in the USA, which attracted considerable amounts of German capital, and hence contributed to a revaluation of the US dollar. This, however, was not sufficient to reduce the imbalances in both the German and the US trade balance. The Bundesbank's attempts to reduce excessive liquidity in the banking system beginning in mid-1988 have been only moderately successful. The monetary target for 1989 was an M3 growth rate of 5%; for 1990 it was 4–6%, which was met.

The Bundesbank has always made it clear that it will not tolerate creeping inflation as a side-effect of the German economic unification process. However, growth of M3 was out of control in 1992 and overshot the 3.5–5.5% target considerably. Only in early 1993 did M3 growth decrease and this gave the Bundesbank the chance to lower interest rates.

Compared to international standards, interest rates in the FRG used to be low (see Tables E30, E31). German unification changed this significantly because of high domestic capital demand,

inflationary pressure and a deficit in the balance of payments. The discount rate reached an all-time record level of 8.75% in July 1992. Under pressure of recession in Germany and abroad, the Bundesbank had only lowered it to 6.75% by July 1993 – much too reluctantly as critics say. What the Bundesbank wants to demonstrate is its determination to defend price stability. The Bundesbank perceives trust in the DM as the major reason for low long-term interest rates (see Figure 2.3), which in real terms are only about 2% now.

Figure 2.3 Interest rates , 1980–93.

Source: European Economy Statistical Annexe, Table E27; *Sachverständigenrat* (1992, Table 6*) ; Deutsche Bundesbank (*Monthly Reports*, Tables VI.5, VII.6).

Long-term rates are more important for investment decisions than the short-term rates which the Bundesbank could try to drive further down. The insistence on price stability has also historic roots (Weimar experience) and is going to be one of the German contributions to the emerging European Economic and Monetary Union.

Over the last 20 years the DM has been revalued against almost all other currencies with the exceptions of the Yen and the Swiss Franc. Compared with the currencies of the 18 most important industrial nations, the DM has been revalued by about 20% over the last eight years (see *Monthly Reports* of the Bundesbank, Table X.10). The exchange rate of the DM within the European Monetary System remained almost unchanged until 1992. This was primarily due to the success achieved by the other EC countries in coping with inflation. The turmoil in the EMS in 1992 resulted in a revaluation of the DM. The US dollar-DM exchange rate had been declining throughout the 1970s, then recovered in the early 1980s (due to *Reaganomics*) and peaked in 1985. Since then the devaluation trend has been dominant, with significant fluctuations. By the end of 1992 the US dollar had been devalued against the DM by about 50% within eight years. This was good for German tourists but forced hard decisions on exporters, especially the automobile industry (e.g. BMW and Mercedes-Benz building plants in the USA).

In mid-1993 the DM lost some of its credit, and its role as a stabilising force within the EMS has become uncertain. Some European currencies and the US dollar were revalued against the DM. Moreover, the weakness of the DM provided central banks in France, the Netherlands and Belgium with the chance to take the lead in decreasing discount rates – and the Bundesbank followed. In this new arrangement, price stability is no longer forced on other countries by the Bundesbank, but they have more responsibility themselves.

Germany's international reserves amount to 70 billion ECU (net), higher than that of Japan or the USA. 60% are in foreign currencies, primarily US dollars. Gold reserves, valued at the low original purchasing costs, amount to 6.8 billion ECU, their market value is about 25 billion ECU. The DM's role as an international reserve currency increased considerably during the 1980s. Among the international reserve currencies the DM is second to the US dollar with a share of about 20%.

2.5 INTERNATIONAL RELATIONS

2.5.1 Foreign trade by industry and country

The FRG's foreign trade volume (exports and imports) is about 9% of the world trade (France and UK 5.5% each). From 1958 to 1991 the share of German exports to EC countries increased from 37.9% to 53.8% (see Tables E32, E33). The share of exports to all other regions decreased with the exception of Japan. 54.5% of German imports came from EC countries in 1991. The proportion from all other regions, with the exception of Japan, declined; for example, the imports from developing countries from 23.9% to 10.8%. Germany's major trading partner is France (exports of 43 billion ECU and imports of 38 billion ECU). France is followed by Italy and the Netherlands on the export as well as on the import side. Despite Germany's strong export position, no EC nation receives more than a quarter of its imports from Germany (e.g. the Netherlands 23.5%, France 20.7%). The countries most dependent on German imports are Austria and Switzerland. The FRG shows a trade deficit with only a few countries, such as Japan (11 billion ECU), the Netherlands (3.4 billion ECU) and the developing countries (4.5 billion ECU). Eastern Europe, until recently, had only a share of less than 5% in the FRG's foreign trade. The trade volume may increase significantly in the future; so far the euphoria caused by the unexpected transformation to market economies in Eastern Europe has not been borne out in business records.

Exports are concentrated in four sectors: automobile industry (17%), machinery (15%), chemicals (13%) and electrical and electronic engineering (12%). Imports are less concentrated: chemicals amount to 9% of imports, electrical and electronic engineering to 10%, textiles to

9%, automobiles to 11%, oil, gas and petroleum products to 8%, agricultural products to 5% and food to 6%.

An increasing share of exports is in technology-intensive goods. Germany's share in world trade of technology-intensive goods was 18% in 1991 (USA 18%, Japan 20%). Industries like textiles and leather are losing market shares to international competitors. But even traditionally strong industries like automobiles and machine tools feel increasing pressure from foreign competitors and hence are more inclined to support (European) protectionist measures. Existing protectionism (especially in coalmining, steel, agriculture, food, textile) cost the FRG billions of DM and thousands of jobs. Protectionism does not pay off, even in terms of jobs. However, well-organised special-interest groups block any moves to more rapid structural change.

2.5.2 Balance of payments

From 1982 to 1991 the current balance was in permanent surplus reaching a peak in 1989 at almost 55 billion ECU, i.e. 4.9% of GDP, and was still 38 billion ECU in 1990 for united Germany (see Table E34). The surpluses resulted exclusively from the surpluses in the trade balance (68 billion ECU in 1989). No significant surpluses occurred in the service balance primarily because Germans spent about 15 billion ECU per year as tourists abroad. The balance of unrequited transfers (transfers by foreign workers and payments for international organisations and grants) showed significant deficits. Related to the surpluses in the current balance during the 1980s were large exports of capital, e.g. 68 billion ECU in 1989.

German unification changed the proportions in the German balance of payments significantly. In 1990 imports increased by more than 10% and in 1991 by 16%. At the same time growth rates for exports were 3% and 0.5% respectively. Hence the high surplus in the trade balance evaporated. In addition the service balance

became negative because of increasing tourism (20 billion ECU deficit in 1992) and lower net capital incomes from abroad. As a consequence the balance of payments has been in deficit since 1991. The deficit is about 15 billion ECU (1% of GDP). Within a period of only three years, Germany changed from a net capital exporting nation to a capital importing nation (68 billion ECU capital export in 1989, 53 billion ECU capital import in 1992). Germany now depends much more on the trust of international investors and is more vulnerable to shifts of international capital flows.

German direct investment abroad increased to almost 19 billion ECU in 1990 and was more than 50 billion ECU over the three-year period 1990–92. Foreign direct investment in Germany was only 8 billion ECU during that period. These figures have been interpreted as flight of capital and have raised concerns about the attraction of the FRG to investors. However, much of the German direct investment abroad complements increased exports. It is marketing- and sales-oriented rather than production-oriented. In total, German direct investment abroad at the end of 1992 amounted to about 125 billion ECU, the largest part of it (about 40%) in the USA.

2.6 SPECIAL ISSUES

2.6.1 German unification: costs and consequences

The single most important challenge which Germany is currently facing is the integration of the east German states. German integration is part of the historic transformation in Eastern Europe, especially in the Soviet Union, and hence part of the integration of a larger Europe. From the peaceful revolution in the GDR in autumn 1989, this process accelerated to a breath-taking speed. After opening the border and the wall in Berlin, the next important step was the currency union which came into being on 1 July 1990. The first problem was choosing a proper conversion rate for Mark into DM which would safeguard people's assets and income without ruining the competitiveness of the East German economy (wages, interest on debt). The compromise solution was as follows: -

- Wages 1:1. Average wages were 1,200 Mark per month (West Germany 3,500 DM per month) and productivity was 30–40% of that in the old West German states.
- Pensions 1:1. As the average pension in the GDR would have been 380 DM additional provisions were necessary here.
- Bank deposits and debt 1 DM: 2 M, except for an amount of 4,000 M per capita which was exchanged 1:1.

As of 3 October 1990, the GDR ceased to exist. The East German states joined the FRG in accordance with Article 23 of the Grundgesetz. If the economic integration process is successful, Germany's position as an economic superpower will be significantly reinforced, maybe by 20%. However, in order to make German integration an economic success story, a large number of difficult problems have to be resolved during the next few years.

First of all, private property rights have to be restored in order to stimulate investment and to attract West German and foreign capital. Most of the land, the buildings and the firms (*Kombinate, Landwirtschaftliche Produktionsgenossenschaften*) were public or social property and have to be privatised. All private property which was expropriated after 1949 is to be returned to the former owners if they claim it. Only in special cases will this restitution be replaced by financial compensation. This procedure considerably delays and blocks investment, especially because an efficient administration and jurisdiction are only just emerging. In early 1993 only 15% of the more than 2 million restitution claims had been settled. The state enterprises which made up 90% of the economic activity of the former GDR have been converted into a huge public institution, the *Treuhandanstalt (THA)*, which is organising their privatisation. The THA should not give priority to first redeveloping firms but rather leave this task to private investors. However, this principle has not

worked well because most firms were in a disastrous condition and attracted no private investors. Therefore, in many cases privatisation was almost identical to complete shutdown. The consequence of this policy was that within a very short time most of East German industry disappeared. Only very recently, under the pressure of increasing mass-unemployment, was the principle of privatisation changed and the federal government now intends to save 'industrial cores' in the new states. As of February 1993 more than 11,000 THA-firms with 1.5 million jobs have been sold. The THA is still responsible for 1,250 firms and 240,000 employees. THA activity is due to end in 1994. Remaining firms will then be reorganised into holdings with more entrepreneurial freedom of decision but continuing high subsidies. The remaining THA debt will be taken over by the federal government (*Erblastenfonds*).

The creation of new firms has been successful only in some sectors like house construction, handicraft and services. A revival of entrepreneurial 'animal spirits' (J. M. Keynes) in the new states needs time, education and capital. In addition, superior competition from the West is a severe barrier to entry for start-ups.

Price reform has made progress but will continue. All subsidies, for example for housing, energy and transportation have to be abolished or reduced in order to reach realistic, i.e. cost-oriented, prices and to end shortages (sellers' markets). Consumer prices increased by more than 20% in the new states in 1991, primarily because of higher rents and energy prices. During 1992 the inflation rate dropped to 8%. Excluding rents and energy prices, the inflation rate is no longer higher than in West Germany. The high inflation rates in 1991 and 1992 cut incomes in real terms and had negative consequences for the negotiations on wage increases and the amount of government subsidies. However, in the area of price changes the worst seems to be over.

Unemployment will be the single most important problem for many years. Most products and production technologies in the GDR economy were not competitive in the international market in which firms had to survive from one day to the next. Most firms had no chance of coping with this challenge, particularly given a management which had no idea of what a market economy was all about and consumer preferences turning radically towards Western products. In addition, East European markets broke down with the dissolution of the Soviet Union. Shortly after unification, unemployment in the new states began to increase dramatically and was 1.2 million in early 1993 (15%). However, this number tells less than half the truth. The number of people in short-time work, retraining, job creation schemes, early pension programmes, etc. amounted to 1.6 million. About 500,000 people living in the new states commute to the West. In fact the unemployment rate is now more than one-third and in some regions is close to 50%. While GDP in the new states was increasing by 6.8% in 1992 (growth rate for 1993 is estimated at 4%), industrial production was still decreasing. Only about 750,000 of the former 3.3 million industrial jobs are left now, one third of them in THA-firms. To overcome the disastrous labour market situation:

- **It is necessary** to continue direct and indirect subsidisation of jobs in the new states (wage subsidies, active labour market policy, employment guarantees in THA-firms). A special instrument to keep unemployment rates down are *Beschäftigungsgesellschaften* (employment companies) which provide jobs and practical training, e.g. cleaning up industrial sites or renovating buildings. They are highly subsidised by the labour administration. Not only does it pay for most of the wage costs, but it also participates in operation and equipment costs.
- **It is necessary** to increase labour productivity which was only one-third of the West German level in 1991 and is currently about 40%. Costs per labour unit are almost twice the West German. Therefore, wage increases have to be moderate and more capital investment to modernise industry and infrastructure is necessary. Significant tax incentives have been established in order to attract private inves-

tors. The moderate success of these programmes will further decline because of overcapacity in the West.
- **It is necessary** to retrain and equip with qualifications the labour force on a large scale, beginning at the shop floor and extending right up to top management. This is not possible without government involvement and government support for private initiatives.

German unification has caused huge deficits in public budgets. For many years to come transfer payments from West to East Germany will amount to more than 50 billion ECU annually (2% of the West German GDP). When this dimension of the unification challenge was finally acknowledged by the federal government in 1992, it was clear that debt financing could not be the solution but taxes had to be increased and government expenditure in the West had to be cut. The only controversy in the talks on a *Solidaritätspakt* (solidarity agreement) is now the burden sharing. The German Unity Fund, which raised 68 billion ECU from the (old) FRG states and the capital market was not sufficient to cope with the problems nor did the programme '*Aufschwung Ost*' provide enough stimulus. Estimates state that 500 billion ECU are required to rebuild the East German rail, road, and telecommunications systems. To raise such amounts of money in an acceptable period of time, it is necessary to delegate some of these traditional government tasks to private investors.

The GDR regime left behind an environmental disaster of huge and not yet fully explored proportions. Among the consequences of this disaster are the following:

- the need for immediate closure of some industrial plants (because of highly toxic or dangerous waste products, e.g. in the chemical industry and nuclear power plants);
- the need for investment in end-of-pipe technologies, such as scrubbers for brown coal power plants and purification plants for drinking water;
- the urgent need to clean up hazardous waste dumps, which over the years have also provided a cheap method of getting rid of West

German hazardous waste. About 60,000 contaminated sites have been identified and await treatment. Most of the costs – estimated at 100–300 billion ECU – will have to be covered by public funds.

A preliminary evaluation of the experience with German integration teaches some lessons which might be valuable beyond the German case of transforming a planned socialist economy into a capitalist market economy.

- Hopes for a relatively painless spontaneous transformation have been destroyed. Even in optimistic scenarios (6% average annual growth of real GDP in the new states) it will take 25–30 years to catch up with West German incomes. The importance of institutions, infrastructure and attitudes which need considerable time to change has become very clear. Their adaptation takes much longer, is more costly and causes much more pain than most of us expected.
- Capital stock, infrastructure and the environment are in a much worse condition than the official statistics suggested and than in part has been believed in the West. Therefore, there is no valuable public property substance that can be given to the people in order to make the new competitive private property environment more attractive to them.
- Job losses are much higher than expected because of high 'hidden umemployment' (unemployment on the job), the superiority and over-capacities of the capitalist world's industries. Only flexible exchange rates (devaluation) or flexible wages could provide protection. Neither option was available in the German case – the latter because low wages would induce a migration wave to West Germany.
- Government has to play an important role in the transformation process. Most importantly, it has to define credible transformation goals and steps towards those goals and it has to support industrial restructuring. It is necessary to privatise and to break up the large enterprises in order to establish a new middle class. But many of the new firms will run at a much

smaller size and with few employees (niche markets). Therefore, additional investors have to be attracted from outside (e.g. by general subsidies on investment) and some core industries will have to be subsidised until they approach world-market standards.

In conclusion, system transformation is much more complicated and costly than expected for the countries under transformation – and it does not leave the 'rest of the world' unaffected but causes structural change there too (e.g. conversion of the military-industrial complex, new international division of labour). It is important not to underestimate the costs of transformation because unfulfilled promises are a support for reactionary forces.

While the FRG may successfully take care of the former GDR, it would be overstreched if it also had to take care of the rest of Eastern Europe. Germany's aid for Russia amounted to 40 billion ECU from 1989 to 1993 (e.g. for house construction for returning troops, export guarantees) – debt relief as negotiated in the 'Paris Club' not included (another 4 billion ECU). Germany is the largest creditor of Russia (about 50% of all foreign debt, followed by the USA with about 20%). The EC and other OECD countries should increase their support for the transformation in East Europe because this will prevent a revival of the old political forces and contribute to saving a lot of money in defence expenditure (peace dividend). Currently most Western nations are too much pre-occupied with their own problems and pay too little attention to the explosive situation in the former Soviet Union. The Bank for Economic Recovery and Development in Eastern Europe is a first step in forming a strategy like the Marshall Plan.

2.6.2 The ecological challenge: towards sustainable development

Environmental policy has been an important issue with considerable impact on the German economy for more than 20 years. During this period quite a number of acute ecological problems have been resolved. Pollution of rivers and lakes has been reduced, air quality improved, toxic substances are handled with more care. The number and extent of environmental regulations have increased, for example, on emission control, waste water, chemicals, noise, biotechnology, but little has been done to minimise costs by applying economic instruments which are less restrictive to innovation than the command-and-control approach. German industry spends more than 10 billion ECU each year, about 120 billion ECU during the last 20 years, on environment protection. However, even in traditional fields of environment policy a lot of problems are still unresolved. NO_x emissions have not been reduced, in summer ozone concentration exceeds the standards, millions of Germans are drinking water which does not comply with EC-standards, most toxic dumps remain to be redeveloped. Waste reduction has been delayed for years. Now there is a shortage of suitable dumps and new incineration plants have been wrecked because of residents' resistance. Hence (illegal) waste exports occur almost out of necessity. Nature is on the retreat: 120 hectares are lost each day to land-settlement, woodlands continue to die (*Waldsterben*) and the list of endangered species grows longer.

The global challenges of climate change and depletion of the ozone layer add a new dimension to environmental policy not only in Germany. As the UNCED conference in Rio 1992 made clear, all highly industrialised countries will have to change their patterns of production and consumption and have to find a path for sustainable development. With respect to the Rio conference the German government formulated the goal to reduce CO_2 emissions by 25–30% before 2005 (base 1987). While official government statements still stick to that goal, no active policy measures have been implemented so far. The link between GDP and CO_2 emissions (see Figure 2.4) is still too strong and the increase in energy efficiency too slow. Coping with the economic crisis seems to be more important today. In consumers' and voters' opinions, environmental issues no longer have the highest priori-

ty. Enterprises are still in the process of catching up with the environmental consciousness of consumers and with government regulations. However, more and more enterprises accept the responsibility for their products from cradle to grave and have restructured the production process and the product portfolio.

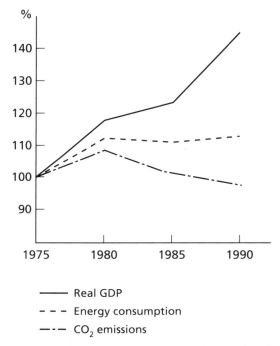

Figure 2.4 GDP, energy consumption and carbon-dioxide emissions (1975 = 100).

Source: Sachverständigenrat (1992, Tables 43*, 89*, 91*) and author's calculations.

In conclusion, German environmental policy has neither resolved the problems which high domestic burdens demand nor has it adequately responded to global challenges. It is often argued that a more consequent German environmental policy would endanger the international competitiveness of German industry. Although this argument is hard to prove, the implementation of German environmental policy would be made easier if international solutions, e.g. an EC energy tax, provided a level playing field.

2.6.3 International competitiveness: is Germany's attraction as a business location declining?

Years of high surpluses in the trade balance suggested that the international competitiveness of Germany was excellent. Now, with the additional burden of the new states and new competitors in Eastern Europe, no one can neglect the challenge any longer. Statistical evidence, e.g. on direct investment, tells only part of the truth. Confidence is even worse and most firms – even SMEs – have plans for shifting some of their activity abroad. Germany is a country where production is expensive and there is little chance to change this fundamentally. Therefore, Germany must focus on reinforcing its strengths. The most important strengths of the German economic system may be summarised in the following three points:

- a qualified labour force at all levels of employment (from the shop floor to the research laboratory) with a unique work ethic and know-how;
- a highly developed infrastructure making mobility, communication and distribution easy;
- social, political, and monetary stability reducing the uncertainty in calculating the return on investments.

The main problems of the German economic system seem to be:

- rigid institutions defended by well-organised interest groups (in part, the other side of the stability coin);
- high costs of labour, social security, energy, environmental protection and high taxes, in sum, costs which are higher than those justified by the advantages of the system. (When the proportion of labour costs is 10:1, e.g. compared with Poland, it is hard to justify this);
- diseconomies resulting from agglomeration (real estate and housing costs, traffic congestion, shortage of landfills).

All of the problems are closely related to the strengths of the system. This sounds paradoxical,

but is due to the German mentality of overdoing things, the tendency to become too sophisticated, too perfect. The most severe aspect of declining German competitiveness is the vulnerability of our specific product portfolio. Middle-technology goods are increasingly provided by newly industrialised countries in a comparable quality but less expensively. Know-how in these markets has become an international public good and individual property rights will not be defended successfully. The high-tech markets in which Germany used to be most successful, tend to become niches – too small as industrial bases. Moreover, German industry has lost contact with the leaders in some high-tech markets of strategic importance like microelectronics, telecommunications or biotechnology. And while the industrial base seems to be eroding, service industries (especially knowledge-intensive ones) prefer locations outside Germany. There is no lack of advice on how to stop the German decline. Some of the most popular suggestions are:

- redefine government activity: reduce costs of social security, deregulate and privatise to give more opportunities to entrepreneurial activity;
- take advantage of the chances of a new division of labour in a larger Europe: global sourcing and manufacturing outside Germany may contribute to economic strength;
- produce less sophisticated, over-engineered, but nevertheless high-quality products;
- find more flexible labour market solutions;
- stabilise and extend social consensus mechanisms (informal groups of conflicting parties, technology assessment, etc.).

Production will be profitable in Germany only for firms who rely on those particular resources which Germany can offer: a highly qualified and motivated labour force, an excellent infrastructure, a differentiated industrial structure with innovative and reliable suppliers, a market place with high purchasing power, social consensus (as evidenced, for example, by the very few working days lost through strikes), and an attractive natural environment. Purchasing power will increase further in years to come, because throughout 40 years of peace and sound money management an enormous amount of wealth has been accumulated. Consumers will become more discerning and competition more intensive as the efforts to deregulate and to open markets continue.

2.7 TRENDS AND DEVELOPMENTS

Germany faces a period of crisis and hard choices. For years to come the German economy will be dominated by the efforts to adapt to a new international division of labour brought about by the fundamental changes in Eastern Europe. The process of German unification will add more problems than stimulating effects to the German economy at least in the short term. Increasing deficits will raise pressure for budget cuts and important investments in the future, such as R&D expenditure, investment in education and environment protection, will be among the victims. Only in the longer term will the stimulating effects emerging from 'new brains' and entrepreneurs predominate. As a former front-line state, Germany is among the nations which will be major beneficiaries of the dividends of peace. Moreover, the role as a bridgehead in East–West trade may contribute to Germany's prosperity when a new international division of labour has emerged.

Today Germany is not addressing its future problems with vigour. Major effort will be necessary to redefine the role of government and to control costs in order to meet increasing international competition. However, Germany does not have the choice of a defensive cost-reduction strategy. Germany as a nation – or rather as a region within the global economy – must be aware that it, like most of its firms, is located at the high-quality high-price end of the market spectrum. Furthermore, it is no longer in the position of an imitator adapting to trends originating abroad. Germany is expected to participate in a world-leadership role. This opens up new opportunities but also implies unknown risks. Pioneers often face high costs and it may

be more convenient instead to be a 'fast second'. Germany has not yet lived up to the demands of this new role. Major deficiencies in social innovations are in the field of an energy-saving restructuring of the economy, the redefinition of the role of labour (becoming more flexible, retraining, more participation) and of social security (more private initiative) as well as the implementation of a culture of social dialogue on the consequences of new technologies. In this respect economic policy in other EC countries, such as Denmark or the Netherlands, is more 'modern' than in Germany.

Germany has always played an active role in the European integration process and the government was among the major protagonists of the Maastricht Treaty. However, there are serious objections against this step in the integration process. First, there is the fear of sacrificing the stable DM. Then there is an uneasy feeling about delegating more and more decision making to an anonymous bureaucracy in Brussels. The gap between decision making and democratic control gets wider and people are not willing to accept this. Is subsidiarity enough to preserve regional identity? While there is a broad consensus that European integration is still a good idea, there is considerable doubt on how to proceed further (two-speed Europe, deepening versus widening, etc.). In its present condition Germany no longer is the paragon of the EC and it is doubtful whether it will be able to fulfil the Maastricht convergence criteria by the end of the decade.

There is no doubt that, so far, almost nowhere in the world has a better combination of economic and social justice been found than in Germany. But the existing 'Model Germany' is not sustainable: its high performance is still based on too high an energy consumption and too high a level of environment pollution. If the whole world were to adapt to those standards, ecological collapse would be the consequence. Environmental problems have added a new dimension to the 'big trade-off' (A.M. Okun) between efficiency and equality. Global leadership should deal with this new 'magic triangle'. Politicians from all parts of the political spectrum are now debating the transformation of the German economic system into a social-ecological market economy. The vision is that of a peace economy: minimum military power, resolution of social conflict and harmony with nature. This is the new challenge which will, hopefully, be addressed more consistently once the haze of German unification has evaporated.

2.8 BIBLIOGRAPHY AND SOURCES OF INFORMATION

Literature

Biedenkopf, K. (1990): The Federal Republic of Germany: Old Structures and New Challenges, in: Calleo, D. P./Morgenstern, C. (eds.): *Recasting Europe's Economies: National Strategies in the 1980s*, Lanham, NY/London, 79-99

Bundesminister für Wirtschaft (various years): *Jahreswirtschaftsbericht der Bundesregierung,* Bonn

Deutsche Bundesbank (various years): *Geschäftsbericht* (Annual Report), Frankfurt/Main

Fels, G./Furstenberg, G. M. v. (eds.) (1989): *A Supply-side Agenda for Germany*, Berlin

Giersch, H./Papué, K.-H./Schmieding, H. (1992): *The Fading Miracle: Four Decades of Market Economy in Germany*, Cambridge

Graskamp, R. et al. (1992): *Umweltschutz, Strukturwandel und Wirtschaftswachstum*, Essen

Lampert, H. (1988): *Die Wirtschafts- und Sozialordnung der Bundesrepublik Deutschland*, 9th edn., München

Monopolkommission (1992): *Neuntes Hauptgutachten 1990/1991*, Baden-Baden

OECD (various years): *Economic Survey Germany*, Paris

OECD (1993): *Environmental Performance Reviews: Germany*, Paris

Sachverständigenrat zur Begutachtung der gesamtwirtschaftlichen Entwicklung/Council of Economic Experts (various years): *Jahresgutachten* (Annual Report), Wiesbaden

Sinn, G./Sinn, H.-W. (1993): *Kaltstart. Volkswirtschaftliche Aspekte der deutschen Vereinigung*, 3rd edn., München

Statistisches Bundesamt (various years): *Statistisches Jahrbuch für die Bundesrepublik Deutschland*, Stuttgart/Mainz

Sources of information

Arbeitsgemeinschaft deutscher wirtschaftswissenschaftlicher Forschungsinstitute, Poschingerstr. 5, 81679 München

Bundesanstalt für Arbeit, Regensburger Str. 104, 90478 Nürnberg

Bundesministerium der Finanzen, Graurheindorfer Str. 108, 53117 Bonn

Bundesministerium für Wirtschaft, Villemombler Str. 76, 53123 Bonn

Bundesverband der Deutschen Industrie (BDI), Gustav-Heinemann-Ufer 84, 50968 Köln

Deutsche Bundesbank, Wilhelm-Epstein-Str. 14, 60431 Frankfurt

Deutscher Gewerkschaftsbund (DGB), Hans-Böckler-Str. 39, 40476 Düsseldorf

Deutscher Industrie- und Handelstag (DIHT), Adenauer Allee 148, 53113 Bonn

Presse- und Informationsamt der Bundesregierung, Welckerstr. 11, 53133 Bonn

Statistisches Bundesamt, Gustav-Stresemann-Ring 11, 65189 Wiesbaden 1

Umweltbundesamt, Bismarckplatz 1, 14193 Berlin

CHAPTER 3

France

Kirk Thomson

3.1 INSTITUTIONAL AND HISTORICAL CONTEXT

3.1.1 Introduction

France has a republican and centralised form of government. The present constitution, the Fifth Republic, dates from as recently as 1958 and, as amended in 1962, provides the directly elected President with considerable powers. He alone appoints the Prime Minister and other members of the government, and even if traditionally he leaves the day-to-day running of affairs to the Prime Minister, while defining the general pattern of policy himself, he can, and frequently does, intervene directly in the decision-making process. Laws must be passed by the separately elected *Assemblée Nationale*. When both President and Assembly majority come from the same side of the political spectrum the legislative process functions normally. Since presidential elections take place every seven years and assembly elections every five, it is possible that situations of institutional conflict may arise. This can have repercussions in the domain of economic policy as was seen in the 1986–8 period of '*cohabitation*' when the socialist President Mitterand felt obliged to appoint a right-wing government led by Jacques Chirac. The more recent period of cohabitation, which began with the appointment of the Balladur government in 1993, has seen a much easier working relationship between a left-wing President and a right-wing Prime Minister than was the case with Chirac.

Until recently, French politics has been marked by a high degree of ideological division. The election of the socialist candidate, François Mitterand, in 1981 was regarded with concern both inside and outside France because the programme on which he was elected, the *Programme Commun*, was one of radical change and was the centrepiece of an uneasy alliance with the then powerful Communist Party. The influence of the ideological left has virtually disappeared, as far as economic policy is concerned, since the early 1980s and is now replaced by a large consensus regarding the general thrust of government policy.

French economic policy during the 1980s and 1990s can be divided into two broad periods with the second and longer of the two showing several modifications of a secondary nature. The first years of the incoming socialist government with Mauroy as Prime Minister were a period of reflation and increased state intervention coming at a time when other industrialised economies were following deflationary policies to counter the effects of the second oil shock. The second period, starting in 1983, was marked first by the austerity measures accompanying the devaluation of March of that year, and subsequently by the introduction of the policy given the general name of competitive disinflation. In the post-1983 period, priority was given to bringing French inflation levels down to those of Germany, the maintenance of the value of the French franc at a stable level in the European Monetary System, the introduction of far-reaching reforms in the banking and financial system, and the preparation of the French economy for participation in European economic and monetary union. With the exception of disagreements on policy towards the state-owned sector, the changes of majority in 1986, 1988, and 1993 have not been accompanied by major shifts in economic policy. French commitment to the structures adopted at Maastricht remains the keystone of economic policy, and the only radical departure introduced by the incoming Balladur government has been the privatisation programme.

3.1.2 Policy developments in the last decade

The reflation policy of 1981–82

The main elements of this policy were an expansion in demand brought about by a number of measures :

- increases in the minimum salary, the *salaire minimum interprofessionnel de croissance (SMIC)*, which raised purchasing power considerably in 1981 and 1982;
- increases in various social benefits;
- increases in public investments: housing; aid to the private and public sectors;
- increases in public employment;
- reduction in the working week to 39 hours and an extra week's paid holiday as well as a lowering of the age of retirement.

These measures had a number of characteristics.

- The government made no effort to reduce taxes in order to encourage demand.
- Most of the measures were irreversible in nature, e.g. increases in public employment, increases in the SMIC, early retirement, investments in nationalised enterprises.
- The combination of new taxes on higher incomes and the nature of the other measures involved an important net redistribution effect.

Although the policy of the Mauroy government ensured a moderate rate of growth in 1981 and 1982, it also produced a rapidly growing balance-of-payments problem and a series of exchange rate crises (October 1981, June 1982 and March 1983). These crises resulted in devaluations and accompanying measures (in particular the wage and price freeze in the summer of 1982) which culminated in a fundamental policy shift in 1983.

The 1983 policy change

The austerity measures introduced in 1983 were designed to reduce aggregate demand in order to bring the balance of payments back into equilibrium. Behind this turnaround lay the constraint of the European Monetary System which is based on the assumption of stable exchange rates. The measures involved three main elements :

1 a compulsory loan of 10% of households' previous tax payments and a special tax of 10% of taxable income to finance the social security system;
2 reductions in public expenditure and incentives to encourage savings;
3 tighter foreign exchange controls.

These measures combined to reduce gross domestic product (GDP) by 0.6% in 1983 and by 0.4% in 1984 and contributed largely to the substantial reduction in the balance-of-payments deficit in 1983 (this latter improvement was aided by other elements, particularly the excellent results of the food and agricultural exports for that year).

Austerity and recovery, 1984–90

The period following 1983 was marked by a degree of homogeneity, despite the March 1986 to May 1988 right-wing interlude. The priority in the 1983–5 period was to reduce inflation and to restore company profits. In terms of budgetary policy the main objectives were to reduce the total level of tax and social security payments and to keep the budget deficit below 3% of GDP. These two objectives were reached, thanks partly to the reduction in oil prices which affected growth, and tax revenue from 1986 onwards.

The period of 1987–90 was one of recovery marked by higher rates of investment and growth but continuing difficulties regarding unemployment and the balance of trade.

Following 1983, both inflation and the restoration of business profits were closely associated with the policies pursued by the various governments. The price and wage freeze of June 1982 was an attempt to break the spiral relationship between wage and price increases. In 1983 the government went further in its attempt to achieve '*desindexation*' by calling on employers and unions to negotiate annual salary increases in line with a norm fixed in accordance with national objectives instead of quarterly increases which anticipated impending price increases. Negotiations were to be based upon the total payroll of the enterprises rather than on specific salaries, and any increases designed to compensate for a difference between the norm and the inflationary outcome had to take account of the situation of the economy as a whole and of the enterprise. This policy was effective and was reinforced from 1985 to 1986 by the depreciation of the dollar and the fall in oil prices (which allowed business to re-establish profit margins).

A combination of growth and government austerity similarly brought about an improvement in public finances. From 1985, budgetary and fiscal policy were aimed at reducing the total tax and social contribution burden and reducing the deficit. In 1985 and 1986 net tax reductions balanced reductions in expenditure, but from 1987 economic recovery brought about a spontaneous increase in revenue. This coincided with the impact of previous austerity measures which limited the spontaneous growth in expenditure.

New economic problems, 1991–93

The 1991–3 period has been one of slow growth and rising unemployment. Growth (GDP at 1980 prices) fell from 4.1% in 1989 to 2.2% in 1990 and 1.0% in 1991. The slight improvement in 1992 (1.8%) masks a slowdown at the end of the year with recession predicted for 1993. Industrial production has started to decline and unemployment to rise. In this context it is no surprise to note increasing doubts being expressed with regard to the exchange-rate policy followed over the last ten years and the high domestic interest rates this policy implies.

3.1.3 The 'dirigiste' tradition

In considering the French economy, it is important to remember that the relatively recent party political consensus regarding economic policy is developing on the basis of a much older tradition regarding the formulation and implementation of such policy in France. In this respect two elements need to be kept in mind.

1 France has a tradition of centralised economic and public administration, and administrative dominance of the economy goes back as far as Colbert and Louis XIV. The development of indicative planning at the end of the Second World War was a modern manifestation of an old established reflex rather than an exciting innovation and the painstaking dismantling of the system of controls over the past few years represents a dramatic, although as yet partial, change. Whether recent movements towards more independence in business decision making have been matched by a fundamental shift in French management attitudes, however, has been questioned by certain observers of French management culture.

2 Very close links exist between the various ministries responsible for the economy and their professional staff, on the one hand, and the leaders of the business community (especially in banking, insurance and the major public and private enterprises) on the other. Leading professional civil servants complete their career in a '*corps*' attached to a ministry and are recruited from specialised and highly selective '*grandes écoles*' run independently from the university system, e.g. the *École Polytechnique*, the *École des Mines* and the *École des Ponts et Chaussées*. Large public and private firms try to recruit either experienced civil servants or young graduates coming from these engineering schools and the resulting close interpenetration of administrative and

industrial technocracies has no equivalent in the Western world. That interconnection helps to explain the close co-ordination and mutual trust which exists between administrative and industrial strategies in key sectors.

In considering French economic policy, then, it is important to remember that:

- Despite ideological differences, particularly in the early 1980s, there has been a strong consensus among the decision-making elite, and the political establishment in particular, regarding interventionist policies and national economic objectives;
- Behind the public political debate a relatively homogeneous corps of highly trained engineers, administrators and managers, sharing a common social and educational background, has been responsible for implementing policy both in the public and the private sectors.

3.2 MAIN ECONOMIC CHARACTERISTICS

3.2.1 Population and labour

Latest estimates (January 1993) put the total population of metropolitan France at 57.5 million, implying a continuation of the growth trend of 0.5% per annum which marked the 1980s. In 1992 the fertility rate slipped slightly to 1.73 children per woman. This is well below the replacement rate of 2.1, but among the higher rates in Europe. Future trends indicate further declines. With a crude birth rate of 12.9 per thousand and a death rate of 9.1 per thousand (1992) and an inward migration estimated at 90,000, the French population will continue to grow slowly but will also continue to age .

The geographical distribution of the French population shows expansion in three areas, Île de France (Paris and its region), Rhône-Alpes, and the south (particularly Languedoc-Roussillon and Provence-Alpes-Côte d'Azur). The northern industrial regions are zones of emigration and the rural regions of central France have become areas of real population decline. Paris

and its region is the home of nearly 19% of the population (10.7 million), up from 18.5% in 1982. The second largest urban agglomeration is that of Lyon (1.3 million) followed by Marseilles (1 million).

Total working population in 1991 was 24.6 million. With an overall participation rate of 55% (as a percentage of the over-14 population), France was very close to the EC average. Within this figure the male rate was 64% and the female 46% in 1991 (see Table 3.1).

Table 3.1 Participation rates by age and sex (%)

	1980		1991	
Age	Male	Female	Male	Female
15–24	52.7	43.1	38.6	31.6
25–49	97.2	65.2	96.1	74.9
50–54	92.9	55.4	89.5	64.6
55–59	81.0	48.0	68.5	45.6
60–64	47.8	27.7	19.7	16.0
65 +	8.4	3.4	3.5	1.5
All age groups	71.0	44.4	64.2	45.9

These figures reveal several trends. The decline in the participation rate of young people of both sexes reflects both the desire for more secondary and higher education, and the desire to postpone entering the labour market. Youth unemployment in France has remained high throughout the 1980s. Another feature common to all industrialised economies is the growth in female employment. A third feature is the marked decline in participation rates of males over 50 under the impact not so much of the retirement age at 60 but rather that of early retirement schemes representing a form of hidden unemployment.

Employment structure

The main changes in employment in France have taken place progressively as the economy has

Table 3.2 Domestic employment by sector (%)

Year	Agriculture/ Fishing	Industry Total	Manufac- turing	Commerce and market services	Insurance/ Finance	Non-market services
1970	13.3	28.0	23.7	28.3	1.8	18.6
1980	8.6	27.0	21.8	32.6	2.5	21.9
1991	5.7	20.7	17.3	38	2.7	25.4

adjusted structurally (see Table 3.2). Employment in agriculture fell from 13% in 1970 to 5.7% in 1991. Manufacturing employment peaked at 5.3 million in 1974 (24%) and fell to 3.9 million (17%) in 1991. Dramatic falls in employment took place between 1982 and 1989 in major traditional industries such as coalmining (down from 56,300 to 27,000), iron and steel (from 150,000 to 98,000) and shipbuilding. The service sector expanded from 49% of employment in 1970 to 66% in 1991. In the same period, employment in education expanded by 19%, health by 16% and government administration by 11%. Salaried workers represented 86% of the working population in 1990.

Of the 3 million self-employed workers, approximately one-half is in the commercial services sector (retail distribution, hotels and restaurants, garages), some 600,000 in agriculture, and nearly 400,000 in consultancy and the liberal professions.

Unemployment

One of the major economic and social problems in France throughout the 1980s and early 1990s has been the continuing high rate of unemployment. Table 3.3 reveals the relative stability of the situation as well as the temporary improvement in the late 1980s which has been followed by the present deterioration.

Unemployment rates tend to be considerably higher for females (12.2%, 1991) than for males (7.2%) and conceal a hard core of long-term unemployed (37% of the total in 1991). The long-term unemployed and the high proportion of youth unemployment have been the main centres of preoccupation.

Another striking feature of the labour market concerns the nature of labour contracts. Over 20% of female employment is in part-time jobs. The total figure in 1992 was 2.8 million part-time employees as opposed to 2 million in 1982.

As elsewhere, regional disparities in the geographical distribution of unemployment appear relatively stable. When, in December 1991, the national average level of unemployment was (9.5%), the lowest figures were Alsace (5.2%), Franche Comté (7.8%) and Île de France (7.9%), whereas the highest rates were found in Languedoc-Roussillon (14%), the Nord-Pas-de-Calais (12.6%) and Provence-Alpes-Côte d'Azur

Table 3.3 Unemployment by age, 1975–92 (%)

Age group	1975	1980	1986	1988	1990	1991	1992
15–24	8.9	15.0	22.8	20.4	16.6	18.0	19.3
25–49	2.9	4.3	8.2	8.4	7.9	8.3	9.0
50 +	2.7	4.6	7.1	7.5	6.6	7.0	7.9
All age groups	4.0	6.3	10.4	10.0	8.9	9.4	10.2

Source: INSEE

(11.8%). A detailed explanation of the situation of each region involves taking into account all the variables affecting the labour market, that is to say, growth in employment, changes in generations, migration and occupation rates. The regions in the south of France have seen a large increase in employment opportunities over the past ten years but this growth trend has been compensated for by greater than average increases in female occupation rates (also the case in the north) and lower decreases in youth occupation rates. In the case of Lorraine and the Nord-Pas-de-Calais, whereas both regions have been affected by the loss of employment in traditional industries, the former has been able to compensate by migration across the frontier, while the latter has not had this possibility. The fortunate position of Alsace is explained by employment growth and by job opportunities across the frontier. In other words the local unemployment rate in France is not a reliable indicator of economic health and can only be explained by taking into account all the variables affecting labour market adjustment.

The causes of unemployment in France

With a working population growing at almost 200,000 per year in the 1980s, and, despite a lower forecast rate of increase of 120,000 in the coming years, the essential problem in France has been the failure of the economy to generate enough new employment. The general link between economic growth and unemployment can be seen in the 1988–90 period when with annual growth around 4% per year 700,000 new jobs were created and unemployment declined. Despite the improvement, unemployment as a whole remained high, marked, as mentioned above, by a relatively stable one-third of hard core long-term jobless and a high level of youth unemployment.

A number of explanations for this situation have been put forward. None of these explain more than a part of the problem, but they do suggest that remedies will be complex, various, and long term. It is generally agreed that whereas demand deficiency has been associated with increases in unemployment at certain periods (after the first oil shock and in the early 1980s) the major cause of unemployment has been classical in nature, and we must therefore look at the various sources of rigidity in the French labour market.

A first element is the minimum wage legislation embodied in the SMIC (*salaire minimum interprofessionel de croissance*), which in July 1992 was fixed at FF 5,630 per month. Although econometric studies of the impact of the SMIC on total employment have been relatively inconclusive, it would appear to have affected youth and unskilled unemployment. Indeed many government employment programmes tacitly acknowledge this in allowing young people to be employed at rates below the SMIC. A related problem is the high 'tax-wedge' on labour caused by the high level of social security contributions, which are substantially higher in France than in comparable economies.

The long duration of unemployment benefit and the initially high replacement ratio (rising to 84% for those earning the SMIC) tend to postpone active job search. The socially desirable guaranteed minimum income (*revenu minimum d'insertion* or RMI) may have similar adverse effects.

There would appear to be a mismatch problem, indicated by the high levels of unemployment among the unskilled in general, and the poorly qualified school-leavers in particular. This is compounded by a low level of geographical mobility even among those looking for work for more than a year. Much of the debate over educational policy in recent years has been concerned with how to prepare those in secondary and post-secondary education for the labour market with various forms of professional training.

The numbers of long-term unemployed have caused concern that they become marginalised creating a so-called hysteresis effect. As people become progressively more difficult to employ, they are not only a problem in themselves, but they also fail to have a moderating effect on wage levels in general.

Employment policies

Policies designed specifically to deal with the unemployment problem have taken a variety of forms over the past decade but have aimed at stimulating the demand for labour, especially the young and the long-term unemployed, at reducing the supply of labour through early retirement and encouraging extended schooling and by reducing the mismatch problem by a variety of training schemes.

Labour market expenditure is relatively high in France. In 1989 it stood at 2.65% of GDP against an OECD average of 2.02%. The effectiveness of these policies can always be questioned in view of the high and durable rate of general unemployment. On the other hand, a recent study of employment policies over the 1974–88 period by the OFCE claimed that in 1988 the various policies enabled some 230,000 people to avoid unemployment. At this time 140,000 were involved in some kind of training scheme or public service employment, about 60,000 took early retirement and 23,000 were in special employment schemes in the private sector with relief from social security payments.

Since unemployment started to increase again in 1990, existing schemes have been expanded and new ones introduced, again targeting the long-term unemployed and the poorly trained young. At the end of 1992, 1.6 million people were involved in training schemes or subsidised employment, of one form or another. The '*contrats-emploi-solidarité*' provided part-time work in the public sector for some 400,000 people. Originally intended for young unemployed people, this programme has been redirected towards the long-term unemployed and offers part-time employment for a limited period at a salary based on the SMIC. Also for the long-term unemployed, are the '*contrats de retour à l'emploi*' (100,000 participants) which relieve employers from social security contributions and '*actions d'insertion et de formation*' which are vocational training courses. Similar batteries of support measures exist for young people, such as exemption from social security contributions for several months when hiring young unemployed

workers, and extensive training programmes. Whereas these measures can be seen as unavoidable if those categories of unemployed most in difficulty are to be helped, it is recognised that only economic recovery, combined with reforms which will reduce the rigidities mentioned above, can bring down unemployment as a whole.

3.2.2 Output and growth

Following the Second World War, output grew rapidly in France and commentators often refer nostalgically to the period from 1945 to 1973 as the '*trente glorieuses*'. From 1969 to 1973 real GDP was growing at around 6% per year. The quadrupling of oil prices in 1973 checked this hectic expansion and coupled with associated anti-inflationary policies led to a period of relatively slow growth and worsening unemployment.

The sentiment of economic frustration in these years provided the background for the left-wing victory in 1981 and the Mauroy government with its policy of expansion and economic reorganisation. Unfortunately the measures introduced in June 1981 (raising the SMIC, increasing social benefits and public sector employment) were not only virtually irreversible, they also came into force when other countries were pursing restrictive policies. Domestic demand grew by 4% in 1982 and quickly produced a widening trade deficit. Although restrictions were introduced in the summer of 1982, it was not until March 1983 that the government felt able to announce a major change in policy alongside a devaluation of the franc. The new policy, announced to accompany the third franc devaluation since the change of government, was aimed mainly at slowing the growth in French domestic demand by cuts in public expenditure and strict budgetary discipline in the period 1984–7. A restrictive monetary policy and low wage norms were introduced and adhered to. Although foreign trade was restored to balance and inflation brought steadily down, the growth rate also suffered considerably. Growth dipped to a low of 0.7% in 1983 and did not pick up until the second half of 1987.

Whereas the biggest contribution to growth in 1986 came from increased household consumption stimulated by the fall in energy prices, in 1987 and 1988 investment became increasingly important. Growth in 1988 and 1989 accelerated, but slowed sharply from the middle of 1990. All the components of demand weakened, particularly business investment. In 1991 overall growth was around 1.2%. This was noticeably higher than the OECD average and was largely due to export demand from the newly unified Germany. If growth in 1992 showed an improvement at 1.8% this was largely due to export growth in the early part of the year. The slowdown in other European economies affected France in the latter part of the year and combined with weak domestic consumption and declining investment to produce negative growth in the last quarter. Latest forecasts for 1993 are for decline in GDP rather than growth. The forecasts produced by INSEE for 1993 have been progressively reduced from 2.6% in the summer of 1992 to –1% by mid-1993.

3.2.3 Consumption, savings and investment

The growth in household consumption has shown a rapid deceleration over the past four years (1989 3.3%; 1990 2.9%; 1991 1.5% and 1992 1.9%). Over the past two years consumers have not attempted to borrow or to use their savings to compensate for slower increases in the purchasing power of their disposable income. Growth of disposable income was 2.0% in 1992, 1.8% in 1991, 3.2% in 1990 and 3.9% in 1989.

Consumption is being held back as households seek to reduce their level of debt, and the savings rate remains at a relatively high level. Personal savings levels began a steady decline in the late 1970s to reach a low point in 1987 at 10.8% of gross disposable income. By 1991 this had risen to 12.7% where it stayed in 1992. Although the rate is well down on the figures for the 1970s which varied between 18% and 20% the question is whether this recent rise represents a lasting phenomenon. A sense of insecurity regarding employment and the future

financial situation is widespread. In addition, high real interest rates and a wide range of highly accessible new financial products may be stimulating the propensity to save at a time when the wealth effect of reductions in real estate prices exercises an influence in the same direction.

The period of rapid growth in the 1950s and 1960s was one of high rates of investment in France. According to the OECD, investment averaged 23% of GDP between 1960 and 1973. Business investment declined from the relatively high figures of the early 1970s to reach a low in 1984. The subsequent improvement was related to the improvement in business profitability as wages growth was brought under control and demand increased (see Table 3.4).

Table 3.4 Business investment, 1970–92

Year	Business investment as percentage of value added	Business profit ratio[1]
1970	22.1	30.8
1975	19.4	27.0
1980	19.4	25.8
1985	16.9	28.4
1987	17.6	31.9
1989	18.8	33.4
1990	18.8	32.6
1991	17.1	31.7
1992	16.7	32.6

[1] Gross operating surplus as percentage of value added.

(*Source* : INSEE, *Comptes de la Nation* and *Notes de Conjoncture*)

While if business profits over the past three years have remained healthy, business decisions in 1991 and in 1992 have been dominated by pessimism regarding market strength. The continuing high level of interest rates is another contributing factor at a time when capacity utilisation rates have declined. Manufacturing investment declined by 8.4% in 1991 and by 12% in 1992. Similar declines are forecast for 1993. The investment rate of the national enterprises

Table 3.5 Business productive investment (% change over previous year), with weighting as for 1991

	1988	1989	1990	1991	1992
National enterprises (15%)[1]	3.0	−1.4	3.2	7.4	0.0
Competitive sector enterprises (85%)	11.5	10.1	4.6	−5.3	−4 to −5
Agriculture (5%)	12.6	9.2	−4.6	−9.2	−4.0
Manufacturing (33%)	10.3	6.7	10.6	−8.4	−12
Commerce/Services (43%)	12.0	13.6	2.1	−2.2	−1 to −2
Building and civil engineering (4%)	17.6	3.7	−2.6	−6.5	−8
All enterprises	10.2	8.3	4.4	−3.5	−4 to −5

[1] National enterprises (*Grandes Entreprises Nationales*) are state-owned enterprises mainly in transport and energy production.

remained stable in 1992 after the increase in 1991 (Air France fleet renewal and the TGV). Changes in investment in the main sectors are given in Table 3.5.

3.2.4 Inflation

France has had a tendency to be more inflation-prone than many of her European partners, in particular Germany. Although a widespread use of indexation protected the economy from many of the harmful effects of inflation, the setting up of the European Monetary System made a reduction of French inflation rates to West German levels absolutely imperative.

Inflation peaked at 15% in 1974 after the first oil shock. Having been reduced to an annual rate of around 9.5% by the policies of Raymond Barre in the late 1970s, inflation again accelerated from mid-1979 as a result of the second oil shock. Contrary to the deceleration which followed the events of 1973 the situation now worsened partly as a result of the policies of the Mauroy government. Prices continued to rise at over 13% until mid-1982. The price freeze of the summer of 1982 checked the upward trend and heralded a downward movement under the combined impact of a radical change in government policies, salary restraint and subsequently the downward movement in the dollar, oil and raw material prices.

Since the difficulties of the early 1980s the policy of competitive disinflation has been the keystone of French economic policy. The strategy has aimed at slowing down inflation and restoring a competitive edge to the economy. It is based on four principal elements: a monetary policy aimed at mastering inflation; a sound budgetary policy; tight control over costs to ensure a competitive position in European markets; structural reforms designed to create a dynamic and competitive environment. The ultimate aim has not been to obtain a low rate of inflation or a stable currency as ends in themselves but to ensure that costs in real terms are as low as possible enabling French producers to sell proportionately more on the domestic and export market than competitors. Clearly such a policy is significant within the context of European integration and the setting up of EMU. A crude indicator of the success of this policy is given is Table 3.6.

Table 3.6 French inflation rate and differential with Germany and the EC average

	France	France–EC	France–Germany
1983	9.6	1.2	6.4
1985	5.8	−0.2	3.6
1987	3.1	−0.1	2.9
1989	3.6	−1.5	1.5
1991	3.2	−1.8	−0.2
July 1992	3.0	−1.7	−1.1

Another indicator of the success of this policy has been the survival of the French franc within the ERM without devaluation despite a series of speculative attacks. This policy has also contributed to the recovery in the balance of trade. Improvements in productivity combined with low increases in nominal labour costs have meant that unit labour costs have been increasing more slowly in France than elsewhere in the EC. In the period 1987–91, for example, unit wage costs in France were increasing at roughly one-half the EC average. As a result of this improved performance France has been able to improve export market share in the EC from 15.5% in 1987 to 17% in 1992.

On the other hand, it would be unrealistic to suggest that this policy is without its critics. Associated with the disinflation and the maintenance of the franc in the ERM, interest rates have been maintained at historically high levels, and this has helped curb consumption and investment, and thus contributed to high French levels of unemployment.

3.2.5 Industrial market structure

In 1991 production of goods and services in France was supplied by 2.18 million enterprises of various types, in addition to around 1 million agricultural producers, some 40,000 financial establishments and 250,000 organisations providing non-market services (classified as public if more than 50% of their funds are government provided, and otherwise classified as private). This picture and changes since 1987 are summarised in Table 3.7.

Table 3.7 Number of production units (thousands)

	1987	1991	1991 (%)
Market sector			
Industrial commercial and			
service enterprises	2,028	2,187	63
Agricultural producers	1,059	994	29
Financial establishments	36	40	1
Total	3,123	3,221	93
Non-market sector			
Public organisations	116	116	3
Private organisations	117	113	4
Total	3,356	3,470	100

Of the enterprises in the market sector just over 90% had less than 10 employees of which the great majority were in the market services, construction and commercial sectors. As a whole, these very small enterprises provided 32% of total employment and 21% of value added. Outside the tertiary and building industry, very small enterprises were involved in industrial activities requiring specialised know-how rather than capital (e.g. printing, cabinet making, metal-working and electronics). In terms of geographical distribution such businesses are found throughout France, but with a relatively larger proportion in the rural and semi-rural areas of the South of France.

Half of the small and medium-sized businesses in France (10–499 employees) operate in the tertiary sector, mainly because of the smaller amounts of capital required (see Table 3.8). Another 16% are in the construction industry. As a general rule these enterprises suffer from a major financial disadvantage compared to larger enterprises. Their short-term debts are relatively larger (58% of total debt as opposed to 34% for large businesses). A larger proportion of their debt comes from the commercial banks (19% as opposed to 5%). Associated with these problems of financial structure, small businesses are obliged to provide longer credit to their customers (64 days on average) than the larger ones (20 days).

The proportion of employees in small and medium-sized enterprises (SMEs) in the industrial sector has increased over recent years rising from 42% in 1980 to over 50% in 1989. There are two main reasons for this trend. First, the decline in manufacturing employment has meant that certain larger firms have fallen into the SME category. Secondly, larger firms tended to reorganise some of their activities by setting up subsidiaries or using sub-contractors. It is the larger industrial SMEs which tend to be members of groups and it is this 15% which produces 46% of the turnover.

Since it was observed in the late 1980s that the SMEs were generating more recruitment than larger companies, a special aid package was launched by the government (the *Plan PME*) in September 1991. Its aim was to help SMEs

Table 3.8 Employees in enterprises of various size by sector (%)

		No of employees	
	Less than 10	*10–499*	*More than 500*
Manufacturing industry	7	46	47
Construction	32	54	14
Commerce and other services	30	36	34
All sectors	22	42	36

Source: Eurostat

increase their equity capital through tax concessions, and included a number of non-tax measures, such as a limitation on time allowed for payment of bills.

The degree of concentration in French manufacturing has depended on market structure and barriers to entry. Manufacturing tends to have a high degree of concentration (as measured by share of total industry turnover of the four leading enterprises). At the other end of the scale, baking in France is still largely in the hands of self-employed producers. In the armaments industry, the four leading enterprises produce 89% of the total industry turnover. In textiles the share of the four leading enterprises is 7.5%.

3.2.6 Productivity and growth potential

France's stock of productive capital has grown more slowly in the past decade than that of its main competitors, with the exception of the UK. Average age of capital stock, for example, increased from 12.2 years in 1980 to 13.4 years in 1987. The situation improved in the late 1980s with an increase of nearly 3% in 1989, but it slipped back to an increase of 2.7% in 1991 with noticeably less expected in 1992. The working population, on the other hand, is increasing at around 0.6% per year (average increase 1988–91). Productivity growth for the economy as a whole has been close to 3% per year in the 1980s (added value per hour of labour), and around 3.7% in manufacturing industry. In 1990 and 1991 productivity declined both in manufacturing and in services as employment adjusted with a noticeable lag to the decline in demand. Latest figures are given in Table 3.9. The recov-

ery in 1992 took place as labour adjustments adapted to declines in production.

Table 3.9 Labour productivity (% change)

	1987	*1988*	*1989*	*1990*	*1991*	*1992*
Manufacturing industry	3.4	7.6	4.1	0.9	–0.8	2.7
Market services	2.2	1.3	1.3	–1.4	0.4	1.7

Source: INSEE: Note Conjoncture, March 1993

According to the OECD (Survey France 1990), the growth rate of potential output, taking into account these trends in labour and capital growth, is about 2.75% per year. If growth of above 3% is to be sustained then faster growth of capital stock will be required.

One aspect of productivity growth which has caused much debate in France concerns the alleged relationship between low growth in employment (a growth of 0.2% per year between 1979 and 1990 in France, compared with an average growth of 1.1% for the rest of the G7) and a relatively high overall rate of productivity growth (1.8% per year in France as opposed to 1.3% for the OECD Europe). In the case of the United States productivity only increased by roughly 1% per year, whereas employment increased at a rate of 1.6%. However, it can be argued that the French situation requires an analysis which separates manufacturing from services. One explanation for the level of employment in French manufacturing is the late acceleration in growth of output which only started in 1988 (whereas the recovery started in 1983 in other equivalent economies). When the downturn intervened in the second half of 1990, French manufacturing had not had the time to recruit large numbers. In the case of services, while in the period 1979–90 French productivity increased by an average of 1.4% per year (as opposed to 0.9% for the G7), employment only increased by 1.6% per year (as opposed to 2.2% for the G7). In this area the non-market added value is calculated on the basis of salaries paid. The relatively high level of minimum salary in France exaggerates the real level of productivity and has tended to discourage employment. In addition, special low-salary employment encouraged in public services by official employment policies does not show up fully in official statistics as it can be classified as training. Hence low productivity/low salary employment in the services has been discouraged and, probably, underestimated.

3.3 GOVERNMENT INVOLVEMENT IN THE ECONOMY

As is the case in other developed economies, the role of the state has expanded in France in recent years. This role remains considerable despite recent policies designed to liberalise major sectors of economic activity.

3.3.1 Fiscal policy

Public expenditure has increased steadily in France since the Second World War in absolute and in relative terms. Between 1950 and 1990 as a proportion of GDP, public expenditure increased in real terms by a factor of 7.2 whereas GDP increased by 5. As a percentage of GDP, government expenditure increased from 33.3% to 51%. The first oil price shock marked the biggest change. Until 1973 public expenditure increased at a rate slightly higher than the economic growth rate. Between 1974 and 1984 the difference was much greater as the rate of economic growth fell. Since 1985 the public

expenditure share of GDP has been held stable as a result of restraint on public expenditure and improved growth. Much of the increase in the recent period has been caused by social transfers and by increases in interest payments on government debt.

Tax and social security contributions have grown from 28.3% of GDP in 1950 to 43.8% in 1990. In this period, whereas taxes increased by 4 points, social security contributions increased by 11. The total level of compulsory contributions, varying between 43% and 44%, remains high and only a major policy change will bring the total tax burden down to the European average of 41%.

Fiscal policy over the past 15 years has gone through a number of marked phases. From mid-1976 to 1980 priority was given to the fight against inflation and the maintenance of the franc exchange rate. The incoming socialist government launched a policy of reflation in 1981 which involved mainly increases in expenditure rather than tax cuts. The cost of the various measures came to 1.45% of GDP in 1982 and while they were successful in improving growth and creating employment, the effects on the trade balance and the exchange rate were negative.

In March 1983 the third devaluation of the franc since 1981 was accompanied by expenditure cuts, tax increases and a compulsory loan, in order to reduce the deficit by FF 37 billion. Since this crisis, budgetary policy has not been active. From 1982–6 the stated policy was to reduce the deficit to 3% of GDP and to this was added in 1985 the objective of progressively reducing the tax and social security contribution. From 1986, tax reductions for enterprises and households were added as an objective.

When the total deficit began to fall after 1985, the improvement in economic growth enabled governments to satisfy all objectives. In the period 1986 to 1990 the government borrowing requirement fell from FF 138 billion to under FF 90 billion (2.7 to 1.4% of GDP). Public expenditure, as a percentage of GDP, fell from 51.4% to 50% in the same period. Tax cuts amounting to FF 170 billion were introduced in the period benefiting households (direct taxes and VAT) and business (corporation tax). Unfortunately the falling off of growth from 1990 has meant that budgets since that year, enshrined in the annual Finance Acts (*Loi de Finance*) have successively failed to meet their objectives. The 1991 Finance Act provided for a reduction in the deficit to FF 81 billion in 1991, assuming a growth rate of 2.7%. With a lower growth rate, the 1991 result was a deficit of FF 132 billion equivalent to 1.9% of GDP. The same problem arose in 1992. The Finance Act envisaged a deficit of FF 90 billion and assumed a growth rate of 2.2%. The final government deficit was around FF 230 billion. If the social security deficit is included, the general borrowing requirement for 1992 came to FF 270 billion or 3.8% of GDP.

The situation regarding French public finance has not been the cause of great concern so far, since the level of national debt is not particularly high in comparison to that of other EC Member States. On the other hand, the level of interest payments is rising steadily and the budget for 1993 will certainly lead to another large deficit unless corrective measures are taken. The Finance Act for 1993 provided for a deficit of FF 165 billion assuming a growth rate of 2.3%. In view of the recession in 1993 the probable deficit will be around FF 365 billion. The rapidly deteriorating economic situation caused the new government to introduce a number of corrective measures (tax increases and expenditure cuts), the aim of which was to bring the probable deficit down to a more reasonable figure.

Between 1982 and 1992 the national debt rose from 17.8% of GDP to 28.7%. The reason for this significant increase is the series of deficits which have accumulated throughout the 1980s and 1990s. With a primary deficit of some FF 40 billion for 1992 the level of debt will continue to rise after slowing in the period 1988 to 1992. High interest rates coupled with slow growth imply this burden will increase throughout the 1990s and this will act as a significant constraint, bearing in mind that some 30% of the negotiable debt is held by non-residents.

Taxation

The tax system in France has a number of particular features that merit attention in addition to the relatively large total tax burden and the high proportion of social insurance contributions.

Personal income tax is highly progressive, takes considerable account of family size and exempts a high proportion of potential tax payers. In fact in 1988 only 54.54% of households paid income tax. Despite reductions in recent years, top rates are among the highest in Europe. Payments are consequently highly concentrated, and in 1986 the first 10% of households paid 64% of income tax. On the other hand, this effect is compensated for by the fact that virtually all households pay social insurance contributions. Consequently, although an average production worker in 1988 paid 7% of his income in income tax, he paid 17% in social insurance.

Tax on corporate profits has been reduced to replace the tax incentives previously used to encourage investment. Standard corporate income tax was reduced from 50% to 42% and the tax on undistributed profits was reduced in 1990 from 39% to 37%. Special tax credits still exist for business start-ups and for investment in enterprise zones.

VAT is the main source of tax revenue in France. This situation is likely to remain unchanged even if such a tax is by its very nature regressive. Widespread opposition to any extension of income tax from trade unions and similar pressure groups and considerable administrative difficulties (tax avoidance, an overburdened tax administration, and lack of any structure for collection of income tax at source) combine to make any shift away from VAT and towards income tax a gradual process. The government has reduced the number of VAT rates from five to three and has reduced the top rate from 33.3% to 25%. The standard rate is 18.6%. Excise duties are lower in France than elsewhere.

Local taxation in France is rather complex and varies considerably. There are four local direct taxes. Three are paid by households as occupants and are based on rental value with, as of 1990, a limit of 4% of household income. A business tax produces 45% of local authority revenue.

3.3.2 Regional policy

Although France is a country with marked cultural and geographical diversities, it has not suffered to the same extent as some of its neighbours from regions afflicted by marked and lasting economic difficulties. In 1988, for example, with a national unemployment rate of 10.1% the two worst-hit regions were Languedoc-Roussillon with 13.6% and the Nord-Pas-de-Calais with 13.5%. The most favoured region was Alsace with 6.8% followed by Rhône-Alpes and Limousin with 8.2%.

Since 1963, the *Delegation à l'Aménagement du Territoire (DATAR)* has been responsible for implementing policy designed to deal with two main problem areas; those isolated agricultural regions particularly hit by the exodus from the land and certain areas hit by structural industrial change, particularly the former steel-producing and shipbuilding centres. An example of this kind of activity was the creation of three enterprise zones in 1987 in Dunkerque, La Seyne and La Ciotat to deal with the problems caused by the closure of local shipyards. Businesses starting up in the zones were given a ten-year exemption from all corporation taxes provided they created sufficient numbers of new jobs.

The main role of DATAR has been considerably modified in recent years by two major developments. First, the development since 1975 of the Community regional policy, including the existing aids to agriculture distributed by FEOGA. DATAR co-ordinates the application for and the distribution of aid coming from these and other Community funds. Second, the *Law of Decentralisation* in 1982 gave considerable new powers to the Regional and the Departmental Councils. These changes led to a series of State–Region planning contracts from 1984. The preparation and negotiation of these *Contrats de Plan* was entrusted to DATAR. In the early months of 1989 a second series of five-year contracts was signed with the regions for a global sum of 52 billion francs. Three main priority themes were picked out for attention : development of the road network, training and research, and economic and social support for small businesses and rural areas in difficulty.

3.3.3 Industrial policy

French governments have not hesitated to implement active industrial policies aimed at promoting growth, improving competitiveness or simply preserving employment. Such direct involvement in industrial and commercial life goes back to the period of Colbert and Louis XIV. The instruments used have covered a wide range, from full state ownership, protected monopolies, mixed-capital enterprises, state subsidies and protection, through to a vigorous defence of national industrial interests in international trade negotiations. Business leaders consider the close relationship with government that must accompany such support to be quite normal, and politicians of all sides regard the vigorous defence of French commercial interests as a natural part of their responsibilities. Seen in this light, the wave of nationalisations undertaken by the socialists in 1981 and 1982, the aim of which was to reorganise and revitalise French manufacturing, is better interpreted as a particular, if anachronistic, form of industrial policy rather than as an ideologically inspired change with the past.

Although the state was already involved in the economy through mixed-capital enterprises, or state-owned enterprises, the first major expansion of public ownership took place in the period of reconstruction after 1945. The main commercial banks and the insurance companies were nationalised to further economic recovery and the Renault interests suffered the same treatment but because of the owning family's collaboration during the war years. Economic planning was introduced to play a co-ordinating role. The 1960s was a period of particularly active industrial policy with the state encouraging industrial reorganisation in the search for 'national champions' and helping manufacturing investment through its control of the financial system. This was also the heyday of French indicative planning.

The nationalisations of 1982 represented a major change of gear. After the wave of nationalisations the public sector in manufacturing included 20% of employment, 24% of turnover, 33% of investment and 33% of exports. The aim was to use the nationalised enterprises as the spearhead of the campaign to improve export performance and reduce unemployment. Whereas investment in private industry declined to below 10% of added value, the public sector rate was 16.5%. Accompanying this investment, which came in the form of loans and capital grants, the public enterprises signed medium-term planning contracts with the government. After 1985, however, the difference between the public and the private sector was considerably reduced. Industrial assistance was reduced, and earlier attempts to influence strategy through sectoral plans were allowed to fall into abeyance.

Despite the increasingly non-interventionist climate of the 1980s there were several major examples of industrial restructuring involving publicly owned enterprises. The French steel industry was successfully reorganised in the form of Usinor-Sacilor in 1984 and 1986. Production of chemicals was concentrated around Rhône-Poulenc, Elf, and Total. As late as 1991 proposals were put forward to reorganise some of France's technology enterprises around Thomson and CEA-Industrie (these were shelved in 1992).

By 1988 industrial policy had become more neutral. Priority was given to the establishment of a competitive environment favourable to business expansion and to the improvement of profitability. This involved a range of policy changes mentioned elsewhere, such as the removal of price controls, steady reductions in company profits tax and the removal of the structure of managed and subsidised bank loans which had been such a feature of the French capital markets. While the prospect of preparing French industry for the approaching single European market, and the increasing opposition from the European Commission to state subsidies to industry were part of the background to this change, support in France for an industrial

policy remained widespread. The failure of the Maastricht conference to accept an active industrial policy at Community level in the EMU programme was widely criticised.

The role of the European Commission, in particular that of the DG4 handling competition, was to be seen in several matters involving industrial policy in France. Limitations on the government's ability to write off loans made to Renault, the insistence that added competition be introduced in air transport to accompany the merger of Air France with UTA and Air Inter, as well as the rejection of the purchase by Aerospatiale and Alenia in October 1991 of De Havilland, all served to limit freedom of action.

Nevertheless, the 11th Plan underlines the need for an active industrial policy as an essential part of economic policy for the coming five years. It seems unlikely that French policy-makers will entirely convert themselves to the concept that industrial strategy is best left to enterprises and that government planners have no role to play, and the close relationship which has always existed between officialdom and business leaders will continue to function.

3.3.4 The public sector and privatisation

Even if, as mentioned in the preceding section, the expansion of public ownership into competitive industry in 1982 formed a part of industrial policy, it was nonetheless controversial. One of the reasons for much of the hostility was the scale of the operation. The principal transfers concerned 38 banks and finance houses and five major industrial groups (Alcatel-Alsthom, Pechiney, Rhône-Poulenc, Saint-Gobain and Thomson). The steel producers Usinor and Sacilor were already in state hands. The state had majority shareholdings in Bull, Dassault, ITT France and Matra. The list, of course, does not include Renault and the *Grandes Entreprises Nationales* (EDF, GDF, Charbonnages de France, SNCF, RATP, Air France, Air-Inter and the PTT, enterprises covering energy, public transport and telecommunications), which were already under state control, as were the main banks and insurance companies.

To the extent that the nationalisations allowed the government to invest massively in industrial concerns in desperate need of funds, the policy was a success. But early attempts to influence the management of the manufacturing enterprises were quickly abandoned and as the enterprises recovered their independence so the logic of nationalisation became less and less apparent.

The right-wing government from 1986 to 1988 set out to privatise most of what had been taken over in 1982. Although the Chirac privatisation programme was interrupted by the October 1987 stock market crash and electoral defeat in 1988, and only 40% of their plans were completed, substantial inroads into the public sector were made. Among the most notable privatisations were TFI (television), the banks Suez, Paribas, Société Générale and the CCF, and the industrial groups Saint-Gobain, Alcatel-Alsthom and Matra. Since then official policy has been to allow neither reductions nor expansions of the public sector although the policy was modified in 1991 to allow partial privatisations provided the state maintained a majority.

Despite the privatisations, public enterprise has remained important in France. Estimations by the *Centre Europeen d'Entreprise Publique* put the share of the public sector in the French economy at 24% in 1985, 18.3% in 1988 and 18% in 1991. In 1990 the public sector still represented nearly 14% of manufacturing employment, 50% of the banking sector, 40% of insurance, 78% of energy, and virtually 100% of air transport and telecommunications.

The period from 1988 to 1993 has seen many public sector innovations such as the association between Volvo and Renault (which was changed to a '*société anonyme*' for the purpose) and a major reorganisation of the chemicals industry under public control. But pressure on public finances has had two major effects. The first has been to restrict access to new funds for the public enterprises which has been dealt with by some sophisticated financial engineering (non-voting certificates of investment, for example) and by the support in the form of shareholdings and loans from the public sector banks and insurance companies (for example, BNP and Air-France). In September 1991 it was decided to relax the restrictions on privatisations provided the state retained a voting majority. Sales of public assets involved shares in the bank Credit Local de France, the petrol companies Elf and Total and to a greater extent Rhône-Poulenc. The proceeds from these sales, some FF 13.5 billion, were to be used partly to pay for employment policies and partly to provide fresh capital for other public enterprises.

Under these circumstances the basic question of the relevance of state ownership becomes all the more pressing. If the public enterprises lack capital why should they not be allowed free access to the financial markets? If certain enterprises continue to make losses should they be cross-subsidised by the more successful ones? If the public enterprises are managed independently, in what way does state majority ownership contribute to efficiency? In view of these questions, it is hardly surprising that one of the first policy innovations of the Balladur Government was to announce its relaunch of the privatisation programme, interrupted in 1988. The privatisation law passed in 1993 went further than the plans in 1986, however, and, when completed, will leave France with a rather more typical public sector composed of energy utilities and land transport.

3.3.5 Indicative planning

One aspect of government intervention in the economy which has attracted much attention and controversy is the system of economic planning which has operated since 1946.

As introduced into France by Jean Monnet, planning was not ideological. It dealt with the enormous practical problems of an economy devastated by the war. The planning system was also indicative rather than imperative and set out to provide a series of quantified macroeconomic objectives for the period in question. The difficulties of the 1970s made such quantification impossible and in the 8th Plan, Raymond Barre limited the plan to a statement of areas in which effort was necessary, the '*programmes d'action prioritaire*'. In July 1982 a reform of the planning system created two stages. First, a law was to be passed defining the broad strategy and objectives. Second, the means required to achieve these ends would be set aside in a series of *contrats de plan* signed by the state and the various regions and major enterprises involved. The preparation of the plan was entrusted to a *Commissariat Général du Plan* with no powers beyond that of organising debates between the various partners concerned; the detailed work was carried out by commissions and committees who are responsible for a particular problem area. The technical support has become progressively more sophisticated and nowadays various scenarios are examined with the help of computer simulations.

The 9th Plan (1983–8) was prepared on the basis of the new two-stage procedure outlined above. Like the 8th Plan it lacked precise macroeconomic objectives. Contracts were signed in 1983 and 1984 with the enterprises of the public sector and with the regions, but this second stage of the planning procedure and the contracts with publicly owned firms and the regions could not bring about a real renaissance of the planning system. The public enterprises increasingly needed their independence in formulating and applying business strategy and any funds to be made available to the regions depended more on the limitations imposed by budgetary restraint than on the plan.

The whole planning process had become so unpopular with those favouring a liberal approach to the economy, that the incoming Chirac government seriously considered abolishing the *Commissariat Général du Plan* altogether. But this did not discourage the Socialist government in 1988 from returning to the planning process. The legislation approving the 10th Plan was duly voted in in July 1989. Designed to cover the period 1989–92, the plan had two main priorities. One objective was to modernise the French economy in such a way that the country could benefit fully from the creation of the Single Market. The other main priority was to restore a high level of employment. This improvement was to be brought about by a number of processes.

For example, ensuring that, although salary earners were to benefit from economic growth, improved rates of investment should be encouraged so as to provide new jobs. Training and education were to be improved to help the 18–25 age group. Employers' social costs were to be held steady to avoid further increasing the cost of labour and the conditions of employment were to be reorganised in ways favourable to the creation of stable jobs.

The strategy of the 10th Plan was based upon a number of 'construction projects' (*grands chantiers*) or priority areas in which government activity was to concentrate throughout the period of the Plan. In this way even if the 10th Plan, like its immediate predecessors, lacked quantitative objectives, it provided a coherent framework for government policy over the medium term and in this respect it fully reflected the Prime Minister's approach to the relationship between Plan and day-to-day economic policy. These projects involved improving education and training, investing in research and raising the competitiveness of French industry, ensuring the maintenance of social solidarity, improving the regional and urban environment and improving the quality and performance of the public services.

The latest plan, the 11th, published in April 1993, bears a marked similarity in its general approach to the current economic problems of France to that outlined by the incoming Prime Minister, Balladur. The Plan states, for example, that there is no real alternative to the general thrust of economic policy which France has followed for the past ten years. If France must remain in the EMS the fight against unemployment and the associated evil described as 'social exclusion' must be the main priority. The search for solutions to this problem involves strengthening European integration in order to better prepare France for the world economy and this cannot be envisaged without strengthening social cohesion. At the international level the Plan calls for new structures making it possible to improve co-ordination of the global economy. A strong Europe is seen as an essential vehicle if France is to have any real influence in international economic developments. To this end the Plan calls for the establishment of the single currency and the closer co-ordination of European economic policies. In this area, industrial policy should not be neglected, and agriculture will need continued support both because of its economic importance and its role as an element of regional policy.

Within France it is considered necessary to reconcile a competitive economy and social cohesion. Improved economic performance is not enough in itself if the cost is high unemployment. To overcome the unemployment problem, attitudes must be changed in business and employment must become the priority in public policy. This will mean using all the policy variables such as reducing the burden of social costs, training, developing employment in the tertiary sector, as well as appropriate social policies. It is interesting to note that the 14 reports, which form the basis of the 11th Plan, prepared under the authority of the Socialist government, coincide closely with the general principles of policy announced by the new Conservative leadership – another example of the wide consensus regarding general objectives which pervades the current French approach to economic policy.

3.3.6 Competition policy

In the period of reconstruction, following the Second World War, France built up a wide range of price controls in an attempt to deal with inflationary pressures. Until the early 1980s economic policy was generally interventionist and more concerned with establishing protected 'national champions' with a view to reconquering the domestic market than with the fostering of a competitive business environment. In view of the disappointing results of this policy and with a changing approach to economic management in mind the decisive step was taken in December 1986. Virtually all remaining price controls were removed and to counterbalance this freedom the *Conseil de Concurrence* (Competition Council) was set up.

The Competition Council has wide powers to investigate, make recommendations, and to impose sanctions where necessary. The Council can issue orders and impose fines of up to 5% of turnover. The Council may be petitioned by businesses, by the Minister of Finance, by the courts, by professional and by consumer associations. While regretting the lack of vigour with which the various non-governmental bodies make use of its powers to investigate restrictive practices, the Council noted in its most recent report for 1991 an increase of petitions of 20% over the previous year.

A number of specific restrictive practices are expressly forbidden. The abuse of dominant position is condemned although not monopoly situations in themselves. Most cases of such abuse concern efforts to restrict market access through unfair pricing or other attempts to keep competitors out of a particular market. Other restrictive practices expressly condemned are refusals to sell, collusion in price-fixing and the artificial maintenance of retail prices, while predatory pricing is curbed by the ban on selling below cost. Another area to which the Council has paid particular attention is that of collusion in the case of public procurement. In November 1989, for example some 80 major public works contractors received fines amounting to FF 166 million for conspiring to fix prices on public contracts and in January 1990 43 suppliers of electrical materials were fined for similar offences.

With regard to potentially anti-competitive aspects of mergers and take-overs, the Council can be requested to look into proposed or actual mergers which involve a horizontal or vertical control of more than 25% of the market or which involve an annual turnover of FF 7 billion. In 1991 four such cases of market concentration were submitted to the Council which suggested action to rectify the anti-competitive implications in each case.

On a wider level the position regarding anti-competitive business concentration is complicated by the role of community competition law in certain respects and by the continuing large scale of state involvement in industry in others.

3.4 FINANCIAL SYSTEM

The development of the French financial system from the 1960s to the present can be seen in outline as a progressive movement from a system where business finance came essentially from bank and state-controlled credit to one based on modern financial markets. Until quite recently, the French system featured extensive credit controls, specialised lending circuits, and large-scale use of subsidised credits for favoured sectors. Recent changes towards a more market-directed approach have taken place for several reasons – the government borrowing requirements resulting from the deficits of the early 1980s, the internationalisation of and technical developments in the banking industry, the desire to see Paris play a leading role as an international financial centre, and the prospect of monetary integration in the European Community.

3.4.1 Banking system

The banking system as a whole falls under the dual control of the Minister of the Economy, Finance and the Budget on the one hand and the Governor of the Banque de France, the central bank, on the other. This control is exercised through a number of regulatory bodies starting with the *Comité de Règlementation Bancaire* (Bank Regulation Committee) which lays down the regulations governing the banking sector, and the *Comité des Établissements de Credit* and the *Commission Bancaire* which together monitor the banks and other financial institutions operating under the Bank Act and enforce the appropriate regulations. The banks themselves are members of the *Association Française des Banques*.

There are 412 (1991) registered banks in France but most are members of a limited number of banking groups or are branches or subsidiaries of foreign banks. The three leading commercial banks are the Banque Nationale de Paris, the Credit Lyonnais (both still nationalised) and the Societé Générale. Together they control 22% of the branches in France and each has a string of specialised subsidiaries in the banking and financial sectors. Other important banks are the Banque Parisbas and Banque Indosuez which specialise in major business clients and international banking, the Credit Industriel et Commercial and the Credit Commercial de France.

In addition there are major networks of mutual and co-operative banks of which the Credit Agricole Mutuel, the Banques Populaires and the Credit Mutuel all have national importance. The Credit Agricole, originally, as its name implies, set up to provide banking services to farmers has a pyramid structure of local, regional and national levels of representation and control. It now operates throughout France and caters for all types of customer. The network of Banques Populaires originally specialised in the needs of small businesses but now functions as a general commercial bank as does the network of the Credit Mutuel.

The Caisses d'Epargne operate a system of savings banks throughout France. Although they increasingly provide banking services their particular feature is that the bulk of their funds is managed by a specialised institution, the Caisse des Depôts et Consignations. The CDC manages these funds and those of other state-controlled pension and social security funds using them to finance local government investments and social housing projects. The post office, the PTT, also offers savings bank facilities.

Other specialised banking institutions include the Credit Foncier de France, providing home loans financed by long-term borrowing, the Credit National, providing medium and long-term finance to industry and the Banque Française de Commerce Exterieur.

The Banque de France

Set up in 1800 and nationalised in 1945, the Banque de France is the central bank. Legislation introduced in 1993 by the new government provides for greater independence for France's central bank, which will have, in future, the sole responsibility for defining and implementing monetary policy. The four principal functions of the Banque de France are to define and implement monetary policy, to control and regulate the banking system, to manage the means of payment and the foreign reserves, and to act as banker to the state.

3.4.2 Monetary policy

If the overall objective of monetary policy is to achieve price stability, this has taken on a new dimension in France since 1983. The policy of competitive disinflation has involved the stabilisation of the franc within the European Monetary System. In practice this means stabilising the French franc/German mark exchange rate and since 1987, and despite the recent turmoil, the rate has been unchanged. Interest rates have been manipulated to combat speculation and to prevent the French franc from hitting its floor. A second objective has been to limit the growth of money supply to an agreed level, defined first in terms of M2 and since 1991 in terms of M3.

Exchange rate policy

The French exchange rate policy has been operated within the framework of the European Monetary System since March 1979. Three devaluations of the franc (October 1981, June 1982 and March 1983) associated with France's relatively higher inflation rate at that time led to a period of stability until April 1986. In this period the main elements of the policy of competitive disinflation were put in place aimed at supporting a stable exchange rate and a strong franc. The currency realignment of April 1986 and the German mark revaluation of January 1987 led to the long period of stability within the EMS broken only by the crisis of September 1992.

This stability has been maintained thanks to low inflation and is associated with high rates of interest and an expansion of the money supply limited to a range of 4% to 6% per year. Despite the fact that French inflation is now below that of Germany a certain interest rate differential remains. At present the nominal long-term differential is 0.4%. It will probably fall to 0.2% in the coming months. By the end of April 1993 the short-term risk premium on the Euro-franc

had disappeared. The fact that the franc survived waves of speculative attacks in September and December 1992 and January 1993 is evidence that the underlying strength of the French economy did not justify devaluation. Since then exchange rate stability has enabled the Banque de France to bring its intervention rates down to 9% and 8%.

The instruments of monetary policy

The Banque de France uses two rates to influence short-term market rates – the intervention or tender rate (*taux des appels d'offres*) and the repurchase rate (*taux des pensions de 5 à 10 jours*). Short-term rates fluctuate between these two limits, although the tender rate is used as the main indicator.

The Bank intervenes in the inter-bank money market to influence bank prime rates in the desired direction. Indeed, the removal of interest rate subsidies, restrictions on interest rates and the desegmentation of the financial markets which took place in the mid-1980s, mean that changes in official rates are quickly transmitted to all bank lending rates. Funds are lent at the intervention rate to the inter-bank market at twice-weekly auction sessions. This is the lowest rate at which the Bank lends to the markets and therefore forms the floor rate.

The repurchase rate is normally 0.5% to 0.75% above the intervention rate. Lending is available permanently against certain types of securities at this rate, on request. The market will only have a reason to borrow at this rate when it is below the 24-hour market rate. Consequently the repurchase rate sets the upper limit to the market and is comparable to the German Lombard.

The Bank can organise special auction sessions if it feels the need to inject liquidity into the market to keep rates down or can borrow from the market if it wants to tighten rates. Open market operations can also be used by the Bank to influence rates but so far little use has been made of this technique. The Bank's stock of Treasury Bills (*Bons du Trésor*) is too limited to enable it to have a major influence on rates.

The banks have to maintain a specified minimum of their reserves at the Bank in the form of special deposits (*reserves obligatoires*). The proportion and nature of these deposits will be determined by the Bank and as they do not receive interest they can be expensive in terms of lost interest. The higher the ratio, the higher the cost of credit. By reducing the level of special deposits the Bank has sought to persuade the commercial banks not to raise their base rates at times when the defence of the franc made it necessary to raise money market rates.

The participants in the money market

At the centre of the inter-bank market are the Bank of France and the principal market operators (*Operateurs Principaux de Marché or OPM*), of which there are 25. These are all leading banks. Loans can be from 24 hours to ten years but most are under two years with a special interest in three-month loans.

The *Trésor* (Treasury) uses the market to fund the government's borrowing requirement and to balance short-term differences between revenue and expenditure. The growth in the size of the national debt and the modernisation of its management has been one of the principal backdrops to the modernisation of the Paris financial market. First, there has been a process of simplification. The Trésor now issues only three forms of debt:

- the BTF (*bons du Trésor à taux fixe*) with a maturity of four to 52 weeks, issued at a discount
- the BTAN (*bons du Trésor à taux annuel*) with a maturity of two to five years
- the OAT (*obligations assimilables du Trésor*) with a maturity up to 30 years.

These investments correspond more closely to international norms than the previous forms of government bonds. The dealing in these bonds required the establishment of an appropriate market structure, and starting in 1986 a group of market makers, the *specialistes en valeurs du Trésor (SVT)* was designated, now consisting of some 15 banks and specialist houses. Appropri-

ate measures were also taken to ensure the proper functioning of the secondary market.

Businesses will also use the money market for borrowing and lending. Borrowing can be in the form of short-term loans or the issue of *billets de tresorerie* (commercial bonds).

Among the largest investors on the Paris money markets are the OPCVMs (*organismes de placement collectif en valeurs mobilières*) or mutual funds. Until recently the money markets were attractive to private investors for fiscal reasons and Paris witnessed a phenomenal growth in various money market mutual funds (*SICAV monétaires*).

Capital markets: new interest in the Bourse

Until recently the French system was based upon intermediation, meaning that savings were collected by the financial intermediaries, who then made these funds available to enterprises and the state.

In the 1980s this began to change as a result of a variety of developments – fiscal changes, the rapid expansion of unit trusts (*société d'investissement à capital variable (SICAV)*) and managed funds (*fonds commun de placement (FCP)*), higher real interest rates. Since the early 1980s, then, the Paris market has been characterised by rapid growth and many far-reaching regulatory and technical changes which have made the market intensely competitive in both domestic and international trading.

There have been several institutional changes. A second market was introduced in 1983 to cater for smaller companies, and a financial futures market, the *Marché à Terme d'Instruments Financiers (MATIF)*, in 1986.

3.5 INTERNATIONAL RELATIONS

The general growth of international trade and increasing integration into the European Community have ensured a growing importance for exports and imports in the French economy. France is the world's fourth largest exporter of manufactured goods coming behind the USA,

Germany and Japan but ahead of Italy and the UK, and is the second largest exporter of services.

3.5.1 Foreign trade

Foreign trade by sector

The French foreign trade position improved considerably in 1991 and 1992. Despite an international environment marked by recession and by slow growth there was an overall improvement in 1991 and a trade surplus in 1992. Export growth was stimulated by demand resulting from German unification and by an improvement in price competitivity. In 1991 unit wage costs in the manufacturing sector went up by 3.4% in France, but by 7.4% on average in the seven main trading partners. In 1992 this advantage was accentuated. The increase in France was 0.8% as opposed to 5% in the partners. As a result France was able to improve its overseas market share despite a marked deceleration in German imports (+18% in 1991 and +2.7% in 1992).

On the other hand the slow-down in the French economy has reduced the demand for imports. Imports increased by 15.2% in 1989, by 3.3% in 1990, by 2% in 1991 and by 1.8% in 1992. The impact was particularly noticeable in manufactured goods since domestic French demand for such products declined as a result in a fall in household consumption and industrial investment.

In 1991 the trade deficit improved to FF 30 billion and in 1992 a surplus of some FF 28 billion is expected, with a manufactured goods surplus of some FF 9 billion.

The balance of trade in manufactured goods

In 1987 the trade in manufactured goods went into deficit for the first time since 1969. Coming after a period of satisfactory results the 1987 deficit of FF 10.7 billion was a cause of considerable concern. A number of explanations have been put forward to explain this reversal.

1 As a result of the first oil crisis, French exports to OPEC countries increased and although this represented a logical response to the trade situation created by the two oil price increases, it left France in a rather vulnerable position when, from 1982 onwards, OPEC countries began reducing their imports.

2 In the early 1980s rates of commercial and other non-physical investment (for example, R&D) dropped, leaving France poorly placed to benefit from the economic recovery when it came. This failure made itself apparent in a fall in French market share in the OECD countries. In 1986 and 1987, for example, French exports to this area grew by 4.7%, whereas local demand grew by 7.9%. The difficulty is not simply one of price. In the period 1980–3 French export price competitiveness improved by 12% but market share grew by only 1%. The problem stems from a lengthy period of underinvestment as compared with France's main trading rivals.

3 Several French commentators have drawn attention to the fact that French industry has failed to develop sufficient points of specialisation (apart, arguably, from armaments and agro-food products). Only in the field of perfumery and luxury goods can French exporters be considered to have a dominant position.

4 Finally, the OECD attributed a large part of the responsibility to various government policies. Industrial policies in the late 1970s and early 1980s meant that considerable aid went to ailing industries in the hope of preserving employment and reconquering the domestic market, rather than accelerating inevitable readjustment. Export credits may have had the unintended effect of encouraging French exporters to pay too much attention to less solvent markets.

The recent improvements in the French position would appear to come from three sources:

- the improvement in levels of investment in French industry

- the beneficial results of the policy of competitive disinflation combined with the steady value of the franc in the EMS
- an increase in market share in the late 1980s and early 1990s in the OECD area and a movement away from the less buoyant markets elsewhere.

Nevertheless, it must also be remembered that the improvement in 1992 and 1993 reflects the recession. The lower levels of investment and the slowdown in household consumption imply lower levels of imports.

Trade in agricultural and food products

France is the world's second largest food exporter and trade surpluses have shown an upward trend since 1980. The surplus slipped back to FF 44.5 billion in 1991 but 1992 is expected to show an improvement. The main strengths of France are in cereals, dairy products and alcoholic beverages. Despite France's natural advantages it is generally accepted that the CAP has played a significant role in stimulating French exports in this area.

Services

Commercial services provide regular surpluses of some FF 50 billion. Tourism is the largest source but technological services are also important. The latter includes civil engineering contracts, engineering consultancy, nuclear reprocessing and management services on projects such as Airbus Industrie.

The geographical structure of foreign trade

The overall trend in the geographical structure of France's foreign trade has been similar to that of most of her EC partners showing the increasing importance of intra-community trade. Since 1958 the proportion of trade with the EC partners has more than doubled (see Table 3.9).

As the figures in Table 3.9 indicate, in the last decade France's exports have concentrated on the more prosperous but competitive OECD markets. Exports to OPEC countries declined from 7.4% in 1985 to 3.4% in 1991. To some extent some of France's difficulties in the 1980s stemmed from conscious policies called for in the 7th Plan (1975) to develop trade with the oil-surplus countries. Coupled with traditional links with sub-Saharan French-speaking Africa this policy left France with a relatively large share of trade with economies which suffered difficulties after the mid-1980s.

France's main export markets in 1991 were in Europe with Germany (18.1%), Italy (10.7%) Benelux (8.8%) and the UK (8.7%) at the head of the list. The same list represented France's main suppliers.

In 1991 and in 1992 there was a noticeable improvement in France's trading position with her EC partners, despite the fact that the deficit with Germany increased in 1992. The impact of German unification has been to encourage French exports and has considerably reduced France's traditional deficit with Germany. Increases in deliveries to the United States under the Airbus programme helped reduce the trade deficit by FF 10 billion. On the other hand the deficit with Japan remains at a high level.

Table 3.9 Foreign trade by zone (%)

	1980		1985		1991	
	Exports	Imports	Exports	Imports	Exports	Imports
EC	55.4	49.5	53.7	55.8	61.4	57.9
Other OECD	15.3	17.5	20.1	18.9	16.9	22.3
Non-OECD	29.3	33.0	26.2	25.4	21.7	19.8

Source: Douanes Françaises

3.5.2 Foreign investment

The 1980s witnessed, particularly after the period 1984–5, a rapid increase in foreign direct investment. French industry participated fully in this process but with a certain delay due to a later improvement in company profits and the removal of exchange controls in 1985. This trend is a reflection of the globalisation of business strategy in general, and as far as France is concerned, a strategy of preparation for the European Single Market.

French foreign direct investment fluctuated around FF 20 billion between 1980 and 1985 and then increased to reach FF 147.6 billion in 1990 (see Table 3.10). In the next two years investments decreased as enterprises felt the need to assimilate their acquisitions and maintain their financial stability in a deteriorating economic climate.

Table 3.10 French foreign direct investment (billion FF)

1981	1985	1986	1987	1988	1989	1990	1991	1992
25.1	20	36.2	52.3	76	115.2	147.6	115.8	94

Source: Banque de France

The direction of this flow of investment shows a concentration on the OECD economies in general, and on the EC in particular (see Table 3.11).

Table 3.11 French foreign direct investment by area (%)

	EC	Other OECD	Non-OECD
1980–1985	23.5	52.7	23.8
1986–1991	59.3	35.2	5.5

Source: Banque de France

There is an obvious link, in the internationalisation of business strategy, between direct investment abroad and exporting. It comes as no surprise, then, that the control of French foreign subsidiaries is concentrated in the hands of a small number of industrial groups (16 groups provide 50% of total foreign employment) and that 71% of total foreign employment is in the OECD area. The US has the largest number of French subsidiaries (1,500), followed by France's main European trading partners (Germany 1,200 subsidiaries, UK, 1,000, Spain and Benelux each 800 and Italy 660). Outside this area, Africa is the most important (1,300) with the largest numbers in Morocco and the Ivory Coast.

Foreign direct investment in France has also increased significantly since the mid-1980s but a noticeable imbalance remains. In 1990 the total was FF 49.3 billion as opposed to an outward investment of FF 147.3 billion. A number of reasons are given to explain why France remains a relatively less attractive economy for foreign direct investment. If salary costs, levels of taxation, and other costs of investment are not a direct handicap, foreign investors indicate other problems. Mediocre foreign language skills, lack of mobility, shortages of certain categories of highly skilled labour and inadequate training facilities for categories of labour below the *'grande école'* elite are often cited in the labour area. The administrative apparatus of central and local government is often perceived as being unfavourable to incoming investment. Despite recent efforts to speed up administrative procedures the system is still seen as *'dirigiste'* and burdened by complex rules interpreted by a multitude of compartmentalised civil servants.

3.5.3 Balance of payments

The French balance of payments is drawn up on the same accounting principles as that of other countries and must be analysed in terms of current account and long- and short-term capital payments. One element of confusion in the presentation of French trade statistics involves the apparent discrepancy between the trade balance as reported by the French customs authorities (*les Douanes*) and the trade balance in the balance of payments. There are some significant corrections involved. First, the customs authorities record exports and imports for metropolitan France excluding the various overseas territories and departments. Integrating the trade of these areas into the balance of payments increases the apparent trade deficit by between 20 and 30 billion francs. Another correction involves the inclusion by the customs (excluded by the balance of payments) of imports and exports which do not involve payment or transfer of ownership. An element in integrated industrial programmes affecting imports in particular the exclusion of such transfers improves the figures by FF 8 to 10 billion. Finally customs figures are collected on an FOB basis for exports and a CIF price for imports. The balance of payments uses FOB for both, correcting the customs import figures by 4% in 1990.

The French current account has been in deficit throughout the 1980s and 1990s except for a slight surplus in 1986 (see Table 3.12). The crisis year, however, was 1982 when the current account deficit expanded from a deficit of 0.8% of GDP in 1981 to one of −2.2%. This was the single principal cause of an abrupt change in macroeconomic policy involving the introduction of a series of austerity measures. The deficit declined to −0.9% in 1983 and −0.2% in 1984. Since 1987 the deficit has fluctuated around −0.5% of GDP.

Table 3.12 Current account (balances in FF billion)

	1986	1988	1990	1991	1992
Merchandise	−19.1	−50.4	−70.3	−49.8	+9.2
Services of which	31.0	27.4	23.2	17.5	10.3
transport, insurance	−3.1	0.6	−12.6	−13.2	−12.2
technical services	22.4	13.0	14.9	19.2	15.4
revenues	−7.7	−2.1	−17.5	−28.7	−44.6
tourism	22.2	24.2	43.2	51.0	56.5
Other goods and services	32.5	34.5	38.9	40.2	41.6
Unilateral transfers	−31.7	−40.3	−44.4	−41.4	−45.4
Current balance	12.7	−28.8	−52.7	−33.4	15.7

The main features of the current account over recent years have been a deteriorating trade balance which has improved significantly since 1990, and a declining surplus in services. The main trends in the latter area are an increase in France's surplus on tourism and a growing deficit on revenues paid abroad reflecting, in turn, the weight of foreign investment in France and high prevailing interest rates (see Table 3.12). The deterioration in 1992 concerning unilateral transfers was to a large extent exceptional involving payments of some FF 10 billion related to the Gulf War. Apart from this negative item there was an improvement as payments to the EC went down and compensation through the CAP increased. Private transfers, consisting mainly of payments from immigrant workers, remain stable at around FF 14 billion.

Capital movements include transfers (associated with cancellation of debt) and long- and short-term elements. With regard to direct investment the deficit has tended to decline since 1990 under the combined effect of a reduction in French direct investment abroad and an increase in foreign investment in France. Similarly foreign portfolio investment in France has remained at a high level despite a fall from the peak in 1990. In 1992 there was a noticeable increase in foreign purchases of government securities, as compared to 1991. These capital movements were affected by the September monetary crisis. Detailed figures for the second half of 1992 are not yet available but for the first five months the net figures for long-term capital were (all in billion francs): July −18.1, August −10.3, September −52.5, October +59.7, November +43.1.

3.6 SPECIAL ISSUES

3.6.1 The social security system

Established in its present form in 1945, the '*Securité Sociale*' is regarded both as politically sacrosanct and as being in need of urgent reform. Essentially, the social security system, which covers hospital and medical care, family allowances, and retirement pensions is suffering from two underlying trends. First, expenditure on health care is rising inexorably, and, secondly, demographic trends indicate that the already heavy burden of retirement pensions will increase dramatically as the population ages significantly in the next 20 to 30 years.

Expenditure on unemployment benefits, which constitutes a separate problem, suffers from a different logic. With a replacement ratio of 60%, as opposed to an EC average of 70% and with further curbs planned after reforms in the unemployment compensation system in the summer of 1992, expenditure on unemployment benefits has been kept down. Despite a 50% increase in the number of unemployed between 1981 and 1993 expenditure as a percentage of GDP only increased from 1.59 to 1.85. On the other hand, early retirement expenditure, which is an employment-related phenomenon is included in the statistics on general retirement.

Amending the social security system is rendered difficult by its complexity. It is composed of three levels. First, there is the *regime de base* which provides basic compulsory protection available to all. This is complemented by various industry-wide systems based on collective agreements. Finally, there is a range of optional schemes (in many cases optional in theory rather than practice) which provide extra cover. The finance for the various services provided comes to an overwhelming extent from contributions from employers and employees. However, deficits of the basic regime came to FF 15.7 billion in 1992 after FF 16.6 billion in 1991 and FF 9.6 billion in 1990. Deficits are being caused by the combination of slow growth and unemployment (which reduce contributions) and continuing high levels of expenditure. The other specialised organisations responsible for managing other sections of the social security, such as the *UNEDIC* (unemployment benefits), also report large provisional deficits which will be absorbed by the state. In 1992, the deficit on health care came to FF 6.3 billion and that on retirement pensions to nearly FF 18 billion. Official estimates fear that 1993 will see a general social security deficit of FF 60 billion unless substantial corrective measures are taken.

The causes of these problems are the increasing consumption of health care services, on the one hand, and an ageing population, on the other. Neither of these trends, of course, is unique to France. According to OECD estimates the dependency ratio (population over 65 as a percentage of the population 15–64) will increase from 21.9% in 1980 to 23.3% in 2000, 30.6% in 2020 and 38.2% in 2040.

In the spring of 1991 the authorities prepared a White Paper on retirement pensions which summarised the present situation and made a number of suggestions. When the government established the right to retirement at 60 years in 1982 it made a popular but costly innovation. Changes to the system of indexation in 1982 and 1987 made minor improvements but the White Paper's recommendations went further. It suggested a reorganisation of the multitude of various pension schemes now operating and two possible measures to reduce the cost of pensions. One would involve raising the number of years' contributions required for a full pension from 37.5 to 41 or 42, and the other was to calculate entitlements on the basis of the average of the 25 highest annual salaries rather than the 10 highest at present. Current negotiations are aimed at introducing the first of the two changes. While not necessarily endangering the principle of retirement at 60, it does mean that those who reach 60 but who have not made enough contributions would be obliged to postpone retirement. No effort has yet been made to introduce compulsory systems based on capitalisation.

Expenditure on health care has increased much faster than growth in GDP and public expenditure on health in France is higher than other leading OECD members. The increase in expenditure has continued inexorably. In 1991 it reached 9.1% of GDP after 8.8% in 1990. Various measures have been introduced during the past decade to reduce the share of this expenditure covered by the social security (the principle remains one of repayment for treatment consumed, rather than the provision of free treatment) from 76.5% in 1980 to 73.6% in 1991. On the other hand, there still seems to be no general reform of the system in view and the government continues to aim at various agreements which will limit the growth in expenditure.

3.6.2 Agriculture and the question of reform

Although the proportion of the French working population employed in agriculture has been in steady decline for many years, and is now approaching the level found in other industrialised countries (5.6%), the industry remains of major importance. The reasons for this importance are economic and political. France remains Europe's leading producer of wheat, maize, wine, beef and veal, poultry meat and milk. Food exports represent 12% of total French exports and with an annual trade surplus of around FF 50 billion provide a considerable contribution to the balance of trade. On the other hand the decline in the farming population is associated with a fall in farm incomes and fears regarding the depopulation of rural regions. Since the peasant roots of modern France are generally regarded as being of importance to the stability of French society and part of the national heritage, the main professional farming union, the FNSEA, is able to appeal to wide popular sympathy and represents a very powerful lobby.

The average age of the farming population is also considerably higher than that of the working population as a whole (in 1990, 46.3 years in farming as opposed to 38 years outside). The departure of the older generations into retirement will probably cause a rapid fall to some 700,000 in the next five years. French farming has also seen a more rapid decline in salaried farm workers (−73.6% between 1954 and 1982) than in independent farmers (−63.7% in the same period). At the same time the rapid decrease in the number of small farms has been associated with the abandonment of marginal farms in many areas and the absorption of others into larger units. In the 1980s the average farm size increased from 23.4 to 28.1 hectares.

In this environment the adoption of the reform of the Common Agricultural Policy in May 1992 was bound to cause considerable doubt and argument in France. As the essence of the Macsharry Reform is to combine substantial cuts in guaranteed prices and the setting aside of arable land, the impact on French farm incomes is the subject of controversy. The system of compensating for the cuts in price support by direct aids in the case of cereals, and the various accompanying measures, in particular the French accompanying plan of July 1992, have created a complex situation. The French plan involves aid in the form of tax concessions, support to farmers heavily in debt, as well as investment subsidies to new farmers and extensive stock raisers. Official estimates (*Economie et Statistique*, May 1992) claim that French agricultural production will rise by 5% over the next five years instead of the 10% which the previous policies would have caused. On the other hand, thanks to the accompanying measures, farm incomes should rise by 7% instead of 5% without the reform.

The reaction to the reforms is complicated by the diversity of farming and the diversity of the various measures. Average farm income declined by 5.9% in 1992 but this global fall covers a wide disparity. Cereal producers saw incomes increase by 15% while vegetable producers saw their incomes decline by 50%.

3.7 FUTURE PROSPECTS

The assessment of France's overall economic position in early 1993 is inevitably complicated by the rapid deterioration of growth prospects and the budget deficit. The distinction must be made between the underlying strength of the economy, and the difficulties created by the present conjuncture.

Since 1983 French economic policy has been characterised by the strategy aiming at slowing inflation and improving the competitivity of the economy, known as competitive disinflation, and by a process of structural reforms. Both of these aspects of policy had as their overall objective improving France's position in an increasingly integrated European economy. This commitment to Europe is particularly visible in the banking and capital market reforms undertaken since 1985 and culminating in the recent proposals to make the Banque de France independent of government control. It is also to be seen in French determination to maintain the franc at its 1987 value without devaluation, throughout the recent crisis in the European Monetary System.

A number of major successes have been achieved. Despite several attacks since the summer of 1992 the franc has not been devalued. Whereas inflation was running at up to 14% at the start of the 1980s, after 1987 it stabilised around 3%. Combined with a low increase in wage costs and exchange rate stability the French economy enjoyed improved international competitiveness. From the period 1987–8 French export performance improved with her share of European exports rising from 15.5% in 1987 to 17% in 1992. From 1991 the trade balance improved leading to a surplus in 1992. The growth rate of the French economy also improved relatively so that in 1991 and 1992 it was performing better than the EC average.

Although few commentators would criticise the overall macroeconomic policy stance of recent years, several major problems remain. The main one is the high and persistent rate of unemployment. Improvements in this area can only be long term.

The recent downturn has been caused by external factors. The economic slowdown among France's trading partners led to an increasing lack of confidence in French industry about market prospects, and a consequent drop in business investment. It is not sure whether recent interest rate cuts and strong profits will be enough to ensure a recovery in business investment in France before a general European recovery sets in.

The immediate future of the French economy is determined less by the gains of recent years and the underlying strength of the economy and more by the probable fall in GDP in 1993 and the impact on public finances. Attempts to bring down this deficit will reduce the role of the automatic stabilisers and run the risk of deepening the recession.

The main hope for an improvement in 1993 and in 1994 comes from the downward trend in interest rates since the September 1992 crisis. It is to be hoped, but it is by no means sure, that this effect, combined with measures taken by the incoming Conservative government, will lead to an improvement in business confidence and a recovery in business investment. Even optimistic forecasts consider stagnation in 1993 will be followed by only moderate recovery in 1994. Unemployment will continue to rise into 1994.

3.8 BIBLIOGRAPHY AND SOURCES OF INFORMATION

INSEE (monthly): *Economie et Statistique*
INSEE (1989): *Les Entreprises à l'épreuve des années 80*
INSEE (1993): *La France des Entreprises*
INSEE (1993): *La France et ses régions*
INSEE (annual): *Rapport sur les comptes de la nation*
INSEE (annual): *Tableaux de l'économie française*
Jeanneney, J.M. (1989): *L'économie française depuis 1967*, Editions du Seuil, Paris
Ministère de L'Economie (monthly): *Les Notes Bleues de Bercy*
OECD: *Economic Survey: France*
Pebereau, M. (1985): *La Politique Economique de la France*, (3 vol.), Armand Colin, Paris

Useful sources of information

Banque de France, 39, rue Croix-des-petits-Champs, 75001 Paris. Tel: (1) 42 92 42 92
Centre Français du Commerce Extérieur, 10, avenue d'Iéna, 75783 Paris. Tel: (1) 40 73 30 00
Chambre de Commerce et d'Industrie de Paris, 2, rue de Viarmes, 75001 Paris. Tel: (1) 45 08 39 20
INSEE (Institut national de la statistique et des études économiques), 18, boulevard Adolphe-Pinard, 75675 Paris Cedex 14. Tel: (1) 45 40 01 12
La Documentation Française, 31 quai Voltaire, 75007 Paris. Tel: (1) 40 15 70 00
OECD, 2, rue André-Pascal, 75775 Paris Cedex 16. Tel: (1) 45 24 82 00

CHAPTER 4

Italy

Andrea Fineschi

4.1 INSTITUTIONAL AND HISTORICAL CONTEXT

4.1.1 Institutional framework

Italy is a parliamentary democracy, with the government chosen not directly by the electorate, but requiring the support of parliament (the Chamber of Deputies and the Senate). Government stability depends on the electoral system of proportional representation in one of its purest forms, which explains the continual presence of numerous political parties in parliament. With the exception of 1948–53 – the period immediately following the approval of the constitution and during which the Christian Democratic Party had an absolute majority in parliament – Italy has had a succession of coalition governments for the entire post-war period and these governments have been extremely unstable.

The most important changes in the composition of the political structure occurred in the early 1960s and during the second half of the 1970s. In the first period, the Socialist Party participated for the first time in a coalition government (in which its majority partner was, and continues to be, the Christian Democratic Party). In the second half of the 1970s, a national unity government was formed with the support of the Communist Party. Political scientists have defined the Italian democratic system as a 'locked' democracy, in that it is one of the few systems in the industrialised world which has not operated with alternating governments.

The nature of the political system has a number of important economic consequences. First, the necessity to form coalition governments from among the main political groupings representing diverse interests in society, and the instability of these coalition governments, have resulted in a preference for monetary policy (carried out by the more stable financial institutions) over other tools of economic policy. Fiscal policy has rarely been used in a 'radical' way (as it was used, for example, by other countries after the oil crisis) owing to the excessive fragmentation and instability of executive power, though it has been used as a short-term expedient.

The need to reconcile differing political interests has thus been a major determinant of policy choice in post-war Italy. For example, it was no coincidence, that, in the early 1950s, economic policy was clearly oriented towards deregulation of the market and a refusal to accept Keynesian policies and yet, at the same time, large-scale state enterprises were developed in several essential sectors of the economy. Nor is it fortuitous that in recent years, during which a 'return to the free market' economic policy was supported officially, the size of the state enterprise sector has been reduced only marginally and continues to be a major and distinctive characteristic of the Italian economy. These are contradictions which emerge out of political compromise.

In addition, the Italian administrative structure is characterised by a fragmented system of self-governing local units (regions, provinces and boroughs) whose power is restricted by the fact that finance is controlled by central government. Furthermore, prior to 1993, the members of those local administrations, with an electorate of over 5,000 inhabitants, were also elected by a system of proportional representation, which has meant that they too have been very unstable. This power structure has made both the day-to-day running of the local authorities and the implementation of new economic policy measures by central government particularly complex. Furthermore, the presence of a plurality of decision-making centres, with their inherent instability, has made the exercise of consistent cyclical economic policy difficult. The proportional electoral system and coalition governments are largely responsible for Italy's poor performance in relation to public finance management in recent decades and certainly a cause of the disastrous state of public debt. Increasing public expenditure would have been an obvious policy choice in the face of economic difficulties following the oil shocks of 1973–4 and 1979–80; but a strict fiscal policy would have destroyed coalition governments in which component parties represented different social interests and different regions of the country.

In spite of the instability of coalition governments, until recently Italy experienced a relatively stable political majority in terms of the parties which supported the government. Electoral results, the formation of governments since the period immediately after the Second World War and the emergence of the 'Cold War' were all influenced by what is usually called 'factor K' – a '*conventio ad excludendum*' from government of the Communist Party, a party which was the most representative of the Italian working class. It is not difficult to understand why the change in international politics, the end of the 'Cold War' and the disintegration of the Soviet Union, had a major influence on the Italian electorate. This change in attitudes is clearly due to the downfall of Communist leadership in East European countries and in the former USSR and the consequent disappearance of the 'factor K'. The 1992 parliamentary elections and, more importantly, the local elections which followed overturned the traditional majority.

The Parliament no longer expresses the people's real political preferences which have altered very substantially in the space of just one year. If the electoral rules used in the past were used today, the major parties would receive a much reduced level of support, new parties would emerge and parliamentary representation would be more fragmented, making it more difficult to form stable central and local governments. In this context, at the beginning of 1993, a new law was passed which changed the electoral system for the *Comuni* (town administrations). Under the new law the Mayors of *Comuni* with an electorate of over 15,000 inhabitants are elected directly by the citizens (and the majority system is extended to *Comuni* with less than 15,000 inhabitants) and new rules provide for more stable local government. Moreover in April 1993 a referendum established, with a very large majority (more than 80%), a change in the electoral rules in favour of a majority system in elections for the *Senato*. The result of this referendum was interpreted politically as clear support for the introduction of new rules (i.e. a majority system) for the other chamber (the *Camera*) also. Parliament is now working on the new electoral rules. When the new law is passed it is anticipated that elections will result in a marginalisation of the traditional government parties.

The possibility, under a new electoral system, of different political forces alternating in the government of the country, should also help to achieve a reduction in political 'corruption', a phenomenon which intensified among politicians and businessmen in the 1980s in the field of public works. The process of change in the institutions is also determined by the pressure of an enormous public debt and the hope is, supported by recent international economic research in the field, that Italy will be successful in reducing public debt in a context of more stable and authoritative governments, made possible by the new electoral majority law.

4.1.2 Political structure and trade unions

The nature of the political structure of Italian democracy has also had repercussions on the relationships among the workers' organisations and the relationship between the workers' organisations and the government. The organisations which represent the interests of workers and employers certainly have a strong influence on the economy, as is normal in countries with liberal-democratic political structures.

Organised labour in Italy is currently represented by three main trade unions (*CGIL, Confederazione Generale Italiana dei Lavoratori*; *CISL, Confederazione Sindacale Italiana dei Lavoratori* and *UIL, Unione Italiana Lavoratori*) which are organised according to productive sector, rather than by occupation. These three trade unions are well supported with a high level of membership among workers. However, in recent years, a number of small unions have emerged which are occupationally based and independent of the three major unions.

The origin of the main trade unions can be traced back to the various political parties to which they were linked. For example, the CGIL was linked to the Communist and Socialist parties and the CISL to the Christian Democratic party. It is difficult to forecast the consequences the current political upheaval (see section 4.1.1) will have on the structure of trade unions but it is clear that the political stance of the trade unions will have to take the appearance of new political parties into account.

The link between unions and political parties has been made more complex by inter-party relationships. This, together with the fact that the Communist party was excluded from government while its supporters and members formed a majority in the CGIL (the largest union), explains the reluctance on the part of the unions to assume a unified position with regard to the economic policy of the government. This was especially true when large-scale social agreements were proposed by the government. In other words, the political origins of the trade unions and the exclusion from government of a party which a large number of trade union members supported (the Communist party) have determined to a great extent the relationship between the government and the trade unions.

The strength of the unions and their ability to

represent the Italian workers depends to a large extent, as in all industrialised countries, on a range of factors: the stage of economic development, the level of unemployment, the firm size and the mix of industrial sectors. Other factors influencing the workers' negotiating power are specifically related to the Italian economy: the ownership of the company (privately or state), the political climate and criteria which influence the employment of large numbers of people in public administration, and most important of all, the state of political relationships between the main unions and the government.

4.1.3 Social policy

The principal areas of social policy are health care, workers' insurance against industrial accidents and workers' pension schemes. The national health system provides free assistance for all those (Italian citizens and foreign residents) who demand its services. Established during the 1970s, it operates through a system of local health centres *(Unità Sanitarie Locali (USL))* and is financed by transfers from the state to the regions, and then from the regions to each centre. Pensions are paid on the basis of an assessment of salary over recent working years through *INPS (Istituto Nazionale per la Previdenza Sociale)*, an institute financed by the compulsory contributions of the workers and employers. Another institution, *INAIL (Istituto Nasione per l'Assicurasióne contro gli Infortuni sul Lavoro)*, also financed by the workers and employers, provides for workers in case of accidents at work.

The state system for the unemployed operates differently from those in the countries of North and Central Europe. There are varying levels of assistance for workers. Those receiving the greatest degree of protection are generally the workers in large firms, who, because of the social and political importance of mass dismissals, receive the services of the *cassa integrazione guadagni* scheme (a wage-related unemployment benefit scheme which pays over 70% of the last salary). It applies both for ordinary cases, such as a temporary lay-off, and where much longer periods of unemployment are involved. Workers dismissed by small firms and people looking for their first jobs are given much less protection. If they are registered as unemployed, they are eligible for only a small benefit for a comparatively short period.

4.1.4 Market regulations

Three different institutions supervise market competition in the Italian economy. The *Autorità garante della concorrenza e del mercato* has general responsibility for ensuring markets are competitive. Another institution, the *Autorità garante per l'editoria*, supervises market competition in the specific field of the media. The Bank of Italy is responsible for overseeing competition in the banking and (partially) in the insurance sector.

The country's anti-trust law is not based on the (neo-)classical model of perfect competition; the dominance of companies is evaluated in accordance with EC anti-trust law with reference to European and world markets and the assessment as to whether competition rules are infringed is no longer made simply according to company size but rather on the basis of the actual market power that a company or group of companies possesses. Thus, even though FIAT produces almost all Italian cars, it is not considered to occupy a dominant market position unless it acquires this by colluding with foreign companies.

The level of competition in the manufacturing sector is quite satisfactory if compared with that prevailing in European countries, a result largely due to the liberalisation of foreign trade. Nevertheless protected sectors continue to exist, especially in the service sector, and some Italian economists think that this is one of the major causes of the higher level of inflation frequently experienced by the Italian economy.

The law limiting firms in the field of the media regulates a situation in which the TV market is essentially divided between the State (*RAI, Radio Televisione Italiana*) and the private corporation *Fininvest,* and in which the press (mostly daily papers) is controlled by a handful of large publishing groups, often owned by the important industrial groups. In the TV sector, market competition is significantly constrained by the existence of a duopoly (RAI and Finivest). The main function of this law is to consider simultaneously the two kinds of information and then to limit the market power of the companies in the whole market.

The extent of market competition in the banking sector is actually less than satisfactory. Nevertheless, the objective of achieving more competition needs to be reconciled with the fact that banks have to be large in order to compete in the European market. The free entry of the European banks into the Italian system (since the beginning of 1993) is supposed to create more intense competition. A boost to the expansion of Italian credit institutions is expected to come from a new banking law, recently passed by parliament, which allows Italian banks to make medium and long-term loans in addition to the short-term loans to which they were previously restricted.

4.1.5 Historical context

During the late 1960s and early 1970s Western economies were characterised by significant levels of social conflict both in relation to the distribution of income and industrial relations. In Italy, compared with other Western countries, this was a long-lasting and deep-rooted conflict, especially in the 1970s, when a rediscovered sense of trade union unity gave workers' organisations a strong negotiating position.

The prices of raw materials began to increase at the end of the 1960s, followed by an unexpected and sudden rise in the price of oil (1973–4). These price increases hit the Italian economy when it was already suffering deep social conflict. The agreement between the trade unions and the major employers' organisation (*Confindustria*) on linking wages to the rate of inflation (the 1975 working agreement on the reform of the *scala mobile*, which was later extended to the public administration sector, was considered by the *Confindustria* to be an instrument for lessening the conflict over the distribution of income and for improving industrial relations. It was also welcomed by the trade unions as it gave automatic protection to real wages against sharp price increases (including those of imported goods affected by the constant devaluation of the lira). Even if the agreement did succeed in maintaining the purchasing power of wages in the face of high inflation, it did not achieve significant success in terms of improving industrial relations until the formation of the national unity government in 1975–6.

Exchange rate depreciation and expansionary fiscal policy simply dampened down the bitter social conflict of the 1970s and postponed resolution of the problem to a later date. During the 1970s public sector savings, the difference between fiscal revenues and current expenditure, which had been in surplus during the preceding period, moved into deficit. The debt grew progressively as social security and health legislation caused a sharp increase in public spending in the mid-1970s at a time when there was a loss of potential revenue due to delays in introducing tax reform. A more rigorous fiscal policy would certainly have accentuated the conflict in society in the years following the first oil shock. However, the systematic devaluation of the lira meant that the vicious circle of price and salary increases did not halt economic growth and this also helped to reduce social conflict. From 1977, the trade unions became less aggressive (during the period of the national unity government, 1976–9). This, together with a foreign exchange policy which was oriented towards a strong national currency *vis-à-vis* the dollar (the currency in which raw materials and energy supplies were paid for), yet floating with regard to other European currencies, meant that in the late 1970s, there was less inflation, a recovery in investment and an improvement in the foreign trade balance.

The second wave of oil price increases (1979–80) hit Italy when its economy was in a phase of strong growth, which continued until the second half of 1980 thus making it difficult to control inflation and accentuating the trade deficit. The delay in adjusting to the international economic cycle worsened the problem of inflation and foreign debt.

In the late 1970s and early 1980s there were significant changes in Italian monetary, financial and foreign exchange policy, and in the general orientation of economic policy, reflecting changes which had occurred in the world economy. In 1979 Italy joined the European Monetary System, which further constrained Italian economic policy and removed a great deal of its discretionary power to influence the value of the currency. Italy, by joining the European Monetary System, suffered a worsening of its foreign commercial accounts as the German mark became, year by year, undervalued in relation to the lira; however, this can also be seen as an anti-inflation policy, as it was an indication from the government to the employers and unions that increases in prices would not be accompanied by a policy of devaluation of the lira.

In 1982 the central bank 'divorced' from the treasury with the adoption by the monetary authorities of a measure which relieved the Bank of Italy of the obligation to act as 'buyer of last resort' at the auctions of public debt bonds. This measure was the clearest sign of the change in the policy of financing the public debt, which shifted from the system of financing the debt by issuing public debt bonds (outside the market) through the banking system, to one of financing the debt largely through the market itself. As a consequence both of the divorce between the central bank and the treasury and entry into the European Monetary System, Italian real interest rates increased sharply in the early 1980s, reaching levels above those of the 1970s and indeed of other countries in the industrialised world. This elevated real interest rate increased the cost of servicing the public debt and was a major cause of the marked increase in the deficits on the public sector account.

In 1983 parliament passed a measure which changed the method of calculating the relationship between salaries and the rate of inflation. In itself this measure had only a moderate effect; it was important, however, in that it announced future government policy and showed that the government intended to adopt a hard line in relation to both inflation and the unions (the CGIL was not aligned to government policy). In the early 1980s the major companies took action to reduce the negotiating power of the trade unions inside the factories. These included dismissals of workers who belonged to extremist organisations, the movement of workers from one place to another, and measures to lay off thousands of workers for varying periods of time. In this the companies were helped by the part played by the white-collar workforce, whose salaries had been hit, both by the introduction of the *scala mobile* which had had the effect of levelling out salary differentials and also by the fiscal drag caused by prolonged and persistent inflation which was not compensated for by adjustments in the rates of tax. Of particular importance, was the march of the 40,000 in Turin (the city of FIAT) organised by the white-collar workers.

During the 1980s there was a sharp reduction in social conflict according to all the indicators (see Figure 4.1) and this was one of the major

reasons for the recovery in profitability of the major companies, especially those where the trade unions were traditionally the strongest. At the beginning of the 1980s the economic situation of the major companies was poor. The level of external debt of the companies was high in relation to their internal financial resources, and the return on investment was low. In 1983–4, however, a new phase of recovery began to have a positive effect on investment and profits.

With increasing pace, the recovery continued uninterruptedly up to the end of the 1980s. While, during the first phase of recovery, investment was largely devoted to the modernisation of capital equipment (a period of company restructuring), in the late 1980s investment was channelled into the expansion of productive capacity. The change in the economic performance of the major Italian companies was a characteristic of the 1980s. This development was of more than purely economic significance; its influence extended into the political arena, owing to the considerable power that the major companies have in forming economic policy.

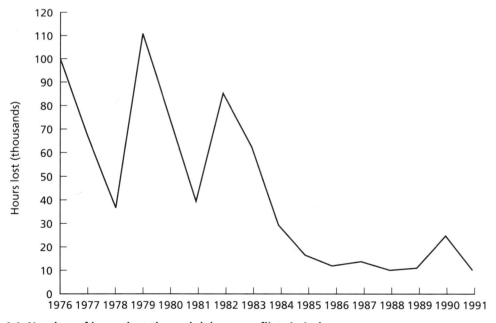

Figure 4.1 Number of hours lost through labour conflicts in industry.

Source: ISTAT.

The period of growth came to an end in the early 1990s when the effects of the world economic depression began to impact on Italy. The devaluation of the national currency inside the EMS in September 1992, immediately followed by the lira's exit from the EMS (leaving the currency floating freely in the market) brought an end to the policy started in the late 1970s. The impact of devaluation was immediately positive in terms of the current balance. Moreover, it has not resulted in increases in prices due to the low level of domestic aggregate demand. The rate of inflation in mid-1993 was actually around 4%, the lowest level for 25 years.

4.2 MAIN ECONOMIC CHARACTERISTICS

4.2.1 Gross domestic product

The estimation of the gross domestic product (GDP) is especially difficult in the case of Italy because of the significant quantity of products and services traded within the 'black economy' which escape measurement by *ISTAT* (*Istituto*

Centrale di Statistica). Examples include people who have several jobs but are only officially registered in one, people who are not legally employed, and people who work at home and are thus able to avoid paying taxes. Twice in the last 20 years, ISTAT's estimates of national income have been revalued to take black market activity into consideration. This means that it is difficult to provide valid time series data for the national income in recent years. However, the data for the 1980s can be considered fairly reliable due to the recent estimates of ISTAT which incorporate the black economy.

From 1984 to 1990 Italy experienced a phase of relatively high growth (see Figure 4.2) in comparison with the disappointing performance of the early 1980s. However, the trend moved clearly downwards once more at the beginning of the 1990s.

Italian performance is in line with those of most industrialised countries but it is interesting to note the time lag by which the Italian economy experienced the effects of the second oil shock (a lag responsible for the delay in recovery in the early 1980s) and the uninterrupted phase of growth in the second part of the 1980s. The aver-

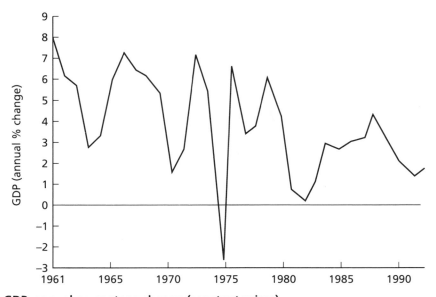

Figure 4.2 GDP: annual percentage change (constant prices).

Source: Statistical Annexe, Table E19 and *Annual Economic Report of Commission of European Communities* (1992).

age rate of growth in the period 1981–90 was 2.2%, not a bad result if we consider the extremely poor performance of the economy in the 1981–3 period. If we consider per capita GDP measured in PPS (Europe, excluding East Germany = 100), the Italian level in 1992 is 103.5 (see Table E20). This outcome should be interpreted as an extraordinarily good performance by Central and Northern Italy, given the marked difference in per capita income existing between the South and the Centre–North (see section 4.6.1).

4.2.2 Employment and unemployment

The prolonged upturn in GDP during the 1980s failed to alleviate the problem of unemployment in Italy as a whole. While most of the North and Centre of the country experienced full or near-full employment, the South (the regions south of Rome) and the islands (Sicily and Sardinia) continued to suffer high (and rising) unemployment. Since the mid-1970s the Italian working population (due to the post-war birth explosion and the increase in active population which typically follows a phase of intense urbanisation) has grown faster than new jobs have been created, leading to a steady increase in unemployment over the period since the mid-1970s (see Figure 4.3).

In the late 1980s, data relating to Italy as a whole shows that the increase in official unemployment was not only halted, but that the level

actually fell slightly (see section 4.6.1 on the trends of unemployment in the different regions). The onset of recession in 1990, however, saw unemployment resuming its upward path. As in other EC countries, young people, women and less qualified people are the most likely groups to be affected by unemployment. The level of unemployment in the North of the country is low even compared with the best performing European economies. The trend of unemployment in the South of Italy is linked to deficits in public finances; there is a strong relationship between employment in the South and public expenditure. Overall unemployment rose again at the beginning of the 1990s, reflecting the world recession and also the restrictive fiscal policy necessitated by the huge public debt. The tendency for large companies (those with over 500 employees) to implement a policy of almost continuous reduction in the size of their workforce has been counteracted, in varying degrees, by job creation in small and medium-sized firms. The fact that the latter are more numerous in the North and Central areas helps to account for the contrast in unemployment levels between these areas and the South.

The employment structure in terms of the relative shares of the three traditional sectors of production (agriculture, industry and services) has broadly followed the usual patterns for industrialising economies. Table 4.1 shows the evolution through time of sector employment, indicating the speed with which the structure of the Italian economy has been transformed from a largely agricultural economy in the early 1950s to a mature industrial economy with (in 1988) less than 10% of its workforce in the primary sector. It is also interesting to note that the proportion of people currently employed in industry is much lower than at its peak at the end of the 1960s. This reflects a distinct feature of the more recently industrialised economies, which have quickly adopted modern labour-saving techniques. It is also interesting to note that Italy has proportionally fewer industrial workers than a number of countries, in particular Germany and Japan, which have maintained a high proportion of industrial workers owing to

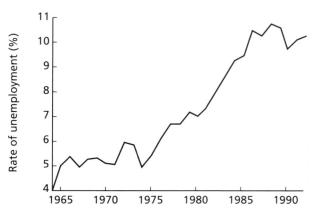

Figure 4.3 Percentage rate of unemployment.

Source: European Economy, Statistical Annexe, Table E17.

an especially good trading performance in manufacturing. Italy has still a high proportion of agricultural workers in comparison with most industrialised countries, a fact explained, on the one hand, by the slow process of industrialisation in the South and, on the other, by the labour-intensive nature of agricultural cultivation in Italy.

Table 4.1 Employment by sector (%).

Sector	1954	1966	1981	1988	1992
Agriculture	39.9	24.9	13.4	9.9	9.5
Industry	32.8	40.7	37.5	32.5	29.2
Services	27.3	34.4	49.1	57.5	61.3
Total	100.0	100.0	100.0	100.0	100.0

Source: ISTAT

4.2.3 Consumption and savings

Consumption has been a fairly stable factor in aggregate demand. However, the items consumed have changed a great deal in the post-war period and especially in the last two decades. There has been a reduction the share of spending devoted to foodstuffs and an increase in that going to services. This development, as well as the changes in the composition and type of products consumed followed the same pattern as those of countries which experienced industrialisation at an earlier date.

The level of total savings as a proportion of income is particularly high in Italy. Among other industrialised countries, Japan is the only country which has a higher savings/income ratio. The explanation is found in the fact that family savings are especially high in comparison with other countries. Italy and Japan are also similar in that they both have a large number of family firms and it is common for the savings of these firms to be counted as family savings, even though they are really company savings. However, even if the figure for family savings is corrected to take this into account, the level of family savings remains high, and this can probably be explained by the importance of the family in Italian society, in comparison with most industrialised countries where the family unit has a relatively smaller economic role.

Company savings during the 1980s once again returned to high levels and, as a consequence, the generally high levels of self-financing among firms have been restored. This trend has been caused, to a degree, by higher profits. A high rate of company profits has always been the policy of the Central Bank, not only because it is an extremely strong stimulus to investment but also because a high level of company self-financing means that the companies have greater flexibility in decision-making than would be the case if they were financed externally.

4.2.4 Investment

In order to evaluate Italian investment trends in the 1980s it is necessary to consider the various investment items and leave aside investment in real estate, as trends in the latter depend on very specific factors which are usually dissimilar to the motivations for other types of investment. Investment in plant and machinery is particularly significant in terms of industrial performance. This item has been consistently positive in the period since 1983, particularly in the second half of the 1980s, owing to the growing proportion of investment expenditure devoted to expanding productive capacity. The company investment trend in the 1980s (plant and machinery) has been especially impressive and as a proportion of the GDP reached a post-war high. If total investment as a proportion of GDP for the 1980s is less than that of the 1950s or the early 1960s, this is largely due to the fact that there has been less investment in the housing sector and by the state.

The total investment trend (excluding investment in real estate) is more in line with other industrialised countries and this is largely due to a relatively low level of investment in the construction sector. If we breakdown the figure for investment in the construction sector, it is possible to see that investment by industry in new factories has returned to a high level in the late 1980s and the modest overall figure is due to trends in the state sector (roads, ports, drains, etc.), the level of spending on which has been restricted by financial constraints.

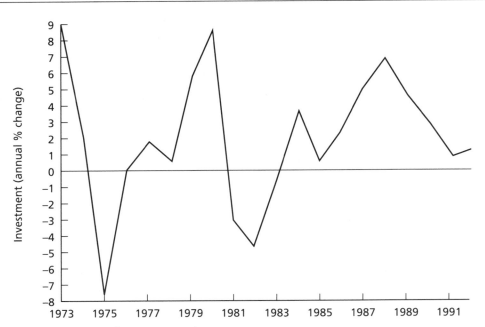

Figure 4.4 Investment: annual percentage change.

Source: European Economy, Statistical Annexe, Table E19 and *Annual Economic Report of Commission of European Communities* (1992).

The decrease in investment in the early 1990s is clearly shown in Figure 4.4, which also depicts an apparent tendency for the reduction in investment during downturns to be less accentuated than was the case in the past. This suggests a change in the behaviour of firms faced with an economic downturn.

4.2.5 Inflation

Inflation in Italy, in the 1970s and the 1980s, has been closely related to the oil price trend as well as to the negotiating strength of the trade unions. The inflation rate, which was particularly high following the first major hike in oil prices (1973–4), was gradually reducing during the second half of the 1970s and then took off once more at the beginning of the 1980s. After 1984, it began to decrease and the downward trend subsequently accelerated as a result of the large reduction in the price of oil and the sharp fall in the dollar in 1985 (see Figure 4.5). When Italy became a member of the European Monetary System in 1979, it was forced to abandon

the earlier practice of systematically devaluing the lira; a change which exerted a further downward influence on the rate of increase in prices in the 1980s.

In the period following the oil shocks, price rises were experienced by most countries of the Western world, but the level of Italian inflation was particularly high in comparison with other industrialised countries. Although price rises have remained relatively high, the inflation rate differentials between Italy and other major economies were significantly narrowed during the second half of the 1980s and in the first months of 1993 Italian inflation was in line with that of its major European trading partners in spite of a significant devaluation of the Italian lira against the major currencies. Inflation is expected to rise in the future (because of devaluation of the lira) as aggregate demand increases again. At the moment, however, the increase in import prices is balanced by the weakness of trade unions in the labour market (due to high unemployment) and by the freeze imposed by government on civil servant salaries.

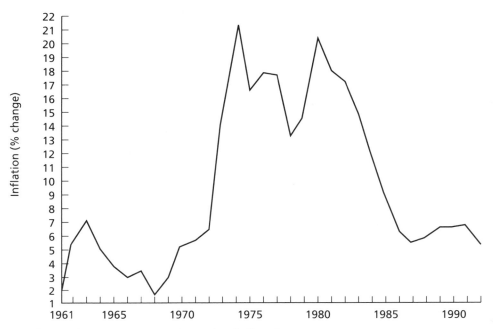

Figure 4.5 Inflation (private consumption price deflator).

Source: European Economy, Statistical Annexe, Table E27.

4.2.6 Market structure

The majority of Italian private companies (small and large) are owned by families. A small group of families own a significant proportion of the largest private companies, resulting in a substantial concentration of economic power. This ownership characteristic has restricted the development of the stock-exchange market (see also section 4.4.1). State-owned firms constitute a considerable element in many industrial sectors. The extent of state ownership, especially in heavy industry, is partly explained by state intervention to save from failure a number of banks (and of firms owned by those banks, see also section 4.4.1) in the years of the great depression after 1929. In addition, a large number of firms were established or purchased by the state in recent decades to create or maintain employment, especially in the South.

The Italian productive structure, when analysed according to firm size, presents unusual characteristics for an industrialised economy, because of the presence of a large number of small and very small firms (see section 4.6.2). Nevertheless, the output of 'modern' sectors (i.e. those with a high rate of technological development) has, in recent decades, come to account for an increasing proportion of the total. The productive structure is also characterised by the importance of the so-called 'mature' or 'traditional' industrial sectors. These are industries in which technology appears to have reached the point where further improvement is restricted and thus are industries which are relatively easy for countries in earlier phases of industrialisation to enter. The particular role still played by the traditional sectors in the Italian industrial structure (see also section 4.6.6), despite the high labour costs typical of an advanced economy, gives rise to the need for a better definition of the term 'traditional sectors'. On the basis of recent Italian experience, it can be observed that product differentiation, design and flexibility play so important a role in a number of 'traditional industries', that it is entirely possible for countries with high labour costs to compete successfully against those with low labour costs.

4.2.7 Income distribution

The pattern of income distribution changed during the 1980s as a result of an increase in the profits of major companies and a much reduced rate of increase in wages compared with the preceding decade (see section 4.1.5).

The state paid a much higher volume of interest on public debt bonds because of the debt 'demonetisation' policy which led to the issue of a higher volume of state bonds. The higher real rate of interest affected the distribution of income because the financial 'rentiers' took advantage of the situation and since most of the bonds are owned by the relatively well-off sections of the population, the change in public debt financing redistributed incomes towards the higher income classes.

In addition, from the geographical point of view, there was an increase during the 1980s in the per capita income gap between the South and the Centre–North of the country; a kind of territorial income redistribution (analysed in greater depth in section 4.6.1). More recently in 1992, government, in order to cut public expenses, decided to put an end to increases in public sector wages (including the increases paid for the passage from one career group to another due to time) and to halt the application of *scala mobile*, in all the sectors of the economy. These actions will undoubtedly have an impact on income distribution in the ensuing period.

4.3 GOVERNMENT INVOLVEMENT IN THE ECONOMY

4.3.1 Expenditure, revenues and public debt

During the last two decades, public expenditure has increased at an average annual rate which is above that of the EC average, and above all economically advanced European countries. If we consider public expenditure by the general government of EC countries as a percentage of GDP (see Table E28) in 1992 only Denmark's public expenditure (58.5%) is higher than that of Italy (55.4%). However, this level of expenditure has not been accompanied by the required improvement in the services offered to the public and industry. There are two principal reasons for this development: poor productivity in the public ser-

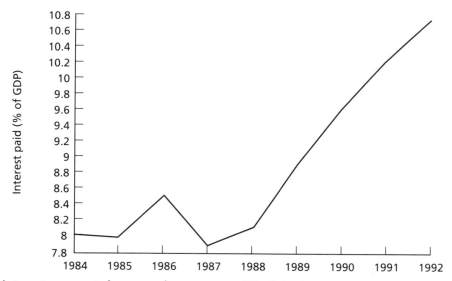

Figure 4.6 Interest payments by general government (% of GDP).

Source: European Economy, Statistical Annexe, Table E9.

vice sector and restrictions on increased expenditure on social services and state investment. Expenditure on social services has been somewhat contained. The reason why expenditure on public services and investment has increased only marginally is that the increase in public expenditure on transfers and the fast rise in the level of interest paid on public debt have accounted for most of the public expenditure budget. (see Figure 4.6)

A sharp increase in state expenditure occurred in the second half of the 1970s and the early 1980s and has basically been due to transfers to families and firms as well as the payment of interest on the state debt bonds. A large part of the growth in the public debt in the 1970s is explained by the fact that there was a lag between the increase in expenditure and a corresponding rise in revenues due to a delay in putting tax reforms into practice. The accumulation of an extremely high level of public debt has been accompanied by increasing servicing costs, something which emerged as a problem in the 1970s. Expenditure on debt interest payments rose sharply in the early 1980s due to a change in the way the debt was serviced. As the debt was serviced in the market the rates of interest naturally rose sharply.

In recent years there has been a tendency for the public debt to decrease when calculated net of interest as a percentage of the GDP. This reflects the containment of public spending. However, the total gross public debt is still rising (see Figure 4.7) owing to the increasing expenditure devoted to interest payments and this actually represents the major negative characteristic of the Italian economy.

4.3.2 Industrial policy

During the 1980s Italian industrial policy concentrated mainly on promoting the process of 'restructuring' among the major industrial companies (see section 4.5.1), especially those which were the focus of the bitter social conflict of the 1970s. There were also serious problems with state enterprises (the main state enterprises affected were *IRI* (*Istituto per la Ricostruzione Industriale*) *ENI* (*Ente Nazionale Idrocarburi*), and *EFIM*, which suffered serious losses. The state facilitated the recovery of profits and investment by transferring, in various ways, financial resources to industries (including subsidies to production, payment for workers laid-off for short/long periods, and support for technological innovations) and these measures have eased the social conflict which normally accompanies a policy of industrial restructuring.

The policy of privatisation, widely practised during the 1980s in other European countries, has been applied only to a limited extent in Italy. The most famous case is the successful sale of the Alfa Romeo car company by IRI to FIAT; but a number of important attempts at privatisation have failed. For example, the sale of the wholesale food group SME in the mid-1980s (the largest company owned by the State in the food sector) failed because of political disagreements. Even the attempts to find agreement between public and private sector firms, to create mixed groups strong enough to be competitive in the European and international markets, have not been successful. In fact, in the telecommunications sector, an attempt at agreement between IRI and FIAT broke down, and in chemicals a company created by ENI and the Montedison group turned out to be impracticable. The reasons for these failures can be traced to disagreements between the parties who make up the

Figure 4.7 Gross debt of general government (% of GDP); Average annual level of debt.

Source: European Economy, Statistical Annexe, Table E9.

coalition governments, because such economic decisions have significant repercussions in terms of the power of the political parties especially when state ownership determines in many ways the electoral power of the parties forming the coalitions (see also section 4.1.1).

Despite the problems, privatisation of state-owned firms remains one of the most important targets of government policy. In the first place it offers a means of reducing the size of the transfer of financial resources from the state to state-owned enterprises for purposes of covering operating losses. Such actions should also help government regain the confidence of the most relevant 'rating houses' and international finance companies who consider privatisation as a means of achieving a recovery in Italian public finances and whose disapproval of past policy in this field contributes to the instability of the country's financial markets and its currency. Achieving privatisation is made a difficult task by the extent of the financial problems afflicting the major private Italian companies and the reluctance of foreign industrial groups to purchase Italian state-owned assets, given the unstable economic and political environment. These are problems from the perspective of the buyers. For the seller (the state), the problem is one of how to sell the heavily loss-making industrial companies *as well as* those with budget surpluses and at the same time avoid the risk of being left with the financially weak companies, having lost the possibility of cross-subsidising these via profits from stronger companies.

4.3.3 Environmental policy

The causes of environmental pollution in Italy are those typical of any industrialised country: industrial processes, the use of chemicals in agriculture, the expansion in both the quantity and quality of consumer commodities and an overuse of the soil for construction. The level of environmental pollution depends on the ability of public administration to face the problem and, from this point of view, Italy has room for improvement. Different types of pollution characterise the different regions of Italy. The South does not suffer the consequences of massive industrialisation but experiences pollution problems related to ineffective urban and land planning overuse of soil resources and ineffective arrangements for dealing with waste materials. Local government has been ineffective in relation to these issues and indeed has contributed to the environmental problems. The North of Italy and the industrialised parts of the country, on the other hand, suffers from the effects of intensive industrialisation. A very large share of Italian industrial production is located in the Po valley and the problems found there are those of any other industrialised country. Air pollution in the towns and cities is a general problem, resulting from the excessive use of private cars, which, in turn, reflects the inadequacy of public transport.

The economic effect of environmental pollution is higher when the value of what is damaged is higher. This is certainly the case in Italy, where architectural and artistic patrimony is enormous. The Ministry of Environment was created only in 1986. The guidelines of environmental policy involve the identification of environmental problems in specific areas (the environment triennial plan operates in eleven fields and/or projects) and the selection of the appropriate policy instruments to reach those targets. The problem with environmental policy is that firms, of course, do not welcome charges and taxes on polluting activities because of their consequences on the costs of production and government efforts in this direction receive only limited support in parliament in the face of intense lobbying against such measures. Reducing environmental pollution through economic incentives has thus far not been seriously attempted.

4.4 FINANCIAL SYSTEM

4.4.1 General system

In order to understand the Italian financial system we need to bear in mind the savings patterns in the various sectors of the economy (families, firms, the state and the foreign sector). In net terms the household sector has traditionally been largely in credit, firms in deficit and the state sector also increasingly in deficit (since the beginning of the 1970s). The balance on the foreign sector has been more erratic and closely linked to market forces.

The current structure of the financial institutions in Italy is basically that which was outlined in the 1936 Banking Laws, although the process of liberalisation of the European Monetary System and developments at a European level have influenced, and will increasingly influence, the characteristics of the system. The central aspect of the system – the separation of banks and companies – was essentially designed to avoid the possibility of collapses of the major banks caused by the bankruptcy of key companies (as happened in the early 1930s). Banks are not permitted to own companies and there are no '*banche miste*' as in Germany or France (see also, for the very recent period, section 4.4.2).

In brief, the financial system has operated in the following way. Companies finance themselves directly by means of shares and debentures, indirectly by means of banks (short-term credit) or by credit institutions (*Istituti Speciali di Credito*) (medium- and long-term credit). The Italian stock exchange has a limited role in the financing of industry, owing to the relative lack of institutional investors and the large proportion of small firms which, by their very nature, do not depend on stock-exchange financing. The main cause of the limited number of institutional investors is to be found in the way in which the national insurance system is organised. This is almost exclusively state-run and characterised by the making of payments on the basis of earnings in the same time period. This explains the modest flow of savings coming on to the stock market. The attempt, in the mid-1980s, to create a financial system which was capable of giving a greater impulse to the stock market (with the regularisation of the 'investment funds'), though promising in its initial phase (due to the then buoyant share prices), eventually proved unsuccessful because of a lack of important 'institutional' investors.

The state finances its deficit by issuing public debt bonds and by drawing upon a special current account which it holds with the central bank in accordance with strict legal limits. The public debt bonds are bought by the general public and the Central Bank, which as already mentioned, is no longer obliged to act as a 'buyer of last resort' at the auctions of public debt bonds. Recently the public debt bonds have increasingly been sold to foreign buyers. Local public administrations have the opportunity of financing their own investment through the '*Cassa Depositi e Prestiti*' (Deposits and Loans Institute), a financial institution that was derived from the French financial experience. It is a section of the Treasury and uses deposits collected by the Italian Post Office. However, its role in financing local authorities has diminished as savers have shown a preference for holding their savings in banks rather than the Post Office.

The above mentioned *Istituti Speciali di Credito*, the institutional role of which is financing companies in the medium and long term, obtain their funds through issuing bonds which are bought mainly by the major banking institutions and, to a lesser extent, by other financial institutions such as insurance and finance companies. There are also credit institutions specialising in making medium- and long-term loans to particular economic activities, such as agriculture, public works and land credit. In practice, the system has allowed an occasional exception to the 'separation rule'. For example, the *Mediobanca* is a medium and long-term credit institute which operates also as a merchant bank for major companies.

4.4.2 Banking system

Banks obtain funds through customers' deposits and pay interest both on deposit and current accounts. Most of the major Italian banks are state-owned, a situation which arose because of the intervention of the State to save a number of private banks involved in the bankruptcy of companies in the early 1930s. Until very recently, the various types of banks in Italy were categorised according to the way in which they collected funds and by the type of financing in which they specialised. The development of the banking system, has in fact, involved a significant reduction in the differences between the various types of banks in terms of how they operate. A network of banking services throughout the country is guaranteed by local credit institutions as the large banks are generally located in the major towns.

The banks became the centre of the financial system which grew out of the 1936 Banking Law; a position that has been consolidated over the post-war period. The main reasons for this change were:

- the progressive marginalisation of the Post Office as a means of saving;
- the increase in the number of banks throughout Italy;
- the growth of local banks;
- the progressive growth of the public debt;
- the increasing placement of bonds and shares in the banks' portfolios (from the state, state organisations and special credit institutions);
- the marginal role undertaken by the stock exchange in financing industry.

Between the mid-1960s and the end of the 1970s – due to indirect pressure known as 'moral suasion' from the Bank of Italy and/or a 'pegging' policy (a policy directed) at maintaining low interest rates), or directly because of the administrative measures of the monetary authorities – banks progressively acquired more of both state bonds and bonds issued by the special credit institutions. The monetary authorities laid down minimum proportions of bank deposits to be held in the form of bonds. On the other hand, the banks, in the same period, were doing well as their interest rates on deposits were above those of the other short- and medium-term financial institutions, so families preferred bank deposits to other ways of saving. Thus, the banks were the centre of the financial system because not only did the bulk of family savings take the form of bank deposits, but also banks were the source, directly or indirectly, of more or less every kind of loan operation.

The differentiation of credit institutions according to the relative length of time-deposits and periods of loans was the reasoning behind the *Banking Law* of 1936, a guarantee of stability in the banking system. Nevertheless, in practice, banks were involved extensively in the provisions of medium- and long-term loans (buying the bonds issued by '*Istituti Speciali di Credito*' and a large number of state-issued bonds) and the stability of the system was based on the control exerted by the Bank of Italy on the financial institutions.

This situation was considerably modified at the beginning of the 1980s. The divorce of the Central Bank from the Treasury, associated with the government decision to finance its deficit through the market, implied a marked change in the role of the banks, with their function as mediators in the savings market diminished. This development was caused basically by the keen competition from public debt bonds with their high net returns. The process of weakening the role of banks can be easily understood in quantitative terms by looking at the composition of family portfolios (the way in which families save their wealth). The structure of household portfolios shows that the quantity of public debt bonds has increased sharply and this has been accompanied by a decrease in the percentage of family wealth held in bank deposits.

The European Community Directive relating to banking (scheduled for introduction in 1993) will end Central Bank control over banking activities in Italy. In addition, foreign banks will be able to operate freely on Italian soil. In December 1992 a new banking law was passed which changed quite radically the structure of banking intermediaries. As a result no distinction is now made between banks in relation to the short, medium and long term. Any credit institution can operate as a short-, medium-, or long-term credit institution providing it observes central bank rules relating to 'prudent' conduct of their operations. As a consequence, the major banks will probably be induced to extend their activities to the entire spectrum of credit activities and there is a growing tendency in Italy for banks to take over credit institutions specialising in activities different from those in which they are currently engaged.

In addition, the traditional prohibition (a requirement of monetary authorities and not a rule established by law) of banks participating in the ownership of firms seems to have been reconsidered recently. The '*Considerazioni finali*' of the '*Governatore*' of the Bank of Italy (May 1993) states that the Bank of Italy will promote the right of banks to share the ownership of 'non-financial' firms with limits determined by the patrimony of the banks, their profits and the quality of their management. It is too early to evaluate the consequences of the measure announced by the Bank of Italy, but it is possible to foresee a quite radical change in the entire financial system.

4.4.3 Monetary policy

Italian monetary policy during the 1980s can be regarded as both a cause and a consequence of the main economic policy choices made in Italy during the late 1970s and early 1980s: specifically, membership of the EMS and the demonetisation of the public debt. Joining the European Monetary System involved the imposition of a more rigorous monetary policy in order to contain exchange rate fluctuations within internationally fixed constraints. The demonetisation of the public debt (made possible bv the 'divorce' between the Central Bank and the government) allowed the central bank to recover its autonomy in controlling the money supply. As a consequence (and, of course, as a result of the lower rate of price increases) the Bank of Italy has been able to follow a more restrictive policy on money supply. This is clear from Figure 4.8 showing the annual percentage change of M2, which includes savings deposits which have a high degree of 'liquidity' in Italy. To better understand Figure 4.8 it is necessary to bear in mind that in the first years of EMS the 'central parities' of European currencies changed frequently and not marginally and that monetary policy in terms of quantity of money was allowed to become restrictive in nominal terms over a number of years in accordance with the decrease in the rate of inflation.

The higher interest rates caused by the more restrictive monetary policy and the demonetisation of the public debt have had uneven effects on the different business sectors, because large firms in particular took advantage of the lower level of the 'prime rate' and the ease of access to international financial markets characterised by lower interest rates. The higher real interest rates determined by a more restrictive monetary policy were also supposed to operate positively on public expenditure because of the higher cost of financing public debt.

4.5 INTERNATIONAL RELATIONS

4.5.1 General remarks

Throughout the 1980s the balance of trade was in deficit. Trends on the foreign accounts are determined both by inherent factors and specific policy measures. At the beginning of the 1950s Italy radically changed its international economic policy, transforming itself, in a very short space of time, from a highly protected to a relatively free economy, at least in regard to trade in products and services. Entry into the Common Market accelerated this process. The lack of natural resources, the fact that Italy began to industrialise at a later date than many other countries

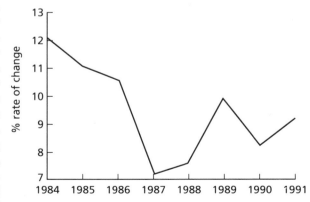

Figure 4.8 Money supply (M2): annual percentage rate of change.

Source: European Economy, Statistical Annexe, Table E9 and '*Relazione annuale*' (1993) of the Bank of Italy.

and because its industrialisation has been focused on international markets, has had and still has a dual effect on the economy. These factors have created a strong stimulus for technological innovation by companies yet, at the same time, have acted as a permanent brake on the expansion of the economy. As Italy does not have much in the way of natural resources, any expansion in production must, by definition, be accompanied by an increase in imports of raw materials, and energy supplies and, as a consequence, every expansionary phase must be accompanied by an increase in the exports of goods and services or by inflows of capital.

In the first phase of industrialisation after the Second World War exports increased rather more than imports owing to the low level of Italian wages and salaries combined with an entrepreneurial ability with respect to the adoption of modern technology in a number of industrial sectors. There was a surplus in the balance of payments including services: receipts from tourism and remittances sent home by emigrants led to a diminished foreign debt. Apart from a brief period (1963–4), this trend generally continued until the end of the 1960s. The first oil crisis worsened the problem of the balance on

international accounts but the policy of continually devaluing the lira, which started at the beginning of the 1970s and was pursued until 1979 when Italy joined the EMS, allowed Italian industrial products to maintain competitiveness in the international market.

4.5.2 Recent trends

Membership of the European Monetary System brought a halt to the policy of adjusting the rate of exchange to internal price rises. If the new policy had positive effects in terms of containing inflation (through lower prices of import of raw materials and foreign commodities), it also adversely affected the Italian trade balance, especially in comparison with the German D-Mark area countries (see Figure 4.9). In the 1980s the balance of trade was continually in deficit and the current account worsened. Recently, besides the items which traditionally feature among Italian imports (raw materials, energy supplies and agricultural products) there has also been a net import of energy produced by neighbouring countries. The positive balance on invisible items was insufficient to compensate for the deficit in the balance of trade. Tourism, which in

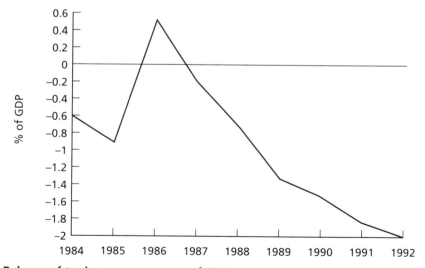

Figure 4.9 Balance of trade as a percentage of GDP.

Source: European Economy, Statistical Annexe, Table E9.

the past contributed in a major way to balancing the current account, is gradually becoming less and less important because the rise in per capita income in Italy has led to more Italians travelling abroad, while the higher cost of living in Italy compared to the earlier period has deterred foreign visitors.

In the 1980s the balance of payments became dependent on the net inflow of capital, attracted by the high real interest rates in Italy. The rates have been generally above the EC and international averages. The need to have interest rates at a sufficiently high level to permit an overall balance in foreign accounts comes as a direct consequence of the use of exchange rate policy as an instrument for controlling inflation (something very close to the policy of the USA).

It seems likely that trade deficits during the 1980s were largely caused by the worsening of trade with the German D-Mark area and especially Germany itself. The German mark and the currencies with which it is linked have been, inside the EMS, undervalued with respect to most European currencies, including the Italian lira. The rules established within the European Monetary System have significantly reduced room for discretion in exchange rate policy on the part of national governments.

In 1992 the turbulence in world financial markets had a marked influence on a number of currencies and especially on the Italian lira. After a devaluation of the lira inside the EMS (and an unsuccessful attempt to maintain the new parity) both the Italian and British governments opted to remove their currencies from the EMS. Floating in the market the lira's value fell substantially in comparison with the major world currencies. As expected the current balance, after a short lag, improved substantially (a 10,000 billion lira surplus is forecast for 1993) and with no sign of undesirable consequences, in terms of inflation in mid-1993. It is difficult to say if and when inflation is likely to be affected by the lira's devaluation; we have to await a recovery of production and employment to evaluate the cause–effect relationship of the substantial devaluation of the currency on the rate of inflation.

4.6 SPECIAL ISSUES

4.6.1 The economic dualism

Every European economy has specific characteristics, even if there is a strong tendency with development of European economic integration for differences to diminish. Territorial dualism and the special role played by the small and medium-sized industries in the production system are two special characteristcs of the Italian economy. Italy is characterised by a marked dualism compared with other advanced industrial countries. The economy has experienced two phases of intense industrialisation, the first at the turn of the century and the second in the period since the Second World War. The first phase concerned a small area, almost exclusively the industrial 'triangle' of Milan, Turin and Genoa. The second, although more widespread, still did not include part of the South of Italy and the islands.

The strong territorial dualism in terms of differences in per capita income between the most and the least advanced regions decreased in the period following the Second World War. The difference, nonetheless, still exists and from the mid-1980s statistical measures show that the North–South divide has once more begun to widen. The growth of income in the South of the country, the *Mezzogiorno*, though continuing, has in recent years been markedly lower than that in the North.

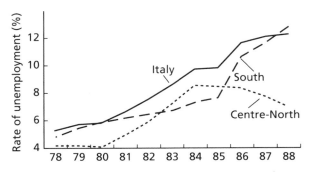

Figure 4.10 Rate of unemployment (number of unemployed persons actively seeking employment) in three regions of Italy.

Source: Bank of Italy, *Relazione annuale* (1993).

A case study of the research office of the Bank of Italy (published in 1990) makes a systematic comparison of the South's economic performance with that of the Centre-North. In particular, it is important to underline the data relating to per capita income in the South as compared to the Centre-North. In the 1980–4 period, the South's per capita income was 57.8% of the North's, while in 1987 the proportion had dropped to 54.9%. Employment in the South of Italy also fell during the 1980s. If the employed labour force is indexed at 100 in 1980, it averaged 98.4 in the period 1980–4 and by 1987 had fallen to 87.7.

There has been a slight reduction in the South's share of the total number of people employed in the nation as a whole, but there has been a larger overall increase in the population of working age in the South. Figure 4.10 clearly shows that, while the unemployment in the Centre-North has fallen since 1984, it has increased rapidly in the South during the same period. In 1988 the official unemployment figure in the South was 20.6% and female unemployment was 32.7%. It should be noted that the percentage of females available for work was extremely low; only 25% of women in the South are in the labour force.

In many respects the economic situation of the South is contradictory. Family consumption in the Mezzogiorno has increased continuously. If the per capita consumption is indexed at 100 in 1980, it reached 113.8 in 1987. The value of investment in the construction sector (excluding housing) has grown in absolute terms in the South and has, in fact, grown relatively more than in the North. Moreover, investment in machinery has not been below that in the Centre-North. The individual productive sectors are more capital-intensive in the South and by quite a long way, partly due to the presence there of state-owned heavy industry and also to the phenomenon known in economic literature as the *Leontieff paradox*, according to which it is not infrequently observed that there is more capital-intensive production in less developed countries. Public spending is distributed in Italy largely according to population distribution and so the per capita public spending in the South (both for state investment expenditure and state expenditure on services) continues to be a great deal higher than revenues.

The average rate of growth of bank deposits, post office savings and bank investments is higher in the South than in the Centre-North. In the South, bank investments have fallen as a pro-

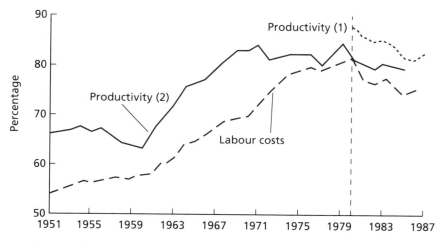

Figure 4.11 Productivity and labour costs in industry: South as a percentage of Centre-North. (1) Revised national accounts; (2) Data corrected according to Cassa Integrazione from 1970 on.

Source: Bank of Italy digest of SVIMEZ and INPS data.

portion of bank deposits, but this has been due to an increase in bank deposits (the role of the banks in the South has maintained its primary importance) rather than a fall in bank loans.

Figure 4.11, which shows the relationship between the South and the Centre-North with regard to productivity and cost of labour in industry, suggests, to a certain degree, why the position of the South has worsened. The efficiency of industrial production processes in the Mezzogiorno is decidedly inferior to those of the Centre-North. Although the cost of labour is lower in the South (by 15% to 20%, according to estimates) and the cost of indebtedness is also lower (due to the more intensive use of credit facilities in the South), these advantages are eroded by lower productivity levels. Industry in the South is thus less productive and the gap in productivity between the South and the North, which had previously diminished, in recent years once more widened. There is no one definitive explanation for this phenomenon and the various theories are often contradictory. Some scholars take the view that the gap is widening because of the government assistance given to the industries in the South (credit and tax benefits) which allows them to survive, even though they are not really competitive. Other economists believe that the total amount of services offered by the government to the industrial sector (infrastructure and administrative services) is so low that the costs of industries in the South are decidedly higher (an explanation based on transaction costs). Another group of industrial economists believes that there are environmental diseconomies: the industrial sector is not well integrated and lacks important links and this causes high relative costs. Although the above factors are important, they do not give a complete explanation of the lower productivity in the South. In fact, many other regions of Italy have experienced industrialisation in the last decades and have experienced similar difficulties.

Those economists who believe that the problems of the economy in the Mezzogiorno are not purely of an economic nature, but can be largely attributed to social and political causes, would seem to have a case. The lower productivity of some of the firms can be put down to the lack of competition: for example, those firms which operate with state contracts, or where potential competitors are not able to operate due to the unsatisfactory level of 'public order' and/or strong political influences in determining the contracts. In some areas of the South the presence of the public sector in the running of companies producing goods and services means that management are more concerned with maintaining employment levels (and filling the jobs with people of the same political or social background) rather than with efficient management. Finally, the economic grounds for the running of a company are not the same as in the rest of Italy as many companies are exploited by 'organised criminal groups' and not infrequently controlled by these groups. This discourages potential competition and entrepreneurial activity. Unemployment in these areas is considered (in line with a traditional interpretation) one of the reasons why there is an extremely high level of organised crime in Campania, Calabria and Sicily, although it would be an overstatement to attribute a direct cause–effect relationship to these variables and it is difficult to establish the direction of the causation.

The difficulty of working in the South leads to the phenomenon of 'exit' (as one famous social scientist has called it) of entrepreneurs and managers, as well as of the more skilled workers. This point is a particularly serious factor as those who do 'exit' are often the most talented, skilful and enterprising; the people more likely to change the existing state of things.

The process of European integration could also accentuate difficulties which already exist in the weakest part of the Italian economy, the Mezzogiorno. It is difficult to predict the effect of the process of integration on areas with different levels of economic development. The outcome of the process of integration depends on the growth potential of the most backward areas and the ability of the most advanced areas to absorb workers from the poorest regions. The present rate of unemployment in a large part of Europe (especially of young people and women) does not allow us to be optimistic about the possibility of absorbing workers from the South of Italy into other EC countries and/or the North of Italy. At the same time, the type of economic development in the most advanced Italian and European economic areas requires a specialised workforce that, if it were to come from the South of Italy, would result in a further impoverishment of the South itself as well as a worsening in the Mezzogiorno prospects for future growth.

We still need to assess whether the South of Italy will be able to offer investment opportunities for companies from the most advanced areas of Europe when the single market is acheived and in what measure the southern Italian companies will be affected by the increased integration of the European market. The answer to the first question involves assessing whether the companies from the advanced European countries will be more able to exploit the development opportunities in the South of Italy than those from the North of Italy have done in the past. The most realistic answer seems to be a negative one, if we reflect upon the comments on the Mezzogiorno economy made above. The potential for economic development in a large part of the South is limited by the existing environmental conditions (widespread organised crime and inefficiency in the public administration system) which hampers the development of the entrepreneurial ability which is present in the South. It is doubtful that the European companies will be able to do better than the entrepreneurs from the South and the North-Centre regions have done up till now. It is likely, in fact, that the ex-Communist bloc countries of Eastern Europe will offer better investment opportunities (especially lower wages) than many regions of the South of Italy.

With regard to the second question, it is difficult to see how the process of European integration, and the accompanying increase in competition, will produce a result which is any different to that produced by the intense competition during the 1980s. As the latter phenomenon widened the gap between the South and the North, European integration will probably also further increase the gap. It must be underlined that the problem of closing the gap between the South and the North (through expanding the productive capacity of the South of Italy) is one which will have to be resolved, above all, by the South of Italy itself, through the removal of the factors which have for so long hindered development. These problems are beyond the scope of economics and their answer can only be found in institutional and political policies.

4.6.2 The role of small firms

The second aspect of the Italian economy worth a special mention is the extemely important role that small companies have played (and continue to play) in the development of Italian industry. A large number of small and medium-sized firms were created during the Italian industrial boom in the 1950s. In the 1960s it seemed that the 'natural' development of the industrialisation process would have given rise to an increase in company size as well as a movement from the traditional sector to industries which are, on the basis of historical experience, more typical of an advanced industrial society. However, the 1970s were characterised not only by a proliferation of small firms (accompanied by the fact that many large companies ran into difficulty) but also by the particular vitality of the more traditional industrial sectors (ones in which technology is 'assumed' to be 'mature' and amenable only to slow improvement) especially in the regions characterised by small firms.

The contribution that these small companies have made to the development of the Italian economy is multi-faceted and includes income and employment creation (see Table 4.2) as well as a significant addition to exports. The contribution that they have given to employment in manufacturing industry can be seen from Table 4.2, which contains the data taken from the general statistical surveys undertaken by ISTAT every ten years. In 1981 the number of people employed in small firms (both those with less than 10 employees and those with 10–49) actually exceeded both the number of people working in large plants (more than 500 employees) and the number working in medium-sized plants with 100 to 499 employees. The increase in the proportion of total employment found in manufacturing firms with between 10 and 49 employees was especially marked.

From the geographical point of view the industrial triangle has followed the national trend. In the NEC, North-East-Centre (or the 'Third Italy' as it is often called) the 'very small' and 'small' plants have developed much faster than the medium-sized and large plants. The SCI, Centre-South and Islands, has exhibited a trend which stands in contrast to that in the nation as a whole, with a reduction in the number of workers employed in very small companies and an increase in the large companies.

The phenomenon described above has given rise to a lively and prolonged academic debate. There are two main positions. The first interpretation suggests that the economic development and the particular prominence of small companies can be linked to a single pattern of growth that originates from the regions which have a key role in Italian capitalism and manifests itself in different ways according to the social-geographical conditions found in the various areas. This line of thought has two sub-theories. The first underlines the difficulty experienced by large companies in adapting to conditions of increased instability and change which have affected the national and international markets since the 1970s and the encouragement this gives to 'externalisation' of production to smaller, more flexible subcontracted firms. The second indicates a defensive strategy in which the large companies have reacted to the growth in power of organised labour in the 1970s, and which is based on the decentralisation of production to smaller factories which are less unionised and, therefore, have lower labour costs and more flexible work practices. Following the reduction in the number of people employed in the large companies, union power has, in general, diminished. Both the explanatory positions underline, however, the dominant role of major companies and the dependent one of the small firms.

The second interpretation gives importance to the autonomous aspect of the development of

the small companies. This is based on a number of theories, the best known is the theory which is captured in the phrase 'small is beautiful' which has been linked to the desire for independence of the post-1968 generation. More useful, perhaps, is the theory which stresses the inherent strengths in the integrated systems of small companies which operate in a restricted industrial area ('industrial districts' in the terminology of Alfred Marshall) and benefit from economies of scales that are external to the single firms but internal to the group of firms which constitute the industrial district. The existing industrial districts benefited, in the beginning, from a pool of pre-existing skilled craft labour and latent entrepreneurial ability, often related to the types of agriculture traditionally adopted in those areas and in the organisation of the agricultural sector in the period before industrialisation, and created a unique form of industrial development.

Table 4.2 Percentage composition of employment in manufacturing firms by size of plants

Number of employees	1951	1961	1971	1981
Less than 10 employees	29.7	25.3	20.3	22.8
10–49	14.7	19.6	21.9	26.0
50–99	8.3	10.5	10.8	10.1
100–499	21.1	22.5	23.2	21.3
500 and more	26.2	22.1	23.8	19.8
Total	100	100	100	100

Source: ISTAT, ten-year census.

It seems that there is no single adequate explanation for the fact that there are so many very small and small companies in Italian manufacturing industries. The decentralisation of the production of the large companies into smaller operational units, the persistence of small companies in the backward industrial environments and integrated systems of small companies are all economic phenomena which are to be found in the Italian economy. However, it should be pointed out that while the decentralisation of production capacity from large to small-scale units and the persistence of small companies in areas which have experienced a slower process of industrialisation are part of an international phenomenon, the integrated systems of small companies in delimited industrial districts are a unique phenomenon. This type of organisation of production certainly does not seem to be transitory or cyclical nor simply a response to the state of industrial relations in the major companies. Rather, it is a special and persistent characteristic in the development of Italian industrialisation, which is able to offer developmental paths, which are, at least in part, different from those experienced by countries which were industrialised at an earlier period. It is a phenomenon which is attracting the interest of foreign scholars of industrial economics.

4.7 FUTURE PROSPECTS

Now that the prolonged phase of economic growth during the 1980s has come to a halt, it is an appropriate time to consider whether we can expect a new phase of growth in the near future, how strong such a recovery would be and, more generally, what the main factors likely to influence future performance would be. As the Italian economy is closely linked to international markets, the performance of the other major economies, especially the USA, Japan and Germany, severely affect the Italian economy. This is not the place to consider the possible developments in the world economy, but it is important to consider the possible consequences of the further integration of the Italian economy into Europe in the 1990s.

In the economic field we have to examine two different aspects of European integration. Without political integration, the objective of European unity is condemned to (at least) partial failure because the creation of a free trade area is clearly insufficient by itself to achieve the target. Nevertheless, there are many fields where political unity could be reached (a common foreign affairs and defence policy, for instance) with meaningful consequences and the idea that

monetary unification is the decisive step towards political unity may prove unjustified.

On the basis of the experience of steady liberalisation of the economy during the whole of the post-war period (liberalisation in the early 1950s, entry into the Common Market, progressive liberalisation of capital movements with foreign countries and the acceptance of a single European market), one could argue that the choices with regard to the liberalisation of the Italian economy on the international market have generally brought positive results: stimulating innovation in production processes and forcing Italian companies to learn how to operate in international markets. Without underestimating the possible difficulties of adaptation for some sectors (especially credit and finance companies) to the 1993 liberalisation process, it is possible to envisage that a more extensive liberalisation (as indicated in the most recent European agreements) will have a positive influence on many sectors of the Italian economy; some sectors which lack competitiveness at present should become more competitive in a freer market environment than in a protected one. There will probably be a marked phase of modernisaton as the presence of the state sector in the market – a presence that often cannot be justified and has, in fact, delayed modernisation – is reduced in scale. It is also probable that the co-ordination of the fiscal and monetary policies necessary for European integration will lead the state to act in a more prudent way, given that harmonisation needed for integrating the European market will result in a reduction in the margins of discretion in the management of the national debt.

The process of monetary unification offers the prospect of a different scenario. A forced effort to reach monetary unification may turn out to be a disaster for the weaker countries and for the project of European integration itself. For the Italian economy we have to consider two different aspects: the external constraint and limits on the government's ability to reduce the public debt.

The new phase of European integration which started with the creation of the European Monetary System, the final steps of which are set out in the Maastricht Agreement, has produced contradictory effects on the Italian economy. The positive effects were, in the early 1980s, as predicted and desired by those political and economic groups who were in favour of the Italian membership of the European Monetary System, namely an external limit to the determination of prices and a stricter discipline in determining internal industrial relations, two aspects negatively influenced by the policy of continuing devaluation of the exchange rate of the national currency.

The tendency of EMS to limit the extent and frequency of changing parities between European currencies has resulted, on the other hand, in unsustainable external limits being imposed on the Italian economy (as well as on other weaker economies outside the D-Mark area). The weaker European countries are keen to remove the external constraints because of the necessity to promote industrialisation of the poorest areas of their countries. One of the most noticeable features of the development of the Italian economy in the 1980s was certainly the fact that the lira was strong in international markets (due to the high rates of interest) which created inflows of foreign capital, and the search for finance on foreign financial markets by Italian operators. The capital account surplus allowed the economic system to operate at a high level of activity even though the current account was in deficit. In certain respects therefore the Italian situation reflected, on a reduced scale, a feature of the American economy.

As has been mentioned above, the high level of net interest rates is one of the main causes of the disastrous situation represented by the public sector accounts, both in relation to the level of public debt (which is slightly above the current level of GDP) and a very high budget deficit (about 10% of the GDP); this has also resulted in unsatisfactory performance in terms of some expenditure items, in particular public investment. A reduction in the net rates of interest seems to be one important way (though not the only one) to balance public sector accounts.

Economic policies for dealing with the difficulties of the Italian economy at the end of the 1980s were influenced significantly by the inter-national context. The growth in the German economy has for most of the 1980s been slower than that of the Italian economy as the German authorities have taken special care to keep inflation at a low level. This policy is usually traced back to the consequences of high inflation in the period immediately after the First World War, but that could be better explained in terms of the role of the major German banks as owners of industrial firms and the risk of instability of financial markets on the entire German economy. German policy and the creation of the European Monetary System in maintaining exchange rate stability among European currencies, given the higher inflation rate in the Italian economy in the 1980s, caused a large deficit for Italy in its trade with Germany. This situation could have been rectified, in the context of Italian participation in the EMS, by means of either a tighter price control policy in Italy or a higher growth rate in the German economy (involved in the process of unification of the country), or both. It is rather obvious that the second solution would have been preferable for the Italian economy, since this would have moved the commercial accounts back into balance without Italy having to pay the price of a strong anti-inflationary policy. If this had happened, the Italian economy would have obviously benefited. But this was not the case. The process of unification was a new development which caused the West German economy to grow faster for a short period, but the re-emergence of inflation put a halt to German growth.

In this context the steps agreed at Maastricht would appear not to be in the interests of economic growth in Italy and the other weaker European economies. The choice made by the Italian government temporarily to leave the EMS, prompted by the wish to avoid the dissipation of the country's foreign currency reserves, must be regarded as a sensible decision. Eminent economists of both the Monetarist and Keynesian schools have argued that the lira's withdrawal from the EMS would not be regarded as merely a short-term expedient, but a long-term position based on a realistic view of the implications of participation in the EMS.

4.8 BIBLIOGRAPHY AND SOURCES OF INFORMATION

Autorità garante della concorrenza e del mercato (1992): *Rapporto al presidente del consiglio dei ministri*, Tipografia dello stato, Rome

Bagnasco A. (1977): *Tre Italie: la problematica territoriale dello sviluppo italiano*, Il Mulino, Bologna

Banca d'Italia (1991): *Relazione annuale del Governatore alla assemblea generale ordinaria dei partecipanti*, May, Rome

Banca d'Italia (1990): 'Il sistema finanziario nel Mezzogiorno', numero speciale dei *Contributi all'analisi economica*, Rome

Becattini G. (ed.) (1987): *Mercato e forze locali: il distretto industriale*, Il Mulino, Bologna

Cavazzuti F. (1986): *Debito pubblico e ricchezza privata*, Il Mulino, Bologna

Confindustria (1990): *Rapporto annuale a cura del Centro Studi Confindustria*, May

Commissione CEE (1987): *Le regioni della Comunità allargata*. Terza relazione periodica sulla situazione socio-economica e sullo sviluppo della Regioni della Comunità, Luxembourg

Fineschi A. (1991): 'Alcune osservazioni sulla politica monetaria e sul tasso di cambio in Italia negli anni ottanta', *Quaderni di economia, statistica e analisi del territorio*, Messina

Fuà G./Zacchia C. (eds.) (1983): *Industrializzazione senza fratture*, Il Mulino, Bologna

ISTAT (1992): *Annuario di contabilità nazionale*

Istituto Nazionale per il Commercio Estero (1989): *Rapporto sul commercio estero*, Rome

Mediocredito Centrale (1989): *Indagine sulle imprese manifatturiere*, Rome

Ministero del Lavoro e della Previdenza Sociale (1989): *Rapporto 1988. Lavoro e politiche della occupazione in Italia*, Rome

Ministero dell' Ambiente (1992): *Relazione sullo stato dell' ambiente*, Istituto poligrafico della Stato, Rome

Rapporto annuale (1993) dei governatori delle banche centrali europee

SVIMEZ (1990): *Rapporto sul Mezzogiorno*, Angeli, Milano

Sylos Labini P. (1986): *Le classi sociali negli anni' 80, Laterza*, Bari

Valli V. (1988): *Politica economica. I modelli, gli strumenti, l'economia italiana*, La Nuova Italia Scientifica, Rome

CHAPTER 5

United Kingdom

Ian Stone

5.1 INSTITUTIONAL AND HISTORICAL CONTEXT

5.1.1 Political background

The United Kingdom consists of the countries of Great Britain (England, Scotland and Wales) together with the province of Northern Ireland. It is a constitutional monarchy of long standing; the constitution itself is not a written one, but is formed by elements of statute, common law and convention. Supreme legislative authority resides in Parliament, which is divided into two Houses, the Lords and the Commons. The former, which consists of a mixture of senior Church of England bishops and hereditary and appointed life peers of the realm, revises and amends laws emanating from the democratically elected Commons. Although the Lords can make a useful contribution to the law-making process, its power is restricted to delaying enactment of legislation.

The UK electoral system is based on the principle of 'first past the post'. Each of the country's 650 constituencies returns one member to the Commons, and the leader of the party with the largest number of Members of Parliament at a general election is by tradition asked by the monarch to form a government. A clear majority for any one party gives substantial powers to the executive of government to pursue its legislative programme during its term of up to five years. Since 1945, the government has been formed by one of two parties, Labour and Conservative.

The fact that smaller parties with a significant proportion of the vote are under this system poorly represented in terms of Parliamentary seats has led to increasing pressure for a change in the electoral system to one of proportional representation. However, parties are usually more inclined to pursue this idea when in opposition than when they themselves are in power, with the result that the UK system continues to be distinct in terms of its system of political representation compared to the prevailing form among EC states.

The attitude of the present (Conservative) government to the European Community and the place of the UK within it is well illustrated by the debate over the Maastricht Treaty. The EC is seen primarily in its economic dimension; there is resistance to the idea of political union and no commitment to the concept of 'Social Europe'. Indeed, the latter is seen as interfering with the free operation of markets (while also giving the UK possible competitive advantage through non-participation). Perhaps because of the 'island mentality' and the UK's historical development – particularly the 'special relationship' with the USA – there is a strong nationalist outlook which is sensitive to loss of sovereignty. 'Subsidiarity', however, is a concept the government is more keen to employ in relation to Europe than domestically, where the principle runs against its inclination to centralise power and to resist any devolutionary pressures, whether from Scotland and Wales, the English regions, or local authorities.

5.1.2 Economic background

The post-war period up to the late 1970s was characterised by a consensus between the two main political parties over economic policy. Both adhered to the notion of a mixed economy of private and public enterprises, with regulation of markets, the use of Keynesian demand-management policies, and the maintenance of the welfare state. The election of a Conservative government led by Margaret Thatcher in 1979 marked a departure from this well established pattern as the government introduced a radical policy programme aimed at reversing Britain's economic decline. The high degree of centralisation of power made it possible for the Thatcher governments in particular to make sweeping changes in respect of economic policy and institutions during the 1980s.

The economy had functioned poorly by OECD standards during the 1960s, lagging in terms of the main performance indicators. It also suffered from 'stop-go' cycles, whereby attempts to expand demand, and thus increase output and employment, repeatedly led to a rush of imports and balance-of-payments difficulties, followed by deflation. The problems of the 1970s were appreciably worse. Although it retained (through the Commonwealth) special links with its former colonies, Britain's post-war economic interests moved increasingly towards Europe, culminating in membership of the European Community in 1973. This opened the economy to increased competition, which, combined with the first OPEC oil shock of the following year, led to rising unemployment, serious balance-of-payments difficulties and high inflation. The interventionist policies deployed with apparent effectiveness during much of the post-war period – aggregate demand management mainly through fiscal adjustments, backed up by a prices and incomes policy – became less effective in the face of structural changes occurring in the international economy. After a period when intervention in the economy was intensified (during the Labour administration of the second half of the 1970s) the electorate opted for what, was in terms of UK post-war experience, a radical alternative approach to economic management. Voters have sustained their general support for this approach through four general elections, although other factors – the Falklands War, the re-drawing of constituency boundaries, opposition splits and right-wing domination of the popular press – have contributed to Conservative electoral successes.

Since 1979, the Conservative governments led by Margaret Thatcher and (from 1990) by John Major, have pursued policies founded on an economic and political philosophy of free enterprise, emphasis on market-based allocation of resources and a rejection of the notion that government should act as a prime mover in the economy. The principal focus of stabilisation policy during this period has been inflation. The main weapon against it has been monetary policy. This was pursued initially through controlling the money supply, and subsequently by reliance upon the interest rate policy and exchange rate targeting (including entry into the European exchange rate mechanism (ERM)). Central to the macroeconomic policy has been the Medium Term Financial Strategy (MTFS), setting out for a number of years targets for monetary growth, the Public Sector Borrowing Requirement (PSBR) and money GDP, based on the notion that medium- to long-term policies can be used to affect expectations and thus influence inflation outcomes. Fiscal policy has consisted of an attempt to balance the budget at a reduced level of government spending, with a view to creating scope for tax reductions to encourage enterprise. Over-expansion of the economy in the mid-to-late 1980s led to deflationary measures (higher interest rates) giving rise to the second major recession within a decade. In late 1992, with inflation under control, the government, faced with rapidly rising unemployment, gave priority in its stabilisation policy to promoting recovery. It has, in contrast to the recession of the early 1980s, run a significant counter-cyclical budget deficit, and sterling's forced exit from the ERM in 1992 allowed a sharp reduction in interest rates.

To complement the hoped-for non-inflationary macroeconomic framework, economic strategy since 1979 has embodied an attempt to improve the output responsiveness ('supply-side') of the economy. This emphasis is exemplified by the microeconomic policies relating to the labour market. Reductions in rates of income tax have been introduced to stimulate work effort; successive social security reforms have sought to reduce the disincentive effect of benefits on willingness to accept low-paid jobs; and legislation has been passed to limit the activities of trade unions and thus their power to increase real wages. Other supply-side measures include reducing taxes on business, 'liberalisation' of markets through the abolition of controls, reduction in subsidies to industry, and privatisation.

5.2 MAIN ECONOMIC CHARACTERISTICS

5.2.1 Population and labour supply

As in other EC countries, the rate of UK population growth has fallen markedly over the postwar period. While the total increased from 50.3 to 55.9 million in the two decades to 1971, a further rise of only 2.8% (to 57.4 million) had occurred by 1991 (Table E14). The UK civilian labour force (i.e. those in work and the unemployed) has been increasing at a faster rate than the population, rising from 24.9 million in 1971 to 28.2 million in 1990 (i.e. by 13%). This growth, combined with a rise in female activity rates, has more than compensated for the labour force effects of the fall in the male participation rate resulting from rising numbers staying on in education, more early retirements, and the phenomenon of 'discouraged workers' who have dropped out of the labour force on losing hope of finding employment. The male activity rate, which stood at 81% in 1971, was down to 74% in 1991, but this still represented 16 million workers (up slightly from 15.9 million in 1971). In contrast, female participation rates have risen, from 44% to 53% over the same period (12.6 million workers, up from 8.9 million in 1971), reflecting smaller family size, labour-saving household devices, the structural shift from

manufacturing to services, and changing social attitudes.

At 49.1% of total population in 1990, the UK's civilian working population is the highest in the EC (average 45.7%) apart from Denmark (Table E15). This reflects the high activity rates for both males and females. A further rise in the female participation rate is expected; combined with a continuing rise in the population of working age, this will lead to a further expansion in the UK civilian workforce to 28.9 million by 2001.

The increased role for females in the labour force has been accompanied by a significant increase in part-time working. Almost a quarter of all jobs fall into this category. In 1989 42% of female workers were part-time, compared with 8% among males. The particularly rapid growth of service sector employment in the UK over the 1980s was a major factor in this development, since it is in this sector (notably distribution, hotels and catering) that many of the part-time jobs were created. During 1983–8, the increase in the number of part-time jobs (1.4 million) was almost twice the number of full-time jobs created (0.8 million). Thus, while males in the UK work significantly longer hours than their European counterparts, working hours among women are at the lower end of the EC spectrum.

5.2.2 GDP and output growth

The 1980s real growth performance was noticeably better than that of the 1970s which, following the expansionary boom of 1970–3, subsequently averaged below 1% per annum. During 1981–90 the average real rate of GDP growth was 2.6% – better than the EUR12 economies (2.3%), though behind both the USA (2.9%) and Japan (4.2%) (Table E19). Indeed, the UK average of 3.7% growth in real terms over 1983–8 represents the highest sustained rate of increase since 1949–54. Outwardly this constitutes a dramatic turnaround in the performance of the UK economy, given that it had by far the lowest real rate of growth among the EUR 12 in both the 1960s (EUR 12 average 4.8%, UK 2.8%) and the generally more difficult 1971–80 period (EUR 12 average 3.0%, UK 1.9%).

It cannot be argued that the performance of the UK economy has significantly improved in terms of its long-term growth trajectory. The appearance of excess demand pressure in 1988 led to deflationary action by government and a slowing of growth relative to other European nations. In the recession of the early 1990s – as in that of the early 1980s – UK output fell more than in the rest of Europe (Table E19). The severity of recessions since the late 1970s – in both cases reflecting excessive application of deflationary measures – cancelled out many of the gains from the better performance of the intervening years.

The improved record during much of the 1980s has thus not been of sufficient magnitude to alter significantly the UK's relative position in terms of per capita GDP. Even in the late 1980s – that is, before the latest recession – UK output per head was significantly behind not only the USA and Japan, but also the other major economies of West Germany and France; while being roughly on a par with Italy. By 1990, UK per capita output was on a par with the EUR 12 average; the same relative position as in the late 1970s (Table E20). Moreover, there has since 1990 been a deterioration in the UK's comparative position, albeit a partly cyclical one.

5.2.3 Employment structure

In terms of labour demand, the main feature of change since 1971 has been the dramatic fall in manufacturing employment. Employment (including the self-employed) in this sector fell by a third during 1971–90 (from 8.2 to 5.4 million), and stands at just over 20% of total employment. A substantial proportion of the fall was concentrated in the period 1979–81, when the effects of world recession were intensified in the UK by tight monetary and fiscal policies, contributing to a reduction of over a million, or 13.3%, in manufacturing employment in just two years. The contraction in manufacturing has been more than balanced in aggregate terms by the expansion in service employment, which grew over 1971–90 by around 5.1 million (from 13.1 to 18 million). The proportion of employ-

ment in services (68.3%) is among the highest in the EC and significantly above the EUR 12 average of 61% (Table E16).

There is considerable variation among the different activities within the service sector. The male-dominated transport and communications sub-sector has contracted, while other sub-sectors – distribution, hotels and catering; banking, finance, insurance and business services; and 'other services' – have all shown significant growth. Proportionately large falls have occurred in the number of people engaged in agriculture (down from 0.8 to 0.6 million) and in the energy and water supply industries (0.8 to 0.45 million), though in absolute terms the contraction is small alongside the scale of changes in manufacturing and services. Agriculture, as Table E16 shows, accounts for only 2.2% of civilian employment, the lowest in the EC.

5.2.4 Unemployment

In the UK, as in the EC in general, the average rate of unemployment during the 1980s was more than double that of the 1970s. Unemployment rose steadily from the 1960s level of under 2% to 3.8% in the 1970s, and 9.7% in the 1980s (see Table E17 and Figure 5.1). This latter figure is similar to the EC average, though above that for the USA and nearly four times Japan's. Unemployment in the UK rose especially rapidly in the recession of the early 1980s, from 1.1 million (4.6%) in 1979 it moved upwards until 1986, when 3.1 million people (11.4%) were registered unemployed. With restructuring and strong recovery of output, the rate subsequently came down to below the EUR 12 level, reaching 7% in 1990 (Table E17), before the onset of yet another recession saw the rate begin to rise once more. Unemployment officially stood at 2.9 million at the end of 1992, equivalent to 10.4% of the workforce. With recovery underway in 1993, unemployment actually – and unexpectedly, given that it normally lags behind output change – fell slightly in the period to June.

The official rate of unemployment is normally substantially higher for men than for women (e.g. 12.9% and 5.1% respectively in June 1992).

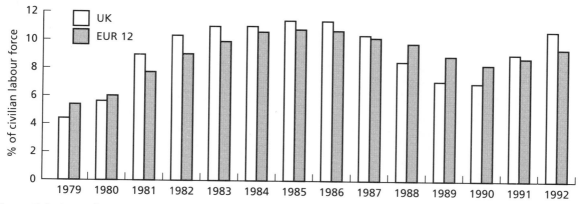

Figure 5.1 Annual unemployment rates, UK and EC average (1979–92).

Source: European Economy, Statistical Annexe, Table E17.

Gender differences in unemployment are exaggerated in UK statistics, however, because the unemployment count includes only those successfully claiming unemployment benefit, and married women make up a significant proportion of those seeking work but not eligible for benefit. Estimates of unemployment based on international (ILO) definitions – counting persons who are without work but available for employment and who have actively sought work in recent months – derived from the Labour Force Survey give rates for men and women of 11.7% and 7.5% respectively for mid-1992. Moreover, comparisons of UK official unemployment rates over time are misleading due to a number of changes in the official definition of unemployment during the 1980s, most of which have had the effect of reducing the official unemployed total.

5.2.5 Productivity and wages

The productivity performance of the UK economy, which was especially poor in the 1970s, showed significant improvement during the 1980s and was hailed by supporters of 'Thatcherite' polices as vindicating the government's approach to economic management and particularly its emphasis on supply-side policies. In fact, there is considerable debate as to the nature and longer-term significance of the productivity 'miracle'.

Table 5.1 Output per person employed in the major industrialised countries (av. annual % change)

	Manufacturing			Whole economy		
	1960 –70	1970 –80	1980 –88	1960 –70	1970 –80	1980 –88
UK	3.0	1.6	5.2	2.4	1.3	2.5
USA	3.5	3.0	4.0	2.0	0.4	1.2
Japan	8.8	5.3	3.1	8.9	3.8	2.9
FRG	4.1	2.9	2.2	4.4	2.8	1.8
France	5.4	3.2	3.1	4.6	2.8	2.0
Italy	5.4	3.0	3.5	6.3	2.6	2.0
Canada	3.4	3.0	3.6	2.4	1.5	1.4
G7 Av.	4.5	3.3	3.6	3.5	1.7	1.8

Source: HM Treasury, *Economic Progress Report*, No. 201, April 1989.

Since 1960 all OECD countries have suffered a decline in productivity growth as represented by increases in real output (all sectors) per employed worker (see figures for 'whole economy' in Table 5.1). In the 1960s, when the average percentage increase in productivity among the large industrial (G7) economies was 3.5% per annum, the UK rate of 2.4% was well behind that of Germany, Italy, and France. OECD figures for the 1970s show the UK rate (1.3%) running at less than half the annual averages in the other three large EC economies. However, the increase in the UK rate during 1980–8 – to an average of 2.5% per annum – is very much against the downward trend affecting virtually all OECD countries, and is comfortably above the average for the largest seven industrial economies (1.8%). Only Japan (2.9%) performed better than this.

In manufacturing alone, as Table 5.1 shows, the UK's average annual rise in output per person employed, at 5.2%, is easily above the next highest figure (USA 4%) for the major industrial economies (G7 average 3.6%). It is widely argued that this reflects a number of factors. The 1970s was characterised by labour hoarding in manufacturing which could not be sustained in the context of deep recession and an over-valued currency in the early 1980s. The least competitive firms were squeezed out of existence, while many of those which survived did so only by tackling over-manning, restrictive labour practices and forms of work organisation which hampered efficiency. A large reduction in the size of the labour force, combined with more intensive use of the labour retained – achieved through reorganisation, new technology and changing work practices – is the main explanation for the better productivity performance. It was *not* (as will be shown below) the result of a significant shift in the level of investment in new plant and equipment or skills formation.

Productivity growth in the 1980s was higher for manufacturing than the whole economy because the former experienced a much sharper fall in output and employment in the early 1980s, and because recovery saw manufacturing output rise at a faster rate than other sectors. The performance is less impressive according to figures which relate to similar points in the business cycle, rather than trough-to-peak years. Certainly, output growth per head in the whole economy began to flatten out from around 1987, while that for manufacturing started to fall in 1990. Much of the output gain in manufacturing (13% in 1980–9) has been wiped out by the subsequent recession, bringing down with it the average annual productivity growth rate. Higher investment levels are needed if the improvement since the 1970s is to be maintained in the 1990s,

and if the gap between the UK and foreign competitor productivity (recently estimated to be 30% for West Germany and 35% Japan) is to be narrowed.

The 1980s productivity increase had only a limited effect in enhancing the economy's international competitiveness, due to the continuing high level of British wage and salary increases, which occurred in spite of the decline in union power brought about by legislation and the effects of structural change. The UK economy has long been characterised by upward pressure from wage and salary costs, and the trend was steeper in the 1980s than the 1970s. The faster rate of earnings growth was mainly the result of buoyant profit levels, improved productivity and skilled labour shortages, rather than union militancy. From 1982 through to 1990 the growth of average annual earnings was steady at 7% to 9%, responding little to either reductions in the inflation rate or slackening of the labour market. The recession has since reduced earnings rises to a 25-year low; but in 1992–3 they continued to increase at a rate (4%) faster than inflation.

The effect of this enormous rise in costs per worker was offset by the increases in labour productivity. While in the 1970s, when productivity growth was low, unit labour costs tracked the path of wage and salaries quite closely, in the 1980s higher productivity gave rise to a sharp divergence between wage costs and unit labour costs. Real unit labour costs actually rose slightly over the period 1980 to 1990 in the UK, while its main trading partners (apart from the USA) all experienced significant falls (Table E23). Gains in productivity were absorbed in real earnings' growth to a much greater extent in the UK, compared to the USA, Japan and West Germany. The UK has thus only been able to narrow the gap in competitiveness through a relative fall in the exchange value of sterling.

5.2.6 Inflation

The UK suffered relatively high rates of inflation in comparison with its trading partners during the 1970s, and although its relative position improved in the 1980s, by the end of the decade the problem had re-emerged, giving the lie to the view that inflation had been 'conquered' (see Figure 5.2). The annual increase in retail prices of below 4% in the 1960s (the same as the EUR 12 average (Table E27)), was accelerating in the early 1970s even before the first oil shock – and high import prices in general – helped push the rate up to 24% in 1975. The rate fell back to 9% by 1978, giving an average for 1971–80 of 13.3%, which was above the EC average (10.7%), and substantially higher than that for West Germany and France, though not Italy, which is similarly inflation-prone.

The second oil price hike, relaxed monetary controls, and VAT increases contributed to a sharp rise in the inflation rate at the end of the 1970s, with the Retail Price Index (RPI) reaching 18% in 1980. 'Eliminating' inflation was declared the principal aim of the incoming Conservative government in 1979 and the chief weapon for achieving this was control of money supply growth. Tight monetary policies were enforced in the early 1980s, reducing inflation to 5% by 1984. The policies were instrumental in bringing about the deep recession of the early 1980s, which itself had the effect of reducing inflationary expectations, while rising unemployment and trade-union reform weakened the power of labour. These circumstances combined to bring UK inflation rates down near to those of its main trading partners during the mid-decade period. The rate subsequently increased once more, with the RPI rising to over 10% in 1990. Some economists see this as the inevitable outcome of the relaxation of monetary control, when the government switched to the exchange rate as its policy target. Others, however, interpret it as simply a reflection of excess demand and changing labour market conditions. The deflationary measures adopted from 1988 had the effect of once more bringing the inflation rate down to low levels; in early 1993, the RPI was below 3.5%.

In technical terms, official inflation figures have been affected by interest rates, which in recent years were first raised to protect the pound and subsequently lowered to promote recovery. Such changes affect the RPI via interest paid on house mortgage loans. With a large owner-occupier sector in the UK, this can have a significant impact upon the RPI (compare, for instance, the standardised figure of 5.6% for 1989 in Table E27 with the RPI level of 8%) and the government has recently begun to issue statistics on inflation which exclude the cost of mortgages ('the underlying rate'). The official argument for this is that such interest-induced changes are unrepresentative of the 'true' rate of inflation; opponents say that to exclude the cost of home ownership from the measure of cost of living makes the latter unrepresentative, because mortgage repayment takes a large proportion of many incomes. More recently, the underlying rate has been substantially above the (generally more volatile) RPI figure, reflecting the impact of a sharp fall in interest rates upon the latter.

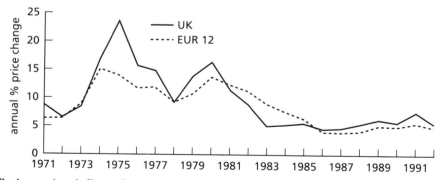

Figure 5.2 Inflation: price deflator for private consumption.

Source: European Economy, Statistical Annexe, Table E27.

5.2.7 Consumption, savings and investment

Consumption

Consumer spending is by far the largest component of total expenditure; larger, proportionately, in the UK than in virtually all the EC economies. Certainly, its expansion was central to growth during the second half of the 1980s. As a proportion of GDP, it began the 1980s at around 60%, rising rapidly from 1986 to 65% in 1989 and 1990. Altogether, this represented a real increase of 40% over the decade, compared with a rise in expenditure-based GDP of 27% over 1980–90. By contrast, public expenditure on goods and services was tightly constrained during the decade, and steadily fell back from around 22% of GDP in 1980 to 19% in 1990 (a rise of just 9% in real terms).

The growth in consumer spending in the 1980s is, in part, explained by the growth in personal sector incomes. The largest component of this is wages and salaries, which rose steadily in the second half of the 1980s (earnings rose at an annual rate of 8.6% during 1986–90, compared with average consumer price rises of 6.0% per year). Aided by reductions in rates of income tax – part of the government's supply-side strategy –

the average annual rate of growth in post-tax personal incomes was roughly 7% to 8% over the decade, with the real rate of post-tax income growth reaching as high as 5% in the late 1980s.

Savings

The proportional rise in consumer spending is also related to the steady fall in the personal *savings* ratio (saving as a percentage of personal disposable income). This rose steadily through the 1970s, reaching 13.5% in 1980; it then fell sharply to a low of 4% in 1989. The expansion of credit as monetary restrictions were relaxed in the mid-1980s, through making it easier for households to borrow, contributed to the fall in savings. On the demand side, lower expected rates of inflation also encouraged spending as households feel less need to replenish money reserves when these are not being eroded by rapid inflation.

The trend to reduced saving has also been ascribed to the 'wealth effect', whereby, as property prices and shares values rose faster than inflation over the 1980s, people with such assets felt wealthier and thus less inclined to convert income into wealth through saving. The late 1980s saw a particularly rapid rise in house prices, which rose from their long-term price-

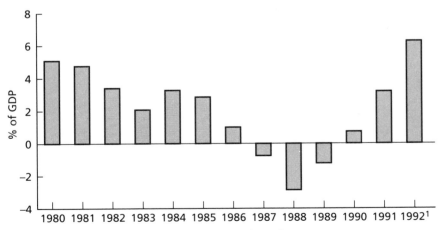

Figure 5.3 UK personal sector financial surplus (% of GDP).

Source: European Economy, 1993, p. 87.

earnings ratio of 3.5 to a peak of 4.8 in 1989. It is a feature of the UK economy in comparison with other EC countries that there is a high proportion (around 70%) of households in owner-occupation. The steady rise of owner-occupation has been encouraged by tax relief on mortgage interest, exemption from capital gains tax, restrictions on private rented accommodation which have discouraged supply and (more recently) by the availability of up to 100% mortgage finance. As house-owners saw the value of their chief asset rise significantly, the general response was to use this equity as security for further loans to finance further consumption (see Figure 5.3).

This helps explain why consumer expenditure over the period 1984–90 grew faster than personal disposable income, contributing to over-heating of the economy at the end of the 1980s. Since then, the situation has gone into reverse. Deflationary measures (higher interest rates) have had a particularly sharp effect in terms of the housing market, and falling house prices have left many home-owners with a problem of 'negative equity', where the value of the property is below the value of the mortgage outstanding. Falling assets values, together with uncertainty over employment, has led to consumer reluctance to spend, reflected in the upward trend in the personal savings ratio since 1990. Lack of confidence on the part of consumers has been a central feature of the early 1990s recession.

National saving is, of course, the sum of private (personal and company) and public saving, and the 1980s decline in personal saving was offset by an increase in company saving and a steady fall in the level of dis-saving by the public sector (e.g. it recorded a positive level of savings in 1988). Thus, *total* savings as a percentage of GDP turned out to be relatively stable over the 1980s. As Table 5.2 shows, however, the savings level overall in the UK is lower than that of other major economies, with the exception of the USA.

Table 5.2 Comparisons of annual average national saving as a percentage of GDP

	USA	Japan	Germany	France	Italy	UK
1975–84	18.5	31.8	19.6	22.5	24.2	17.1
1985–90	15.0	33.0	24.0	20.5	20.8	16.3

Source: OECD, *Economic Outlook*, June 1992.

Investment

Investment, gross domestic fixed capital formation (GDFCF), has increased proportionately more over the 1980s than consumer spending, though it is less important as a component of demand, equivalent to only around 30% of consumer expenditure. GDFCF, which was fairly stable as a percentage of GDP during the first half of the 1980s (around 16%), thereafter rose steadily to 19.9% in 1989 and 19.2% in 1990. The 1990 figure, however, was below the level in the late 1970s, and below the EUR 12 average of nearly 21% (Table E21). Nonetheless, the UK record in investment, which has been poor in EC terms for decades, did show signs of improvement during the second half of the 1980s, when some convergence of rates took place.

'Total business investment' (accounting for some two-thirds of GDFCF) involves the trading sector of the economy; it includes nationalised industries but excludes private investment in dwellings and general government investment. This vital aspect of investment was generally static in real terms during 1973–9, fell sharply in the early 1980s, but increased markedly thereafter to reach levels in the late 1980s which, as a proportion of GDP, were the highest for almost two decades. It has since fallen back once more. Manufacturing is a relatively small part of total business investment – a quarter in 1990, compared to over a third in 1970. Investment in manufacturing was relatively static in the 1980s, and its share of business investment has thus continued to fall even as the total has risen. This reflects ongoing structural changes within the economy in favour of the financial sector and distribution, and provides support for the argument that any improvement in the productivity performance during the 1980s was largely the result of labour intensification.

Another important feature is the noticeable shift in the pattern of investment expenditure since the early 1980s in favour of the private sector. Private sector investment as a proportion of GDP steadily increased from 11% in 1977 to nearly 17% in 1989. The equivalent share of general government investment and public corporation investment over the period 1977–90 fell from a combined total of 6% to 2.6%. This reflects privatisation and government attempts to reduce public spending.

5.2.8 Income distribution

Income in capitalist societies is generally unevenly distributed, and it takes a combination of progressive income taxes and welfare benefits to reduce the inequality. In practice, UK post-war experience indicates that redistribution of post-tax incomes via direct taxes has tended to be more from the top towards the middle-income groups, rather than towards the bottom; it is effectively left to the welfare benefits to effect an improvement in the post-tax position of the poorer groups.

Since 1979, however, Conservative governments have sought to reform taxation and reduce the burden of direct taxation in line with its supply-side strategy. This has been done by a combination of increased tax thresholds and cuts in marginal tax rates. By 1988, the standard rate of income tax had been cut from 33% to 25%, and the maximum rate on earned income from over 80% down to 40%. Such changes are of little assistance, however, to those either below the tax threshold or paying little tax; while being of considerable benefit to the better-off groups previously in high tax brackets. Benefit changes, by comparison, have been modest; most were indexed in line with prices, which for state retirement pensions meant a shift away from the previous practice of linking pension increases to the rise in the higher of prices and earnings.

Recent research on income distribution has shown that the distribution of pre-tax earnings of full-time employees widened over 1979–88.

While the overall rise in earnings was 145%, the percentage increase was graded by decile from 114% for the poorest to 150% for the ninth and 185% for the top decile. The share of original income going to each of the lowest three-fifths of households thus fell between 1979 and 1988 (taken together, from 35% to 30%), while that of the top one-fifth of households rose from 43% to 50%. The combined tax and benefit changes are calculated to have caused the top 10% of earners to be £80 per week better off in 1992 than they would have been under the 1979 tax and benefit regime; the bottom 10% actually paid more in tax and received less in benefits than would have been the case in 1979. Studies which allow for tax and benefit changes show that disposable income is less unevenly distributed than original income, but that it has changed in favour of the better-off in society. The bottom three-fifths, together accounted for 40% of disposable income in 1979, compared to 36% for the top fifth; the corresponding figures for 1988 were 35% and 42%.

The incidence of poverty in the UK is relatively high compared with similar EC economies. Adopting the EC definition (expenditure of household less than 50% of the EC average) gives a percentage below the poverty line of 15.9%, which is just on the average for the EC as a whole (excluding Luxembourg) in 1985. The UK stands ahead of Greece, Ireland, Spain and Portugal, but well behind both the smaller EC economies of Belgium, Denmark, and the Netherlands (average 3%) and the larger economies of West Germany (7.1%), France (12.1%) and Italy (13.9%).

5.3 PRODUCTION AND MARKET STRUCTURE

5.3.1 Output structure

The contribution of individual sectors to overall growth in output has changed as the economy has evolved structurally. The largest change involves the contraction of the output share of manufacturing (down by over eight percentage points over 1972–88 to less than a quarter of GDP), and the rise in that of services, from 55% to over 63% (Table 5.3). Finance-related activity has been the main contributor to the expansion in the service sector, with an output (including net interest receipts) equivalent to over 18% of GDP in 1990. Agriculture has continued its relative decline, while the figures for energy in the table reflect the development of North Sea oil and gas, including the fall in oil prices after 1985.

Table 5.3 Contribution to UK GDP by industry (%)

Sector	1972	1975	1980	1985	1988	1990
Agriculture	2.7	2.6	2.0	1.7	1.4	1.5
Energy and water	4.8	4.9	9.3	10.1	5.6	5.1
Manufacturing	30.7	28.1	25.4	22.6	23.7	22.4
Construction	6.9	6.9	5.8	5.6	6.5	7.6
Services	55.0	57.6	57.5	60.0	62.8	63.4

Source: UK National Accounts '*Blue Book*', CSO, various years.

5.3.2 Industrial structure by firm size

In 1987 there were 2.5 million firms in the UK; 96% of these employed less than 20 people and accounted for 36% of total employment. Of 140,000 manufacturing enterprises in 1989, 96% employed less than 100 workers. These – largely single-establishment independent companies – account for just under one-fifth of manufacturing output. Enterprises with 100 to 1,500 employees – making up only 3.2% of the total number – contribute 29% of output, while the remaining 54% of output is produced by just 395 large enterprises with 1,500+ workers (0.3% of all enterprises). The 20 largest enterprises alone have, between them, 1,300 establishments which together produce one-fifth of UK manufacturing output. In employment terms, firms with under 100 workers account for a quarter of the total for manufacturing, while the largest 395 firms alone employ 57%.

The structure has changed over the last decade in favour of smaller-sized enterprises. The share of manufacturing employment of firms with less than 200 employees increased from 28% to 40% during 1978–89; while in firms with less than 100 employees the share increased from 17.3% to 24.3%. During the 1960s and 1970s large enterprises were favoured by government and mergers were encouraged in the interests of achieving scale economies. Since 1979 the official position has shifted, and emphasis has been given to promoting the formation and growth of small firms. A range of support measures was introduced, including payments to the unemployed who start their own business, improved access to finance, and special tax relief for investors in small firms. These measures, in combination with changes in markets, technology and business organisation, undoubtedly contributed to a significant change in the size structure of UK enterprises.

The last decade has seen a large rise in the number of businesses registering for VAT (up by nearly 400,000 during 1979–89), while the incidence of self-employment increased from 2 million in the late 1970s to 3.2 million in 1990. Self-employment as a proportion of total employment rose steadily from around 8% in the 1970s to 13.2% in 1989. In keeping with broader structural trends, the vast majority of these businesses are engaged in services (distribution, catering and repairs) and construction, rather than manufacturing.

5.3.3 Production specialisation

UK competitive strengths are characterised by their breadth rather than their depth, with the top 50 industries accounting for a low proportion of total exports in comparison with other leading industrial nations. In industry, strengths include chemicals, petroleum, pharmaceuticals, paints, engines, defence goods, electrical generation equipment, aircraft and textile fibres, together with consumer packaged goods (food and drink, household products and cosmetics) and household furnishings (porcelain, ceramic products and carpets). The UK is, as a result of foreign investment, also competitive in the manufacture of semiconductors and computers, cars, and electrical and electronic consumer goods including televisions. UK industry is less strong in office products, textiles/clothing, mechanically based consumer products, and most machinery industries. Beyond manufacturing, there are significant clusters of activity in publishing, recording, information products and software, as well as in finance and trade-related activities (money management, retailing, auctioneering and global trading, international legal and insurance activities). Many of the industries which enjoy a competitive advantage are related to luxury, leisure, entertainment and wealth, and often involve niche market products. Car production illustrates this: apart from Rolls-Royce and Jaguar, British firms lead in the racing car market; competitiveness in production models increasingly relies upon foreign companies.

5.3.4 Multinational business

Most large firms operating in the UK are multinational enterprises, with extensive activities overseas. The British economy is more internationalised than its EC neighbours: in the 1980s it was second only to the US as the source of overseas investment by multinational companies, and is exceeded only by the USA and Canada in terms of the stock of foreign investment. Indeed, among the 100 largest manufacturing firms in the UK (in output terms), 20 are foreign-owned. Altogether, in 1989, 1,350 of the manufacturing enterprises – under 1% of the total, but accounting for 21.5% of total sales and 15% of employment – were in foreign ownership. In 1987, over half of the foreign sector's manufacturing employment, and two-thirds of its output, were American, though the balance has shifted to some extent in recent years with expanded direct investment by Japan (one-third of its investment in the EC has come to the UK) and the Far East, and by EFTA countries seeking access to the EC market after 1992.

Foreign interests tend to be concentrated in the medium and high research-intensive sectors, with proportionately high representation in chemicals, mechanical engineering, electrical and electronic engineering, motor vehicles, instruments and office machinery. In some sectors (notably computers, consumer electrical and electronic goods, cars, and North Sea oil)

foreign producers are dominant and are a crucial element in the turnaround in UK trading performance in relation to these items. New foreign manufacturing investment has been much encouraged since 1979, partly as a means of introducing into the economy new work practices and manufacturing techniques. Combined with entry via acquisition, this has caused the foreign sector to grow rapidly in recent years. While strong foreign interest is found in some non-manufacturing sectors such as banking (see below), most service sector areas of activity are domestically owned.

5.4 GOVERNMENT INVOLVEMENT IN THE ECONOMY

5.4.1 Public expenditure

Public expenditure (on goods and services and transfer payments) rose as a proportion of GDP over the 1960s and 1970s. In the wake of the first oil shock, general government (central and local government) spending reached 49% of output in the mid-1970s before falling back to around 45% in 1979. Although a rising share of public expenditure was a trend widely shared among industrial nations (the UK figure being slightly below the EUR 9 average), in the context of a poor domestic economic performance, there were many who supported the incoming Thatcher government's aim of 'rolling back the frontiers of the state'. The public sector was regarded by the Tory government as a burden on private sector business (i.e. it 'crowded out' private sector investment) and a restriction on the consumer's freedom to choose. Policies were introduced aimed at progressive reduction of spending, both in absolute terms and as a share of GDP.

The measures deployed since the late 1970s to bring this about have included tighter controls on public spending, reductions in the size of the state sector through privatisation, and the pursuit of 'value for money' in public spending. During the 1980s the Medium Term Financial Strategy was a key weapon in the attempt to force public spending proportionately onto a downward path. This involves the preparation, annually, of cash expenditure plans covering a four-year period. Under the previous system, where planning was in terms of goods and services provision, higher expenditure resulted when inflation exceeded the anticipated rate. By the late 1980s, around 60% of public expenditure was 'cash limited'; the rest was 'demand led', i.e. determined by take-up rates for benefits and services. Cash limits for individual departments have also exerted downward pressure on public-sector wages and the number of public employees. The introduction in 1992 of a 'control total' for non-cyclical items of spending marks a further tightening of control. Under this system, government sets a level of real spending which is below the underlying real rate of growth and ministers of each department have to argue for their share of the set total.

In spite of persistent government attempts to reduce public expenditure, the state sector proved stubbornly resistant to such attempts at pruning – although the UK was more successful than most EC economies in this respect (see Table E28 and Figure 5.4). Public expenditure was still (including net lending less privatisation receipts) equivalent to around 46% of GDP in 1985, although it did subsequently fall to 38% of

GDP in 1988 and 1989. For the 1980s as a whole, general government expenditure did rise in real terms (by 12.6%), albeit at a relatively slower pace than previously. Only in 1987–8, i.e. *after* economic recovery, did the ratio of general government spending to GDP fall below its level when the Thatcher government took office, leading to the conclusion that this was due more to rapid economic growth than to curbs on expenditure. Since the late 1980s, the impact of the recession on unemployment and social security benefits (demand-led elements of spending) has pushed public expenditure back up to around 45% of GDP (Table E28). The rise also reflects, to some extent, a modification in government's attitude towards public expenditure and the contribution it can make both counter-cyclically and in social and economic terms (e.g. infrastructure, such as road building).

The composition of public spending has changed significantly over the decade, with the largest departments increasing their share. Social Security, accounting for 31% of public expenditure by function (mainly transfers) in 1990, grew more than a third in real terms, as did Health, which accounts for 14%. Expenditure in both departments is influenced by rising numbers of elderly in the population. Of the other departments, Defence (12% of total spending) and

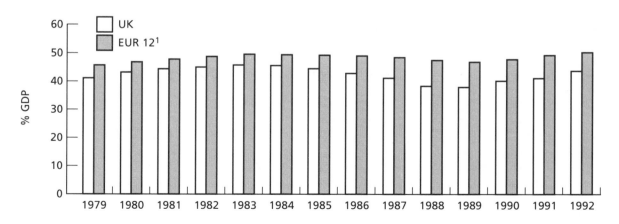

[1] EUR9 for 1979 and 1980

Figure 5.4 Total expenditure of general government (% of GDP).

Source: European Economy, Statistical Annexe, Table E28.

Education and Science (14%) have both increased their share, while Law and Order, though relatively small in absolute terms (6% of total spending), has grown faster than any other department. Transport has remained unchanged, while the budgets of Trade and Industry, Housing and Energy have all fallen in real terms, reflecting reduced state subsidies to industry and the shift of public assets (including nationalised industries and council houses) into private hands.

Defence – alone among the four largest spending areas – has experienced significant cuts recently. The largest proportional expenditure cuts have been in the smaller budget heads; government is finding it difficult to make further reductions since these would have to focus on the large spending areas. Social security spending cuts are difficult given high unemployment and rising numbers of pensioners; rising numbers of children and students make education a hard target, and the nature of demand and supply conditions relating to health makes it peculiarly difficult to make cuts in the National Health Service. Spending on health in the UK is, in any case, lower as a share of GDP (6.1% in 1990) than in other major economies. A backlog of necessary capital spending (the reduction in which was one means of cutting state spending in the 1980s) add to the government's problems in reducing its expenditure in the 1990s.

5.4.2 Revenue sources

In spite of the avowed intention of successive Conservative governments to reduce the burden of taxation, it has remained persistently above its 1979 level. This is substantially due to 'fiscal drag', whereby the rate of income growth exceeds that of prices, by which tax rates are adjusted. However, the burden is relatively modest by international standards; as, indeed, was actually the case in 1979. With total tax revenues (including social security contributions) equivalent to 43% of GDP in 1989, the UK share was ninth among OECD countries, below Germany (45%), France (51%), and considerably behind the Scandinavian countries, particularly Denmark (62%) and Sweden (66%). Britain is not over-taxed compared to other countries.

The UK differs from other OECD countries in that income tax as a share of GDP has tended to fall. This partly reflects the government's wish to shift tax from a direct to an indirect basis. Income tax and social security contributions amounted in 1989 to 44% of tax revenues, compared to 59% in France and 65% in West Germany. Top marginal rates of income tax have been substantially reduced since 1979, and in 1989 were below those in all major economies, though the highest rate applies at a comparatively low income in the UK. The standard tax rate, however, is relatively high by international standards, while the tax threshold is low in comparison. It remains the government's objective – PSBR permitting – to reduce the standard rate from 25% to 20%.

The reduction in the higher rates of tax and the relative shift away from direct taxation is part of a programme of tax reform, a principal aim of which is to stimulate work effort and entrepreneurial activity. It is thus not surprising that in terms of equity the changes are regressive (see section 5.2.7). It has yet to be convincingly demonstrated that reducing tax for the higher income earners has actually resulted in greater work effort. The changes also reflect the view that the punitive tax rates of the 1970s caused the tax base to shrink, as people sought ways of avoiding tax, and of increasing their non-money income (e.g. company-provided cars which were tax exempt).

The same problem afflicted corporation tax in the 1970s, when high marginal tax rates and extensive deductible investment allowances encouraged companies to manipulate balance sheets, so that many large companies paid very little tax in the UK. This, too, has been simplified, and many allowances phased out. A reduction in the tax rate, in stages, from 52% to 33% (25% for companies earning less than £100,000 per annum) has been introduced since 1979. UK company taxation is now attractively low compared with other countries, though the phasing out of capital allowances has made the 33% figure a deceptively modest one. In 1991–2, corporation tax contributed 9% of total revenue.

The UK, like other countries, has placed increased emphasis upon National Insurance contributions as a source of revenue. Although this is technically not a tax, it has the same effect upon disposable income as income tax. The contribution of NI is noticeably smaller as a proportion of the GDP than its equivalents in either Scandinavia or France and Germany, but it still accounts for over 16% of government revenue. Indirect taxes have increased in importance. VAT, the rate of which was raised from 8% to 15% in 1979 (and then to 17.5% in 1991) currently contributes 16% of revenue. This tax is broadly proportional (except for the top 20% of earners) because zero-rating applies to most food, reading matter, public transport, children's clothing and footwear, medicines and (until 1994) domestic heating fuels. Excise duties (on petrol and fuel oils, tobacco, alcohol, betting and gambling), principally aimed at raising revenue, contribute a further 10% to revenue; apart from Denmark and Eire, this represents a higher proportion than elsewhere in the EC.

Finally, there is local authority taxes, which have had a political significance out of all proportion to their contribution to revenue. In the late 1980s, the government replaced a property-based system of local taxation (the Rates) with the Community Charge (or Poll Tax) uniformly levied on adults living in the local authority area. In spite of exemptions, this was regarded as unfair (in that it affected low- more than high-income earners) and was expensive to administer. The tax also created tensions between central government and local authorities who felt their spending needs were greater than those implied by central government calculations based on the 'standard spending assessment'. The funding framework relating to local government meant that authorities which exceeded central government spending guidelines (often in urban areas with significant economic and social problems) had to make disproportionate increases in the level of Community Charge and much higher than anticipated tax demands. Public dissatisfaction with the tax led to its replacement (from 1993) by the Council Tax, which is based on property valuation bands, with a reduced rate for single adult households.

The Community Charge episode was just part of central government's attempt during the 1980s to control the spending and activities of local government. Under the guise of acting to reduce the scope of government, a real centralisation of power occurred. There was also an important (party) political dimension to this, in that the main targets of this policy were the Labour-controlled urban areas. In the end, the misjudgements over the Poll Tax discredited Margaret Thatcher, who was closely associated with its introduction, and contributed significantly to her replacement as Prime Minister by John Major. It is nonetheless the case that, within the unitary state, Britain's local governments are weak in relation to the centre, and have become even weaker in the last decade or so. As a result, they have little power to influence the local economic environment; a situation which stands in contrast to that in most EC states.

5.4.3 The PSBR and the National Debt

The Public Sector Borrowing Requirement (PSBR), or difference between revenue and expenditure, which rose precipitously during the early 1970s from less than 2% of GDP to almost 10% in 1976, has shown a clear downward trend in the 1980s. Table E29 shows that while the average annual net borrowing figure in the UK during 1971–80 (3%) was very close to that of the EUR 9, in the 1980s it was substantially below the EC average (1.7% compared with 4.2%). This was lower than West Germany's figure and second only in the Community to Luxembourg.

Indeed, aided by substantial privatisation proceeds ('negative spending') and unexpectedly high tax receipts, the PSBR itself became negative in the late 1980s (see Figure 5.5). This was the first time this had occurred since 1971, and it meant that the PSBR was converted to the PSDR, or Public Sector Debt Repayment. The PSDR, which was £15 billion (3% of GDP) in 1988–9, was used to reduce the National Debt, which, allowing for liquid assets of the public sector, was down to £150 billion (28% of GDP) in 1991. Since 1970, the scale of the reduction of the National Debt is rivalled only by Luxembourg; on average in the EC, Debt has increased by 50%. Although it was contemplated in the late 1980s that the Debt could disappear altogether within 20 years, in fact the PSDR rapidly evaporated as expenditure increased due to rising unemployment. The PSBR was back to over 5% of GDP in 1992, and the projected PSBR for 1993–4 is around £50 billion (equivalent to over 8% of GDP). Nevertheless, while the size of Debt is of concern to some EC governments – Belgium, Greece and Italy, in particular – the UK government is aided in operating a counter-cyclical deficit for a number of years by the relatively small National Debt (net debt stands at under 30% of GDP).

5.4.4 Industrial policy

Radical changes have occurred since the 1970s in UK policy towards industry. The Labour government of 1974–9 emphasised interventionism; its industrial strategy attempted to bring together employers, the unions and government to plan for industrial growth. It established a National Enterprise Board, extended state ownership through nationalisation, instituted planning agreements with industry, sought to develop industrial democracy, and introduced a range of financial subsidies for firms, sectors and problem regions. During the 1960s and 1970s, expenditure on subsidies increased substantially: whereas in 1965 it amounted to 2% of GDP and 4% of government expenditure, by 1975 the respective figures were 4% and 8%.

The interventionist approach was replaced in the 1980s by a policy of increased reliance upon markets. Supply-side policies, aimed at reducing the level of dependence upon the state and encouraging an 'enterprise culture', have included denationalisation of publicly owned industries (privatisation), deregulation (removal of restrictions under which firms can supply particular goods and services), contracting-out of public services to private firms, reductions in the range and levels of sectoral and regional subsidies to industry, and support for new and small businesses (see sections 5.3.2, 5.4.5/6). Corporatist institutions of economic management have been closed down or downgraded. In accordance with this strategy, since 1979 the annual level of real spending on subsidies to industry has fallen, and in 1990 was equivalent to just 1.2% of GDP and 3.1% of public expenditure.

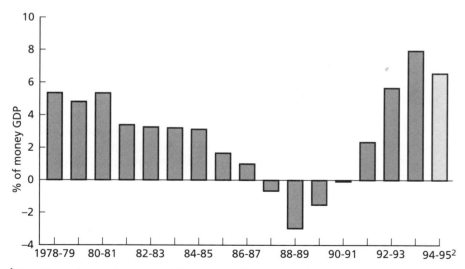

¹Negative values indicate a public sector debt repayment
²Projection

Figure 5.5 Public sector borrowing requirement (including privatisation proceeds).

Source: HM Treasury, *Financial Statement and Budget Report,* various years.

5.4.5 Privatisation

In 1979, the state sector of industry, the public corporations, accounted for 9% of GDP and 7.3% of employment. While the major programme of nationalisation occurred in the early post-war years, when coalmining, railways, gas and electricity were taken into public ownership, further (less systematic) nationalisation took place in the 1960s and 1970s, largely of industries in long-term decline (steel, shipbuilding) and individual firms facing bankruptcy, such as British Leyland and Rolls-Royce. Since 1979, the trend has reversed, with ownership of most of these industries reverting to the private sector – either as private sales to companies (e.g. Rover Group, Vickers Shipbuilding), sales by share offer (e.g. British Gas, British Telecom, the Central Electricity Generating Board, local electricity boards and the water companies, and non-utilities such as British Steel and British Airways), or flotations of government holdings (e.g. in British Petroleum, British Aerospace). By 1992, the output share of nationalised industries had diminished to 3% of GDP and 2.9% of employment. Further privatisation plans exist for British Rail, British Coal and the Post Office, which will virtually complete the process as far as the large publicly controlled entities are concerned.

Although the state assets were often sold at prices significantly below their market value, cumulatively during 1979–92 proceeds amounted to £42 billion (not counting those from the sale of council houses, worth over £17 billion during 1979–89). They have had a significant impact upon government finances – reducing the PSBR in the late 1980s by around 1.5% of GDP – though at the expense of a future contribution to revenue from income streams of profitable industries. There is some doubt, however, over the extent to which privatisation has widened the private shareholding base through its sales by share offer; many people purchased shares only because short-term capital gains were virtually guaranteed by undervaluation.

Government argues that privatisation results in improved efficiency due to competitive forces and profit targets. In fact, the programme has been criticised for transferring utilities to the private sector as single units with a considerable degree of monopoly power, rather than breaking them down into smaller competing entities. Apart from the practical difficulties of achieving the latter, the government recognises that monopoly companies are attractive to buyers, and the successful denationalisation of these industries took precedence over the pursuit of competitive markets. Consequently, regulatory machinery has had to be developed to monitor (quality) and control (prices) the denationalised public-utility monopolies, e.g. British Gas (regulatory agency OFGAS) and British Telecom (OFTEL). These agencies impose a pricing rule known as RPI-X (retail prices index minus a percentage figure below the general inflation rate), which is the ceiling on the annual increase in the firm's prices. Even so, the privatised utilities have been criticised for excessive profits and over-charging.

While the privatised companies have been able to improve the efficiency of their operations (e.g. British Steel, now highly competitive within the EC), and have been given an advantage over state-controlled counterparts elsewhere in the EC in diversifying their activities and developing new products (e.g. British Telecom's global network service for multinational business), some side-effects of privatisation are apparent. Privatisation of electricity, for example, has impacted seriously upon the coal industry, in that it has resulted in cheap imported coal and North Sea gas being substituted in power generation for coal from British mines. UK coal reserves are substantial and, in deep-mining terms, efficiently produced. An energy strategy would take account of the finite nature of gas reserves, the fact that large subsidies are given to nuclear power generation, and the balance-of-payments' impact of imported coal. In the absence of such a policy, the dictates of the market have resulted in a major contraction of the mining industry. Plans were announced in October 1992 to close 31 pits out of the 50 in operation. In spite of public disquiet, prospects for the industry, and for the communities dependent on mining for employment, look bleak.

Other types of privatisation can be identified. One is 'contracting-out', whereby provision to public bodies (e.g. local authorities, central government departments, publicly owned schools and hospitals) of certain goods and services is switched from the public bodies themselves to private firms through competitive tendering. Examples include catering, refuse collection, maintenance functions, and even prison services. Another involves the removal of restrictions on competition, or 'deregulation' of markets. The ending of legal monopolies granted to suppliers of particular services – e.g. the legislation limiting competition in the provision of bus and coach passenger transport – has been seen as an aspect of privatisation in the 1980s, as has deregulation of the Stock Exchange (examined below).

Where it has been decided that the state would have to remain not just the main purchaser, but the chief provider of services, attempts have been made to introduce competition between different state providers, e.g. between schools and between hospitals. In health, an internal market has recently been created, whereby the General Practitioner functions as the equivalent of the private-sector consumer, 'buying' for those patients registered with him/her treatment offered by a variety of hospitals competing for this business. Hospitals are being encouraged by government to 'opt-out' of the control of the District Health Authorities and become semi-independent Trust Hospitals, accountable to the Department of Health. These compete for business against private and DHA hospitals and, for some minor operations, even the GPs themselves.

5.4.6 Regional policy

Regional policy was an important element of industrial policy in the 1960s and 1970s. As a proportion of public expenditure, regional spending in the late 1970s was double that in most other European countries. Regional aid was principally directed at the peripheral regions – Scotland, Wales, Northern England and Northern Ireland – where the traditional industries of coalmining, shipbuilding, steel and textiles, were in decline. Regional economic diversification was pursued by encouraging companies to establish factories in 'Development Areas' (DAs) by means of investment grants, subsidies and tax concessions and by restricting development in the South and Midlands. It resulted in the creation of an estimated 500,000 jobs in DAs over the period 1955–78, mainly through diverting growth from the 'successful' regions, and led to convergence between peripheral and core regions in employment and income. Regional policy was criticised, however, for the high cost per job created, its lack of selectivity (e.g. supporting investments which would have occurred anyway), its relative neglect of services and indigenous enterprise, and for encouraging the establishment of 'branch plant economies', largely restricted to assembly activities and prone to closure during company rationalisations.

The policy has been radically reformed since 1979. Automatic investment grants to companies in DAs have been phased out; discretionary aid is available for projects which maintain employment or create additional jobs in an assisted area. Emphasis is given to assisting the 'indigenous sector' – local small and medium-sized firms – through investment grants and innovation support, and subsidies for use of consultancy services in marketing, design and manufacturing systems.

The area eligible for regional assistance has been reduced; it now contains 15% of the employed population compared with 45% in the 1970s. Apart from Northern Ireland (for which there are special provisions), the policies focus on sub-regions – mainly major conurbations in the north and west – plus underdeveloped rural areas such as the Scottish Highlands & Islands. A substantial proportion of assisted areas have 'intermediate' status, and are not eligible for the full range of assistance, though they do qualify for EC (ERDF) aid.

Although the revisions may make regional intervention more cost-effective, the reduced regional policy budget – down from £2 billion in 1976 to £300 million in 1992 (1990 prices) – has undoubtedly weakened its capacity to significantly reduce regional differences. It has been argued that a 'North–South Divide' exists in the UK, and that it has been intensified since a more market-oriented approach to regional economies was adopted. Job loss through manufacturing decline mainly hit the North and West (even extending down to the West Midlands, centre of the engineering industry), while the services-based expansion of the 1980s was located disproportionately in the South, particularly around London. The North–South employment gap widened from the mid-1970s through to the late 1980s, with 1989 unemployment rates in the regions of the 'North' ranging from 7.3% to 9.9%, compared to 3.6% to 4.5% in the 'South' (UK = 6.3%).

The recent recession, however, reversed the pattern of previous downturns, with the South experiencing faster rises in unemployment than nationally. In early 1993, unemployment in the South East – traditionally the region of lowest unemployment – was very near the national figure (10.5%). One explanation for this is that the rise and fall in house prices was most marked in the South, and its prominent part in fuelling the consumer boom was mirrored in the subsequent collapse in asset values and spending. In fact, employment in the South is expected to recover relatively quickly, given its significant structural advantages, e.g. a high proportion of its population which is skilled and educated, a favourable industry mix, the higher order functions it undertakes within the UK productive system, a high rate of new firm formation and a favourable location in relation to the EC's economic core.

Finally, it should be noted that there has been a diversion of spatially defined assistance towards the inner cities. Urban spending has risen in real terms from £300 million to £1 billion since 1982. Manufacturing contraction in (particularly inner) urban areas has prompted a range of targeted initiatives. These include Enterprise Zones (which offer tax advantages and reduced planning controls in run-down areas) and Urban Development Corporations (which approach urban renewal in their defined areas through infrastructure investments, site assembly, and by 'levering in' private money in development schemes). These (and other) urban policy initiatives have been criticised for concentrating on property development, for their limited impact in providing jobs for those living in the vicinity, and for the fact that the specific agencies established to undertake regeneration activity have displaced local authorities in this role.

5.4.7 Competition policy

Monopoly is defined as one firm (or group of firms acting in concert) accounting for 25% or more of the relevant regional or national market. These may be referred for investigation to the Monopolies and Mergers Commission (MMC) by the Office of Fair Trading or Minister for Trade and Industry. Mergers can be subjected to similar investigation where they involve 25% or more of market share, or the takeover of assets valued at £30 million or above. The latter criteria allows investigation of vertical and conglomerate mergers. It is the purpose of the MMC, an independent body, to determine whether the referred monopoly or proposed merger operates (or is likely to operate) against the public interest, and to recommend appropriate action to the Minister. 'Public interest' is defined to include not only the maintenance and promotion of competition and consumer interests relating to price, quality and choice, but also the promotion of technical progress and international competitiveness. In contrast to practice in the USA and elsewhere, UK policy is not based on the presumption that monopoly is undesirable; it recognises that there are potential benefits (e.g. scale economies and technical progress) to set against the costs of reduced competition, and accordingly each case is examined on its merits. Additionally, the *Competition Act* of 1980 recognised that 'anti-competitive practices' of individual firms (including public sector entities) can 'restrict, distort or prevent competition'.

Relatively few monopolies or mergers have been subjected to investigation; for those which have, the process is slow, and governments have been reluctant to impose formal conditions, usually preferring to accept voluntary assurances from the companies involved. The policy has not changed significantly either the structure or conduct of industry, though the possibility of referral has tended to modify behaviour, particularly in relation to horizontal mergers. Government argues that capital markets function generally in an efficient manner, transferring assets to the companies and management best equipped to make use of them, and that merger decisions are thus best left to the market. Indeed, since 1984 references have been based predominantly on the possible effect of a merger on competition.

Restrictive practices are controlled through the Restrictive Practices Court (part of the judiciary). Restrictive agreements (e.g. on prices or market sharing) have to be registered, and are presumed to be against the public interest unless a case can be made before the court for exemption, e.g. that the restrictive agreement provides substantial benefits to consumers, or that its removal would result in unemployment or reduced exports. This apparatus was effective in removing restrictive agreements underpinning the extensive system of cartels existing in the 1950s, but by the 1980s the effectiveness of the legislation in detecting and tackling such behaviour was seriously questioned. Legislation prohibiting producers from fixing minimum retail prices for their goods has proved particularly effective and fixed prices for goods in all UK shops have virtually disappeared (with the exception of books and medicines).

A competition policy review in 1988 recommended major changes to restrictive practices legislation, involving a new competition authority, with stronger enforcement powers, to administer legal penalties for any agreement with anti-competitive effects. On mergers, the *Companies Act* of 1989 provided for a formal system of pre-notification of mergers, and for those companies not receiving automatic clearance includes provision for the Secretary of State to grant conditional permission for mergers (in exchange for specific undertakings) without reference to the MMC.

The national competition policy is increasingly influenced by the EC. The Community policy relating to cross-border mergers, which came into force in 1990, means that large mergers will increasingly fall within the ambit of European competition policy (Article 85). Already the Commission and UK merger policy have come into conflict, e.g. over the takeover by British Airways of British Caledonian. Although the deal was previously granted approval by the MMC, the Commission insisted that, in the interests of European competition, conditions (the selling-off of particular routes) should be attached to the takeover. The Commission also intervened recently to reduce the amount of state aid offered as part of the deal by which British Aerospace acquired the state-owned Rover Group.

5.5 FINANCIAL SYSTEM

5.5.1 Financial institutions and markets

The UK financial sector comprises banks (retail and wholesale), discount houses and non-bank financial intermediaries (deposit-takers such as building societies and the National Savings Bank, together with insurance companies, pension funds, investment trusts and unit trusts). The system has undergone radical structural change as a result of extensive deregulation, concentration (via mergers), functional 'de-specialisation', and internationalisation, resulting in more competition between institutions over a wider range of financial activities.

The banking sector

The Bank of England, a public sector body since 1946, is central to the financial system. Its Banking Department functions as banker to government and to banks in general. The Bank's role includes implementing monetary policy through influencing interest rates in the bill market, using direct controls and restricting bank credit; it regulates the issues of notes and coins, manages the issue of government stock, and intervenes for government in the foreign-exchange market; and it also exercises general supervision over the banking system and acts as 'lender of last resort' to banks. Its supervisory role has recently been strengthened so that it acts to ensure the adequacy of banks' capital reserves, that an acceptable ratio of primary liquid assets to deposit liabilities is maintained, and that each bank's exposure to risk of loss on foreign-exchange markets is in line with its capital base.

Banking is dominated in terms of lending and depositing in sterling by the 'retail banks'. These are the London clearing banks – dominated by the 'Big Four' (Barclays, Lloyds, the Midland and NatWest) – and those with extensive branch networks, such as the Scottish and Northern Ireland clearing banks, and one or two others including Trustee Savings Bank and Girobank. They mainly deal in individually small transactions, and accounted for just over half the sterling liabilities of the banking sector as a whole in late 1990. The rest was accounted for by banks which concentrate on large sums (wholesale transactions), such as merchant banks and overseas-owned banks. Merchant banks have diversified their activities away from their former role as acceptance houses (guaranteeing repayment of commercial bills), towards provision of advice for companies on matters such as mergers and takeover, financial reconstructions, underwriting of new share issues, and portfolio management. The separation of deposit banking and investment banking has now virtually ended, since all the large British and overseas deposit banks have either acquired an existing merchant bank, or themselves built up a facility in this field.

Overall, foreign currency business is the largest component of banking, with overseas currency denominated liabilities totalling £640 billion in 1990, compared with £528 billion in sterling accounts (GDP = £480 billion). The growth of foreign currency business has been mainly in the wholesale banking sector, and, within that, overseas banks (accounting for 87% of transactions in 1990). Japanese and European banks have become increasingly prominent. Japanese banks commanded a third of the foreign currency market in 1990, two-and-a-half

times the US share. The number of banks from both Europe and Japan increased during 1980–90 (by one-third and a half respectively); a reflection of the growth of the Eurocurrency market and financial deregulation in the UK. In terms of combined sterling and foreign currency liabilities, the foreign element of the monetary sector is nearly 60% of the market, and the position of London as a major financial centre (with 24% of international bank lending in the late 1980s) depends substantially on the contribution of overseas banks, of which there were some 480 in 1990, compared with Frankfurt and Paris, its main rivals, with 250 and 270 respectively.

Non-bank financial institutions

Non-bank financial institutions (NBFIs) include pension funds, building societies, unit and investment trusts, and insurance companies and fulfil a range of specialist functions. The largest category is building societies, total sterling deposits of which in 1990 were equivalent to three-quarters of those of banks. Their prime purpose is to take deposits and lend money for house purchase (via mortgages). The *1986 Building Societies Act* freed them from many of the previous restrictions on their activities, allowing them to extend their range of services into insurance, pension fund management, and investment. Societies now offer chequing accounts, credit cards, and other facilities previously associated with banks. The distinction between banks and building societies has narrowed from the banks' side also, as the latter have significantly expanded mortgage loan provision. Keen competition now exists between them for deposits and business.

Insurance companies are important within NBFIs because of the vast sums – particularly for life insurance – accumulated over long periods and invested so as to meet claims and earn profits. In 1990, estimated funds were put at £248 billion. While in the 1970s insurance companies preferred (fixed-interest) government securities, the balance in the 1980s has favoured commercial and industrial shares, both UK and overseas, which now make up half the assets.

The improvement in UK equity returns is a factor in this development, together with the abolition of capital controls in 1979. Pension funds have increased at an even faster rate than insurance since the 1960s, and accumulated funds in 1990 amounted to £340 billion. Two-thirds of this is held in the form of ordinary shares (including a significant increase in overseas company shares since the ending of exchange control) and property. Insurance and pension funds have built up a large ownership stake in UK industry. With merchant banks, the NBFIs owned in 1986 three-quarters of ordinary shares by value, compared to under 40% in 1963, when individuals held the majority of shares. The portfolio decisions of the NBFIs thus affect considerably the share prices, and on balance add to their volatility.

The money market

The money market is where financial institutions borrow and lend wholesale funds for terms of up to one year. The primary money market, the discount market, is centred upon the activities of seven discount houses, the official function of which is to discount Treasury bills of exchange, the weekly issue of which they underwrite. They purchase the bills by taking surplus funds on a short-term low-interest basis from the banking sector. Increasingly, discount houses also provide short-term finance for companies by discounting commercial bills. In addition to its role in maintaining liquidity in the banking system, the discount market is important to the conduct of monetary policy, since it is through buying and selling bills in this market that the central bank influences the amount of cash in the system and therefore short-term interest rates.

In addition to the discount market, there are a number of other sterling money markets, known collectively as secondary or parallel markets. The largest is the inter-bank market, in which banks lend directly to each other. Similarly, large companies lend to each other in the inter-company market. There is also the building society market, the sterling CD (Certificate of Deposit) market and, since 1986, the sterling Commercial Paper market.

The capital market

The capital market is where new long-term finance is raised by the private and public sector via the sale of securities (also known as stock or bonds, and – in the case of government securities – 'gilt-edged' stock) and new share issues; it is also where trading of existing stock and equity (ordinary shares) is conducted. This activity is centred upon the International (formerly London) Stock Exchange (ISE). An existing company can raise funds on the Stock Exchange by becoming a 'public' company and obtaining a full ISE quotation. This involves complying with certain rules and offering a minimum proportion of shares to the general public. It is a costly process and smaller/new companies have found it easier to gain admittance to the Unlisted Securities Market, which has less exacting rules.

Until 1986, there were two main groups of ISE participants: stockbrokers, who acted for individual and institutional clients to buy/sell stocks and shares on a commission basis; and jobbers, who held stocks and shares on their own account and dealt with the brokers according to the market. Stock Exchange rules maintained this separation of functions, as well as restricting ISE membership. The system had its defects: in particular, fixed commissions paid to brokers (which penalised large institutional and small individual investors alike), and limits on the scope of member firms to increase their capital resources. With an increasing amount of share trading bypassing the ISE (through direct dealing), cheaper international trading available in the New York stock market (due to the effect on commissions of deregulation and computerised dealing), and the threat of a Restrictive Practices investigation into its commission rates, deregulation was a logical development. 'Big Bang', as the October 1986 deregulation of the ISE was dubbed, introduced negotiable commissions, reduced restrictions on outside ownership (and capital resources) of member firms, replaced the system of brokers and jobbers with broker-dealers who deal directly with the public, largely replaced the partnerships with corporate members, and computerised the dealing through the Stock Exchange Automated

Quotations system (which has decentralised the process, and led to virtual desertion of the trading floor). Capital market deregulation has necessitated an increase in investor protection, exercised through the Securities and Investment Board.

As a result of Big Bang, large financial corporations have moved into the stock market – several of them international firms – resulting in half London's brokers being foreign-owned. The market has become more competitive, with much lower commissions on large deals. The new technology has enabled London to participate fully in the trading on global securities, and the merger of the SE and the International Securities Regulatory Organisation in 1986 (to produce the International Stock Exchange), has resulted in a unified market for dealing in international shares. This has been important in maintaining London's position, alongside New York and Japan, in the 'Golden Triangle' of security dealing. The UK financial sector currently has comparative advantages in that institutions and markets elsewhere in Europe are more regulated and less developed; in the longer-term competition from the latter is likely to increase significantly.

5.5.2 Banks and industrial finance

It is a long-standing criticism of the UK banking sector that it has failed to provide adequate finance for industry. In the bank-based systems of France and West Germany, the banking sector does play a major part in the financing of industry, while the securities market is poorly developed and plays a relatively minor role. Bank-based systems foster close relations between banks and their large customers; the former often have a substantial equity stake in the company and are well placed to provide financial support for new products and expansion. The UK financial system, like that of the US, is basically a market-based one; its securities market is active and provides a major part of the finance for industry, while the banking sector role is less prominent. UK banks do not generally buy shares in companies; institutions are the major holders of indus-

trial equities. UK companies thus meet long-term capital needs mainly by selling shares, or through the sale of fixed-interest securities to individuals or non-bank financial institutions. UK banks finance firms via loans and overdrafts, providing mainly short-term (working) capital. Thus, one survey has shown that the average original maturity of long-term loans in the UK was only one-third of the seven to eight years average in France and West Germany.

There are important implications arising out of UK financing arrangements. Reliance on the equity and securities market for long-term finance results in a preoccupation, on the part of companies, with short-term profit and dividend goals. This is because poor performance can lead to a fall in the share price (and thus value) of the company, making it vulnerable to takeover by predators. The encouragement to short- over long-term decision-making can undermine a company's development. Moreover, while institutional shareholders have been criticised for not using their influence to ensure firms are managed efficiently and enterprisingly, industrial restructuring within the bank-based system is often initiated and orchestrated by the banks, and 'constructive' mergers are more common as a result.

A trend towards closer links between banks and industry is underway in the UK, with greater use of industrial experts by banks, and greater willingness to take equity in promising companies. The growing influence of foreign banks has been important in this process, as has the integration of banking and the securities business. The gaps in the UK market in the provision of funds for risky ventures and smaller firms have to some extent been filled in recent years by the Unlisted Securities Market, the Third Market (now abolished), the Business Expansion Scheme, and the emergence of a number of private companies specialising in the provision of venture capital company (e.g. 3i).

5.5.3 Monetary policy and the money supply

The Medium Term Financial Strategy has provided the framework for monetary policy over the last decade. It was the government's view that excessive monetary growth (i.e. exceeding that of real output) was the primary cause of inflation and the MTFS aimed to keep money growth broadly in line with the growth in nominal output and income. Interest rates and PSBR were used to control monetary growth as measured by $£M_3$ (stock of cash and sterling bank deposits – interest and non-interest bearing – held by UK residents). Higher interest rates were used both to restrain private-sector lending and enable the funding of the PSBR by selling government debt to the non-bank public. Banks were thus unable to increase their holdings of public-sector assets, restricting their ability to create deposits and thus expand the money stock. Reductions in the PSBR (via fiscal means) were necessary because of its direct impact on the growth of $£M_3$.

The 1980 MTFS set targets for $£M_3$ which would progressively fall over the period to 1984. However, the government failed to keep the money stock within the set ranges, and overshooting problems led eventually to abandonment of the practice of announcing targets. Indeed, the nature of the target itself was subject to considerable change. Up to 1982, government used $£M_3$ as its target measure, then widened it to include other measures. During 1984–7 M_O (notes and coin held by banks and the public) and $£M_3$ were the chosen targets. In 1987, M_3 was abandoned, leaving just M_O.

Nonetheless, although actual MTFS targets were exceeded, the growth in money supply in the UK was similar to that in France and Italy (though twice as high as in West Germany) during the first half of the 1980s. The period 1985–8, however, saw a rapid increase to around 20% – double the EUR 12 rate, and two to three times that in Germany, France, Italy and Spain. This substantially reflects the fact that interest rates, which were a principal weapon for the control of the money supply, were used increasingly from the mid-1980s to influence the exchange rate; 'Monetarism' was effectively dead.

Why was it so difficult to achieve monetary targets? Partly because of the existence of a range of substitutable monetary assets, so that control over one form of 'money' led institutions and individuals to make increased use of forms which were not subject to control. It was also due to structural changes occurring within the financial sector, for example, reduced differences between banks and building societies, and competition between them, resulting in increased holdings of assets in interest-bearing deposit accounts. Changes in behaviour also had an impact; in particular the increased insensitivity of private-sector borrowing to interest rates.

5.6 External economic relations

5.6.1 Balance of payments

The current account

The UK is a relatively open economy, with exports of goods and services averaging 26% of GDP (1981-90). Next to West Germany (30%), this is the highest among the large EC economies (France 23%, Italy 21%, and Spain 20%), although it is some way behind the smaller economies. Over the post-war period, an increasing proportion of UK output has been traded overseas, with a particularly sharp rise occurring in the years immediately following EEC entry in 1973.

Geographically, UK trade has in recent decades reversed its historical dependence upon sales in developing countries (the share of which fell from 37% to 16% over the period 1955–90) and the former major Commonwealth nations (Australia, New Zealand and Canada), in favour of trade with advanced non-Commonwealth industrialised economies, and especially those of the EC. Thus, while the general trend within the EC has been for intra-community trade to take up an increasing share of the total imports and exports of Member States, this is most dramatic in the case of the UK. In 1958 only 22% of UK trade was with EC countries; the figure in 1991 was 56%, although this was still (with Denmark and Germany) proportionally the lowest among EC countries (EUR 12 62%) (Table E32). In terms of the UK's relative share of EC countries' trade, in

1991, UK goods and services accounted for 6.5% of total imports by EC countries – some way behind the respective market shares of West Germany (14.3%), France (9.6%) and the Netherlands (8.2%), though similar to those of Italy and Belgium/Luxembourg. As a market, the UK took 7.4% of Community exports, making it the third most important market after Germany (14.5%) and France (11.2%) (Table E33). Germany, accounting for nearly 15% of imports and 14% of exports, is the UK's most important trading partner (followed by the USA (11% and 12%)).

The commodity composition of UK trade has also changed radically (see Table 5.4). In the 1950s the UK was essentially an importer of primary products (77% of imports in 1955 consisted of food, basic materials and oil) and an exporter of manufactures (80% of the total in 1955). A massive deterioration in the non-manufacturing side of the balance of payments resulting from the Second World War made it necessary for the UK to run a substantial manufacturing trade surplus (equivalent to 11% of GDP in 1951).

The non-manufacturing visibles account moved from a deficit in the early 1950s equal to over 13% of GDP, to a position of virtual trade balance in the 1981–5 period (Table 5.4). This transformation reflects a number of developments, including falling real costs of food and raw material imports, increased domestic food production due to technical advances and subsidies, the switch from natural to synthetic production materials, and changing output composition in the economy as a whole. Nonetheless, though falling as a proportion of GDP, foodstuffs and raw materials have remained in overall deficit, and it is the exploitation of North Sea oil which has done most to improve the non-manufacturing visible account, mainly through the conversion of the £4 billion oil trade deficit in the mid-1970s into a *surplus* of £8 billion in 1985. The oil surplus has since diminished as both output (down by a third) and the price per barrel have fallen; from 21% of exports in 1985, oil accounted for 7% in 1990.

UK trade in manufactures has also undergone significant change. While the share of finished and semi-finished manufactures in total exports (by value) has remained at around its 1955 level of just above 80%, the share of these goods in imports has increased from 23% to 78% in 1990. UK trade is now characterised by the exchange of manufacturing goods and services with other advanced industrial nations. The economy is thus more exposed than previously to overseas competition, and this has been linked to the other major trend, namely the gradual disappearance of the manufacturing surplus. From the massive surpluses of the 1950s, the surplus

Table 5.4 UK visible trade balances by main categories (% of GDP)

	Manufac-tures	Food, drink, tobacco	Basic materials	Fuels	Total non-manufg	Visible balance
1951–60	+8.4	−5.6	−4.6	−0.7	−10.8	−2.4
1961–70	+5.6	−3.4	−2.0	−1.0	−6.4	−0.8
1971–80	+3.4	−2.2	−1.5	−1.8	−5.4	−2.1
1981–85	−0.2	−1.1	−0.9	+1.9	−0.1	−0.2
1986	−1.7	−1.2	−0.7	+0.8	−1.1	−2.7
1987	−2.1	−1.1	−0.7	+0.8	−1.0	−3.0
1988	−3.8	−1.1	−0.8	+0.3	−1.6	−5.3
1989	−3.3	−0.8	−0.6	+0.2	−1.2	−3.4
1990	−2.0	−0.8	−0.5	+0.2	−1.1	−3.4

Source: NIESR, *The UK Economy* (1990) Table 19; updated using *'Pink Book'* (CSO, 1991).

as a proportion of GDP fell to 5.6% in the 1960s, and then 3.4% in the 1970s, before vanishing altogether in 1982 (see Figure 5.6). By 1988, the deficit on manufacturing trade was over £14 billion, equivalent to 3.8% of GDP (Table 5.4). While in 1960 the UK accounted for 17% of world manufacturing exports – similar to West Germany with 19%, but well above France (10%) and Italy (5%) – in 1991 the figure was down to just 9% (compared to West Germany 20%, France 10% and Italy 8%).

The UK has traditionally had a current account surplus, with the positive balance on invisible items (earnings from sale of services, together with interest, profits and dividends from overseas assets) more than sufficient to offset visible trade deficits. The period since 1970 has seen a departure from this pattern. Poor export performance combined with oil price rises to push the current balance into deficit during 1973–7. When North Sea oil came on stream in the late 1970s, the current account moved sharply back into surplus, reaching £6.9 billion in 1981; even the visible balance was positive during 1980–4. Since then the situation has been reversed. With a growing manufacturing deficit, and a fall in the oil surplus, a domestic consumer boom (at a time when the considerably diminished UK manufacturing sector was operating at near full capacity) made matters worse by sucking in imports. In 1989, the visible trade deficit reached £24.6 billion. The surplus on invisibles has been insufficient since 1986 to cover the visibles deficit, and in 1989 – after allowing for the invisibles surplus of nearly £4.2 billion – the current account was still £20.4 billion in the red. This has fallen slightly since (visibles deficit £10.1 billion in 1991; current account deficit £4.4 billion), but in the context of a severe recession this represents a problem. Whereas previously recession tended to move the current account back into surplus, this has not happened in the early 1990s.

The capital account

Direct investment overseas grew dramatically during the second half of the 1980s (from £5.4 billion in 1983 to £21.5 billion in 1989) causing a significant rise in the gross stock of UK-owned foreign assets, which stands second only to that of the USA. Some of this investment has entailed switching manufacturing production to overseas sites, and has contributed to the poor manufacturing growth performance at home. Direct inward investment into the UK also surged over this period. From a negative amount in 1984, the inflow of investment increased in leaps to reach £19 billion in 1990, partly reflecting attempts by USA and Far Eastern companies to gain a foothold in the post-1992 single European market. In recent years 60% of US and 40% of Japanese investment into the EC has come to the UK. Following the ending of exchange controls

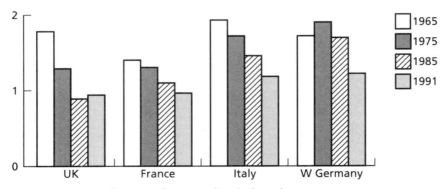

Figure 5.6 Export–import ratios for manufactures. (1 = balance)

Source: OECD data.

in 1979, major asset holders have sought to increase their rate of return and diversify their portfolios by the acquisition of foreign securities. Outward flows of portfolio investment by UK residents increased sharply in the 1980s, and they exceeded inflows by around a half during 1980–91.

5.6.2 The exchange rate

Since the move from fixed exchange rates to a 'managed' float in 1972, the general trend in the value of the pound has been downwards, with periods of depreciation being followed by only partial recovery. In terms of the effective exchange rate (based on a basket of currencies weighted by share of UK trade) the index fell sharply from 150 in 1972 to 100 in 1976. Sterling recovered quite strongly to 120 in 1981 and fell by a quarter to around 90 in the period to 1991. The UK's exit from the Exchange Rate Mechanism (ERM) in 1992 signalled another quite sharp fall (see Figure 5.7). A relatively poor UK trade performance, together with the country's generally higher inflation rates, has been behind this long-term pattern of movement in relation to other currencies; in the shorter term, variation during the 1980s resulted from the government's use of the exchange rate as a key tool of macroeconomic policy.

Since the abolition of UK capital controls in 1979, interest policy has played an increasing role in exchange rate management, with the adjustment of short-term rates being used to influence the net flow of speculative funds ('hot money') into the country and thus demand for the currency. Even so, for almost a decade following 1976, interest rates were adjusted principally with reference to domestic monetary conditions. The high exchange rate of the early 1980s, through making imports cheaper in terms of pounds, helped in the fight against inflation. Beginning in 1982, when inflation was considered to be under control, the government made use of short-term interest rates – backed up by central bank buying and selling of sterling – to keep the pound steady at a lower level and provide an expansionary boost to the domestic economy. In mid-decade, monetary policy shifted decisively towards the exchange rate, in recognition of the fact that exchange rate depreciation was an important mechanism by which domestic inflation was increased, and in the hope that tying the value of sterling to a low-

Figure 5.7 Sterling exchange rate index (1985 = 100).

Source: HM Treasury, *Financial Statement and Budget Report,* 1993–4.

inflation economy (West Germany), would – by emphasising the government's commitment to low inflation – influence expectations and thus help to control price rises. From 1985, interest rates were used to ensure sterling 'shadowed' the German DM, initially at £1:DM3, later increased to DM3.20. This was an unofficial exchange rate target, but nonetheless represented a return to a fixed-rate regime.

Problems arose because the interest rate was the main lever for influencing *both* domestic money supply and the value of the exchange rate. The Chancellor of the Exchequer during this period, Nigel Lawson, has been criticised for overheating the economy, resulting in the rise in inflation during the late 1980s. His monetarist critics argue that shadowing the D-Mark (involving lowering of interest rates to prevent the pound rising above its target value) led to an excessive increase in domestic money supply, which subsequently came through into inflation figures; they insist that higher, not lower, interest rates were needed during the shadowing period.

High interest rates were used during 1988–91 to halt the rise in inflation. The interest rate squeeze was maintained for too long, however, resulting in an especially severe recession. The fact that, when the UK eventually joined the ERM (in October 1990) it did so at what turned out to be too high a rate (£1:DM2.95) is partly to blame for prolonging the squeeze. With German interest rates held relatively high as a result of re-unification borrowing, the UK found itself during the early 1990s in a position of needing to reduce interest rates to promote recovery, while being unable to do so and remain within the ERM band of 6% around the central rate. The UK government was reluctant to devalue sterling within the ERM so soon after joining. In the event, the turmoil in European exchange markets in late 1992 led to the pound being withdrawn from the ERM and allowed it once more to float. During 1993, its value has settled at around £1:DM2.45 as interest rates have fallen to their lowest for more than two decades.

The 'Lawson boom' has prompted debate over whether the UK should have an indepen-

dent central bank with a statutory obligation to pursue price stability. At present, the Bank of England is constitutionally part of the government and is expected to provide a monetary stance that accommodates overall macroeconomic objectives; this is in contrast to the situation in Germany, where the Bundesbank, because of its independent status, is in a position to neutralise an over-expansionary fiscal policy.

5.6.3 The value of sterling and manufacturing

A major influence over the UK exchange rate during the 1980s has been the production of North Sea oil. This improved the current account dramatically in the late 1970s and so exerted strong upward pressures on the pound. In so doing it reduced the competitiveness of the non-oil tradeable sector, principally manufacturing, causing it to decline seriously. An exchange rate influenced by oil – and subsequently maintained at a high level to help control inflation – helps explain why the ratio of imports to total manufacturing output increased by 31% between 1979 and 1989, reflecting a rise of 99% in manufactured imports.

There was, during the 1980s, much debate over the significance of a currency boosted by oil and the related deficit in the manufacturing trade balance (the so-called 'Dutch disease'). To some economists, the worsening manufacturing balance reflected simply a shift in the UK's comparative advantage; other sectors – agriculture, services and oil – all becoming relatively more important within the economy. Thus the shift in the manufacturing trade balance reflected market forces working through the exchange rate, as UK manufactures were priced out of some markets by the higher value of the pound. The process, which has taken place over a long period, was simply accelerated in the early 1980s. The appropriate response to oil-induced exchange rate appreciation, it was argued, was to use oil proceeds to build up assets overseas *via* portfolio and direct foreign investment. This was facilitated by the abolition of exchange controls in 1979, which led to an increase in outward portfolio investment by banks and non-bank intermediaries from an average of £400 million in the second half of the 1970s to £15 billion per year during 1983–91. With UK outward direct investment overseas over 1981–6 around double the level of incoming investment, the UK became one of the world's largest net creditor nations. This stock of assets is expected to provide a continuing source of income as the oil surplus declines, while the currency depreciation accompanying the loss of oil revenue will provide an opportunity for other sectors – such as services (in which the UK has a comparative advantage), but possibly a leaner and fitter manufacturing sector also – to expand their exporting role.

An alternative view is that the manufacturing trade performance reflects government neglect of the sector, particularly during 1979–82, when high interest rates and an overvalued pound compounded the problems UK producers faced due to world recession. Proponents of this view argue that the contraction forced upon manufacturing was inappropriate given an oil surplus known to be only temporary. They contend it is unrealistic to expect to be able to switch in and out of manufacturing, and are sceptical that invisibles will be able to compensate for the falling oil surplus and manufacturing decline – particularly since (1) many traded services are linked to manufacturing, (2) only 20% of services are traded internationally (compared to 50% for manufactures), and (3) barriers to trade in services are significant. While the UK is the largest exporter of financial services, many UK service sectors are actually in deficit (e.g. travel and tourism, sea transport, and civil aviation) and the invisibles balance has been declining as a share of GDP (from 2.5% in 1986 to below 1% in 1990). This group of economists argue that oil proceeds should have been directed towards a programme of industrial regeneration, or – given the lack of profitability in manufacturing at the time – into investments in infrastructure (communications, education and training) with positive long-term effects on industrial competitiveness as oil production declines. The extent to which they

fuelled a consumer boom – which itself ended in tears – is regarded as a wasted opportunity to strengthen the economic base.

Sterling has now been substantially devalued. Growth is firmly on the policy agenda, and for the first time in a decade, government is positively affirming the value of manufacturing. Nevertheless, Government's willingness to intervene on industry's behalf should not be overstated and its ability to do so has been reduced in recent years by privatisation and by EC rules. The onus for the response by manufacturing to the opportunities arising from a competitive pound rests with the private sector, which has to prevent price competitiveness being eroded by wage and salary increases. Price, of course, is not the main criterion of success for many traded products, and developments in the skills' base and product innovation are vital elements of manufacturing success. The 'special issues' examined below relate to developments which are needed to underpin such a strategy.

5.7 SPECIAL ISSUES

5.7.1 Investment in research and development

One area crucially affecting future industrial competitiveness is Research and Development (R&D). The UK has been falling behind its trading partners in terms of investment in relevant R&D. This is reflected in the fact that, almost regardless of industry, the UK has tended increasingly to export lower-value, less R&D-intensive products ('mature' technology), and to import high-value new technology items. Many of its exports are thus in areas where world demand is growing relatively slowly, as well as being more open to competition from newly industrialising countries.

In terms of industrial structure and specialisation, the UK should be an R&D intensive economy, comparable to the USA, Japan, Germany and Sweden. Yet, in 1990, UK R&D investment was equivalent to 2.2% of GDP, compared with 2.8% in both West Germany and USA and 2.9% in

Japan. The UK real rate of growth of industrial R&D was virtually the lowest in Europe during 1967–85, and at the end of the period the level of *industry-financed* R&D was only half that of Germany and Sweden, and lower than Belgium, the Netherlands and France.

The situation is not helped by the relatively high concentration of R&D effort on defence industries. While the total government-funded R&D spending as a share of GDP was in 1987 higher than in some EC countries – and virtually identical to that in Germany – a relatively large proportion (around one-half) was devoted to defence-related projects. This is a similar proportion of GDP (0.5%) to that going on defence-related R&D in France, but it is far higher than the equivalent figure for Italy, Germany and Sweden. The spin-off to the wider industrial economy from this expenditure is limited, due to the specialised nature of defence products, and security-related restrictions on the diffusion of resulting technological developments. Civilian non-military R&D intensity increased rapidly in the leading industrial nations during the 1980s, as did investment in fundamental research (e.g. in the universities). In both these areas research intensity declined in the UK; in spite of the country's relative strengths in relation to the latter type of research, spending cuts have undermined its capacity. Continuing weakness in this area will restrict UK participation in the growth of trade in high technology products.

5.7.2 Education and training

The tendency to concentrate on lower technology products is linked also to the comparatively poor UK performance in education and training. R&D is unlikely to be fully exploited unless management and workforce have the appropriate skills. The fact that in a recent report the UK was placed 22nd out of 23 industrialised countries in respect of the overall quality of its workforce gives credence to the view that the UK is caught in a low-skill/low-technology vicious circle. In the late 1980s, compared to most other advanced industrial nations, Britain produced fewer graduates overall, had a smaller stock of

scientists relative to the population, and a lower output of engineers and technologists. Recent research has shown that UK school children show a lower level of achievement in science than children of the same age in 17 other countries studied. The UK is the only major nation where the majority of pupils leave full-time education or training at the age of 16, with the result that a larger proportion of the UK labour force have less upper-secondary education than in other major economies. The low-level of educational attainment is not offset by higher levels of work-based training. A recent EC survey showed that only 38% of the UK workforce has experienced training, compared to 50% in Portugal and 80% in France. UK firms devote on average just 0.15% of turnover to training compared to 1% to 2% in Japan, Germany and France.

Government has taken action in relation to these shortcomings. The *1988 Education Act* provided for a National Curriculum in schools, with regular testing of standards. The objectives of such initiatives, however, have been confused with others, such as reducing the role of local authorities in education, making the system more responsive to the market and reducing public spending. In respect of training, government initiatives – particularly the establishment of a network of local Training and Enterprise Councils – give a central role to the private sector. However, the relatively low level of public financial support for this scheme makes it unlikely that it will offer sufficient incentive to bring about the major expansion in private training required. At a time when it would seem to be appropriate for government to be expanding its real expenditure on training, spending has been reduced in recent years. The National Council for Vocational Qualifications was set up in 1986 to accredit and standardise qualifications in line with practices elsewhere in the EC. This has yet to have a significant impact. If Britain is to have a training system to rival that, say, in Germany, then tuition fees for vocational and educational training (leading to National Vocational Qualifications) will have to be a public responsibility and employers will need to be obliged to intensify their training of staff.

In education and training – as in other important areas, such as transport infrastructure – the preference during the 1980s for private market-based decisions over collectivist solutions has limited spending in areas where competitor states have been prepared to commit public resources towards the achievement of long-term strategic advantage. Free market economists would argue that 'government failure' can lead to misplaced investment which is wasteful of resources, and that problems cannot always be solved by throwing money at them. Certainly, problems to do with education and training are to some extent cultural in nature. But what about market failure? The government's insistence upon reliance on the market in key areas of resource allocation has frequently caused too short-term a view to be taken, resulting in structural weaknesses and the loss of long-term opportunities for growth and development.

5.8 ASSESSMENT AND FUTURE PROSPECTS

As the economy pulls out of its second major recession in a decade, questions remain as to the likely strength and duration of the recovery and indeed the economic performance over the rest of the 1990s. The PSBR is expected to be equivalent to over 8% of GDP in 1993–4, and the current account deficit has remained high in spite of the recession and 3 million people unemployed. There is a danger that the boost given to the economy by low interest rates and devaluation of sterling may re-fuel inflation or cause imports to be sucked into the economy worsening the balance-of-payments. In either situation, deflationary measures are a likely response and the 'stop-go' cycle which has dogged the UK economy for decades will continue to apply, albeit more due to monetary than Keynesian interventions. There is the possibility, of course, that, because the UK business cycle is out of phase with that of other EC economies, the demand boost through trade will be muted, and that this – together with the need to reduce spending or raise taxes in order to tackle the very high PSBR – will give rise to a weak recovery. Whatever the case, meeting Maastricht convergence targets is a long way down the road as far as the UK economy is concerned. That this currently applies to EC economies in general postpones any decision on whether the UK will be in the slower lane of a 'two-speed Europe'.

As to longer-term economic performance, a clearer perspective of the impact of the Thatcher period has emerged. The UK economy has undoubtedly been transformed in a number of respects during the 1980s, but not necessarily its capacity for sustained and higher rates of growth. Increased flexibility in labour and other markets cannot compensate for structural deficiencies such as the relatively small size of the manufacturing sector, comparatively low levels of skill formation and overall educational attainment, weak industrial R&D, and an unmodernised transport infrastructure. Efforts are being made by government to address some of these issues; it is unfortunate that the opportunities to do so in the 1980s were frequently missed, and that oil revenues were largely used for consumption rather than investment. Manufacturing – at least in the rhetoric – has recently been moved to centre stage. It needs to remain there, for without a sustained effort at promoting this sector of the economy, the UK will find it hard over the long haul to match the performances of its main competitors.

5.9 SUGGESTED READING AND SOURCES OF INFORMATION

UK government/Official publications

Bank of England Quarterly Bulletin, Economics Division, Bank of England, London EC2R 8AH

Economic Trends (monthly plus annual supplement), Central Statistical Office, PO Box 276, London SW8 5DT

Economic Briefing (three times per year), available free from Central Office of Information, Hercules Road, London, SE1 7DU

OECD: *The UK economy*, Economic Surveys, Paris

Central Statistical Office: *United Kingdom in Figures*, available free from Press and Information Office, Great George St., London SW1P 3AQ

General books on the UK economy

Artis, M.J. (ed.): *Prest & Coppock's The UK Economy: a manual of applied economics*, latest edition Weidenfeld & Nicolson, London

Curwen, P. (ed.) (1992): *Understanding the UK Economy*, 2nd Edn., Macmillan Education, Basingstoke

Griffiths, A., Wall, S. (eds.) (1993): *Applied Economics*, 5th Edn., Longman, Harlow

Michie, J. (ed.) (1992): *The Economic Legacy 1979–92*, Academic Press, London

Smith, D. (1992): *From Boom to Bust: Trial and Error in Economic Policy*, Penguin, London

Journals

British Economy Survey (twice yearly), Longman, Longman House, Harlow, Essex, CM20 2JE

Business Briefing (monthly), Chambers of Commerce; available from Border House, High St., Chester, CH3 6PK

Economics (quarterly), the Economics Association, 41–3 Boltro Road, Haywards Heath, West Sussex RH16 1BJ

Lloyds Bank Economic Bulletin (monthly), available from Economics Department, Lloyds Bank, 71 Lombard St., London EC3P 3PS

National Institute Economic Review (quarterly), available from 2 Dean Trench St., London, SW1P 3HS

The Economic Review (5 issues per year) Philip Allan, Market Place, Deddington, Oxford OX5 4SE

CHAPTER 6

Spain

Milagros García Crespo
Arantza Mendizábal
Marisol Esteban

6.1 INSTITUTIONAL AND HISTORICAL CONTEXT

In analysing the institutional framework and historical context of the Spanish economy there are two years which are of great importance.

- In 1978 the Constitution was approved and the democratic system, suspended since the 1936–9 Civil War, was re-established. Two aspects of the Constitution are particularly relevant: first, the adoption of the market economy model in the context of an *état de droit*, and second, the transition from a very centralised economic and political system towards a high degree of decentralisation. Spain was divided up into 17 Autonomous Communities responsible for many aspects of local economic activity.
- The year of 1986 is significant since it marks the recognition of Spain as a member of the European Community. This relatively late entry is being compensated for by the determination of Spain to catch up in the European integration process. Nowadays Spain appears to be one of the EC countries most committed to 'Europe'.
- EC integration required the Spanish government to eliminate, over a transitional period of six years, the complicated system of protectionism which historically had influenced and conditioned the evolution of Spanish industry.

Entry into the EC coincided with a period of economic growth which seemed to offer the prospect of reducing the high levels of unemployment which had prevailed in the Spanish economy since mid-1979. Unfortunately, the current recession has increased the unemployment rate, once again, to the dangerous level of 20%.

6.1.1 The Franco period

The new economic model embodied in the Constitution substantially modified the economic management system which prevailed during the 40 years of Franco's dictatorship. The Franco period falls into two main periods, from 1939–59 and 1959–75.

The 1939–59 period was characterised by (a) the creation of an autarchic economic system, (b) extensive public intervention in the economy, (c) an international black-out, and (d) the relatively minor importance of international trade activities. During this period, basic goods were rationed, productivity levels and per capita income decreased significantly, and there were no institutional channels through which working-class claims could be negotiated. The civil war and its aftermath meant that the production levels of 1936 were not regained until 1951, when US financial assistance flowed in following the installation of US military bases in Spain. In

1955 Spain was accepted as a member of the United Nations

The beginning of the second period (1959–75) was marked by the '*1959 Stabilisation Plan*'. This Plan signalled a new economic approach involving greater use of the market mechanism and thus initiated a slow and somewhat belated process towards liberalisation of both internal activities and external relations. In the event, it proved easier to replace strict state control of the economy with a more liberal approach than to give up the authoritarianism and centralism so entrenched in post-war Spain. The liberalisation process involved the entry of the Spanish economy into the OECD as well as the devaluation of the peseta and the acceptance of foreign investment into the Spanish economic system.

This liberalisation process made limited progress due to entrenched protectionist interests and privileged financial circles for several industrial sectors. Pressure for protectionism was exerted by the main enterprise groups, and as late as 1968 the average customs duty for industrial goods reached 31%. Customs duties were high for an extensive range of imports.

Alongside the rise of protectionism and the preservation of the national market for home production, a period of economic growth commenced in 1960, with sharp increases in real GDP growth rates (averaging 8.6% during 1960–5). Simultaneously, the period saw fixed capital investment increase at a rate of 14% per year. This growth was underpinned by migrant-worker remittances and revenue from tourism which provided the necessary foreign currency to pay for the structural trade deficit and generated surpluses in the balance of payments.

During this period a contradiction manifested itself between the economic development, characterised by growth and capitalist concentration, and the politics of the Franco regime. A distinct socio-economic change occurred since the sharp economic growth (in terms of GDP increases) was not followed by the development of a welfare state and a democratic political system.

In 1964, indicative planning was initiated, inspired by the French model. The three 'four-year plans' (1964–75) consisted basically of macroeconomic forecasts, which were compulsory for the public sector and indicative for the private sector. These plans introduced a certain rationalisation into public sector activities. However, as the 1960s progressed and the protectionist system was erected and extended, GDP increases weakened, with an average annual growth rate of 5.9% between 1968 and 1973 (see Table E19), and a lower rate of fixed capital investment (7.4%) (see Table E26). At the same time, inflation, which had been under control in the 1960s, was allowed to increase reaching 11% in 1973 (see Table E27). The period of expansion was artificially prolonged throughout 1974, even though there was an international economic crisis and most industrial countries had already adopted restrictive measures in their economies to counteract the effects of the sharp increases in oil prices.

With the death of Franco in 1975 the period of economic growth came to an end and the process of political transition towards democracy began, even though the country was in the middle of serious economic problems.

6.1.2 The transition towards democracy

The 1973 oil crisis did not modify the economic strategy pursued by the Spanish government. Not only did it fail to adapt to the recession, but it continued to implement an expansive policy relying on currency reserves and borrowing capacity in anticipation of eventual international recovery. Thus, the Spanish economic cycle ran counter to international trends; GDP increased by 5% in 1974 (see Table E19), but there was a pronounced trade deficit and the rate of inflation rose to 17% (see Table E27). Neither output (by using restrictive policies) nor the level of prices (by modifying the exchange rate) were adjusted. On the contrary, an excess of productive capacity was generated leading to reductions in productivity levels and an associated increase in average costs and prices. As a consequence, external debt rose and foreign reserves were significantly reduced.

These trends in the major economic indicators continued and even worsened over the following years, so that by the end of 1977 the inflation rate had risen to 35%. The government was eventually forced to undertake a set of corrective short-run economic measures, together with others of a structural and institutional nature.

Inflation was brought under control by the management of public sector expenditure, liquid assets in the hands of the private sector and controls over wage increases. Simultaneously, unemployment levels began to rise (see Table E17). In 1978, GDP increased by 1.4% (see Table E19) while unemployment rose by a further 300,000.

The adoption of the market economy model in the context of an *état de droit* in 1978 meant at last the recognition of political parties as the expression of political pluralism together with the acceptance that both trade unions and employers' associations had a legitimate contribution to make to the defence and promotion of their economic and social interests. This late development explains the limited role of trade unions in economic life, and the difficulties encountered when negotiating with the employers' associations who lost the privileges enjoyed in Franco's dictatorship. This is an expression of the fact that Spain is a country only recently introduced to democratic practice.

In addition, the 1978 Constitution led to a new territorial organisation of the state, since it recognised the right of historical nations and regions to autonomy. This has resulted in a high degree of political decentralisation.

The public sector has a significant presence in the economy, accounting for 43.3% of GDP by 1990, a level which is expected to grow to 46.5% by 1993 (see Table E28). Not all the activities generated by public expenditure are carried out by central administration, however. In this context, it is necessary to differentiate at least two levels of administration: 'central administration', i.e. the administration of the central state, other autonomous public organisations and the social security system (whose budgets are approved and operations controlled by the central Parliament) and the 'territorial administrations', which are made up of 17 Autonomous Communities and the local administrations (local and provincial authorities). The autonomous Parliaments of the Autonomous Communities and governing bodies of local administrations are responsible for establishing their own budgets and activities.

The decentralisation of public expenditure, measured in terms of the amount administered by Autonomous Communities, has significantly increased since 1984 (see Table 6.1), as a consequence of the transfer of responsibilities from central administrations and the increasing role of local authorities in the Spanish political system. Yet, the distribution of public expenditure still remains far from the desired distribution of 50, 25, 25. Nevertheless, it is clear that the decentralisation process has been pursued at a pace not met by any other Western political structure.

Table 6.1 Public expenditure by administrative level (%)

Year	Central state	Autonomous communities	Local authorities
1984	75	13	12
1992	69	19	12

The responsibilities transferred to the Autonomous Communities range from health, culture and education to housing, urban planning, roads and other infrastructures, several elements of industrial policy and training programmes, and even tax control in some communities (e.g. Navarre and the Basque Country).

6.1.3 Spain's entry into the EC

Although Spain had been trying over a long period of time to integrate itself into the EC, it was not until 1978, with the transition towards democracy, that its candidacy was taken seriously into consideration by Brussels. The first and very important consequence of entry into the EC was the need to dismantle the protectionist system behind which Spanish industry had traditionally sheltered. From that moment onwards, the need to improve the competitiveness of Spanish production and the urgent need to carry out the restructuring of many industrial sectors became a priority for economic leaders.

This need to undertake a restructuring of the production system came at a time of recession lasting from 1979 to 1985. During this period GDP grew at an average annual rate of only 1.5%, with a positive contribution from the foreign sector, a stable level of internal consumption and a negative rate of investment (see Tables E19 and E26). This demand and production crisis led to the loss of over 1 million jobs – over 3 million people unemployed, equal to an unemployment rate of more than 20% by 1985 (see Table E17). Furthermore, the inflation rate remained close to 10% (see Table E27). The weak economic activity together with an increased demand for social services affected both the income and the expenditure of the public sector, public deficit thus reaching 6% of GDP by the mid-1980s.

While experiencing these severe economic difficulties Spain became a member of the EC in 1986. Right from the start, the Spanish economy embarked on a period of expansion that gradually seemed to overcome the most important economic problems. Yet, the economic cycle had turned again by 1990, along with international economic activity, and all major economic indicators showed a negative trend in mid-1993 that would continue for some time (see Table E6). Unemployment was maintained at 16.7% on average in 1992, but the last data for the last quarter of 1992 and the first months of 1993 showed an unemployment rate of over 20%. Similarly, attempts to control public deficit (4.3% of GDP in 1992) and the deficit of the balance of trade (3.3% of GDP in 1992) failed dramatically. Finally, inflation showed no sign of falling and remained over 6% in mid-1993, even though reducing inflation had become the major objective of economic policy.

6.2 MAIN ECONOMIC CHARACTERISTICS

6.2.1 Human resources

Population

The Spanish population in 1992 amounted to 39 million (see Table E14). The country experienced the process of *demographic transition* (the shift from high death and high fertility rates to low death and low fertility rates) later than Northern European countries. This has produced a radical change in the age pyramid which has gradually become narrower at the base and wider at the peak.

While birth rates in the 1960s and early 1970s were relatively high in the context of a period of intense economic growth, they dropped drastically over the late 1970s and 1980s. Nowadays, Spanish demographic trends mirror general trends in Northern and Central Europe. The reasons for this change are not clear; while the economic crisis and the subsequent insecurity have had an impact, other changes in society and attitudes are also considered important. Nevertheless, the major economic consequences of this change will only be noticeable in twenty years' time.

Although low in numbers, a steady flow of immigration was observed during the 1980s, mainly from South American and North African countries. This development is in contrast with the traditional emigration trends.

Previous trends towards concentration of the population in the large metropolitan areas (Madrid, Barcelona, Valencia) have continued at the expense of central rural areas. At the same time, traditional areas of population growth, such as Bilbao, in the Basque Country, have lost population due to the crisis in their industrial base. The regions where population has grown at the fastest rate are located in the triangle between Madrid and the Mediterranean coast.

Active population

During the 1960s there was a significant increase in the active population, approximately one million people over the decade, representing 38% of the total population by the end of the period. This increase in the active population, however, was not accompanied by the generation of a sufficient number of jobs, which in turn provoked a slight increase in unemployment.

The industrialisation process of the 1960s caused a shift of the labour force from the agricultural sector towards industry and service activities. However, these sectors were unable to absorb the workers flowing from agriculture. The alternative and effective safety valve for the Spanish economy was the constant emigration to Northern and Central European countries. This process continued until 1974 when the international economic crisis brought it to an end (see Table 6.2).

Table 6.2 Spanish migration to Europe (1959–74 (number of migrants)

Year	Emigration	Immigration	Balance
1960–64	658,848	254,068	+404,780
1965–69	324,784	216,584	+108,200
1970–74	462,276	396,400	+65,876
1975–79	69,089	336,500	−267,411
1980–85	99,246	91,006	+8,240

Source: Instituto Español de Emigración.

Throughout the recession, the entire industrial sector was seriously affected. This was exacerbated by the closure of foreign labour markets to Spanish workers, leading to a severe increase in unemployment levels, and a stabilisation in labour-market participation rates. Although the economic recovery of 1985 together with demographic factors (the baby-boom of the 1960s) have resulted in a steady increase in the numbers of the active population, Spanish levels remain lower than the EC average, especially for women (below 30%). Recently, major institutional changes have been introduced to facilitate the integration of women into the labour market.

Employment

Throughout the 1975–85 crisis period, employment decreased by more than 2 million jobs, falling to 10.5 million jobs in 1985. Since that year, with the economic recovery, 1.8 million net jobs have been generated (see the annual percentage change in Table E6), even though by the beginning of 1993 jobs had once again begun to disappear. Self-employment has remained stable, while waged jobs have accounted for most of the employment growth. Both the public and private sector have contributed to this employment recovery, the private sector being the most dynamic.

Ongoing structural change means that employment in agriculture continues to fall (11.8% of total employment in 1990; see Table E16), even though the contribution of agriculture is still significant compared to EC average levels.

Industrial employment (33.4% of total employment in 1990), on the other hand, dropped drastically during the late 1970s and early 1980s, but during the period 1987–90 experienced a relative recovery. The construction sector, in particular, showed up very strongly indeed with a 51% increase in employment in the period 1985 to 1990 due to the activity generated by the Olympic Games of Barcelona, the International Exhibition of Seville and several programmes of public infrastructure by both central and regional governments. Since 1991, however, all industrial sectors have been losing employment in varying degrees.

The service sector has made the greatest contribution to employment generation in the economy and, in 1990, accounted for 54.8% of total employment. Throughout the 1980s and early 1990s service employment, both in market and non-market sectors, has steadily increased, though at a slower pace in the recent past.

Unemployment

The fact that the post-war demographic explosion took place in Spain in the 1955–65 period (ten years later than in the rest of Europe) has meant that the entry of a large number of young people into the labour market together with the late integration of women into the labour market have intensified the effects of employment loss during the decade from 1975 to 1985. Unemployment levels reached a peak of 3 million people (21.6%) in 1985 (see Table E17). With the economic recovery of the late 1980s, unemployment levels steadily fell, but by the beginning of 1993 the unemployment rate had again surpassed the psychological barrier of 20%, bringing the issue of unemployment to the centre of political debate.

Unemployment figures show an irregular distribution by age and sex. The rate for women (24% in 1992) is significantly higher than that for men (11% in 1992). There is discrimination in the labour market against women, not only in terms of the number of jobs available but also in terms of salary levels and working conditions. By age group, youth unemployment is by far the most acute, even though in relative terms it is this group which showed the fastest recovery. Better employment opportunities offered by the labour market as well as the trend to remain longer in the educational system are responsible for this development. The high unemployment rate for young people may be due to both the fact that, in periods of crisis, starters are in a very unfavourable position and that, due to neglect in the public sector, employment programmes specially oriented to the young are not very developed in Spain. The relatively lower rate of unemployment among the older age groups is due to an extensive use of early retirement practices.

6.2.2 Major production indicators

Gross domestic product (GDP)

The economic crisis beginning in the mid-1970s seriously affected the entire economic system as can been seen from GDP performance for that period (see Table E19). Between 1975 and 1980, Spanish GDP grew at rates significantly lower than other developed countries. However, in the 1981–4 period, a time of general recession, GDP

increased at comparable rates. In recent years, the Spanish economy has been growing again at the highest rates among the EC countries. Intense growth in terms of per capita GDP, not seen since the Spanish economic boom of the 1960s, has been experienced again since 1986.

During the 1955–74 period, when the Spanish economy underwent the fastest economic growth of its history, employment and production structure changed drastically. The importance of the primary sector diminished in favour of industry, and more especially in favour of construction and service activities.

Later on, with the economic crisis, the proportionate loss of agriculture and industry was significant, as the service sector expanded to account by 1985 for over 50% of total employment and more than 55% of GDP. While the reduction of the primary sector in relative terms may be seen as part of the process of modernisation of the economy, the fall in industrial activity can be explained both by the crisis in the sector and a restructuring of production. The contribution to GDP of the secondary sector fell by more than five percentage points.

There were also important changes in the structure of industrial production. Table 6.3 analyses this transformation, breaking up industrial activities into 25 industrial sectors and classifying them into three main groups: strong, medium and weak demand at the international level. According to this classification, Spanish industrial structure both in 1970 and in the more recent past, presents the characteristics of a developed country of intermediate level, with a reduced proportion of strong demand industries, an important presence of medium demand activities and still a significant number of weak-demand industries.

However, the recent past shows an increase in strong demand sectors (over 3 percentage points between 1970 and 1986) with the growing presence of two new sectors – office equipment and computers and electronic material – and the reduced importance of electrical machinery and chemistry. The group of medium demand sectors has increased its share in total production by 4.4 percentage points in the same period. This increase is due mainly to the automobile sector, machinery and equipment, foodstuffs and oil refineries. The group of weak demand sectors has lost its share falling by 7.7 percentage points since 1975. This fall is of a general nature with the exception of steel activities, and relates especially to shipbuilding, leather, clothing and shoes.

This development allowed Spain to achieve an industrial value-added growth rate which, compared to that of the EC countries, was similar from 1975 to 1985 (higher from 1976 to 1980, and lower from 1981 to 1985). The rapid increase in internal demand from 1985 onwards, with the recovery of private consumption and especially investment, gave rise to outstanding industrial growth, well above the average for European countries.

Table 6.3 Structure of industrial production, 1970–86 (%)

Sector	1970	1986
Strong demand sectors	11.2	14.5
1 Aircraft	0.2	0.4
2 Office equipment and computers	–	0.6
3 Electrical equipment and components	3.1	3.4
4 Electronic material	–	2.0
5 Precision instruments	0.3	0.4
6 Pharmaceutical products	1.0	1.5
7 Chemistry	6.6	6.2
Medium demand sectors	49.0	53.4
8 Rubber and plastics	2.8	3.1
9 Automobiles	4.8	8.2
10 Mechanical equipment	3.8	4.1
11 Railway transport equipment	0.5	0.2
12 Other transport equipment	0.4	0.3
13 Foodstuffs, drinks and tobacco	21.4	22.9
14 Oil refineries	10.4	10.2
15 Paper	5.0	4.5
Weak demand sectors	39.8	32.1
16 Steel	5.7	8.5
17 Non-ferrous metals	2.7	1.6
18 Shipbuilding	1.8	0.7
19 Metallic products	4.5	6.0
20 Non-metallic mineral products	4.2	3.7
21 Wood and cork	4.3	3.1
22 Textile	5.9	3.4
23 Leather	1.2	0.7
24 Clothing and shoes	7.9	3.4
25 Other manufacturing industries	1.5	0.9
Total industrial sectors	100.0	100.0

Table 6.4 Contribution of service activities to the generation of gross value added, 1987 (%)

Commerce, maintenance and repairs	26.21
Services to firms, other services and domestic services	15.51
General services of public administration	12.27
Credit and insurance	11.87
Restaurants, hotels and bars	11.86
Renting of buildings	11.57
Transport	7.41
Health	6.60
Education and research	5.93
Communications	2.91
Total services	100.00

The service sector exhibits three main characteristics in Spain:

- it has been the most dynamic in terms of employment generation and production growth,
- it is the main sector in terms of its share of GDP and total employment;
- little is known about its main structural characteristics since any study on service activities in Spain encounters countless limits imposed by the available statistics.

A detailed analysis of the contribution of different service activities to the generation of gross value-added can be found in Table 6.4. According to this division, the most important sectors by the late 1980s were: commerce, maintenance and repairs; general services of public administration; and services to firms, other services and domestic services.

The activity branches with the highest growth rates during the 1980s were: air transport, communications and public administration services, each increasing by over 4% per annum at constant prices. At the same time, there were some branches which remained fairly stable, such as commerce, maintenance and repairs, railway transport and passenger transport by road. A small number of activities have contracted during the period, such as marine transport, and the private activities of education and health, which contrast with the significant increase in public activities in these areas. In conclusion, it should be noted that the economy's dependence on the service sector is not caused by public services financed through the public budget (the relative weight of which is four percentage points lower in terms of GDP than the EC average), but rather that the importance of the service sector is derived mainly from the key role of tourist activity in the economy and the relative weakness of the industrial sector.

Consumption and saving

In the last 15 years private consumption has exhibited considerable stability; from high initial levels, it increased its share of GDP by two percentage points in 1981–4. From 1985, however, private consumption has gradually declined as a proportion of GDP towards EC average levels – thus liberating resources for saving. Public consumption has shown a steady upwards trend, and thus has had a moderately counter-cyclical effect, though it has not reached the levels experienced by other European countries.

The level of savings has developed according to consumption requirements. Thus the savings level is depressed during the hardest years of the crisis, since lower levels of production and employment loss made it necessary to dedicate a higher percentage of resources to consumption. Since the economic recovery of the late 1980s, economic measures have been taken by the government to encourage internal saving and restrict consumption, both to control inflation and reduce the deficit in the balance of trade.

Gross fixed capital formation

The development of gross fixed capital formation appears to be very different from that of most EC countries. This aggregate, in Spain, fell in the period 1975–84 with a sharp recovery after 1985. Since the mid-1970s public investment has worked in a counter-cyclical way, maintaining its share of the GDP in the critical years. Undoubtedly, private investment has been critically influenced by macroeconomic conditions.

Table E26 shows some interesting results. The average annual increase in gross fixed capital formation during the 1961–70 period reached 11%, almost double the average rate of the twelve EC countries. Subsequently, in the depression of 1975–85, it experienced a sharp decline, rising again to the highest in the EC by 1989 (13.8% against an EC average of 7.3%). The possibility of Spanish economic growth approaching average European levels depends crucially upon the capacity to generate investment. In fact, investment growth after 1985 was linked to a great extent to the expectations generated by the entry into the Community, and was assisted both by fiscal measures and a significant increase in foreign investment.

Nevertheless, as can be seen in Table E6, the investment growth rate has been declining since 1990, and current estimates show a decrease from the last quarter of 1992. The reasons behind this development have to do with current financial conditions and negative expectations on the part of investors linked to the international economic recession.

Income distribution

The distribution of national income is important because of its effects upon social welfare and also because it affects the dynamics of growth itself. In Spain, the change in income levels and distribution has been rapid and far-reaching.

The per capita income of the Spanish population increased from 337 US dollars in 1960 to 2,275 US dollars in 1974. During the recession, real income grew very slowly at an annual average rate of 1.2%, and real per capita income at 1.16%. This situation has changed markedly since 1985, and in 1992 per capita income in Spain amounted to 77.5% of the EC average. The income expansion and the radical change of the productive structure were accompanied by particular problems. In the first place, economic growth did not generate enough employment, thus resulting in the migration of over two million people in search for work abroad. Another feature was the lack of a modern public sector able to satisfy the collective needs of the country and to correct the uneven distribution of rent and wealth.

While per capita income growth is important, a key question is how it has been distributed among different social groups. The limited information available in Spain (see Table 6.5), shows that despite a gradual but constant trend towards greater equality between 1974 and 1987, the Spanish income distribution model is still characterised by great income inequalities between social groups. In 1987, the share of the bottom 20% amounted to only 6.85% of total household income as against 43.75% for the top 20%.

Table 6.5 Cumulative distribution of final household income, 1974, 1980 and 1987

	1974	1980	1987
Top 20%	51.95	44.28	43.75
Top 40%	71.10	65.82	65.29
Top 60%	85.48	82.10	81.37
Bottom 40%	14.52	17.90	18.63
Bottom 20%	4.94	6.39	6.85

Source: Fondo de Investigación Económica y Social.

Distribution by factor income

An interesting analysis of the various aspects of income distribution can be made by studying the respective income shares of labour, capital and entrepreneurial activities. The Bank of Bilbao provides useful information on this area, which is summarised below.

1 The relative importance of wages and salaries grew until 1980, but have gradually decreased thereafter. Two facts have contributed to this apparently surprising situation: (a) the higher level of social security contributions which have been applied to finance the increasing social benefits, especially after 1975; and (b) the reduction in the number of employed people (more than 1.5 million people between 1975 and 1985).
2 The capitalisation process of the Spanish economy together with the obsolescence of

the productive system has led to an increasing level of amortisation as a percentage of GDP (12% in 1985).
3 In the development of mix rents (rents from self-employment activities), the fall of agricultural rents contrasts with the maintenance of rents of other professionals and private entrepreneurs.
4 Capital rents have shown a behaviour consistent with economic development. In contrast to the stability of incomes from rented accommodation, both firms' savings and interests and dividends fell during the crisis to increase again after 1985.

6.2.3 Wages and productivity

Real labour costs rose significantly from 1970, especially from 1974 until 1980. This has been primarily the result of the performance of wages and salaries. Net real wages over the 1970s grew constantly because of the strength of trade unions throughout the political transition. During the 1980s, however, the rate of increase has been systematically reduced. However, a factor which has prevented labour costs falling further is the growth of social security contributions which have gradually accounted for a bigger share of total labour costs. The further increase in social security contributions at the end of 1992 has reinforced this trend (see Table E23).

As far as productivity is concerned, during the 1960s a sharp increase in labour productivity took place, mostly in the industrial sector. Since 1975, the increases in productivity have been mainly due to employment reduction, as firms have attempted to offset wage increases.

Until 1973, the performance of labour costs and productivity ran a parallel course while in the 1973–9 period a pronounced gap developed as a consequence of the sharp increases in real labour costs and the stagnation of productivity. Since 1980, the gap between the performance of labour costs and that of productivity has been reduced enabling the recovery of working profits. On the one hand, labour costs have decreased due to a lower rate of wage increase; on the other, the increases in productivity of industrial activities have also made their contribution. However, productivity increases have not been the result of an increase in production levels, which have remained stagnated, but the outcome of a reduction in industrial employment and the closing down of a large number of unproductive firms. It was only as recently as 1985 that real economic recovery took place with increases in production without significant reductions in employment levels.

Nevertheless, the competitiveness of the Spanish economy in the European market, in terms of nominal unit labour costs, remains problematic if one takes into consideration the range of labour-intensive sectors which are still predominant in the economy.

6.3 GOVERNMENT INVOLVEMENT IN THE ECONOMY

6.3.1 Fiscal policy

The public sector inherited from Franco's dictatorship was small, centralised and extremely interventionist. The welfare state as known in most European countries did not exist, and thus health, education, social benefits or the provision of infrastructure were and still are under-developed.

In the first two years of the political transition, until 1977, economic policy in general was not a concern for the political leaders, even less budgetary policy. Between 1977 and 1982 an expansive fiscal policy was implemented, manifested in a sharp increase in public expenditure (see Table E28). It must be remembered that the crisis provoked the adjustment of many private and public firms, with the transfer of costs from the private to the public sector through subsidies and other financial transfers to firms. Simultaneously, there were major increases in taxes and social security charges in order to finance unemployment benefits to an increasing number of unemployed workers. As a result of this passive adaptation to the crisis, the necessary fiscal and financial reform process was postponed, financing public expenditure via increasing

deficits, mostly covered directly by the Bank of Spain (see Table E6).

Thus, when the Socialist party came to office in 1982 the budgetary situation was characterised by a large public deficit (5.6% of GDP), caused by the absence of fiscal reform, the demographic and financial crisis of the social security system, the costs of economic restructuring and the outburst of social claims which had been suppressed during the dictatorship period.

It was necessary to re-establish the basis for future economic growth, the only way to create new employment. In order to attain this, the entire economic system had to be stabilised and modernised. Briefly, the major tasks were: (a) to restructure public firms, (b) to balance the social security budget, and (c) to decentralise public income and public expenditure, as ordered by the 1978 Constitution.

The *1984–1987 Medium-term Economic Programme* put forward a general reduction in real wages, a very restrictive monetary policy, and a budgetary policy designed to reduce the public deficit at a time when industrial restructuring was to have important effects on the budget. The income raised through the tax system was to be primarily directed at the objective of deficit reduction. Fiscal policy was to take second place behind wage control policy and the demands of monetary policy.

Throughout the 1977–82 period, public expenditure increased ten percentage points, going from 27% to 37% of GDP (see Table E28). Between 1982 and 1992 public expenditure continued to rise slowly to peak at 44.8% of GDP.

This contrasts clearly with other EC countries. Despite this sharp increase in public expenditure, Spanish levels are still low compared to EC average levels. Moreover, while most of the other countries built up the welfare state during the period of economic expansion after the war, Spain has had to attempt this task in the middle of economic recession.

Public income has experienced a clear boost, going from below 25% of GDP in 1975 to 40.5% in 1992. This is due to the increase in tax income that went from 25% of GDP in 1982 to

36.2% in 1992 after a much needed tax reform. Yet, it still remains five percentage points below the EC average.

The performance of the public deficit (see Table E29) can be divided into four different periods:

1 Between 1977 and 1982, the public deficit went from 0.6% to 5.6% of GDP.
2 Between 1982 and 1985, the efforts to control it were unsuccessful, and it reached a maximum of 7% of GDP.
3 Between 1985 and 1989, the public deficit dropped constantly until it was 2.8% in 1989.
4 Since 1989 the public deficit has remained over 4%, in line with the EC average.

Analysis of the performance of the three most important budgetary variables shows that the stabilisation objective has not been attained to a great extent. If integration into the Community requires the co-ordination and convergence of economic policies, Spanish budgetary policy should be directed at selectively increasing the dimension of the public sector and improving the financial position of the tax system by combating tax evasion in order to reduce the structural deficit.

The deficits registered in the last decade have considerably increased the size of the public debt and interest payments by the government (see Table E6). The level of public debt in Spain (if measured in per capita terms) is not high compared with the rest of the EC countries, and only a small part is financed on the international financial markets.

Every international economic organisation evaluated positively the evolution of the Spanish public budget in the 1980s. On the income side, fiscal pressure was increased avoiding, however, significant increases in per capita fiscal pressure. In addition, entry into the European Community in 1986 obliged Spain to introduce a VAT system which subsequently entailed a radical reform of the entire indirect tax system. The growth of public expenditure was restrained while the number of people who benefited from social services was augmented by increasing the efficiency of the system. Moreover, this general appraisal

appears to be even more favourable if one considers that, during the period, restructuring and re-industrialisation measures absorbed more than one billion pesetas.

Spanish economic recovery started in 1985 when the public deficit reached 7% of GDP. This level of deficit was justified by the need to finance public expenditure dominated by transfers to families and firms, with investment just reaching 5% of total expenditure. The key factor that explains the reduction in the deficit to 2.8% of GDP in 1989 was the economic recovery which allowed the expenditure related to the economic restructuring of the 1980s (subsidies and benefits) to diminish and the income via taxes to increase. The current recession has brought the opposite effect and control of the public deficit is proving difficult for the government.

The above developments partially explain the Spanish gap in terms of public facilities and services, as in Italy, where there is a clear contrast with most European countries. In order to attain a satisfactory level of public facilities, is it necessary to increase public expenditure? To answer this question, one must take into account that what in Western Europe is known as 'a rejection of State intervention' is a phenomenon which appeared when public expenditure represented more than 50% of GDP since 1980. Spanish public expenditure level (44.8% of GDP in 1992) is still far from that level. This contrast in policy has allowed Europe to enjoy a much better level of infrastructure, public facilities and services than that which exists in Spain, a factor that may hinder Spanish development in the future.

6.3.2 Industrial policy

It is common nowadays to describe the economic crisis experienced by all developed countries after 1974 as a structural crisis, especially affecting industrial systems and strategies. Sectors such as shipbuilding, steel works or household equipment, characterised by standardised and unsophisticated technology and a less highly qualified workforce and labour intensive processes, faced substantial excess capacity in all industrialised countries.

The crisis focused, in general terms, on those sectors in which the Spanish economy had specialised during the 1960s and where most of its efforts had been concentrated. As a consequence, of increasing costs resulting from oil price increases, among other things, together with the emergence of the so-called 'Newly Industrialised Countries' (NICs) in the international context, Spain lost its relative advantage in those sectors.

In this context, while most of the countries affected by the crisis reacted rapidly adapting their productive structures to new market demands by reducing productive capacity and channelling resources towards new activities, Spain reacted slowly. This contributed to further losses of competitiveness at the international level. This situation notwithstanding, industrial policy, between 1975 and 1982, was aimed at stimulating export activities and supporting foreign investment as a way of combatting the excess capacity and the shortage of internal investment, without paying any attention to technological issues. Moreover, the absence of an adequate macroeconomic policy together with the passivity of most of the economic agents – directly affected trade unions and entrepreneurs – made the implementation of a determined strategy of industrial restructuring even more difficult. The measures adopted during this period were merely defensive, in an attempt to adapt to the crisis and, therefore, to freeze the sectors most directly affected. This was based on the belief in the soundness of the industrial structure prior to the crisis as an adequate foundation for the future recovery of the Spanish economy.

Clearly in contrast with the strategy just described (which, nevertheless, comprised some measures to solve the most acute problems of certain big firms), industrial policy from 1982 was primarily aimed at facilitating industrial restructuring. This policy was carried out in the context of the '*Restructuring and Re-industrialisation Law*' of July 1984, aimed at the so-called 'mature' or 'traditional' sectors. These sectors were: steelworks, shipbuilding, textiles, electronic components, shoes, electrical equipment for

the automobile sector, fertilisers, iron-alloys, foundry products, copper products, etc. The main objectives of this law and strategy were:

1 to adapt industrial supply to new market conditions, with the subsequent reduction in excess capacity in order to secure an adequate level;
2 to rationalise production processes, which implied both technology modernisation and a shift in production specialisation;
3 to improve the financial structure of the firms affected; and
4 to halt the de-industrialisation process undergone by the Spanish economy since the beginning of the crisis, i.e. to introduce a programme of re-industrialisation.

Behind these objectives lies an attempt to raise the competitive level of these firms to meet European standards and to re-establish Spain's position in the new international market that emerges from the crisis.

The most relevant instruments which support this restructuring process are:

1 *labour measures*: mainly early retirement facilities and improved unemployment benefits and conditions for people made redundant by restructuring firms;
2 *financial measures*: grants and subsidised credits to firms, equity participation by the public sector;
3 *regional measures*: appropriate regional incentives to mitigate the geographical impact of the restructuring process since the firms affected presented a high degree of geographical concentration. Thus the 'Urgent Re-industrialisation Areas' were created to enhance the re-employment opportunities of redundant workers;
4 *measures to support technology development*: the provision of finance and other services to generate R&D activities among industrial firms; and
5 *measures to support small and medium-sized enterprises*: assistance by providing long-term finance and stimulating the emergence of

joint strategies (e.g. common marketing or R&D strategies).

By 1988, restructuring plans had almost been completed, with generally satisfactory results. 791 firms had been included within these plans (683 in the textile sector alone, but one must take into consideration the varying size of firms in different sectors), with a total investment of 650 thousand million pesetas and an employment reduction of approximately 84,000 jobs (out of an original workforce of 280,000 workers). Most of the restructured sectors show a clear recovery tendency (productivity increases, financial soundness, profits), even if for some sectors, e.g. steel or shipbuilding, the results fall short of the objectives.

Now that the restructuring of traditional sectors has officially come to an end, Spanish industrial policy revolves around three major areas.

1 Spain's full membership of the EC since 1992, means that Spain must make a supreme effort to adapt the productive structure to the new competitive requirements if Spanish industry wants to compete as an equal with other European firms. In a 'Europe without barriers' the temptation to rely on protectionism (the reserve of the national market for products which do not find a market abroad) no longer exists.

2 Technological innovation has become a central element in facing not only the above challenge, by increasing productivity levels, but also in guaranteeing continuous economic recovery in the long run.

3 In recent years a substantial effort has been made to attract direct foreign investment with the double objective of helping in the process of technological innovation and complementing internal savings, which have been insufficient since the 1960s to finance the process of economic growth in Spain. Obviously, this last strategy entails the risk of further increasing the dependence of Spanish industry on assistance from abroad, which is already a matter of concern to many critics.

6.3.3 Social policy

As discussed above, there are close links between fiscal policy and the expansion of social expenditure. The aim of this section is to discuss the structural reform of the social security system in Spain. This process has resulted partially from fiscal difficulties but also by the obvious need to build up a welfare system.

Before covering a survey of the reform process, it seems appropriate to explain briefly the main features of the social security system before the crisis. This analysis will highlight sharp differences between Spain and most countries within the Community, which in turn will allow us to understand the relevance and difficulties of the current reform.

The creation of the social security system

The 1964 '*Social Security Law*' and related developments in 1967 marked the beginnings of the social security structure which is now under reform. The aim of this Law was to build up a fee-based social security network which would guarantee a package of retirement pensions, health services, unemployment and disablement benefits, following the German model. The beneficiaries, according to the chosen system, were the wage-earning population, and, through special schemes, several other working groups on account of the particular characteristics of the sector or working conditions. (e.g., mining workers)

From the financial viewpoint, the system had to meet its needs through social dues paid by workers and employers (mainly the first group) and state contributions. Nevertheless, the system was financed up to 95% through social dues.

Until 1972, when a legal reform took place, the level of protection was fairly weak, for the system's financial resources were insufficient. More importantly, and despite this financial shortage, the system was obliged to generate an important volume of savings to finance other activities, apart from those to do with social assistance.

The 1972 reform aimed at radical change. An improvement in the level of protection was to be provided through better management of the available income and an increase in state contributions. This would generate sufficient resources to finance the desired expansion in social expenditure. However, these objectives were not achieved because of the impact of the economic crisis. As early as 1977, the policy response to the crisis imposed serious restrictions on the expansion of social expenditure. The reform of the social security system was to be implemented on the basis of an immature social security structure in which, for example, the guaranteed average retirement pension was below the average official minimum wage.

The 1977–85 transition period

Until the *Social Security Reform Law* of 1985, governments tried to solve the financial problems of the system by working on three different fronts. On the income side, a general reduction in employers' contributions, consistent with a more general strategy of wage restriction, was undertaken together with an increase in state transfers to sustain the system. On the expenditure side, the strategy focused on two lines of action. On the one hand, attempts were made to improve the management of the system, thus cutting down current expenditure levels. On the other, social expenditure was simply frozen. Between 1977 and 1986, with the exception of the expenditure linked to unemployment, total expenditure on the social security system increased by less than 1% of GDP. In 1976, the social expenditure/GDP ratio was 12.3%, while in 1985 this figure had dropped to 11.8%. This development is especially relevant since it took place at a time when a significant restructuring process was taking place in the economy with the subsequent increase in social needs and demands.

The issue of unemployment benefits deserves special attention because of the sharp increase in unemployment levels as we have already seen. Legal changes to the system sought to diminish the level of expenditure by making it harder to gain access to unemployment benefits. As a result of these legal changes, it is estimated that since 1985 only 30% of the unemployed have been entitled to get unemployment benefits. This situation can only be understood if one remembers the important role played by the family as a supportive and protective network in Spanish society.

The current reform

The 1985 *Reform Law* contemplated a whole range of legal changes with the objective of controlling the expansion of social expenditure on retirement pensions. It was an explicit recognition that the financial crisis of the social security system could not be solved by larger state contributions, and was reinforced by general government concern with the size of the public sector deficit.

The next step in the reform came with the 1987 *Budget Law*. From this moment, state transfers to the social security system were to be used to finance health expenditure. Pensions were to be financed exclusively from social contributions. A complementary step had already been taken in 1985 with the regulation of pension funds, thus allowing the private sector to enter into a sector previously reserved for the state.

The final step in this reform came in 1991. It refers to what in Spainish are called 'not paid for' pensions or welfare pensions, that is the pensions received by those people who are not entitled, for various reasons, to get a pension from the traditional system.

Despite these reforms, the system came under pressure again in 1992, because of the increase in the level of unemployment, which obliged the government to increase employers' contributions to the social security system and to restrict considerably the access to unemployment benefits. These changes, known in Spain as the *decretazo*, have met with tough opposition both on the part of trade unions and employers' associations.

6.3.4 Labour policy

Developments in the labour market during the 1980s/early 1990s can be split into three clearly defined periods: 1980–5, with a massive reduction in the number of jobs; 1985–91, with a distinct recovery in employment, and the period from mid-1992 in which employment began to fall again, as we have already discussed. Thus, employment levels and general economic performance have run parallel to each other over the entire period. Improvement in employment levels and economic recovery seem to go hand-in-hand, despite the labour policies implemented to improve employment conditions. An analysis of the labour market, however, would be incomplete without mentioning the significant changes in labour force management that have taken place over these years, especially, those changes aimed at increasing the flexibility of the labour market. There are also structural changes which bring the Spanish labour market more into line with those of most European countries, even though common problems appear to be more severe, given the specific features of Spain's economic development model.

The emergence of a democratic system in the late 1970s brought major changes to labour management strategies, such as the recognition of the right of trade unions and employers' organisations to sign collective labour agreements within the different sectors of the economy. However, the real basis of labour policy in Spain is defined by the 1980 *Employment Law* and the 1980 *Workers Statute*, which developed the general rights written down in the Constitution. Both laws modified significantly the previous legal network, through the introduction of a considerable degree of flexibility into labour relations management by allowing the option of signing part-time contracts and contracts for a limited time period in all sectors of the economy and for any worker.

The result of these changes has been the design of a whole range of flexible contracts, which have given the Spanish labour market the highest degree of flexibility in the entire Community. By the end of 1989, 26% of all wage jobs were being carried out under part-time contracts. Furthermore, almost all the jobs linked to the recovery were associated with different forms of temporary contract. In 1992 only 8% of new contracts were signed on a permanent basis. An increase in this degree of flexibility, and associated job insecurity, was not foreseen, nor were the serious macroeconomic consequences, in terms of demand and employment movements. In fact, at the beginning of 1993, with recession biting and the rate of unemployment over 20%, the government modified the legislation, extending the length of the minimum length of the temporary contracts from three to four years, in an attempt to reduce the rate of increase in unemployment.

Finally, it is necessary to mention here those labour policies aimed at adapting labour force qualifications to new job requirements. This strategy has been designed by the 'General Council of Occupational Training' made up of representatives of workers, employers and the administration. It has been carried out through 'National Training Programmes', financed by the administration and compulsory contributions from employers, and other programmes implemented by the autonomous governments and financed through their own budgets. The expansion of occupational training activities since 1986 has been both a consequence of the availability of the financial resources of the European Social Fund and of the internal concern over labour qualification levels. The issue of 'training' is becoming the central topic of concern, as it is recognised that the qualification shortage faced by many sectors may hinder future economic growth and employment generation.

6.4 FINANCIAL SYSTEM

6.4.1 Institutions, markets and the most relevant financial assets

The Spanish financial market has undergone constant change since 1975. Its major characteristics have become very similar to those of other national markets within the European Community.

In the traditional system, the presence of public institutions in the market was led by the Central Bank, *Banco de España*, and the *Instituto de Crédito Oficial (ICO)* which oversaw several (state-owned) banking institutions, each one specialising in financial transactions for specific economic activities such as industry, shipbuilding, agriculture, etc.

The activity of these banks remained at low levels compared to that of the private sector. However, their importance was due to the fact that they distributed the public resources earmarked for investment.

By the early 1960s, the private banks were divided by law into two groups, commercial and industrial. The purpose was to encourage bank specialisation, either on financial transactions related to industrial investment (industrial or business banks), or on banking for day-to-day transactions of private persons and firms (commercial or deposit banks). In practice, owing to the particular characteristics of Spanish economic development, private banks became 'mixed', half-industrial and half-commercial, rather than specialised. In this sense, private bank lending to companies, mainly for investment plans, constitutes an important feature of the Spanish economy for it also took place in the form of banks acquiring majority interests in many of those firms.

The 'Big Six' Spanish banks, namely Bilbao-Vizcaya, Central, Banesto, Hispano-Americano, Popular and Santander, ignoring their associated institutions, accounted for more than 60% of peseta bank credits. Foreign banks were allowed to establish branches under severely restrictive regulation in 1978.

As the industrial crisis deepened throughout the late 1970s, a bank crisis occurred in Spain. From 1978 to 1985, 58 private banks failed – representing 27% of total bank liabilities. According to experts, the major causes of this crisis are to be found in the real system crisis and in management errors ranging from unorthodox practices (the RUMASA case is a good example) to general undervaluation of financial assets due to high inflation rates and failures of enterprises.

Also remarkable is the lack of legal devices to enable the Banco de España to supervise banking activities. The very first measures were taken in 1978, when the problems arose. Since then, there have been several initiatives extending Central Bank control and power over dubious institutions. Simultaneously, there has been a need for other banks to co-ordinate and co-operate, also with the authorities, in order to prevent the crisis from worsening (the much feared 'domino effect'). Therefore, the *Corporación Bancaria* was created. This is a banking institution jointly owned by the private banks and the Banco de España, which took control over some failing banks so that it could sell them after re-establishing their profitability.

During the 1980s Spanish financial institutions underwent several major changes. In the private banking system, as a consequence of the crisis and other inter-bank relations, a process of mergers began with total support from the public authorities. However, it has resulted so far in only two really important amalgamations, namely that of the Banco de Bilbao and the Banco de Vizcaya, thereafter called Banco Bilbao-Vizcaya, and in 1991 that of the Banco Central with the Banco Hispano Americano, thereafter called Banco Central-Hispano. The Caixa de Barcelona and the Caixa de Pensiones, are still in the process of merging.

The *Cajas de Ahorros*, owned by local authorities, have evolved from their ancient savings-bank role to their present full banking business; the volume of their deposit liabilities now represents more than 40% of the entire system. The merger of the two major *Cajas de Ahorros* – the Caixa de Barcelona and the Caixa de Pensiones – has resulted in the first credit institution in Spain in terms of the volume of deposits. The *Cooperativas de Crédito*, operating locally, are private institutions initially created for aiding regional development and presently operating as banks.

Similarly, in recent years conditions of entrance and restrictions on the activities of foreign banks have been relaxed, preparing the transition to the liberalisation of capital flows in 1993. In this sense, usual comparisons between domestic and foreign institutions based on absolute figures are not relevant and other criteria such as business profitability or growth ratios per employee tend to suggest a certain superiority of foreign competitors.

Finally, other financial intermediaries have to be considered as well, like insurance, leasing and factoring companies or pension funds, which have grown under the control of private banks. They have supplied the necessary funds in the absence of a developed financial market outside the banking system.

The *Sociedades Mediadoras en el Mercado de Dinero*, money market intermediary firms, are non-banking monetary institutions which operate between banks and other agents selling and buying various short-term assets.

The money market, based on the Central Bank operations with reserves, includes inter-banking and other monetary intermediaries' transactions with short-term financial assets. The efficiency of this market is very important to money supply control as policy measures are spread to the economy through the credit strategy changes (reactions) of involved money market institutions. In this sense, the authorities have already completed the scheduled plan for developing this market and improving its efficiency and have shifted their attention to the stabilisation of the capital market.

The stock exchange market (*Bolsa de Valores*) had been underdeveloped in Spain because of traditional interrelations between financial and industrial capital. Similarly, capital markets were restricted to long-term credit institution loans. The relatively low levels of revenues and savings and the role of financial intermediation performed by banking institutions, were the causes of the limited importance of the stock exchange market in the Spanish economy until the 1980s. Since 1985, capital inflows from abroad and the change in Treasury deficit funding have been contributing to the strengthening of the stock exchange market. Nevertheless, this has not been achieved easily because of the problems created by the antiquated market organisation: i.e. transaction timetables (less than 15 minutes for each group of assets), market accessibility (brokers had to be civil servants), market integration (strictly speaking, there were, and still

are, four different stock exchange markets in Spain at Madrid, Barcelona, Valencia and Bilbao, where the same security may have four different prices, one in each market), and the lack of advanced technological support for processing and transmission of information and the decisions of agents.

Unlike London, with its famed 'Big-Bang' approach to the technological *aggiornamiento* of the stock exchange, the Spanish government favoured a gradualist approach, beginning with the creation of a treasury bill market where there were no 'physical' transfers of titles but accounting records on the books of the institutions involved (*Mercado de títulos de deuda pública anotados en cuenta*). This was a crucial step if we consider the importance of public sector financial flows in the economy. As private agents and banking institutions were getting used to the new system, mostly in money market payments, the reform of the stock exchange continued with the extension of the application to the transactions in other financial assets. The *mercado continuo* (continuous market) was born, in which trade begins at 9.00 a.m. and ends at 5.00 p.m. for all assets.

In accordance with the step-by-step approach adopted by the government, firms and other borrowers on the stock exchange were allowed to trade their issues either on the continuous or on any of the four markets until the end of 1992. The task of surveying the solvency and fair play of the agents is carried out by the *Comisión Nacional de Valores*, which replaced the old organisation after the reform.

The main financial assets traded on those markets are short-term treasury bills (*Pagarés* and *Letras del Tesoro*), commercial papers issued by major firms and various bonds and mortgage securities offered by credit institutions.

The reform of the financial system has also affected the public sector. In 1991 the *Corporación Bancaria Argentaria* was created as a publicly owned share-company to compete in the market with the rest of the financial institutions. It has integrated the Banco Exterior de España and the three traditional public banking institutions (Banco Hipotecario, Banco de Crédito Agrícola, and Banco de Crédito Local) that have belonged to the *Instituto de Crédito Oficial (ICO)* since 1988. On the other hand, the Banco Exterior de España has absorbed the Banco de Crédito Industrial, while a 'financial agency for development' has been set up within the *ICO* to carry out government's economic policy.

As a result of the reform, the public sector carries out its activities through *Argentaria*, a financial holding company which aims to become one of the major financial groups, while the *ICO* works as the governmental agency. The *Argentaria* group is undergoing a process of reform to adapt its proceedings to the general regime of the Spanish banking system, even if some of its members continue to distribute subsidised loans to specific projects such as housing construction and some investment activities undertaken by local administrations.

It has to be remembered that the traditional state financial flows to these banks ceased on Spain's entry into the EC. Since 1986, public banks have continued to carry out long-term investments, but have financed them in the market, for state financing is no longer allowed. In order to carry out their activities, public financial institutions need to be able to generate profits. With this in mind 25% of *Argentaria*'s capital will be sold on the stock exchange market by the middle of 1993, opening the way towards privatisation in the future.

6.4.2 Monetary policy in the 1980s

Since the Spanish Socialist party took office in 1992, monetary policy has tended to reduce the pace of money supply growth by means of the relevant instruments related either to Central Bank activity in the money market (i.e. leading to increases or decreases in the reserve balances of credit institutions), or to different legal devices of credit control called *coeficientes*, obligatory rates to be maintained between different parts of their balance sheet by domestic banking institutions. This system has usually been described as a fractional reserves system, where monetary policy is applied on a two-tier basis. The changes

in monetary (intermediary) targets result from the Central Bank changing the monetary base, the quantity of central money or reserves, forcing the credit institutions to change their credit policy in order to respect, among other things, the obligatory cash/reserve ratio. Nevertheless, these latter instruments are being removed while another policy step is taken towards state monetary neutrality and private banking freedom.

The 'traditional' method of state monetary intervention in Spain was the imposition of domestic interest rates, uncompetitive in foreign markets. In addition, restrictions on international financial transactions were usual in order to prevent foreign competitors from penetrating Spanish financial markets.

In that sense, the monetary policy applied by the Socialist government has changed both internal and external conditions for financial activity. With regard to national money market excesses of liquidity, it was more difficult to establish monetary control by means of an operative target (namely, the growth of Central Bank reserves) before 1985 owing to unorthodox Treasury financing and, thereafter, as a result of intervention on foreign exchange markets (where the peseta was appreciating under the pressure of capital inflows).

For this reason, the monetary authorities have implemented a number of measures of general economic policy aimed at the modernisation of the Spanish economy, which involve at least the following interrelated objectives:

1 To reinforce competition in the financial market, in order to increase general efficiency in national financial markets and also to counter-balance the pressure on interest rates caused by public sector borrowing requirements.

2 To improve monetary policy efficiency: active policy on money supply rather than on interest rates, and a strong belief in free-market efficiency, even in financial payments generated by public sector deficit, are the major elements of this strategy. The intervention of monetary policy authorities takes the form of

bids by credit institutions for reserve credits or treasury bills to the Central Bank, which usually determines the total tradable amount and distributes it to each institution depending on the interest rate offered or demanded.

3 To reinforce market liberalisation without endangering national credit institutions' stability and solvency, in the context of the European single market.

Financial innovations, like the new financial products or institutions mentioned above, have been developed by the Treasury and other financial institutions, to help in the creation of new financial markets, in order to obtain resources directly from particular sources for financing expenses in excess of revenues. Financial desintermediation can be seen as the main feature of the changes undergone in domestic monetary policy, for it expresses government's commitment to improving the general efficiency of and competition in the financial system at large.

During the 1980s, and due to financial innovation, the definition of the money supply under control (intermediate objective) has been enlarged, from ancient near-money aggregate (M3 or *Disponibilidades Líquidas*, bank money) to M4 (M3 plus other short-term assets issued by the Treasury or major firms on the money market). The main reason was the lack of accuracy of price movement forecasting based on M3 performance in the early 1980s. The development of new financial products, in the short term, and the emergence of non-banking financial institutions, trading in these products on the markets, shifted the patterns of portfolio distribution, so that near-money assets were no longer included uniquely among bank liabilities and their performance did not reflect the total monetary buying power in the economy.

According to monetarist theory, the level of price inflation is determined by the level of M4, also called *ALP*, liquid assets in the hands of the private sector. Over recent years, many factors have intervened to maintain a high rate of money supply growth: public sector deficit, high rate of economic growth (increasing aggregate demand) and foreign capital inflows.

As already said, by the end of the 1980s, improvements in general economic indicators (unemployment, inflation, reduced public sector borrowing requirements, investment) encouraged the government to ease legal restrictions on banks' credit operations by reducing all reserve ratios. The legal cash ratio, fixed at 5% with a maximum of 7%, is a good example. In spite of this last measure, interest rates are still very high and the causes of this are not clear to experts. In addition to the alleged role of the public sector, namely the impact of public sector borrowing upon the level of interest rates, another factor may be the importance of international financial interdependence.

The strength of monetary growth and the relative inefficiency of short-term fiscal policies, given the public sector deficit, induced the authorities to use restrictive monetary policy as the most important anti-inflationary instrument. Government and Central Bank officials estimate yearly the growth in M4, based upon real growth and inflation forecasting. Taking into account the current fluctuation of monetary variables, monetary authorities do not intervene to correct the rate of M4 growth if it stays within the ceilings, defined within a 1.5% range around the target rate. However, it was not until early 1990 that monetary targets were being respected without heavy intervention on the part of monetary authorities. This intervention has been seen, generally, as the major cause of the high interest rates prevailing in the Spanish market.

Finally, in 1992, the Bank of Spain was given full autonomy by the government to draw up and carry out monetary policy. Thus, the government anticipated the full autonomy of Central Banks agreed by those countries willing to participate in the third stage of the European Monetary Union.

In an open economy, with free movement of capital and with the commitment to restricting the fluctuation of exchange rates achieved by Spain since its integration into the EMS in 1989, the stability of exchange rates has become the only possible function of monetary policy. Taking the current circumstances of the

European economy into account, the objective of exchange rates' stability limits the use of interest rates in national economic policies.

Exchange rate levels in foreign currency markets seem to rely on international capital flows rather than current account balances. Therefore, interest rates, together with tax regulations on capital revenues, constitute a necessary tool for guaranteeing stability in the exchange market.

Consequently, the Spanish government hesitates before reducing national interest rates fearing domestic credit expansion, which may fuel price inflation, current account imports and foreign capital outflows which, in the presence of a current account deficit, may endanger exchange-rate stability and the financial soundness of the whole Spanish economy.

As long as the adjustment problems of the major European economies remain, it is difficult to envisage a change in monetary policy. Nevertheless, it seems possible to accept a downward gradual adjustment of nominal, and perhaps real, interest rates, if inflationary pressures diminish. This development, however, would also require an increase in national saving rates – especially motivated by better performance from the public sector – so that the pressure on lending would be reduced.

Apart from the decrease resulting from lower inflation rates, the only additional factor affecting a reduction in interest rates in the Spanish economy lies in the reduction of expectations of future devaluations due to an eventual tightening of the fluctuation range within the EMS. As there is still some time to take on this compromise, this line of action does not seem very likely in the short term.

Monetary policy for 1993 has been designed with stability in mind, allowing a range of increase in *ALP* of 4.4% to 7.5% in practice, compatible with a nominal increase in GDP of 6%. The fluctuation range of three percentage points seems flexible enough for the objectives to be achieved. Any departure from the objectives will be evaluated in terms of its short- or long-term nature and in terms of its relation to expenditure decisions or merely its financial character.

As far as interest rates are concerned, the fact that in Spain they remain three percentage points above average European rates is well known. Their future reduction is influenced by the uncertainty and instability in the exchange markets and the behaviour of domestic prices. Thus, any eventual reduction in interest rates will be gradual, for the EMS has not returned to lasting stability after the disturbances of late 1992. Germany is indicating signs of recession through high interest rates; there remain serious doubts in the market over the permanence of stabilisation policies in the presence of high increases in unemployment; and, finally, there are still two currencies outside the EMS, with depreciation rates that some report as unfair competition. As long as these circumstances remain, the exchange market will prevent any relevant change in the interest rates from taking place.

In the Spanish context, the sharp decrease in economic activity since late 1992 has led some experts and social and political forces to call for a reduction in interest rates in the context of an expansionary economic policy. However, Spanish monetary authorities believe that an expansionary monetary policy would worsen current economic imbalances. Besides, they also consider that the current monetary policy has to be accompanied by a restrictive expenditure policy and a moderate increase in costs, especially labour costs.

6.5 INTERNATIONAL RELATIONS

6.5.1 Trade policy

Unlike other countries in Western Europe, Spain did not undertake a rapid process of liberalisation in foreign trade after the end of the Second World War. It was not until 1959 that the Stabilisation Plan initiated a slow process of foreign liberalisation, after twenty years of 'economic autarchy'. This fact and the absence of political democratic liberties until the end of the 1970s excluded Spain from the process of European integration. Thus, and despite the fact that in

1970 a Preferential Agreement was signed with the Community, Spain did not become a member until 1986. It is, therefore, necessary to analyse first the main characteristics of Spanish trade policy before the end of the 1970s, and then to discuss the major changes caused by integration into the EC.

The most important feature of the tariff protection system of the Spanish economy was its complexity, due to continuous modifications in the 1960 tariff system. In spite of this, the liberalisation process resulted in a significant decrease in tariff barriers, which went from an average of 16% in 1960 to 7% in 1974, to increase slightly in the second half of the 1970s, and decrease again during the 1980s to reach 5.5% just before the entry of Spain into the EC.

In addition to the tariff system, several 'trade regimes' co-existed (trade of state, bilateral, global and exempted) which made distinctions between imports depending on the type of goods or their origin, establishing import quotas and restrictions. In 1960, only 40% of total imports came under the category of 'exempted trade', but in 1974 this percentage had increased to 85%, while the 'trade of state' (the most restrictive category) had become marginal by 1965.

This protectionist network was complemented by the *Impuesto de Compensación de Gravámenes Interiores (ICGI)* (Tax to Compensate for Internal Taxation), theoretically introduced to tax import products as home products, but which in practice meant a protection level of 2 or 3%.

At the same time, Spanish authorities designed several instruments to support export activities, which in many cases concealed dumping practices. Thus, together with special tariffs for goods in transit, credits to exports, export insurance and other instruments, a very special form of tax reduction for exports was at work. This reduction was an adjustment at the border in line with the ICGI. While this tax overestimated Spanish indirect tax levels, it also overestimated tax reductions. So, in fact it was a concealed subsidy to exports. Hence, some fiscal adjustment at the border, theoretically neutral, became in practice

a very important instrument of Spanish trade policy over the years.

The integration of Spain into the EC has introduced many changes in the regulations of Spanish trade policy. In essence, this has involved the substitution of the general regime in force in the EC for the complex web of fiscal and tariff protection previously in place. This, has resulted in a reduction in the level of protection available to much of Spanish production and a significant loss in competitiveness in several industrial sectors such as steel or shipbuilding. The Common Tariff System with countries outside the EC and the progressive elimination of tariff barriers in relation to other Community members, represent a most important innovation for the Spanish economy. Thus, at the end of the transitional period, the end of 1992 according to the Accession Treaty, Spain became a full member of the tariff union.

Taking into account the structure of Spanish foreign trade, this means that more than 75% of total imports, which come from Community countries or other countries with which the Community has signed preferential agreements, will enter Spain exempt from any tariffs or duties. Moreover, tariff barriers have been significantly diminished for the remaining 25% of imports, because Spanish tariffs prior to integration were three points above Community levels on average. In sum, full integration has resulted in a substantial reduction in the level of protection for the Spanish economy. The first effects of this end in tariff barriers are already noticeable, in the form of a significant increase in imports. In the 1986–90 period imports grew at an average annual rate of 17.5% in volume terms.

6.5.2 The structure of foreign trade

The territorial structure of foreign trade

Western Europe has always been the most important market for Spanish exports and, in a smaller proportion, it has been the major supplier of the Spanish economy (see Tables E32 and E33). This fact has been reinforced during the

1980s, especially as a consequence of the integration into the EC. Thus, in 1992 more than 70% of total exports went to other countries within the Community, while a slightly lower percentage of total imports (60.7% in 1992) came from them. The rest of the countries of Western Europe only account for 5% of total Spanish exports and 6% of its imports. These percentages are surpassed by the USA which ranks first in both cases among non-European developed countries, despite the fast increase in imports from Japan. Yet, exports to Japan only account for 1% of total exports.

During the 1980s, among developing countries, both in terms of imports and exports, a clear downward trend can be observed in the participation of OPEC countries, due to the fall in oil prices which has reduced their buying capacity. The loss of importance of the Latin-American countries is also significant. This traditional market has fallen from accounting for 8% of total exports in 1980 to 3% at the end of the decade. The foreign debt crisis is the origin of this development since it has limited their opportunities to pay in any foreign currency. Nevertheless, in the early 1990s, a revival has taken place (trade with Latin-America represented 4.3% of total foreign trade in 1992) due to favourable economic conditions in several countries of the Latin-American Region. Imports arriving from Latin-America have also been reduced in percentage terms, mainly because they are energy goods. On the other hand, the newly industrialised countries (NICs) of the Asian Coast still account for a small part of Spanish imports and exports (2.1 and 2.9% respectively in 1992), even though their growth rate has been very high in recent years.

The volume of trade with countries which come under the 'trade of state' system is unimportant in the Spanish economy. Imports remained at around 3% of the total during the 1980s, whereas exports fell gradually to approximately 2% at the end of the decade.

The concentration of Spanish foreign trade in the EC market is so pronounced that the largest four countries (France, Germany, Italy and the UK) accounted in 1992 for 54.5% of total Spanish exports and 49.3% of its imports. France ranks first as far as sales are concerned, while Germany is in first position in relation to purchases. Portugal, Spain's neighbour, deserves special attention since, despite its relatively limited economic potential, it receives more than 7.5% of total Spanish exports. Thus, Spain is Portugal's second most important trading partner, just behind the powerful German economy. In fact, Portugal is the only country in the European Community for which imports from Spain are significant at all (15.8% of its total imports in 1991, followed at a great distance by France with 4.9%).

The sectoral structure of foreign trade

With regard to imports, Spain has always had three major sources of foreign trade dependence: energy products, intermediate products and capital goods. In the first group, the lack of oil resources leaves a clear imprint on Spanish imports. In 1981, energy imports represented 42% of total imports, having risen steadily from 1974 onwards, when they doubled in value compared to the previous year (25% against 13% in 1973). After 1981 a noticeable fall took place, and while in 1985 they still amounted to 36% of the total, in 1990 they were only 11.7%. Obviously, this development has been clearly influenced by oil price levels.

Intermediate products, in contrast to energy products, represented 40% of total Spanish imports in 1981, steadily increasing their share throughout the decade to reach a peak of 47% in 1988 and decrease again to 37.7% in 1990. The fact that a sizeable part of imported intermediate products are of an agricultural nature needs to be highlighted. In the industrial sector, almost every sector shows a high level of dependence on foreign intermediate goods.

Capital goods have significantly increased their presence in the structure of Spanish imports in recent years. In 1981, they represented just over 9% of total purchases to foreign markets; in 1985 11% and in 1990 they were 38.1% of the total. This is a good indicator of the high level of technological dependence of Spanish industry.

Finally, consumer goods accounted for 12.1% of total imports in 1990. It is interesting to highlight the rapid increase in the pace of purchases from abroad for direct consumption since the integration into the European Community, especially in the automobile sector.

On the exports side, intermediate goods, other than energy products, play the major role in Spanish trade, since they represented in 1981 almost 49% of total exports, and they were still 43% in 1990. The other main export sector in 1988, consumer goods (37% of total exports), accounted in 1990 for only 12%. Within this group, foods gradually lost their share, while durable consumer goods increased their importance. The automobile sector is responsible for over 75% of durable consumer goods' exports. As far as capital goods are concerned, a change in trend can be observed from 1988 onwards. They represented just below 12% of total exports in the 1980s but by 1990 exports of capital goods amounted to 38.8% of the total.

The joint analysis of foreign trade by geographic area and type of product shows that the trade pattern with industrialised countries is very different to that with developing countries. Spain exports in relative terms more consumer goods to the OECD countries and capital goods and intermediate products to developing countries. Among exports to the Community countries, durable consumer goods (especially cars) dominate; non-durable consumer goods constitute the most important item of exports to the USA; and food items are the major component of sales to Japan. Among developing countries, the export of capital goods becomes more relevant to Latin-American countries than other markets.

With regard to imports the Spanish economy gets capital goods from OECD countries, from whom it buys most of its durable consumer goods. From the developing countries, Spain purchases raw materials, especially energy products, with the exception of the NICs from whom durable consumer goods are mostly obtained.

Nevertheless, different studies on the impact of EC integration on Spanish exports show a decrease in the traditional comparative advantage of Spanish industry in natural-resource or labour-intensive products, in favour of products with high economies of scale and to a lesser extent product differentiation or scientific knowledge. This evolution together with the high concentration of trade in the OECD area must be taken into account to develop an export policy in the future based not so much on competition via prices, but on aspects such as design, higher quality and better marketing services.

6.5.3 The balance of payments

Despite the fact that the openness of the Spanish economy is still below the Community average, the growth rate in goods and services exports has been surpassed during the 1980s by only two other EC countries, Ireland and Portugal. However, Spain endures a lasting trade deficit (see Table E34), that traditionally was covered by surpluses in the balances of services and transfers. During the 1980s this trade deficit reached problematic levels between 1980 and 1983, due to the oil crisis, and after 1988 as a consequence of the integration into the EC together with the economic recovery. The recession starting at the end of 1992 has again decreased this deficit due to a lower level of imports.

The positive results of the balance of services derive mainly from the income from tourist activities, that represent over 60% of total income from services. On the other hand, investment income and technical assistance have always displayed a negative balance, because of the dependence of the industry on foreign technology and investment.

The balance of transfers always shows a positive result, due to emigrants' remittances. The presence of more than a million Spanish people in Europe contributed to compensating the deficit in the balance of trade, even if it was in a smaller proportion to the receipts from services.

Because of this compensatory effect of services and transfers, the current account balance occasionally displays surpluses, and, in any case, significantly smaller deficits than the balance of trade. In fact, once the impact of oil price increases in the early 1980s had been overcome in 1984, 1985 and 1986, Spain showed a surplus in its current account balance. However, in 1988 (see Table E6), the deficit on the current account represented approximately 1% of GDP, rising to over 3% from 1989 onwards.

Previous examples of this situation can only be found in the mid-1970s, after the first oil crisis. However, in the last few years, the performance of the oil market could not be better. The increasing trade deficit is associated with a declining surplus in services. It is difficult to ascertain the extent to which the worsening situation in the balance of trade (see Table 6.6) is the consequence of the economic recovery in the late 1980s, the integration into the European Community, or other factors. In any case, it does not seem possible to continue with this situation in the long term, especially after the loss of reserves at the end of 1992.

A positive assessment of this deficit suggests that this foreign debt supports the financing of the investment process which in the medium term will improve the production system which, in turn, will enhance the competitive position of Spanish products. A negative view, however, considers that this deficit may generate foreign payment difficulties in the long run, strangling future economic growth.

Table 6.6 Cover rate of Spanish foreign trade (exports/imports x 100%)

Year	Total trade	Trade with the EC
1985	81	115
1986	78	93
1987	70	81
1988	67	77
1989	62	73
1990	63	74
1991	63	75
1992	65	76

Source: Calculated from data published by the *Dirección General de Aduanas.*

In any case, the inflow of long-term capital, especially abundant since 1987, is financing this deficit on the current account. Thus, the balance on current account and long-term capital has been positive since 1983. If the positive balance on short-term capital is added, an increase in reserves can be observed.

While direct investment (around 60% of total long-term capital inflows in 1990) is reasonably stable, portfolio investment (which accounted in the same year for 20%) is highly volatile. Moreover, it does not seem possible, in the context of the monetary convergence process introduced by the Treaty of Maastricht, that the Spanish economy can maintain for a long period of time a significant differential in interest rates, with the subsequent loss of attractiveness for long-term capital. Therefore, and without unnecessary alarm, even if the current trade deficit does not cause problems in the short run, it must be considered as one of the major concerns for future economic strategy.

The increase in currency reserves led to the strengthening of the peseta after 1987 even though it is not a hard currency – this did not prove helpful for Spanish exports. This position of the peseta was consolidated by the integration of the Spanish currency into the European Monetary System in mid-1989. Since this coincided with the large trade deficit, the decision has been controversial. On the one hand, it helps to finance the deficit since it guarantees a stable currency to foreign capital, which ensures profitability levels. On the other hand, it does not support the reduction in the trade deficit, which lies at the root of the deficit on the current account. In addition, the interest rate differential necessary to attract foreign capital and maintain the exchange rate, may impose severe deflationary pressure on the domestic economy.

In fact, in the context of the continuing 'crisis in the European Monetary System' of 1992/3, and despite serious attempts by the Central Bank to support the peseta by reducing currency reserves significantly, the peseta has been devalued twice by a total of 11%. Some analysts argue that the peseta is still overvalued if the relative competitive position of the Spanish economy is taken into account.

6.6 SPECIAL ISSUES

6.6.1 The future of agriculture

The future of Spanish agriculture within the EC is still full of uncertainties, despite the apparent popularity of Spanish products among other EC members. Spain has the greatest agricultural potential of the Southern European countries, but severe natural deficiencies (climate, altitude) work hand-in-hand with structural problems, related to distribution and the size of agricultural firms (too small in the North, too large in the South and Centre), to make the problem of integration a difficult one. These issues may limit the future competitiveness of several sectors and regions of Spanish agriculture since other EC countries do not suffer from these problems, as the difficulties faced by many agricultural firms since the full integration into the EC in 1993 seem to demonstrate.

Differences in the main production structures explain the contrast between Spanish areas of specialisation in agriculture and those of other EC countries. EC agriculture is primarily oriented towards cattle raising, while vegetable production is dominant in Spanish agriculture. Moreover, Spanish productivity is significantly lower for most products (1.5 times less than the EC average and four times less than those countries with the highest levels of productivity – Belgium and the Netherlands – in 1992). Nevertheless, it has to be acknowledged that differences in productivity are less significant in agriculture than in other sectors, since products are highly distinctive. Thus, competitiveness depends less on prices than on quality and services offered by products of different origins. In sum, many Spanish products seem to be highly competitive against Mediterranean products – EC and non-EC – especially, wine, oil, fruits and vegetables.

The integration into the EC has provoked a thorough and yet unfinished restructuring process of modernisation and the merging of small firms to enable them to compete with the more powerful European companies. Over a period of six years, the sector has gone from operating in a traditional environment to coping with a general liberalisation of frontiers and markets, with a resulting loss of 500,000 jobs. Per capita income has increased, but more as a consequence of a decrease in people working in agriculture than a rise in production value. Spanish per capita income in agriculture in 1989 amounted to 6,872 ECUs while the EC average reached 18,372 ECUs.

The new Common Agricultural Policy (CAP) will have diverse effects upon Spanish agriculture depending on the specialisation and level of development of different regions, but it will generally intensify the need for restructuring to enable Spanish agriculture to reach the necessary size to be competitive and to participate in the production–distribution–industrialisation process at EC level.

The agro-industrial sector in Spain is limited in size, even though a high and increasing percentage of total sales in the sector is concentrated in the hands of a small number of firms. However, the average firm, by volume of sales, differs greatly from the average firm operating in the EC market.

Among big firms, the level of direct foreign investment has increased over the recent past, covering most activities. The employment and productive structure of these Spanish subsidiaries is similar to those of national companies, but their strategies in terms of foreign trade and technological innovation differ greatly. From a geographical perspective, the location of Spanish agro-industry seems to favour demand factors, which works against less developed traditional agricultural regions.

6.6.2 Tourist trade

The tourist trade represents a major source of economic wealth in Spain, resulting both from internal but mainly external demand. By the mid-1980s, foreign visitors to Spain exceeded 40 million per year. Estimates in 1993 show that this sector accounts for over 8% of GDP and 10% of total employment. Moreover, since the 1960s, income from tourism has been a crucial feature in the Spanish economy, for it has worked as a counter-balance in the balance of payments, compensating for the traditional deficits in the balance of trade necessary to undertake the process of industrialisation and modernisation of the economy.

Geographically, this sector is highly concentrated in a number of the Spanish regions – the Balearic Isles, the Mediterranean Coast and the Canary Isles – where it has been a driving force of economic development. Spanish tourism originates primarily from the EC: France, Portugal, the United Kingdom and Germany being the most important countries (in the mid-1980s tourists from these four countries accounted for over 70% of total foreign tourists).

The development of the Spanish tourist sector has been highly dependent upon the standards of living of EC citizens. Thus, this sector grew steadily from the 1960s (when the Liberalisation Plan and some political changes made Spain a more attractive country for tourists) until 1973, due to the effects of the international crisis. The economic recovery of the 1980s resulted in a period of strong growth in terms of number of visitors, income, employment, etc. However, by 1989–90 the sector experienced a substantial reduction in its activities linked, it seems, not to an absolute decrease in demand but to a shift of demand away from Spain and directed to other Mediterranean countries. In this respect, the military and political crises faced by some traditional competitors in East Europe and North Africa in the recent past have worked in Spain's favour. The tourist industry recovered in 1992 and is expected to expand further in 1993/4.

Despite this development, the tourist trade in Spain is in the midst of a severe crisis and in need of profound restructuring. This situation is influenced by changes in demand but is mainly the result of the way in which the sector has been developed since the 1960s.

The sector developed, without any special attention from the public sector, in accordance with the desire of the private sector both to increase supply and to attract demand. This growth focused on short-term benefits without any clear long-term strategy. It was not until 1990 that the government recognised the need

to undertake a reform of the sector and initiated the preparation of the 'White Book of Tourism' which eventually defined the major strategies to be undertaken by both the public and private sector to adapt the Spanish tourist industry to the challenges it faces.

The major issues to be confronted are:

- a high concentration of tourist activities in some months of the year, mainly in the summer;
- sun and beach tourism accounts for over 80% of total demand with a clear underdevelopment of other types of tourism (cultural, professional) despite the existing clear potential;
- the comparatively low price/quality relationship of tourist services in Spain (hotels, restaurants, leisure facilities);
- the environmental disasters in many tourist areas and the underdevelopment of public services and facilities;
- the lack of a clear and co-ordinated policy between central and autonomous governments together with the lack of adequate marketing abroad of Spanish tourist attractions.

Despite these major problems for the trade, the prospects for the sector seem to be positive because of the obvious Spanish potential for tourism and the well-developed structures and traditions of the industry. Following the advice contained in the 'White Book', there are already indications of a shift towards diversification, entrepreneurial management and a co-ordination of public and private strategies to improve the quality of services, with extended training schemes and capital investment.

6.7 CONCLUSION AND FUTURE PROSPECTS

Three elements commit Spain to a future as an integrated member of the European Community: the *Treaty of Accession*, signed in Madrid in June 1985; the *European Single Act*, signed in Luxembourg in February 1986; and the integration of the peseta into the European Monetary System in June 1989.

By signing the Treaty of Accession, Spain accepted the Community's rules and practices. However, this was to be accomplished over a transition period of seven years, so that full integration was achieved at the end of 1992. This process of the integration of Spain into the European Community was soon effected by the signing of the European Single Act, and reached its full momentum with the entry of the peseta into the Monetary System in the summer of 1989. An exchange rate of 65 peseta/1 mark was fixed, with a 6% fluctuation band, similar to that of the Italian lira, in recognition of the inflationary pressures within the Spanish economy. The rapid decisions adopted by the Spanish government were undoubtedly eased by the favourable attitude of Spanish society as shown by the polls on European issues.

As already stated, the economic liberalisation of the 1960s made it possible for Spain to enjoy the benefits of economic growth. However, the pace of past liberalisation was constrained by political priorities and was very dependent upon favourable internal conditions. By contrast, economic liberalisation in the 1980s was driven by the requirements of integration into the European single market. This obliged Spain to accept a very precise timetable and to implement it without hesitation or failure. Participation in the construction of the European union requires Spain to be rigorous both in the process of opening up to external markets and the maintenance of the internal equilibrium, in co-ordination with the rest of the European economies.

The desire of Spain to become a European country, in the sense of a modern liberal economy, compels the entire society to accept substantial social and economic reform in order to close the development gap between it and the richer members of the Community. Between 1986 and 1991 the Spanish economy achieved sustained expansion, with an annual cumulative rate of increase of GDP over 4%. In these six years, average per capita income rose from 72.8% to 79% of the European average. Simultaneously, the government established closer control of the major macroeconomic variables – thus making significant progress towards the

linked objectives of real and nominal convergence.

This convergence trend has been halted since 1992. In order to continue the approach to European GDP average values, both internal policies and efforts and European help are needed. This task is not an easy one; even with the favourable forecast of Spanish GDP growth exceeding the EC average by 1% per annum, income convergence will only have reached 88% of EC level by the year 2000.

Since the re-establishment of democracy, all governments have displayed a strong commitment to integration into the European Community. With the setting up of the European Union in Maastricht, the EC countries have taken a further step in the direction of integration. In response to the Maastricht initiative, the government announced a new convergence programme for the Spanish economy; however, this has encountered serious opposition from various forces within Spanish society.

The first issue at stake is whether Spain wants to be in the group of countries that will implement the third stage of the European Union. This would entail substantial effort, but offers prospective benefits from full and irreversible integration into Europe. Besides, if this effort is not carried out over the next four or five years, it will have to be undertaken anyway later on, to correct the major macroeconomic imbalances in the economy.

Among the conditions established by the Treaty on European Union, Spain only fulfils the public debt/GDP requirement, which is estimated for 1993 at 48.2%. With regard to inflation, the gap between Spanish and EC levels widened in 1992. This was largely due to the impact of indirect taxation on the consumer price index – a transitory effect which should allow further convergence in 1993. The public deficit condition established by the Treaty has not been fulfilled. Progress is being made, however, and the public deficit has moved from 0.2 points above the European average in 1991, to a predicted 0.2 points below for 1993.

The basic framework set up by the Government to achieve the convergence conditions depends upon two key assumptions: a revival of the international economy from the second half of 1993, and a growth rate in the Spanish economy of 1 or 1.5% above the Community's average (i.e. a domestic growth rate of between 3 and 4%).

The measures designed in the programme of convergence of the Spanish economy may be split into two groups: those aimed at reaching the objectives agreed in Maastricht for the nominal convergence (macroeconomic policies) and those helping in the process of real convergence by deregulating and liberalising product and factor markets (structural policies). Nevertheless, both types of policies are clearly interrelated as can be seen when one analyses them in detail.

6.7.1 Macroeconomic policies

In order to achieve the nominal convergence both monetary policy and fiscal policy are considered.

Monetary policy

The prime objective is the stability of exchange rates. The programme requires the convergence of interest rates, the reduction of inflation and an increase of savings rates – especially in the public sector.

Fiscal policy

The overriding aim is the control and reduction of the government deficit, since it affects inflation rates and interest rates in the long term. The objective is to reduce the public deficit to 1% of GDP by 1996, when the Treaty fixes a maximum of 3%.

The reduction in public deficit of almost 3.5 points in five years means an average annual rate of decrease of 0.7 points. This decrease is to be achieved by a reduction in the growth rate of public expenditure, that would increase less than the GDP. Thus, public expenditure would stabilise around 37% of GDP to grow thereafter at a similar pace. With this change, the financial requirements of the central administration

would go from 3.3% of GDP in 1992 to 0.75% in 1996. Simultaneously, the territorial administrations have also acquired a similar commitment, reducing their borrowing requirements from 1.1% of GDP in 1992 to 0.25% in 1996. In sum, the total borrowing requirements of public administration would go from 4.4% of GDP in 1992 to 1% in 1996. Notwithstanding this objective, which foresees a decrease in all expenditure items, a major objective of the programme is to maintain public expenditure in infrastructures around 5% of GDP.

As far as public income is concerned, there is a commitment to maintain individual fiscal burdens at 1993 levels, when the reforms of direct and indirect taxation are fully operative. From that year onwards, income increases can only be generated by economic growth and better management.

6.7.2 Structural policies

The programme clearly identifies 'market rigidities' as the major obstacle preventing Spain from convergence, in welfare terms, with the rest of Europe. In this context, several structural reforms are given priority.

The labour market

With the aim of unemployment reduction in mind, the programme considers that the structural reforms needed should be directed to enhance the flexibility of the labour market. Three major areas are selected: first, the removal of the barriers that prevent functional and geographical mobility of workers; second, the setting up of incentives among unemployed people to stimulate active job-search; and third, the enhancement of labour skills by the reform of the training system.

Economic deregulation

The most important source of structural inflation has been the strictly regulated sectors of the economy which have enjoyed several norms and regulations that work as effective barriers to entry, as well as numerous agreements establishing market shares, common-pricing, and restrictions to production, distribution and investment. The programme commands the Court for the defence of competition to draw up the necessary measures to overcome this situation. In fact, this represents a major attempt to set up an operative competition policy in Spain, which so far has been lacking.

Liberalisation

This is directed at several domestic sectors such as telecommunications, transport, credit and insurance institutions, etc.

Are there any alternatives to this policy of convergence? There is no obvious alternative to the structural microeconomic measures directed at improving competition and flexibility levels of labour, capital and technology markets. This is the most urgent task, since major divergences with European competitors are to be found in these areas, rather than the features of major macroeconomic imbalances. Therefore, the answer has to focus on these last measures.

There are two major options for action. On the one hand, the government can carry out an expansive fiscal policy instead of reducing the public deficit. This has been the option followed by Italy in recent years. The problem lies in the fact that if expansion is carried on for a long time, there is a risk of generating a cumulative interaction between debt financing, interest rates and public deficit. If this course of action is taken, interest rates might well increase to over 16% – thus creating severe difficulties for public debt finance.

On the other hand, the peseta might be devalued to improve competitive levels and thus increase exports. The EMS prevents Spain from undertaking this policy, unless it can be shown that the internal or external monetary situation cannot be maintained any longer. However, the recent changes to the operating rules have created scope for greater flexibility.

Neither the first option, by stimulating internal demand, nor the second one, through export stimulus, seem likely to correct Spain's imbalances. The most appropriate option remains the fiscal/monetary stance outlined in the government's convergence programme. The central aim is to change the mix of expansive fiscal policy and restrictive monetary policy to a more restrictive fiscal policy that might allow for a more flexible monetary policy, enabling a possible reduction in interest rates – thus helping in the process of economic recovery. In order to achieve the growth objectives estimated in the programme, a moderate increase in real wages has to take place at the same time as significant increases in employment and internal saving capacity. The fulfilment of these conditions appears to be a difficult task. The increase in nominal wages foreseen by the programme is set below that experienced in recent years. This will mean difficult negotiations with trade unions, especially as the level of employment is full of uncertainties, because, in recent Spanish experience, employment growth has occurred only with GDP increases over 3%. It does not seem easy either to improve the rate of savings if the recent behaviour of consumers is taken into account.

Nevertheless, the major obstacle encountered by the programme of convergence has been the lack of support on the part of economic, social and political forces. The positions taken by both trade unions and entrepreneurs' organisations appear to be clearly divergent.

Trade unions do not consider the 'nominal convergence' as a priority, while entrepreneurs agree on the need to reduce public deficit, but want a general and immediate deregulation of the labour market and a reform of the social security system.

In the political arena, there is no agreement since the major opposition force, the conservative party, is making the privatisation of public companies its major priority, and maintained an ambiguous position during the discussion of the programme in Parliament, without offering an alternative.

The new government emerging from the general elections of June 1993 will have to clarify these uncertainties and to secure the necessary support to overcome this economic and political challenge.

This future task will be favoured by the recent positive developments in which there has been a process of intense recovery which has surprised many. It is generally agreed that the integration into the EC has accelerated industrial investment and capitalisation processes and the economy is now better equipped to compete in the future single market. Simultaneously, foreign investment has boomed and this is a major factor in explaining the current recovery.

However, earlier in this chapter we characterised Spain as an intermediate economy whose competitiveness has been based primarily upon a comparative advantage in terms of labour costs. Thus, and despite these positive prospects, the future single market incorporates major concerns for the Spanish economy. These concerns arise from the lower technological level of Spanish firms, which may endanger external equilibrium, as well as from the process of fiscal harmonisation and the prospect of higher wage and social demands. This may result in greater fiscal pressure or an increase in public deficit, as a consequence of rising expenditure levels.

Nevertheless past experience suggests that liberalisation has always produced very positive effects on the Spanish economy, and this encourages an a priori optimistic attitude towards the impact of European integration – even if it means an increase in competition for Spanish sectors and firms.

6.8 BIBLIOGRAPHY AND SOURCES OF INFORMATION

Bibliography

The following books provide more information on the issues discussed in this chapter as well as a very complete bibliography on each section.

Garcia Delgado, J.L. (ed.)(1990): *España. Economía*, Espasa Calpe, Madrid.

Ruesga, S.M. (ed.) (1989): *1993. España ante el Mercado Unico*, Ediciones Pirámide, Madrid.

Tamames, R. (1990): *Estructura Económica de España*, Alianza Editorial, Madrid.

Among the periodicals that provide up-to-date information on Spanish economic issues the following may be recommended:

Economía Industrial, published by the 'Ministerio de Industria y Energía', Castellana, 160, 28046 Madrid, Tl. 34-1-4588010.

Información Comercial Española, published by the 'Ministerio de Comercio', Madrid.

Papeles de Economía Española, published by the 'Confederación Española de Cajas de Ahorros', Padre Damián, 48, Madrid, Tl. 34-1-4586158.

Sources of information

Banco de España, Servicio de Publicaciones, Alcalá 50, Madrid, Tl. 34-1-4469055.

Consejo Superior de las Cámaras Oficiales de Comercio, Industria y Navegación de España, Claudio Boello, 19, 28001 Madrid, Tl. 34-1-2752307.

Dirección General de Aduanas, Guzmán el Bueno, 137, Madrid, Tl. 34-1-2543200.

Instituto Nacional de Estadística (INE), Paseo de la Castellana, 183, 28071 Madrid, Tl. 34-1-2799300.

Ministerio de Economía y Hacienda, Paseo de la Castellana, 162, 28046 Madrid, Tl. 34-1-4588664.

The smaller EC countries

CHAPTER 7

The Netherlands

Frans Somers

7.1 INSTITUTIONAL AND HISTORICAL CONTEXT

In terms of income and number of inhabitants, the Kingdom of the Netherlands is the largest of the smaller EC countries. The country is a 'constitutional monarchy', meaning that the powers of the monarch are clearly limited by the constitution. The function of the King or the Queen as head of state is more or less symbolic; in fact, a system of parliamentary democracy clearly prevails. The most important body of the Parliament, the Lower House (Second Chamber), is elected by a direct proportional system, with a rather low electoral threshold for political parties. The government, headed by a prime minister, is appointed by the parties in the Lower House who after elections manage to form a coalition, which (normally) will command a majority.

7.1.1 Political fragmentation

As in Italy, there are numerous parties represented in Parliament, reflecting the highly fragmented nature of Dutch society. In the past, political differences were not only determined by socio-economic interests but also religious distinctions between Roman Catholics and the various Protestant denominations.

Throughout the present century, the Dutch have coped with the religious differences by dividing society into a number of strictly separated blocs, capable of peaceful coexistence with each other. Every group – religious or ideological – had its own (publicly financed) educational establishments, clubs, newspapers, trade unions and political party. This way, dangerous confrontations between religious groups were avoided and class conflicts reduced as well. Socio-economic antitheses were partly replaced by religious ones.

The significance of religion in Dutch society has diminished sharply since the 1960s. This development has been reflected in the decreasing size of the religion-based political parties. The most important ones merged in 1980 to form one united Christian Democratic Party (*CDA – Christen Democratisch Appel*). Nevertheless, it is generally the case that no single party has an absolute majority in Parliament, which means that all governments are based on coalitions of at least two parties. The Dutch society, consisting of *minorities* only, is a very pluralistic one. Major parties represented in Parliament – apart from the centrist Christian Democrats – are the left-wing Social Democrats (*PvdA*) and (liberal) Democrats (*D'66*) and the right-wing Liberal Party (*VVD*). The Christian Democrats are generally to be found in power, governing on the basis of a coalition with either left-wing or right-wing parties.

7.1.2 Welfare state

Religion is probably also one of the major factors that contributed to the strong expansion of the *welfare state* in the Netherlands. Parties based on religion, which were always in the centre of political power, had to reconcile the conflicting social and economic interests of their members, of employers and employees alike. One way of dealing with conflicts is to develop a wide variety of social security provisions, which protect workers against the hardships of a market economy. Although, therefore, direct government intervention in the Dutch economy is fairly limited, government involvement is quite high because of the very extensive social security system. This system provides generous benefits for many groups in society, including the unemployed, pensioners, sick and disabled workers and in general for every person without means of subsistence. Virtually no one is excluded; the Dutch welfare system provides 'care from cradle to grave'. It is the main reason why an underclass and social exclusion did not emerge in the Netherlands. The Dutch welfare state contributed to a large extent to an integrated society without extreme social tensions and extreme crime rates. It is assumed to be a major explanation for the social and political stability in the country. The latter can be considered as a positive element for the business environment as well.

The social security system clearly has its price too, however. It has given rise to a huge public sector, which many argue has negative effects in terms of restraining development of the business sector, economic growth and employment. The problems became especially noticeable in the early 1980s, when the economy was in crisis, and the system was overburdened with claims. In 1983, total government expenditure amounted to 61% of GDP, a higher share than for all other EC countries in that respect (Table E28). Since then, successive Dutch governments have implemented strict austerity policies, aimed at reducing the size of the public sector and the overall burden of taxes and social security contributions. Decreasing the size of the public sector will remain a major issue for governments in the coming years, particularly as high taxes have a negative impact on Dutch competitiveness within the rapidly developing European internal market.

7.1.3 Trading nation

Another characteristic of the Netherlands, deeply rooted in its history, is the dominant position of trade and its related services in the economy. The central location of the Netherlands in Western Europe, at the mouth of the rivers Rhine, Meuse and Schelde, and surrounded by countries like England, Germany and France, created the optimal conditions for developing a trading nation. In its 'golden age' in the 17th century, Holland was one of the most important maritime nations. Nowadays, the seaport of Rotterdam is the biggest in the world, and is not only of importance for the Netherlands but also for the adjacent parts of Germany and generally as a transshipment harbour for bulk products and container transport. Schiphol (Amsterdam) Airport belongs in the top five European airports in terms of passenger and freight traffic handling. International distribution and transport services are thus prominent industries. In addition, the country has long been an international centre for financial and other trade related services.

Because of the fertile soil and the favourable climate, Dutch agriculture has always been a successful part of the economy. This sector has been developed by a rather unique combination of private farming, co-operation between producers, scientific research institutes and the government, and a good educational system. Manufacturing industry, on the other hand, has never played a dominant role in the Dutch economy.

7.1.4 Open economy

Because of its strong orientation to trade, the Dutch economy is one of the most open economies in the world. Exports and imports of goods and services amount to about 55% of GDP. Within the EC this figure is only surpassed by Belgium and Luxembourg. This openness, however, makes the Dutch economy very vulnerable to external developments such as recessions and especially protectionism. That is why it is of vital importance for the country to support free trade. For that reason, the Netherlands has always strongly advocated economic integration;

together with Belgium and Luxembourg it established a customs union in 1944 (*Benelux*) and it has been a member of the European Community right from the start in 1958. Its main competitive advantage lies in its geographical position, which can be best exploited in a Europe without frontiers.

7.2 MAIN ECONOMIC CHARACTERISTICS

7.2.1 Gross domestic product

Dutch performance in the field of growth in recent decades has not been particularly impressive. Before the first oil shock of 1973 real growth rates were on average about 5% per year, slightly ahead of the average of the twelve countries, which nowadays form the European Community. During the stagnation period of 1974–83 the real GDP growth rate dropped to 1.6%, which was below the EC average of 1.9%. In the period of economic recovery from 1984–90 the average growth rate of 2.7% was again surpassed by the average EC rate of 2.9% (Table E19 and Figure 7.1).

Moreover, between 1970 and 1991 the Dutch population increased by 15.6%, almost double the rate of growth for the EC as a whole (8.8%).

The combined result of these developments was that the Netherlands has been losing its place as one of the richest EC countries. GDP per head of population (average = 100) fell from 113.0 in 1970 (third highest) to only 101.7 in 1991 (seventh place; Table E20). The country has been overtaken by countries like Belgium, Italy and Denmark. The main reasons for the deterioration of the Dutch position are the vulnerability of the economy with respect to international disturbances and the inability of the highly developed welfare state to cope with economic crises and mass unemployment and to generate enough jobs. These subjects will be discussed in more detail in sections 7.3 and 7.5.

7.2.2 Population and employment

The Netherlands is a very crowded country with in 1992 15.2 million people living on 42,000 km². The population density of 362 inhabitants per square kilometre – the highest within the EC – puts great pressure on natural resources and the environment. Land is very scarce and the country is confronted with a serious pollution problem.

Although the figure for the labour force as a percentage of total population is in line with the EC average (see Table E15), the participation rate is rather low if measured in terms of full-

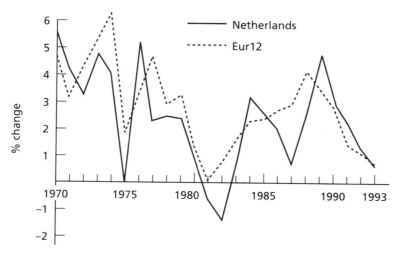

Figure 7.1 GDP at constant market prices, 1970–92. (National currency; annual percentage change.)

time jobs. Employment in 1990 (in terms of worker years) as a percentage of the population between 15 and 64 years was equivalent to 49% in the Netherlands, 57% in France, 61% in Germany, 62% in the United Kingdom and 67% in Denmark. Only countries like Ireland, Spain and Greece show lower or similar levels of employment. Labour participation is clearly an issue of concern in the Netherlands. The difference between the figures in terms of persons and those in working years is caused by the high degree of part-time employment, especially among women.

Important factors contributing to the modest participation rate (in terms of working years) are:

- The low participation rate of women. Until the 1960s Holland was a quite conservative country, with clear distinctions between the role of both sexes. Since then, many cultural changes have taken place, which have resulted in more and more women taking paid jobs. The process is continuing; women still have some way to go before they catch up with males and also with women in other EC countries.
- The relatively high number of (long-term) *unemployed* and – even more important – the large number of *disabled workers*. Holland is striking for the sheer size of its disabled population; particularly given that it is one of the world's best performers in terms of health indicators. The way the social security system is operated (considered below) provides a major explanation for this phenomenon.

The above two factors, in turn, are heavily influenced by the *low employment level*. The Dutch economy does not generate an adequate number of jobs. This situation discourages women from joining the workforce and puts upward pressure on unemployment and the hidden unemployment component in disablement.

Major explanations for the low employment level are:

1 Structural problems. The profitability of the Dutch business sector has been relatively low for a long period. Labour costs have been high, mainly due to high taxes and social security contributions. Although profitability recovered strongly during the upswing in the second half of the 1980s, it still remains a matter of great concern. New recessions can easily result in new upward pressures on labour costs via increasing social security contributions. Apart from this, Dutch firms are too heavily involved in industrial activities with a rather low or moderate technological content. Demand growth is rather weak for these sectors.

2 The social security system and the functioning of the labour market. The social security system offers little incentives for people to re-enter the labour market. Most of the unemployed receive benefits – if they have to maintain a family – on the net social assistance (welfare) level, which is practically the same as the net minimum wage. Disablement schemes are frequently used as an alternative to unemployment benefit programmes. The programme offers an easy route for firms wishing to reduce the size of their workforce; poorly performing workers can – if they are prepared to co-operate and after a period of sickness – be declared partially or totally disabled. The origins of disablement do not necessarily have to be related to the workplace itself: sport accidents, psychological problems or a deterioration of general health equally qualify. So, in contrast to general practice in most other countries, both professional and social risks are covered by the disability insurance laws. In 1993 the Netherlands expects to have 0.95 million persons receiving disablement benefits, compared to a total workforce of 7.3 million and a population of 15.2 million. In reality the disablement programme contains a huge unemployment component. Moreover, unemployment and disablement programmes hardly push people to search for new job opportunities or to participate in (re) training schemes. There is a strong tendency to stay for a long time, or even permanently, in the social security system (a phenomenon

known as the 'social security trap'). As noted, the social security contributions necessary to finance the programmes drive up labour costs, causing structural problems in turn.

3 Rigidities in the labour market. The Dutch labour market does not work very efficiently. Reasons for this are:

- The high level of minimum wage, preventing the labour market from clearing at the lower end. This means that an excess supply of low-skilled workers will not be eliminated by decreasing wages to levels appropriate for these categories.
- The strongly centralised collective bargaining system, in which employers associations, trade unions and the government participate, results in rather inflexible wage levels which adapt only slowly to new market conditions.
- Lay-off restrictions, allowing firing of employees by employers only in case of 'economic necessity'.

The lack of efficiency in the labour market is also indicated by the relatively strong sectoral mismatch. Persistent unemployment exists alongside a substantial number of vacancies.

4 Sensitiveness to cyclical disturbances. The Dutch economy generally responds sharply to (international) recessions, as in the beginning of both the 1980s and the 1990s. While this can be explained partly by the high degree of openness of the economy, the generous social security system plays its part. During recessions labour costs rise quickly because of the rapidly augmenting social security claims. This usually leads to a decline in competitiveness, an increase in the public deficit and/or erosion of the profitability of the business sector; especially if the recession persists for any length of time.

Unemployment and disablement do not have only negative aspects. The other side of the coin is that labour productivity is very high in the Netherlands; internationally it is only surpassed by the productivity of US workers. This situation is partly due to the inherent selection process of the social security system.

7.2.3 Consumption, savings and investment

Private and collective consumption (in terms of GDP) in the Netherlands have been below the EC average for a considerable time (see Tables E21 and E24). Investment, however, has been generally in line with the EC average during the last decade (Table E25). The difference in the use of GDP is made up by the high export surplus of the Netherlands (equivalent to 5.1% of GDP, see Table E21), indicating that the Dutch economy normally has a huge national savings surplus.

Business investment recovered strongly in the 1980s averaging around 20% during the decade. Although this rate seems normal by international standards, there are nevertheless some worries about this figure. First, compared to Japan (more than 30% in the beginning of the 1990s) and other fast developing East-Asian countries this proportion is rather low. Second because of its extreme openness, international competitiveness is of vital importance to the Dutch economy. One of the strongest features of the Netherlands is its high labour productivity, which is expected to offset high labour costs. Investment should be a major instrument in achieving this goal.

Government involvement in the economy is considered to have been unhelpful in this respect. Too large a part of government expenditure has been used for consumption. These expenses have been financed in a substantial part by revenues from natural gas, which alternatively could have been used to finance government spending on infrastructure for instance, or on (subsidies for) Research & Development. The present Dutch government has decided, however, to give more priority to investments in infrastructure, which will partly be financed by means of a special 'Natural Gas Fund'.

Finally, it should be noted that massive government borrowing to finance the public deficit may have caused the 'crowding out' of private investment.

Another factor contributing to the moderate investment ratio is the large and persistent national savings surplus. According to the OECD, outward investment in 1990 represented 4.5% of GDP, the highest proportion among all OECD countries and roughly equal to the business savings surplus in that year. The Netherlands has become an important foreign investor, with a net creditor position of around 26% of GDP in 1989. With the exchange rate firmly pegged to the Deutschmark, no correction can be expected from a strong appreciation of the guilder. However, it would be much more beneficial for the Dutch economy if part of the national savings surplus was invested in the domestic economy, especially in light of the fact that a substantial part of the labour force is unemployed. In response, over the last decade or so successive Dutch governments have pursued policies designed to improve the general investment climate by promoting wage moderation, reducing taxes, deregulation, etc.

7.2.4 Wages and prices

The level of wages and prices is of crucial importance to the competitiveness of the Dutch economy. Since the economic crisis in the early 1980s, Dutch governments have given priority to policies aimed at *moderating wage increases*. Part of this approach was an attempt to decrease the collective burden of taxes and social security contributions. In line with these policies, employers and unions agreed in 1982 to give job creation priority over wage increases. In addition, more room was created for decentralised wage negotiations and wage differentiation at branch and company level.

These policies appear to have been quite effective. In the second half of the 1980s productivity rose much more than real wages, resulting in a reduction in real unit labour costs. This reduction was more marked than in most other EC countries, Japan and the US. Holland was only surpassed by Portugal, Ireland and Spain in this respect (see Table E23).

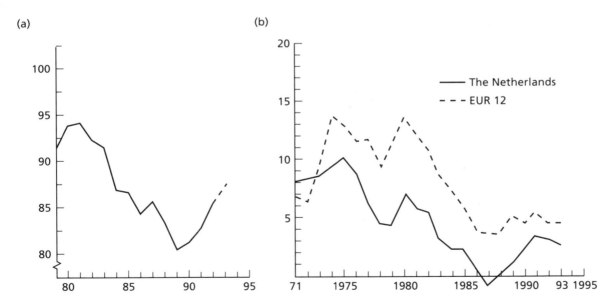

Figure 7.2 (a) Wage share in value-added (non-energy) business sector; (b) Inflation (price deflator private consumption).

Source: (a) *Centraal Economisch Plan 1993*; (b) *European Economy*, No. 54. 1992/1993 estimates.

The wage share in value-added of the (non-energy) business sector decreased from 94.2% in 1981 to 80.4% in 1989 (see Figure 7.2(a)), leading to a significant recovery in the capital share in value-added and the profitability of firms. For all that, the hourly labour costs in industry are still very high; by the end of the 1980s, within the EC, Holland was only surpassed by Germany. On the other hand, the country is, as noted above, the best performer in terms of labour productivity within the EC.

In relation to *the reduction in inflation*, the Netherlands has been even more successful (see Figure 7.2(b) and Table E27). The country had by far the lowest inflation in the 1980s, even surpassing Germany. The gain in competitiveness resulting from decreasing unit labour costs and a negative inflation differential *vis-à-vis* other industrialised countries has been partly offset, however, by repeated revaluations of the guilder. Nevertheless, good progress has been made, resulting in a steady increase in investment and employment.

Forecasts for the first half of the 1990s, on the other hand, are rather gloomy. The wage share in value-added is expected to rise again (and business profitability to fall), erasing a substantial part of the progress made in the 1980s. Moreover, since 1990 inflation has begun to rise once again and the Central Planning Bureau predicts a considerable increase in unemployment.

7.2.5 Economic structure

As can be seen from Table 7.1, services (market and non-market) are by far the most important economic activity in the Netherlands. In terms of employment it is the biggest service sector of all EC countries.

The relative size of the service sector is a reflection of the importance of the Netherlands as a trading nation and distribution centre and of the fact that a relatively large proportion of national income is devoted to non-market services like health care, education and social services.

Table 7.1 Sectoral shares for value added, employment and labour productivity growth, 1990[1]

	Value added	Employment	Labour productivity growth, 1974–90 av
Agriculture and food	10.0	10.2	4.7
Manufacturing	19.3	18.4	3.3
Energy	6.8	1.5	0.7
Construction	7.2	8.7	0.8
Market services	45.9	46.3	1.8
Non-market services	10.8	14.9	0.2
Total	100.0	100.0	2.0

[1] Because of the use of different statistical definitions, the figures in Table 7.1 differ from the (standardised) figures presented in Tables E16 and E22.

Source: Netherlands Scientific Council for Government Policy (1993), *Shaping Factors for the Business Environment after 1992.*

Figure 7.3 illustrates the prominent role of the Netherlands as a distribution centre and transit port. The port of Rotterdam and Schiphol airport play a crucial role in this transit trade. The Netherlands likes to present itself as 'the' *Gateway to Europe*, as part of an effort to attract investors from outside the EC. Apart from direct trade services, like harbour facilities, transport and communication, the country has obtained a strong position in other business services, e.g. financial services and information technology. A comparative advantage of the Netherlands, apart from its geographical location, is its strong international orientation. Most Dutch people speak several foreign languages and are used to international contacts. With the growing internationalisation of the world economy this is clearly an advantage.

The role of *manufacturing industry* is more modest in the Netherlands. The most important industries are chemicals and electrical, metal and mechanical engineering. The chemical sector, the biggest one in terms of value added, is heavily involved in bulk products and very

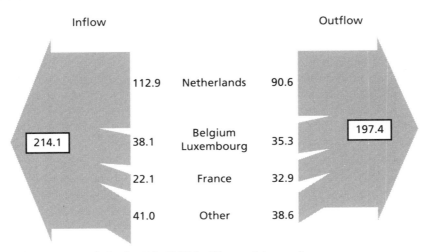

Inflow   Outflow

	Netherlands	
112.9	Netherlands	90.6
214.1		197.4
38.1	Belgium Luxembourg	35.3
22.1	France	32.9
41.0	Other	38.6

Figure 7.3 Flows of transit goods in the EC; 1987 (millions of tonnes).

Source: Miljoenennota 1993/CPB Onderzoeksmemorandum 97.

much internationally oriented. In addition, oil refineries are found around the port of Rotterdam. The geographical location of the Netherlands and its efficient transport facilities (e.g. its waterways) explain to a great extent the development of these industries. Major Dutch firms in this field with headquarters in the Netherlands are AKZO and DSM (Chemicals) and Royal Dutch/Shell (oil business). Electrical engineering is the second largest branch of manufacturing industry. It is dominated by Philips, one of the world's biggest producers in this field, which has its headquarters in the Netherlands. The metal and metal products industry occupy the third place (in terms of value added). Small and medium-sized companies dominate this industry.

Generally, it is considered that the technological level of Dutch manufacturing industry is not high enough (see also section 7.5). In the field of Research & Development the Netherlands is a rather average performer. Nevertheless, Dutch efforts have been increased in recent years, after years of underachievement. Expenditure on R&D as a percentage of GDP at the end of the 1980s was lower than in Japan, the USA and Germany, but higher than in most of the smaller countries. Most of the R&D (more than 50%) is realised by 'the big five' Dutch multinationals

(Shell, Unilever, Philips, AKZO and DSM), though their share is decreasing. R&D efforts of the smaller companies are clearly rising.

Agriculture and its related *food industry* constitute the typical success story of the Dutch economy. The Netherlands occupies second position as a world exporter of agricultural products, after the USA. Food products contribute 20% of total exports of goods – the second largest export category. Several factors have contributed to the impressive performance of Dutch agriculture. Natural conditions are quite favourable and private family farming guarantees a high degree of competition and motivation. On the other hand, there is traditionally extensive co-operation between Dutch farmers. For instance, in the field of milk processing, banking, purchasing and selling, farmers operate co-operatives to promote their common interests. Furthermore, with the aid of government sponsorship, research and educational institutes, information services on the one hand and farmers on the other hand closely co-operate.

There are, however, clear threats currently facing Dutch agriculture. First, there are environmental constraints. The pressure on the environment from intensely industrialised agriculture concentrated in a small area are enormous. The sector is confronted, for instance, with a huge manure waste problem, one of the major sources of acidification. Second, there are overcapacity problems, which could persist given EC policies. Changes in the CAP, induced by GATT talks, are likely in the near future, however. Prospects for cattle breeding and grain farming look somewhat gloomy; although forecasts relating to horticulture are more optimistic.

Until recently the *market structure* was not characterised by a high degree of concentration in most industries. Although a handful of large multinationals originated from the Netherlands, small and medium-sized enterprises prevailed. Only in industries like steel, electrical engineering, chemicals, mining and quarrying, aircraft and food and drink does big business dominate. European integration, however, resulted in a strong impulse towards a further concentration. Many mergers have resulted, for instance, in the banking and insurance sector. Competition law is rather weak in the Netherlands, even allowing mergers which virtually lead to a dominant position on the domestic market. For mergers across borders, the much stricter EC regulations apply. Likewise, cartels in the Netherlands are generally not forbidden, resulting in all kinds of co-operation between firms.

Nonetheless, large parts of Dutch industry have remained unaffected by concentration movements so far; small and medium-sized enterprises are still an important feature of the Dutch economy. The total number of enterprises increased from 460,000 in 1985 to 581,000 in 1992; 498,000 of them employed less than five workers and only 4,800 more than 100 workers. SMEs still dominate the commercial and non-commercial services, construction industry, transport and communication, hotel and catering and parts of manufacturing.

7.3 GOVERNMENT INVOLVEMENT IN THE ECONOMY

The Netherlands does not have a tradition of direct state intervention in the economy. The country has never possessed a large state enterprise sector and the government's involvement with industrial and regional policies has always been relatively limited. There are two areas, however, where the government has played a very explicit role, namely in the fields of wage determination and social security provision.

7.3.1 Wage determination

The wage negotiation process in the Netherlands is initially conducted at a central level, where employers associations, trade unions and the government participate in the bargaining process. Sometimes these negotiations result in central agreements. Such agreements contain general guidelines for the subsequent negotiations between employers and employees at industry, branch or (large) company level. The collective labour agreements concluded at this level can be (and normally are) declared binding for all firms by the Minister of Social Affairs and Employment.

The whole process of decision making is based on a neo-corporatist model of tripartite consultation. In fact, co-operation and mutual consultation prevail over conflicts and strikes as a method of decision making. The government influences the bargaining process by means of persuasion and also by manipulating, for example, the rates of payroll taxes and social security contributions. The outcome of the process is intended to be consistent with actual government policy, particularly as the government will be confronted directly with the results, since many benefits are related to the wage level. This means that the level of public expenditure is evidently affected by the outcome of the bargains.

Co-operation between the social partners and government is not only limited to wage negotiations. There are numerous administrative bodies and councils which are run on a tripartite basis. The most important one is *the Social Economic Council (Sociaal Economische Raad – SER)*, consisting of representatives of employers, employees and independent experts assigned by the government. The government has legal obligations to consult this council before taking any decision in the socio-economic field.

The above system of industrial relations was largely established immediately after the Second World War, although its roots stem from even earlier. The dominance of religion in the social and political field offers a major explanation for the emergence of this neo-corporatist system. In recent decades it has weakened, however. The major advantage of the system is that it is a rather efficient method of bargaining, avoiding class conflicts and devastating strikes. Moreover, it offers the government a clear instrument for influencing the economy. On the other hand, it lacks flexibility and does not always produce results with are in line with the prevailing market conditions. It is expected that, over the coming years, the system will be loosened so as to give more room for flexibility and decentralisation.

7.3.2 The social security system and the public sector

As mentioned above, the core of the Dutch welfare state is a comprehensive statutory system of social security. The construction of this system took place largely during the 1950s and 1960s: a time of high economic growth and virtually no unemployment. The high birth rates resulted in a favourable demographic composition, with relatively few pensioners. The population was assumed to be pretty healthy. It was not foreseen at that time that the system would have to cope with mass unemployment and an ageing population. On the contrary, it was anticipated that the number of persons entitled to social security benefits would be limited. For instance, when the *Disablement Benefit Act* came into force in 1968, it was only expected that at most 100,000 persons (in the long run) would be eligible for an allowance.

From the moment that the economic crisis of the 1970s set in, it became clear, however, that the system would be overburdened with claims. As a result, the total expenditure of general government went up very rapidly (see Figure 7.4). Almost all the rise from 42.4% of GDP in 1970 to 61.0% in 1983 can be explained by the rise in

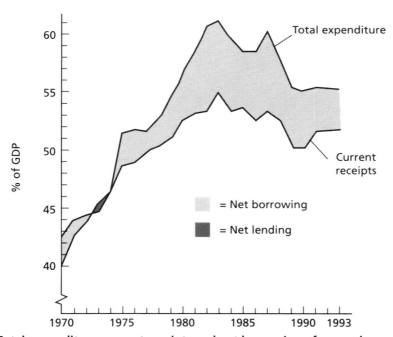

Figure 7.4 Total expenditure, current receipts and net borrowing of general government, 1970–92.

Source: Eurostat, European Economy 1993, No. 54 (see also Tables E28 and E29). 1992, 1993: estimates.

transfer incomes (including interest payments). Current receipts increased, though by a smaller amount, causing the public deficit to rise (to 6.4% of GDP in 1983).

Nevertheless, payroll taxes, social security contributions (and other taxes) had to be substantially increased in order to fill the gap. This in turn drove up labour costs, undermining Dutch competitiveness and the profitability of firms, causing further unemployment and so on. Although the origins of the recession were mostly external (the oil shock, international monetary and trade problems), the problems were made much worse by the structure of the Dutch economy. It is understandable, therefore, why successive governments, since the first centrist-right government under Prime Minister Lubbers came into power in 1982, have made budget cuts, reductions in social security expenses and public deficits their first priority. The substitution of the right-wing liberals by left-wing social democrats did not make any difference in this respect.

The need to bring down public expenditure and the public deficit was furthermore reinforced by the European integration movement in general and the Maastricht Treaty of 1991 in particular. According to the EMU convergence criteria, the public deficit should be reduced to 3% of GDP and the national debt to 60%. Holland seems to be on target to achieve this. The public deficit is estimated to become 3.25% in 1993 and the national debt – currently about 80% of GDP – has ceased to rise. Nonetheless, public finance is and will remain a matter of concern for Dutch governments.

7.4 FINANCIAL SYSTEM

7.4.1 Financial markets

Traditionally, Amsterdam has been an important financial centre. Although its stock market is rather small compared with London, Paris or Frankfurt, it is quite large in relation to the size of the country. In the early 1990s the capitalisation of shares amounted to almost half of the

Dutch GNP, while bonds amounted to another 50% GNP. After the UK (with a total stock market capitalisation of around 75%) the Netherlands has by far the highest proportion of investment financed through the stock market. In France, Germany, Italy and Spain (with respective stock market capitalisations of approximately 21, 22, 12 and 18% in that period) financing through the banking sector is much more important. The bond market is mainly called upon by the government to finance its budget deficits.

In addition to the stock market there is a parallel market providing access to venture capital for smaller firms. In the early 1980s Amsterdam lost a considerable part of the business to its competitors, mainly to London. Since 1986, however, several measures have been taken to deregulate the market and to increase efficiency and to reduce the costs of financial intermediation. Part of the trade has returned in recent years.

On the demand side, the stock market is strongly dominated by four large international firms (Royal Dutch, Unilever, Philips and AKZO). They account for about 40% of total share turnover. The bond market is dominated by the government, which absorbed, for instance, 78% of net bond lending in 1991.

On the supply side of the capital market, institutional investors like insurance companies, pension funds and social insurance funds are the major players accounting for 45% of total net supply in 1991. The banking (23.5%), foreign (15%), and household and business sector (14%) are far less important. The dominant position of institutional investors stems partly from the high degree of contractual savings in the Netherlands. This is also the major reason why the Netherlands has a very high savings ratio (see sections 7.2 and 7.5).

Although the banking sector is not the most prominent participant in the capital market it is nevertheless quite well developed. It shows a high degree of concentration. The two largest banks (in terms of balance sheet total), the Algemene Bank Nederland (ABN) and the Amsterdam-Rotterdam Bank (AMRO) merged in 1991 to form the new giant ABN AMRO. In 1990, the so-called 'structure policy' rule forbidding mergers between banks and insurance was liberalised. Henceforth only a declaration of 'no-objection' from the Central Bank (*De Nederlandsche Bank – DNB*) is required. This change enabled a merger in 1991 between the second largest bank, NMB-Postbank, with a large insurance group, the Nationale Nederlanden, into a new financial conglomerate called Internationale Nederlanden Groep bv (ING-bank). The third bank, RABO, obtained a large stake in another big insurance group. The top three banks (ABN AMRO, ING and RABO) now have between them well over 80% of the combined balance sheet total of the country's banking sector. Compared with other banks in the EC they are still only middle-sized.

7.4.2 Monetary policy

The main objective of monetary policy in the Netherlands is the maintenance of internal and external stability of the national currency, the guilder. In the last decade the stress has shifted more and more towards exchange rate stability, however. There are two basic reasons for this. First, external relations are of major importance to the Dutch economy. A stable guilder, strictly pegged to the Deutschmark, is an absolute condition for stable trade relations. Second, the ability to control inflation by monetary policy has diminished very significantly in the last decade. The liberalisation of capital markets and the marked increase in international capital mobility loosened the grip of the monetary authorities on the money supply, especially the external component of it. Besides, it would appear that a substantial increase during the second half of the 1980s in the national liquidity ratio (M2/net national income), which was the old target variable of monetary policy, did not really result in an upward pressure on inflation. The business sector used the newly created liquidity mainly to increase its financial soundness. The relation between the money supply (M2) and inflation seems, therefore, rather weak.

In fact, the Netherlands has already had a de facto monetary union with Germany for ten years, with the guilder firmly pegged within a margin of ± 1% to the Deutschmark. The justification for this policy is twofold. First, Germany is by far the most important trading partner for the Netherlands, counting for almost 30% of its total exports. Second, the German authorities have a very strong commitment to price stability. This guarantees – via a stable guilder–mark exchange rate – a stable price level in the Netherlands as well. The exchange rate policy is backed up by a policy which aims to control domestic money creation. This policy should prevent problems of excessive money growth, leading to large capital outflows and hence downward pressure on the exchange rate. Last but not least, the Treasury and the central bank agreed in 1981 to avoid monetary financing of the public deficit.

The main policy instrument used for exchange rate stability is the interest rate. The Dutch central bank (*De Nederlandsche Bank, DNB*) closely follows the German interest rate policy. Only in special circumstances, e.g. in 1992 and 1993 when the guilder was very strong, does the central bank alter the interest rates independently of the Bundesbank. In addition to changes in the official interest rates (e.g. discount rates), DNB mostly uses open-market operations to influence market interest rates. Open-market operations in combination with mandatory cash/reserve requirements and mandatory deposits at the central bank can also be used to squeeze the monetary base of the banking sector, which will prevent excessive domestic money creation.

To conclude this section, it can be seen that the Dutch monetary authorities have been very successful with respect to both external and internal price stability. Inflation in the Netherlands has been the lowest of all EC countries in the last decade, even lower than Germany. The Dutch guilder is – together with the mark – the strongest currency in the EC. The country will probably easily satisfy the EMU criteria in this respect.

7.5 INTERNATIONAL RELATIONS

As has been noted, The Netherlands has an extremely open economy. The average (goods

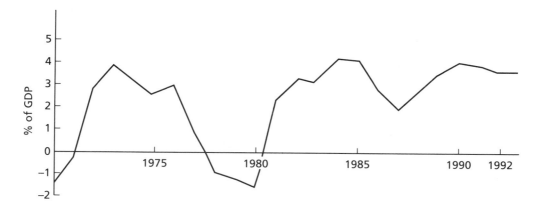

Figure 7.5 The Dutch current account balance, 1970–93. Surplus (+) or deficit (–) as a percentage of GDP. 1992, 1993: estimates.

Source: European Economy, 1993, No. 54.

and services) exports level amounted to 48.7% in the 1970s and went up to 57.5% in the 1980s. The corresponding figures for the average import levels were 47.1% and 53.2%. As a result, the country normally has a large and persistent current account surplus (see Figure 7.5).

Part of the current account surplus is due to the extraction of natural gas, which is an important export good and also a substitute for energy imports. But even when energy is excluded, there usually remains an impressive trade and current account surplus. Although the latter surplus is usually substantially offset by a huge capital account balance deficit (meaning an outflow of money), the overall balance of payments in most years shows a surplus. That is one of the reasons why the Dutch currency, the guilder, has tended to revalue against the ECU.

The traditional low inflation rate together with high productivity are the main causes of the competitiveness of Dutch industry. The Dutch position was, however, severely affected by the steep increase of labour costs in the early 1980s, caused by the combination of an economic depression and generous social security provisions (see section 7.3). Since then, Dutch competitiveness has improved substantially, especially in the second half of the 1980s. The

Netherlands was the most successful of all EC countries in bringing its relative unit labour costs down (measured in a common currency): from 100 in 1980 to 80.5 in 1991 (index figures). Government austerity policies and wage moderation are the major explanations for this achievement. Dutch unit labour costs remain a matter of concern, though, because labour costs once more started to rise quite sharply during the recession in the early 1990s.

7.5.1 Geographical orientation and composition of trade

The bulk of Dutch exports (76.2% in 1991) is directed at other EC countries. The emergence of the EC had a clear effect on this trade diversion: in 1958 only 58.3% of total exports went to the twelve states which now make up the EC. The neighbouring countries are by far the most important trading partners: 29.3% of total exports go to Germany, 14.2% Belgium/Luxembourg, 10.6% France and 9.3% the UK (see Table E32). The same holds, more or less, for imports, although the percentage of imports originating from EC countries (60% in 1991) does not match the export figure (76.2%). Germany is the largest exporter to the Netherlands (23.5%) followed by Belgium/Luxembourg (13.0%), the UK (8%) and France (7%) (see Table E33).

The composition of the Dutch commodity exports is as follows: 23.5% machinery and transport equipment, 19.7% food and drink, 16.1% chemicals, 14% manufactured goods, 9.9% energy, 5.5% raw materials and 11.8% other goods (1991). A striking feature is the high proportion of food, drink, energy and raw materials (together 34.6%) in total exports; in addition, a substantial part of the chemical products consists of basic bulk products. There are some serious concerns about the specialisation of Dutch industry, e.g. that it is too focused on primary products with a rather low technological content. If Dutch industry wants to maintain its strong export position, it needs to shift towards more knowledge-intensive, high-tech production. Investment would be a key factor in this process.

7.6 SPECIAL ISSUE: ENVIRONMENTAL POLICY

For a number of reasons, environmental issues play a very important part in the Netherlands. First, the Netherlands is a very small and over-crowded country. As a result the pressure on the environment from economic activities, especially from manufacturing, agriculture, transport and buildings is very high. Second, Dutch industry consists substantially of activities which involve energy-intensive and polluting processes. This applies especially to the chemical industry, which produces noxious emissions and toxic waste, and to the highly industrialised agriculture, with its enormous manure waste problem and its very intensive use of fertilisers. Third, there is a growing awareness on the part of the Dutch population of environmental problems, resulting in strong political support for environmental policies.

As a result, the second Lubbers government introduced in 1989 the so-called *National Environmental Policy Plan (NEPP)*. This plan aimed at achieving 'sustainable growth', which would not lead to a depletion of natural resources and

environmental damage. It argued that the full costs of production and consumption should be borne by the present generation; unpaid environmental bills should no longer be transferred to future generations.

Measures were proposed designed to prevent the passing on of external costs by levying taxes on polluting activities. To avoid an excessive use of natural resources, an energy tax was proposed as well. However, the second Lubbers cabinet, had to resign in late 1989 because the Parliament did not agree with the proposed financing of the NEPP. The third Lubbers government (backed up by Christian Democrats and Social Democrats) came up with a revised plan though one with similar aims: the *National Environmental Policy Plan Plus (NEPP-Plus)*. The '*NEPP-Plus*' merely constitutes a strategic framework for environmental policy, while concrete action and related costs are incorporated in an annually revised *Environmental programme*, which has an advancing horizon. The expected total costs for 1995 amount to about 17 billion guilders (around 3% of GDP).

The stress in the *NEPP-Plus* has been put on market-conforming measures rather than on rules and regulations. Undesirable behaviour should be discouraged by financial instruments, such as levies and taxes. The basic idea involves the internalisation of external costs. A hotly debated issue in this respect has been the introduction of the so-called *ecotax*, which is designed to decrease the use of energy and noxious emissions (e.g. CO_2-emissions). In order to prevent an increase in the collective burden, it was proposed to decrease the taxes levied on labour. This policy should result in a shift from polluting and energy-intensive production to a more labour- and knowledge-intensive one. Employment should benefit from this policy as well.

Many questions have been raised, however, regarding the effectiveness of such a tax. Either it will generate enough revenue to replace revenue lost as a result of lower payroll taxes, but it will have no effect on the behaviour of industry and consumers then; or it will result in a change in this behaviour, but in this case the tax receipts will not replace revenue lost from lower payroll taxes.

Notwithstanding this discussion, it is very risky for a small country like the Netherlands to deviate too much from the policies in the surrounding countries. Such policies can significantly distort competition. That is why the Netherlands has been fiercely promoting the idea of a combined CO_2/Energy tax within the framework of the EC. This is done on the grounds that such a tax would avoid distortion of competition and is in the general interest given that acid rain and the greenhouse effect and many other forms of pollution do not stop at borders. The idea of an EC ecotax has been adopted by the EC Commission in the meantime as a cornerstone of the strategy aimed to reduce carbon-dioxide emissions.

7.7 FUTURE PROSPECTS

The future prospects of the Dutch economy appear moderate. The strong points are political stability, a low inflation record, the current account surplus and the strong and stable currency, the reduced budget deficit and the international orientation of the economy. The country would be one of the first candidates to enter the EMU (though its national debt is far too high still).

Unfortunately, there are structural imbalances as well. The most important are the low labour participation, the still high level of public expenditure and collective burden, the functioning of the social security system and, last but not least, the technological level of Dutch industry.

Recent governments, however, have shown their determination to reduce the size of the public sector and to restructure the social security system. If future governments succeed in doing so and, in addition, manage to create a more favourable environment for investment, it might be expected that labour participation too will increase. In that case there should be room for qualified optimism.

7.8 BIBLIOGRAPHY AND SOURCES OF INFORMATION

Official publications

Ministry of Finance: *Miljoenennota* (annually)
Central Planning Bureau (CPB): *Macro Economische Verkenning* (annually)
CPB: *Centraal Economisch Plan* (annually)
De Nederlandsche Bank: *Jaarverslag* (annually)
Central Statistical Office (CBS): *Statistisch Jaarboek* (annually)
Netherlands Scientific Council for Government Policy (1993), *Shaping Factors for the Business Environment in the Netherlands after 1992*
OECD, *Economic Surveys, The Netherlands* (annually)
Commission of the European Communities: *Country Studies, The Netherlands* (annually)

Other publications

Buunk, H. (1992): *De economie in Nederland*, Wolters-Noordhoff, Groningen
Compaijen/Den Butter (1991/1992): *De Nederlandse economie* (4 volumes), Wolters-Noordhoff, Groningen
CPB, FKSEC (1992): *A Macro-Econometric Model for The Netherlands*, Stenferd Kroese, Leiden
Koopmans, Wellink, Woltjer, De Kam (1991): *Overheidsfinanciën*, 7th edn. Stenferd Kroese, Leiden/ Antwerpen
Somers, F.J.L. (1993): *De economie van het overheidsbeleid*, Wolters-Noordhoff, Groningen

CHAPTER 8

Belgium/Luxembourg

Ian Stone

8.1 INSTITUTIONAL AND HISTORICAL CONTEXT

8.1.1 Political background

Belgium was formed as a European nation in 1830, when Dutch-speaking Flemings and French-speaking Walloons forged an alliance in opposition to Dutch (William I's) autocratic rule. The new buffer state kingdom was supported by other European powers and its neutrality guaranteed under the *Treaty of London* (1839). In spite of the understanding that the government should be made up of identical numbers of French and Flemish-speaking ministers, the act of governing has been rendered complex by a regional and linguistic split between the two large regions of Flanders and Wallonia, superimposed upon a conventional left–right span of views (Socialists, Christian Democrats, Liberals) in both communities. Belgium today remains an uneasy union of linguistically distinct regions to which power is being devolved in stages.

Political difficulties arising out of communal differences between the Flemings in the north of the country and the Walloons in the south – and the particular interests of Brussels (the French-speaking enclave in Flemish territory) – have eventually forced the process of devolution. Beginning in 1970 and still underway, devolution entails the effective dismantling of Belgium's unitary state. How far this process will go is still unclear. The Minister-President of the Flemish government, Mr Van den Brande, recently caused a storm when he argued that the reform of the Belgian state should evolve from a federation of regions and communities into two states within a confederal system. Yet there are powerful voices opposed to even taking federalism too far and several large anti-separatist demonstrations have been staged in recent months. Against the strident tones of separatist and nationalist politicians there is a clear majority in favour of federalism.

The 1980 regionalisation laws, which came into effect in 1982, involved the splitting of the country into three communities (French, Flemish and German-speaking) with responsibility over matters relating to the individual (education and culture), and into three geographically defined regions (Flanders, Wallonia and Brussels), each with powers relating to their specific territory. However, while Wallonia has separate councils to represent the region and the community, the Flemish communal and regional assembly and government are one and the same thing. Since 1988, Brussels has achieved similar status, having attained its own directly elected assembly and executive. The executives of these entities are autonomous from central government and have the power to prepare bills which, if they are passed by the assembly, become law.

The constitutional changes of 1970 and 1980 progressively pared away central government responsibilities, leaving just foreign affairs, defence, the constitution, social security, law, monetary policy and some elements of fiscal policy. The third (and final) phase of constitutional reform, drawn up in 1988, was directed towards the transfer of further spending powers to the regions and communities, including public works, research, communications, environmental protection, local economic development and energy. In addition, this reform sought to introduce direct elections for the Flemish and Walloon assemblies, to reform the upper house of parliament (the Senate), and to divide responsibility for international relations among the different institutions. The current four-party coalition of Socialist and Christian Democrat groups from each community commands only a simple majority, rather than the two-thirds of seats needed to carry through constitutional reform, and agreeing a workable formula in terms of the details of the reforms has been difficult.

For the analysis contained in this chapter, it is not possible to identify a consistent grouping of regions, since various forms of economic union exist with neighbouring states. Apart from being an EC member since the inception of the Comunity, Belgium is a signatory to a 1958 treaty of economic union with the Netherlands and Luxembourg (Benelux). Particularly close relations exist with Luxembourg, however. These are formalised through *BLEU (Belgium and Luxembourg Economic Union)*, involving parity of currencies, integrated foreign trade and payments and a joint central bank. In keeping with common practice, therefore, this country study incorporates Luxembourg – both as a separate section and within the section on trade and payments (where its statistics are integrated with those of Belgium).

8.1.2 Economic background

The Belgian economy performed well in the decade or so up to the time of the first oil shock. The country's central position within the EC, together with its well developed transport network, skilled labour force and government investment incentives, attracted substantial inward investment. An industrial structure developed which was notable for its concentration on a limited number of sectors and specialisation in standardised semi-finished goods. It was also highly dependent upon imported energy (80% in the early 1970s), with the result that it was badly affected by the oil price shocks of the 1970s, and Belgium's terms of trade deteriorated markedly. International competitiveness fell sharply as wage costs rose due to continued indexation, high pay awards and increased social security contributions. The public sector deficit increased as revenues declined and spending to combat unemployment – including the subsidisation of declining sectors – escalated. Moreover, the attempt to hold purchasing power at an artificially high level caused the balance of payments to move sharply into the red.

In 1982 the Socialists in the coalition were replaced by the Liberals. In recognition of the fact that consumption-supporting policies had become unsustainable, a new phase of policy was embarked upon; one which placed emphasis on encouraging enterprise. Central to this was the restoration of competitiveness through the devaluation (by 8.5% within the ERM) of the Belgian franc. To limit the acceleration of inflation, devaluation of the currency was combined with the introduction of an incomes policy and price controls. Public spending was reduced and the corporate tax burden eased. The austerity programme gave rise to a significant improvement in profit levels, encouraged a strong investment phase and generally improved economic performance during the later part of the 1980s. However, while most of the economic indicators have bounced back robustly since the mid-1980s, the economy still seems to be dogged by a stubbornly high rate of unemployment and by the level of public spending and indebtedness. Dealing with each of these problems is made more difficult by the recession conditions of the early 1990s.

8.2 ECONOMIC CHARACTERISTICS AND TRENDS

8.2.1 Gross domestic product

Belgium's overall real growth performance in the 1960s was, at almost 5% per year, fractionally ahead of the average annual EUR 12 rate, and the pace of expansion was maintained during the early 1970s (Table E19). From 1975 onwards, however, the growth became both erratic and, over the run of years, clearly below that of the EUR 12 average. Over the period 1975 to 1987, there were only three years in which the Belgian economy grew at the EUR 12 rate or above, and the average for these years was below 1.5% per year. This period encompasses the 1980s' austerity measures which paved the way for stronger growth performance during 1988–90, when the annual rate (4.1%) once more ran ahead of the EUR 12 average. Recession in its main export markets has contributed to slower expansion in the 1990s, with the rate falling to 1% in 1992 and 0.5% (forecast) in 1993.

GDP per head is somewhat above the EC average, by around 6% in 1992 (Table E20). This marks a gradual improvement over the period since the 1960s, when per capita income lagged behind all but one of the original EC Six. Belgium's average income is now bettered only by Luxembourg, (West) Germany, France and (marginally) Denmark.

8.2.2 Labour market and unemployment

Belgium is a small country, 280 kms across at its widest point, with a population of 9.9 million and a density of 325 persons per km². The population is divided unevenly between the different regions, with the largest share in Flanders (58%), followed by Wallonia (33%) and Brussels (9%). It has one of the lowest birth rates in the EC and numbers have risen only slowly (about 0.1% per annum during the 1980s). However, in spite of this, and a low rate of immigration since the mid-1960s, the population of working age has shown a pronounced increase and it is only because of a declining labour participation rate that the labour force has grown slowly over the past two decades (0.11% per year during the 1980s).

The civilian workforce of 4.12 million is relatively small in proportion to the total population (41% in 1990 compared to EUR 12 average of nearly 46%) and very substantially below the levels found in Denmark, UK and Germany in particular (Table E15). Male participation rates, which have long been below other EC countries, fell faster than elsewhere in the 1980s to finish the decade some eight percentage points below the EC average. Rising female participation rates have not eliminated the difference, and the 62% participation rate overall at the end of the 1980s was still some four percentage points below the EC average (and 14 points lower than in the UK).

Out of a total civilian employment force in 1990 of 3.72 million, only a small proportion (2.7%, second only to the UK within the EC) is engaged in agriculture, forestry and fishing. Industry accounted for nearly 29% of the total, of which nearly three-quarters of a million workers are in manufacturing (21% of total employment). While industry in general is a smaller employer in Belgium than in the EC as a whole (28.7% compared with 32.5%), the employment share of services, at 68.5%, is among the highest in the Community and well above the EUR 12 average of 61% (Table E16). Belgian public sector employment, although falling back slightly in recent years, is up by 40% compared with 1970 and stands at 0.9 million, or just under one-quarter of total employment.

The trends in participation rates reflect structural changes both in the economy and labour market policies. The decline in industrial employment and expansion of job opportunities – many of them for part-timers – in services has favoured women. Indeed, the growth in total employment in the 1980s was entirely due to an increase in part-time employment (which has doubled since 1975). Legislation giving part-time workers the same rights (e.g. social security) as full-time workers has encouraged the growth of part-time working. At the same time, other government policies contained labour supply growth in the 1980s, e.g. compulsory education (up to the age of 18) and early retirement schemes, and the latter were particularly important in encouraging males to withdraw from the labour force.

Even though growth in the labour force has been slow, unemployment is a persistent problem, reflecting the low rate of growth of employment since the mid-1970s (partly the result, it is widely argued, of the disincentive to job creation of the large tax wedge) and significant labour market rigidities (to which government policies have contributed). Belgium's unemployment rate of 10.7% during the 1980s was slightly higher than the EUR 12 average (9.6%). However, the rate fell during the course of the 1980s from its post-oil shock peak of 12.5% in 1984 down to 7.8% in 1990. The economy's relatively strong performance over these years (with an estimated 161,000 jobs created in the period 1984–9), combined with early retirement schemes, enabled Belgium to finish the decade with a jobless rate officially below the EUR 12 figure of 8.3% (Table E17). This situation still applies, although the rate crept up to over 9% by late 1992 with the onset of recession. These are, of course, standardised EC rates; Belgian official statistics put unemployment somewhat higher, at 12.4% in early 1993.

The unemployment level is strikingly uneven in its geographical distribution (see section 8.6) and includes a large proportion of long-term unemployed. In 1988, 78% of the unemployed had been without work for over a year – by far the highest among OECD countries – giving rise to problems of workers being cut off from the labour market and erosion of their skills. The problem is particularly acute among females, who made up 61% of the unemployed in 1989; a notably large proportion (by EC standards) of these are long-term unemployed married women. Female unemployment (12.2% in 1992) is slightly higher than the EUR 12 average, while – chiefly due to the withdrawal schemes – unemployment among males is more than two percentage points below the Community average (5.5% as against 8.1%).

In recent budgets, the government has been giving increasing attention to eliminating rigidities in the labour market. This includes the introduction of a system whereby each unemployed person under the age of 46 who has been out of work for nine months is given a 'guidance plan' involving vocational training and employment schemes. Belgian unemployment programmes have tended to be generous and easily accessible; now checking whether unemployed persons are genuinely available in the labour market is being intensified, as part of a policy of introducing more stringent entitlement criteria. There is also concern now that early retirement policies are encouraging experienced employees to leave the labour force at a time when there are fewer new entrants, with not only budgetary, but possibly supply-side implications for the economy. The response has been to institute a gradual rise in the early retirement age.

8.2.3 Consumption and investment

Private consumption as a percentage of GDP increased in the decade up to 1985, from 60% to 65.5%. Since that time it has been cut back, and stood in the early 1990s at 63%, which is only slightly above the EUR 12 average since 1980 (Table E24). This change has resulted from the government's austerity policies, which had as their aim the redistribution of income from the personal to the corporate sector in order to redress the balance between investment and consumption.

Investment has recovered since its collapse during 1979–83. During the 1960s and 1970s, gross fixed capital formation rates were consistently around 22%. By 1985 they had fallen to 15.6%. As a result of some of the largest gains in investment achieved anywhere in the EC in the late 1980s, by 1990 the annual overall investment rate was once more above 20% of GDP. Prominent within this was private non-residential fixed asset formation, which grew by 15% in 1988 and over 17% in 1989, compared to a percentage change for the EC as a whole which peaked at 10% in 1988. This performance is widely held to reflect the impact of wage restraint and improved terms of trade upon corporate profitability, combined with reductions in the company tax burden.

8.2.4 Wages and prices

To safeguard competitiveness and jobs, wage indexation and free wage negotiations were suspended for a number of years following the 1982 devaluation. Restraint of pay levels in the public sector was also exercised, with the effect of limiting earnings growth to half the levels achieved in the private sector. Real unit labour costs, which increased markedly in the 1970s, fell sharply in the years following 1982, and for the 1980s as a whole exhibited a greater fall than that recorded by EUR 12, USA or Japan (Table E23). Concern to maintain international competitiveness is built into Belgium's institutional framework relating to pay settlements. Under the terms of legislation introduced in 1989, the bipartite Central Economic Council has to monitor the economy's competitiveness against its main competitors. If the situation is deemed to have deteriorated, and the social partners (employers and unions) cannot agree on remedial action, then the government may take action (ultimately intervening in the wage indexation system).

Although labour costs per employee in common currency terms have been smaller in Belgium than the average for its EC partners during 1987–92, unit labour costs – that is, labour costs per unit of output – have increased at a rate somewhat above those in the neighbouring countries (which account for 60% of BLEU trade). This has recently given rise to expressions of concern from manufacturing associations over a wage cost gap with France and the Netherlands put at 25% and 15% respectively.

Wage controls have contributed to the achievement of low inflation levels (and vice versa). The annual rate increase in prices prior to the early 1980s' devaluation stood at around 8%, which was reasonable by EC standards but somewhat above the levels of neighbouring trading partners (Table E27). Tight policies in the period following devaluation led to low rates of inflation (just over 1% per annum) during 1986–8 which were shared only by West Germany, the Netherlands and Luxembourg. The late 1980s expansionary period saw the rate rise to just over 3%, which is very much in line with the main EC trading partners and still below the EUR 12 average of almost 5%, while in the early 1990s inflation has been comfortably below the EC average.

8.2.5 Market structure

In terms of output, agriculture contributes just over 2% of gross value added in the economy, the smallest in the EC next to the UK. The average size of holding is small (70% are under 20 hectares), and there is a concentration on livestock products and horticulture. No significant mining activity is undertaken, following the recent closure of the remaining loss-making coal mines. Manufacturing in 1989 accounted for 23% and services 65.5% of GDP. The contribution of services to output in Belgium is higher proportionally than anywhere in the EC apart from Denmark, and reflects in part the country's central role within the EC, NATO and multinational company administration, as well as significant levels of activity in areas of finance and transport/distribution.

Traditional industries such as iron and steel, non-ferrous metals, textiles and heavy engineering nowadays make a relatively small contribution to industrial output (around one-sixth). The sectors which now dominate manufacturing are chemicals (including bio-technology and pharmaceuticals), light engineering and food and drink. Belgian producers have increasingly concentrated upon the processing of raw materials and the production of semi-finished goods. The country has relatively limited capability in the areas of electronics (including computers), robotics and instrument engineering.

Belgium's strategic location and open economy – together with equal treatment accorded nationals and foreigners alike with respect to investment incentives, taxes and business laws – have encouraged significant levels of direct investment from overseas. Foreign corporations operating in Belgium account for one-third of all employment, with the largest proportion of investment coming from the US ($7.2 billion or 40% of the total in 1988). A most notable target of inward investors has been car assembly; between them Ford, GM, Renault, VW and Volvo employed around 44,000 workers in 1990. The development of Brussels as an important financial centre has also attracted foreign operators.

The economy is dominated by a small number of relatively large companies which, by means of an elaborate structure of holding companies and operational units, play a major role in almost every sector of industry, finance and trade. GBL (Groupe Bruxelles Lambert) and Société Génerale de Belgique are examples of such organisations; the latter is the country's largest with interests in almost a third of the corporate sector. Although the commercial banks are legally prevented from holding investments directly, they are closely involved with industrial and finance corporations through a system of interlocking shareholdings.

8.3 GOVERNMENT INVOLVEMENT IN THE ECONOMY

In Belgium, as in other countries, total expenditure by general government has risen as a proportion of GDP over time. This was especially the case after the oil shocks, when the state tried to maintain consumption despite a decline in real income, resulting in expenditure rising to 58% of GDP in 1981. It has since been progressively reduced to around 51%, which is only a percentage point or so above the EUR 12 level (Table E28). This reduction in expenditure has enabled the government to cut its net borrowing requirement, which rose through the 1970s to reach a high of 13.5% of GDP in 1981. Belgium's 1992 level of borrowing (equivalent to over 6.9% of GDP), although much reduced, is still high in that it is exceeded only by countries notorious for their inability to control public expenditure, Italy and Greece (Table E29), and means that government bond issues are a major factor in the Belgian capital market.

Part of the problem of the government deficit arises out of the sheer scale of accumulated public debt which, at 121% of GDP in 1992, is virtually double the average debt of EC members (see Figure 8.1). Not all of the threefold rise in

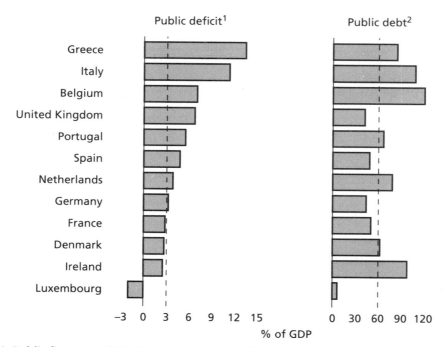

Figure 8.1 Public finances of EC Member States (1992).

1 Net financing requirement of general government as a percentage of GDP.
2 Harmonised public debt as a percentage of GDP.

Source: derived from National Bank of Belgium, *Report 1992*, p. 23

gross debt since 1970 is due to spending itself; the OECD estimates that half the gross debt is attributable to the 'snowball effect', i.e. the continued rise in the stock of public debt as a proportion of GDP in spite of a primary expenditure surplus, due to the burden of interest charges on the cumulative deficit. The primary balance of government has been transformed since 1981, when there was a deficit of 8.4%. More recently, as Table 8.1 shows, the net financing capacity (excluding interest charges) of government has been consistently in surplus (around 4% during 1987–92). However, annual interest payments equivalent to 11% of Belgium's GDP result in the government being left with a large net financing requirement. Government is aware of the need to bring the public deficit down to below 3.5% of GDP, in order to ensure the continuous reduction in the gross debt to GDP ratio and to escape from the situation where the burden of the stock of debt crowds out other public expenditure. Achievement of the Maastricht targets of PSBR (3%) and gross public debt (60%) is a long way off, particularly in the context of generalised recession, rising unemployment and welfare spending pressures.

There is limited scope for reducing the net borrowing requirement through increasing tax levels. Although the comparatively low revenue contribution from indirect taxes (including VAT) suggests opportunities for raising revenue, Belgium's overall tax burden is quite high with a larger proportion of GDP taken as tax (44.7%) than the EC on average (41.6%). In particular, taxes on household incomes and employers' social security contributions are both high by EC standards. Taxes on capital (corporate profits, property, estates) are more moderate when allowance is made for exemptions and deductions (which reduce the effective tax rate from 39% to 21%). However, given that the exemptions and reductions are specific instruments of policy (i.e. to encourage employment creation, investment, regional development and the attraction of headquarters functions of international companies), government is reluctant to interfere with these incentives. High marginal tax rates – the maximum personal rate is 58% – and inefficient administration has led to evasion and a substantial black economy. This helps explain why tax revenues in the 1980s have tended not to keep pace with income growth.

Cutting expenditure is also difficult. A significant reduction in public investment has been achieved over the course of the 1980s. However, the scale of this fall – from 3.6% of GDP in 1980 down to 1.4% in 1990 – makes only a relatively small contribution to solving the problem and yet threatens the quality of the country's infrastructure. There has been a substantial reduction in subsidies to business in the 1980s, mainly attributable to reduced aid to steel and shipbuilding. Belgium remains a heavy subsidiser by EC standards. This is due, however, to subsidies

Table 8.1 Net financing requirement of general government, Belgium 1987–92 (% of GDP)

	1987	1988	1989	1990	1991	1992
1 Revenue	49.2	47.5	45.9	46.6	46.6	47.0
2 Expenditure excluding interest charges	45.9	44.0	42.0	41.4	42.6	42.6
3 Net financing capacity excluding interest changes (= 1–2)	3.3	3.5	3.9	5.2	3.9	4.3
4 Interest charges	10.8	10.3	10.6	11.0	10.6	11.2
5 Net financing requirement (= 3–4)	–7.5	–6.8	–6.7	–5.8	–6.7	–6.9

Source: National Bank of Belgium, *Report 1992*, p. 76.

to retirement and medical-insurance programmes in the rail and coal sectors; otherwise subsidies are similar to levels elsewhere in the EC. Operating and investment subsidies have been reduced in respect of railways and ceased in relation to coal following the final closure of the mines. Heavy restraints on the pay of the nearly 20% of the employed workforce in the general government sector may prove a false economy, given the impact this policy is reputed to have had upon morale and effectiveness.

Social expenditure has tended to rise at a faster rate than the EC average, due to rapid increases in unemployment benefits, pensions and health expenditure. OECD figures show that during 1970–83 social expenditures rose from 13% to nearly 22% of GDP, with the subsidy (i.e. allowing for contributions) to the social security system increasing from 3% to 8.4% of GDP. While improvement in the labour market combined with spending controls helped the state reduce social expenditures to 18.7% in 1989 (and the subsidy to 4.7% of GDP), at the end of the 1980s, spending on social benefits as a percentage of public expenditure (excluding interest), at 52%, was still much higher than elsewhere (especially the United Kingdom 33%, West Germany 38%, and the Netherlands 40%).

Like other major EC economies, the government has found it especially difficult to curb health care spending. This is publicly financed and is not subject to market constraints; demand has increased due to pressure from both suppliers and consumers and its share of GDP rose during 1988–92 from 5.7% to 6.5%. Despite the rise, as a proportion of GDP, health care expenditure in Belgium is somewhat below the level in most of its EC neighbours.

8.4 FINANCIAL SYSTEM

Belgium and Luxembourg are joined in a monetary union; the currencies have parity and circulate freely in both states. The central bank, the *Bank Nationale de Belgique* (50% state-owned), is responsible for conducting monetary policy on behalf of the government. It administers interest rate policy largely through the manipulation of interest on Treasury certificates and, following a new banking law introduced in 1988, can require private banks to deposit with it compulsory reserves as circumstances dictate.

Reflecting its position as the location of the EC Commission headquarters, as well as numerous other public and private headquarters functions, Brussels has become a major financial centre within Europe. In particular, it has developed as the principal banking centre for private sector use of the ECU. Many foreign financial institutions have been attracted to the city, especially by the absence of regulations on capital movements. The Belgian banking sector is the most internationalised in the EC, after Luxembourg and the UK. Nearly half the total assets of the banking system – and two-thirds of the interbank business – is in the hands of foreign operators. In 1960, 67 out of 83 banks were domestically owned and controlled; in 1990 only 21 out of 86 were entirely in the hands of nationals. Belgian banks are not large in international terms; the biggest (Génerale Bank) only just figures in the world's top 100.

The Brussels stock exchange, while significant in terms of the number of foreign securities quoted, is relatively small and unmodernised, and restricts the further development of Brussels as a financial centre. Deregulation of financial markets, the further reduction of the withholding tax on bonds and dividends, and new financial instruments designed to attract foreign savers have been suggested as a means of increasing the volume of business carried out on the Brussels stock exchange.

The government has been engaged in recent years in deregulating the country's financial markets, with the aim, partly, of reducing its debt service costs and bringing monetary policy mechanisms (and the effectiveness of monetary intervention) into line with practices elsewhere in the Community. This has been done essentially by putting tight limits on the government's direct access to Banque Nationale credits and by enhancing competition in the market for public debt. Belgian banks effectively have had the monopoly over the market for government debt, since non-residents and resident non-financial businesses have not been allowed to buy Treasury certificates. The 1991 reforms involve weekly public auctions of Treasury certificates which will be available for purchase by others besides Belgian and Luxembourg financial intermediaries. The changes should both boost competition for government debt and lead to the development of a more active secondary market in public short-term debt.

8.5 INTERNATIONAL RELATIONS

8.5.1 Foreign trade

Due to the customs and economic union (BLEU), trade and payment accounts are amalgamated with those of Luxembourg. The economy is an extremely open one, with imports and exports each being equivalent to more than 60% of GDP (a proportion only exceeded within the EC by another small economy, the Netherlands). The high level of integration with other EC economies is reflected in the fact that 75% of exports from BLEU are to other member states. The main trading partners are the neighbouring continental countries of Germany, France and the Netherlands, which accounted for 57% of Belgium-Luxembourg's exports and 55% of imports in 1991 (Tables E32/33). Raw materials, energy and intermediate products make up a significant share of the imports, with an estimated 40% import content in exported items. There is still a significant proportion of relatively low value-added items (non-ferrous metals and iron and steel products). Predictably, in the case of such a small economy, imports of finished manufactures and capital goods (machinery and equipment) are also significant.

8.5.2 Balance of payments

Increased competitiveness has been the basis of an improved current account position since 1980, when the deficit on visible and invisible trade reached 4% of GDP. The deficit was elimi-

nated by the mid-1980s, when the economy recorded its first current account surplus since 1976. The surplus in 1991 was equivalent to 2% of GDP. As Table E34 shows, trade in goods makes a marginal contribution to this surplus in comparison with that in services which, although smaller in aggregate value (around a quarter of that involved in merchandise trade), has consistently been in surplus over the 1980s. Freight and insurance in particular are important net earners of service income.

The capital account has benefited from financial reforms aimed at modernising and opening up the markets. The result of these changes – together with increased general confidence in the currency – has been to make the holding of franc assets more attractive, reversing the previous pattern of large outflows of investment in securities. Foreign takeovers of Belgian companies in the late 1980s, and strong investment by foreign companies has led to an improvement in net direct investment flows.

8.5.3 The exchange rate

The main instrument of monetary policy in Belgium is the exchange rate within the Exchange Rate Mechanism. Pegging the Belgian franc to the D-mark has been central to the anti-inflation policy, which has been aided by small upward re-alignments within the ERM since devaluation in 1982. Independent use of monetary policy within the country is prevented, however, since interest rates have to be set so as to maintain exchange rates within a range (unilaterally set in 1990 at a tight ± 0.5% around its central parity) regardless of the implications for domestic monetary growth. This explains the emphasis upon maintaining international competitiveness, and the institutionalised approach to wage determination described earlier. The close relationship between currencies also gives rise to a close relationship in terms of short-term interest rates. Since the adoption of the hard franc, an adverse short-term interest rate gap with the D-mark of 5.1% in 1980 has disappeared altogether. The same cannot be said of longer-term interest rates, however, which, due to the scale of government debt, include a risk premium over D-mark bonds.

8.6 SPECIAL ISSUE: PROBLEMS OF DEVOLVED REGIONAL ECONOMIES

The process of gradual devolution of powers from national to sub-national units was outlined in section 8.1. This section outlines the nature of the two main regions, and draws attention to the structural characteristics and problems confronting the respective governments of the new economic entities.

8.6.1 Flanders

The Flemish-speaking region of Flanders – the upper half of Belgium minus a small pocket carved out of its southern flank by Brussels – is the dominant region in modern Belgium. It has 58% of the population, 60% of the output, and annual output growth in the 1980s (2.9%) which outstripped both national and EC rates. Industrial conversion of the textile and coal-mining areas in this region has been relatively successful, contributing to a 30% increase in industrial production over 1984–90. Flanders thus acquired a large proportion of Belgium's new jobs during the 1980s, which helps account for the fact that the region's unemployment rate (officially 10.3% in early 1993) is much lower than that in Wallonia (19.5%) and Brussels (17.2%).

Flanders' regional structure is simpler than Wallonia's, due to the fusing of responsibilities relating to 'region' (local economic planning and development, agriculture, energy, environment, transport, public works and housing) and those of 'community' (education, culture, broadcasting), which remain separate in Wallonia. Central government has delegated to the regional authorities responsibility for the 'national' sectors, so-called because they have tended to rely on subsidies. Flanders benefited from the fact that the expensive process of restructuring the textiles sector (modernising and slimming down the industry from 100,000 to 50,000 employees) was undertaken before the transfer of responsi-

bility, though the regional government has itself undertaken the closure of remaining coal mines in Limburg, preferring to use the resources tied up in subsidies to diversify the local economy.

Support for new enterprise is a feature of the industrial policy, and is reflected in the activities of the *Flemish Investment Company (GIMV)*, which concentrates its assistance on helping successful companies to grow through interest rate rebates, seed money for investment and provision of equity capital (the latter often temporary with buy-back arrangements on terms agreed in advance). The regional government has also set up the *Inter-University Micro-Electronics Centre (IMEC)*, to link universities and business in diffusing ideas and know-how into industry.

The growth performance of recent years is only partly the result of such initiatives and support. Its populace, by EC standards, is noted for being disciplined, well-educated, multi-lingual and enterprising. Flanders has also benefited from its diverse spread of industries – including chemicals, carpets, food processing, mechanical engineering, non-ferrous metals and the larger part of Belgium's car assembly capacity. The share of industry in terms of contribution to output (31% in 1989) and employment (33%) is significantly higher than the national average. Services accounted for just 61% in 1989; particularly important within which is transport and communications. This revolves significantly around Antwerp (Europe's second largest port) and nearby Ghent and Zeebrugge, the combined activity of which contributes 10.4% to Flanders' output.

8.6.2 Wallonia

The French-speaking region of Wallonia is smaller in population (3.2 million) and less successful economically than its northern neighbour. Traditional industries of steel, glass, coal, electrical engineering, textiles and metalworking were proportionately more important in this part of Belgium, and their steady decline has hit the region hard. Industry's contribution to total employment, which amounted to 52% in 1961, had fallen to 26% in 1990 (compared with 33%

for EUR 12). No longer is the major part of the workforce employed in a small number of large companies; small and medium-sized enterprises are much more in evidence today. The coal mines are now closed and the much slimmed steel industry is largely state-owned. The legacy of the past lives on, however, in the low new firm formation rates often found in old industrial areas, and the reputation for militancy, which is slow to fade.

There are developments in new industries, including biotechnology, aerospace, new materials and pharmaceuticals, and the region has strengths in other sectors (notably chemicals, and paper, printing and publishing), but with inward investment favouring Flanders, new job creation in industry has been slow. Indeed, large firms in the traditional sectors still provide the overwhelming bulk of the region's exports. Service sector employment has increased sharply and now contributes 71% of Wallonia's jobs. The number of these new jobs, however, has not been sufficient to fully replace the 103,000 industrial jobs lost in the 1980s; in contrast to the situation in Flanders, Wallonia's economy recorded a small overall fall in employment during the decade. Thus, in spite of a virtually static population over the period since before the war, the registered unemployment rate is double that in Flanders, and the ratio between the regions worsened significantly from Wallonia's perspective in the second-half of the 1980s. Moreover, there are local black spots, mainly the former mining areas, with significantly higher rates than the average for the region. Inter-regional migration (and even inter-regional commuting) between Wallonia and Flanders is restrained by linguistic barriers among other factors – another rigidity affecting the labour market.

Walloons see regionalisation as an opportunity to remedy the decline of their economy. They feel that national policies have not allowed them to benefit from their position at the heart of the 'industrial triangle' of western Europe. The region's industrial strategy is directed at developing the region's technological base and diversifying its industries. Inward investment is

encouraged, and the *Walloon Regional Investment Company (SRIW)* provides start-up funds and equity capital for new firms on a selective basis, while also propping-up existing loss-making companies of strategic value so they can restructure their activities. An important aspect of the industrial strategy is the attempt to increase the degree of processing of the region's basic commodities (steel and agricultural products) in Wallonia itself; the pattern hitherto has been for firms in Flanders to add this value.

Wallonia's GDP per head is around 20% below the level for Belgium as a whole (and the EUR 12 average). Regional autonomy is likely to have the effect of worsening the position of Wallonia *vis-à-vis* its richer neighbours to the north, since the redistributive role of the central government is to be at least reduced and possibly phased out altogether. Indeed, one of the forces behind the constitutional reforms has been the political dissatisfaction in Flanders over subsidising its poorer counterpart. A transitional arrangement on central funding will be of help until the late 1990s, providing for a modest transfer of resources from Flanders and Brussels to Wallonia. Even after that, it is currently envisaged that social security will remain a national responsibility.

8.7 FUTURE PROSPECTS

Figures given in Table 8.2 indicate that both Luxembourg and Belgium perform relatively well in terms of meeting the convergence criteria established at Maastricht. At the end of 1992 Luxembourg fully met all four of the criteria; Belgium met three but was a long way short of doing so in relation to the dual criteria on public finances. Given the weight of its cumulative debt and the current recession conditions, the Belgian government will find it exceedingly difficult to meet the public finance criteria in the short to medium term. Certainly, there will continue to be great internal budgetary pressure on its level of social security provision. Conversely, from an external perspective, it would be to Belgium's advantage if social security pro-

Table 8.2 Position of EC member states in relation to convergence criteria, 1992. (Figures in bold indicate criteria met)

	Inflation[1]	Public finances		Interest rates[4]	Exchange rates (end 1992)	Number of criteria met in full
		(a) Deficit[2]	(b) Debt[3]			
France	**2.8**	**2.8**	**50.1**	**8.6**	Yes	4
Luxembourg	**3.1**	**−2.0**	**5.9**	**7.8**	Yes	4
Denmark	**2.1**	**2.6**	62.2	**9.0**	Yes	3
Belgium	**2.4**	6.9	121.0	**8.7**	Yes	3
Ireland	**3.1**	**2.5**	98.1	**9.1**	Yes	3
Netherlands	**3.8**	3.8	78.3	**8.1**	Yes	3
Germany	**4.0**	3.2	**44.0**	**8.0**	Yes	3
United Kingdom	**3.8**	6.6	**41.9**	**9.1**	No	2
Italy	5.1	11.1	108.4	11.9	No	0
Spain	5.9	4.7	**48.4**	12.1	No	0
Portugal	9.1	5.4	66.7	13.2	No	0
Greece	15.9	13.2	84.3	–	No	0
EC	4.3	5.3	62.3	9.6[5]		
Convergence criterion	4.0	3.0	60.0	10.7		

[1] Percentage rate of increase in consumer prices.
[2] Net financing requirement of general government as a percentage of GDP.
[3] Harmonised public debt as a percentage of GDP.
[4] Average of long-term yield rates.
[5] Excludes Greece.

Source: National Bank of Belgium, *Report 1992*, p. 26.

vision were generally raised throughout the EC (via acceptance of the social chapter), since the country operates with comparatively high indirect labour costs but low direct labour costs.

While the Belgian economy's openness and integration with its larger neighbouring states makes it virtually powerless in the face of economic downturn, the fact that the country's producers are already exposed to international competition should leave the economy well-placed to benefit from further integration among EC states (and enlargement of the Community). For such opportunities to be fully exploited unit labour costs will need to be kept under tight control, especially since maintaining cost competitiveness via manipulation of the exchange rate is largely ruled out. Recent OECD projections of Belgian labour cost increases above those in neighbouring economies raise questions about the economy's future competitiveness and ability to attract vital inward investment. It is likely that improving the functioning of the labour market will be a particularly important aspect of economic policy in the coming years.

8.8 LUXEMBOURG

Created as an independent state in 1815, the Grand Duchy of Luxembourg is a constitutional monarchy with legislative power vested in its elected Chamber of Deputies and executive power delegated by the monarch to chosen ministers. The population of this tiny country is close-knit, with a fierce national pride. It has been a partner in the economic union with Belgium since 1921, and was an original member of the EC. The smallest member state in population terms, with just 382,000 inhabitants (of whom over a quarter are foreign nationals), Luxembourg is highly dependent upon trade, with 95% of its GDP exported. It is very successful economically. Despite its size, Luxembourg contributed nearly 40% to the BLEU current account surplus in 1990; the country's GDP per head is the highest in the EC (30% above the EUR 12 average, Table E20); the annual growth rate in the 1980s (3.4%) was comfortably above that of EUR 12 in general (2.3%) and the core EC economies in particular; unemployment is virtually non-existent at less than 2% (Table E17); and its government, alone in the EC, does not need to borrow to cover expenditures (net lending equivalent to 2% of GDP (see Table 8.2). Economic performance has improved since the 1970s substantially as a result of important structural shifts in the productive base.

The industrial sector, which accounted for some 45% of GDP in 1970, has declined in importance and contributed only around 30% of total output by the late 1980s. Within industry, iron and steel – long the mainstay of the economy and accounting for a third of GDP and half of all employment in the 1950s – has gradually diminished in overall importance and now stands at only 8% of output. Tax exemptions and investment subsidies have been used since the 1960s to encourage a diversified industrial structure, and new areas of activity have been developed, notably chemicals, engineering, plastics, glass and aluminium. ARBED, the largest steel group, has as a company been actively involved in the diversification programme. Luxembourg does not offer significant inducements to inward investors, and has benefited from relatively few such projects in recent years.

The main development over the past three decades has been the growth of the service sector. Apart from the increase in employment in services associated with rising incomes, the sector has expanded on the basis of more outward-oriented activities including the Euro institutions (Parliament, Investment Bank and Court of Auditors), media developments (broadcasting and film-making), shipping registration, and finance. The latter is of prime importance and now accounts for 15% of GDP and nearly 20% of tax revenues. Since the 1970s, Luxembourg has established a leading role in Eurocurrency markets and in offshore D-mark deposits. A liberal legislative and regulatory system – including lenient reserve requirements, an absence of stamp duty on security transactions, the lack of a withholding tax on dividend or interest payments for non-residents and rigorous banking secrecy – have been important factors in the emergence of the Duchy as a major financial centre. Location and facility with languages are the natural advantages offered to investors. In 1991 it had over a thousand registered financial institutions – nearly 200 of them foreign – employing nearly 16,000 (more than double the figure for 1980). While Luxembourg's share of Eurocurrency transactions declined in the 1980s, new areas of business, including private client banking and investment fund management, have emerged to take its place.

Policy-makers are cautious about the country becoming as dependent upon financial services as it was previously upon steel. They are concerned that harmonisation within the EC may undermine Luxembourg's competitive advantage and are well aware of the Commission's disapproval of the prized secrecy laws. Active encouragement of technologically-based industries is part of a conscious effort to diversify the economic base. The healthy state of the public accounts (a reflection of high incomes and low unemployment) has allowed the government to carry out improvements in infrastructure and to bring down the rates of personal income tax and corporation tax, both of which have been somewhat above EC levels in general. The government is, as ever, careful in its handling of revenue; recognising that its ageing population will increasingly impose demands in the form of pensions, health care and social security.

Skilled labour shortages should not constrain production potential; foreign labour is not discouraged from settling in the country (27% of the resident population is foreign) and there is an increasing number of '*frontaliers*' (the 30,000 Belgians, French and Germans who daily commute into the Duchy). Indeed, with a fertility rate only three-quarters of that needed to maintain the population, such inflows have more significance in Luxembourg than for any other European state. This is simply the labour market dimension of a more general feature of the Benelux zone; namely, that the local components are extensively involved in broader functional regions which are spread across national boundaries. As such, this part of Europe offers insights into the concept of a 'Europe of regions' and how it might evolve.

8.9 SUGGESTED READING AND SOURCES OF INFORMATION

Barclays Bank: *Country Reports, Belgium* (1992) and *Luxembourg* (1991), Economics Department, London

Bughin J: Benelux in Dyker D. (ed.), (1992): *The National Economies of Europe*, Longman, London 126–59

Economist Intelligence Unit (1991): *European Community: Economic Structure and Analysis*, EIU Regional Reference Series, London, Belgium 40–57, Luxembourg 127–32

European Commission (1993): *Portrait of the Regions*, Dir-Gen for regional policy/statistical office, Vol 1, Luxembourg

European Commission (1993): *European Economy: Annual Economic Report for 1993*, Dir-Gen for economic and financial affairs, Luxembourg (see Belgium in section on the national economies)

Gay F.J.: Benelux, in Clout H. D. (ed.) (1987): *Regional Development in Western Europe*, 3rd edn., David Fulton

Gay F.J., Wagret P. (1987): *Economie des Payes du Benelux*, Presses Universitaires de France, Paris

National Bank of Belgium (1993): *Report 1992*, Brussels

OECD (1990/1): *Belgium and Luxembourg Economic Surveys*, Paris

See also:

Financial Times, London (periodic *Surveys*)
Kredietbank, Brussels (*Monthly Bulletins*)

CHAPTER 9

Denmark

Richard Bailey

9.1 REGIONAL CONTEXT

There is a common tendency in post-war economic writing to treat Sweden, Norway and Denmark, together with Finland, as parts of the same 'Scandinavian Experience'. This is justified by reference to important common features – political characteristics, social ideas and economic institutions – deriving, in part at least, from the common experience of a shared history. Perhaps the single feature which identifies these countries as a 'group' is the particular form of institutional structures and policies identified with *welfare capitalism*.

In the course of the 20th century, European countries have been continuously exploring alternative structures of socio-economic organisation to deal with the intractable problems of conflict and co-ordination between the 'social', 'political' and 'economic' spheres of human activity. The outcome, in post-war Europe, was the emergence of a number of variations on the theme of the mixed economy. In this context, Scandinavia developed a socio-economic discourse and an institutional structure which was quite sharply differentiated from those of other economies – this has become known as the '*negotiated economy*'. The policy approach emphasised the formulation of a flexible strategy for socio-economic development based on consensual agreement derived from a continuous dialogue between firms, governments, local authorities and interest organisations.

In the current Danish context, this is illustrated in the recent evolution of industrial policy.

From the mid-1980s there emerged a network of institutional investors, public authorities, private firms and trade unions – a loosely articulated grouping known as the *Forum for Industrial Development*. This became a central player in a number of restructuring initiatives during the late 1980s and early 1990s (see Pedersen *et al*). These semi-formal structures of private policy-making also exist in the labour market where collective agreements established in the leading sectors of the economy become the accepted norm, or the determining framework, for general arrangements in the labour market as a whole.

While there are important common features in institutional structures and policy priorities within Scandinavia, the Nordic countries do exhibit important variations. Subtle political differences and widely varying factor endowments have combined to produce different policy responses to both internal and external circumstances.

9.2 STRUCTURES AND INSTITUTIONS OF THE ECONOMY

With a land area of 43,000 km^2 and a population of just over 5 million, Denmark is one of the smallest countries in the European Community. Geographically, the country consists of the peninsula of Jutland and 500 islands located between the peninsula and Sweden. The two main islands are Funen and Zeland; the capital city, Copenhagen, is located on the latter and has historically held a vital strategic position controlling access to the Baltic sea route.

The natural resources of the country consist of little more than productive farm land and an extended coastline. It is not surprising, therefore, that farming and fishing have long been primary occupations of the local population. In spite of this there has been a strong trend towards urbanisation, with 86% of the population currently classified as living in urban areas.

Over a quarter of Danish citizens live in the Copenhagen conurbation, the remaining urban centres being relatively small with no towns in excess of 200,000 population. With the exception of Copenhagen, most of the centres of urban population are located on the peninsula.

International openness, measured by a high trade/GNP ratio, has been a characteristic feature of the Danish economy since the 19th century when agricultural production became increasingly orientated toward the needs of the UK market. Throughout the first half of the 20th century, Denmark experienced only modest industrial development, based largely on the increasing commercialisation of agriculture. However, as may be seen from the employment statistics in Table 9.1 rapid changes from the late 1950s onwards radically reshaped the structure of the Danish economy.

Table 9.1 Changing structure of employment (%)

Sector	1955	1973	1981	1991
Agriculture	21.8	9.5	7.2	5.8
Industry	34.9	33.8	29.3	27.2
Services	43.3	56.7	63.3	67.1

Source: OECD Labour Statistics.

The Golden Age of the 1950s and 1960s represents a 'second industrial revolution'. There was an impressive expansion in the traditional sectors of textiles, shipbuilding and food-processing, together with the emergence of a group of medium-sized, high value-added niche market producers in areas such as furniture, electrical engineering and pharmaceuticals. The industrial expansion in the 1960s led to a dispersal of manufacturing away from Copenhagen to south and west Jutland, and this, together with the emergence of agricultural co-operatives in the food processing industry, contributed to the increasing urbanisation of the population.

While social and political realignments reflected these developments, traditional interest groups of agriculture and industrial labour remained strongly represented in political life. As a consequence, economic strategy reflected a series of social compromises and was geared to ensuring that the distributional consequences of structural change were politically acceptable. The expanding role of the state, a high level of commitment to full employment and the development of increasingly comprehensive welfare provision, were essential features of this process.

The industrial dimension involved a regulative and redistribution role for the state which ensured that some sheltered sectors of the economy absorbed a large share of available resources. The small industrial base and high productivity growth in manufacturing meant that the resource shift from agriculture was mainly to the service sector (see Table 9.1). During the 1960s and early 1970s full employment was maintained through state-financed infrastructure investment, plus rapid growth in construction and state employment. As a consequence, taxation to finance the expansion of state activity, transfer payments and sectoral support policies, rose steeply during this period.

In general the 1960s was characterised by rapid growth, low unemployment and rising real incomes. Very high levels of taxation remained politically acceptable so long as they were accompanied by sustained income growth. The combination of high private and public consumption, however, meant that continued growth of the manufacturing export sector became increasingly dependent on external finance. The net effect of this was the emergence of a chronic structural deficit on the balance of payments, which, by 1972, produced a foreign debt equal to 56% of annual exports and 13% of GNP.

The structural vulnerability of the Danish economy was cruelly exposed by the events of the early 1970s. The impressive industrial development of the 1960s had been accompanied by an increasing dependence on energy, and by 1973 over 88% of fuel consumed was imported oil. The deterioration of the terms of trade caused by OPEC policies resulted in the government facing serious adjustment problems. The institutional structures of the welfare economy and the political commitment to full employment led to severe inflationary pressures.

With the exception of agriculture, productivity growth in the 'tradeable' sector of the economy experienced a decline in the 1970s and 1980s compared with the pre-1973 period (*OECD Survey 1990/1:* Table K). Macroeconomic policies geared to maintaining levels of employment, combined with a high degree of wage rigidity, resulted in high inflation rates, declining international competition and periodic currency devaluation. During 1973–80 the Krona depreciated against the D-mark from 2.27 to 3.1 (K to Dm); this, combined with a degree of appreciation against the £ and $, contributed to the shifting geographical pattern of Danish trade described below.

9.3 MAIN ECONOMIC CHARACTERISTICS

9.3.1 Human resources and the labour market

Denmark has a population of 5.1 million, which for all practical purposes may be viewed as static, with no significant changes during the 1980s. The changing pattern of civilian employment has been outlined above and shows an increasing concentration of employment in public and private sector service activity.

As in other Nordic countries labour participation rates are very high. In Denmark these have risen strongly in the last two decades from 60% to 80% of the working age group, and currently stand 10% above the OECD average. The growth in labour participation has been the primary source of labour supply growth at a time of low population growth and limited labour migration. All of this growth is accounted for by increased female participation and may be largely explained by the nature of the welfare state which provides both positive support for female employment and expanding job opportunities in traditional areas of female employment. This is also reflected in the level of part-time employment – standing at 23% of total employment. Self-employment represents 15% of the labour force and is, in part, a reflection of the importance of the personal services sector.

9.3.2 Output and productivity growth

In the two decades following the oil shock, GDP growth has been about 0.5% below the EC average (Table E19). Allowing for labour force changes and increasing participation rates, the major causal problem appears to have been the slow growth in labour productivity. Explanations of productivity slow-down are complex and problematic; in part, this may be a natural consequence of convergence and structural evolution in a country which had already attained high levels of real income. One element explaining slow growth of overall labour productivity is to be found in the explosion of public sector/service sector employment in the 1970s and early 1980s. On the basis of differential sector productivity growth, the OECD estimates that GDP growth would have been significantly higher had Denmark maintained sectoral employment shares closer to the OECD average (*OECD Survey 1989/90* p.42).

9.3.3 Prices, wages and unemployment

Denmark, together with other EC countries, has experienced an almost uninterrupted rise in unemployment levels since the early 1970s: annual average unemployment for each of the last three decades being 1.0%, 3.7% and 7.5%. This does not compare unfavourably with the average for the other EC countries (see Table E17); however, inter-country statistical comparisons of this sort are notoriously unreliable and at best offer only indications of broad trends.

Ostensibly, wages are determined by central bargaining between trade union and employer organisations. National agreements are negotiated bi-annually and cover about 30% of manual workers; however, these agreements tend to have an extended impact on general wage negotiations. This can be most clearly seen in the process of establishing reductions in working hours. Unlike the majority of European countries, Denmark does not have a statutory maximum working week; however, collectively bargained maximum hours (currently 37 hours per week) have become established as a 'norm' for both union and non-unionised employees. More generally, trade union bargaining has been based on a 'solidarity wage policy', which has had the objective of securing higher relative increases for the low-paid workers. The result of this has been a considerable compression of wage differentials to a level which is currently among the lowest in the OECD area. Market forces intrude into this structure and modify outcomes via decentralised negotiation at the firm level; this has generated substantial 'wage drift', through which skilled workers seek to protect differentials by bargaining for increases above the central norm.

The institutional structures of the labour market have produced a set of working conditions and a system of unemployment compensation, which together have contributed to severe problems of market inflexibility resulting in structural unemployment. The average replacement ratio (the ratio of unemployment benefit to wages) rose rapidly through the mid-1970s and, although it has fallen slightly since, it remains high by international standards. The net effect has been to produce an uncomfortable unemployment/inflation trade-off, with an OECD estimate for NAIRU (non-accelerating inflation rate of unemployment) of 8% (*OECD Survey 1989/90*). Problems of labour market restructuring are likely to persist throughout the 1990s – as an ageing labour force faces continuing technological and market changes.

Price inflation has been progressively reduced during the 1980s, falling from 12% in 1981 to 2.2% in 1992 and a predicted 1.6% for 1993.

While this compares favourably with the other core EC countries (see Figure 9.1), it has been achieved at the cost of high and rising levels of unemployment. Government commitment to a 'hard currency' and the associated financial restraint have provided the essential background for the successful anti-inflation policy, which has also combined a number of supply-side measures to increase labour market flexibility.

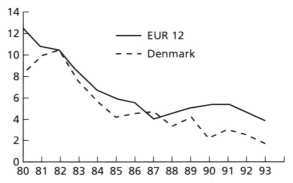

Figure 9.1 GDP deflator for EUR 12 and Denmark.

Source: European Economy, Statistical Annexe, Table E23.

9.3.4 Production, firm size and market structure

Some reference has already been made to changes in the pattern of production in the post-war years. Since the 1960s, changes in the distribution of economic activity within the private sector have been influenced by a number of factors, most notably energy price changes, membership of the EC and the increasing social concern with environmental issues. During 1966–89 agriculture's share of value-added fell from 10.2% to 6%, while that of manufacturing contracted slightly from 25% to 23%; in compensation, the services sector expanded from 64% to 70%. Within these broad categories, the main sectoral expansion has been financial/business services which grew from 11% to 24% of value-added (*OECD Survey 1990/91*, Table K).

The impression that the country has moved from 'pre-industrial to post-industrial' society while missing out the intermediate stage is perhaps somewhat misleading, in view of the fact that Denmark has, since the 19th century, had a commercially orientated agricultural sector. However, the small and relatively narrow industrial sector combined with a large market and non-market service sector does represent a uniquely Danish response to the changing global environment. This has created problems in terms of economic management; in particular, the balance of payments has become increasingly sensitive to changes in aggregate demand and to movements in the terms of trade.

Manufacturing industry is dominated by the small/medium sized firm, although, as indicated below, there has been a progressive shift from small to medium-sized. In 1971 76% of the manufacturing workforce was employed in firms with fewer than 50 employees, while only 1% was employed by firms with over 500 employees. By 1987 the comparable figures were 27% and 22% respectively.

Danish industry is frequently described as being 'niche-orientated', that is to say firms and groups of firms focus on specialised sectors within global industries – establishing leading positions in the global market. An illustration is pharmaceuticals, where Novo Nordisk is one of only three producers of insulin and is also a world leader in the production of industrial enzymes. A further instance, from the building industry, is Rockwool – one of the four leading world producers of mineral wool and a dominant player in the market for building insulation. Similar examples can be found in food-processing, where Danish firms account for 43% of world exports of bacon and 16% of exports of frozen fish fillets. Shipping and ship-building represent another area in which careful targeting on specialist products has enabled the six major Danish yards to position the country as the third largest shipbuilding nation after Japan and Korea.

There was a rapid growth of mergers and acquisitions during the late 1980s and early 1990s as Danish industry became more internationally orientated in preparation for the enhanced opportunities of the 'single market'. This process was also reflected in increased for-

eign investment flows during the same period – Danish firms being part of the small band of non-German capitalists making acquisitions through the Treuhand (see section 2.3).

9.3.5 Consumption and investment

The share of private consumption in GDP is low by EC standards and represents the culmination of a gently falling trend observable over the past three decades (see Table E24). This is mirrored by high levels of public consumption and the associated high levels of forced savings (taxation). Gross Fixed Capital Formation (GFCF) has fallen below the EC trend during the 1980s; at least part of this may be explained by fluctuating levels of residential construction and the generally high interest rates throughout the period. In the last years of the 1980s the increase in profit share contributed to investment stability in the face of low levels of capacity utilisation. However, the ratio of GFCF to GDP remains below the average for the core EC countries and may have contributed to the relatively poor productivity performance (see Table E25).

9.4 GOVERNMENT INVOLVEMENT IN THE ECONOMY

A broad measure of the extent of government involvement in the economy is indicated by the government expenditure/GDP ratio. In the 1950s this ratio was one of the lowest of the European countries, but between 1953 and 1973 public consumption and transfer payments grew more rapidly than in any other European state. By the mid-1970s, employment in the public sector exceeded that of the manufacturing sector and Danish citizens became the most heavily taxed of the western world.

The 1980s witnessed political changes commonly described as a 'welfare backlash'. In 1982, a conservative-led coalition government was elected with a 'medium term economic strategy' which combined policies to rein back welfare spending, reduce direct taxes and restore competitiveness in the manufacturing sector. The policies have met with a considerable measure of success: economic growth averaged 3.5% per annum between 1982 and 1986. The government budget deficit of 9% GDP (1982) was converted to budget surplus of 2–3% of GDP by the end of the decade. Major reform of the income tax system reduced the maximum rate from 73% to 68% and at the same time removed allowances which had enabled a range of interest costs to be set against taxable income. In spite of these efforts, government expenditure as a percentage of GDP, and the associated level of public consumption, remain the highest of all the EC countries (see Tables E21 and E28). State control of public expenditure is made more difficult because of the high degree of administrative devolution to counties and municipalities. Much of the social expenditure on 'merit goods' such as education, health, social services and public transport is under the control of local authorities, who collectively account for 56% of final government expenditure. The actions and attitudes of local authorities indicate a continuing political commitment to the 'welfare state strategy'.

9.4.1 Prices and incomes policies

In the short run, the problem of inflation may be viewed in terms of two inter-related dimensions – the management of aggregate demand and the institutional structures of the labour market which determine the relationship between wages and productivity growth. Danish governments have periodically sought to contain the cost-push pressures by intervening in the centralised wage negotiation process. The 1980s saw a strategic shift in the government approach to the wage bargaining process with the imposition of statutory ceilings, but in recent years this has given way to a more informal system of influence on the key collective agreement, negotiated bi-annually between the employers' organisation (*Dansk Industri*) and the industrial union cartel (*CO Industri*). There is some evidence that this intervention has had an impact on moderating wage increases. The impact of recent wage agreements appears to have halted the compres-

sion of skill differentials and thus marginally reduced the structural element in unemployment.

9.4.2 Industrial policy

Danish governments may be regarded as having a 'light touch' in terms of industrial intervention. In manufacturing, the only sector gaining significant financial support has been shipbuilding and even here direct subsidy is being eliminated. Government subsidy to private industry is less than 1% of GDP and is one of the lowest in the EC countries. During the 1980s there has been a shift away from the traditional defensive strategy of supporting vulnerable sectors towards export promotion and technological development. There is modest government support for a 'technology development programme' targeted on small firms.

In contrast to the above, the main beneficiaries of government subsidy and support have been the public utilities, especially the social infrastructure activities of housing and public transport. Rent controls and subsidies for housing associations combine with tax relief for owner-occupiers to produce a highly regulated and subsidised housing sector. As in the case of the UK, this, it is argued, results in significant misallocation of resources and inhibits geographical mobility.

Direct subsidy for public transport amounts to some 9% of the sector's value-added; additionally, VAT exemption and officially approved competition and price fixing agreements provide further support for the sector. In the energy sector, natural gas is subsidised by the granting of exemptions from the high energy taxes imposed on other energy sources. Justification for this sectoral support is that it represents an essential part of the government's comprehensive strategy of environmental protection (see section 9.7).

9.4.3 Regional policy

Changes in the geographical distribution of employment during the 1970s, which involved a relocation of industrial expansion into the Jutland peninsula at the expense of the urban conglomeration on Zeland (Copenhagen), was facilitated by a series of administrative reforms and financial incentives. Local government reform, together with the *National and Regional Planning Act* of 1973, established a framework for the development of regional planning and public service provision based on the 'counties'. This political and financial devolution facilitated the shift away from the metropolitan 'growth pole' towards a more balanced pattern of industrial development.

Regional balance has not been an important political issue in the 1980s and active regional policies, in the form of soft loans for industrial location, have been gradually phased out. However, there still remain some incentives in the form of capital and training grants for firms locating in areas of high unemployment. The *Small Islands Assistance Act* (1983) addressed the problem of depopulation of the small islands and the government transport subsidy supports ferry communication links which facilitate mainland commuting.

9.5 BANKING AND FINANCIAL STRUCTURES

The post-war years witnessed an extended process of consolidation within the commercial banking system as local banks were increasingly absorbed into nationally and regional based branch networks. A similar process took place with regard to the savings banks and mortgage credit institutions.

The financial markets remain compartmentalised although there has been some movement towards integration via co-operation and mergers between banks, insurance companies and mortgage institutions. The bond market is extremely large and is a unique feature of the Danish financial system. This market is the primary source of funds for mortgage refinance and public borrowing. Bond issues are the equivalent of 120 to 130% of GDP, much higher than other EC countries. In contrast, the stock market

is small and only limited corporate finance is raised through equity issues.

Nationalbank (the Central Bank) exercises control over the commercial banking system with the traditional instruments of bank rate and open market operations. Historically, these were supplemented by a variety of 'deposit agreements' and credit ceilings. As in other Western economies, the inflationary experience of the 1970s led to a review of the relaxed attitude taken to money supply growth. Control of liquidity has not been an easy task in an open economy where there has been a progressive relaxation of controls on capital account transactions. However, a series of changes since 1985 have led to improved mechanisms of credit control through the switch from lending ceilings to formal deposit arrangements. Banks are now required to maintain a credit balance with the Central Bank which in turn issues 'certificates of deposit'. Banks can obtain loans against such certificates up to 90% of their nominal value at an interest rate fixed by the Central Bank. Growth of bank deposits can now be controlled by varying the placement requirements.

The overriding objective of monetary policy has been to keep the exchange rate within its ERM limits and interest rates have been directed towards this end. In essence, current and future monetary policy stance crucially depends on the international environment and the actions of its immediate neighbour, Germany.

9.6 INTERNATIONAL RELATIONS

For Denmark, both history and geography have for long dictated an internationally orientated economic strategy. However, since the early 1970s, trade as a share of GDP has grown quite slowly – exports rising from 31% of GDP in 1970 to 35% in 1988. Although there has been continued growth in agricultural exports, manufacturing exports have become an increasingly important element of the trade account. In 1991 manufactures represented 67% of merchandise exports compared to 15% for agricultural products.

The other Nordic countries, the United Kingdom and Germany have traditionally been the primary focus for Danish exporters. However, the nature of the evolution of Danish manufacturing has led to an increased dispersal of exports throughout the richer markets of the developed world while agriculture has found expanding markets in the Middle East. In 1958, 53% of exports went to three countries, UK, Germany and Sweden, but by 1991 this total had fallen to 38%. The largest decline has been in trade to the UK which fell from 25% to 10% of total exports. Although the German share of exports has increased and now represents by far the largest single market for Danish goods, membership of the EC has not resulted in any trade diversion. In the period 1982–8, Denmark's intra-EC exports grew by 4.2% per annum while extra-EC trade grew by 5%. Denmark has the distinction of being the only EC country for which intra-community trade has actually decreased as a proportion of total trade – from 59% to 54% between 1958 and 1991 (see Table E32).

9.6.1 Balance of payments, external debt and exchange rate policy

A major policy concern of the 1980s has been the intractable problem of Denmark's external debt. It is something of a puzzle that one of the richest countries in the industrialised world should have a debt profile more normally associated with a developing third world country. This situation stems from 26 years of continuous current account deficits, which produced, in 1988, a debt/GDP ratio of 40% and a debt/export ratio of 130%. The last four years have witnessed an improvement in the trade position, with a strong growth in exports contributing to a surplus on trade account and a rough balance on the current account. This has been achieved through a modest growth in private saving and the virtual elimination of the government deficit. The current account surplus achieved in the early 1990s produced a decline in foreign debt and debt-service costs. With a continued improvement in private sector savings and tight budgetary policy,

there is an expectation that the net foreign debt will be eliminated by the end of the decade.

An important dimension of Danish economic policy has been the strict adherence to 'hard currency stance' implied by the government's commitment, effective since 1984, to maintain the krona as a 'core currency' within the narrow band of the EMS/ERM currency grid. This, together with supportive fiscal and monetary policies, contributed to the progressive reduction in inflation illustrated above. However, in spite of strong economic fundamentals (as measured by Maastricht criteria) the krona has been subject to a number of speculative attacks during the recent period of exchange market instability. The exit of sterling and the lira from the ERM, the subsequent float of the Swedish and Norwegian currencies, together with the devaluation of the Irish punt and Spanish peseta, caused a significant appreciation of the Danish currency against the currencies of some of its major trading partners. This has produced a substantial decline in short-term competitiveness and an additional deflationary impulse which seems likely to depress GDP growth over the next year.

9.7 SPECIAL ISSUES

9.7.1 Research and development

In the early to mid-1980s Danish R&D expenditure averaged about 1.1% of GDP, compared with the EC average for core countries (including Denmark) of 2%. There has been some modest improvement in the late 1980s, but Danish R&D is still low in comparison to other rich EC/OECD countries. While such low levels may be partly explained in terms of industrial structure and the dominance of the small firm, it has worrying implications for future trends in manufacturing competitiveness.

The nature of Danish manufacturing industry is such that success depends on being close to the technological frontier of product and process development, which in turn requires that firms sustain in-house or networked research and development activity. Government encouragement has come in the form of a 'technology development programme' which provides consultative support and financial assistance for risk-capital projects in small firms. The general aim has been to provide incentives for firms to introduce new technology more rapidly and ensure long-term competitivness in export markets.

9.7.2 The environment

Environmental issues have for some time held a high position on the Danish political agenda. In areas such as air pollution, hazardous waste and nature conservancy, Denmark has led the way in setting standards and implementing regulatory controls. Drinking water pollution, in part a consequence of the fertiliser and pesticide use stimulated by CAP incentives, has been tackled by the *1987 Aquatic Environment Plan* which set progressive abatement targets on nutrient emissions into water. Energy conservation measures are implemented via a combination of regulation, high energy taxation and financial support for energy-saving investment. There is increasing awareness that environmental quality is simply a matter of domestic policy. International linkages mean that environmental quality is an international public good, and as such, can only be effectively addressed at an international level. Danish initiatives in pollution control has resulted in levels of regulation and taxation which weaken the cost competitiveness of domestic firms. This has led some Danish companies to locate overseas, action which has encouraged the government to advance the case for common environmental policies within the EC.

9.7.3 Energy

The heavy reliance on oil as a primary energy source has been progressively reduced over the last two decades. However, owing to the Danish rejection of the use of nuclear power, this has involved the substitution of imported coal for oil as a means of electricity generation, with a consequent impact on levels of air pollution. This conflict with environmental objectives produced policy responses which emphasised energy-saving measures and the rapid development of indigenous sources of oil and natural gas. Danish oil and gas extraction from the North Sea expanded rapidly in the 1980s and gas is gradually substituting for coal in electricity generation as well as being used as a direct energy source.

The success of energy-saving policies combined with the nature of Danish industry has resulted in the country achieving a low level of energy intensity in total output. Between 1972 and 1989 energy use per unit of GDP declined by 30%, giving Denmark one of lowest energy/GDP ratios of the OECD countries.

9.7.4 Denmark and the EC

It is 20 years since Denmark made its somewhat reluctant entry into the EC. The virtual demise of the European Free Trade Area (EFTA) and Denmark's close trading links with the UK, left the country with little option. When Norway and Sweden failed to follow the Danish lead, the traditional Nordic political and economic linkages appeared to be under threat. Subsequently the trading pattern, which obliged Denmark to move with Britain, changed radically as Germany became the principal focus for the country's exports. In spite of the EC entry split, the Nordic connection has remained strong, with expanding levels of trade flows, cross-border inter-firm mergers and inter-governmental co-operation.

While business and agricultural interests remain committed to EC membership, popular suspicion of the EC as an undemocratic decision-making institution, combined with the realisation that Danish political priorities regarding the environment and social welfare were not necessarily shared by other EC countries, produced the politically unexpected 'No' vote in the Maastricht referendum. The Government worked hard to overturn the referendum decision and, with the help of concessions negotiated at the Edinburgh Summit in December 1992, achieved a reversal of the decision in a subsequent referendum in May 1993. However, the lack of affinity with the south of Europe and an underlying fear of German domination are likely to continue to colour Danish attitudes toward further EC integration. If prospective accession negotiations result in the successful entry of the other Scandinavian countries, the Danish position within the EC will be considerably strengthened. Such a widening of EC membership would significantly shift the decision-making axis to the North, and fundamentally alter the development priorities and political agenda of the Community as it enters the 21st century.

9.8 BIBLIOGRAPHY

Economic Intelligence Unit (1992): *'Denmark' in European Community: economic structure and analysis* (Regional Reference Series)

OECD (1989–92): *Economic Survey – Denmark*, Paris

Johansen H.C. (1987): *The Danish Economy in the 20th Century*, Croom Helm, London

Pedersen O.K. *et al* (1992): 'Private Policy and the Autonomy of Enterprise', in *Journal of Economic Issues*, Vol. 36, No.4 D

CHAPTER 10

Portugal

Richard Bailey

10.1 INSTITUTIONAL AND HISTORICAL CONTEXT

A brief history of this small but long-established European state is necessary in order to understand and appreciate its current economic condition and circumstances. For a short period in the late 15th and early 16th centuries, Portugal was the centre for the pioneering 'voyages of discovery' which led to the great expansion of European economic power in the centuries which followed. The protracted conflict over the establishment of trading empires, which characterised the 300 years following the discovery of the Americas, crucially influenced Portugal's subsequent development.

The country was established as an independent kingdom in 1140, but Phillip II of Spain reunited the crowns in 1580 with the practical objective of consolidating the vast empires of the two countries. However, the reverses experienced by Spain during the Thirty Years' War created the opportunity for Portugal to re-establish its independence in 1640. There followed a period of pre-industrial capitalist development, under the leadership of the Duke of Erceira, but this was cut short by the *Methuen Treaty* of 1703. This Anglo-Portuguese treaty, while providing Portugal with valuable political support in struggles with her continental neighbours, had the effect of locking the country into a relationship of political and economic dependence on Britain for the next 200 years.

For much of the 20th century (1928–68) Portuguese development was dominated by the pro-feudalist and anti-liberal vision of one man – Antonio de Olivera Salazar. Salazar's dictatorship was profoundly anti-developmental and ardently nationalistic; consequently, throughout the 'Golden Age' of post-war development, Portugal remained in semi-isolation. Although the country was a founder member of NATO and subsequently became a member of EFTA, economic and industrial development was narrowly focused on strengthening and sustaining the links, with its remaining colonies. Until the mid-1970s, industrial development proceeded within the context of a hierarchical, autocratic social structure, and the main focus of economic development was on the traditional sectors of textiles, clothing, ceramics, and the agricultural processing industry.

The country experienced some modest output growth in the 1960s and 1970s but infrastructure investment and welfare services were largely neglected. There was no convergence with the richer more developed economies of continental Europe and per capita incomes remained at around a quarter of the EC average. This contrasts with Spain, its immediate neighbour, which achieved some significant convergence, with per capita income growing from 33% to 58% of EC average. In summary, during the two decades of the 1960s and 1970s Portugal remained a semi-detached peripheral economy of Western Europe.

Following Salazar's withdrawal from public life in 1968, the dictatorship lost much if its direction and, more importantly, the support of the military. An army coup in April 1974, backed by widespread popular support, set Portugal on a path of modernisation. Initially this ushered in a decade of political confusion and radical economic change. The 1970s saw the nationalisation of vast swathes of industry, business and financial services, the collectivisation of significant sections of agriculture, and the granting of independence to all the remaining colonies of the empire. Somewhat surprisingly, this period also saw the enactment of a Parliamentary Constitution and stumbling progress towards a democratic multi-party system.

The inherent difficulties of structural modernisation have, until recently, been exacerbated by the political instabilities associated with frequently changing minority governments. The needs of social and political modernisation were given particular urgency by Portugal's application and subsequent entry into the European Community in November 1985. The mid-1980s saw a gradual consolidation of power by the 'centrist' Social Democratic Party (*PSD*), led by Anibal Cavaco Silva. The *PSD* finally achieved single party majority rule in 1987, on the basis of a reformist programme with an emphasis on market-oriented policies and extensive privatisation.

10.2 MAIN ECONOMIC CHARACTERISTICS

10.2.1 Population and labour force

The resident population of Portugal was 10.4 million in 1991, approximately half a million of which live on the two island groups of Madeira and the Azores. The level of urbanisation is low – around 30% – with the main concentrations of urban population in the areas around Lisbon, Sintra, and Setubal in the mid-west of the country, and Oporto in the North. Population statistics are complicated by the fact that about 4 million nationals are resident outside the country, which gives rise to significant migration flows. Historically, the country has experienced net emigration, but this was dramatically reversed in the mid-1970s when, as a consequence of colonial independence, the domestic population increased by 8% in two years. Approximately one million Portuguese live and work in other EC countries, France being the principal destination of migrant workers. Income reparations from expatriates amount to some 10% of GDP and contribute significantly to Portugal's balance of payments (equivalent to 20% of current receipts).

10.2.2 Employment and the labour market

The sectoral employment pattern diverges quite markedly from the EC norm, with 18% of the civilian labour force employed in agriculture, 35% in industry/construction and 46% in services (see Table E16). During the 1980s, employment in manufacturing remained broadly stable while agricultural employment declined by some 20%; at the same time, there was a 40% expansion of employment in public administration, trade, banking and personal services (*OECD Survey 1991/2* Table E).

Current unemployment levels are low in comparison with other EC countries; while unemployment averaged 7–8% in the early to mid-1980s, the level fell to 4–5% in the late 1980s and early 1990s. However, because of high levels of underemployment in agriculture and some parts of the public sector, the absolute level of unemployment is not a good indicator of labour market disequilibrium. The unemployment figures do not take account of those on temporary contracts or short-time working; if these figures were to be included Portugal's unemployment level would be closer to the EC average. Both male and female participation rates are low; in part, this may be a consequence of the extended 'black economy' and the limited coverage of unemployment insurance schemes.

OECD estimates suggest that the levels of real wage flexibility are high, responding rapidly to changing demand conditions. This combines with a high level of employment rigidity, resulting from legislative restriction on dismissal. Consequently, labour market adjustment is initially via wage movement while employment response is subject to a significant lag. Real wages declined quite sharply during 1981–4 in response to a contraction in domestic demand and subsequently rose modestly over the remainder of the decade. Labour costs are low, about one-third of Spain's and a quarter of the EC average. However, the labour force tends to be short of industrial skills and there is a need for sustained investment to enhance the level of human capital and increase employment flexibility in the labour force.

10.2.3 Output and inflation

Portugal remains a poor country by EC standards; with a per capita GNP of $466, incomes are about a quarter of the EC average. However, apart from the disruptive years of 1974/5 and 1982/3, when external shocks combined with internal instability, the country has experienced sustained growth in real GDP throughout the 1970s and 1980s. This has produced some degree of real income convergence (see Figure 10.1).

The major problem during this extended period of adjustment has been the inability to contain the inflationary pressures which frequently characterise a modernising economy. As can be seen from Figure 10.2, the Portuguese inflation rate remains substantially above the average for EC economies. Although both exhibit a declining trend during the 1980s, Portugal has experienced sharp and erratic price movements.

During the last twenty years inflation has averaged 17% per annum, which was well above the EC average. Following IMF-inspired stabilisation programmes in the early 1980s and EC membership in 1986, the inflation record has improved somewhat and there is evidence that, following a series of reforms of the financial sector, the government is gaining a measure of control over domestic monetary aggregates. Government commitment to price stability was reinforced by the decision to replace the crawling-peg exchange rate system, which had accommodated the inflationary pressures, with participation in the European Exchange Rate Mechanism (ERM).

10.2.4 Consumption, savings and investment

Private consumption has traced a somewhat erratic path over the last decade. The late 1970s

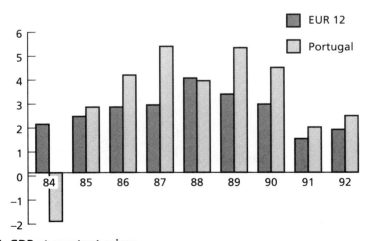

Figure 10.1 GDP at constant prices.

Source: European Economy, Statistical Annexe Tables E1 and E12.

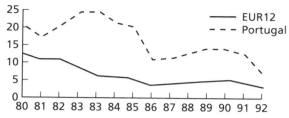

Figure 10.2 GDP deflator.

Source: European Economy, Statistical Annexe Table E27.

and early 1980s were characterised by a very high savings ratio and low and sometimes negative growth in private consumption. Following EC entry, falling tariffs and rising real incomes combined to produce an air of confidence which produced a sustained consumer boom, with the savings ratio falling from a high of 28% in 1985 to 22% in 1990. Private consumption has grown on average between 4–5% per annum in the early 1990s, fuelled by the strong growth in real wages. Consumption growth is set to slow down in 1993, as the government seeks to restrict wage growth in the public sector.

Table 10.1 Gross fixed capital formation

	1985–7	1988–9	1991	1992	1993
GFCF as % of GDP	22.7	26.5	25.5	25.4	26.0
% change	7.2	8.8	2.8	3.6	3.3

Source: European Economy, No. 54.

In spite of high real interest rates, there has been a sustained growth in fixed investment since 1985 (see Table 10.1). This reflects the pressing need both to enlarge and modernise the capital stock. Much of the investment has been in the form of capital-widening projects in infrastructure and services which have had a positive impact on employment. However, the continuing need for capital-deepening to enhance industrial productivity will produce increasing amounts of labour displacement.

Investment volumes have been substantially boosted by the rapid growth of foreign direct investment (see section 10.5.2).

10.2.5 Agriculture

Agriculture represents one of the key problem areas of the Portuguese economy. It is characterised by low productivity, employing about 19% of the labour force and producing about 6% of GDP. The sector provides shelter for extensive underemployment, supported by a generous government subsidy of producer prices. These subsidies are due to be phased out by 1996, which means that efficiency must improve substantially if farm incomes are not to fall sharply. In 1987 average labour productivity in agriculture was only 16% of the EC average and crop yields varied from 37% to 71% of European averages. Part of the problem derives from the land tenure system which has produced excessive division into non-viable small land holdings in the North, and equally inefficient large co-operative farms in the South. Some 50% of all farms have less than one hectare of land and 94% have less than 20 hectares. In addition, the sector suffers from low infrastructure investment, an inefficient distribution system, poor education levels (45% of farmers said to be illiterate) and inadequate agricultural extension services.

In spite of the large areas of agricultural land and favourable climatic conditions, Portugal cannot meet its domestic food requirements, half of which is met by imports. A land reform initiative has started the process of the progressive privatisation of the large co-operative farms and capital investment has been raised significantly through EC structural support programmes. As yet this has produced little in the way of positive results; labour productivity and crop yields are about one-third of the EC average and extensive structural reform will be required to convert the sector from subsistence to commercial agriculture.

An exception to the above is forestry, an important sub-sector of agricultural activity. Forestry and the associated processing industry have expanded rapidly in the last decade. Portugal is the world's largest exporter of cork (harvested from the cork oak) and a significant net exporter of pulp products. The total area under forest cultivation is 3.7 million hectares, and, although cork oak plantations are the dominant crop, there has been a rapid expansion of eucalyptus tree plantations which are becoming an increasingly important source of raw material for the paper product industry.

10.2.6 Industry

The industrial sector of the economy is quite large; the manufacturing shares of both gross value-added and civilian employment are marginally above the EC average (see Tables E16/22). Including energy and construction, industry accounts for 35% of employment, 37% of GDP and 90% of exports.

The sector is characterised, however, by an increasingly dualistic structure. The major source of employment is in traditional small-scale labour-intensive manufacturing industries dominated by textiles, clothing and footwear, a legacy of the pre-revolution period. This stands in contrast to a rapidly growing sub-sector of large capital-intensive manufacturing and processing firms which are either state-owned or, increasingly, local subsidiaries of multinational corporations. An important and expanding sector is paper and pulp processing which is dominated by four large, vertically integrated, conglomerates. Over half the annual output of 800,000 tonnes of pulp is produced by Portucel, a state-owned corporation, while the remaining production is controlled by British and Swedish multinationals.

The heavy industrial sector generally is dominated by state-owned and foreign-owned firms: in 1986, ten of the top twenty-five companies were state-owned, eight were foreign-owned and seven were private. Multinationals such as Rio Tinto Zinc, Stora and BAT have focused on resource processing (paper and pulp), while others, such as Ford/VW, are developing component sourcing activities. The government is moving towards the privatisation of many of the state monopolies in heavy industry, but progress is slow (see section 10.3.2).

Textiles appear to be the most exposed and vulnerable sector of manufacturing industry. It is also a very important element of the country's industrial base, providing 28% of manufacturing employment and contributing 30% of the country's exports earnings. The industry is characterised by low-technology low value-added products which compete at the highly competitive end of the world market. The market in the 1990s is characterised by continued expansion of supply capacity fed by the low-cost producers from the Far East and Eastern Europe. Portuguese industry must modernise if it is to survive in this market environment.

Heavy investment is required to raise capital intensity and maintain competitiveness in the spinning and weaving sub-sectors, while modernisation in the final product sectors is required to improve quality and move products upmarket. The sector is already experiencing considerable employment contraction and is the focus of EC-financed industrial restructuring. The difficulties of structural adjustment and contraction are exacerbated by the high level of geographical concentration, with most of the industry in the North and Central regions.

10.2.7 The informal economy

As in many transitional developing economies the informal or 'black' economy represents an important element of economic life. As these activities are undeclared – and thus untaxed – they are by their nature very difficult to quantify. In the rich economies of the EC the unmeasured black economy is variously estimated to be between 5–8% of GDP; in Portugal some commentators put the figure in the region of 15–20% of GDP. The construction industry is a major source of unmeasured economic activity, as is tourism and the craft manufacture of tourist artifacts. The plethora of regulations and controls which have traditionally circumscribed legitimate business processes, together with an eccentric and inequitable system of income taxation, have, in the past, provided strong incentives for the expansion of unrecorded economic activity.

10.3 GOVERNMENT INVOLVEMENT IN THE ECONOMY

In spite of strong growth in the private sector in recent years, the legacy of the 'nationalisation experiment' of the mid-1970s has meant that the state continues to account for nearly 40% of GDP. In certain sectors, such as metals and heavy engineering, its weight is overwhelming. Even in the private sector, legislative and bureaucratic controls on the economy remain extensive and contribute to an unnecessarily high level of transaction costs. The government took an important step towards rationalisation of bureaucratic regulation with the establishment of a new *Commercial Code* in 1987, but much still remains to be done.

10.3.1 Government revenue and tax reform

Traditionally tax revenues have represented a small but growing proportion of GDP, rising from 26% in 1979 to 36% in 1991. The narrow tax base has been insufficient to support growing government expenditure and since 1974 the country has experienced continuous budget deficits. The Public Debt/GDP ratio quadrupled between 1974 and 1988 when it reached a peak of 74%. In past years, much government spending has been financed by 'implicit taxation' – low-interest forced lending by the state-owned banks to the government together with traditional inflationary finance.

In an effort to improve fiscal efficiency and control the inflationary tendency of public finance, the country has embarked upon a far-reaching programme of tax reform. The aim has been to widen the tax base and to reduce the opportunities for tax avoidance. The introduction of VAT in 1986, followed by income tax reforms in 1989, have combined to provide a stronger fiscal multiplier and to increase the horizontal equity of the system. In 1991 tax receipts contributed just over 94% of government income: of this, social security payments and indirect taxes contributed 62% and direct taxes on households and corporations contributed 32% (calculated from *OECD Survey 1992*, Table 13). The general easing of the financing constraint enabled the government to advance reform of the financial markets, including a deregulation of interest rates. The combination of improved revenue structures and sustained growth of GDP has produced a modest decline in the Debt/GDP ratio which now stands at 70%, marginally below the EC average.

As part of the 1992–4 convergence programme, the 1993 budget contained a general government deficit target of 4% of GDP based upon tight current expenditure limits and a commitment to the control of public sector wages. Monetary policy is dedicated to support the participation of the escudo in the ERM (see Section 10.4.1).

10.3.2 Privatisation

The process of privatising the very large public sector depended on the mobilisation of substantial political support to amend the 1976 Constitution which explicitly outlawed the sale of public assets. Amendments to the Constitution in 1988 and 1989 allowed first for partial privatisation (private/public partnership) and finally for full privatisation. The main activity to date has been in the financial services sector where some banks and insurance companies have been sold to the private sector. In addition, there has been successful privatisation of the brewery sector and some progress toward restructuring the heavy industrial sector in preparation for a return to private ownership – notably cement, petro-chemicals and steel.

10.3.3 Structural reform

Following EC entry in 1986, there was a general recognition of the need to modernise and adapt agriculture, industry and commerce to face the increased competition resulting from the 1992 Single Market. The backbone of the far-reaching programme of industrial restructuring is the '*Specific Programme for Industrial Development in Portugal*' (PEDIP). This programme is funded from private investors, the Portuguese government and the EC – the latter funding coming from community structural and regional funds. Between 1988 and 1992 $2 billion has been channelled through PEDIP for industrial modernisation. Key areas of funding have included: infrastructure investment, professional training, capital investment and advisory support services for improving productivity and product quality. Advisory support services are provided by specially created 'centres of competence' which are providing international expertise in areas such as information technology, manufacturing logistics and financial management for both established firms and new business projects.

Active labour market policies are being implemented as part of the modernisation process. The main thrust of these policies is towards occupational training and subsidies for job creation. With an illiteracy rate variously estimated at between 15 and 20%, raising the general level of education and the occupational skill profile of the workforce is a key ingredient of the government's modernisation strategy. Substantial disbursements from the European Social Fund have been earmarked for adult training and the general development of human resources.

10.3.4 Policies for prices and wages

National minimum wage legislation was introduced in 1974 as part of a general policy of improving conditions for the least favoured groups of the labour force. Currently, only about 3% of the workforce are directly affected by statutory wage provision. The majority, about 80%, are subject to collective agreements or civil service statutory regulation, thus leaving a not insignificant group without collective wage regulation.

The government has developed a non-statutory prices and incomes policy based upon the *Economic and Social Agreement (acordo economico e social)*. The process involves a negotiated pact between employers, trade unions and the government which sets pay targets for wage negotiations in the public and private sectors. In 1992 the collectively agreed pay limit was 9.75%, with a government pay target of 8%. This was part of a package which included improvements in the minimum wage, income and mortgage tax relief. Future negotiations of the pact are likely to be subject to increasing strain, as negotiations will take place against a background of accelerated industrial restructuring, rationalisation and job losses.

10.3.5 Regional policy

Regional divisions between the North and South are a long-established feature of the country. The 1974 revolution reflected and reinforced these differences; the more highly politicised South moved down the path of nationalisation and collectivisation, while ownership structures in the North – family firms and peasant landholdings – remained largely untouched. Present regional policy is administered by the *Ministry of Planning and Terratorial Co-ordination* and is targeted on improving communication linkages between the North and South. Considerable emphasis is placed on the Lisbon–Oporto coastal axis, to the neglect of the underdeveloped eastern interior. The continuing processes of structural adjustment will impact differentially on the regions, creating a need for more focused regional policy in the future. The existing structures of centralised administration are likely to face increasing demands for regional devolution as economic imbalances become more marked.

The autonomous island regions of Madeira and the Azores present particular development problems due to their size and location. The strategy has been to negotiate free trade zone status within Portugal and the EC. Madeira has already used this status to advance its position as an offshore financial centre, capitalising on its traditional role as a link between Europe and South America.

10.4 FINANCIAL SYSTEM

Following the 1974 revolution the stock exchanges of Lisbon and Oporto were closed and almost the whole of the financial sector was nationalised – commercial banks, saving banks, insurance companies and agricultural credit institutions, the only significant exceptions being the four foreign-owned banks.

Government control was exercised via a network of direct controls; the only financial instruments available to the private sector were bank and savings deposits which were mobilised to provide funding for the government and state enterprises. In essence the whole of the private and public sectors were financed by the banking sector; in 1984 99% of households' financial assets consisted of sight or term deposits with the banking system. Since the mid-1980s there has been a major effort to revitalise and modernise the financial system, to create a competitive market environment with the flexibility necessary to underpin the processes of economic development. In 1987 banks were authorised to issue marketable certificates of deposit and subsequently there has been a progressive deregulation of interest rates on credits and deposits. The removal of credit ceilings and administered interest rates are aimed at the establishment of market discipline and the price rationing of credit for both the private and public sector. In the past, credit ceilings not only subsidised government borrowing but also protected the inefficient state-owned banks, which now face a much more threatening competitive environment. There has been a partial privatisation of some of the state institutions and the formation of a number of new private banks. This, together with the increasing presence of foreign banks, has radically increased competition and stimulated reform within those institutions remaining in state ownership.

The Stock Exchanges of Lisbon and Oporto were re-opened in 1982, but the market is small, with the shares of only 30 companies being continuously traded. Market activity is dominated by trade in government bonds and securities, which were introduced in 1986 and now finance a substantial proportion of government debt. Some progress is being made to widen the market by improving the administrative structures and reducing transaction costs of market activity. As yet the market is too 'meagre'

to enable the government to float significant amounts of privatisation stock.

10.4.1 Monetary and exchange rate policy

The various measures of liberalisation and the introduction of financial markets and institutions have created new problems of money market management. The increased liquidity, following the removal of quantitative restrictions, has been partly absorbed by sales of government securities, but in spite of this there was significant liquidity growth in 1991/2. Interest rates, both real and nominal, have risen in the 1990s and this in turn has contributed to capital inflows and a tendency for currency appreciation.

The authorities decided to abandon the crawling-peg system of currency management in 1990, first shadowing and then joining the ERM in April 1992. In addition to the inflation discipline which this action imposed, membership of the ERM offered substantial benefits from reduced exchange rate variability, especially for a country whose currency is not used extensively in international trade and where the financial sector is underdeveloped. However, the continuing high level of domestic inflation, albeit declining relative to other Community countries, led to a substantial real appreciation of the escudo in terms of unit labour costs. The currency turmoil in September 1992 which resulted in the withdrawal of sterling and the lira from the ERM led to a further deterioration in competitiveness; when, in November, Spain sought a devaluation within the ERM – Portugal was obliged to follow the Spanish move.

Given the current level of underdevelopment in the Portuguese economy, the decision to opt for a non-accommodating exchange rate regime has introduced a valuable dimension of financial discipline. However, it has also simultaneously removed an element of policy flexibility for a country facing severe burdens of structural adjustment.

10.5 INTERNATIONAL RELATIONS

10.5.1 Trade and the balance of payments

The geographical pattern of Portugal's trade has changed radically over the last 30 years. This is particularly noticeable with reference to the destination of exports. Traditionally, Portuguese exports had been oriented toward its colonial territories, but the 'end of the empire' in the 1970s and EC membership in the 1980s have combined to switch trade to EC markets; three-quarters of merchandise exports are now destined for the EC compared to less than half in the 1970s. Of particular importance has been the growth of trade with Spain, which, although only a small proportion of total trade, has more than doubled in the last five years. Following many years' separate development, EC membership appears to have stimulated a process of Iberian integration. However, tensions still remain, stimulated by the persistence of a strong bilateral trade imbalance in favour of Spain, and high levels of Spanish corporate investment in the Portuguese market.

In spite of substantial growth of exports, the sustained growth in domestic demand has resulted in rapid import growth and a continuous trade deficit throughout the 1980s. The 'services' account has consistently provided a positive net balance: this derives from high earnings from tourism and emigrants' remittances (the latter representing the equivalent of some 10% of GDP). The current account deficit has widened from 3–4% of GDP in the mid-1980s to 8–9% of GDP in the early 1990s. This may be represented as a natural feature of the process of economic development and is easily financed by a combination of EC Structural Fund transfers and foreign direct investment.

10.5.2 Foreign direct investment

FDI has made a major contribution to the country's economic development since the mid-1980s. Over recent years FDI flows have averaged between 3 and 4% of GDP. The combination of low labour costs, EC investment incentives and a favourable local tax regime provides an attractive environment for foreign investment. This activity seeks to capitalise on the high rates of return obtainable in the domestic market where there is a dearth of local competition, as well as to establish export oriented production platforms. With the exception of Belgium-Luxembourg, Portugal has the highest level of FDI/GDP of any EC country; foreign firms are now operating in most sectors of the economy and are particularly well represented in finance, real estate and business services [*OECD Survey 1992, Table 9*]. FDI represents a vital means for achieving economic modernisation: it represents an important channel for knowledge transfer, a source of much needed financial capital and a competitive stimulus for domestic firms.

10.6 PROSPECTS AND FUTURE DEVELOPMENT

Portugal's entry into the EC followed nearly two centuries of virtual isolation from European affairs. Since 1977, when the country first made an application to join the EC, there has been a radical shift towards West European values and socio-political structures. This has been followed by sustained structural adjustment in the economy but there remains a long way to go if significant economic convergence is to be achieved. Net resource transfers via EC structural funds seem set to continue through the 1990s but pressures on key sectors of the economy, notably agriculture, will increase as full EC integration is completed between 1993 and 1996. The real challenge facing the economy in the remaining years of the 20th century derives from the competitive pressures generated from the simultaneous completion of the single market and the end of the transition period for EC accession. Successful integration will depend upon the country's ability to sustain 'supply-side' improvements, notably: continuing privatisation, financial liberalisation, increased flexibility of the labour market and extended administrative reform.

While progress is being made in most of the above areas, reform of the bureaucracy is a central problem which remains to be addressed. Portuguese public administration is rule-bound, inefficient and extensively overmanned. Public administration employment, excluding health and education, is 6.6% of the working population, compared to 5% in the UK and 4.5% in West Germany. Public bureaucracy grew rapidly in the 1970s, and in part, provided a means of absorbing the large numbers of returning colonial administrators.

An essential requirement for the transformation to a modern market economy is the elimination of the overload of regulation and restriction, together with the associated bureaucratic structures and attitudes which have accumulated over the long period of pre-democratic dictatorship. Improvements in the attitudes and efficiency of the civil service require the creation of a meritocratic system of promotion, proper training and rational pay structures. In view of the substantial political power and influence exercised by the civil service, this will represent a real challenge to a modernising government.

10.7 BIBLIOGRAPHY

European Commission: *European Economies* OECD (1988–92): *Economic Surveys: Portugal*, Paris

Economic Intelligence Unit (1992): 'Portugal' in *European Community: Economic Structure and Analysis* [Regional Reference Series]

Bliss, C. & de Macedo, J.B. [eds.] (1990): *Unity with diversity in the European Economy:The Community's Southern Frontier*, Cambridge University Press

Corkill, D. (1993): *The Portuguese Economy since 1974*, Edinburgh University Press

Hudson, M. (1989): *Portugal to 1993, Investing in a European Future*, Economic Intelligence Unit Special Report No. 1157

CHAPTER 11

Greece

Ian Stone

11.1 POLITICAL AND HISTORICAL CONTEXT

The country regarded as the ancient centre of European civilisation is now on the economic and political periphery of Europe. It is the only EC state without a frontier with another Community member, and in many respects it more closely resembles its Balkan neighbours than its EC partners. Psychologically it is part of the West and for decades has looked in that direction for its military and economic support; yet geographically it is in the East and significant elements in the society are ambivalent to the Western state and its institutions. Communism's collapse presents a challenge to the nation's social and political cohesiveness in terms of the fragmentation of neighbouring states and the reassertion of cross-border ethnic divisions. It also, however, deprives Greece of much of its strategic importance for the West, thus undermining its eligibility for special treatment and support enjoyed throughout the post-war era. It is within this context that government has been attempting to bring the Greek economy – in terms of its structures, management and performance – into line with that of other EC member states.

The USA exerted considerable influence in the 25 years following World War II, by virtue of its loans, foreign investment and political support for the only non-communist country in Europe, east of Austria. European influence increasingly displaced that of the US in the period following the 1967–74 dictatorship by 'The Colonels'.

Democracy was restored in 1974, when the centre-right New Democracy Party was elected to power, and it was out of a concern to nurture the fledgling democracy that Greece (after a period as an associate member) was admitted as a full member of the European Community as part of its 'second enlargement' in 1981. The year of entry coincided with the election to office of the *Panhellenic Socialist Movement (PASOK)* under Andreas Papandreou. State corruption scandals, unfulfilled promises and poor economic performance led to a swing back to the liberal-conservative *New Democracy* party in 1990, albeit with a virtual balance in terms of parliamentary seats.

Three decades of being excluded from power had sharpened political differences between the Left and Right in Greek politics; the Socialist governments of the 1980s were, perhaps understandably, keen to institute radical change. By adopting an extensive programme of nationalisation, they attempted to add the role of entrepreneur to the traditional indirect forms of state influence on the economy based on subsidies, licensing, and price and income controls. The use of increased public spending and an enlarged public sector to redistribute income and employment in favour of *PASOK* supporters, was a marked feature of the early 1980s. At the very point when – learning from experiences in the 1970s – other EC states were turning away from such policies as nationalisation and maintaining employment through supporting 'lame duck' industries and by fiscal expansion, Greece embraced them. The inefficiency of state enterprises together with intensified external competition associated with full EC membership combined to produce low real growth and declining investment. The economy ended the 1980s with significant macroeconomic imbalances and widespread structural problems. At the time of the 1990 election, inflation was running at 23%, the current account deficit was equivalent to 7% of output and the PSBR stood at 22% of GDP.

Recognising foreign creditors' increasing reluctance to finance the ailing consumer-oriented economy, the New Democracy government introduced stabilisation measures, together with a wide-ranging package of liberalising reforms (including deregulation and privatisation) designed to alter expectations and economic behaviour. The *Medium Term Adjustment Programme*, covering 1991–3 and supported by an EC loan of 2.2 billion ECUs, was aimed principally at reducing the size of the public sector (and the PSBR), bringing down inflation, and improving the balance of payments. Short-term deflation was to be combined with medium-term growth through improving the economy's supply-responsiveness. Slippage in the programme's implementation led to its extension to 1994 and more active government efforts (via a convergence plan) to move towards targets embodied in the Maastricht Treaty. Priorities in the adjustment programme also shifted, with more weight assigned to a wholesale reform of both taxes and the public sector.

The New Democracy government has been trying to signal an end to the conditions which applied in the 1980s; henceforth, the economy will be run on the basis of non-accommodating policies. Businesses now have to rely on efficiency gains rather than subsidies, low-interest bank loans and devaluations; labour has to accept wages in line with its productivity. Such changes are regarded as a prerequisite for improved economic performance and a resumption of the Greek economy's convergence towards EC standards.

11.2 STRUCTURAL CHARACTERISTICS AND TRENDS

11.2.1 Population and labour market

The population of Greece stands at 10.2 million. While population is declining in the majority of EC states, in Greece – as in Ireland, Portugal and Spain – numbers are rising. The rate of increase has fallen since the 1970s, however, from over 9% in the 1970s as a whole, to only half that rate in the 1980s. The yearly growth rate during 1985–90 was 0.56% compared to an EC average of 0.27%. Projections indicate a rise of over 14% for 1980–2010 compared to 4.3% for the EC as a whole.

The labour force has increased in recent years at more than 1% per year, and the forecast for 1980–2010 is for a rise of 25% (compared to the EC average of under 9%). Currently, the labour force in Greece amounts to 4 million, with 3.7 million officially employed in 1990. At 39.5% of total population, Greece's participation rate is well below the EC average of 45.7% (Table E15). The country has a history of substantial emigration during the post-war period, particularly during the 1960s. In the 1970s, 9% of the workforce was working abroad (mainly in Germany, but also in the UK), providing remittances sufficient to purchase almost a quarter of imports, but depriving the economy of skills. Migration has since fallen away considerably, with the changed labour market conditions in host economies. One estimate of the number of emigrants for the 1980s put the figure at 150,000 (around 3% of the labour force), although there are some 4 million people living outside the country who are Greek-speaking or think of themselves as Greek.

The previously rapid transformation from a rural to industrial economy slowed dramatically in the 1980s, reflecting attempts to decentralise administration and industry and increased farm investment and support. Some 25% of all jobs were still in agriculture in 1990; a proportion markedly above that in the EC as a whole (6.6%; see Part E, Figure E.2). The comparative backwardness of the economy is also revealed in the proportion of the employed population engaged in services, which at 47% in 1990, falls well short of the percentage for the EC (61%). Manufacturing, with 20% of employment, is also somewhat below the overall EC figure of 23%, while construction and mining account for 5% and 2% of jobs respectively.

The official figure for unemployment over the period 1983–90 was 7.6%. The official rate for the 1970s (average 2.2%) was half that prevailing in the EC as a whole; even during 1981–90, Greece achieved an average figure which was below that for the EC as a whole (9.8%). The most recent rise is understandable in terms of lay-offs in the state-controlled sector and reduced hoarding of labour among private sector firms. Urban areas (Athens and Salonica) record higher rates than the rest of the country (10% as against 6.5% in 1991). It should be remembered that Greek unemployment figures are comparatively low by EC standards for a combination of reasons, including the method of statistics collection and availability of casual employment in agriculture and the urban informal sector 'the black market'. There is a large difference between these administrative measures and those based on labour force surveys. The latter suggest that the true level of unemployment is double the official figure.

11.2.2 Gross domestic product

In economic terms Greece performed well in the 25 years leading up to 1980, recording a rate of economic growth for the period second only to that of Japan among OECD nations. In the 1960s, real growth in GDP averaged 7.6% per annum; the lower rate of growth between 1971 and 1980, 4.6%, was actually slightly greater than the rate recorded by Japan (and considerably above the average of 3% in the EC). This achievement was based on investment by Greek and US companies encouraged by a package of financing arrangements, export incentives and protectionism. The performance in the 1980s, however, was comparatively poor: real GDP growth averaged only 1.5% for the decade, compared with the EUR 12 figure of 2.3% (Table E19). In the

1980s the economy suffered from exposure to international competition (as a result of full EC membership), capital flight by Greek nationals (in response to the policies of the Socialist government) and a diminished supply of funds from Western banks. Greece's performance was such that it fell to the bottom of the OECD growth league. The country was overtaken in terms of GDP per head by Portugal in 1989, thus making it the poorest EC state, with GDP per head equivalent to less than half (48%) of the EUR 12 average in 1992 (Table E20). While it is true that the size of the 'black market' means that the published figures do not fully reflect the level of Greek average income, the country's relative position has clearly deteriorated.

11.2.3 Consumption and investment

Government policy during the 1980s contributed significantly to the situation where an increasing share of output was devoted to consumption (private and collective consumption of general government), partly at the expense of investment. Private consumption rose from 64.6% of GDP in 1980 to over 70% in the early 1990s (Table E24). Given that the current average for the EC is 61%, and the next highest total is 64% (the UK), Greece is well out on its own in terms of the share of output devoted to private consumption. Further, in respect of collective consumption of general government, Greece also has the second highest proportion in the EC (21.2% compared to 16.4% in 1990) (Table E21).

The proportion of output devoted to gross fixed capital formation was lower in the late 1980s than it was for any of its EC partners; although this has since recovered slightly, Greece is still very much at the low end of the EC range. Discouraged by uncertainty over fiscal policies and a marked fall since the mid-1970s in the gross operating surplus, investment in the Greek economy fell from the range of 21–27% during the 1970s to 17–18% during the second half of the 1980s. Moreover, the actual level of consumption and investment has only been sustained by net inflows of goods and services from abroad equivalent to over 11% of GDP (the highest in the EC; see Table E21).

11.2.4 Wages and prices

The Greek economy's performance in relation to inflation is noticeably poor compared with that of its EC partners. High wage demands in the wake of the Colonels' dictatorship forced up real wages at rates twice the improvement in productivity. Inflation indexation of pay, introduced in 1982, subsequently added to the wage–price spiral. During 1981–90, annual inflation averaged 18.5% (EUR 12 = 6.5%) (Table E27). The only other EC economy with average 1980s inflation of above 10% was Portugal, though it performed markedly better than its Greek counterpart over the second half of the decade. Again, the performance since 1980 represents a sharp deterioration compared with the 1970s, when there were no fewer than five of the EUR 12 countries, including the UK and Italy, which had higher inflation rates than Greece's (13.2% for the period 1971–80). Collective agreement on private sector pay, combined with a pay freeze for public sector workers and a fall in inflation, has decelerated sharply the rate of increase in compensation per head over the recent period (see Figure 11.1).

11.2.5 Industry and market structure

Currently, agriculture contributes just over 15% to output, manufacturing, mining and energy 21%, construction 7% and services 57%. The agricultural sector, with 25% of the labour force, is characterised by generally low productivity, while the reverse is the case in relation to services, the substantial contribution of which is closely associated with the importance of shipping and tourism.

Agriculture is markedly more important in Greece than in all other EC economies (Table E22), and accounts for over 30% of exports. The sector, however, performs poorly in terms of EC productivity levels – reflecting the fact that some 70% of farms are less than five hectares in size. Some regions, such as Macedonia-Thrace in the

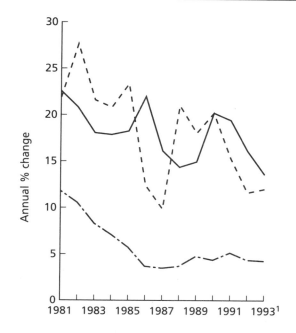

- - - - Nominal compensation per employee (total economy)

——— Inflation (private consumption deflator)

—·— EUR12 inflation (private consumption deflator)

[1] 1992–93 forecast

Figure 11.1 Trends in inflation and pay, 1991–3.

Source: European Economy, Annual Economic Report, 1993, p. 55

North and Thessaly in central Greece, are reasonably well-suited to agricultural development. These zones have higher than average farm sizes, a substantial share of the country's irrigated land and agricultural mechanisation, relatively fertile soil, and access to consumer markets for their tobacco, wheat and cotton crops. Agriculture is much less developed in mountainous and island areas, which make up respectively three-quarters and one-fifth of the land area. In such areas, farms are generally small and fragmented, soil fertility is poor and transport costs high. Greek meat and dairy producers have found it hard to compete at home with Northern EC competitors, while 'Mediterranean' crops like olives and vines have been exposed to competition for markets from Spain and Portugal. Considerable investment has been made in the agricultural sector during the 1980s – both by the Greek government and through the EC's Integrated Mediterranean Programmes – including marketing (establishment of co-operatives), storage facilities and irrigation extension.

Mining makes a relatively small contribution to output. Apart from bauxite and magnesite, accessible non-energy natural resources are not especially abundant. Energy resources, however, are hardly more substantial. Production of lignite, which in the 1970s supplied two-thirds of thermal energy, has been in decline, and oil and gas from the (one) offshore well is also now running down, leading to an increasing dependence upon imported oil, coal and direct imports of electricity from Albania (for peak requirements). Schemes such as a gas pipeline from Russia, shipment of liquid petroleum gas from Algeria and natural petroleum gas from Iran have all figured in recent plans for future energy provision. While Greece's overall energy requirement is low by EC standards, it is growing faster than elsewhere in the Community, yet the government has invested almost nothing in the last decade in projects to develop hydro-electric thermal, solar or wind-power sources. The substantial – and largely unexploited – hydro-electric potential is likely to become more significant in overall energy production. Similarly, there is considerable potential for development of solar power; Greece is the EC's most active market for solar installations, mainly for water heating.

Manufacturing – the output of which grew by only 2.5% over the decade to 1990 – accounted for a smaller share of GDP in 1990 than it did in 1960. The sector has never really developed in high-technology areas such as electronics and aerospace; its main areas of specialisation have been in labour-intensive and resource-processing activities. These include textile, clothing and shoe manufacture; food processing (canned, frozen and dehydrated fruits and vegetables); drinks (wine and Metaxa brandy); cement production; metal manufacture (nickel, steel and aluminium); chemicals and petro-chemicals, including fertilisers; and plastic household arti-

cles. Many of these sectors were built up during the period of protection, frequently by foreign companies, though Greek families – particularly those engaged in shipping – have diversified into shipbuilding, oil refining and other industrial activities, just as they have into airlines and tourism. The 1980s saw many manufacturing plants struggling to survive in a more competitive environment. The nationalisation of a substantial number of large enterprises has not been helpful in terms of achieving the efficiency improvements required for international competitiveness. This applies particularly to heavier industries affected by energy supply problems: in spite of plentiful bauxite reserves, production of aluminium continues only because its electricity is subsidised (the same situation applies in relation to nickel production). Cement, which is successfully sold overseas (mainly to the Middle East), is something of an exception to the general pattern; the coastal location of limestone being a major advantage.

The government is currently attempting to sell off its industrial plants as part of its privatisation programme (see below). Apart from the state-owned enterprises, many of the larger plants are in the hands of foreign companies; the only Greek-based multinational, as such, is Petzetakis, engaged in making plastic tubing products. Beyond this sector of industry, Greek manufacturing is characterised by a multiplicity of small and medium-sized family-owned companies. This applies particularly in relation to food processing and clothing, and the expanding sub-contract sector, where nationals returning from overseas have established factories making components for larger companies located elsewhere in Europe. In the mid-1980s, less than 1% of industrial establishments employed more than 50 people and 94% employed fewer than ten. Typically, firms tend to be under-capitalised, over-reliant on bank lending for their financial resources and limited in their adoption of modern business techniques.

Within services, shipping and tourism are of major importance. Shipping has been built up in the post-war period and the fleet largely consists of general cargo and container ships, tankers and cruise ships owned by shipping families such as

Onassis, Niarchos, Vardinoyannis and Carras. Government tax policies in the 1980s led some owners to register their ships outside the country; only around half the fleet now fly the Greek flag (although this is still equal to around 40% of EC tonnage, and constitutes the world's third largest merchant fleet after Liberia and Panama). Tourism also developed during the post-war period as modern communications and rising European incomes allowed the country to capitalise on its climate, beaches, islands and archaeological sites. Investment in tourist facilities has more or less kept pace with demand, and a significant increase in the numbers of marinas, golf courses and casinos is under way. Foreign companies have been active in this sector; they possess considerable advantages in terms of their multinational networks of agencies and airline links. Their chief means of access is through purchasing existing hotels and facilities – a strategy which reflects the extent of the bureaucratic obstacles confronting those wishing to establish greenfield ventures. A host of private family-run hotels caters for the cheaper end of the market.

Elsewhere in the service sector, small firms dominate. There are no really large trading companies in Greece; instead, a large number of medium-sized and small firms operate, often on a fairly local scale. This is partly a reflection of the fact that bank credit to commerce has been discouraged for many years by the central bank; credit for wholesalers usually comes from manufacturers, who have better access to bank credit. While some supermarket chains have emerged in recent years, most retailing is in the hands of small independent traders.

11.3 GOVERNMENT INVOLVEMENT IN THE ECONOMY

11.3.1 Government spending

In contrast to the situation in the EC overall, where general government expenditure as a percentage of GDP remained constant at around 48% during the 1980s, a dramatic increase in the size of government spending took place in Greece (from 40% in 1981 to 54% in 1991). Of the EC nations, only Denmark and the Netherlands have larger percentages of general government expenditure. This development has been accompanied by a rising government deficit which has, in turn, increased the size of the national debt.

During the 1970s, the general government financial deficit, though increasing, was in line with OECD trends and magnitudes and averaged only around 1.7% of the GDP for the decade. Government accounts sharply deteriorated with the oil price shock in 1980, and the situation worsened over the decade. The deficit quadrupled as a proportion of GDP during the 1980s, to stand at 20% in 1990 (compared to only 4% for the EUR 12) (Table E29). The general government debt stood at 106% of GDP in 1992 (up from 63% in 1985); on a wider measure of government activity, the public sector's debt has been put at 130%. This led to debt-servicing problems in 1991, resulting in government rescheduling (on top of previous action such as capitalisation of debt interest). Table 11.1 shows the rapid rise in interest payments associated with this debt.

Table 11.1 Net borrowing, gross debt and interest payments of general government, 1981–92 (as a % of GDP)

	1981	1982	1983	1984	1985	1986	1987	1988	1989	1990	1991	1992
Net borrowing	10.6	9.4	8.9	10.1	13.6	12.0	11.6	13.8	17.7	18.6	15.2	13.4
Gross debt	33.0	37.0	41.0	48.0	63.0	65.0	73.0	80.0	86.0	95.0	101.0	106.0
Interest on debt	3.2	2.6	3.4	4.6	5.3	5.7	7.2	7.9	8.2	11.9	12.8	14.6

Source: European Economy, Annual Economic Report, various issues.

In an effort to reduce spending the government has in recent years introduced a wage freeze for public sector employees, as well as adopting a policy of replacing only one out of every two members of staff leaving public sector jobs and taking steps to reduce spending on pensions (Greece spends 50% more on pensions than the average OECD country, measured against national income). Spending on defence, at over 6% of GDP, is also high by EC standards, but it is difficult for government to reduce this given the political uncertainty in the region.

11.3.2 Revenue sources

The size of the public sector deficit reflects a combination of, on the one hand, growth of government subsidies, generous welfare policies and the poor performance of many of the public enterprises, and on the other, the erosion of the tax base. The latter problem is associated with the very large size of the unofficial or 'black economy' in Greece, variously estimated to be the equivalent of between 30 and 50% of the GDP. There is major tax evasion among many sections of Greek society, amounting to an estimated loss of revenue for the state equivalent to around 10% of GDP. Although the problem is thought to be worst among the wealthy, professionals, small entrepreneurs and farmers, it is considered in Greek society in general almost a matter of *philotimo* (honour) to avoid taxes, wherever possible.

This has prompted the New Democracy government's reform of the tax system, which includes penalties for evasion, incentives for inspectors, and computerisation of government tax records. The government backed away from introducing a notional income tax based on lifestyle in the face of determined resistance from professional groups; tax inspectors do have the power, however, to inspect financial papers and credit card accounts where they find inconsistencies between declared incomes and lifestyle. The compulsory introduction of cash registers has done little to prevent the practice whereby those in self-employment or partnerships offer regular clients two prices, one with

and one without a receipt. In 1992 lower rates for most tax payers were announced in the hope that this will encourage payment, while also contributing to the strengthening of the supply-side of the economy. Increases in indirect taxes (e.g. petrol) have also been introduced.

11.3.3 Industry policy

Current policy towards industry differs sharply from that which applied in the 1980s, when nationalisation was central to the strategy for industrial development. This policy failed for a number of reasons, including a shortage of appropriate managerial personnel, lack of effective and independent supervision, immoderate recruitment according to political criteria (i.e. buying support through public sector jobs), promotions based on political connections rather than ability, and the priority given to pay increases over investment. The nationalised concerns became increasing loss-makers as the 1980s proceeded. In the 1990s the emphasis is on the private sector, and many public enterprises are scheduled for privatisation (see section 11.3.4). As in the past, the government operates low interest loans to small and medium-sized manufacturers, though the earmarked proportion of bank deposits for this purpose has been reduced and the interest charged on the loans has been raised. The rate of corporation tax was reduced in the 1992 reforms to a uniform 35% (from its previous range of 42–50%), with distributed profits not taxed again as personal income.

11.3.4 Privatisation

The nationalised sector of the Greek economy has grown in phases over the post-war period. Foreign-owned utilities and oil production facilities were taken into public ownership after the withdrawal of the Axis powers in 1944; the right-wing government in the mid-1970s nationalised various enterprises, among them banks, shipyards, chemical fertiliser plants, ammunitions works and Olympic Airways; and a further round of state acquisitions of private productive commercial and industrial enterprises took place in the early 1980s. A programme of privatisation was launched in 1990, with the aims both of confronting the budgetary problem and dismantling a long-standing system and mentality of dependence on the State which had become even more entrenched in the 1980s. Initially, the list included 27 debt-burdened companies which had come under state control in the 1980s. The programme has grown in size since then, however, and includes government asset holdings in the state-controlled banks, shipyards, mines, hotels and insurance companies; the list of companies for privatisation now extends to over 200. In addition, the government wants to sell stakes of up to 49% in state-owned utilities, transport companies (including Olympic Airways), and some defence industries, and has drawn up plans for the disposal of some 300 public entities attached to various ministries ('quangos'), many of which only survive because (like the utilities) they are a useful outlet for patronage appointments.

Progress in carrying through the programme has been slow. In 1991 only 19 companies were privatised (or liquidated), almost all of these small. Since then, although the sale was recently finalised of AGET-Heracles (Europe's largest cement exporter), a number of obstacles have contributed to delays in achieving privatisation. These include legal claims by previous owners, problems in co-ordinating the different public bodies involved, disagreements over the market value of firms and strong political and labour union opposition based on fears of job loss in subsequent rationalisation.

11.3.5 Regional policy

Over 50% of industrial capacity is to be found in the Athens–Port Piraeus conurbation, where 30% of the country's population is located. The noticeable concentration of economic activity in the conurbation relative to the rest of the country has attracted the concern of government. The other significant manufacturing centre is Thessaloniki. Efforts have been made by the authorities to decentralise manufacturing from Athens to the provinces and islands, but success has been limited by high transport costs and the difficulty of creating external economies outside the main centres; manufacturing has tended to develop near to an established market.

Following legislation on development assistance completed in 1983, the proportion of state grant available for a project has been determined by a combination of factors, including location and type of investment. Crudely, in defined zones around Athens and Thessaloniki, schemes only qualify for aid if they meet environmental, energy saving or technological criteria. A series of four further zones have been defined in which progressively higher grant awards apply. The highest awards – up to 50% of project costs – are available in the northern frontier areas and the islands on the eastern border. Tourism is a valuable source of employment to islands without significant development alternatives, and development of tourist infrastructure (e.g. marinas, golf courses, conference centres) is an important element of regional policy.

11.3.6 Markets and competition policy

Greek citizens have long been used to government intervention in markets. The Ministry of Commerce exercised extensive discretionary powers to control prices, grant licences, establish marketing boards and allow monopolies for some products. The tight regulation related to financial markets is a good example of the state's role (see section 11.4). Gradual liberalisation from the late 1960s onwards was reversed in the 1980s, with the re-imposition of price controls; deregulation resumed in the late 1980s, and accelerated with the change of government in 1990. By 1992, excluding EC-determined agricultural prices, fixed or controlled prices remained on products and services equivalent to 13% of consumers' expenditure (most notably, rents, electricity and petrol). In general, however, price levels on the controlled items do not deviate significantly from market levels.

Apart from state-controlled areas, a large number of organised trades and professions enjoy privileged status in the sense that regulations on competition allow incomes which are to a great extent economic rent rather than payment for productive work. Moreover, due to effective lobbying, this power increased in the 1980s, when laws were passed to further increase barriers to entry. Public sector trade unions, as well as professional groups and trades, were notable beneficiaries of such legislation during this period. Thus, for example, there are regulations in force which prevent the establishment of a bakery near to another (and restrictions on the sale of bread from other shops), while competition between petrol station operators is practically non-existent, allowing the operation of a system of restrictive opening hours.

Those expecting deregulation to result in significantly greater competition have so far been disappointed. In a country where the dominant firms and organised trades exert considerable influence, the authorities responsible for ensuring competition have made few inroads. Procedurally, the Competition Committee makes rulings on cases forwarded to it by the Directorate of Market Research and Competition and advises the Ministry of Commerce on sanctions. For a number of reasons, the system does not function effectively, however. There is a shortage of qualified personnel to analyse firms' accounts, consumer associations are weak, and the Ministry has tended to treat organised interests with great leniency.

11.4 FINANCIAL SYSTEM

The financial system in Greece is poorly developed and inefficient by EC standards. Traditionally, Greek business has been a family activity and securities accounted for barely 1% of finance to private companies during the 1980s. State-owned institutions accounted for 80% of loans made in 1992: 70% of the total by the National Bank and Commercial Bank; and the rest via the Agricultural Bank, Mortgage Bank and Industrial Development Bank. There is no clearing system, and the transfer of funds between banks is slow. State banks still operate a pass-book system, rather than cheque books; none of them operate a credit card system. Competition is limited, par-

ticularly in relation to bank-loan terms, which are subject to oligopolistic price fixing. The large spread between interest rates and deposits on loans (11 percentage points in 1991) has permitted inefficiency, with overmanning contributing substantially to the high operating costs. Like other public institutions, the banks have been a target for patronage appointments, and there is a general shortage of skilled personnel able to develop new financial products. Strictly financial criteria have often not been the basis of lending activity.

Private banks benefit from the large interest rate spread established by the state banks, and a number of new ones have entered the market in recent years. New entrants include a number of foreign institutions bringing the total number of overseas-owned banks to over 20. With lower operating costs, the new banks have been very profitable, while gradually building up their market position via new and specialised financial products (shipping lending, mortgage loans, consumer credit) and the quality of the service they offer. However, it takes time to build up a network of branches, and this – together with the absence of a clearing system – is undoubtedly to the competitive advantage of the established major banks relative to private and foreign institutions. Thus, inefficient banks have survived and lenders and borrowers alike are penalised by the high costs of banking (rates for working capital, including taxes and commissions, reached 33% in 1991).

The Greek financial system has been affected by changes introduced in recent years. The Bank of Greece has been active in trying to improve the functioning of the country's financial markets, and is putting pressure on the government to reduce its deficits by paring back its access to privileged sources of funding. Thus, the system whereby banks were obligated to hold an investment ratio of Treasury Bills equivalent to 40% of the increment of deposits is being phased out altogether, and banks have also been allowed to convert their stock of obligatory bill holdings into negotiable bonds of varying maturity. This has been an attractive option, given the pegging of the interest rates on such bonds to twelve-month Treasury Bills. In a further act of liberalisation, the banks' obligation to earmark 9% of the increment on deposits to finance public enterprises has been abolished.

These changes have allowed banks to diversify their portfolios and clear the way for the use of open-market operations (previously rendered impossible by the narrowness of the government securities market which forced the Bank of Greece to rely on more direct controls such as investment rationing). Both banks and non-bank residents are increasingly holding a more diversified portfolio of assets, and are thus becoming more receptive to changes in the relative prices of these assets. Monetary policy has also been facilitated by the imposition of greater central bank control over sources of bank liquidity (for example, overdrafts on accounts held with the Bank of Greece).

While the process of liberalisation has extended to include some freeing of capital movements and changes which allow Greek residents to have bank accounts in foreign exchange, established banks themselves are beginning to respond to a more competitive environment. Interest spreads have come down and new management in the state-controlled banks – personnel with extensive experience in foreign banks – are instituting investments in automated telling machines, strengthening dealing rooms and developing new financial products. However, efforts to achieve market determination of lending rates have been hampered by the high PSBR, which is the principal influence over the cost of credit and the money supply.

11.5 INTERNATIONAL RELATIONS

Greece's external trade sector is smaller than the EC average, with only Spain and Italy exporting a smaller share of output. Exports were equivalent to 22% of GDP in 1990, compared to an EC average of nearly 29%, though the share of exports in GDP grew faster (at 5% per year) in Greece in the 1980s than in the EC as a whole. The EC provided a market for 64% of total Greek exports in 1988 and 60% of its imports. The current main commodity exports are textiles and clothing (28% of total), food, drink and tobacco (26%), metals (9%) and oil products (7%). Germany is the principal market for Greek exports (24% of all exports in 1991), followed by Italy (17%), France and the UK (both 7%) (Table E32). Imports are dominated by manufactured goods, including machinery and transport equipment, which comprise 53% of all incoming items, with food and mineral oils accounting for 13% and 8% respectively. Germany (20%), Italy (14%), France (8%) and the Netherlands (6%) are the main sources of imported items (Table E33).

During the 1960s and 1970s the pattern of Greek exports shifted from minerals and agricultural products to finished manufactured products and semi-processed goods. This trend reflected the emphasis placed in that period upon industrial development and was assisted by a barter trade agreement with Eastern bloc states and by a 1% levy on bank loans which was used to subsidise exports. The fact that both of these trade-assisting devices disappeared when Greece joined the EC, helps to explain the sharp decline in manufacturing performance since the 1970s. While the export performance of industry deteriorated in the 1980s, Greeks showed an increasing appetite for imported consumer and manufactured goods; they now buy three times as many goods from the outside world as they manage to sell to it (exports in 1992 were $6 billion, compared to imports of $19.8 billion, a gap equivalent to 17% of GDP).

Due to the weakness of Greece in terms of merchandise exporting, it is normal for the balance of payments to show a substantial deficit in its visible trade and a sizeable surplus on invisibles. Even so, the net position is one of substantial and long-running deficit on current account. The average annual deficit was equivalent to around 5% of GDP during the period 1980–91. In this respect, at least, the economy's performance is not worse than that in the 1970s, when a similar-sized average deficit was recorded. The size of the external debt, however, has risen substantially since 1981 (when it stood at 22% of GDP) and in 1990 it was equivalent to 35% of GDP.

Invisibles are a particularly important element in Greece's current account, reflecting the significance of migrant remittances, tourism and shipping in the economy. Tourism is a major activity and the main foreign currency earner. The 9.3 million tourist arrivals in 1990 contributed $4.1 billion in overseas earnings; even in the recession of 1992 visitors brought in $3.3 billion. Money remitted home by Greeks living abroad contributed a further $2.4 billion to the invisible account in 1992 and earnings overseas from shipping amounted to $2 billion. Proportionately, the invisibles trade, at around 11% of the GDP, is roughly twice the EC average.

Transfers from the EC are another important means by which the deficit on the trade account is covered. The amount of transfer in 1992 was around $6 billion ($4 billion in structural aid, farm support, etc. and a further $2 billion in 'cohesion' money). This is a large transfer – equivalent to 9% of GDP – important not only for its balance-of-payments contribution, but also in terms both of infrastructural developments to which it is contributing (such as underground railway systems in Athens and Salonika and a tourist-oriented park and culture zone in Athens) and the government's budgetary situation.

Exchange rate

Greece is not a member of the Exchange Rate Mechanism, although the drachma is included in the currency basket of the ECU. It has thus been possible for the authorities to allow the exchange rate to depreciate to reflect, among other things, the higher rate of inflation relative to trading partners. The extent of depreciation in the 1980s has been very significant. In terms of ECU per national currency unit, the drachma depreciated from an index of 100 in 1979 to 29 in 1989 – only Portugal (down to 40 in 1989) can rival this deterioration – and fell by a further 11% against the ECU in both 1990 and 1991. The current government policy is to maintain a rate of currency depreciation which is less than the adverse inflation differential against trading partners. While this has the advantage of helping to reduce inflationary pressures in the economy, it also implies a cumulative loss of international competitiveness.

11.6 SPECIAL ISSUES

A number of further issues of significance can be identified.

Improvements in economic infrastructure

The need for improved economic infrastructure was recently highlighted when the inadequacy of transport and telecommunications facilities was cited as a factor in the failure of the Greek bid for the 1996 Olympic Games. The country's railway system is badly in need of modernisation; road links, particularly North–South, are inadequate; and the telephone system is lacking in standardisation and there are long waiting times for new connections. A number of key projects have been held up as a result of short-term political horizons, including an extension to the Athens underground system (badly needed given the problems of congestion and pollution in the capital city), the new city airport, and water supply improvements. These investments, and others in a substantial infrastructure modernisation programme, are important in the context of attempts to develop Greece as an upmarket tourist destination, particularly given the increasing competitiveness of neighbouring Turkish resorts across the Aegean. They are also important in that they are substantially funded by the EC and will thus help the balance of payments as well as providing a source of employment at a time of rising joblessness.

Public sector inefficiency

Public sector inefficiency is another area of concern, not least because of the fiscal pressures facing the government. The sector's inefficiency has given rise to wasteful duplication. The low quality of education and health services are widely supplemented with private provision;

defective public transport encourages the use of cars and contributes to widespread external costs in the form of congestion and pollution. Efficiency is hampered by the fact that in many branches of the public sector posts are filled by political appointments; a practice which has contributed to a very substantial problem of overmanning. Far from achieving its target of trimming 50,000 (10%) from the civil service payroll by 1993, an EC report noted that the numbers actually increased in 1991 (by over 4%). Recognising that failure to make progress on such structural reforms will make it increasingly difficult for Greece to obtain further instalments of EC funding – given the stiff terms attached to the special loan – the government is (as already noted) monitoring closely public sector recruitment and insisting on one replacement only for every two people retiring. There is an urgent need for a change in the philosophy and culture of the public sector, towards an emphasis upon efficiency and effectiveness in pursuing national rather than sectional objectives.

Political uncertainty

Political uncertainty relating to the developments in surrounding countries is also an important issue facing Greece. The break-up of the Soviet bloc has exacerbated Greek fears and suspicions of the territorial ambitions of its neighbours. In particular, it has been concerned at the recognition of Macedonia, the former Yugoslav republic adjoining northern Greece, which has led to a re-surfacing of nationalistic tendencies inside Greece itself. While developments in neighbouring former communist bloc countries raise the possibility that Greece may in the future be burdened by immigration from strife-torn areas, at a broader level, the forms of economic association between such low labour cost countries and the EC may undermine the attractiveness of Greece as a target for inward investment. Equally, of course, the changes affecting the Balkans potentially give Greece a new political and economic focus, e.g. trade and investment in neighbouring states, especially Bulgaria

and Albania. This may alter the Greek perspective on the EC, since membership of the Community would no longer be the country's sole source of combatting isolation. There is now the possibility of Greece finding a distinctive role in the south-east corner of a more homogeneous Europe.

11.7 FUTURE PROSPECTS

The recent period has seen some improvement in underlying conditions in the Greek economy. Government borrowing, inflation, and the current account have all been moving in the right direction. However, progress has fallen behind the targets set by the adjustment programme, particularly in relation to the public borrowing requirement – which in 1991 was still equivalent to 17% of GDP – and inflation (16% in mid-1992). The economy is a long way from achieving Maastricht Treaty targets.

If Greece is to become a Western-style economy, a prolonged and sustained effort to bring about structural change and performance improvement is needed. This will involve far-reaching changes in expectations and behaviour in both political and economic spheres. Responsibility for this task now falls to the PASOK government returned to power in October 1993. The New Democracy government did not make its task any easier by attempting to eliminate outdated regulations and to introduce free markets into a context which lacks a modern institutional environment and appropriate rules of conduct. Although Greece is under external pressure to achieve significant change in the nature and character of the economy, the new government's will to carry through such policies will be severely tested over the coming years. East European countries might do well to study the Greek experience of full membership of the EC; they may well conclude – as many observers in the EC now do in relation to Greece – that for some economies a prolonged period of associate membership holds greater economic advantages than full membership status.

11.8 SUGGESTED READING

Barclays Bank (1989 and 1992): 'Greece' in *Periodic Country Reports*, Economics Department, London

Carter, F.W.: 'Greece', in H.D. Clout (ed.), (1987): *Regional Development in Western Europe*, 3rd edn., David Fulton, London

Economist Intelligence Unit (1991): 'Greece' in *European Community: Economic Structure and Analysis*, London, pp 69–98

International Communications Network (1992): *Greece 1992: Doing Business in Greece* (published annually), Athens

Jouganatos, G.A. (1992): *Development of the Greek Economy, 1950–91*, Greenwood Press, London

OECD (1991): *Economic Surveys 1990/91: Greece*, Paris

Survey of Greece, The Economist, 22 May 1993

Tsaliki, P.V. (1991): *Greek Economy: Sources of Growth in the Post-war Era*, Praeger

CHAPTER 12

Ireland

William Glynn

12.1 INSTITUTIONAL AND HISTORICAL CONTEXT

Ireland is an island on the western fringe of Europe and is composed of 32 counties. A brief overview of Irish history will shed light on economic developments.

Ireland was a colony of the United Kingdom for almost 800 years. Its value to the UK was primarily defensive; for many years England feared a French or Spanish invasion through Ireland. An industrial revolution failed to take place to any significant degree due to a number of factors: Ireland was a convenient off-loading point for UK manufactured goods; a political decision was made to keep Ireland a poor agricultural country, and hence dependent on the UK; the Famine (1845–51) decimated the population through disease and emigration. Emigration has remained a feature of Irish life ever since.

In 1921, 26 of the 32 counties were made independent of the UK, and became known as the Republic of Ireland in 1949. The remaining six counties form Northern Ireland, which is part of the UK. The Republic comprises the main part of the island, with a land area of 70,283 km².

Ireland has been a member of the United Nations since 1955, but is not a member of NATO. In 1973, Ireland became a member of the EC, at the same time as Denmark and the UK.

While Ireland's industrial base has expanded significantly over the last 25 years, it is considered a developing economy by international standards. Agriculture, although declining in importance, is still an important sector. The modernisation of the Irish economy dates almost entirely from the post-war years. Real increases in economic growth did not emerge until the late 1950s.

Because of the underdevelopment of many aspects of the Irish economy, and the close trading ties with the UK, comparisons between UK markets and trends and the Irish context are common. However, while similarities between the two markets do exist, there are fundamental economic and cultural differences.

12.2 MAIN ECONOMIC CHARACTERISTICS

12.2.1 Population

The 1986 Census recorded the population of the Republic as 3,540,000. The annual rate of population increase dropped from 1.1% per annum in the period 1971–9 to 0.6% per annum between 1986 and 1989. This decrease was caused by a declining birth rate and increasing emigration. In 1989, emigration ran at approximately 30,000 per annum. This trend has been reversed somewhat due to the perceived upswing in the Irish economy, which has led to the return of many emigrants. The emigration trend has radically affected the age structure and geographical distribution of the Irish population. Figure 12.1 indicates population distribution among the four main regions of Ireland – Leinster, Munster,

Connaught, and Ulster. Leinster encompassing the Dublin area, lies in the South-east, Munster occupies the South, Connaught accounts for the Western region, while Ulster comprises the North – both the Republic and the six counties of Northern Ireland.

Due to the emigration factor, it is difficult to predict future population levels. Assuming low emigration (less than 20,000 per annum), population levels are likely to grow by 37.69% between 1990 and 2020, giving a population of 4,808,000. Trends since 1979 indicate an ageing population, with approximately one-half over 28 years of age. This is in line with current European trends, and barring unforeseen developments, will result in 50% of the population being over the age of 34 by the year 2000. At present, population density, at 51.4 per km^2, is the lowest in the EC.

12.2.2 Employment and the labour force

The lack of employment is one of the major problems of Ireland. Nevertheless, until the 1980s, unemployment remained at acceptable levels, mainly because (the growth in) the labour force was constantly reduced by continuous emigration. However, in the mid-1980s, unemployment rose to the extremely high level of more than 18%; and after a small dip in the late 1980s, it increased again during the recession in the

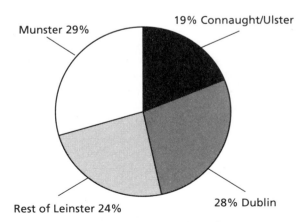

Figure 12.1 Population by area (1991).

early 1990s. Although reinforced by short-term cyclical effects, unemployment is at present chiefly caused by underlying structural problems, such as a steady employment reduction in agriculture, inadequate job generation in the manufacturing and service industry sectors and fiscal barriers to efficient job creation. The latter consists, among others, of a high tax wedge and generous unemployment compensation. In addition to the inadequate level of employment generation, emigration rates have decreased. The industrialisation programme, which started in the 1970s, was rather successful in terms of attracting inward investment, but failed to provide high rates of employment growth. Because of its weak position, the traditional labour-intensive indigenous industrial sector did not produce employment growth either.

In the early 1990s unemployment was rising rapidly again (see Table 12.1). As in the early 1980s, 1993 is forecast to show a further deterioration in employment levels due to adverse exchange rate developments, particularly in traditional industry sectors. Any upturn in the financial market will not be reflected in employment figures until 1994, as much of the movement is likely to take place at the end of 1993. Preliminary estimates from the 1992 Labour Force Survey show that there was no change in the numbers employed between April 1991 and April 1992 – 1,126,000 for both periods (see Table 12.1). A rise of 7,000 in the services sector has offset declines of 3,000 in agriculture and 4,000 in traditional industries, mostly construction. Further decreases in the sectors of agriculture and in traditional industry are expected in 1993, while a decline in the services sector is also anticipated, resulting in a possible overall reduction of 2,000 in the total 'at work' figure.

The rate of increase in unemployment for 1992 is unclear. The Labour Force Survey indicates a rise of 19,000 in unemployment in the year ending April 1992. The Live Register, however, records an increase of 31,000 for the same period. The low estimate of net immigration may explain the divergence.

Table 12.1 Employment and unemployment: annual averages (000s)

	1990	1991	1992	1993
Working population				
Agriculture	160	152	149	146
Industry	321	319	315	312
Services	645	655	662	666
Total at work	1,126	1,126	1,126	1,124
Unemployed	185	216	235	256
Labour force	1,311	1,342	1,361	1,380
Unemployed rate (%)	13.4	15.1	17.1	18.5
Live register	225	254	285	315

Source: ESRI Quarterly Economic Commentary, Autumn 1992.

12.2.3 Output and inflation

In line with European trends, Ireland's economic growth slowed markedly in 1992. However, in spite of an international slump and the difficult trading conditions caused by the Gulf War and its aftermath, GDP (measured on an expenditure basis) increased by 2.5%. GNP growth rose to 4.5%, due mainly to a sharp decrease in profit repatriations.

Growth in manufactured exports was 3.5 times that of other Irish export markets. This reflects a change in recent trends, which showed domestic demand driving expansion. Trends in exports and imports show a surplus.

While Ireland's performance compares favourably with that of other countries, it has not resulted in the much needed employment gains.[1] A recent National Economic and Social Council (NESC) report suggests an explanation: transfer pricing, regarded as rampant in the pharmaceutical, electronic, and manufacturing sectors, has created the illusion of high exports, output and productivity growth in Ireland. The reality is that Ireland is being used as a tax haven by multinationals, whereby transfer pricing is used to move world-wide profits to a low-tax location, i.e. Ireland.

[1] In the OECD, average ouput growth in 1992 was only 1.2%, while the EC average GDP growth was 1.5%.

This explanation is consistent with the EC Commission's revised forecasts for the Community economy, which places growth on a Community-wide basis for 1993 at almost zero; the Commission further concedes that this forecast is most probably optimistic.

12.2.4 Consumption and savings

The early 1980s recorded a major slump in consumer spending due to recessionary conditions. Growth did resume in the second half of the decade, but was modest, averaging 2% per annum in real terms. Throughout 1988–9 Ireland experienced a mini spending boom, funded by savings, credit, and current incomes. Rising unemployment, combined with the deepening UK recession, halted this. The 1990 National Accounts' estimate of personal consumer expenditure was correspondingly low; the retail sales index for the same year masked the sharp deceleration of growth in consumption (see Table 12.2). Consistently high real interest rates, combined with rising unemployment and slow international recovery, have resulted in low levels of consumer confidence. Savings ratios have consequently risen, and are expected to remain high. This obviously affects growth in consumer spending. The rise in interest rates and continued currency uncertainty caused a downturn in personal consumption levels during the last quarter of 1992, resulting in a total increase in personal consumption of 6% for 1992. Growth in personal consumer spending for 1992 is estimated at 2.75%.

Personal spending in the first quarter of 1993 was inhibited by economic uncertainty and high interest rates. However, renewed growth is expected to emerge during the second half of the year. The value of personal consumption is estimated to increase by 4.25% during 1993, with an 0.25% reduction in the savings ratio. Predicted low price increases mean that personal consumption volumes will rise by approximately 3%. The negative trend in consumer spending experienced in the 1980s is, however, likely to resurface, given rising unemployment figures.

Table 12.2 Consumption indicators

	Annual percentage change						
	1988	*1989*	*1990*	*1991*	*1992(a)*	*1992(b)*	*1993**
Consumption value							
NIE 1990 personal consumption	6.4	7.6	3.7	3.5	–	6.0	4.8
Retail sales index, value	4.8	9.2	4.8	1.8	5.6	5.5	4.3
Divergence	1.6	–1.6	–1.1	1.7	–	0.5	0.5
Consumption volume							
NIE 1990 personal consumption	3.6	3.7	1.1	0.3	–	2.7	3.0
Retail sales index, volume	2.1	4.7	2.7	–0.2	3.2	2.7	2.5
Divergence	1.5	–1.0	–1.6	0.5	–	0	0.5
Consumer prices							
NIE personal consumption deflator	2.7	3.8	2.6	3.2	–	3.2	1.7
Retail sales index deflator	2.6	4.3	2.0	2.0	2.4	2.6	1.8
Consumer price index	2.1	4.0	3.4	3.2	3.4	3.2	1.5

NB: 1992(a) – Annual percentage change to date
1992(b) – Annual percentage change forecast
1993* – Annual percentage change forecast

Source: The Economic & Social Research Institute (ESRI) Quarterly Economic Commentary, Autumn 1992.

The volume of public consumption has increased over the past two years, reflecting wage commitments made under the *Programme for Economic and Social Progress (PESP)*, and the increased demand on social services due to the rise in unemployment. Growth in the non-pay component is expected to form the bulk of increased public consumption throughout 1992/3. Net public expenditure on current goods and services is expected to fall in line with 1992 budget projections, showing an increase of 7.5% in value and 1.5% in volume. A similar value rise is anticipated in 1993. This, combined with a relatively higher pay deflator, suggests a volume increase of approximately 1%. While lower than the average public expenditure levels of recent years, it does not reflect a return to the severe spending cuts experienced in the late 1980s.

Following trends in other OECD countries, Irish savings ratios have increased substantially since the mid-1980s. Accordingly, consumer spending has risen only marginally, even though personal disposable incomes have grown by 3% in real terms. Inflation dropped from 3.4% in 1990 to 3.2% in 1992. GDP growth in 1992 was projected at 2.5% – a percentage point above the anticipated EC average. However, due to increased profit outflows, GNP was lower, at 1.5%.

12.2.5 Industrial structure

The economy, once predominantly based on agriculture, is now more oriented towards services and manufacturing industry. Growth in non-agricultural areas of employment is expected to continue. The services sector accounts for 54% of GDP, while manufacturing, mining, and utilities account for 36%. The remaining 10% is comprised of agricultural activities, the focus of which is dairy farming and the breeding of livestock. Agriculture comprises 15% of total exports, while the production of electrical machinery and chemicals account for 40% of exports.

Gross agricultural output in 1993 is expected to rise by 2% in volume due to livestock and crop increases. Because of a decrease in input volumes, the expected increase in the volume of gross agricultural output could be in the region of 5%. Growth is likely to cease in 1993 due to CAP and GATT requirements. However, as input volumes continue to decline, little change in gross agricultural output is expected in 1993.

1992 saw an upward trend in production volumes for manufacturing industries in general (for the first eight months of 1992 an increase of 10.75% was observed). The devaluation of sterling has resulted in reduced order books. Continued pressure on both the exchange rate and interest rates will have an adverse effect on industrial production levels.

Slower growth in manufacturing production will result in a decline in exports of manufactured goods in 1993. Initial forecasts for manufacturing growth were in the region of 4%. It is likely, however, that this will have to be revised downwards given recent economic developments. Whatever growth occurs will come from advanced industrial sectors. It is predicted that the traditional industrial sector will remain static. Output for the broad industry sector in 1993 is estimated in the region of 3.5%

1992 service output volumes are estimated to have risen by 2%. The situation for 1993 is affected by tight budgetary controls, although tourism may pick up from a relatively quiet year in 1992. Increases of 2% in the volume of total service sector output for 1993 are predicted.

12.2.6 Costs and competitiveness

Given the UK's predominance as Ireland's trading partner, it is essential that Irish enterprise maintains a competitive cost advantage with sterling.[1] Before the currency crisis, exchange rates averaged £ sterling 1:IR£0.96 in favour of sterling. Even with devaluation, the Irish punt is trading at a level higher than sterling. This poses major problems for Ireland's export trade. While recent trends have shown an improvement in hourly earnings and unit wage costs in the manufacturing sector, this has been due to the strengthening of Ireland's position against a single country – the UK. This strengthening was, with hindsight, due

---

[1] The UK accounted for 43.2% of Ireland's total imports in 1992, and 33.8% of Ireland's total exports during the same period. Germany was Ireland's second largest trading partner, accounting for 11.7% of Irish exports.

to the overvaluation of sterling, and as such, misleading. Current and future wage increases must be offset by relative gains in productivity in all sectors of the economy, if further competitive loss relative to other EMS narrow-band countries is to be avoided.

Currency effects will result in slower wage rises than those set out in the PESP guidelines – for the private sector, at least. Aggregate wages, salaries, and pensions are forecast to rise by 5.25% over 1992, although public sector earnings have risen slightly faster, and will continue to do so in 1993 under the terms of the PESP. Employment stagnation, combined with the exchange rate situation suggest that aggregate earnings will rise by approximately 5% in 1993. The rise in gross personal income is expected to slow from 6.25% in 1992 to 4.5% in 1993. Personal disposable income is forecast to rise by 6% in 1992 across all forms of income. The 4.5% rise forecast for gross personal income in 1993, however, is expected to be confined to non-agricultural incomes. The personal savings ratio remained constant in 1992. A forecast 0.25% drop in personal savings in 1993 reflects projected changes in the composition of income over the coming year.

12.3 GOVERNMENT INVOLVEMENT IN THE ECONOMY

12.3.1 Fiscal policy

Fiscal policy is aimed at reducing the Debt/GNP ratio. The 1991 Budget estimated exchequer borrowing at 1.9% of GNP. In reality it reached 2.1%. Net borrowing reached IR£231 million. Overall, the Debt/GNP ratio fell to below 105% from 109% in 1990. However, non-capital supply services were IR£130 million above the Budget estimate. This was due to a sharp increase in unemployment and a subsequent increase in health and social welfare payments.

The 1992 Budget held the current budget deficit to within IR£40 million of the 1991 figure. Overall Exchequer Borrowing Requirements were set at IR£590 million (2,4% of GNP).

The Budget for 1993 indicates a movement away from government intervention in business. This is in response to industrial lobbying for the creation of a competitive environment. The increase in minimum wage levels is viewed by some economists as a backward step as regards the creation and maintenance of competitive advantage, particularly given the recent currency crisis. While the present Budget does not actively increase competition, it does largely confine indirect taxes to the domestic sector. The ability of the Budget to impose radical fiscal policies on the Irish economy in an attempt to contain, and indeed, shape, the effects of the past six months of financial chaos caused by artificially sustained German interest rates and an international recession, has been severely hampered by two factors:

- the impact of the public sector debt burden, and,
- constraints imposed on taxation policy by the EC single market.

The government has introduced an additional 1% income levy on all incomes over IR£9,000 in an attempt to reduce exchequer borrowing (exchequer borrowing is estimated at IR£760 million for 1993, or 2.9% of GNP). This is aimed at stimulating economic activity and reducing interest rates. Such action is based on the assumption that Irish interest rates are within the control of the Irish government. The truth is that Irish interest rates in 1993 were dictated by instability in the ERM, not by the level of exchequer borrowing.

The main criticism of the 1992 Budget is that it failed to address seriously the unemployment problem. The restoration of spending power to those with jobs, combined with the widening of the differential between the net income of those with low-income jobs and those receiving government benefit, has yet to happen. While the need to maintain the standard of living of those without employment is not questioned, there are serious question marks over policy decisions which appear to discriminate against those earning above IR£9,000 per annum. In effect this policy, in its present form, will create a disincentive to work.

The current budget deficit and the Exchequer Borrowing Requirement (EBR) are predicted to remain within their original targets, i.e. in the region of IR£250 million and IR£500 million respectively, with the EBR not exceeding 2.3% of GNP. Trends in international currency and capital markets will make 1993 a difficult year for Ireland. Poor employment prospects mean that pay increases in the private sector will be constrained. Price inflation will be lower than it has been for some years, and tax buoyancy will be weak. Non-tax revenue is also expected to reflect this weakness. The increase in total revenues for 1993 is not expected to exceed 3%. Expenditure will rise due to previously agreed wage rises for the public sector under the PESP, rising unemployment, increased annual interest rate charges, and the cost of devaluation subsidies to businesses. The value of net current expenditure is anticipated to rise by more than 8%. In order to keep the EBR to IR£800 million, it will be necessary to restrict current spending to under 6%. This will necessitate the abandonment or postponement of development programmes scheduled for 1993.

12.3.2 Monetary and exchange rate policy

The main objective of monetary policy is to keep inflation as low as possible through maintaining a firm exchange rate within the EMS. This, combined with the continued absence of sterling from the EMS, its subsequent devaluation, and increasing speculative pressure on the punt, resulted in the devaluation of the Irish currency in the first quarter of 1993. This event took place despite the high interest rates at that time.

Domestic demand, however, will be severely affected by high interest rates. Should such a trend continue, it will render any forecasts of growth invalid. The principal factor in a determination of Irish short-term interest rates lies in the perception of the stability of the Irish currency. This is inextricably interwoven with the more general perception, and, indeed, future, of the ERM. The establishment of a credible exchange rate is essential if interest rates are to be reduced.

The reduction of German interest rates would facilitate the subsequent reduction of Irish interest rates – as it would for other EC members. German interest rates were 8% in mid-1993.

There is a growing perception that there is a fundamental change taking place in the German interest rate strategy. It is widely anticipated that the discount rate will fall in the near future; this expectation has had a positive effect on the activities of Irish investors, with sales of government bonds now in excess of IR£600 million since the start of the year. This strong inflow of funds into the economy has pushed external reserves close to IR£3.5 billion and National City Brokers (NCB) predict that the underlying level of reserves will continue to grow.

12.4 INTERNATIONAL RELATIONS

12.4.1 International trade

Imports of consumer goods and industrial materials rose in 1992, while those of capital goods and agricultural materials declined. Import prices declined in general throughout 1991, thus implying that the rise in value was accounted for by a rise in the volume of imports. A volume increase of 4.25% was predicted for 1992, with a value increase of 3.5%. Table 12.3 indicates these increases and the composition of total imports. The forecast for 1992 indicated an increase of 4% in value and 4.5% in volume.

The volume of imports is expected to reflect a marginally faster increase due to increased UK competitiveness and a more import-intensive composition of final demand. While the sterling devaluation did result in lower import prices, the subsequent devaluation of the punt has redressed this somewhat. Prices of imports from other sources are likely to increase, particularly with the expected increase in the strength of the US dollar. The fall in the annual unit value of total imports is forecast at approximately 0.5% for 1993, with the projected increase in the value of visible imports at 4.5%. The volume of total imports for goods and services in 1993 is estimated at 4.75%, as is that for visible imports. The value of imports of goods and services is projected at 4.5%.

Available export statistics predate the currency crisis, and indicate a value increase of 13.25%.

Table 12.3 Imports of goods and services

	1991 £m	% change Vol.	% change Val.	1992 £m	% change Vol.	% change Val.	1993 £m
Capital goods	1,814	−1.5	−1.5	1,787	4	3	1,841
Consumer goods	3,620	5	4.5	3,783	5.5	4.5	3,953
Intermediate goods							
Agriculture	466	−2	−5	443	−3	−3.5	427
Other	6,871	6	5	7,214	5	5	7,576
Other goods	83	3.5	3.5	86	0	0	86
Total visible	12,853	4.25	3.5	13,313	4.75	4.25	13,883
Adjustments	−188	–	–	−180	–	–	−180
Merchandise imports	12,665	4.5	3.75	13,133	4.75	4.25	13,703
Tourism	699	6	9.5	765	5	6.75	816
Other services	921	3	6	976	3	5	1,025
Imports of goods and services	14,285	4.5	4	14,874	4.75	4.5	15,544

Source: ESRI Quarterly Economic Commentary, Autumn 1992.

The devaluation of sterling, combined with the currency crisis, has led to a deterioration in Irish competitiveness relative to that of the UK on a scale hitherto unknown. Subsequent estimates of the likely effects on exports indicate a loss in export value. It is inevitable that, with the continued cost differential, a percentage of UK orders will be lost due to a reduction in profitability. This implies a decrease in the volume of exports in 1993. As the UK is Ireland's major trading partner with regard to traditional manufactured goods, the increased competitiveness of UK exporters in third markets will not affect Irish export volumes to any great extent, as Irish exporters do not trade directly with these markets. Overall, the volume of manufactured exports to the UK is likely to remain static in 1993. Lower average prices are, however, likely to lead to a fall in the value of exports in the region of 5%.

Irish market share in other European countries is expected to continue a pattern of modest growth. It is anticipated that the modern industrial sector will account for most of this expansion, resulting in volume increases of 6%, and 7% increases anticipated in value levels.

12.4.2 Balance of payments

The surplus on trade in goods and services in 1992 is expected to be in the region of IR£3,600 million; this takes into account balance of trade adjustments and a slight deterioration in the service balance. This surplus is expected to be maintained in 1993, although there will be a slight weakening in the trade balance.

An increase in the value of high-technology exports by multinational companies (MNCs) since mid-1991 suggests that a substantial increase in the amount of expatriated profits will be evident for 1992. Predicted slower growth in export values effectively means that profit expatriation for 1993 will also be slower. The national debt interest paid abroad is expected to remain constant throughout 1992 and 1993.

A high level of capital outflows will ensure the continued rise in credit flows. It is anticipated that forecast increases of 8.5% and 3.75% in net factor outflows will be confirmed. A decrease in intervention-related transfers is expected to result in a significant fall in net transfers from the EC in 1992. This is despite an increase in structural funds. However, the surge in 1992's trade surplus is sufficient to ensure that the total current account shows a significant surplus, in spite of negative net transfers and equally negative movements in net factor outflows. 1993's current trade account surplus is likely to show a slight decrease, although it should still account for over 8% of GNP (IR£2.25 million).

12.5 CONCLUSIONS AND FUTURE PROSPECTS

Ireland's economic growth in 1992 significantly outpaced OECD and EC averages. This was despite recession in the UK, one of Ireland's major trading partners, and in spite of an international economic downturn. The Irish economy was on course to achieve growth in the region of 3%, export levels were strong, and personal consumption was recovering from previously stagnation. This was, however, before both the devaluation of sterling, which has effectively reduced Irish competitiveness, and subsequent steep rises in interest rates. Any assessment of the Irish economy must take into account the high degree of interaction between the Irish and British economies. Due to Ireland's small size and the relatively high level of trade between the two countries from Ireland's point of view, any developments in the UK have a knock-on effect in Ireland. For 1992, growth is anticipated to be in the region of 2.5%, the annual increase in the consumer price index is placed at 3.25%, while annual average employment levels are expected to remain static.

Prospects for 1993 are heavily dependent on the exchange rate and interest levels. Should the current high interest rates persist indefinitely, the likely outcome for 1993 is economic stagnation, while a further rise would undoubtedly cause a full-scale recession. A rapid reduction in interest rates (through the restoration of confidence in the currency) is essential if this situation is to be avoided, and indeed, if economic growth is to be resumed. Given that Ireland is in effect a small open economy, it is buffeted by international events in the economic arena, with very little in the way of protection.

Another key challenge facing Ireland's economic development is the creation of employment throughout the next decade. A decline in emigration has resulted in an increase in the labour force, which, in turn, has led to increased unemployment (currently at 21%). Ireland's demographic profile means that annual growth in the domestic labour force will continue for a number of years.

Ireland's macroeconomic policy, focusing on low inflation, fiscal responsiblity, and a commitment to exchange rate stability, aims at developing competitiveness and assisting employment objectives. Low inflation rates, compared to those of Ireland's trading partners, are essential if rapid employment growth is to be achieved. Cost competitiveness of goods and services must be improved, particularly since the recent loss of competitiveness brought about by the devaluation of the Irish punt. The programme for Economic and Social Progress (PESP) had, prior to the current economic crisis, agreed on wage rises in both public and private sectors. While the need to keep pace with EC rises in standards of living is undeniable, there is an accompanying need to safeguard the Irish industrial base and its competitiveness. This means that, relative to competitor countries, Irish incomes should be slower to increase.

International recovery, albeit slow, will offer opportunities for faster export-led growth to those with competitive and innovative advantage. The maintenance of industrial peace, exchange rate stability, moderate cost development, and fiscal responsibility should translate into increases in Irish output and investment, which, in turn, will result in increased employment and prosperity.

12.6 BIBLIOGRAPHY

Irish Government Publications Office (1992): *Economic Review and Outlook 1992*, Sun Alliance House, Molesworth Street, Dublin 2

The Economic and Social Research Institute (1992): *Quarterly Economic Commentary*, Burlington, Dublin 4

Lambkin, M., Bradley F. (1993): The Changing Consumer in Ireland. Unpublished working paper. Department of Marketing, University College, Dublin

The Marketing Institute (1992): *The Irish Market: A Profile*, Leopardstown, Dublin 18

Euromonitor (1992): Turnmill Street, London

PART D

International comparisons

CHAPTER 13

International comparisons

Frans Somers

13.1 INTRODUCTION

This final chapter is concerned with international comparisons. There are both remarkable similarities and clear distinctions in the developments in the twelve major European countries.

Section 13.2 deals with the way in which the role of government has been reduced in almost all twelve countries; except for Greece they all show a movement towards market-orientated policies. This development is obviously in line with the overall market orientation of the Community policies. But there are also clear distinctions. Changes in Italy have not been as profound as in the UK for instance, leaving the other countries somewhere in between. The possibility of disparities in policies within the framework of the emerging economic and monetary union is also reviewed.

Sections 13.3 and 13.4 deal with the output, growth and international competitiveness of the twelve countries. Spain, Portugal and Ireland demonstrated remarkable growth rates in recent decades, while growth in the UK has been lagging behind. Furthermore, it will be shown that there are substantial differences in starting positions for the internal market. The opportunities and benefits for the respective economies will be discussed.

Section 13.5 outlines the continued marked differences in financial systems within the EC, especially in the field of financing of firms. The

UK especially, and to minor extent the Netherlands and Belgium, occupy a rather special position in this area. The differences in monetary policies are also discussed.

In section 13.6 a speculative attempt is made to identify possible fields of national specialisation within the framework of the coming reallocation of factors of production within the Community.

In section 13.7 some final conclusions will be drawn. One is the potential shift of relative importance from national states to regions in the future European Community, leaving the significance of national states, nevertheless, for the greater part unimpaired.

13.2 THE REDUCED ROLE OF GOVERNMENT

13.2.1 The return of free-market ideologies

The economic crises of the 1970s and the early 1980s marked a turning point in views on the role of government in the mixed economies of the Western world. The general consensus on state interventionist policies in the Keynesian welfare state broke down.

After the Second World War, social tensions in Europe were reduced considerably by the reaching of a kind of 'historic compromise' between labour and business management. Private enterprise and the freedom of the market were accepted by labour, in return for collective bargaining, social security, income and full employment policies and demand management. For business management this arrangement meant harmonious labour relations, political stability, assured demand and motivated workers. The welfare state enjoyed wide political support from both conservative and progressive parties. Naturally, there were differences in political opinions and aims, but in most West European countries these differences tended to be fairly small. Parties on both the extreme left and extreme right generally attracted a limited number of voters. Only in France and Italy did the Communist parties remain significant; though even in these countries they were unable to gain power. The main exceptions were Spain and Portugal, both ruled by right-wing dictatorships, and both with highly regulated, centralised and autarchical economies with protected interests for vested business groups.

Income and production in Western Europe increased very rapidly in the decades following the Second World War. Average GDP real growth rates amounted to about 5% and unemployment was reduced to low percentage levels. The Keynesian welfare state seemed to enjoy a measure of success in generating prosperity, employment, social security and harmonious industrial relations. Among theorists, a certain degree of consensus emerged; with a majority believing that a regulated market economy would lead to optimal results.

Within this framework of a 'mixed economy', the degree of regulation, however, remained a subject of extensive debate. In Germany, for instance, the idea of planning in any form was widely rejected. France, on the other hand, adopted a system of 'indicative planning', intended to establish a state controlled framework for the market economy. There remained also differences of opinion on the issues of nationalisation of key industries, the extension of social security systems and the size of the public sector in the various West European countries. But the extremes – on the one hand, a free market economy and, on the other hand, a centrally planned economy – were almost completely abandoned as realistic options; instead a convergence of economic policies along the lines of Keynesian theories took place.

There were two main causes for the breakdown of the general post-war consensus on economic policies which took place from the early 1970s: the economic crises and the internationalisation of the economy.

1 The economic crises began in the early 1970s. The rapid economic growth of the post-war decades had started to slow down, mainly because of increasing labour costs, saturation of output markets, surplus capacity and environmental constraints. The economy experienced serious difficulties after the first oil shock in 1973; and after some recovery, further serious problems accompanied the second oil price hike in 1979. Both oil shocks resulted in very rapidly increasing input prices for industry, putting a very strong upward pressure on inflation. This process was reinforced by a rapid expansion of the money supply, resulting in a situation of 'stagflation': a situation of inflation and stagnation combined. The welfare state proved unable to deal with mass unemployment and stagnating economic growth, because these phenomena put a heavy pressure on government expenditure while reducing revenue simultaneously. The social safety net of the welfare state was built for individual cases, not for mass unemployment. Thus, the 1970s was marked by increasing government expenditure, deficits and rising taxes, adding an increased tax burden to already depressed business profitability. Reduced profits meant a deepening of the crisis and gave rise to a vicious circle of lower investment and the closure of firms. Keynesian demand policies were generally not effective in the face of this crisis, because the problems were essentially located on the supply side: rising costs of inputs of energy and labour.

2 The internationalisation of the economy resulted, among other things, in an intensification of competition. Domestic industries

became more exposed to the world economy. Companies were forced to lower costs to compete in world markets, demanding improvements in efficiency and putting downward pressure on wages and labour.

In order to support their industries, governments were inclined to decrease taxes and reduce social security contributions and to relax labour protection.

Another consequence of the increasing internationalisation was the reduced ability of national governments to implement stabilisation policies. To be effective, such policies should be carried out more and more on a global scale, via supranational authority, as yet not in existence.

The above developments paved the way for what could be called a new era in economic theory and practice. Many economists and politicians blame the problems of the 1970s and early 1980s on government involvement in the economy. The welfare state, it is argued, created too heavy a burden for business and resulted in rigidities in many markets, particularly the labour market. Prices were distorted by taxes and subsidies, resulting in misallocation of production factors; profits were squeezed. Finally, governments were inclined to cover their deficits by monetary financing, fuelling inflation in the process. This is not the place to discuss the relative merits of these arguments. Indeed, some can be inverted: the welfare state did not cause high levels of government expenditure and the consequent economic crises, rather economic crises resulted in high levels of government expenditure. Similarly, deficits (e.g. the US deficit) could be seen as acting as a locomotive for the stagnating world economy in the early 1980s instead of slowing it down.

The point is that since the 1970s there has been a strong preference among economists and most governments of the Western world in favour of a return to the principles of the free market. This tendency has been reinforced by the events in Eastern Europe, where the failure of the planned economy became clear.

In practice, free-market principles have not been wholly dominant. It can be argued that an undoubted advocate of the free market, like Ronald Reagan, President of the United States from 1980 to 1988, combined supply-side measures with Keynesian demand policies. In Europe, pollution and other urgent environmental problems called for new regulations. But the general tendency of the last decade is clear. Most Western governments, whether led by Christian or Social Democrats, by Socialists, Liberals or by others, have been in favour of 'more market and less state' ideologies. To a certain degree this is in line with the Community policies in Europe which, as we have seen in Part A, are largely founded on free-market principles. But substantial differences, exist nevertheless, in the approach to the role of government by the various countries in the EC. These distinctions could become important barriers for further integration, particularly to the Economic and Monetary Union (EMU).

13.2.2 Policy shifts in the major EC countries

United Kingdom: sweeping reforms

Arguably it is the *United Kingdom* that has made the most pronounced changes towards creating a more liberal economy. These changes were set in motion when the Thatcher administration came to power in 1979. What has been said above about breaking an existing consensus is especially applicable to the UK. 'Thatcherism' stood for the abandonment of Keynesian demand management, deregulation of labour and capital markets, denationalisation of state enterprises, withdrawal of subsidies to industries, dismantling of labour union power, reduction of government expenditure and taxes and the eradication of the budget deficit. The only goal which has eluded the government has been that of controlling the money supply.

The Thatcher government was able to carry out such sweeping shifts in policy because the British political system normally guarantees that one party will be in power. The replacement of Mrs Thatcher by Mr Major as Prime Minister in 1990 merely meant a continuation of the same policies, albeit that some of them were softened to a certain degree.

Federal Republic of Germany: moderate changes

In comparison with the UK, reforms in the *Federal Republic of Germany* have been moderate. In Germany, too, tax reforms, reductions in the growth of government expenditure, the elimination of the budget deficit, deregulation and some privatisation have been carried out. But, alongside the UK, changes since the beginning of the 1980s have been more gradual. A tight monetary policy and an anti-inflationary stance have been constant factors in German political attitudes ever since the War. The *Bundesrepublic* never experimented with forms of economic planning and established few large state enterprises. Public sector ownership is mainly limited to the holding of private sector company assets by the federal government or the states.

Arguably, the biggest change may have been the shift from short-run stabilisation and full employment to long-run growth policies. Demand management was renounced in favour of supply-side policies. These policies included measures to lower labour and other costs (for instance, by reducing the tax burden), deregulation (e.g. in the field of telecommunication, transport and housing) and privatisation (in the form of selling government assets).

German unification in 1990 called for intensified state intervention. Government expenditure rose considerably and taxes went up. However, the bulk of the money was used to improve the East German infrastructure, to clean up the environment, to restructure East German industry and to create an appropriate institutional framework for a market economy. In other words: increased government intervention is only temporary and is meant to establish the right conditions for a free-market economy. It is in line with the long-term supply-side approach dominating German policy since the early 1980s.

France: role of government still significant

The last decade has also witnessed a remarkable policy shift in *France*. Though France can be considered as a market economy, it has a long tradition of state intervention, which goes back as far as the mercantilist policies of the 17th-century statesman, Colbert (see Chapter 3). Changes took place only after a fruitless attempt during the early 1980s to combat the crises with intensified state intervention. In 1982, which can be considered as a watershed year in French politics, the ruling Socialist government was converted to supply-side politics. To a certain extent it was forced to do so, because the French membership of the EMS effectively prevented the depreciation of the French franc in order to restore competitiveness and reduce the trade deficit. The free market principles of the Community influenced an individual Member State to act according to common principles in relation to a matter which could be considered as one of national sovereignty.

A whole range of measures to strengthen the supply side were implemented, from austerity policies to denationalisation and deregulation. The famous French system of 'indicative planning' was partly dismantled and the rigid French financial markets liberalised (in 1984). Industrial policy shifted from supporting specific industries and enterprises to provision of a favourable overall business environment. Nevertheless, state intervention has not altogether vanished in France. The role of government remains significant when compared with most other Community countries. Privatisations have been limited in extent and large state enterprises still exist.

After an attempt by the right-wing Chirac government in the second half of the 1980s to abolish the planning process completely, the Socialist government, which came into power in 1988, came up with a new Plan. This 10th Plan (the tenth since the War), designed to prepare France for the single market in the period of 1989–92, defines a range of targets, some of which required substantial government involvement. The 11th Plan, launched in 1993 by the incoming right-wing Balladur government, does not deviate from its predecessor's in this respect.

This approach to economic policy is noticeably different from the British one, and also, to a lesser extent, from the German one.

Spain: liberalisation led by state

For different reasons *Spain* is also moving in the direction of a freer market economy. This is mainly caused by Spain's efforts to integrate into the world economy in general, and the European economy in particular. This integration represents a distinct break with the practices of the Franco era. The early Franco period was characterised by extensive and wide-ranging public intervention, the existence of large dominant industrial groups, the complete absence of social concentration and high external trade barriers. The year 1959 marked the initial turning point. Spain became a member of the OEEC (the predecessor of the OECD) in that year and started a liberalisation process by removing controls and relaxing import restrictions. This development gathered momentum after Franco's death in 1975 and particularly after Spain's entry into the European Community in 1986.

The Civil War and the first period of Franco's dictatorship (1939–59) are crucial to understanding why Spain still lags so far behind in Western Europe. The international isolation, monopolistic structure and the rigid state intervention were responsible for a long period of stagnation in the Spanish economy. That is why Spain has been liberalising its highly centralised economy since 1959 and is aiming to convert it eventually into a market-dominated system. Full exposure of the Spanish economy to international competition (which will take place from the beginning of 1993), requires a continued modernisation of industry, enhancement of competitiveness and an increase in productivity. It is quite remarkable, however, to observe that the restructuring of the Spanish economy along market lines has not only been performed by relaxation of controls and regulations, but also to a large measure by state intervention. The state has sought, for instance, to revitalise traditional manufacturing sectors, to stimulate technological innovation, to build a social security system and to remove rigidities in the labour market.

The restructuring measures have met with considerable success since Spain is catching up very rapidly. Compared with other advanced market economies, however, the involvement of Spanish government in industry is still very large. Total financial support for the business sector in the middle of the reconstruction process (in the mid-1980s) rose to over 5% of GDP, which is the highest percentage within the EC next to Italy. A large part of these transfers and subsidies went to public enterprises. They have been only partly reduced since then, preventing the market-determined structural adjustments. Despite a vigorous privatisation programme in the 1980s, Spanish state-owned businesses still accounted for 9% of GDP by the end of the decade. On the other hand, the provision of public services (e.g. health care services, public education and transportation) is still underdeveloped. This could become an important constraint for continuing growth. Generally, an adequate level of these services is considered to be a necessary condition for the functioning of the market; that is why Spanish government, despite a tight budget policy, is intending to give public investment a high priority in the near future.

Italy: a continuing high degree of state intervention

Of all EC countries, *Italy* is probably least affected by the reinvigorated neo-liberal free market ideology of the 1980s. Like France, it has a long tradition of state intervention. General government was responsible for more than a quarter of total investment in Italy in the second half of the 1980s; direct investment of the public sector in a broad sense (including state enterprises and public and semi-public enterprises in which the state has a large stake) accounted for 6.5% of GDP in the period of 1980–7 according to OECD figures. Italy devoted a larger part of its GDP to aiding industry than any other European country in the early 1980s. A substantial proportion of this aid was destined for (not very successful) development programmes for the South of Italy and for the support of ailing industries. Public expenditure, too, increased considerably in the last decade, mainly due to transfers to families and companies and interest payments to service the rising national debt.

Nevertheless, in Italy too, a movement towards the free market can be observed. There has been a shift in industrial policy towards favouring the more advanced and strategic sectors, encouraging R&D expenditure and stimulating export performance. The financial system has been deregulated and capital can move more freely, especially since Italy accepted the Community Directive in this respect which became into force in July 1990.

A beginning has also been made on a programme of privatising state enterprises. The main aims of this policy are the reduction of the public debt and the strengthening of the role of the market in the economy. Public enterprises and the public service sector in general in Italy are notorious for their inefficiency; the discipline of the market is expected to reduce costs and to increase productivity.

As yet, however, this denationalisation process has not gone as far as in the UK, or even France. A large state enterprise sector remains a distinctive characteristic of the Italian economy, accounting for about one-fourth of GDP (against 19% in France). The three major state companies (IRI, ENI and EFIM) employ 550,000 people.

One of the main reasons why major policy shifts in Italy have not been carried out thus far is in the Italian political system. Radical political solutions and economic measures are ruled out by the fragmented political power and the necessity to form coalition governments, as Fineschi points out in Chapter 4. This is a major contrast to the situation in the UK, for instance, where the political system facilitated significant changes. Political reform, which started in 1993, may change this situation, however, providing new opportunities.

13.2.3 Policy shifts in the smaller EC countries

The year 1982 appears to be a watershed year in European politics, at least for the smaller European countries. Left-wing or left-of-centre (coali-

tion) governments were replaced by right-of-centre (coalition) governments in *the Netherlands, Belgium* and *Denmark*. All these governments – in line with the general trend of the 1980s – have shifted their approach away from public intervention, welfare state ideas and Keynesian demand management policies to tight fiscal and monetary policies, wage moderation, inflation reduction, improvement of competitiveness, strengthening of the supply side and other market-oriented policies. Since the mid-1980s governments in *Portugal* (led by 'centrist' Social Democrats) adopted similar policies, especially focusing on privatisation. Even the replacement of right-wing parties by more left-wing ones in later years in some of the countries mentioned above did not really change this trend. Despite the efforts to reach a freer market economy, government influence remained important in these countries; in Denmark and the Netherlands the public sector was only reduced to a limited extent, while Portugal is still characterised by a very large state enterprise sector, accounting for nearly 40% of GDP.

The major exception in the 1980s was *Greece,* which was, from 1981–90, ruled by a Socialist-led government, which put heavy stress on nationalisations, subsidies, licensing and price and income controls. The result was excessive inflation rates and public deficits, declining investment and a stagnating economy. The socialist government was replaced in 1990 by a conservative one, which launched a programme aimed at reducing the size of the public sector, bringing down inflation and liberalising the economy. In 1993, however, the socialists came into power again.

13.2.4 European integration and government involvement in the economy

Does the completion of the internal market and the coming of the EMU require further convergence in economic policies, e.g. in the field of fiscal policies? To a certain extent it must do. Large inflation, wage and productivity differentials between EC countries cannot be offset any more by the national use of the exchange rate mechanism. Large and sustained budget deficits can result in inflationary pressures, which in turn can threaten the common monetary policy of the Community (to be implemented by the future European Central Bank). Fiscal discipline is therefore supposed to be a crucial component of EMU.

With regard to fiscal policies, (more) convergence for indirect taxation and capital income taxation is certainly needed, because these taxes relate to the free movement of goods and capital. According to an EC report of 1990 on the EMU, however, there is no case for an overall harmonisation of the tax systems; Member States will remain free to choose their taxing and spending levels. Tax differentials, especially of income taxes and social security contributions, do not necessarily cause individual citizens to move if higher tax levels are matched by higher public welfare provisions and vice versa. This raises the question of the cost of public goods and services. First, there is the issue of efficiency. An inefficient public sector, as in Italy, will result in higher costs, to be financed by higher taxes. Second, countries with high debts have to devote a relatively large proportion of their budgets to servicing their debts. This means that (as in Italy) their public good provisions will be low compared with their tax levels.

So, a mismatch of taxing and levels of public provisions can be a reason for citizens moving from one country to another in order to maximise their benefits and minimise spending.

In addition to this mismatch, benefits and costs of public goods can spill over from one country to another. This applies, for instance, to transportation and telecommunication provisions and a clean environment.

Finally, diverging redistributive policies can cause spill-over effects if persons with higher incomes are allowed to migrate to countries with low tax regimes and if those entitled to social benefits also have some freedom of choice in selecting a country in which to reside (e.g. after leaving the workforce).

It may be that a complete harmonisation of fiscal policies is not needed. But there are clear limits to the extent to which disparities may occur. In the emerging Common Market, the level of taxing and public goods will be prominent elements in the increasing rivalry between national states. Governments want to offer favourable conditions for business; hence it is most likely that there will be a downward pressure on taxes.

For public goods and services the question is more complicated. On the one hand, a high level of public provision will strengthen national competitiveness; on the other hand, financial constraints (because of lower taxes) and the possibility of cross-frontier spill-over effects will have a negative impact on government spending.

This inclination to lower public provisions may be offset partly by common regulations, which will involve long and complicated negotiations. But the fact remains that the intensified competition in the Common Market, together with the loss of national autonomy, point to a further reduction in the role of government in the EC. This tendency may be reinforced if competition increases due to an economic recession, like the recession of the early 1990s. The traditional instrument of protection cannot be used; hence governments will be inclined to reduce tax burdens in order to enhance competitiveness.

State aid to industry is also under threat. This aid distorts free competition and is one of the barriers to be (at least partly) removed in order to achieve a barrier-free internal market after 1992. It is likely therefore that despite vigorous opposition from countries like France and Italy, EC limits to state aid will be tightened in the near future.

For all those reasons it seems likely that the trend towards a free market economy, which started in the 1970s, will be furthered by the process of European unification.

13.3 OUTPUT AND GROWTH

13.3.1 The overall picture

The period of 1984 to 1990 constituted a period of considerable growth for the European Community, with an average real growth rate of almost 3% (EUR 12). This period was preceded by a strong recession, with average real EUR 12 GDP growth slackening to 0.1% in 1981. So the recovery of the European economy has been remarkable. Nevertheless, European real growth rates still lagged behind the US and Japanese figures. The USA achieved in the same seven prosperous years a real growth rate of almost 3.1%, and Japan 4.6% (see Table 13.1). The worldwide upturn came to an end in the early 1990s when the economies of the Western world slid into recession again, albeit that this recession will probably not be as deep as the previous one. For 1994, a recovery is foreseen, which had started already in the US and the UK in 1993. Although an international trend can be recognised, there are quite noticeable differences between the European countries, however.

13.3.2 The major EC countries

Spain: highest growth rates

Apart from short cyclical disturbances, *Spain* has

shown very high growth rates ever since it began to liberalise its economy at the end of the 1950s. The average real growth rate over the last 33 years was about 4.3%, the highest (together with Portugal and Greece) of the twelve countries of the present EC. For all that, Spain has been confronted with very serious imbalances, in respect of high unemployment and inflation rates, large trade deficits and substantial regional disparities. Its infrastructure and social security system are still underdeveloped. Despite the progress made, Spanish per capita income is still only three-quarters of EUR 12 average.

For Spain in particular, with its economy still on an intermediate level, it will be of vital importance to increase productivity while controlling labour costs. The key factor for the Spanish economy is to enhance competitiveness and to keep real unit labour costs at an acceptable level in order to withstand the strongly increased European competition in the single market.

Table 13.1 Real growth rates, 1960–93

(a) The five major EC countries, USA and Japan

	Germany[2]	France	Italy	UK	Spain	EC[2]	USA	Japan
1961–79	3.7	4.6	4.8	2.6	5.6	4.0	3.5	7.7
1980–83	0.5	1.4	1.5	0.5	1.0	0.9	0.7	3.3
1984–90	2.9	2.5	2.9	3.1	3.7	2.9	3.1	4.6
1991–93[1]	1.6	1.3	0.8	−0.6	1.5	1.1	1.0	2.5
1961–93[1]	2.9	3.4	3.6	2.2	4.3	3.2	2.9	6.0

(b) The smaller EC countries

	Netherlands	Belgium	Denmark	Portugal	Greece	Ireland	Luxembourg
1961–79	4.2	4.0	3.5	5.6	6.4	4.5	3.2
1980–83	0.1	1.3	1.0	2.0	0.7	1.4	1.1
1984–90	2.8	2.7	2.4	3.4	2.0	4.5	4.6
1991–93[1]	1.4	1.1	1.3	1.6	1.6	2.5	1.8
1961–93[1]	3.1	3.2	2.8	4.3	4.3	4.0	3.2

[1] 1993: estimates.
[2] Excluding Eastern Germany.

Source: Table E19/*Eurostat*.

Italy: impressive growth, but slowing down

For *Italy*, too, growth in the last 33 years has been impressive. With an average rate of 3.6%, it is comfortably above the EUR 12 average and surpasses most other European countries, including Germany. But growth has slowed down markedly in the last decade, mainly because the Italian economy lacked balance in a number of respects.

First, there is an immense regional problem, with marked regional disparities between the Centre-North on the one hand and the South (Mezzogiorno) and Islands on the other hand. It could be argued that these disparities constitute an impediment to the further development of the more prosperous parts of Italy. Support for local industries, development plans and unemployment benefits put large claims on the budget already in deficit. A substantial part of the trade deficit is also attributable to the stagnation in the South. Second, servicing the rising national debt and transfers to families and companies are crowding out urgently required public investments in infrastructure and public services. Third, public services in Italy are very inefficient and ill-suited to an advanced economy like the (North and Central) Italian economy. Public education, too, should be upgraded to meet the growing demand for well-trained management. Fourth, wage increases and inflation rates are both too high, resulting in a deterioration of competitiveness and a persistent balance of trade deficit.

Many of the above disequilibria are interrelated with political problems. The highly fragmented and discredited political system existing until 1993 can be held in part responsible for a number of the problems indicated above, for instance for the mismanagement of the public sector. It is to be hoped that the political reforms which have been set in motion in 1993 will result in a new political structure able to come up with radical solutions.

On the positive side, the private sector, especially the small and medium-sized industrial enterprises, has proved itself a strong feature of the Italian economy, and has shown itself capable of adapting to changing conditions. Italian entrepreneurship has proved to be very vibrant and innovative. A substantial reduction in the disequilibria would strongly improve the effectiveness and the overall performance of the Italian economy.

Germany: moderate growth

Growth in the *Federal Republic of Germany* has been very moderate; in the 1984–90 upturn period it occupied a middling position with a real GDP growth rate of 2.9%. From 1960 to 1993 its growth rate of 2.9% put it not only behind Spain and Italy, but also behind France. Until 1990 expansion of the German economy, however, has been very solid and stable and it has been achieved without many imbalances. Inflation rates and the budget deficit have been very modest. Unemployment, however, though relatively low if compared with other European countries, is considered as too high in Germany, especially in the last decade. Another notable disequilibrium consists of the persistent current account surpluses.

Until recently, Germany's economy seemed to be more 'shock-proof' than any other, mainly because of its solid character and its basically sound structure. However, there are three major concerns for the German economy. The first is the high level of costs, especially labour costs. This level can only be maintained if Germany manages to achieve a sustained increase in productivity. The competitive advantage of the German economy lies in its ability to develop quality products with a high-tech content, not in its labour costs. If it wants to keep up with its main rivals, the USA and Japan, it needs to continue to devote a large proportion of its GDP to investment and research and development. Production costs in Germany are forced up also by relatively advanced environmental regulations.

The second concern is fear of loss of German dynamism. The growth of capital formation is rather low for an innovation-driven economy. There are some signs of changing attitudes towards risk-taking and entrepreneurship. New business formation is stagnating and there is a tendency among big firms to co-operate; both factors may be attributed to a decline in domestic competition. Rigidities in the labour and capital markets and a high degree of industry regulation in the field of working and closing hours, entrance requirements and competition rules undermine flexibility, dynamism and ultimately international competitiveness.

The third – and maybe for the moment most important – concern is related to German unification, which took place in October 1990. The integration of the former GDR puts a heavy burden on Germany as a whole, resulting in long-term inflationary pressures, large-scale bankruptcies and increasing unemployment in the eastern part of the country, a rising budget deficit, environmental problems, etc. Although the recession in Germany was postponed because of an expenditure boom right after the unification in October 1990, unification will probably slow down German growth for a considerable period of time. The transformation process requires far more money and time than originally expected, resulting in increased taxes and persistent upward pressures on inflation. This situation in turn restricts room for expansionary monetary policies, which constitutes the main reason why nominal interest rates remained relatively high in the early 1990s in Germany, in spite of a deepening recession. The biggest fear with respect to unification is that a permanent dual economy will arise, causing similar problems as those in Italy. Successful integration, on the other hand, may possibly raise the German long-term growth trend. Because of a catching-up process, East German growth could take off at a later stage and then eventually surpass West German growth, increasing the combined figure. Together with the challenge of the emerging internal market, the unification process may also contribute to a revival of German entrepreneurship and dynamism.

United Kingdom: recovery not founded on a firm base

Long-term growth in the *United Kingdom* has been the lowest of the twelve countries under consideration: only 2.2% from 1960–93. This is basically due to the poor performance of the UK economy in the period preceding the last upswing in the international economy in the 1980s. In the boom period of the late 1980s, the country succeeded in keeping pace with the average trend within Europe. The Thatcher government claimed the credit for this recovery, ascribing it to the return to the market and monetarist and supply-side politics. The British service industry – especially the financial sector – has expanded sharply in the last decade. In the early 1990s, however, the British economy was hit again by a deep, albeit short, recession. The downturn in the business cycle hit Britain first and more severely than most other European countries. Unemployment and the budget deficit increased again to high levels. This reveals that the British economy still exhibits important structural weaknesses.

First, the recent growth has been accompanied by growing imbalances within the economy. Inflation is, despite vigorous attempts to fight it, rather persistent, saving and investment (especially in R&D) remain comparatively low; and regional disparities have increased. Since 1986 the current account has deteriorated and there is now a large deficit. Underlying the latter is the lack of competitiveness of British industry, in manufacturing in particular. There is a tendency for UK manufacturing to concentrate on lower value products, as Stone explains in Chapter 5. A positive element, however, is the high level of direct foreign investment in the UK, Japanese in particular. This development could contribute substantially to a revitalisation and modernisation of British manufacturing, for example in the fields of electrical engineering, office machines and vehicles.

Second, the example of the UK clearly highlights the negative aspects of rigorously implemented monetarist and other market-oriented policies. Public investment in infrastructure has been neglected, with serious consequences for public transport, education, training and the level of R&D. A satisfying level of public provision is arguably a necessary condition for a flourishing private sector. The current insufficient level of public goods is one of the explanations of the deterioration in the competitiveness of British industry. In conclusion although there clearly have been positive developments in the UK economy in the last decade, future prospects for the UK economy do not seem to be especially bright. The recovery of the British economy in the second half of the 1980s was not founded upon a particularly firm base. Some policy adjustments in order to secure long-term growth seem to be necessary.

France: improvements

The *French* economy has made considerable progress in the last decade, after a deep recession in the early 1980s. It appears that it is returning to its long-term growth path characterised by a comfortable overall real GDP growth rate of 3.4% on average over the last 33 years. Generally the French recovery has been attributed in large part to the successful adjustment policies implemented by consecutive governments since 1982. In the second half of the 1980s there has been an impressive increase in exports and investment, which has restored the growth momentum. French macroeconomic policy succeeded in achieving low inflation rates and budget deficits, wage moderation, a balanced current account and a stable currency. The result of this strategy of 'competitive disinflation' has been the strongly improved position of French industry, particularly in export markets. Thanks to its overall improvement in supply conditions, France succeeded in gaining increased market shares in export markets recently. Although the French economy is confronted with international recession as well, which considerably depresses its performance in the short run, it may be expected that growth rates will pick up soon, if the international economic situation improves.

The French economy also has its weaknesses, however; unemployment being the most important. After reaching a peak in the mid-1980s of well over 10%, unemployment has proved to be rather persistent, even in times of output expan-sion. Mid-1993 unemployment soared again up to a provisional record of around 12%. Rigidities on the labour market seem to be the major reason for this development. The inadequate educational system is another reason. The high institutional minimum wage probably has contributed to the high unemployment among low-skilled workers and a capital-deepening investment trend. Another matter of concern is the high value of the French franc, caused by the nominal exchange rate adjustments of some important trading partners (notably the UK, Italy and Spain) in recent years. This has eroded French competitiveness. The policy of a stable exchange rate relationship with the D-mark also limited the room for interest reductions, which could be useful in pulling the country out of recession.

In general terms, however, the overall picture for France looks pretty sound. Notwithstanding the effects of international business cycles the French economy should be capable of resuming its long-term upward trend.

13.3.3 The smaller EC countries

The Netherlands

The Netherlands is an average performer in terms of output, with a long-term growth rate in line with the average EUR 12 rate. Of all EC countries, the Netherlands was most severely hit by the economic crisis of the early 1980s. The most important problem for the country is the high levels of labour costs and taxation, mainly caused by high social security expenditure. Particularly in the 1970s and early 1980s these costs squeezed profits and hence depressed investment. Other factors negatively influencing output are the rigidities in the labour market and the low level of labour participation. Since the early 1980s economic policy has been aimed at redressing these problems; and although some progress has been made, there is still a long way to go.

The Dutch economy has also some remarkable strong points, however. Inflation rates are among the lowest in the world, the currency is very strong and closely pegged to the German mark, competitiveness has been sharply increased, the current account shows persistent surpluses and the budget deficit has been reduced to acceptable levels. With a combination of strong international orientation and the favourable central location of the country, the Netherlands appears to be well prepared for further European integration and the internationalisation of the economy.

Belgium

Belgium is also a moderate performer with respect to output growth, with a long-term growth rate just on average. It is an extremely open economy (the most open within the EC, apart from Luxembourg); that is also the reason why it is forced to score well in terms of competitiveness, currency stability and inflation. The country is characterised by major imbalances as well, however, such as a very high national debt, high public deficits, high labour costs, a large tax wedge, and – last but not least – regional disputes and disparities.

Servicing the gross debt of general government (around 135% of GDP in 1993), mainly created in the 1970s and 1980s, puts a heavy burden on the government budget, causing an upward pressure on taxes and depressing government investment in infrastructure. Labour market disequilibria put a constraint on future economic growth as well. The central location of Belgium (like the Netherlands) and its international orientation will be a clear advantage for the country in the near future.

Denmark

Mainly because of the weak growth rates in the 1960s and 1970s Denmark is a poor performer in terms of output growth. This can be explained in part because of the high starting level in the 1950s. Another reason appears to be the slow growth in productivity, caused by the high levels of public sector expenditure and non-market services employment. Within the EC, Denmark has by far the largest public sector (in terms of both revenue and expenditure as a percentage

of GDP) which has a negative effect on the development of the private sector. Attempts to reduce government involvement in the last decade were only partly successful. Another constraint on growth is the rigidities of the labour market, which are caused in part by the (extended) social security system and the compressed wage structure. Unemployment is relatively high.

On the positive side, the Danish cost competitiveness and the international character of Danish industry are to be mentioned. In 1990, the current account went into surplus for the first time in 25 years. The integrating European economy will provide an opportunity for the Danish economy.

Portugal

Together with Spain and Greece, Portugal has shown the highest growth rates in the last three decades, reaching an average figure of 4.3% over the last 33 years. The underdevelopment of the country in the 1950s at the periphery of a developed continent offered plenty of room for growth, of course. The entrance of Portugal into the EC in 1986 has turned out to be quite beneficial for the country to date. Between 1986 and 1993 growth rates remained far above the EC average. Restructuring policies, which were aimed at converting the highly regulated and protected economy into a market-oriented one, have been relatively successful so far. The country received large amounts of money from the EC structural funds and a special status until the end of 1992. Successful real (and nominal) convergence in the future will crucially depend on supply-side improvements like industrial restructuring, privatisation, financial liberalisation and administrative reform. Effective improvements will ensure that the country remains attractive to foreign capital as well, which can make a vital contribution to the development of the country.

Greece

The exceptional average growth rate in Greek long-term output of 4.3% is mainly caused by the fast growth in the 1960s and 1970s. Since then, growth performance has been relatively poor, in spite of the Greek entrance into the EC in 1981 and the substantial aid from EC regional funds. The most important problems for Greece are fiscal imbalances, the public sector inefficiency, high inflation rates, lack of competitiveness and the underdeveloped infrastructure. The two main pillars of the Greek economic policy programme, launched in 1991, are fiscal adjustment and structural reform. Without a successful completion of this programme real GDP growth performance will probably remain weak.

Ireland

Ireland managed to realise impressive growth rates in both the long run and the recent past. Real convergence appears to be under way. The country was quite successful in redressing a number of imbalances in the 1980s, like high inflation rates and huge budget and current account deficits. Furthermore, since the mid-1970s it has introduced an intensive industrialisation programme, aimed among others at attracting direct inward investment. The economy's orientation shifted from predominantly agriculture to services and manufacturing.

The major imbalance is unemployment; Ireland has together with Spain the worst records within the EC in this area. The high unemployment rates are in part explained by the excessive population growth and in part by other factors such as the Irish development strategy. The Irish industrialisation programmes failed to attract labour-intensive industries and to integrate the successful foreign-based sectors with the indigenous sectors.

Continuation of the high Irish growth rates will depend among others on the success of structural reforms aimed at the supply-side of the economy, like tax reforms, reduction of state intervention in business and the creation of a more competitive environment.

Luxembourg

The long-term growth rates of Luxembourg are about average for the last three decades. In the 1960s and 1970s Luxembourg was an underperformer, mainly because of declining manufacturing industries. In the last decade, however, the country outpaced all other EC countries with a growth rate of 4.1% (see Table 1.4(b)). It has become a major international financial centre and is engaged in many international service activities. It shows outstanding records in almost every macroeconomic field and per capita income is the highest in Europe. Future growth prospects look very favourable as well.

13.3.4 Real convergence in the Community?

For a successful economic integration to be achieved, a certain degree of nominal and real convergence is needed. Nominal convergence was discussed in Chapter 1 (section 1.2.2, Table 1.1). This section addresses itself to real convergence. Has the Community witnessed a reduction in real income disparities in recent decades? Generally, the per capita incomes in purchasing power standards are taken as the most important indicator to evaluate this question. Real GDP growth is corrected for population increase in this case. In Figure 13.1 the development of real per capita GDP from 1973–93 of a number of selected countries is shown.

Of the four least developed countries (Greece, Portugal, Spain and Ireland) Ireland, Spain and Portugal made remarkable progress from 1986 onwards. This was also the year Portugal and Spain entered the Community. The efforts of these four countries to catch up with the Community average standard of living are supported by the Community's structural funds and national restructuring policies. Average income in Ireland has already been on an upward trend since 1973 (the year of entrance of that country into the EC). So far, EC membership appears to have been beneficial for these three countries. Nevertheless, there is still a long way to go before they meet the average living standard. For Greece it is a different story. Since its entry into the Community in 1991, the situation has deteriorated, despite heavy support from structural EC funds. The gap between Community and Greek per capita GDP has been widened considerably since that time.

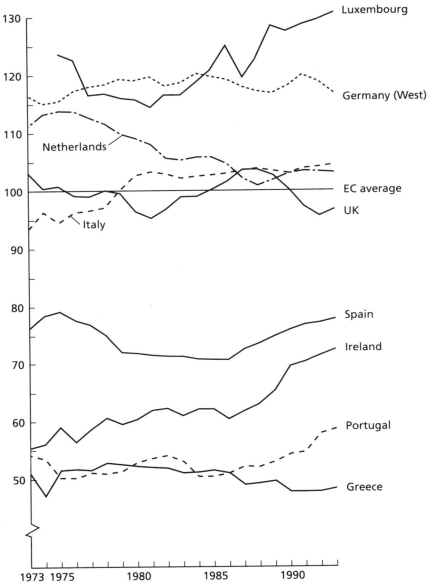

Figure 13.1 Gross domestic product at current prices per head of population, selected countries, 1973–93 (PPS; EC average (East Germany excluded) = 100).

Source: Table E20/Eurostat

From Figure 13.1 some trends with respect to the more advanced countries can also be identified. The Netherlands and the UK show clearly a downward trend. For the Netherlands, this is due to the combination of an average real income growth and an above average population increase. If the country wants to keep up, it should augment its labour participation rates. The UK-curve reflects the very moderate increase in real GDP; only in the late 1980s was a sharp improvement realised. Italy made indisputable progress, particularly around 1980 and has surpassed both the UK and the Netherlands. Luxembourg's success story is clearly demonstrated in the graph; the country is by far the richest in Europe today. Finally, (West) Germany shows stable development at a high level, which only came into jeopardy after German unification in 1991.

13.4 PRODUCTIVITY AND COMPETITIVENESS

13.4.1 The overall picture

National competitiveness is affected by inflation, unit labour costs and productivity growth in relation to exchange rates. It is usual to consider these factors as they relate to tradeable goods and services. The competitiveness of the European economy as a whole improved strongly in the 1980s; even relative to Japan and the USA. In the case of Japan, this is largely explained by the appreciation of the yen over the decade. By the mid-1980s the dollar too increased very strongly in value, which had a very negative impact on US competitiveness. From 1986 onwards the dollar depreciated dramatically to reach in 1992 a level even lower than that reached a decade earlier. This fall has, nevertheless, only partly offset the competitive advantage of the European economy acquired during the 1990s *vis-à-vis* the USA; nor did the reversal of the trend of decreasing nominal labour costs in the early 1990s so far.

Considerable progress has thus been made, mainly due to very moderate wage increases and sharp rises in productivity. The modest wage development can be attributed (at least partly) to a Phillips curve effect: unemployment and the unfavourable economic conditions of the beginning of the 1980s considerably reduced the bargaining power of the trade unions and hence resulted in limited wage demands. Labour productivity rose because of the lay-off of workers in company rationalisation measures and the capital-deepening investment policies implemented by employers in response to the economic crisis in the early 1980s. As a result the real unit labour costs of the total European economy decreased by 7% between 1980 and 1992, compared to 1.8% in the USA and 7% in Japan (see

Table E23). The real labour cost reduction contributed significantly to the improvement of company profits.

More relevant for the degree of competitiveness, however, are the unit labour costs of exported goods and services. If we take the double-weighted[1] nominal unit labour costs of the total economy in a common currency (relative to 19 industrial countries) as a standard, then the competitiveness of the EC countries as a whole rose by 22.7% between 1980 and 1989; since that year, however, it has fallen again to a level of 12% in 1992 compared with 1980. So a considerable part of the gains were lost again in the early 1990s. In the same period (from 1980–92) American competitiveness improved only by 1.1% (mainly due to the fall of the dollar) while Japanese competitiveness fell by 27.8%.

13.4.2 The major EC countries

For individual European countries their national degree of competitiveness is much more important, however, especially since more than 60% (on average) of their exports is going to other Member States of the Community. If we look at the figures of the five major EC countries, striking differences can be observed (see Figure 13.2).

Competitiveness in *France* and (to a lesser extent) *Germany* clearly improved in the 1980s. This can be explained by sharp increases in productivity and moderate wage rises. For Germany, this trend has been reversed in the early 1990s, however.

Spain and the *UK* made an impressive start in the first half of the decade, but fell back in the second half mainly due to inflationary pressures. The growth of annual earnings has been quite considerable in the UK and was not balanced by productivity growth. The deterioration of competitiveness in that country came only to an end in the early 1990s, mainly because of the slow down of wage increases due to the recession and the depreciation of sterling in 1992. Again it explains Britain's hesitation to participate in the EMS (and the European integration process in general),

---

[1] Weighted for geographical orientation and basket composition.

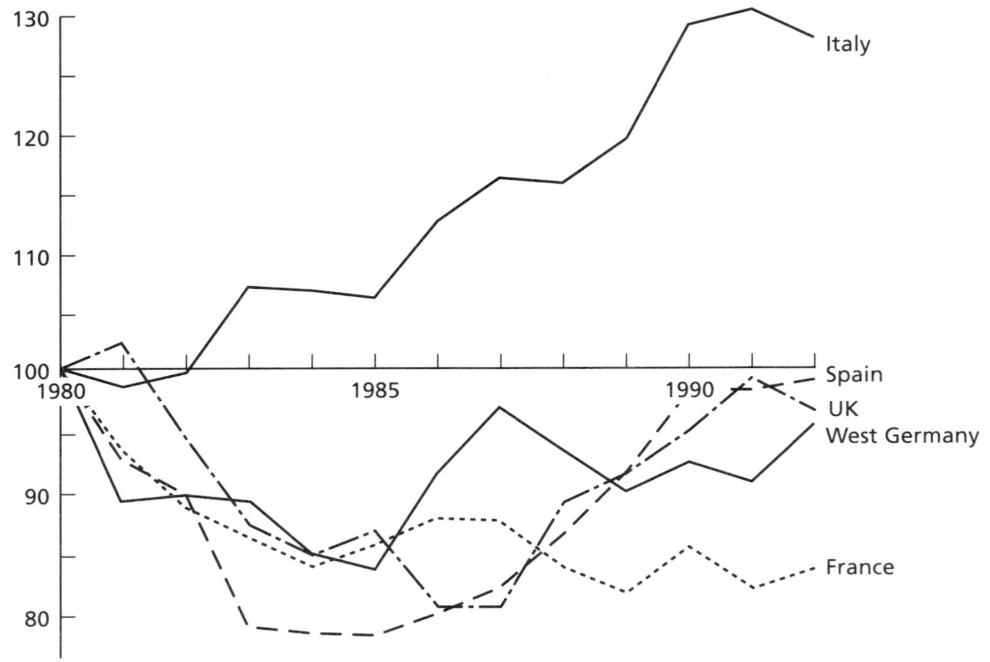

Figure 13.2 Nominal unit labour costs of the major EC countries in a common currency (USD): total economy. Relative to 19 industrial countries; double export weights. 1980–92.

Source: European Economy, No. 54, table 53

because the UK's membership will largely rule out use of the exchange rate instrument.

Inflationary pressures in Spain in the late 1980s were mainly caused by the demand side. Buoyant demand in an economy operating near capacity resulted in a gradual overheating and hence in a tendency for inflation to rise. The weakening of demand in the early 1990s, however, has not yet resulted in a substantial reduction in inflation. Despite the rising level of unemployment, the rise of labour costs did not stop. It appears that wages respond very slowly to deteriorating labour market conditions in Spain. The badly functioning social dialogue is one of the reasons for this. Only through the repeated devaluations of the peseta in 1992 and 1993 has the negative trend in Spanish competitiveness been stopped.

Italy's experience is quite different. Its sharp deterioration in competitiveness in the last decade compared to other European countries

seems to be dramatic; but this is a too black-and-white conclusion. Admittedly, for the Italian economy as a whole, wage increases were higher than improvements in productivity. After a marked diminution of pay rises at the beginning of the decade, provoked by the unfavourable economic circumstances, wage inflation picked up again in the second half of the 1980s. This can be explained by the regained strength of the trade unions, the continuing rise in social security transfers and the relative overall high level of inflation in Italy. Only after the depreciation of the lira in 1992, did the decrease in competitiveness stop.

The problem, however, is that Italy should perhaps in this respect not be treated as one country. While wage negotiations are centralised and on a national level, productivity improvements are certainly not. There are marked disparities between the Northern and Central areas on the one hand, and the South on the other. So the increase in labour unit costs in the South has been much more dramatic than in the Centre-North. These variations notwithstanding, concern over Italian competitiveness is justified. Italian industry has lost some market shares recently; a situation which will possibly be aggravated because Italian industry is not particularly strong in those sectors which will benefit most from the completion of the internal market (i.e. the advanced sectors). The removal of internal barriers will also sharpen rivalry in the more mature and labour intensive sectors which are still of great importance for Italy. Decentralisation of wage negotiations, an industrial policy encouraging R&D expenditure and the promotion of education and skills might be the spearheads in a medium-term policy to reverse the negative trend in Italian competitiveness.

13.4.3 The smaller EC countries

Most of the smaller European countries have succeeded in increasing their competitiveness in the last decade (see Figure 13.3).

These results were in general largely due to the effects of crises in the early 1990s and to government policies. In *the Netherlands*, for instance, since 1982 successive governments have pursued policies aimed at wage moderation, reduction of government expenditure and the budget deficit, and a decrease in inflation. To safeguard jobs, trade unions also refrained from excessive wage demands. The impact of a steady increase in the nominal effective exchange rate of the guilder was exceeded by far by the effect of modest real wage increases, causing unit labour costs to go down. In *Belgium*, too, wage increases have been constrained by government policies. In the early 1980s wage indexation and free wage negotiations were suspended and pay rises in the public sector were limited. In 1989, legislation was adopted giving the government ultimate authority to impose wage controls if Belgian competitiveness deteriorates. The conservative-led coalition government, which came into power in *Denmark* in 1982, also put heavy stress on the reduction of the public sector, the cutback of direct taxes, the

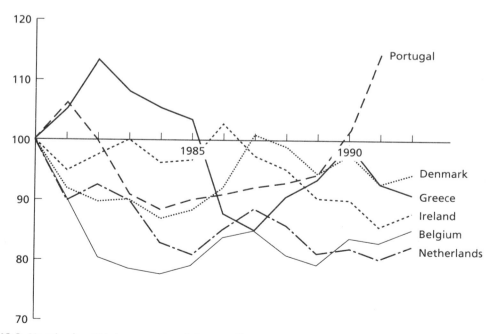

Figure 13.3 Nominal unit labour costs of the smaller EC countries in a common currency (USD): total economy. Relative to 19 industrial countries; double export weights. 1980–92.

Source: European Economy, No. 54, table 53

containment of wage increases and the recovery of Danish competitiveness. As a result, Danish competitiveness initially improved considerably in the 1980s; but it deteriorated again in the second half of the 1980s due to the hard currency policy of the government in combination with persistent inflation differentials. Some progress has been made again since 1990, however.

Portugal was characterised by very high inflation rates in the 1980s. Throughout most of the decade these inflation rates were more than offset by frequent depreciations of the escudo, preventing a deterioration in competitiveness. This development came to an end, however, when Portugal started to pursue an anti-inflationary hard currency policy in the late 1980s, culminating in the membership of the escudo of the Exchange Rate Mechanism of the EMS in 1992. Since then, Portugal's competitiveness has deteriorated very rapidly, due to strong rises in real wages, mainly caused by the tight situation on the labour market and time lags with respect to the falling rate of inflation. A reverse – or at least a slowing down – of this development might be expected from the depreciation of the escudo in 1993.

Although wages and prices in *Greece* have been soaring since the end of the 1970s, competitiveness has, nevertheless, not been worsened in the last decade. This can be explained by the continuous fall of the Greek drachma, which never participated in the ERM. Between 1980 and 1992 the double-weighted nominal effective exchange rate of the drachma has fallen by almost 80% (!), largely offsetting the average yearly increase in nominal compensation per employee of 20% during the last decade.

The improvement of *Irish* competitiveness in the second half of the 1980s was mainly due to very low inflation rates and moderate wage development in relation to productivity. The latter can be explained by the existing social consensus, and the high unemployment rate (Phillips curve effect). Part of the gains of the late 1980s was lost in 1992, however, mainly because the Irish pound did not follow the depreciation of the British pound in that year; instead it devalued almost nine months later. (The UK is by far Ireland's most important trading partner.)

13.5 FINANCIAL SYSTEM

13.5.1 The European financial markets

Financial markets and financial intermediation play an important role in the economy. They provide, for instance, the following services:

- gathering financial surpluses (savings) and channelling these funds to investment opportunities (real and financial);
- allocating financial resources to the most efficient users;
- spreading risks.

The financial sector is also quite important in terms of output and employment. In 1990 it accounted for approximately 7% of total value-added of the Community and for some 3% of total employment. An efficient financial system will obviously enhance economic welfare. The total amount of saving and investment will rise, new business formation will be encouraged and factors of production will be better allocated, increasing their productivity. That is why the Community puts heavy emphasis on the improvement of the European financial system by pursuing the establishment of a common European financial area. Distinct national banking regulations, high establishment costs for new banks, restrictions on foreign acquisitions of or participations in indigenous banks, limitations in cross-frontier activities, exchange controls and other regulatory barriers have segmented the European financial markets and hence prevented their efficient operation thus far.

In line with most other Community policies, the creation of a common financial market is mainly sought via deregulation, removal of barriers and harmonisation of standards and banking licences and, last but not least, in the strengthening of the Monetary System. Considerable progress has been made via the adoption by the European Council in 1988 of the Directive on the complete liberalisation of capital movements, which came effect on 1 July 1990. From that moment on, all restrictions on monetary or quasi-monetary transactions (financial loans and credits, current account, deposit account and stock market operations) were abolished. For Member States facing balance-of-payments difficulties because of this capital liberalisation, the medium-term financial support facility (MTFS) was created, a regulation granting them medium-term loans.

The free movement of capital is one of the cornerstones of the internal market and also a prominent step in achieving the first stage of the EMU (see section 1.2.2). Another important goal at this stage is the enhancement of the exchange rate stability of the Community currencies.

Notwithstanding this trend towards integration of the financial system within the Community, marked discrepancies in financial attitudes and practices can still be observed at present in Europe. Examples can be found in the field of:

(a) the financing of firms
(b) monetary policies
(c) the stances and responsibilities of central banks.

13.5.2 Financing of firms

The financing of firms is dominated by the banks (and special credit institutions) in Germany, Spain, France and Italy. Only in the UK, the Netherlands and Belgium, is the stock market of major importance. Financing of companies through the stock market is also more widespread in the United States and especially in Japan (see Table 13.2).

Table 13.2 Stock market capitalisation, end 1992

	billion ECU	% of GDP
UK	651	81
Netherlands	134	54
France	280	27
FR Germany	320	20
Spain	76	17
Italy	133	14
Japan	1,768	62
USA	3,663	81

In both Spain and Italy, the stock market has been very underdeveloped up till now. This is less the case in Germany and France, where they are of growing importance. The method of company financing is of particular relevance in affecting management attitudes towards risks and profits. On the one hand, financing through stock markets has the advantage of spreading business risks more widely. This can encourage investment involving high risks, because banks are generally reluctant to engage in this kind of business. Another advantage of market-based financing is that the financial vulnerability of companies will be reduced because equity is higher. Furthermore, public information on business will be more widely available because of legal disclosure requirements for firms issuing stocks and bonds. This will enhance public awareness of the capital markets. Against this, it is recognised that security-based finance can result in a preoccupation of management with short-term profits and dividend goals as Stone explains in Chapter 5. Focusing on short-term objectives may have a negative influence on long-term development and performance. Most shareholders (including institutional investors) are not concerned with the running of companies, while banks in general supply expertise if they are financially involved in a company.

If we apply the above remarks to company financing in Europe, we reach the following conclusions. Spain, Italy and arguably German stock markets should play a more prominent role. Well-developed, risk capital markets are lacking in these countries, frustrating new business formation and new venture initiatives. In the UK, by contrast, the dominance of stock market financing prevents business management from achieving long-term goals and objectives, essential for survival and long-term profitability of the companies involved. The best solution may be convergence of the two extreme positions; the UK shifting to long-term finance through banks and the other countries to more security-based financing. There are clear signs that this is happening.

Table 13.3 Financial structure of enterprises in the six largest EC countries (liabilities) (1987)

		Denmark	Spain	France	Italy	UK[1]	NL
1	Net capital	14.1	19.5	9.3	11.7	7.6	8.1
2	Reserves and provisions	28.3	20.2	21.4	21.4	42.7	43.5
3	Total capital and reserves (equity; = 1+2)	42.4	39.7	30.7	33.1	50.3	51.6
4	Medium- and long-term debt	18.3	14.1	23.1	10.2	7.2	16.1
5	Short-term debt	39.3	46.2	46.2	56.7	42.5	32.3
	Total	100.0	100.0	100.0	100.0	100.0	100.0

[1] 1986

Source: Data Base of Harmonised Company Accounts (BACH, DG II, October 1989).

In Table 13.3 some additional figures on the financial structure of enterprises of the six largest EC countries are presented. This table again highlights the prominent role of equity in the financing of British and Dutch firms and the noticeable significance of short-term debt financing, for example, of French, Spanish and especially Italian firms.

Financing through the stock market reduces financial risks. The ratio of indebtedness to equity (a measure of financial soundness) for the UK, the Netherlands and Belgium is only a fraction of the French and Italian enterprises.

13.5.3 Central banks and monetary policies

The stance and responsibilities of central banks vary greatly in the Community. At the one extreme is the German Central Bank. The *Deutsche Bundesbank* is almost completely independent from the German Treasury. Its main goal is to support price stability and the value of the D-Mark. Furthermore, it is supposed to support the economic policy of the Federal Government, but only in so far as this policy does not interfere with its main task. This arrangement reflects the German preoccupation with inflation, originating from Germany's traumatic pre-war experiences. In general, it has proved to be very successful.

In Italy, too, the Central Bank is relatively independent of central government. Since 1982

it has no longer been obliged to act as 'buyer of last resort' of public debt bonds. This 'divorce from the Treasury' was mainly effected in order to ensure a more solid stance of monetary authorities towards inflation, government itself being left too exposed to the effects of unstable political relations and interests. In the Netherlands, the Central Bank is formally subordinate to the Treasury. In practice, however, it is largely independent. It normally adapts to the policies of the German *Bundesbank*.

The German, Italian and Dutch system is in sharp contrast to those of the British, Spanish and French at least up to now. In France, for example, the *Banque de France* is narrowly related to the centralised French state and played an even more important role in the state-induced credit distribution in the past. In the UK, the Bank of England is a public sector body which acts under the (ultimate) authority of the Treasury, so the Bank of England can be considered a policy instrument of the British government.

In Spain, too, there are close links between the banking sector and government; in addition to the Central Bank (*Banco de Espana*) many banks are state-owned.

What does this mean with respect to monetary policy? For the *Bundesbank* fighting inflation is the first and utmost priority. The control of the money supply and interest rates principally serves this goal. Other objectives, like demand management, prevention or smoothing out of recessions, attraction of foreign capital, stabilisation of exchange rates are subordinate. Spain, Italy and Portugal, however, have also used interest rates to support their currency or to attract foreign capital. Even more important is the utilisation by many countries (UK, Spain, Italy) of interest rates as a major weapon against recession, even if this may cause inflation or a downward pressure on exchange rates. This is also one of the major reasons for the disturbances on currency markets in 1992/1993. Basically, these events were caused by differences in the monetary objectives of the countries involved, in part due to different stances and responsibilities of their central banks.

Clearly, nominal interest rate differentials cannot be maintained, once monetary unification occurs. This means that the goals and implementation of monetary policy should be agreed upon internationally. The problem, however, is that apart from convergence problems, the setting of short-term monetary objectives may also be influenced by differences in the phases of the business cycle applying to the various countries. This was clearly the case in 1992 when the UK found itself in the middle of a recession while the economy in Germany was just peaking.

Nevertheless, it has been decided (by the Treaty of Maastricht) that Europe's EMU will have a system of Central Banks (ESCB), co-ordinated by an independent European Central Bank (ECB), whose main objective will be price stability. Germany is an avowed proponent of this set-up. For most other countries the establishment of the ECSB and ECB will mean a radical change in approach to monetary policies. For all Member States it will mean another substantial loss of national sovereignty. The events on the currency markets in 1992 and 1993 do not encourage optimism regarding the realisation of the ECB and ECSB according to plan .

13.6 NATIONAL SPECIALISATION WITHIN THE COMMUNITY

The establishment of the large internal market, which came into effect in January 1993, will almost certainly result in a reallocation of production factors and economic activities, according to each country's specific competitive advantages. This will be the case because most artificial barriers, protecting inefficient industries, have been removed. This raises the question of what the distribution of industries will be in the Europe of the future. Obviously, nothing can be said for sure, but a tentative attempt can be made to identify some future industry patterns in Europe. A higher degree of specialisation can be expected in the field of tradeable goods and services along the lines of a country's or region's strong and weak points.

This raises the question, first of all, of what determines the comparative advantages of nations? It is clear that this question is not simple to answer. According to Michael Porter, in his book. *The Competitive Advantage of Nations*, international successes of a particular (branch) of industry in a certain country are dependent on four factors:

1 costs and availability of factors of production;
2 demand conditions;
3 the presence of related and supporting industries;
4 firm strategy, industry structure and rivalry.

These determinants are strongly interrelated and form a kind of mutually reinforcing system (called a 'diamond' in Porter's terminology). Additional variables influencing the national system, are government and chance. Without relying completely on Porter's system, one can appreciate, that competitiveness is dependent on a whole range of conditions. A large and demanding domestic market, vigorous competition, sufficient scale, favourable physical conditions, a high concentration of related industries, a good infrastructure, entrepreneurship, starting positions and government support play a prominent role. With this in mind, we will try to ascertain some possible fields of specialisation for the EC countries (Table 13.4). The list, which does not pretend to be complete, is principally based on existing dominant positions and future prospects.

Table 13.4 Possible fields of specialisation within the European Community

(a) Major countries

Germany

Services:
  construction services
Manufacturing:
  electrical engineering (electric motors, generators,
    transformers, household appliances,
    telecommunications)
  mechanical and instrument engineering (machinery,
    machine tools and equipment, plant for mines,
    iron, steel)
  motor vehicles and motor vehicle parts and
    accessories
  metal goods
  chemicals

France

Services:
  tourism
  engineering
Manufacturing:
  data processing, office machinery
  motor vehicles, parts and accessories
  aerospace
  nuclear power and hydroelectricity
  electrical equipment
  food
  drink (wine, brewing and malting, soft drinks, water)
  pharmaceutical products
  wool
Agriculture:
  dairy, livestock produce, fruit and
    vegetables

Italy

Services:
  tourism
  design services, fashion
Manufacturing:
  motor vehicle parts and accessories, motorcycles
  textile and leather, footwear and clothing
  furnishing
  jewelry
  machinery, machine tools
  electrical household appliances
  insulated wires and cables
  food industry (manufactured pasta, wine)

United Kingdom

Services:
  financial services (banking, insurance, financial
    intermediation)
  business services (advertising, management
    consulting, accounting, engineering)
  trading services
Manufacturing:
  chemicals (basic, industrial, agricultural)
  pharmaceuticals
  aircraft, aircraft parts and engines
  office machinery, computers and computer parts,
    software printing and publishing
  telecommunication equipment
  electrical plant and machinery and other equipment
  brewing, soft drinks
Energy:
  oil products

Spain

Services:
  tourism
Manufacturing:
  motor vehicles
  oil refinery
  electrical household appliances
  insulated wires and cables
  food and drink products
  footwear, household textiles, clothing
  rubber goods, ceramics
  wine, olive oil
Agriculture:
  fruit and vegetables

(b) *Smaller countries*

Netherlands

Services:
  transport and communication
  trading services
  business services
Manufacturing:
  basis industrial chemicals
  telecommunications equipment
  electronic appliances, radio, TV
  food processing
  shipbuilding
Agriculture:
  dairy products
  horticulture

Belgium

Services
  (international) administration
  transport and distribution
  financial services (banking and insurance)
Manufacturing
  basic industrial chemicals
  food and drink (brewing, malting, water, soft drinks,
    chocolate)
  car assembly
  wool and cotton, carpets, household textiles
  glass and glassware

Denmark

Services:
  transport and distribution
  trading services
Manufacturing:
  pharmaceuticals
  machinery
  medical and surgical equipment
  shipbuilding
  processing of plastics

Agriculture:
  fishing

Portugal

Services:
  tourism
Manufacturing:
  textiles, clothing, footwear
  fish and other seafood, wine
  ceramics
  insulated wires and cables
  paper and pulp

Greece

Services:
  shipping
  tourism
Manufacturing:
  cement
  clothing and footwear
  household textiles
  wool and knitting industry

Ireland

Manufacturing:
  office and data-processing
  telecommunications equipment
  medical and surgical equipment
  pharmaceuticals
  dairy products
  insulated wires and cables

Luxembourg

Services:
  financial services (banking and insurance)
  trading and business services

Specialisation within a particular country in a certain field of industry in this list does not mean that other countries will retreat from this kind of activity; it merely indicates that this country has or will possibly develop a leading position in (branches) of this industry. Moreover, dominant positions can be shared with other countries. Apart from these specialisations, many industries will continue to exist in virtually every country, simply because these industries are hardly able to serve more than local markets (e.g. construction and most services).

The table shows that – in broad terms – it is to be expected that, of the major EC countries, Germany will remain the industrial workshop of Europe, the UK the financial heart, Italy the designing and fashion centre. Similar striking national specialisations cannot be identified so easily in France or Spain; only in tourism do these countries occupy relatively dominant positions. The scope of activities in both countries is fairly broad; France, having clear-cut comparative advantages in capital and R&D intensive sectors, is engaged in industrial activities at a more advanced level and Spain still at an intermediate level. The strength of the French nuclear power and defence industry is partly due to favourable government procurement and state intervention policies and the independent attitude with regard to national defence of consecutive French governments.

The key to the German success is a high level of productivity, quality, reliability. Maintaining and strengthening the German position, which is currently under threat, will crucially depend on R&D, education, social stability, improvement of the labour market and restriction of labour cost increases. German competitiveness in international services (except for construction services) is rather weak. The UK has a leading position in this field. The City of London has become the third financial centre of the world, after New York and Tokyo. Recent technical innovations and deregulation contributed to the reinforcement of the dominant position of the City. London is confronted however, with more and more competition from its continental rivals in Frankfurt and Paris. Commitment to Europe is an essential condition for London to maintain its position. The use of English as a major language of communication may be one of the explanations of the strong presence of the UK in the international business services market.

Italy's powerful position in the area of design, fashion, clothing and related industries can be attributed to the sophisticated demand of the domestic market and the ability to perform this kind of activity in small and medium-sized companies, which are typical of the Italian private sector.

Of the smaller economies Belgium, the Netherlands and Denmark occupy strong positions in the service industry, especially in distribution, transport, communication and trading services. Belgium is leading in the intra-EC sea transport market and the Netherlands in the intra-EC road transport market. The central location of these countries clearly offers them a comparative advantage in this field. In addition, Belgium and Luxembourg have solid positions in the financial services industry; both countries also accommodate the seats of numerous international organisations and companies.

Due to their favourable climate and attractive coasts Portugal and Greece are well placed for tourism. Because of their low wages both countries also have a comparative advantage in labour-intensive manufacturing sectors (such as clothing and footwear). These sectors, however, are characterised by low demand growth and are facing increased competition from developing countries. Without substantial restructuring Greece, Portugal (and also Spain) will lose their competitive advantage in this field. Spain and Portugal are already implementing restructuring policies. Modernisation of the traditional industries should possibly be combined with an improvement in product quality (upgrading), in order to develop non-cost competitive factors. Italy can serve as an example in the implementation of such a policy.

Although wages in Ireland are modest as well, the country has a rather weak position in labour-intensive industries. It does hold a strong position in high-tech manufacturing sectors, however, due to the presence of many multinationals.

A dominant position, once established, tends to reinforce itself. The removal of administrative barriers can act as a further catalyst. The completion of the internal market, therefore, will probably have a positive effect on national specialisation.

13.7 FINAL CONCLUSIONS

In concluding this book, we will return to the subject of the importance of national states within the emerging European Economic and Monetary Union.

The completion of the EMU before the end of this millennium, will mean that monetary and budgetary policies will be carried out chiefly by a central authority, backed up by centrally controlled policies in the fields of infrastructure, education, R&D, the environment, the regions and competition. Important responsibilities remaining with national governments are expected to be the supply of public goods (those without cross-frontier effects), income transfers and redistribution and fiscal policies (in part).

This transfer of power from national to supra-national level means a considerable reduction in national sovereignty and will lead to a reduction in significance of the national states as independent entities.

This development notwithstanding, there will remain substantial geographical differences within the Community. These differences are determined by distinct industry patterns, inequalities in economic development and performance, variations in mentalities, tastes and culture, and will even be reinforced by an eventual higher degree of local specialisation.

With the national states losing influence as economic and political entities, however, regions probably will become relatively more important. Barriers between neighbouring regions will be broken down and cross-frontier contacts intensified.

Regions within nations will possibly be of increasing importance as well. This can apply to differences between rural and urban areas, but also to differences between one urban area and another. New opportunities and increased competition caused by the integrated market may emphasise not only local specialisation, but also disparities and unequal developments between nations. National instruments to adjust these developments will partly be dismantled or transferred to the Community level. The size, effectiveness and degree of differentiation of the Community policy are not yet clear. But despite this expected shift in relative importance from the national to the regional level, national differences will probably remain of great interest, even in a United Europe.

PART E

Statistical information

LIST OF TABLES

SOURCES

All data are derived from official EC publications.

European Economy, No. 54, 1993, Statistical Annexe: Tables E1–E14, E17–E20, E23–E33, E35.

Eurostat: Basic Statistics of the Community, 29th Edn. (1992): Tables E15, E16, E21, E22, E34; Figures E.1 and E.2.

1992 and 1993 figures are estimates and forecasts made by Commission staff using the definitions and latest figures available from national sources and based on data up to February 1993.

SYMBOLS AND ABBREVIATIONS USED

B	Belgium
DK	Denmark
D	Federal Republic of Germany
GR	Greece
E	Spain
F	France
IRL	Ireland
L	Luxembourg
NL	The Netherlands
P	Portugal
UK	United Kingdom
EUR 12	Total of Member States of the EC
–	nil
:	not available
Mio	Million
ECU	European Currency Unit
PPS	Purchasing Power Standard
GDP	Gross Domestic Product
EUR 12–	12 member countries, incl. West Germany
EUR 12+	12 member countries, incl. Unified Germany

Table E1 EUR 12–[1]: main economic indicators, 1961–93[2] (Annual percentage change, unless otherwise stated)

	1961–73	1974–84	1985	1986	1987	1988	1989	1990	1991	1992	1993
1 Gross domestic product											
At current prices	10.2	13.2	8.6	8.6	7.0	8.7	8.5	8.2	6.9	5.7	4.5
At constant prices											
incl. West Germany	4.8	1.9	2.4	2.8	2.9	4.1	3.4	2.8	1.4	1.1	0.7
incl. Unified Germany	:	:	:	:	:	:	:	:	:	1.2	0.8
2 Gross fixed capital formation											
at constant prices											
Total	5.6	–0.3	2.2	4.3	5.5	8.8	7.1	4.0	0.0	–0.1	–1.0
Construction[3]	:	–1.3	–1.7	3.9	3.2	6.8	6.1	3.7	0.5	1.1	–0.5
Equipment[3]	:	1.4	8.0	4.3	8.5	10.6	9.0	4.8	–0.2	–1.3	–1.6
3 Gross fixed capital formation											
at current prices (% of GDP)											
Total	23.2	21.3	19.0	19.0	19.3	20.0	20.7	20.9	20.3	19.8	19.6
General government[4]	:	3.2	2.8	2.8	2.6	2.6	2.8	2.9	2.9	2.8	2.8
Other sectors[4]	:	18.1	16.2	16.3	16.7	17.5	17.9	18.0	17.4	17.0	16.8
4 Final national uses incl. stocks											
At constant prices	4.9	1.5	2.3	3.9	4.0	5.0	3.6	2.8	1.2	1.0	0.3
Relative to 9 other OECD countries	–0.6	–0.8	–1.7	0.2	–0.3	0.1	–0.2	1.3	1.8	0.4	–1.2
5 Inflation											
Price deflator private consumption	4.6	11.3	5.9	3.8	3.6	3.8	4.9	4.5	5.3	4.5	4.4
Price deflator GDP	5.2	11.1	6.0	5.6	4.1	4.5	5.0	5.3	5.4	4.6	3.8
6 Compensation per employee											
Nominal	9.9	13.3	7.0	6.3	5.5	5.8	5.8	7.5	7.2	5.8	4.4
Real, deflator private consumption	5.0	1.8	1.0	2.4	1.8	1.9	0.9	2.8	1.8	1.3	0.0
Real, deflator GDP	4.5	2.0	0.9	0.6	1.3	1.2	0.8	2.1	1.7	1.1	0.6
7 GDP at constant market prices											
per person employed	4.4	2.0	1.9	2.1	1.7	2.5	1.8	1.2	1.2	1.5	1.5
8 Real unit labour costs											
1961–73 = 100	100.0	103.4	99.3	97.8	97.5	96.4	95.4	96.3	96.7	96.3	95.4
Annual % change	0.1	–0.1	–1.0	–1.4	–0.3	–1.2	–1.0	0.9	0.4	–0.4	–0.9
9 Relative unit labour costs in											
common currency against											
9 other OECD countries											
1961–73 = 100	100.0	103.4	84.3	92.4	99.0	97.0	93.9	104.8	102.2	106.9	104.2
Annual % change	1.1	–2.1	–0.3	9.6	7.2	–2.1	–3.2	11.7	–2.6	4.6	–2.5
10 Employment											
incl. West Germany	0.3	–0.1	0.5	0.7	1.2	1.6	1.6	1.6	0.2	–0.5	–0.8
incl. Unified Germany	:	:	:	:	:	:	:	:	:	–1.0	–0.8
11 Unemployment rate[5]											
(% of civilian labour force)	2.1	6.4	10.8	10.7	10.3	9.8	8.9	8.3	8.8	9.5	10.6
12 Current balance (% of GDP)											
incl. West Germany	0.4	–0.2	0.7	1.3	0.8	0.1	–0.1	–0.3	–0.5	–0.6	–0.9
incl. Unified Germany	:	:	:	:	:	:	:	:	–1.0	–1.1	–1.2
13 Net lending (+) or net borrowing (–)											
of general government (% of GDP)[6]											
incl. West Germany	–0.5	–4.1	–4.9	–4.5	–4.0	–3.4	–2.7	–4.0	–4.6	–5.3	–5.6
Incl. Unified Germany	:	:	:	:	:	:	:	:	–4.5	–5.2	–5.4
14 Gross debt of general government[6]											
(% of GDP)	:	46.1	58.5	59.3	60.8	60.1	59.5	59.5	61.4	63.9	66.9
15 Interest payments by general											
government (% of GDP)	:	3.1	4.9	4.9	4.7	4.6	4.7	4.9	5.0	5.4	5.7
16 Money supply (end of year)[6]	12.6	12.6	9.6	9.7	9.6	10.1	11.1	8.5	6.5	:	:
17 Long-term interest rate (%)	7.1	11.7	10.6	8.9	9.0	9.1	9.6	10.9	10.2	9.8	:
18 Profitability (1961–73= 100)	100.0	70.9	75.9	81.9	84.0	88.7	91.9	90.3	88.9	89.7	89.5

[1] Incl. West Germany, unless otherwise stated.
[2] 1961–91 Eurostat and Commission services: 1992–93: Economic forecasts winter 1992–93.
[3] 1974–84: EUR 12 excl. Portugal.
[4] EUR 12 excl. Greece.
[5] 1961–73: EUR 12 excl. Greece, Spain and Portugal.
[6] 1961–73: 1974–84: EUR 12 excl. Greece, Spain and Portugal.
[7] Broad money supply M2 or M3 according to country, 1961–73: EUR 12 excl. Spain, Portugal and United Kingdom.

Table E2 Belgium: main economic indicators, 1961–93[1] (Annual percentage change, unless otherwise stated)

	1961–73	1974–84	1985	1986	1987	1988	1989	1990	1991	1992	1993
1 Gross domestic product											
At current prices	9.2	8.8	7.0	5.3	4.5	6.9	8.6	6.2	4.6	4.7	3.6
At constant prices	4.9	1.9	0.8	1.5	2.0	5.0	3.8	3.4	1.9	1.0	0.5
2 Gross fixed capital formation at constant prices											
Total	5.1	−0.8	0.7	4.4	5.6	15.4	13.7	8.4	0.3	2.5	−3.3
Construction	:	−2.7	−0.6	3.0	3.0	14.7	7.5	7.1	2.0	3.8	−2.8
Equipment	:	3.4	2.3	5.3	7.1	15.9	21.2	10.9	−1.9	0.7	−4.0
3 Gross fixed capital formation at current prices (% of GDP)											
Total	21.8	20.0	15.6	15.7	16.0	17.6	19.3	20.2	19.8	19.9	19.1
General government	:	3.8	2.2	2.0	1.8	1.8	1.6	1.5	1.6	1.5	1.5
Other sectors	:	16.2	13.4	13.7	14.2	15.8	17.7	18.7	18.2	18.3	17.5
4 Final national uses incl. stocks											
At constant prices	4.8	1.3	0.5	2.8	3.8	4.5	5.1	3.5	1.6	1.9	0.6
Relative to 19 competitors	−0.1	−0.5	−2.1	−0.8	0.5	0.2	1.6	0.8	0.8	1.1	0.0
Relative to other member countries	0.0	−0.3	−1.7	−0.8	0.5	0.2	1.6	0.4	0.3	1.0	0.3
5 Inflation											
Price deflator private consumption	3.7	7.6	5.9	0.7	1.9	1.6	3.5	3.1	2.9	2.4	2.8
Price deflator GDP	4.1	6.8	6.1	3.8	2.4	1.8	4.7	2.7	2.7	3.6	3.1
6 Compensation per employee											
Nominal	8.9	9.8	4.5	4.7	1.8	2.4	3.5	7.7	6.8	5.4	4.7
Real, deflator private consumption	5.0	2.1	−1.3	4.1	−0.2	0.9	0.0	4.4	3.8	2.9	1.8
Real, deflator GDP	4.6	2.8	−1.5	0.9	−0.5	0.6	−1.1	4.9	4.0	1.7	1.6
7 GDP at constant market prices per person employed	4.3	2.3	0.2	0.8	1.6	3.5	2.2	2.3	2.2	1.7	1.2
8 Real unit labour costs											
1961–73 = 100	100.0	111.3	108.1	108.2	105.9	103.1	99.8	102.3	104.1	104.1	104.5
Annual % change	0.3	0.6	−1.7	0.1	−2.1	−2.7	−3.2	2.5	1.8	0.0	0.4
9 Relative unit labour costs in common currency											
● Against 19 competitors											
1961–73 = 100	100.0	105.3	87.8	93.2	94.2	90.0	87.9	92.8	92.2	94.5	98.2
● Annual % change	−0.3	−1.5	1.7	6.1	1.1	−4.5	−2.3	5.6	−0.7	2.6	3.9
Against other member countries											
1961–73 = 100	100.0	103.4	91.2	94.5	93.9	90.1	88.8	91.3	91.2	92.5	96.6
Annual % change	−0.8	−0.9	1.9	3.6	−0.7	−4.0	−1.4	2.8	0.0	1.4	4.5
10 Employment	0.6	−0.4	0.6	0.6	0.5	1.5	1.6	1.1	−0.3	−0.7	−0.7
11 Unemployment rate (% of civilian labour force)	:	7.7	11.8	11.7	11.3	10.2	8.6	7.6	7.5	8.2	9.3
12 Current balance (% of GDP)	1.1	−1.6	0.3	2.1	1.3	1.7	1.7	0.9	1.7	1.8	1.8
13 Net lending (+) or net borrowing (−) of general government (% of GDP)	−2.2	−8.3	−9.0	−9.4	−7.5	−6.7	−6.7	−5.7	−6.6	−6.9	−6.2
14 Gross debt of general government (% of GDP)	:	79.0	119.7	123.9	131.0	131.9	127.9	128.3	130.1	132.2	134.3
15 Interest payments by general government (% of GDP)	3.1	6.2	10.8	11.4	10.7	10.3	10.6	10.9	10.6	10.9	10.3
16 Money supply (end of year)[2]	10.1	9.5	7.8	12.7	10.2	7.7	13.3	4.5	5.3	:	:
17 Long-term interest rate (%)	6.5	10.6	10.6	7.9	7.8	7.9	8.7	10.1	9.3	8.6	:
18 Profitability (1961–73= 100)	100.0	65.5	67.9	69.7	75.1	81.7	90.1	85.7	80.3	79.6	76.8

[1] 1961–91: Eurostat and Commission services; 1992–3: Economic forecasts winter 1992/93.
[2] M3H

Table E3 Denmark: main economic indicators, 1961–93[1] (Annual percentage change, unless otherwise stated)

	1961–73	1974–84	1985	1986	1987	1988	1989	1990	1991	1992	1993
1 Gross domestic product											
At current prices	11.7	11.4	8.8	8.4	5.0	4.6	5.2	3.9	4.1	3.5	3.5
At constant prices	4.3	1.8	4.3	3.6	0.3	1.2	0.8	1.7	1.2	1.0	1.8
2 Gross fixed capital formation at constant prices											
Total	6.5	–2.0	12.6	17.1	–3.8	–6.6	–0.6	–0.5	–2.8	–8.3	–1.9
Construction	:	–4.5	8.9	18.0	1.1	–5.5	–5.7	–4.6	–8.1	–4.5	4.5
Equipment	:	2.4	16.2	16.6	–8.9	–8.6	5.7	3.7	2.8	–12.0	–0.6
3 Gross fixed capital formation at current prices (% of GDP)											
Total	24.0	19.7	18.7	20.8	19.7	18.1	17.8	17.7	17.1	15.6	15.7
General government	:	3.3	2.2	1.6	1.8	1.9	1.7	1.7	1.7	1.5	1.6
Other sectors	:	16.4	16.6	19.1	17.9	16.2	16.1	16.0	15.4	14.1	14.1
4 Final national uses incl. stocks											
At constant prices	4.6	0.9	5.4	6.1	–2.2	–1.2	0.4	–0.8	0.1	–0.4	2.1
Relative to 19 competitors	0.1	–0.9	2.3	2.3	–5.5	–5.2	–2.8	–3.0	–0.1	–0.9	1.7
Relative to other member countries	0.2	–0.5	3.3	2.3	–5.5	–5.6	–2.9	–3.7	–1.1	–1.4	2.0
5 Inflation											
Price deflator private consumption	6.6	10.1	4.3	2.9	4.6	4.0	5.0	2.1	2.3	2.1	1.6
Price deflator GDP	7.0	9.4	4.3	4.6	4.7	3.4	4.3	2.1	2.9	2.5	1.7
6 Compensation per employee											
Nominal	10.7	10.6	4.7	4.4	7.9	5.0	3.8	3.4	3.7	3.2	2.5
Real, deflator private consumption	3.8	0.5	0.4	1.5	3.1	1.0	–1.2	1.3	1.2	1.1	0.9
Real, deflator GDP	3.4	1.1	0.4	–0.2	3.0	1.5	–0.5	1.3	0.8	0.7	0.8
7 GDP at constant market prices per person employed	3.2	1.4	1.7	1.0	–0.6	1.8	1.5	2.3	2.2	1.7	1.7
8 Real unit labour costs											
1961–73 = 100	100.0	100.6	93.6	92.5	95.9	95.7	93.8	92.8	91.6	90.7	89.9
Annual % change	0.2	–0.3	–1.3	–1.2	3.6	–0.2	–2.0	–1.0	–1.4	–0.9	–0.9
9 Relative unit labour costs in common currency											
● Against 19 competitors											
1961–73 = 100	100.0	111.4	95.8	101.3	110.7	108.8	104.4	107.5	101.6	102.9	105.4
Annual % change	2.1	–1.5	0.4	5.7	9.3	–1.7	–4.0	2.9	–5.4	1.3	2.4
● Against other member countries											
1961–73 = 100	100.0	109.0	100.3	102.3	109.0	108.3	105.7	104.5	99.7	98.8	101.0
Annual % change	1.7	–0.9	0.9	2.0	6.6	–0.6	–2.4	–1.1	–4.7	–0.8	2.2
10 Employment	1.1	0.4	2.5	2.6	0.9	–0.6	–0.7	–0.5	–0.9	–0.7	0.1
11 Unemployment rate (% of civilian labour force)	:	6.3	7.2	5.5	5.6	6.4	7.7	8.1	8.9	9.5	9.5
12 Current balance (% of GDP)	–2.0	–3.4	–4.6	–5.4	–2.9	–1.3	–1.5	0.5	1.3	3.0	3.0
13 Net lending (+) or net borrowing (–) of general government (% of GDP)	2.2	–2.9	–2.0	3.4	2.4	0.6	–0.5	–1.4	–2.0	–2.3	–2.7
14 Gross debt of general government (% of GDP)	:	37.2	76.8	69.0	65.8	66.8	66.2	66.7	72.2	74.0	76.2
15 Interest payments by general government (% of GDP)	:	4.0	9.9	8.8	8.3	8.0	7.5	7.3	7.3	6.9	7.2
16 Money supply (end of year)[2]	10.6	13.3	15.8	8.4	4.1	3.5	8.3	7.1	6.4	:	:
17 Long-term interest rate (%)	9.0	16.4	11.6	10.6	11.9	10.6	10.2	11.0	10.1	10.1	:
18 Profitability (1961–73= 100)	100.0	72.5	84.2	89.7	81.1	80.7	82.7	82.1	83.3	83.7	84.7

[1] 1961–91: Eurostat and Commission services; 1992–3: Economic forecasts winter 1992/93.
[2] M2

Table E4 Germany[1]: main economic indicators, 1961–93[2] (Annual percentage change, unless otherwise stated)

	1961–73	1974–84	1985	1986	1987	1988	1989	1990	1991	1992	1993
1 Gross domestic											
At current prices	8.9	6.1	4.1	5.6	3.4	5.3	6.1	8.7	8.1	6.1	3.0
At constant prices											
West Germany	4.3	1.7	1.9	2.2	1.4	3.7	3.4	5.1	3.7	1.5	−0.5
Unified Germany	:	:	:	:	:	:	:	:	:	1.9	0.0
2 Gross fixed capital formation											
at constant prices											
Total	4.0	−0.2	0.0	3.6	2.1	4.6	6.5	8.7	6.5	1.7	−1.7
Construction	:	−0.8	−5.6	2.7	0.0	3.1	4.8	5.3	4.1	4.5	0.5
Equipment	:	1.4	9.9	4.3	5.0	6.7	10.0	13.3	9.1	−2.0	−4.0
3 Gross fixed capital formation											
at current prices (% of GDP)											
Total	24.9	20.9	19.5	19.4	19.4	19.6	20.2	21.0	21.6	21.5	21.4
General government	4.2	3.3	2.4	2.5	2.4	2.3	2.4	2.3	2.3	2.3	2.3
Other sectors	20.8	17.6	17.2	16.9	17.0	17.2	17.8	18.6	19.3	19.3	19.1
4 Final national uses incl. stocks											
At constant prices	4.5	1.4	0.9	3.3	2.6	3.6	2.8	4.9	3.1	1.2	−0.5
Relative to 19 competitors	−0.5	−0.5	−2.1	−0.3	−1.0	−0.9	−0.8	2.8	3.0	0.5	−1.4
Relative to other member countries	−0.3	−0.2	−1.7	−0.5	−1.1	−1.1	−0.9	2.7	2.6	0.3	−1.1
5 Inflation											
Price deflator private consumption	3.5	4.7	2.1	−0.3	0.8	1.4	3.1	2.7	3.9	4.1	3.6
Price deflator GDP	4.4	4.3	2.2	3.3	1.9	1.5	2.6	3.4	4.2	4.5	3.5
6 Compensation per employee											
Nominal	9.1	6.1	2.9	3.6	3.2	3.0	2.9	4.7	5.8	5.4	3.6
Real, deflator private consumption	5.4	1.3	0.8	3.9	2.4	1.6	−0.2	2.0	1.8	1.3	0.0
Real, deflator GDP	4.5	1.7	0.7	0.3	1.2	1.5	0.2	1.3	1.5	0.8	0.1
7 GDP at constant market prices											
per person employed	4.0	2.0	1.1	0.8	0.7	2.9	1.9	2.0	1.1	0.7	0.4
8 Real unit labour costs											
1961–73 = 100	100.0	104.0	100.2	99.7	100.2	98.8	97.1	96.4	96.8	97.0	96.6
Annual % change	0.5	−0.3	−0.4	−0.5	0.5	−1.4	−1.7	−0.7	0.4	0.2	−0.3
9 Relative unit labour costs in											
common currency											
● Against 19 competitors											
1961–73 = 100	100.0	108.2	92.5	101.4	107.5	103.6	99.7	102.2	100.5	105.6	110.1
Annual % change	2.3	−2.3	−1.8	9.6	6.0	−3.6	−3.8	2.6	−1.7	5.1	4.3
● Against other member countries											
1961–73 = 100	100.0	108.3	99.6	106.1	110.0	106.3	103.1	101.1	100.2	103.9	110.5
Annual % change	2.2	−1.6	−1.9	6.6	3.6	−3.4	−3.0	−2.0	−0.9	3.7	6.4
10 Employment											
West Germany	0.3	−0.3	0.7	1.4	0.7	0.8	1.5	3.0	2.6	0.8	−1.0
Unified Germany	:	:	:	:	:	:	:	:	:	−1.5	−1.0
11 Unemployment rate											
(% of civilian labour force)	:	4.0	7.1	6.5	6.3	6.3	5.6	4.8	4.2	4.5	6.0
12 Current balance (% of GDP)											
West Germany	0.7	0.7	2.4	4.3	4.1	4.3	4.8	3.5	1.2	0.9	−0.1
Unified Germany	:	:	:	:	:	:	:	:	−0.9	−1.1	−1.1
13 Net lending (+) or net borrowing (−)											
of general government (% of GDP)											
West Germany	0.4	−2.9	−1.2	−1.3	−1.9	−2.2	0.1	−2.0	−3.6	−3.5	−3.9
Unified Germany	:	:	:	:	:	:	:	:	−3.2	−3.2	−3.6
14 Gross debt of general government											
(% of GDP)	:	32.1	42.5	42.5	43.8	44.4	43.2	43.6	45.0	45.9	48.5
15 Interest payments by general											
government (% of GDP)	0.9	2.0	3.0	3.0	2.9	2.9	2.7	2.6	2.8	3.1	3.2
16 Money supply (M3; end of year)	10.9	7.4	5.0	6.6	5.9	6.9	5.6	4.2	6.3	:	:
17 Long-term interest rate (%)	7.2	8.1	6.9	5.9	5.8	6.1	7.0	8.9	8.6	8.0	:
18 Profitability (1961–73= 100)	100.0	72.9	73.3	76.8	75.9	80.5	84.8	88.8	88.2	86.8	84.5

[1] West Germany, unless otherwise stated
[2] 1961–91; Eurostat and Commission services: 1992–3 Economic forecasts winter 1992/93.

Table E5 Greece: main economic indicators, 1961–93[1] (Annual percentage change, unless otherwise stated)

	1961–73	1974–84	1985	1986	1987	1988	1989	1990	1991	1992	1993
1 Gross domestic product											
At current prices	12.5	20.6	21.3	19.4	13.5	20.3	16.6	20.4	21.7	17.3	14.5
At constant prices	7.7	2.5	3.1	1.6	−0.7	4.1	3.5	−0.1	1.8	1.5	1.6
2 Gross fixed capital formation at constant prices											
Total	10.0	−2.2	5.2	−6.2	−5.1	8.9	10.0	5.7	−2.0	0.6	4.5
Construction	:	−3.7	3.1	−0.8	−5.0	9.2	4.0	2.2	−6.4	−3.0	3.0
Equipment	:	0.1	7.7	−12.6	−5.2	8.4	18.1	7.9	3.3	4.5	6.0
3 Gross fixed capital formation at current prices (% of GDP)											
Total	22.7	22.0	19.1	18.5	17.2	17.5	19.2	19.4	18.2	17.5	17.9
General government	:	:	4.4	4.1	3.2	3.2	3.4	3.1	3.6	3.6	3.9
Other sectors	:	:	14.7	14.3	14.0	14.3	15.9	16.4	14.7	13.9	14.0
4 Final national uses incl. stocks											
At constant prices	8.1	1.5	5.4	−1.1	−1.5	6.7	3.8	0.9	2.7	1.1	1.6
Relative to 19 competitors	3.1	−0.3	2.6	−4.6	−4.8	2.2	0.4	−1.8	1.8	0.2	1.0
Relative to other member countries	3.3	0.0	3.3	−4.7	−4.7	2.2	0.5	−2.2	1.2	0.1	1.4
5 Inflation											
Price deflator private consumption	3.5	17.4	18.3	22.1	15.7	14.3	15.2	19.7	18.4	16.0	13.5
Price deflator GDP	4.5	17.7	17.7	17.5	14.3	15.6	12.7	20.5	19.5	15.6	12.7
6 Compensation per employee											
Nominal	10.4	21.5	23.4	12.8	11.4	19.1	18.1	19.7	15.1	12.4	11.3
Real, deflator private consumption	6.7	3.5	4.3	−7.6	−3.7	4.2	2.6	0.0	−2.8	−3.1	−1.9
Real, deflator GDP	5.7	3.3	4.8	−4.0	−2.5	3.0	4.8	−0.7	−3.7	−2.8	−1.2
7 GDP at constant market prices per person employed	8.1	1.5	2.2	1.3	−0.6	2.4	3.0	−1.2	3.5	2.0	1.7
8 Real unit labour costs											
1961–73 = 100	100.0	98.3	107.9	102.2	100.2	100.8	102.6	103.1	96.0	91.5	88.8
Annual % change	−2.2	1.8	2.6	−5.2	−1.9	0.6	1.7	0.5	−6.9	−4.7	−2.9
9 Relative unit labour costs in common currency											
• Against 19 competitors											
1961–73 = 100	100.0	78.8	77.3	65.5	64.2	67.6	69.5	73.7	69.1	67.9	66.2
Annual % change	−3.9	0.6	−1.9	−15.2	−2.1	5.3	2.9	6.0	−6.3	1.6	−2.5
• Against other member countries											
1961–73 = 100	100.0	77.5	82.1	67.5	64.7	68.6	71.3	73.0	68.9	66.8	65.7
Annual % change	−4.4	1.4	−1.8	−17.7	−4.2	6.0	3.9	2.4	−5.6	−3.0	−1.7
10 Employment	−0.4	1.0	0.9	0.3	−0.1	1.6	0.4	1.1	−1.6	−0.5	−0.1
11 Unemployment rate (% of civilian labour force)	:	3.7	7.7	7.4	7.4	7.6	7.4	7.2	7.7	7.7	8.5
12 Current balance (% of GDP)	−2.9	−2.5	−8.2	−5.3	−3.1	−2.0	−5.0	−6.1	−5.1	−3.3	−3.0
13 Net lending (+) or net borrowing (−) of general government (% of GDP)	:	:	−13.6	−12.0	−11.6	−13.8	−17.7	−18.6	−15.2	−13.4	−9.8
14 Gross debt of general government (% of GDP)	:	31.8	62.5	65.0	72.5	80.2	85.9	95.3	100.9	105.6	106.0
15 Interest payments by general government (% of GDP)	:	2.4	5.3	5.7	7.2	7.9	8.2	11.9	12.8	14.6	14.5
16 Money supply (end of year)[2]	18.2	25.4	26.8	19.0	24.0	23.2	24.2	15.3	12.3	:	:
17 Long-term interest rate (%)	:	13.4	15.8	15.8	17.4	16.6	:	:	:	:	:
18 Profitability (1961–73= 100)	100.0	69.0	34.8	43.8	47.7	49.9	44.2	44.3	62.2	74.0	79.8

[1] 1961–91: Eurostat and Commission services; 1992–3: Economic forecasts winter 1992/93.
[2] M3

Table E6 Spain: main economic indicators, 1961–93[1] (Annual percentage change, unless otherwise stated)

	1961–73	1974–84	1985	1986	1987	1988	1989	1990	1991	1992	1993
1 Gross domestic product											
At current prices	14.8	17.7	11.1	14.6	11.8	11.1	12.1	11.2	9.4	7.5	5.7
At constant prices	7.2	1.7	2.3	3.2	5.6	5.2	4.8	3.6	2.4	1.2	1.0
2 Gross fixed capital formation at constant prices											
Total	10.4	−1.6	4.1	9.9	14.0	14.0	13.8	6.9	1.6	−2.0	−1.9
Construction	:	−1.8	2.0	6.5	9.9	12.4	15.1	10.8	4.3	−3.4	−3.3
Equipment	:	−1.3	9.1	15.8	23.2	16.6	12.9	1.4	−2.5	0.2	0.3
3 Gross fixed capital formation at current prices (% of GDP)											
Total	24.6	23.2	19.2	19.5	20.8	22.6	24.2	24.6	24.1	22.6	22.0
General government[2]	:	2.4	3.7	3.6	3.4	3.8	4.4	4.9	5.2	5.1	5.0
Other sectors[2]	:	20.3	15.5	15.8	17.4	18.8	19.7	19.7	18.9	17.6	16.9
4 Final national uses incl. stocks											
At constant prices	7.6	1.0	2.9	5.4	8.1	7.0	7.8	4.7	2.9	1.8	0.4
Relative to 19 competitors	2.7	−0.8	0.1	1.5	4.4	2.5	4.3	2.2	2.3	0.8	−0.4
Relative to other member countries	2.9	−0.5	0.8	1.5	4.5	2.4	4.3	1.7	1.7	0.8	0.0
5 Inflation											
Price deflator private consumption	6.6	16.1	8.2	9.4	5.7	5.0	6.6	6.4	6.3	6.0	5.5
Price deflator GDP	7.1	15.7	8.5	11.1	5.8	5.7	7.0	7.3	6.9	6.3	4.7
6 Compensation per employee											
Nominal	14.6	18.8	9.4	9.5	6.7	6.8	6.3	7.9	8.7	9.0	7.3
Real, deflator private consumption	7.5	2.3	1.1	0.1	0.9	1.8	−0.3	1.4	2.2	2.8	1.7
Real, deflator GDP	7.1	2.7	0.8	−1.4	0.8	1.1	−0.7	0.5	1.7	2.5	2.5
7 GDP at constant market prices per person employed	6.5	3.2	3.7	1.8	1.1	1.7	1.2	0.8	2.1	2.8	2.6
8 Real unit labour costs											
1961–73 = 100	100.0	103.5	94.1	91.1	90.8	90.3	88.6	88.4	88.0	87.8	87.7
Annual % change	0.6	−0.5	−2.8	−3.2	−0.3	−0.6	−1.8	−0.2	−0.4	−0.3	−0.1
9 Relative unit labour costs in common currency											
● Against 19 competitors											
1961–73 = 100	100.0	117.1	101.4	103.8	106.3	112.1	118.7	126.8	127.7	128.7	123.8
Annual % change	1.8	−0.6	−0.6	2.3	2.4	5.5	5.9	6.8	0.7	0.8	−3.8
● Against other member countries											
1961–73 = 100	100.0	113.0	106.7	105.1	104.8	111.2	119.4	122.6	124.6	123.5	119.9
Annual % change	1.2	0.2	−0.4	−1.5	−0.3	6.1	7.4	2.7	1.6	−0.8	−2.9
10 Employment	0.7	−1.4	−1.3	1.4	4.5	3.4	3.5	2.8	0.2	−1.6	−1.6
11 Unemployment rate (% of civilian labour force)	:	10.4	21.6	21.0	20.4	19.3	17.1	16.1	16.3	18.0	19.5
12 Current balance (% of GDP)	−0.2	−1.7	1.4	1.6	0.1	−1.1	−3.2	−3.7	−3.5	−3.7	−3.4
13 Net lending (+) or net borrowing (−) of general government (% of GDP)[2]	:	−2.4	−6.9	−6.0	−3.1	−3.3	−2.8	−4.0	−4.9	−4.6	−4.2
14 Gross debt of general government (% of GDP)	:	20.1	45.2	46.2	46.6	42.9	44.4	44.5	45.6	47.4	49.5
15 Interest payments by general government (% of GDP)[2]	:	0.8	3.1	4.0	3.5	3.4	3.5	3.5	4.0	4.3	4.7
16 Money supply (end of year)[3]	:	18.0	13.8	14.0	15.4	14.4	14.6	15.3	10.9	:	:
17 Long-term interest rate (%)	:	:	13.4	11.4	12.8	11.8	13.8	14.7	12.4	12.2	:
18 Profitability (1961–73= 100)	100.0	71.7	84.5	101.6	108.3	112.4	122.0	123.5	123.5	123.6	120.4

[1] 1961–91: Eurostat and Commission services; 1992–3: Economic forecasts winter 1992/93.
[2] Break in 1985/86.
[3] ALP: Liquid assets held by the public.

Table E7 France: main economic indicators, 1961–93[1] (Annual percentage change, unless otherwise stated)

	1961–73	1974–84	1985	1986	1987	1988	1989	1990	1991	1992	1993
1 Gross domestic product											
At current prices	10.7	13.1	7.8	7.9	5.3	7.5	7.4	5.4	4.2	4.8	3.9
At constant prices	5.4	2.2	1.8	2.4	2.2	4.3	3.8	2.2	1.1	1.9	1.0
2 Gross fixed capital formation at constant prices											
Total	7.5	−0.5	3.4	4.6	5.0	9.6	6.8	3.1	−1.3	−1.5	−0.7
Construction	:	−1.1	−0.4	3.6	3.2	6.7	7.2	2.7	0.6	2.3	0.2
Equipment	:	0.3	10.0	4.3	6.7	10.8	6.4	4.1	−2.5	−4.3	−1.4
3 Gross fixed capital formation at current prices (% of GDP)											
Total	24.0	22.5	19.3	19.3	19.8	20.7	21.2	21.2	20.8	20.0	19.6
General government	:	3.4	3.2	3.2	3.0	3.3	3.3	3.5	3.4	3.4	3.3
Other sectors	:	19.1	16.0	16.1	16.7	17.4	17.9	17.8	17.4	16.6	16.2
4 Final national uses incl. stocks											
At constant prices	5.6	1.6	2.3	4.3	3.3	4.4	3.3	2.6	0.8	1.0	1.0
Relative to 19 competitors	0.7	−0.2	−0.4	0.7	−0.3	−0.1	−0.2	0.0	0.1	0.1	0.5
Relative to other member countries	0.9	0.1	0.2	0.7	−0.3	−0.2	−0.2	−0.5	−0.6	−0.1	0.9
5 Inflation											
Price deflator private consumption	4.8	11.2	6.0	2.9	3.3	2.9	3.6	3.2	3.2	2.6	2.7
Price deflator GDP	5.1	10.7	5.8	5.3	3.0	3.1	3.5	3.1	3.1	2.9	2.9
6 Compensation per employee											
Nominal	9.9	13.8	6.6	4.6	3.7	4.4	4.7	5.0	4.2	4.1	3.9
Real, deflator private consumption	4.8	2.3	0.6	1.7	0.4	1.4	1.0	1.8	1.0	1.5	1.2
Real, deflator GDP	4.6	2.8	0.7	−0.7	0.6	1.2	1.2	1.9	1.1	1.2	1.0
7 GDP at constant market prices per person employed	4.7	2.2	2.1	2.3	1.9	3.4	2.6	1.2	0.7	2.2	1.3
8 Real unit labour costs											
1961–73 = 100	100.0	106.2	104.2	101.1	99.9	97.8	96.4	97.0	97.4	96.4	96.2
Annual % change	−0.1	0.6	−1.4	−2.9	−1.2	−2.1	−1.4	0.6	0.4	−0.9	−0.3
9 Relative unit labour costs in common currency											
● Against 19 competitors											
1961–73 = 100	100.0	93.8	86.4	88.9	88.4	84.8	82.5	86.0	82.6	84.2	86.7
Annual % change	−0.8	−0.8	1.8	2.9	−0.5	−4.1	−2.7	4.2	−4.0	1.9	3.0
● Against other member countries											
1961–73 = 100	100.0	93.0	93.1	92.5	89.6	86.3	84.9	85.1	82.3	82.5	85.9
Annual % change	−1.2	0.1	2.1	−0.6	−3.2	−3.7	−1.6	0.2	−3.3	0.2	4.2
10 Employment	0.7	0.0	−0.3	0.1	0.3	0.8	1.1	1.0	0.4	−0.2	−0.3
11 Unemployment rate (% of civilian labour force)	:	6.0	10.1	10.3	10.4	9.9	9.4	9.0	9.5	10.1	10.8
12 Current balance (% of GDP)	0.4	−0.3	0.1	0.5	−0.2	−0.3	−0.4	−0.8	−0.5	0.1	0.2
13 Net lending (+) or net borrowing (−) of general government (% of GDP)	0.4	−1.6	−2.9	−2.7	−1.9	−1.7	−1.1	−1.4	−1.9	−2.8	−3.2
14 Gross debt of general government (% of GDP)	:	39.6	45.5	45.7	47.2	46.8	47.5	46.7	48.5	50.1	52.4
15 Interest payments by general government (% of GDP)	:	1.6	2.9	2.9	2.8	2.7	2.7	2.9	3.1	3.2	3.3
16 Money supply (end of year)[2]	13.7	13.1	7.4	6.8	9.8	8.4	9.6	8.9	2.5	:	:
17 Long-term interest rate (%)	6.9	12.3	10.9	8.4	9.4	9.0	8.8	9.9	9.0	8.6	:
18 Profitability (1961–73= 100)	100.0	69.0	68.8	76.6	78.8	84.8	89.2	87.5	84.2	86.0	85.9

[1] 1961–91: Eurostat and Commission services; 1992–3: Economic forecasts winter 1992/93.
[2] M3.

Table E8 Ireland: main economic indicators, 1961–93[1] (Annual percentage change, unless otherwise stated)

	1961–73	1974–84	1985	1986	1987	1988	1989	1990	1991	1992	1993
1 Gross domestic product											
At current prices	11.8	17.8	8.4	6.1	7.4	7.9	11.5	6.6	3.8	5.9	4.5
At constant prices	4.4	3.8	3.1	−0.4	5.0	4.9	6.5	8.3	2.5	2.9	2.1
2 Gross fixed capital formation at constant prices											
Total	9.9	1.8	−7.7	−2.8	−3.2	1.5	15.1	10.2	−7.2	1.6	2.2
Construction	:	1.3	−7.1	−4.6	−7.6	1.9	15.1	11.7	−1.4	2.5	3.0
Equipment	:	2.3	−7.4	1.5	0.9	0.1	19.6	7.2	−11.6	0.5	1.2
3 Gross fixed capital formation at current prices (% of GDP)											
Total	21.2	25.9	19.0	18.0	16.4	16.3	17.7	18.6	17.1	16.8	16.7
General government	:	5.1	4.0	3.7	2.7	1.9	1.9	2.2	2.4	2.4	2.4
Other sectors	:	20.7	15.0	14.3	13.7	14.4	15.8	16.4	14.7	14.4	14.3
4 Final national uses incl. stocks											
At constant prices	5.1	2.3	1.1	1.1	−0.2	1.6	6.7	6.3	−0.7	−0.9	2.2
Relative to 19 competitors	1.1	0.7	−1.7	−2.6	−3.9	−3.2	3.2	4.3	−0.6	−1.6	1.5
Relative to other member countries	1.3	1.0	−1.1	−2.7	−3.9	−3.4	3.1	3.9	−1.1	−1.7	1.9
5 Inflation											
Price deflator private consumption	6.3	14.5	5.0	4.6	2.9	2.5	3.7	1.7	3.2	2.9	2.2
Price deflator GDP	7.2	13.5	5.2	6.5	2.3	2.9	4.7	−1.6	1.2	2.9	2.3
6 Compensation per employee											
Nominal	11.3	17.4	8.9	5.3	5.3	6.1	6.2	4.4	4.4	6.3	5.9
Real, deflator private consumption	4.7	2.5	3.7	0.7	2.4	3.5	2.4	2.6	1.1	3.3	3.6
Real, deflator GDP	3.9	3.5	3.5	−1.2	2.9	3.1	1.4	6.0	3.1	3.3	3.4
7 GDP at constant market prices per person employed	4.3	3.5	5.4	−0.6	5.1	3.9	6.6	4.8	2.6	2.8	2.0
8 Real unit labour costs											
1961–73 = 100	100.0	100.2	94.3	93.7	91.8	91.1	86.7	87.7	88.2	88.5	89.8
Annual % change	−0.4	0.0	−1.8	−0.6	−2.1	−0.7	−4.8	1.2	0.5	0.4	1.4
9 Relative unit labour costs in common currency											
● Against 19 competitors											
1961–73 = 100	100.0	95.6	97.8	103.8	98.6	96.3	91.0	90.6	86.3	88.7	93.3
Annual % change	0.4	−0.4	0.7	6.1	−5.0	−2.4	−5.4	−0.4	−4.8	2.8	5.1
● Against other member countries											
1961–73 = 100	100.0	94.1	102.5	105.4	97.9	95.8	91.7	88.3	84.5	85.7	90.9
Annual % change	0.2	0.1	0.8	2.8	−7.2	−2.1	−4.3	−3.7	−4.2	1.3	6.1
10 Employment	0.1	0.3	−2.2	0.2	−0.1	1.0	−0.1	3.3	−0.1	0.1	0.1
11 Unemployment rate (% of civilian labour force)	:	10.3	18.2	18.2	18.0	17.3	15.7	14.5	16.2	17.8	19.2
12 Current balance (% of GDP)	−2.5	−8.4	−3.9	−2.9	1.2	1.5	0.8	1.3	6.0	6.7	6.6
13 Net lending (+) or net borrowing (−) of general government (% of GDP)	−3.8	−10.9	−11.2	−11.1	−8.9	−4.8	−1.8	−2.5	−2.1	−2.7	−3.0
14 Gross debt of general government (% of GDP)	:	76.0	107.9	119.9	120.6	118.2	108.0	101.6	100.9	99.0	98.7
15 Interest payments by general government (% of GDP)	:	6.6	10.3	9.7	9.6	8.9	8.1	8.2	8.0	7.2	7.2
16 Money supply (end of year)[2]	12.1	16.6	5.3	−1.0	10.9	6.3	5.0	15.4	3.1	:	:
17 Long-term interest rate (%)	:	14.7	12.7	11.1	11.3	9.4	9.0	10.1	9.2	9.1	:
18 Profitability (1961–73= 100)	100.0	78.0	100.7	102.8	113.0	116.2	140.4	139.0	133.3	133.5	128.6

[1] 1961–91: Eurostat and Commission services; 1992–3: Economic forecasts winter 1992/93.
[2] M3.

Table E9 Italy: main economic indicators, 1961–93[1] (Annual percentage change, unless otherwise stated)

	1961–73	1974–84	1985	1986	1987	1988	1989	1990	1991	1992	1993
1 Gross domestic product											
At current prices	11.0	20.1	11.7	11.0	9.3	11.0	9.3	9.9	8.8	6.3	5.3
At constant prices	5.3	2.8	2.6	2.9	3.1	4.1	2.9	2.2	1.4	1.1	0.8
2 Gross fixed capital formation at constant prices											
Total	4.7	0.5	0.6	2.2	5.0	6.9	4.3	3.3	0.9	–0.2	–1.2
Construction	:	–1.4	–0.5	1.9	–0.7	2.3	3.9	2.5	1.2	0.4	–0.7
Equipment	:	3.6	1.9	2.6	11.9	11.6	5.1	3.5	0.7	–0.7	–1.6
3 Gross fixed capital formation at current prices (% of GDP)											
Total	24.4	23.3	20.7	19.7	19.7	20.1	20.2	20.2	19.8	19.4	19.3
General government	:	3.2	3.7	3.5	3.5	3.4	3.4	3.4	3.3	3.1	3.1
Other sectors	:	20.1	16.9	16.2	16.2	16.7	16.8	16.8	16.4	16.3	16.2
4 Final national uses incl. stocks											
At constant prices	5.3	2.4	2.8	3.4	4.3	4.7	2.9	2.7	2.2	1.3	–0.2
Relative to 19 competitors	0.4	0.6	0.0	–0.3	0.8	0.2	–0.6	0.1	1.6	0.4	–1.0
Relative to other member countries	0.6	1.0	0.8	–0.4	1.0	0.2	–0.6	–0.4	0.9	0.4	–0.5
5 Inflation											
Price deflator private consumption	4.9	16.6	9.0	6.2	5.3	5.7	6.5	5.9	6.8	5.3	5.8
Price deflator GDP	5.5	16.8	8.9	7.9	6.0	6.6	6.2	7.5	7.3	5.2	4.5
6 Compensation per employee											
Nominal	11.5	19.0	10.1	7.5	8.2	8.8	8.8	10.5	8.7	5.1	4.1
Real, deflator private consumption	6.3	2.0	1.0	1.3	2.8	2.9	2.2	4.4	1.7	–0.2	–1.6
Real, deflator GDP	5.7	1.8	1.1	–0.3	2.1	2.0	2.5	2.8	1.3	–0.1	–0.4
7 GDP at constant market prices per person employed	5.5	1.8	1.7	2.1	2.7	3.2	2.9	1.1	0.7	1.0	0.8
8 Real unit labour costs											
1961–73 = 100	100.0	103.9	101.7	99.3	98.7	97.6	97.2	98.8	99.4	98.4	97.2
Annual % change	0.1	0.0	–0.5	–2.4	–0.6	–1.2	–0.4	1.7	0.6	–1.1	–1.2
9 Relative unit labour costs in common currency											
● Against 19 competitors											
1961–73 = 100	100.0	89.0	95.5	100.9	104.4	103.8	107.1	115.7	116.9	114.5	103.5
Annual % change	–0.3	0.2	–0.6	5.7	3.4	–0.5	3.1	8.1	1.0	–2.0	–9.6
● Against other member countries											
1961–73 = 100	100.0	87.6	103.3	105.0	105.6	105.7	110.7	115.0	117.3	112.7	102.5
Annual % change	–0.8	1.2	–0.4	1.7	0.6	0.1	4.7	3.8	2.0	–3.9	–9.0
10 Employment	–0.2	0.9	0.9	0.8	0.4	0.9	0.1	1.1	0.8	0.1	0.0
11 Unemployment rate (% of civilian labour force)	:	7.1	9.6	10.5	10.3	10.8	10.6	9.9	10.2	10.2	10.6
12 Current balance (% of GDP)	1.4	–0.6	–0.9	0.5	–0.2	–0.7	–1.3	–1.4	1.9	–2.4	–2.4
13 Net lending (+) or net borrowing (–) of general government (% of GDP)	–3.1	–9.3	–12.6	–11.6	–11.0	–10.7	–9.9	–10.9	–10.2	–10.5	–10.2
14 Gross debt of general government (% of GDP)	:	60.9	82.2	86.2	90.4	92.6	95.5	97.8	101.3	106.8	112.2
15 Interest payments by general government (% of GDP)	:	5.4	8.0	8.5	7.9	8.1	8.9	9.6	10.2	· 11.5	12.6
16 Money supply (end of year)[2]	15.4	17.3	11.1	10.7	7.2	7.6	9.9	8.2	9.0	:	:
17 Long-term interest rate (%)	7.0	15.2	14.3	11.7	11.3	12.1	12.9	13.4	13.0	13.7	:
18 Profitability (1961–73= 100)	100.0	64.3	66.6	76.5	80.3	85.5	87.1	83.5	82.3	84.2	84.2

[1] 1961–91: Eurostat and Commission services; 1992–3: Economic forecasts winter 1992/93.
[2] M2.

Table E10 Luxembourg: main economic indicators, 1961–93[1] (Annual percentage change, unless otherwise stated)

	1961–73	1974–84	1985	1986	1987	1988	1989	1990	1991	1992	1993
1 Gross domestic product											
At current prices	8.7	8.8	6.0	8.8	1.9	10.0	13.0	6.2	6.1	4.5	6.2
At constant prices	4.0	1.7	2.9	4.8	2.9	5.7	6.7	3.2	3.1	2.2	2.0
2 Gross fixed capital formation at constant prices											
Total	4.9	−2.1	−9.5	31.2	14.7	14.1	8.9	2.5	9.8	4.5	2.3
Construction	:	−3.1	−2.1	5.7	8.9	8.8	4.6	8.0	7.1	6.0	3.3
Equipment	:	−0.8	−20.5	87.2	18.7	16.1	−16.9	10.9	11.4	3.5	1.7
3 Gross fixed capital formation at current prices (% of GDP)											
Total	26.4	24.5	17.7	22.1	25.5	27.1	27.1	26.9	29.0	29.7	29.6
General government	:	6.2	4.6	4.3	4.9	5.0	4.8	4.7	4.4	4.5	4.7
Other sectors	:	18.3	13.1	17.8	20.7	22.0	22.3	22.2	24.6	25.2	24.9
4 Final national uses incl. stocks											
At constant prices	4.0	1.6	0.1	8.0	4.2	6.8	5.7	5.1	8.4	3.3	2.2
Relative to 19 competitors	:	:	:	:	:	:	:	:	:	:	:
Relative to other member countries	:	:	:	:	:	:	:	:	:	:	:
5 Inflation											
Price deflator private consumption	3.0	7.7	4.3	1.3	1.7	2.7	3.6	3.6	2.9	3.4	4.7
Price deflator GDP	4.4	7.0	3.0	3.8	−1.0	4.0	6.0	2.9	3.0	2.2	4.1
6 Compensation per employee											
Nominal	7.4	9.7	4.2	3.6	4.8	3.1	6.7	6.9	5.4	5.1	6.0
Real, deflator private consumption	4.2	1.8	0.0	2.3	3.1	0.4	3.0	3.2	2.4	1.6	1.2
Real, deflator GDP	2.8	2.5	1.2	−0.2	5.9	−0.9	0.7	3.9	2.3	2.8	1.8
7 GDP at constant market prices per person employed	3.0	1.2	1.5	2.1	0.1	2.6	2.9	−1.1	−0.6	0.7	0.5
8 Real unit labour costs											
1961–73 = 100	100.0	115.9	108.6	106.2	112.2	108.4	106.1	111.4	114.7	117.1	118.6
Annual % change	−0.2	1.3	−0.3	−2.3	5.7	−3.4	−2.1	5.0	2.9	2.1	1.3
9 Relative unit labour costs in common currency											
● Against 19 competitors											
1961–73 = 100	:	:	:	:	:	:	:	:	:	:	:
Annual % change	:	:	:	:	:	:	:	:	:	:	:
● Against other member countries											
1961–73 = 100	:	:	:	:	:	:	:	:	:	:	:
Annual % change	:	:	:	:	:	:	:	:	:	:	:
10 Employment	1.1	0.4	1.4	2.6	2.8	3.1	3.7	4.3	3.6	1.5	1.5
11 Unemployment rate (% of civilian labour force)	:	1.6	2.9	2.6	2.5	2.0	1.8	1.7	1.6	1.9	2.0
12 Current balance (% of GDP)	6.8	25.3	43.8	38.8	30.3	30.8	34.0	34.2	27.9	19.9	18.7
13 Net lending (+) or net borrowing (−) of general government (% of GDP)	2.0	1.4	6.2	4.3	2.4	3.1	5.3	5.0	−0.8	−0.4	−1.0
14 Gross debt of general government (% of GDP)	:	15.4	14.0	13.5	11.9	9.8	8.3	6.9	6.1	6.8	7.8
15 Interest payments by general government (% of GDP)	:	1.2	1.1	1.1	1.2	1.0	0.7	0.6	0.6	0.5	0.5
16 Money supply (end of year)	:	:	:	:	:	:	:	:	:	:	:
17 Long-term interest rate (%)	:	8.0	9.5	8.7	8.0	7.1	7.7	8.6	8.2	7.9	:
18 Profitability (1961–73= 100)	100.0	51.8	63.6	71.9	56.7	68.1	76.8	65.6	57.1	50.9	47.0

[1] 1961–91: Eurostat and Commission services; 1992–3: Economic forecasts winter 1992/93.

Table E11 Netherlands: main economic indicators, 1961–93[1] (Annual percentage change, unless otherwise stated)

	1961–73	1974–84	1985	1986	1987	1988	1989	1990	1991	1992	1993
1 Gross domestic product											
At current prices	11.2	7.8	4.5	2.5	0.4	3.8	6.0	6.5	5.3	4.0	3.4
At constant prices	4.8	1.7	2.6	2.0	0.8	2.6	4.7	3.9	2.2	1.3	0.6
2 Gross fixed capital formation at constant prices											
Total	5.3	−0.9	6.7	7.9	1.5	4.5	4.9	3.6	0.1	−0.4	−0.7
Construction	:	−2.0	−0.1	5.0	1.9	10.3	2.3	0.6	−2.1	0.0	−0.6
Equipment	:	1.3	15.5	10.1	1.9	5.0	5.3	7.6	2.6	−0.8	−0.8
3 Gross fixed capital formation at current prices (% of GDP)											
Total	25.7	20.6	19.7	20.6	20.8	21.3	21.5	21.3	20.8	20.6	20.4
General government[2]	:	3.3	2.6	2.5	2.1	2.1	2.0	2.0	2.0	2.1	2.2
Other sectors[2]	:	16.8	16.6	17.6	18.7	19.2	19.5	19.2	18.8	18.5	18.3
4 Final national uses incl. stocks											
At constant prices	4.9	1.3	3.2	2.1	1.2	1.8	4.6	3.5	1.7	0.6	0.3
Relative to 19 competitors	0.1	−0.4	0.8	−1.6	−2.2	−2.6	1.2	0.7	0.7	−0.4	−0.2
Relative to other member countries	0.3	−0.2	1.3	−1.6	−2.2	−2.7	1.3	0.3	0.3	−0.5	0.1
5 Inflation											
Price deflator private consumption	5.0	6.1	2.2	0.2	−0.9	0.5	1.2	2.3	3.3	3.1	2.7
Price deflator GDP	6.0	5.9	1.8	0.5	−0.4	1.2	1.2	2.5	3.0	2.7	2.8
6 Compensation per employee											
Nominal	11.4	7.2	1.4	1.6	1.5	0.9	0.7	4.1	4.3	4.8	3.3
Real, deflator private consumption	6.0	1.0	−0.8	1.4	2.4	0.3	−0.5	1.8	0.9	1.7	0.6
Real, deflator GDP	5.0	1.2	−0.4	1.2	1.9	−0.3	−0.5	1.5	1.3	2.1	0.5
7 GDP at constant market prices per person employed	3.9	2.1	1.0	0.0	−0.6	1.0	2.7	1.5	0.9	0.9	1.1
8 Real unit labour costs											
1961–73 = 100	100.0	103.5	93.2	94.2	96.6	95.3	92.3	92.4	92.7	93.8	93.2
Annual % change	1.0	−0.9	−1.4	1.1	2.5	−1.3	−3.1	0.0	0.3	1.2	−0.6
9 Relative unit labour costs in common currency											
• Against 19 competitors											
1961–73 = 100	100.0	118.1	97.8	103.3	107.5	104.5	98.3	99.5	97.0	99.8	102.5
Annual % change	2.9	−1.3	−3.0	5.6	4.1	−2.8	−6.0	1.3	−2.5	2.8	2.7
• Against other member countries											
1961–73 = 100	100.0	117.2	102.1	105.3	107.8	105.3	99.8	98.5	96.6	98.2	101.3
Annual % change	2.6	−0.8	−2.9	3.2	2.4	−2.3	−5.2	−1.4	−1.9	1.6	3.2
10 Employment	0.9	−0.3	1.5	2.0	1.4	1.6	1.9	2.3	1.3	0.4	−0.4
11 Unemployment rate (% of civilian labour force)	:	7.5	10.5	10.3	10.0	9.3	8.5	7.5	7.0	6.7	7.6
12 Current balance (% of GDP)	0.5	1.7	4.1	2.7	1.9	2.8	3.5	4.0	3.9	3.6	3.6
13 Net lending (+) or net borrowing (−) of general government (% of GDP)[2]	−0.8	−3.9	−4.8	−6.0	−5.9	−4.6	−4.7	−4.9	−2.5	−3.5	−3.5
14 Gross debt of general government (% of GDP)	:	:	71.6	73.1	75.6	78.8	78.8	78.8	78.3	79.8	81.7
15 Interest payments by general government (% of GDP)[2]	:	3.9	6.3	6.2	6.4	6.3	6.0	6.0	6.2	6.2	6.2
16 Money supply (end of year)[3]	10.3	8.9	10.7	5.1	4.4	10.6	13.7	8.2	4.7	:	:
17 Long-term interest rate (%)	5.9	9.6	7.3	6.4	6.4	6.3	7.2	9.0	8.9	8.1	:
18 Profitability (1961–73= 100)	100.0	74.0	85.2	83.8	76.9	78.2	84.5	86.2	85.3	81.8	80.9

[1] 1961–91: Eurostat and Commission services; 1992–3: Economic forecasts winter 1992/93.
[2] Break in 1986/87.
[3] M2.

Table E12 Portugal: main economic indicators, 1961–93[1] (Annual percentage change, unless otherwise stated)

	1961–73	1974–84	1985	1986	1987	1988	1989	1990	1991	1992	1993
1 Gross domestic product											
At current prices	11.1	23.3	25.2	25.4	17.1	16.0	18.8	19.3	16.5	15.0	9.4
At constant prices	6.9	2.1	2.8	4.1	5.3	3.9	5.2	4.4	1.9	1.7	1.3
2 Gross fixed capital formation at constant prices											
Total	7.9	−1.0	−3.5	10.9	15.1	15.0	5.6	5.9	2.8	3.6	3.3
Construction	:	:	−6.0	8.7	9.4	10.1	3.5	5.3	4.5	2.5	2.8
Equipment	:	:	−4.5	14.2	26.8	23.2	10.0	5.8	1.0	4.8	3.8
3 Gross fixed capital formation at current prices (% of GDP)											
Total	24.1	27.4	21.8	22.1	24.2	26.8	26.4	26.4	25.5	25.1	25.4
General government	2.7	3.2	2.5	2.6	2.7	2.9	3.1	3.9	4.0	4.0	4.0
Other sectors	21.4	24.1	19.3	19.5	21.5	23.9	23.3	22.4	21.5	21.1	21.4
4 Final national uses incl. stocks											
At constant prices	7.3	1.2	0.9	8.3	10.4	7.4	4.3	5.4	4.1	3.6	3.2
Relative to 19 competitors	2.5	−0.5	−1.8	4.3	6.5	2.9	0.7	2.9	3.6	2.9	2.6
Relative to other member countries	2.7	−0.2	−1.2	4.3	6.6	2.7	0.7	2.5	2.9	2.7	2.9
5 Inflation											
Price deflator private consumption	3.9	22.5	19.4	13.8	10.0	10.0	12.1	12.6	11.9	9.1	6.8
Price deflator GDP	3.9	20.7	21.7	20.5	11.2	11.6	13.0	14.3	14.3	13.1	8.0
6 Compensation per employee											
Nominal	10.8	24.4	22.5	21.6	17.9	13.4	12.8	18.7	19.0	14.9	9.9
Real, deflator private consumption	6.7	1.6	2.6	6.8	7.2	3.1	0.6	5.4	6.4	5.3	2.8
Real, deflator GDP	6.7	3.1	0.6	0.9	6.0	1.5	−0.2	3.9	4.1	1.7	1.7
7 GDP at constant market prices per person employed	6.7	2.7	2.8	7.0	4.7	3.9	4.1	3.5	1.0	1.9	1.8
8 Real unit labour costs											
1961–73 = 100	100.0	119.1	104.4	98.4	99.7	97.4	93.5	93.8	96.7	96.5	96.4
Annual % change	0.0	0.4	−2.2	−5.7	1.3	−2.2	−4.1	0.4	3.0	−0.2	−0.1
9 Relative unit labour costs in common currency											
● Against 19 competitors											
1961–73 = 100	100.0	100.4	80.1	81.0	82.0	82.7	83.9	90.2	101.6	115.0	121.0
Annual % change	−0.7	−2.2	1.7	1.0	1.3	0.9	1.4	7.5	12.6	13.2	5.2
● Against other member countries											
1961–73 = 100	100.0	98.1	83.0	81.6	81.1	82.2	84.3	88.3	100.1	111.7	117.8
Annual % change	−1.2	−1.6	2.0	−1.7	−0.6	1.4	2.6	4.7	13.3	11.6	5.5
10 Employment	0.2	−0.5	0.0	−2.7	0.5	0.1	1.0	0.9	0.9	−0.2	−0.5
11 Unemployment rate (% of civilian labour force)	:	6.8	8.8	8.3	6.9	5.7	5.0	4.6	4.1	4.8	5.4
12 Current balance (% of GDP)	0.4	−7.3	0.4	2.4	−0.4	−4.4	−2.3	−2.5	−3.5	−2.1	−4.2
13 Net lending (+) or net borrowing (−) of general government (% of GDP)	0.6	:	−10.1	−7.2	−6.8	−5.4	−3.4	−5.5	−6.4	−5.6	−4.8
14 Gross debt of general government (% of GDP)	:	39.9	70.9	69.5	72.9	75.2	72.1	68.4	68.5	66.2	66.3
15 Interest payments by general government (% of GDP)	0.6	3.3	7.9	9.2	7.8	7.8	7.2	8.1	8.5	9.1	7.9
16 Money supply (end of year)[2]	:	21.7	28.6	26.3	19.7	17.7	10.4	11.3	19.0	:	:
17 Long-term interest rate (%)	:	:	25.4	17.9	15.4	14.2	14.9	16.8	17.1	15.0	:
18 Profitability (1961–73= 100)	100.0	38.1	44.9	53.6	53.0	54.9	60.4	60.8	58.6	59.0	57.5

[1] 1961–91: Eurostat and Commission services; 1992–3: Economic forecasts winter 1992/93.
[2] L: Liquid assets residents.

Table E13 United Kingdom: main economic indicators, 1961–93[1] (Annual percentage change, unless otherwise stated)

	1961–73	1974–84	1985	1986	1987	1988	1989	1990	1991	1992	1993
1 Gross domestic product											
At current prices	8.4	14.4	9.6	7.7	10.1	11.2	9.4	6.8	4.3	3.6	4.9
At constant prices	3.2	1.2	3.7	4.1	4.8	4.3	2.1	0.5	−2.2	−0.9	1.4
2 Gross fixed capital formation at constant prices											
Total	4.6	0.4	4.0	2.4	9.6	14.2	7.2	−3.1	−9.9	−0.4	−0.8
Construction	:	−0.7	−2.4	6.1	11.0	13.4	5.4	−0.6	−8.4	−1.4	−1.5
Equipment	:	1.4	10.7	−0.9	8.7	13.0	11.6	−3.6	−11.9	0.6	0.0
3 Gross fixed capital formation at current prices (% of GDP)											
Total	18.5	18.1	16.9	16.8	17.5	19.1	20.1	19.3	16.7	15.6	15.5
General government	:	3.0	2.1	1.9	1.7	1.3	1.8	2.3	2.2	2.1	2.2
Other sectors	:	15.1	14.9	14.9	15.9	17.8	18.3	17.0	14.5	13.5	13.4
4 Final national uses incl. stocks											
At constant prices	3.2	1.1	2.9	4.7	5.4	8.0	3.3	−0.5	−3.2	0.0	0.5
Relative to 19 competitors	−1.9	−0.8	0.0	1.2	2.1	3.8	−0.3	−3.0	−3.9	−0.9	−0.4
Relative to other member countries	−1.8	−0.5	0.9	1.2	2.4	4.1	−0.3	−4.0	−5.1	−1.0	0.2
5 Inflation											
Price deflator private consumption	4.9	12.6	5.3	4.3	4.4	5.1	5.9	5.3	7.2	5.1	5.1
Price deflator GDP	5.1	13.0	5.7	3.5	5.0	6.6	7.1	6.3	6.7	4.6	3.4
6 Compensation per employee											
Nominal	8.3	14.4	7.6	7.8	6.9	7.8	8.3	9.5	8.9	6.0	3.7
Real, deflator private consumption	3.3	1.6	2.2	3.4	2.4	2.5	2.2	3.9	1.5	0.8	−1.3
Real, deflator GDP	3.0	1.2	1.8	4.2	1.8	1.1	1.1	3.0	2.0	1.3	0.3
7 GDP at constant market prices per person employed	2.9	1.5	2.5	4.0	2.7	1.0	−0.8	−0.2	0.9	1.4	3.1
8 Real unit labour costs											
1961–73 = 100	100.0	101.7	97.0	97.2	96.3	96.4	98.3	101.5	102.7	102.6	99.8
Annual % change	0.1	−0.3	−0.6	0.2	−0.9	0.1	2.0	3.2	1.2	−0.1	−2.8
9 Relative unit labour costs in common currency											
● Against 19 competitors											
1961–73 = 100	100.0	92.1	94.3	87.5	87.5	96.5	99.2	103.1	106.8	104.7	93.4
Annual % change	−1.9	1.0	1.4	−7.2	0.0	10.3	2.7	3.9	3.6	−2.0	−10.8
● Against other member countries											
1961–73 = 100	100.0	87.9	100.8	87.5	84.0	94.4	99.3	97.7	102.8	98.0	87.6
Annual % change	−3.0	2.3	1.8	−13.2	−4.0	12.4	5.2	−1.6	5.2	−4.6	−10.6
10 Employment	0.3	−0.3	1.3	0.1	2.1	3.3	3.0	0.7	−3.1	−2.3	−1.7
11 Unemployment rate (% of civilian labour force)	:	6.5	11.4	11.4	10.4	8.5	7.1	7.0	9.1	10.8	12.3
12 Current balance (% of GDP)	−0.1	−0.1	0.5	−0.8	−2.0	−4.8	−5.4	−4.2	−1.8	−2.7	−3.5
13 Net lending (+) or net borrowing (−) of general government (% of GDP)	−0.6	−3.6	−2.9	−2.4	−1.3	1.0	0.9	−1.3	−2.8	−6.2	−8.3
14 Gross debt of general government (% of GDP)	:	58.6	59.0	58.0	55.8	49.5	43.2	39.8	41.1	45.9	52.6
15 Interest payments by general government (% of GDP)	:	4.5	5.0	4.5	4.3	3.9	3.7	3.4	3.0	3.1	3.8
16 Money supply (end of year)[2]	:	14.0	13.0	15.9	16.4	17.6	19.1	11.5	5.8	:	:
17 Long-term interest rate (%)	7.6	13.2	10.6	9.8	9.5	9.3	9.6	11.1	9.9	9.1	:
18 Profitability (1961–73= 100)	100.0	75.1	91.7	92.7	99.0	102.1	97.5	87.5	85.9	90.0	94.7

[1] 1961–91: Eurostat and Commission services; 1992–3: Economic forecasts winter 1992/93.
[2] M4.

Table E14 Total population (000s)

	B	DK	WD	D	GR	E	F	IRL	I	L	NL	P	UK	EUR 12–	EUR 12+	USA	Japan
1960	9 153	4 581	55 433	..	8 327	30 559	45 684	2 834	50 198	313.5	11 483	8 426	52 372	279 364	..	180 671	94 118
1965	9 464	4 757	58 619	..	8 551	32 060	48 778	2 876	51 987	331.5	12 293	8 511	54 350	292 577	..	194 303	98 851
1970	9 651	4 929	60 651	..	8 793	33 849	50 772	2 950	53 661	339.2	13 032	8 432	55 632	302 692	..	205 052	104 674
1971	9 673	4 963	61 284	..	8 831	34 163	51 251	2 978	54 005	342.4	13 194	8 382	55 928	304 995	..	207 661	105 713
1972	9 709	4 992	61 672	..	8 889	34 471	51 701	3 024	54 381	346.6	13 330	8 364	56 097	306 976	..	209 896	107 156
1973	9 739	5 022	61 976	..	8 929	34 783	52 118	3 073	54 751	350.5	13 438	8 368	56 223	308 770	..	211 909	108 660
1974	9 768	5 045	62 054	..	8 962	35 119	52 460	3 124	55 111	355.1	13 543	8 482	56 236	310 260	..	213 854	110 160
1975	9 795	5 060	61 829	..	9 046	35 487	52 699	3 177	55 441	359.0	13 660	8 737	56 226	311 516	..	215 973	111 520
1976	9 811	5 073	61 531	..	9 167	35 909	52 909	3 228	55 718	360.8	13 773	8 942	56 216	312 637	..	218 035	112 770
1977	9 822	5 088	61 400	..	9 309	36 338	53 145	3 272	55 955	361.4	13 856	9 044	56 190	313 781	..	220 239	113 880
1978	9 830	5 104	61 327	..	9 430	36 749	53 376	3 314	56 155	362.1	13 939	9 105	56 178	314 869	..	222 585	114 920
1979	9 837	5 117	61 359	..	9 548	37 079	53 606	3 368	56 318	363.0	14 034	9 189	56 240	316 058	..	225 055	115 880
1980	9 847	5 125	61 566	..	9 642	37 356	53 880	3 401	56 434	364.4	14 148	9 289	56 330	317 383	..	227 757	116 800
1981	9 853	5 122	61 682	..	9 730	37 726	54 182	3 443	56 508	365.4	14 247	9 358	56 352	318 569	..	230 138	117 650
1982	9 856	5 119	61 638	..	9 790	37 950	54 492	3 480	56 639	365.6	14 312	9 429	56 306	319 377	..	232 520	118 450
1983	9 855	5 114	61 423	..	9 847	38 142	54 772	3 505	56 836	365.7	14 368	9 502	56 347	320 077	..	234 799	119 260
1984	9 855	5 112	61 175	..	9 900	38 311	55 026	3 529	57 005	366.0	14 423	9 577	56 460	320 739	..	237 011	120 020
1985	9 858	5 114	61 024	..	9 934	38 474	55 284	3 540	57 141	366.7	14 488	9 640	56 618	321 482	..	239 279	120 750
1986	9 862	5 121	61 066	..	9 964	38 604	55 547	3 541	57 246	368.4	14 567	9 686	56 763	322 335	..	241 625	121 490
1987	9 870	5 127	61 077	..	9 984	38 716	55 824	3 542	57 345	370.8	14 664	9 727	56 930	323 177	..	243 942	122 090
1988	9 921	5 130	61 449	..	10 005	38 809	56 118	3 538	57 452	373.9	14 760	9 761	57 065	324 382	..	246 307	122 610
1989	9 938	5 132	62 063	..	10 033	38 888	56 423	3 515	57 540	377.7	14 846	9 793	57 236	325 785	..	248 762	123 120
1990	9 967	5 141	63 253	..	10 140	38 959	56 735	3 503	57 661	382.0	14 947	9 808	57 411	327 907	..	251 523	123 540
1991	9 977	5 154	64 083	80 046	10 269	39 025	57 050	3 524	57 796	386.2	15 066	9 815¹	57 561	329 706	345 669	254 284	123 960
1992	9 997	5 167	65 006	80 731	10 350	39 085	57 366	3 555	57 913	385.3	15 188	9 345¹	57 741	331 099	346 825	256 900	124 380
1993	10 017	5 178	65 864	81 468	10 422	39 141	57 685	3 579	58 024	390.3	15 311	9 355	57 927	332 894	348 498	259 290	124 800

¹ Break in 1991–92.

Table E15 Working population and employment (1990)

Country	Civilian working population (000s)	As % of total population	Civilian employment (000s)	% of females
EUR 12	144 542	45.7	131 639	38.4
1 Belgium	4 091	41.1	3 726	40.6
2 Denmark	2 889	56.3	2 653	45.9
3 Germany (FR)	29 829	47.6	27 946	40.8
4 Greece[1]	3 967	39.5	3 671	35.0
5 Spain	15 021	38.6	12 578	32.3
6 France	23 929	42.4	21 733	42.4
7 Ireland	1 294	36.9	1 115	33.3
8 Italy	23 744	41.7	21 123	35.2
9 Luxembourg	167	44.0	165	36.8
10 Netherlands	6 784	45.4	6 268	38.4
11 Portugal	4 694	47.9	4 474	42.6
12 United Kingdom	28 133	49.1	26 187	44.3
13 USA	124 787	49.9	117 914	45.4
14 Japan	63 840	51.7	62 490	40.6

[1] 1989.

Table E16 Civilian employment by main sectors of economic activity (1990) (%)

Country	Agriculture	Industry	Services	Total
EUR 12	6.6	32.5	60.9	100.0
1 Belgium	2.7	28.7	68.5	100.0
2 Denmark	5.7	25.6	68.7	100.0
3 Germany (FR)	3.4	39.8	56.8	100.0
4 Greece[1]	25.3	27.5	47.1	100.0
5 Spain	11.8	33.4	54.8	100.0
6 France	6.1	29.9	64.0	100.0
7 Ireland	15.0	28.7	56.3	100.0
8 Italy	9.0	32.4	58.6	100.0
9 Luxembourg	3.2	30.7	66.1	100.0
10 Netherlands	4.6	26.3	69.1	100.0
11 Portugal	17.8	34.9	47.4	100.0
12 United Kingdom	2.2	29.5	68.3	100.0
13 USA	2.8	26.2	70.9	100.0
14 Japan	7.2	34.1	58.7	100.0

[1] 1990.

Table E17 Unemployment rate[1] (% of civilian labour force)

	B	DK	WD	GR	E	F	IRL	I	L	NL	P	UK	EUR 9[2]	EUR 12	USA[3]	Japan[3]
1960	3.1	1.6	1.0	:	:	0.7	4.7	7.2	0.1	0.7	:	1.6	2.5	:	5.4	1.7
1964–70	2.0	1.0	0.7	5.0	2.7	2.0	5.5	5.0	0.0	1.0	2.5	1.7	2.1	2.3	4.2	1.2
1971	1.7	0.9	0.6	3.1	3.4	2.7	6.0	5.1	0.0	1.3	2.5	2.7	2.5	2.6	6.0	1.2
1972	2.2	0.8	0.8	2.1	2.9	2.8	6.7	6.0	0.0	2.3	2.5	3.1	2.9	2.8	5.6	1.4
1973	2.2	0.7	0.8	2.0	2.6	2.7	6.2	5.9	0.0	2.4	2.6	2.2	2.7	2.6	4.9	1.3
1974	2.3	2.8	1.8	2.1	3.1	2.8	5.8	5.0	0.0	2.9	1.7	2.0	2.8	2.8	5.6	1.4
1975	4.2	3.9	3.3	2.3	4.5	4.0	7.9	5.5	0.0	5.5	4.4	3.2	4.0	4.0	8.5	1.9
1976	5.5	5.1	3.3	1.9	4.9	4.4	9.8	6.2	0.0	5.8	6.2	4.8	4.7	4.7	7.7	2.0
1977	6.3	5.9	3.2	1.7	5.3	4.9	9.7	6.7	0.0	5.6	7.3	5.0	5.0	5.1	7.1	2.0
1978	6.8	6.7	3.1	1.8	7.1	5.1	9.0	6.7	1.2	5.6	7.9	5.1	5.1	5.3	6.1	2.3
1979	7.0	4.8	2.7	1.9	8.8	5.8	7.8	7.2	2.4	5.7	7.9	4.6	5.0	5.4	5.8	2.2
1980	7.4	5.2	2.7	2.7	11.6	6.2	8.0	7.1	2.4	6.4	7.6	5.6	5.4	6.0	7.1	2.0
1971–80	4.6	3.7	2.2	2.2	5.4	4.1	7.7	6.1	0.6	4.4	5.1	3.8	4.0	4.1	6.4	1.8
1981	9.5	8.3	3.9	4.0	14.4	7.3	10.8	7.4	2.4	8.9	7.3	8.9	7.1	7.7	7.6	2.2
1982	11.2	8.9	5.6	5.8	16.3	8.0	12.5	8.0	2.4	11.9	7.2	10.3	8.3	9.0	9.7	2.4
1983	12.5	9.2	6.9	7.9	17.8	8.2	15.2	8.7	3.5	12.4	8.1	11.0	9.1	9.9	9.6	2.7
1984	12.5	8.7	7.1	8.1	20.6	9.7	16.8	9.3	3.1	12.3	8.7	11.0	9.6	10.6	7.5	2.7
1985	11.8	7.2	7.1	7.7	21.6	10.1	18.2	9.6	2.9	10.5	8.8	11.4	9.7	10.8	7.2	2.6
1986	11.7	5.5	6.5	7.4	21.0	10.3	18.2	10.5	2.6	10.3	8.3	11.4	9.7	10.7	7.0	2.8
1987	11.3	5.6	6.3	7.4	20.4	10.4	18.0	10.3	2.5	10.0	6.9	10.4	9.4	10.3	6.2	2.8
1988	10.2	6.4	6.3	7.6	19.3	9.9	17.3	10.8	2.0	9.3	5.7	8.8	8.8	9.8	5.5	2.5
1989	8.6	7.7	5.6	7.4	17.1	9.4	15.7	10.6	1.8	8.5	5.0	7.1	8.1	8.9	5.3	2.3
1990	7.6	8.1	4.8	7.2	16.1	9.0	14.5	9.9	1.7	7.5	4.6	7.0	7.5	8.3	5.5	2.1
1981–90	10.7	7.6	6.0	7.1	18.5	9.2	15.7	9.5	2.5	10.2	7.1	9.7	8.7	9.6	7.1	2.5
1991	7.5	8.9	4.2	7.7	16.3	9.5	16.2	10.2	1.6	7.0	4.1	9.1	8.1	8.8	6.7	2.1
1992	8.2	9.5	4.5	7.7	18.0	10.1	17.8	10.2	1.9	6.7	4.8	10.8	8.7	9.5	7.3	2.1
1993	9.3	9.5	6.0	8.5	19.5	10.8	19.2	10.6	2.0	7.6	5.4	12.3	9.7	10.6	7.2	2.2

[1] Definition. Eurostat
[2] EUR 12 excl. Greece, Spain and Portugal.
[3] OECD.

Table E18 Gross domestic product at current market prices (ECU; Mrd)

	B	DK	WD	D	GR	E	F	IRL	I	L	NL	P	UK	EUR 12–	EUR 12+	USA	Japan
1960	10.5	5.6	68.2	..	3.3	11.1	57.7	1.7	37.6	0.5	11.3	2.4	68.5	278.5	..	487.3	42.1
1965	15.5	9.5	107.3	..	5.6	22.5	92.8	2.5	62.5	0.7	19.0	3.5	94.1	435.6	..	658.1	85.3
1970	24.7	15.5	180.5	..	9.7	37.2	139.8	3.8	105.1	1.1	33.5	6.1	121.2	678.1	..	989.6	199.3
1971	27.2	16.9	205.7	..	10.5	41.3	153.2	4.3	112.7	1.1	38.2	6.7	134.3	752.2		1 048.1	221.8
1972	31.3	19.4	230.1	..	11.2	48.8	174.6	5.0	122.0	1.3	43.9	7.6	143.6	838.8		1 076.8	272.0
1973	36.7	23.3	280.0	..	13.1	59.0	206.6	5.4	135.0	1.6	52.6	9.3	147.5	970.1		1 096.4	337.7
1974	44.8	26.9	318.8	..	15.8	75.4	229.6	5.8	154.3	2.0	64.5	11.3	163.0	1 112.3		1 215.0	395.2
1975	49.8	30.4	336.7	..	16.8	86.7	276.0	6.8	171.2	1.9	71.9	12.0	188.6	1 248.6		1 279.5	411.2
1976	59.7	37.2	398.0	..	20.2	98.1	318.2	7.5	188.0	2.3	87.3	13.9	201.1	1 431.5		1 583.4	502.9
1977	68.1	40.7	451.3	..	22.9	107.1	342.1	8.7	213.0	2.5	100.6	14.3	222.9	1 594.3		1 731.1	607.0
1978	74.6	44.4	502.2	..	24.8	116.8	380.3	10.2	234.7	2.8	110.5	14.1	253.2	1 768.4		1 749.9	765.3
1979	79.4	48.1	552.9	..	28.1	144.7	425.6	11.8	272.2	3.0	117.7	14.8	306.1	2 004.5		1 813.9	737.4
1980	85.0	47.8	583.2	..	28.8	154.3	478.5	13.8	326.0	3.3	124.9	18.1	386.4	2 250.0		1 945.1	762.4
1981	86.6	51.5	610.6	..	33.3	167.3	524.0	16.4	367.4	3.4	130.2	21.9	459,6	2 472.2		2 719.2	1 051.3
1982	82.7	56.9	668.4	..	39.4	184.0	563.8	19.4	411.8	3.6	144.5	23.7	496.2	2 698.7		3 217.8	1 111.1
1983	90.8	63.0	734.9	..	39.4	176.3	591.7	20.7	469.2	3.8	153.8	23.3	516.8	2 883.9		3 812.9	1 333.2
1984	97.5	69.4	782.3	..	43.0	200.6	634.8	22.6	525.4	4.3	162.5	24.3	549.9	3 116.6		4 769.7	1 606.4
1985	105.6	76.7	818.9	..	43.7	218.4	691.7	24.9	559.8	4.6	170.6	27.1	604.6	3 346.4		5 263.7	1 774.6
1986	114.0	84.0	904.7	..	40.1	235.2	745.5	25.7	615.6	5.1	182.8	30.1	571.3	3 554.0		4 298.8	2 028.0
1987	121.1	88.8	960.9	..	40.0	254.2	770.2	26.2	658.1	5.3	188.8	31.8	599.4	3 744.7		3 895.0	2 091.4
1988	128.3	92.1	1 010.4	..	44.9	291.9	815.1	28.2	710.2	5.8	195.9	35.3	706.9	4 064.9		4 104.9	2 452.3
1989	139.5	95.6	1 074.5	..	49.1	345.3	876.9	31.4	790.1	6.5	207.5	41.1	762.8	4 420.4		4 723.9	2 607.6
1990	151.5	101.8	1 178.2	..	52.5	386.9	938.9	33.9	861.8	7.1	223.3	47.0	768.5	4 751.5		4 291.4	2 318.1
1991	159.2	105.3	1 274.0	1 364.8	57.1	426.4	970.3	35.1	930.9	7.6	235.2	55.5	816.5	5 073.2	5 164.0	4 527.9	2 720.4
1992	169.2	110.4	1 372.1	1 486.7	61.1	444.5	1 036.0	37.6	951.3	8.0	248.5	65.2	804.0	5 307.8	5 422.4	4 522.8	2 852.5
1993	180.9	117.7	1 457.2	1 598.2	64.0	445.2	1 103.3	40.3	913.3	8.8	265.5	70.9	779.2	5 446.0	5 587.0	4 995.6	3 176.6

Table E19 Gross domestic product at constant market prices (National currency; annual % change)

	B	DK	WD	D	GR	E	F	IRL	I	L	NL	P	UK	EUR 12– (PPS)	EUR 12+ (PPS)	USA	Japan
1961	5.0	6.4	4.5	:	11.1	11.8	5.5	5.0	8.2	3.8	3.1	5.2	3.3	5.5	:	2.7	12.0
1965	3.6	4.6	5.4	:	9.4	6.3	4.8	1.9	3.3	1.9	5.2	7.6	2.5	4.4	:	5.5	5.8
1970	6.4	2.0	5.1	:	8.0	4.1	5.7	2.7	5.3	1.7	5.7	7.6	2.3	4.7	:	-0.1	10.7
1961–70	4.9	4.5	4.4	:	7.6	7.3	5.6	4.2	5.7	3.5	5.1	6.4	2.9	4.8	:	3.8	10.5
1971	3.7	2.7	3.0	:	7.1	4.6	4.8	3.5	1.6	2.7	4.2	6.6	2.0	3.2	:	2.9	4.3
1972	5.3	5.3	4.3	:	8.9	8.0	4.1	6.5	2.7	6.6	3.3	8.0	3.5	4.3	:	5.1	8.2
1973	5.9	3.6	4.9	:	7.3	7.7	5.4	4.7	7.1	8.3	4.7	11.2	7.3	6.2	:	5.2	7.6
1974	4.1	-0.9	0.3	:	-3.6	5.3	2.7	4.3	5.4	4.2	4.0	1.1	-1.7	1.9	:	-0.6	-0.6
1975	-1.5	-0.7	-1.4	:	6.1	0.5	-0.3	5.7	-2.7	-6.6	-0.1	-4.3	-0.8	-1.0	:	-0.8	2.9
1976	5.6	6.5	5.3	:	6.4	3.3	4.4	1.4	6.6	2.5	5.1	6.9	2.7	4.7	:	4.9	4.2
1977	0.5	1.6	2.8	:	3.4	3.0	3.5	8.2	3.4	1.6	2.3	5.5	2.3	2.9	:	4.5	4.7
1978	2.7	1.5	3.0	:	6.7	1.4	3.4	7.2	3.7	4.1	2.5	2.8	3.6	3.2	:	4.6	4.9
1979	2.1	3.5	4.1	:	3.7	-0.1	3.2	3.1	6.0	2.3	2.4	5.6	2.9	3.5	:	2.6	5.5
1980	4.3	-0.4	1.1	:	1.8	1.2	1.4	3.1	4.2	0.8	0.9	4.6	-2.2	1.3	:	-0.4	3.6
1971–80	3.2	2.2	2.7	:	4.7	3.5	3.2	4.7	3.8	2.6	2.9	4.7	1.9	3.0	:	2.8	4.5
1981	-1.0	-0.9	0.2	:	0.1	-0.2	1.2	3.3	0.6	-0.6	-0.6	1.6	-1.3	0.1	:	1.9	3.6
1982	1.5	3.0	-0.9	:	0.4	1.2	2.3	2.3	0.2	1.1	-1.4	2.1	1.7	0.7	:	-2.2	3.2
1983	0.4	2.5	1.6	:	0.4	1.8	0.8	-0.2	1.0	3.0	1.4	-0.2	3.7	1.6	:	3.5	2.7
1984	2.2	4.4	2.8	:	2.8	1.8	1.5	4.4	2.7	6.2	3.1	-1.9	2.3	2.3	:	6.1	4.3
1985	0.8	4.3	1.9	:	3.1	2.3	1.8	3.1	2.6	2.9	2.6	2.8	3.7	2.4	:	3.0	5.0
1986	1.5	3.6	2.2	:	1.6	3.2	2.4	-0.4	2.9	4.8	2.0	4.1	4.1	2.8	:	2.6	2.6
1987	2.0	0.3	1.4	:	-0.7	5.6	2.2	5.0	3.1	2.9	0.8	5.3	4.8	2.9	:	3.0	4.1
1988	5.0	1.2	3.7	:	4.1	5.2	4.3	4.9	4.1	5.7	2.6	3.9	4.3	4.1	:	3.9	6.2
1989	3.8	0.8	3.4	:	3.5	4.8	3.8	6.5	2.9	6.7	4.7	5.2	2.1	3.4	:	2.6	4.7
1990	3.4	1.7	5.1	:	-0.1	3.6	2.2	8.3	2.2	3.2	3.9	4.4	0.5	2.8	:	0.7	5.2
1981–90	2.0	2.1	2.1	:	1.5	2.9	2.2	3.7	2.2	3.6	1.9	2.7	2.6	2.3	:	2.5	4.2
1991	1.9	1.2	3.7	:	1.8	2.4	1.1	2.5	1.4	3.1	2.2	1.9	-2.2	1.4	:	-1.3	4.4
1992	1.0	1.0	1.5	1.9	1.5	1.2	1.9	2.9	1.1	2.2	1.3	1.7	-0.9	1.1	1.2	2.0	1.5
1993	0.5	1.8	-0.5	0.0	1.6	1.0	1.0	2.1	0.8	2.0	0.6	1.3	1.4	0.7	0.8	2.4	1.5

Table E20 Gross domestic product at current market prices per head of population (PPS EUR 12−; EUR 12− = 100)

	B	DK	WD	D	GR	E	F	IRL	I	L	NL	P	UK	EUR 12−	EUR 12+	USA	Japan
1960	97.5	115.2	124.3	:	34.8	58.3	107.7	57.2	86.6	155.3	116.8	37.2	122.6	100.0	:	182.5	54.1
1965	98.9	117.8	121.9	:	40.9	68.5	109.6	55.6	88.5	133.1	113.4	41.4	113.6	100.0	:	174.6	66.1
1970	101.1	112.2	118.6	:	46.4	72.2	112.7	56.1	95.5	138.4	114.1	46.9	103.5	100.0	:	158.4	88.8
1971	102.1	111.7	118.0	:	48.4	73.1	114.2	56.1	94.1	128.0	114.6	49.1	102.5	100.0	:	157.0	89.6
1972	103.4	112.8	118.0	:	50.5	75.5	113.7	56.8	92.7	130.8	113.2	51.3	102.1	100.0	:	157.6	92.3
1973	103.5	110.1	116.7	:	51.1	76.4	112.6	55.5	93.4	138.8	111.3	54.1	103.5	100.0	:	155.6	92.8
1974	105.9	107.1	115.2	:	48.4	78.5	113.3	56.1	96.5	149.5	113.2	53.2	100.3	100.0	:	151.1	89.7
1975	105.4	107.5	115.6	:	51.5	79.2	114.0	59.1	94.6	123.9	113.7	50.1	100.9	100.0	:	150.5	92.4
1976	106.5	109.4	117.2	:	51.8	77.5	113.6	56.5	96.2	123.0	113.6	50.1	99.3	100.0	:	149.9	91.3
1977	104.2	108.1	117.8	:	51.5	76.9	114.2	58.8	96.5	116.6	112.7	51.0	99.1	100.0	:	151.1	92.3
1978	104.0	106.4	118.2	:	52.7	75.0	114.3	60.5	97.0	116.8	111.6	50.6	99.9	100.0	:	152.1	93.2
1979	103.0	106.5	119.2	:	52.4	72.0	113.9	59.5	99.4	116.1	110.0	51.4	99.6	100.0	:	149.6	94.6
1980	106.4	105.0	119.1	:	52.3	71.7	113.9	60.2	102.5	115.6	109.2	52.7	96.4	100.0	:	146.0	96.5
1981	105.6	104.4	119.4	:	52.0	71.1	114.9	61.7	103.2	114.5	108.0	53.3	95.4	100.0	:	147.7	99.5
1982	106.6	107.1	117.8	:	51.7	71.2	116.3	62.1	102.7	116.5	105.5	53.8	96.6	100.0	:	142.2	101.4
1983	105.7	108.4	118.4	:	50.9	71.1	115.1	60.7	102.0	116.4	105.1	52.6	98.7	100.0	:	143.8	102.1
1984	105.7	110.9	119.7	:	50.9	70.6	113.9	61.6	102.2	118.5	105.7	50.1	98.7	100.0	:	148.0	103.6
1985	104.3	113.1	119.6	:	51.2	70.4	112.9	61.9	102.4	120.2	105.6	50.1	100.0	100.0	:	147.7	105.8
1986	103.1	114.2	119.2	:	50.6	70.6	112.2	60.1	102.6	124.8	104.5	50.6	101.3	100.0	:	146.3	105.2
1987	102.5	111.5	117.8	:	48.9	72.5	111.2	61.5	103.0	119.5	102.0	51.7	103.2	100.0	:	145.5	106.2
1988	103.2	108.7	117.1	:	49.0	73.3	111.2	62.3	103.1	122.3	100.3	51.7	103.5	100.0	:	144.5	108.4
1989	103.9	106.5	116.5	:	49.1	74.5	111.5	64.9	103.0	128.2	101.4	52.6	102.4	100.0	:	142.6	109.8
1990	104.9	105.8	117.6	:	47.5	75.4	111.0	69.0	102.8	127.2	102.4	53.7	100.5	100.0	:	139.0	112.7
1991	105.9	106.0	119.4	102.4	47.4	76.4	110.7	69.7	103.2	128.1	103.0	54.2	97.1	100.0	97.0	134.5	116.3
1992	106.1	106.0	118.7	102.8	47.4	76.7	111.5	70.7	103.5	129.1	102.9	57.5	95.3	100.0	97.1	134.9	116.9
1993	106.2	107.5	116.4	101.7	47.8	77.2	111.9	71.6	104.0	129.8	102.6	58.1	96.2	100.0	97.3	136.7	118.1

Table E21 Use of gross domestic product at market prices (1990) (%)

	Country	National private consumption population	Collective consumption of general government	Gross fixed capital formation	Change in stocks	Balance of exports and imports of goods and services	Gross domestic product at market prices
	EUR 12	61.1	16.4	20.9	0.5	1.0	100.0
1	Belgium	61.9	14.3	20.3	0.3	3.2	100.0
2	Denmark	52.3	24.8	17.7	−0.2	5.4	100.0
3	Germany (FR)	60.2	12.3	21.2	0.8	5.5	100.0
4	Greece	72.3	21.2	19.7	0.3	−11.2	100.0
5	Spain	62.4	15.2	24.6	1.1	−3.4	100.0
6	France	60.3	18.0	21.2	0.5	0.0	100.0
7	Ireland	55.4	15.7	19.1	1.8	8.1	100.0
8	Italy	61.8	17.3	20.2	0.6	0.0	100.0
9	Luxembourg	57.1	16.3	25.3	1.8	−0.5	100.0
10	Netherlands	58.8	14.8	21.5	−0.2	5.1	100.0
11	Portugal	63.1	16.7	26.4	2.7	−8.9	100.0
12	United Kingdom	63.3	19.9	19.2	−0.1	−2.4	100.0
13	USA	67.4	18.1	16.1	−0.1	−1.5	100.0
14	Japan	57.1	9.0	32.6	0.6	0.7	100.0

Table E22 Gross value-added at market prices by branch (1989) (%)

	Country	Agriculture, forestry and fishing	Industry (incl. construction)	Services and general government	Gross value-added at market prices
	EUR 12	3.0	34.4	62.5	100.0
1	Belgium	2.1	30.3	65.5	100.0
2	Denmark[1]	4.6	27.1	68.3	100.0
3	Germany (FR)	1.6	39.4	59.1	100.0
4	Greece[1]	17.0	27.2	55.9	100.0
5	Spain	4.9	35.3	59.7	100.0
6	France	3.6	30.3	66.2	100.0
7	Ireland[2]	10.0	36.7	53.3	100.0
8	Italy	3.6	34.2	62.2	100.0
9	Luxembourg	2.1	35.9	62.1	100.0
10	Netherlands	4.7	32.4	62.8	100.0
11	Portugal	6.3	37.7	56.0	100.0
12	United Kingdom	1.1	34.2	64.8	100.0
13	USA	2.5	27.1	70.5	100.0
14	Japan	2.5	40.2	57.3	100.0

At factor cost
[1] 1988.
[2] 1987.

Table E23 Real unit labour costs[1] for total economy (1980 = 100)

	B	DK	WD	GR	E	F	IRL	I	L	NL	P	UK	EUR 12-(PPS)	USA	Japan
1960	86.9	94.3	92.7	119.0	91.4	92.9	96.8	98.5	81.4	86.5	89.5	97.9	96.4	98.6	99.6
1965	87.8	98.8	94.8	104.0	95.2	93.5	95.4	99.2	86.2	93.7	86.3	98.2	96.7	94.9	95.8
1970	85.9	99.5	96.4	98.5	96.6	92.7	96.0	96.4	78.2	97.3	90.8	99.2	96.4	100.3	88.5
1971	88.4	101.1	97.1	96.8	97.7	93.0	95.9	100.5	85.5	98.8	93.7	98.1	97.3	98.7	92.9
1972	90.1	96.9	97.3	96.0	98.3	92.1	92.3	101.1	85.4	97.7	93.0	98.9	97.3	98.7	93.1
1973	90.8	96.8	98.7	88.9	98.4	91.6	92.1	100.3	79.8	98.9	89.3	99.7	97.5	98.6	94.6
1974	92.9	102.0	101.3	91.3	98.2	94.6	99.6	99.2	82.7	101.0	99.7	105.1	100.0	100.1	99.2
1975	96.8	102.7	101.1	92.5	100.8	98.9	100.3	105.8	101.4	103.3	120.6	108.9	103.3	98.3	104.1
1976	98.2	100.5	99.2	93.1	102.2	98.9	96.9	103.0	97.9	99.9	120.3	104.7	101.5	98.1	103.8
1977	98.7	100.0	99.3	98.2	101.4	99.3	92.5	102.4	104.6	99.5	111.9	99.5	100.4	97.8	103.8
1978	98.7	98.9	98.3	100.9	101.6	98.6	92.4	101.5	100.6	99.5	104.0	98.4	99.5	98.1	102.3
1979	98.8	98.4	97.8	101.8	101.7	98.1	96.7	101.1	99.1	100.3	101.0	97.9	99.1	98.8	101.1
1980	100.0	100.0	100.0	100.0	100.0	100.0	100.0	100.0	100.0	100.0	100.0	100.0	100.0	100.0	100.0
1981	100.6	98.8	100.4	106.4	100.5	100.8	96.5	102.4	102.1	97.3	102.3	99.7	100.7	98.6	99.9
1982	98.5	97.5	100.0	107.4	98.3	100.6	93.5	101.8	97.2	96.0	99.0	97.0	99.6	100.6	99.7
1983	97.7	95.9	97.2	110.1	98.0	99.8	93.7	102.3	94.2	94.1	95.8	95.5	98.5	99.2	99.3
1984	96.8	93.3	95.9	107.9	93.1	98.3	91.7	100.2	91.5	89.7	93.5	96.2	96.9	97.8	97.0
1985	95.1	92.1	95.5	110.7	90.6	97.0	90.1	99.6	91.2	88.4	91.4	95.6	95.9	97.7	94.2
1986	95.3	91.0	95.0	104.9	87.7	94.1	89.6	97.3	89.2	89.4	86.2	95.8	94.5	98.1	93.9
1987	93.2	94.3	95.5	102.9	87.5	93.0	87.7	96.7	94.3	91.7	87.3	95.0	94.2	98.8	93.8
1988	90.7	94.1	94.2	103.5	86.9	91.0	87.1	95.5	91.1	90.5	85.4	95.1	93.1	99.0	92.7
1989	87.8	92.2	92.6	105.3	85.3	89.7	82.9	95.2	89.1	87.7	81.9	96.9	92.2	97.8	92.7
1990	90.0	91.3	91.9	105.8	85.1	90.3	83.9	96.8	93.6	87.7	82.2	100.1	93.0	98.9	92.7
1991	91.6	90.0	92.3	98.5	84.8	90.7	84.3	97.4	96.3	88.0	84.7	101.2	93.4	99.6	92.7
1992	91.6	89.2	92.4	93.9	84.5	89.8	84.6	96.3	98.3	89.0	84.5	101.2	93.1	98.2	93.0
1993	92.0	88.4	92.1	91.2	84.4	89.5	85.8	95.2	99.6	88.5	84.4	98.4	92.2	96.4	91.9

[1] Nominal unit labour costs deflated by the GDP price deflator.

Table E24 Private consumption at current prices (% of GDP at market prices)

	B	DK (ECU)	WD (ECU)	D	GR	E	F	IRL	I	L	NL	P	UK	EUR 12−	EUR 12+	USA	Japan
1960	69.2	62.0	59.4	:	80.3	67.5	59.7	76.6	59.7	54.0	57.9	73.1	66.0	62.3	:	63.7	58.7
1965	64.3	58.9	59.2	:	72.8	67.1	59.0	71.7	59.2	58.2	58.9	67.9	64.1	61.1	:	62.3	58.5
1970	59.8	57.4	58.4	:	69.2	64.0	57.9	68.9	59.5	50.5	57.9	65.9	61.8	59.6	:	62.8	52.3
1961–70	64.3	59.8	59.4	:	72.9	66.1	59.3	72.0	59.6	56.5	58.8	68.6	64.1	61.2	:	62.4	56.5
1971	60.3	55.8	58.7	:	68.0	64.3	57.8	68.0	59.8	54.8	57.3	68.3	62.1	59.8	:	62.7	53.6
1972	60.2	53.4	59.4	:	65.7	63.8	57.7	65.0	60.1	53.6	56.8	64.2	62.8	59.9	:	62.5	54.0
1973	60.6	54.5	58.8	:	63.4	63.5	57.1	64.4	60.5	48.9	56.2	64.8	62.5	59.5	:	61.7	53.6
1974	59.8	54.3	59.7	:	67.7	64.2	57.5	68.4	60.3	46.1	56.3	72.7	63.8	60.2	:	62.3	54.3
1975	61.2	55.5	62.9	:	67.5	64.3	58.7	64.1	62.0	57.8	58.1	77.1	62.2	61.5	:	63.3	57.1
1976	60.9	56.6	62.5	:	65.8	65.7	58.4	64.5	60.8	56.6	58.2	75.0	61.1	61.1	:	63.3	57.5
1977	61.9	56.9	63.1	:	65.9	65.0	58.2	64.1	60.3	59.6	59.2	72.0	59.9	61.0	:	63.1	57.7
1978	61.6	56.2	62.6	:	65.2	63.9	57.9	63.8	59.5	57.9	59.8	68.0	59.9	60.6	:	62.3	57.7
1979	62.8	56.4	62.3	:	63.3	64.5	58.1	65.3	59.7	57.8	60.4	67.5	60.3	60.7	:	62.2	58.7
1980	62.9	55.9	63.1	:	64.6	65.3	58.9	65.8	61.0	58.7	60.6	67.3	60.1	61.3	:	63.1	58.8
1971–80	61.2	55.5	61.3	:	65.7	64.5	58.0	65.3	60.4	55.2	58.3	69.7	61.5	60.6	:	62.6	56.3
1981	65.2	56.0	64.0	:	67.5	66.5	60.3	65.9	61.2	60.9	59.9	69.6	60.8	62.1	:	62.2	58.1
1982	65.6	55.0	64.1	:	67.4	66.2	60.7	59.8	61.5	60.3	59.6	69.6	61.0	62.2	:	64.0	59.4
1983	65.2	54.6	63.8	:	66.7	65.7	60.8	59.6	61.1	59.6	59.8	69.3	61.2	62.1	:	64.9	60.2
1984	64.9	54.5	63.6	:	64.7	64.3	60.8	58.8	61.1	58.1	58.6	70.7	61.3	61.8	:	63.8	59.4
1985	65.5	54.8	63.4	:	65.5	64.1	61.1	59.6	61.4	58.7	58.7	67.9	61.1	61.9	:	64.7	58.9
1986	64.1	55.0	61.9	:	67.4	63.2	60.4	59.9	61.3	56.5	59.2	65.1	62.9	61.6	:	65.3	58.6
1987	64.5	54.0	62.2	:	69.5	63.2	60.9	59.3	61.7	59.2	60.8	64.5	63.0	61.9	:	65.8	58.7
1988	63.0	53.1	61.8	:	68.3	62.6	60.1	58.9	61.4	57.4	59.4	65.1	63.9	61.6	:	65.9	57.9
1989	62.3	52.8	61.1	:	70.4	62.9	59.8	56.9	62.0	54.	58.7	63.5	64.0	61.5	:	65.7	57.7
1990	62.2	52.1	60.8	:	71.4	62.4	60.1	56.0	61.7	55.4	58.6	63.1	63.5	61.2	:	66.5	57.4
1981–90	64.3	54.2	62.7	:	67.9	64.1	60.5	59.5	61.5	58.1	59.3	66.8	62.3	61.8	:	64.9	58.6
1991	62.7	52.5	60.6	64.1	70.3	62.5	60.4	55.8	62.1	57.3	59.4	63.3	63.9	61.5	62.4	67.1	56.8
1992	62.6	52.5	60.0	63.3	70.4	63.4	60.1	55.8	62.6	58.5	59.7	62.3	64.6	61.5	62.4	67.4	57.3
1993	63.3	52.5	60.3	63.4	70.7	63.9	60.2	55.7	63.0	58.9	59.8	63.0	65.1	61.7	62.6	67.4	57.9

Table E25 Gross fixed capital formation at current prices for total economy (% of GDP at market prices)

	B	DK	WD	D	GR	E	F	IRL	I	L	NL	P	UK	EUR 12– (ECU)	EUR 12+ (ECU)	USA	Japan
1960	19.3	21.6	24.3	:	19.0	20.4	20.9	14.4	26.0	20.9	24.8	23.2	16.4	21.4	:	18.0	29.0
1965	22.4	24.1	26.1	:	21.6	24.8	24.2	21.4	22.2	28.0	25.8	22.8	18.4	23.1	:	19.0	29.8
1970	22.7	24.7	25.5	:	23.6	26.4	24.3	22.7	24.6	23.1	26.6	23.2	18.9	23.8	:	18.0	35.5
1961–70	21.9	23.8	24.9	:	21.4	24.3	23.8	20.2	24.6	26.0	26.0	23.4	18.3	23.0	:	18.3	32.2
1971	22.1	24.2	26.2	:	25.2	24.2	24.7	23.6	23.9	28.4	26.0	24.7	18.9	23.9	:	18.5	34.2
1972	21.3	24.6	25.4	:	27.8	25.3	24.7	23.7	23.1	27.8	24.2	27.1	18.5	23.6	:	19.2	34.1
1973	21.4	24.8	23.9	:	28.0	26.8	25.2	25.3	24.9	27.3	23.7	26.8	19.9	23.9	:	19.5	36.4
1974	22.7	24.0	21.6	:	22.2	28.3	25.8	24.6	25.9	24.6	22.5	26.0	20.9	23.7	:	18.9	34.8
1975	22.5	21.1	20.4	:	20.8	26.8	24.1	22.7	24.9	27.7	21.6	25.9	19.9	22.5	:	17.6	32.5
1976	22.1	23.0	20.1	:	21.2	25.3	23.9	25.0	23.9	24.9	20.0	25.1	19.6	22.0	:	17.9	31.2
1977	21.6	22.1	20.3	:	23.0	24.3	22.9	24.8	23.5	25.1	21.6	26.5	18.6	21.6	:	19.3	30.2
1978	21.7	21.7	20.6	:	23.9	23.0	22.4	27.7	22.7	24.1	21.9	27.9	18.5	21.4	:	20.7	30.4
1979	20.7	20.9	21.7	:	25.8	21.9	22.4	30.5	22.8	24.4	21.6	26.6	18.7	21.6	:	21.3	31.7
1980	21.1	18.8	22.6	:	24.2	22.5	23.0	28.6	24.3	27.1	21.6	28.6	18.0	22.0	:	20.2	31.6
1971–80	21.7	22.5	22.3	:	24.2	24.8	23.9	25.6	24.0	26.1	22.5	26.5	19.1	22.6	:	19.3	32.7
1981	18.0	15.6	21.6	:	22.3	22.1	22.1	29.7	23.9	25.4	19.7	30.8	16.2	20.9	:	19.9	30.6
1982	17.3	16.1	20.4	:	19.9	21.6	21.4	26.5	22.3	25.0	18.7	31.1	16.1	20.0	:	18.7	29.5
1983	16.2	16.0	20.4	:	20.3	20.9	20.2	23.1	21.3	21.2	18.7	29.2	16.0	19.5	:	18.5	28.0
1984	16.0	17.2	20.0	:	18.5	19.0	19.3	21.4	21.0	20.0	19.1	23.6	16.9	19.2	:	19.3	27.7
1985	15.6	18.7	19.5	:	19.1	19.2	19.3	19.0	20.7	17.7	19.7	21.8	16.9	19.0	:	19.5	27.5
1986	15.7	20.8	19.4	:	18.5	19.5	19.3	18.0	19.7	22.1	20.6	22.1	16.8	19.0	:	19.1	27.3
1987	16.0	19.7	19.4	:	17.2	20.8	19.8	16.4	19.7	25.5	20.8	24.2	17.5	19.3	:	18.5	28.5
1988	17.6	18.1	19.6	:	17.5	22.6	20.7	16.3	20.1	27.0	21.3	26.8	19.1	20.0	:	18.3	29.9
1989	19.3	17.8	20.2	:	19.2	24.2	21.2	17.7	20.2	27.1	21.5	26.4	20.1	20.7	:	17.7	31.0
1990	20.2	17.7	21.0	:	19.4	24.6	21.2	18.6	20.2	26.9	21.3	26.4	19.3	20.9	:	16.8	32.2
1981–90	17.2	17.8	20.1	:	19.2	21.4	20.4	20.7	20.9	23.8	20.1	26.2	17.5	19.9	:	18.6	29.2
1991	19.8	17.1	21.6	23.2	18.2	24.1	20.8	17.1	19.8	29.0	20.8	25.5	16.7	20.3	20.8	15.4	31.6
1992	19.9	15.6	21.5	23.5	17.5	22.6	20.0	16.8	19.4	29.7	20.6	25.1	15.6	19.8	20.4	15.4	31.1
1993	19.1	15.7	21.4	23.6	17.9	22.0	19.6	16.7	19.3	29.6	20.4	25.4	15.5	19.6	20.3	15.3	31.2

Table E26 Gross fixed capital formation at constant prices for total economy (National currency: annual % change)

	B	DK	WD	D	GR	E	F	IRL	I	L	NL	P	UK	EUR 12– (PPS)	EUR 12+ (PPS)	USA	Japan
1961	12.4	13.9	6.6	:	8.1	17.9	10.9	16.9	11.6	9.0	6.0	6.7	9.8	9.8	:	1.4	23.4
1965	4.1	4.7	4.8	:	12.8	16.6	7.0	10.5	-8.4	-13.9	5.3	10.3	5.2	3.6	:	9.4	4.6
1970	8.4	2.2	9.2	:	-1.4	3.0	4.6	-3.3	3.0	7.5	7.5	11.4	2.5	5.1	:	-3.7	16.9
1961–70	5.8	7.0	4.3	:	9.3	11.2	7.8	9.6	5.1	3.4	6.7	6.9	5.2	6.0	:	3.8	15.7
1971	-1.9	1.9	6.0	:	14.0	-3.0	7.3	8.9	0.2	10.7	1.5	10.2	1.8	3.4	:	5.8	4.4
1972	3.4	9.3	2.6	:	15.4	14.2	5.6	7.8	1.3	7.0	-2.3	14.0	-0.2	3.8	:	8.7	9.7
1973	7.0	3.5	-0.3	:	7.7	13.0	7.2	16.2	8.8	11.8	4.2	10.3	6.5	5.9	:	6.2	11.6
1974	6.9	-8.9	-9.7	:	-25.6	6.2	0.8	-11.6	2.0	-7.0	-4.0	-6.1	-2.4	-2.3	:	-6.0	-8.3
1975	-1.9	-12.4	-5.2	:	0.2	-4.5	-6.8	-3.6	-7.3	-7.4	-4.4	-10.6	-2.0	-5.4	:	-10.7	-1.0
1976	4.0	17.1	3.7	:	6.8	-0.8	2.8	13.6	0.0	-4.2	-2.2	1.3	1.7	2.0	:	6.9	2.7
1977	0.0	-2.4	3.8	:	7.8	-0.9	-1.6	4.1	1.8	-0.1	9.7	11.5	-1.8	1.3	:	11.3	2.8
1978	2.8	1.1	4.3	:	6.0	-2.7	2.3	18.9	0.6	1.1	2.5	6.2	3.0	2.3	:	9.5	7.8
1979	-2.7	-0.4	6.9	:	8.8	-4.4	3.2	13.6	5.7	3.8	-1.7	-1.3	2.8	3.3	:	2.4	6.2
1980	4.6	-12.6	2.3	:	-6.5	0.7	2.7	-4.7	8.7	12.7	-0.9	8.5	-5.4	1.9	:	-6.8	0.0
1971–80	2.2	-0.8	1.3	:	2.8	1.6	2.3	5.9	2.1	2.6	0.2	4.1	0.4	1.6	:	2.5	3.5
1981	-16.1	-19.2	-4.9	:	-7.5	-3.3	-1.9	9.5	-3.1	-7.4	-10.0	5.5	-9.6	-5.0	:	-0.1	2.4
1982	-1.7	7.1	-5.3	:	-1.9	0.5	-1.2	-3.4	-4.7	-0.5	-4.3	2.3	5.4	-1.9	:	-8.7	-0.1
1983	-4.4	1.9	3.3	:	-1.3	-2.5	-3.3	-9.3	-0.6	-11.8	1.9	-7.1	5.0	0.1	:	8.8	-1.0
1984	1.7	12.9	0.3	:	-5.7	-5.8	-2.6	-2.5	3.6	0.1	5.2	-17.4	8.5	0.9	:	15.9	4.7
1985	0.7	12.6	0.0	:	5.2	4.1	3.4	-7.7	0.6	-9.5	6.7	-3.5	4.0	2.2	:	6.9	5.3
1986	4.4	17.1	3.6	:	-6.2	9.9	4.6	-2.8	2.2	31.2	7.9	10.9	2.4	4.3	:	2.0	4.8
1987	5.6	-3.8	2.1	:	-5.1	14.0	5.0	-3.2	5.0	14.7	1.5	15.1	9.6	5.5	:	2.9	9.6
1988	15.4	-6.6	4.6	:	8.9	14.0	9.6	1.5	6.9	14.1	4.5	15.0	14.2	8.8	:	5.0	11.9
1989	13.7	-0.6	6.5	:	10.0	13.8	6.8	15.1	4.3	8.9	4.9	5.6	7.2	7.1	:	2.7	9.3
1990	8.4	-0.5	8.7	:	5.7	6.9	3.1	10.2	3.3	2.5	3.6	5.9	-3.1	4.0	:	-2.8	9.5
1981–90	2.4	1.5	1.8	:	0.0	4.9	2.3	0.5	1.7	3.5	2.1	2.7	4.2	2.5	:	3.0	5.5
1991	0.3	-2.8	6.5	:	-2.0	1.6	-1.3	-7.2	0.9	9.8	0.1	2.8	-9.9	0.0	:	-8.5	3.4
1992	2.5	-8.3	1.7	4.4	0.6	-2.0	-1.5	1.6	-0.2	4.5	-0.4	3.6	-0.4	-0.1	0.6	5.2	-0.7
1993	-3.3	1.9	-1.7	0.3	4.5	-1.9	-0.7	2.2	-1.2	2.3	-0.7	3.3	-0.8	-1.0	-0.5	4.6	1.0

Table E27 Price deflator private consumption (National currency; annual % change)

	B	DK	WD	D	GR	E	F	IRL	I	L	NL	P	UK	EUR 12– (PPS)	EUR 12+ (PPS)	USA	Japan
1961	2.7	3.5	3.5	:	1.1	1.8	3.3	2.3	1.7	0.5	2.4	0.6	2.9	2.8	:	1.3	6.4
1965	4.6	6.1	3.4	:	4.6	9.7	2.6	4.4	3.6	3.4	4.0	4.8	4.9	4.2	:	1.9	6.8
1970	2.5	6.6	4.0	:	3.1	6.6	5.0	12.4	5.0	4.3	4.4	3.2	5.9	5.0		4.4	7.2
1961–70	3.1	5.8	2.8	:	2.5	5.9	4.3	5.1	3.8	2.5	4.1	2.8	3.9	3.8		2.7	5.6
1971	5.3	8.3	5.5	:	2.9	7.8	6.2	9.4	5.5	4.7	7.9	7.0	8.7	6.6		4.8	6.8
1972	5.4	8.2	5.7	:	3.3	7.6	6.4	9.7	6.3	5.1	8.3	6.3	6.5	6.4		3.0	5.8
1973	6.1	11.7	6.7	:	15.0	11.4	7.6	11.6	13.9	4.9	8.5	8.9	8.6	9.2		6.0	10.8
1974	12.8	15.0	7.5	:	23.5	17.8	15.1	15.7	21.4	10.0	9.5	23.5	17.1	14.9		10.5	21.0
1975	12.3	9.9	6.1	:	12.7	15.5	12.1	18.0	16.5	10.2	10.1	16.0	23.6	13.8		8.0	11.2
1976	7.8	9.9	4.2	:	13.4	16.5	10.0	20.0	17.8	9.3	9.0	18.1	15.8	11.7		5.8	9.6
1977	7.2	10.6	3.4	:	11.9	23.7	9.6	14.1	17.6	5.7	6.1	27.3	14.8	11.8		6.5	7.4
1978	4.2	9.2	2.8	:	12.8	19.0	9.0	7.9	13.2	3.4	4.5	21.3	9.1	9.1		7.0	4.5
1979	3.9	10.4	4.3	:	16.5	16.5	10.9	14.9	14.5	4.9	4.3	25.2	13.7	10.8		9.0	3.6
1980	6.4	10.7	5.9	:	21.9	16.5	13.5	18.6	20.4	7.5	6.9	21.6	16.3	13.5		10.7	7.5
1971–80	7.1	10.4	5.2	:	13.2	15.1	10.0	13.9	14.6	6.5	7.5	17.3	13.3	10.7		7.1	8.7
1981	8.7	12.0	6.2	:	22.7	14.3	13.4	19.6	18.0	8.6	5.8	20.2	11.2	12.1		8.8	4.5
1982	7.8	10.2	5.1	:	20.7	14.5	11.8	14.9	17.1	10.6	5.5	20.3	8.7	10.8		5.7	2.7
1983	7.1	6.8	3.3	:	18.1	12.3	9.7	9.2	14.8	8.3	2.9	25.8	4.8	8.5		3.9	2.0
1984	5.7	6.4	2.6	:	17.9	11.0	7.9	7.3	12.1	6.5	2.2	28.5	5.0	7.3		4.1	2.5
1985	5.9	4.3	2.1	:	18.3	8.2	6.0	5.0	9.0	4.3	2.2	19.4	5.3	5.9		3.3	2.2
1986	0.7	2.9	-0.3	:	22.1	9.4	2.9	4.6	6.2	1.3	0.2	13.8	4.3	3.8		2.3	0.4
1987	1.9	4.6	0.8	:	15.7	5.7	3.3	2.9	5.3	1.7	-0.9	10.0	4.4	3.6		4.2	0.2
1988	1.6	4.0	1.4	:	14.3	5.0	2.9	2.5	5.7	2.7	0.5	10.0	5.1	3.8		4.2	-0.1
1989	3.5	5.0	3.1	:	15.2	6.6	3.6	3.7	6.5	3.6	1.2	12.1	5.9	4.9		4.8	1.8
1990	3.1	2.1	2.7	:	19.7	6.4	3.2	1.7	5.9	3.6	2.3	12.6	5.3	4.5		5.0	2.6
1981–90	4.6	5.8	2.7	:	18.4	9.3	6.4	7.0	9.9	5.1	2.2	17.1	6.0	6.5		4.6	1.9
1991	2.9	2.4	3.9	:	18.4	6.3	3.2	3.2	6.8	2.9	3.3	11.9	7.2	5.3	:	4.2	2.6
1992	2.4	2.1	4.1	4.7	16.0	6.0	2.6	2.9	5.3	3.4	3.1	9.1	5.1	4.5	4.6	3.1	2.4
1993	2.8	1.6	3.6	4.1	13.5	5.5	2.7	2.2	5.8	4.7	2.7	6.8	5.1	4.4	4.5	2.7	2.6

Table E28 Total expenditure general government (% of GDP at market prices)

	B	DK	WD	D	GR	E¹	F	IRL	I	L	NL²	P	UK	EUR 9- (ECU)³	EUR 12- (ECU)	EUR 12+ (ECU)	USA	Japan
1960	30.7	24.8	32.5	..	..	..	34.6	28.0	30.1	29.1	33.7	18.5	32.2	32.3	..	..	27.0	..
1965	32.7	29.9	36.7	..	..	..	38.4	33.1	34.3	31.6	38.7	21.5	35.9	36.3	..	..	27.1	..
1970	37.0	40.2	38.7	..	..	21.5	38.9	39.6	34.2	32.5	42.4	23.2	38.8	38.2	..	..	31.6	19.3
1961–70	33.7	32.1	37.1	..	..	..	38.3	33.5	32.8	32.3	39.9	21.8	36.5	36.4	..	..	29.1	..
1970	38.3	42.0	38.7	..	..	21.5	38.1	37.4	32.1	33.2	42.2	23.2	36.8	37.4	..	..	31.6	19.3
1971	40.1	42.9	40.2	..	..	22.9	38.0	38.3	34.3	37.1	43.9	23.0	36.7	38.3	..	..	31.6	20.7
1972	41.0	42.5	40.9	..	..	22.5	38.3	37.0	36.4	37.5	44.4	24.5	37.3	39.1	..	..	31.3	21.8
1973	41.3	40.8	41.7	..	..	22.4	38.4	36.8	35.0	36.4	44.6	23.3	38.1	39.4	..	..	30.7	22.4
1974	41.6	44.8	44.7	..	..	22.6	39.4	45.0	34.4	36.0	46.6	26.4	43.1	41.6	..	..	32.3	24.5
1975	46.8	47.0	49.0	..	..	24.4	43.8	47.0	39.9	48.7	51.5	31.9	44.5	45.5	..	..	34.5	27.2
1976	47.4	46.4	48.1	..	..	25.6	44.3	46.6	37.8	49.4	51.7	36.6	44.4	45.2	..	..	33.4	27.7
1977	49.0	47.2	48.2	..	..	27.1	44.1	44.3	37.7	52.1	51.6	35.2	41.7	44.9	..	..	32.3	29.0
1978	50.4	48.7	47.9	..	..	28.9	45.2	44.8	40.4	51.5	52.9	36.4	41.5	45.6	..	..	31.5	30.5
1979	51.9	51.5	47.8	..	..	30.1	45.6	46.0	39.7	52.6	54.6	35.8	41.0	45.6	..	..	31.7	31.6
1980	53.1	54.8	48.5	..	..	32.5	46.6	50.5	41.9	55.9	56.5	..	43.1	46.8	..	..	33.7	32.6
1971–80	46.3	46.7	45.7	..	..	25.9	42.3	43.6	37.7	45.7	49.8	..	41.1	43.2	..	..	32.3	26.8
1981	58.1	58.6	49.4	..	39.6	35.2	49.2	52.1	45.8	59.8	58.6	41.7	44.4	48.8	47.7	..	34.2	33.4
1982	57.8	60.0	49.7	..	39.6	37.1	50.9	55.0	47.4	57.3	60.5	43.8	44.7	49.8	48.7	..	36.4	33.6
1983	57.4	60.4	48.5	..	41.3	38.4	52.0	54.4	48.6	56.9	61.0	46.1	44.8	50.0	49.1	..	36.8	33.9
1984	56.3	58.9	48.1	..	44.1	38.9	52.5	53.1	49.4	53.6	59.6	46.6	45.3	50.0	49.2	..	35.6	32.9
1985	56.0	58.1	47.7	..	47.9	41.6	52.7	53.7	50.9	51.9	58.5	43.5	44.2	49.9	49.3	..	36.4	32.3
1986	55.6	54.3	47.1	..	47.2	41.9	52.2	53.7	50.7	51.3	58.5	44.6	42.6	49.3	48.8	..	37.1	32.6
1987	54.1	55.7	47.4	..	47.7	40.8	51.7	51.5	50.2	55.2	59.4	43.0	40.8	48.9	48.3	..	36.8	32.8
1988	52.0	58.0	47.0	..	47.9	41.0	50.8	48.1	50.3	52.9	57.6	43.0	38.1	47.8	47.3	..	35.8	32.2
1989	50.8	58.1	45.5	..	49.4	42.2	49.8	41.3	51.4	48.6	54.8	42.9	37.8	47.1	46.7	..	35.8	31.5
1990	50.2	57.2	45.9	..	52.5	43.3	50.3	42.0	53.2	48.9	55.0	44.3	40.0	48.1	47.8	..	36.7	32.3
1981–90	54.8	57.9	47.6	..	45.7	40.0	51.2	50.5	49.8	53.6	58.4	43.9	42.3	49.0	48.3	..	36.2	32.8
1991	51.2	57.1	49.2	49.8	51.5	45.0	50.6	42.2	53.5	49.3	55.2	46.4	40.8	49.4	49.0	49.2	37.7	31.4
1992	51.5	58.1	49.9	50.7	51.2	46.0	51.3	43.2	55.4	50.1	55.1	46.9	43.5	50.7	50.3	50.5	38.7	..
1993	51.3	58.5	50.7	51.1	49.5	46.5	52.2	43.8	55.8	50.6	55.2	45.9	45.1	51.5	51.0	51.1	38.5	..

¹ Break in 1985/86.
² Breaks in 1968/69 and 1986/87.
³ EUR 12 excl. Greece, Spain and Portugal.

Table E29 Net lending (+) or net borrowing (–) general government (% of GDP at market prices)

	B	DK	WD	D	GR	E[1]	F	IRL	I	L	NL[2]	P	UK	EUR 9– (ECU)[3]	EUR 12– (ECU)	EUR 12+ (ECU)	USA	Japan
1960	-2.9	3.1	3.0	..	..	..	0.9	-2.4	-0.9	3.0	0.8	0.6	-1.0	0.6	..	..	0.7	..
1965	-1.6	1.8	-0.6	..	..	..	0.7	-4.3	-3.8	2.8	-0.8	0.3	-1.9	-1.1	..	..	0.2	..
1970	-1.3	2.1	0.2	..	..	0.7	0.9	-3.7	-3.5	2.8	-1.2	2.8	2.4	0.1	..	..	-1.1	1.8
1961–70	-1.5	1.3	0.4	..	..	..	0.4	-3.6	-2.3	1.8	-0.9	0.3	-0.6	-0.4	..	..	-0.3	..
1970	-2.4	4.1	0.2	..	..	0.7	0.9	-4.3	-3.3	3.2	-1.2	2.8	3.0	0.2	..	..	-1.1	1.8
1971	-3.7	3.9	-0.2	..	..	-0.5	0.6	-4.2	-4.8	2.6	-1.0	2.3	1.3	-0.6	..	..	-1.8	1.3
1972	-4.8	3.9	-0.5	..	..	0.3	0.6	-4.1	-7.0	2.3	-0.4	0.9	-1.3	-1.5	..	..	-0.3	0.2
1973	-4.2	5.2	1.2	..	..	1.1	0.6	-4.6	-6.5	3.8	0.8	1.6	-2.7	-0.9	..	..	0.5	0.5
1974	-3.1	3.1	-1.3	..	..	0.2	0.3	-8.2	-6.4	5.3	-0.2	-1.4	-3.8	-2.0	..	..	-0.3	0.4
1975	-5.5	-1.4	-5.6	..	..	0.0	-2.4	-12.5	-10.6	1.1	-2.9	-4.1	-4.5	-5.1	..	..	-4.1	-2.8
1976	-6.3	-0.3	-3.4	..	..	-0.3	-0.7	-8.6	-8.1	2.0	-2.6	-5.9	-4.9	-3.7	..	..	-2.2	-3.7
1977	-6.4	-0.6	-2.4	..	..	-0.6	-0.8	-7.6	-7.0	3.3	-1.8	-4.7	-3.2	-3.0	..	..	-0.9	-3.8
1978	-6.8	-0.4	-2.4	..	..	-1.7	-2.1	-9.7	-8.5	5.0	-2.8	-6.9	-4.4	-3.7	..	..	0.1	-5.5
1979	-7.6	-1.7	-2.6	..	..	-1.6	-0.8	-11.4	-8.3	0.7	-3.7	-6.1	-3.3	-3.5	..	..	0.4	-4.7
1980	-9.3	-3.3	-2.9	..	..	-2.6	0.0	-12.7	-8.6	-0.8	-4.0	..	-3.4	-3.6	..	..	-1.3	-4.4
1971–80	-5.8	0.9	-2.0	..	..	-0.6	-0.5	-8.4	-7.6	2.5	-1.9	..	-3.0	-2.8	..	..	-1.0	-2.3
1981	-13.4	-6.9	-3.7	..	-10.7	-3.9	-1.9	-13.4	-11.4	-3.9	-5.5	-9.3	-2.6	-4.9	-5.0	..	-1.0	-3.8
1982	-11.5	-9.1	-3.3	..	-7.6	-5.6	-2.8	-13.8	-11.3	-1.6	-7.1	-10.4	-2.5	-5.1	-5.2	..	-3.4	-3.6
1983	-11.8	-7.2	-2.6	..	-8.1	-4.7	-3.2	-11.8	-10.6	1.5	-6.4	-9.0	-3.3	-5.0	-5.1	..	-4.1	-3.6
1984	-9.5	-4.1	-1.9	..	-9.8	-5.4	-2.8	-9.8	-11.6	2.8	-6.3	-12.0	-3.9	-4.9	-5.1	..	-2.9	-2.1
1985	-9.0	-2.0	-1.2	..	-13.6	-6.9	-2.9	-11.2	-12.6	6.2	-4.8	-10.1	-2.9	-4.5	-4.9	..	-3.1	-0.8
1986	-9.4	3.4	-1.3	..	-12.0	-6.0	-2.7	-11.1	-11.6	4.3	-6.0	-7.2	-2.4	-4.3	-4.5	..	-3.5	-0.9
1987	-7.5	2.4	-1.9	..	-11.6	-3.1	-1.9	-8.9	-11.0	2.4	-5.9	-6.8	-1.3	-3.9	-4.0	..	-2.5	0.5
1988	-6.7	0.6	-2.2	..	-13.8	-3.3	-1.7	-4.8	-10.7	3.1	-4.6	-5.4	1.0	-3.3	-3.4	..	-2.0	1.5
1989	-6.7	-0.5	0.1	..	-17.7	-2.8	-1.1	-1.8	-9.9	5.3	-4.7	-3.4	0.9	-2.5	-2.7	..	-1.5	2.5
1990	-5.7	-1.4	-2.0	..	-18.6	-4.0	-1.4	-2.5	-10.9	5.0	-4.9	-5.5	-1.3	-3.8	-4.0	..	-2.5	3.0
1981–90	-9.1	-2.5	-2.0	..	-12.4	-4.6	-2.2	-8.9	-11.2	2.5	-5.6	-7.9	-1.8	-4.2	-4.4	..	-2.7	-0.7
1991	-6.6	-2.0	-3.6	-3.2	-15.2	-4.9	-1.9	-2.1	-10.2	-0.8	-2.5	-6.4	-2.8	-4.4	-4.6	-4.5	-3.4	2.4
1992	-6.9	-2.3	-3.5	-3.2	-13.4	-4.6	-2.8	-2.7	-10.5	-0.4	-3.5	-5.6	-6.2	-5.3	-5.3	-5.2	-4.8	..
1993	-6.2	-2.7	-3.9	-3.6	-9.8	-4.2	-3.2	-3.0	-10.2	-1.0	-3.5	-4.8	-8.3	-5.7	-5.6	-5.4	-4.8	..

[1] Break in series 1985/86.
[2] Breaks in series 1968/69 and 1986/87.
[3] EUR 12 excl. Greece, Spain and Portugal.

Table E30 Nominal short-term interest rates (%)

	B	DK	WD	GR	E	F	IRL	I	NL	P	UK	EUR 12–	USA	Japan
1961	4.6	6.3	3.6	..	..	3.7	..	3.5	1.1	..	5.2	4.0	2.4	..
1970	8.1	9.0	9.4	..	..	8.6	..	5.3	6.2	4.0	8.1	8.0	6.3	..
1961–70	5.2	6.8	5.0	..	..	5.4	..	3.7	3.8	..	6.3	5.2	4.3	..
1971	5.4	7.6	7.1	..	..	6.0	6.6	5.7	4.5	4.3	6.2	6.2	4.3	6.5
1972	4.2	7.3	5.7	..	..	5.3	7.1	5.2	2.7	4.4	6.8	5.5	4.2	5.2
1973	6.6	7.6	12.2	..	..	9.3	12.2	7.0	7.5	4.4	11.8	9.9	7.2	8.3
1974	10.6	10.0	9.8	..	..	13.0	14.6	14.9	10.4	5.3	13.4	11.9	7.9	14.7
1975	7.0	8.0	4.9	..	..	7.6	10.9	10.4	5.4	6.8	10.6	7.6	5.8	10.1
1976	10.1	8.9	4.3	..	..	8.7	11.7	16.0	7.4	8.4	11.6	8.8	5.0	7.3
1977	7.3	14.5	4.3	..	-15.5	9.1	8.4	14.0	4.8	11.1	8.0	8.4	5.3	6.4
1978	7.3	15.4	3.7	..	-17.6	7.8	9.9	11.5	7.0	15.5	9.4	8.1	7.4	5.1
1979	10.9	12.5	6.9	..	15.5	9.7	16.0	12.0	9.6	16.1	13.9	10.5	10.1	5.9
1980	14.2	16.9	9.5	..	16.5	12.0	16.2	16.9	10.6	16.3	16.8	13.4	11.6	10.7
1971–80	8.4	10.9	6.9	..	..	8.8	11.4	11.3	7.0	9.3	10.8	9.0	6.9	8.0
1981	15.6	14.9	12.4	16.8	16.2	15.3	16.7	19.3	11.8	16.0	14.1	14.8	14.0	7.4
1982	14.1	16.4	8.8	18.9	16.3	14.6	17.5	19.9	8.2	16.8	12.2	13.4	10.6	6.9
1983	10.5	12.0	5.8	16.6	20.1	12.5	14.0	18.3	5.7	20.9	10.1	11.4	8.7	6.5
1984	11.5	11.5	6.0	15.7	14.9	11.7	13.2	17.3	6.1	22.5	10.0	10.9	9.5	6.3
1985	9.6	10.0	5.4	17.0	12.2	10.0	12.0	15.0	6.3	21.0	12.2	10.2	7.5	6.5
1986	8.1	9.1	4.6	19.8	11.7	7.7	12.4	12.8	5.7	15.6	10.9	8.7	6.0	5.0
1987	7.1	9.9	4.0	14.9	15.8	8.3	11.1	11.4	5.4	13.9	9.7	8.4	5.9	3.9
1988	6.7	8.3	4.3	15.9	11.6	7.9	8.1	11.3	4.8	13.0	10.3	8.2	6.9	4.0
1989	8.7	9.4	7.1	18.7	15.0	9.4	9.8	12.7	7.4	14.9	13.9	10.6	8.4	5.4
1990	9.8	10.8	8.4	19.9	15.2	10.3	11.4	12.3	8.7	16.9	14.8	11.4	7.8	7.7
1981–90	10.2	11.2	6.7	17.4	14.9	10.8	12.6	15.0	7.0	17.2	11.8	10.8	8.5	6.0
1991	9.4	9.5	9.2	22.7	13.2	9.6	10.4	12.2	9.3	17.7	11.5	10.7	5.5	7.4
1992	9.4	11.5	9.5	24.5	13.3	10.4	12.4	14.0	9.4	16.2	9.6	11.1	3.5	4.4

B: 1961–84 four-month certificates of 'Fonds des Rentes'; 1985–88 three-month treasury certificates; 1989–92 three-month interbank deposits. DK: 1961–76 discount rate; 1977–88 call money; 1989–92 three-month interbank deposits. D: three-month interbank deposits. GR: 1960–April 1980 credit for working capital to industry; May 1980–87 interbank sight deposits; 1988–92: three-month interbank deposits. E: three-month interbank deposits. F: 1960–68 call money; 1969–81 one-month sale and repurchase agreements on private sector paper; 1982–92 three-month sale and repurchase agreements on private sector paper. IRL: 1961–70 three-month interbank deposits in London; 1971–92 three-month interbank deposits in Dublin. I: 1960–70 12-month treasury bills; 1971–92 interbank sight deposits. NL: 1960–September 1972 three-month treasury bills; October 1972–92 three-month interbank deposits. P: 1966–July 1985 six-month deposits; August 1985–92 three-month interbank deposits. UK: 1961–September 1964 three-month treasury bills; October 1964–92 three-month interbank deposits. EUR 12: weighted geometric mean; weights: gross domestic product at current market prices and ECU. USA: three-month treasury bills. J: bonds traded with three-month repurchase agreements; certificate of deposit three-months since January 1989.

Table E31 Nominal long-term interest rates (%)

	B	DK	WD	GR	E	F	IRL	I	L	NL	P	UK	EUR 12–	USA	Japan
1961	5.9	6.6	5.9	..	..	5.5	..	5.2	..	3.9	..	6.3	5.7	3.9	..
1970	7.8	11.1	8.3	..	..	8.6	..	9.0	..	7.8	..	9.3	8.7	6.6	..
1961–70	6.3	8.3	6.8	..	..	6.5	..	6.7	..	5.6	..	7.0	6.7	4.8	..
1971	7.3	11.0	8.0	..	..	8.4	9.2	8.3	..	7.1	..	8.9	8.3	5.7	..
1972	7.0	11.0	7.9	..	..	8.0	9.1	7.5	..	6.7	..	9.0	8.0	5.6	6.9
1973	7.5	12.6	9.3	9.3	..	9.0	10.7	7.4	6.8	7.3	..	10.8	9.1	6.3	7.0
1974	8.8	15.9	10.4	10.5	..	11.0	14.6	9.9	7.3	10.7	..	15.0	11.3	7.0	8.1
1975	8.5	12.7	8.5	9.4	..	10.3	14.0	11.5	6.7	9.2	..	14.5	10.5	7.0	8.4
1976	9.1	14.9	7.8	10.2	..	10.5	14.6	13.1	7.2	9.2	..	14.6	10.6	6.8	8.2
1977	8.8	16.2	6.2	9.5	..	11.0	12.9	14.6	7.0	8.5	..	12.5	10.1	7.1	7.4
1978	8.5	16.8	5.7	10.0	..	10.6	12.8	13.7	6.6	8.1	..	12.6	9.7	7.9	6.3
1979	9.7	16.7	7.4	11.2	13.3	10.9	15.1	14.1	6.8	9.2	..	13.0	10.8	8.7	8.3
1980	12.2	18.7	8.5	17.1	16.0	13.1	15.4	16.1	7.4	10.7	..	13.9	12.6	10.8	8.9
1971–80	8.7	14.6	8.0	..	..	10.3	12.8	11.6	..	8.7	..	12.5	10.1	7.3	..
1981	13.8	19.3	10.4	17.7	15.8	15.9	17.3	20.6	8.7	12.2	..	14.8	14.8	12.9	8.4
1982	13.5	20.5	9.0	15.4	16.0	15.7	17.0	20.9	10.4	10.5	..	12.7	13.9	12.2	8.3
1983	11.8	14.4	7.9	18.2	16.9	13.6	13.9	18.0	9.8	8.8	..	10.8	12.3	10.8	7.8
1984	12.0	14.0	7.8	18.5	16.5	12.5	14.6	15.0	10.3	8.6	..	10.7	11.5	12.0	7.3
1985	10.6	11.6	6.9	15.8	13.4	10.9	12.7	14.3	9.5	7.3	25.4	10.6	10.6	10.8	6.5
1986	7.9	10.6	5.9	15.8	11.4	8.4	11.1	11.7	8.7	6.4	17.9	9.8	8.9	8.1	5.2
1987	7.8	11.9	5.8	17.4	12.8	9.4	11.3	11.3	8.0	6.4	15.4	9.5	9.0	8.7	4.7
1988	7.9	10.6	6.1	16.6	11.8	9.0	9.4	12.1	7.1	6.3	14.2	9.3	9.1	9.0	4.7
1989	8.7	10.2	7.0	..	13.8	8.8	9.0	12.9	7.7	7.2	14.9	9.6	9.6	8.5	5.2
1990	10.1	11.0	8.9	..	14.7	9.9	10.1	13.4	8.6	9.0	16.8	11.1	10.9	8.6	7.5
1981–90	10.4	13.4	7.6	..	14.3	11.4	12.6	15.0	8.9	8.3	..	10.9	11.1	10.2	6.6
1991	9.3	10.1	8.6	..	12.4	9.0	9.2	13.0	8.2	8.9	17.1	9.9	10.2	8.1	6.7
1992	8.6	10.1	8.0	..	12.2	8.6	9.1	13.7	7.9	8.1	15.0	9.1	9.8	7.7	5.3

B: State bonds over five years, secondary market. DK: State bonds. D: public sector bonds outstanding. GR: State bonds. E: 1979–87 State bonds of two to four years. F: 1960–79 public sector bonds; 1988–92 State bonds of more than two years. F: 1960–79 public sector bonds; 1988–92 State bonds over seven years. IRL: 1960–70 State bonds 20 years in London; 1971–92 State bonds 15 years in Dublin. I: 1960–84 Crediop bonds; 1985–91 rate of specialised industrial credit institutions (gross rate), from January 1992: public-sector bonds outstanding. NL: 1960–73 3.25% State bond 1948; 1974–84 private loans to public enterprises; 1982–92 five State bonds with the longest maturity. P: Weighted average of public and private bonds over five years. UK: State bonds 20 years. EUR 12: weighted geometric mean; weights: gross domestic product at current market prices and ECU. USA: 1960–88 federal government bonds over 10 years; 1989–92 federal government bonds over 30 years. J: 1961–78 State bonds; 1979–June 1987: over-the-counter sales of State bonds: 1987–April 1989: benchmark: bonds No 111–1988; 1989–92: benchmark: bonds No 119–1999.

Table E32 Structure of EC exports by country and region (1958 and 1991) (% of total exports)

Export of to	B/L 1958	B/L 1991	DK 1958	DK 1991	D 1958	D 1991	GR 1958	GR 1991	E 1958	E 1991	F 1958	F 1991	IRL 1958	IRL 1991	I 1958	I 1991	NL 1958	NL 1991	P 1958	P 1991	UK 1958	UK 1991	EUR 12 1958	EUR 12 1991
B L	:	:	1.2	2.1	6.6	7.3	1.0	2.3	2.1	2.9	6.3	8.5	0.8	4.9	2.2	3.4	15.0	14.2	3.7	3.2	1.9	5.7	4.8	6.4
DK	1.6	0.8	:	:	3.0	1.9	0.2	0.8	1.7	0.8	0.7	0.9	0.1	1.0	0.8	0.8	2.6	1.6	1.2	2.1	2.4	1.3	2.0	1.3
D	11.6	23.7	20.0	22.4	:	:	20.5	23.9	10.2	15.0	10.4	20.7	2.2	12.7	14.1	21.0	19.0	29.3	7.7	19.1	4.2	13.7	7.6	14.5
GR	0.8	0.6	0.3	0.8	1.3	1.0	:	:	0.1	0.7	0.6	0.7	0.1	0.6	1.9	1.8	0.6	1.0	0.6	0.4	0.7	0.6	0.8	0.9
E	0.7	2.5	0.8	1.9	1.2	4.0	0.2	1.7	:	:	1.6	6.4	0.8	2.3	0.7	5.1	0.8	2.5	0.7	14.9	0.8	4.1	1.0	4.1
F	10.6	19.1	3.0	5.9	7.6	13.1	12.8	7.5	10.1	18.8	:	:	0.8	9.5	5.3	15.2	4.9	10.6	6.6	14.4	2.4	11.0	4.7	11.2
IRL	0.3	0.4	0.3	0.5	0.3	0.4	0.4	0.1	0.3	0.3	0.2	0.4	:	:	0.1	0.3	0.4	0.6	0.3	0.5	3.5	5.1	1.1	1.0
I	2.3	6.0	5.3	4.8	5.0	9.1	6.0	16.7	2.7	10.7	3.4	11.1	0.4	4.3	:	:	2.7	6.4	4.3	4.0	2.1	5.8	3.1	7.2
NL	20.7	13.7	2.2	4.8	8.1	8.4	2.0	3.4	3.2	3.9	2.0	4.7	0.5	6.6	2.0	3.2	:	:	2.5	5.7	3.2	7.9	5.3	6.3
P	1.1	0.7	0.3	0.6	0.9	1.1	0.3	0.3	0.4	6.2	0.8	1.4	0.1	0.5	0.7	1.5	0.4	0.7	:	:	0.4	1.0	0.8	1.3
UK	5.7	7.7	25.9	10.3	3.9	7.6	7.6	6.8	15.9	7.1	4.9	8.9	76.8	32.0	6.8	6.7	11.9	9.3	11.3	10.8	:	:	5.9	7.4
Total intra-EC trade	55.4	75.2	59.3	54.1	37.9	53.8	50.9	63.5	46.8	66.4	30.9	63.6	82.4	74.4	34.5	59.0	58.3	76.2	38.9	75.1	21.7	56.3	37.2	61.6
Other European OECD countries	8.7	6.4	16.6	23.8	22.7	17.9	10.3	9.7	12.4	5.2	9.0	7.4	0.9	5.7	18.9	11.6	11.9	7.5	5.1	9.9	9.1	9.4	13.7	11.4
USA	9.4	3.8	9.3	4.8	7.3	6.3	13.6	5.6	10.1	4.6	5.9	6.0	5.7	8.7	9.9	6.9	5.6	3.8	8.3	3.8	8.8	11.0	7.9	6.4
Canada	1.1	0.3	0.7	0.5	1.2	0.8	0.3	0.6	1.3	0.6	0.8	1.0	0.7	1.0	1.2	0.8	0.8	0.4	1.1	0.8	5.8	1.6	2.3	0.8
Japan	0.6	1.2	0.2	3.6	0.9	2.5	1.4	1.0	1.7	0.8	0.3	2.0	0.0	2.3	0.3	2.2	0.4	0.9	0.5	0.9	0.6	2.2	0.6	2.0
Australia	0.5	0.2	0.3	0.4	1.0	0.5	0.1	0.8	0.3	0.2	0.5	0.5	0.1	0.6	0.8	0.6	0.7	0.4	0.6	0.2	7.2	1.3	2.4	0.6
Developing countries of which:	18.0	10.0	9.3	9.0	20.9	11.0	7.2	13.5	18.4	18.6	46.9	16.7	1.6	5.4	26.2	14.3	17.6	7.8	42.3	7.4	33.6	15.8	27.4	12.8
OPEC	3.3	2.1	2.3	2.1	4.8	3.2	0.9	3.7	2.6	3.3	21.3	4.2	0.2	1.3	7.5	4.8	4.5	2.1	2.0	0.6	7.0	4.9	7.6	3.5
Other developing countries	14.7	7.9	7.0	6.9	16.1	7.8	6.3	9.8	15.8	15.3	25.6	12.5	1.4	4.1	18.7	9.5	13.1	5.7	40.3	6.8	26.6	10.9	19.8	9.3
Rest of the world and unspecified	6.3	2.6	4.3	3.1	8.1	5.4	16.2	5.9	9.0	3.7	5.7	2.6	8.6	2.2	8.2	4.6	4.7	3.0	3.2	2.3	13.2	2.9	8.5	3.8
World (excl. EC)	44.6	24.8	40.7	45.9	62.1	46.2	49.1	36.5	53.2	33.6	69.1	36.4	17.6	25.6	65.5	41.0	41.7	23.8	61.1	24.9	78.3	43.7	62.8	38.4
World (incl. EC)	100	100	100	100	100	100	100	100	100	100	100	100	100	100	100	100	100	100	100	100	100	100	100	100

D: 1958: West Germany; 1991: unified Germany.

Table E33 Structure of EC imports by country and region (1958 and 1991) (percentage of total imports)

from	B/L 1958	B/L 1991	DK 1958	DK 1991	D 1958	D 1991	GR 1958	GR 1991	E 1958	E 1991	F 1958	F 1991	IRL 1958	IRL 1991	I 1958	I 1991	NL 1958	NL 1991	P 1958	P 1991	UK 1958	UK 1991	EUR 12 1958	EUR 12 1991
B L	:	:	3.8	3.3	4.5	7.9	3.3	3.4	1.8	2.9	5.4	10.2	1.8	2.2	2.0	2.0	17.8	13.0	7.3	4.1	1.6	4.4	4.4	6.6
DK	0.5	0.6	:	:	3.4	2.2	0.7	1.1	1.3	0.7	0.6	0.9	0.5	0.9	0.4	1.0	0.7	1.1	0.3	0.8	3.1	1.9	2.0	1.4
D	17.2	22.3	19.9	23.1	:	:	20.3	19.4	8.7	16.1	11.6	20.7	4.0	8.0	12.0	20.9	19.5	23.5	17.6	14.8	3.6	14.7	8.7	14.3
GR	0.1	0.2	:	:	0.1	0.6	:	:	0.2	0.2	0.2	0.3	0.0	0.0	0.4	0.8	0.2	0.2	0.1	0.1	0.2	0.3	0.3	0.4
E	0.5	1.4	0.7	1.1	0.4	2.5	0.1	2.2	:	:	1.2	4.9	0.0	0.5	0.4	4.4	0.4	1.4	6.8	15.8	1.0	2.2	0.9	2.8
F	11.6	14.9	3.4	5.9	8.4	12.2	5.4	7.8	11.6	16.1	:	:	2.9	5.1	5.5	14.7	2.8	7.0	7.7	11.9	2.7	9.2	4.4	9.6
IRL	0.1	0.6	0.0	0.6	0.1	0.8	0.0	0.0	0.0	0.5	0.0	1.0	:	:	0.0	0.2	0.0	0.7	0.0	0.4	2.9	3.7	0.9	1.2
I	2.1	4.3	1.7	4.0	4.8	9.2	8.8	14.2	1.8	9.8	2.7	11.0	1.4	2.4	:	:	1.8	3.4	3.7	10.3	2.1	5.4	2.7	6.8
NL	15.7	17.9	7.3	7.2	8.1	11.8	4.8	6.0	2.6	3.9	2.9	6.6	1.8	3.4	3.0	5.7	:	:	3.7	6.1	4.2	7.6	5.2	8.2
P	0.4	0.4	0.3	0.8	0.1	0.8	0.1	0.1	0.3	2.8	0.2	1.0	0.0	0.4	0.1	0.3	0.2	0.6	:	:	0.4	0.9	0.3	0.8
UK	7.4	7.9	22.8	7.8	6.4	6.4	9.9	5.4	3.5	6.8	3.5	7.6	56.3	46.2	6.4	7.7	7.4	8.0	6.1	7.6	:	:	5.4	6.5
Total intra-EC trade	55.5	70.5	60.0	54.2	36.3	54.5	53.7	60.3	31.8	59.8	28.3	64.2	68.9	69.1	30.2	57.7	50.7	59.0	53.4	71.9	21.8	50.1	35.2	58.6
Other European OECD countries	7.7	5.8	18.6	23.6	15.2	14.9	11.5	7.6	8.4	6.0	6.7	7.3	3.4	4.8	13.1	10.9	7.2	6.8	8.6	6.3	8.7	11.8	10.1	10.4
USA	9.9	6.1	9.1	5.8	13.6	6.1	13.7	4.3	21.6	7.9	10.0	8.3	7.0	15.1	16.4	5.6	11.3	8.1	7.0	3.4	9.4	12.5	11.4	7.7
Canada	1.4	0.6	0.2	0.5	3.1	0.7	0.8	0.3	0.5	0.5	1.0	0.8	3.0	0.7	1.5	0.9	1.4	0.9	0.5	0.6	8.2	1.6	3.6	0.8
Japan	0.6	3.7	1.5	3.1	0.6	5.3	2.0	6.7	0.7	4.4	0.2	2.9	1.1	3.8	0.4	5.4	0.8	5.4	0.0	2.9	0.9	5.7	0.7	4.3
Australia	1.7	0.3	0.0	0.3	1.2	0.3	0.3	0.1	0.8	0.2	2.4	0.3	1.2	0.1	3.0	0.4	0.2	0.4	0.9	0.1	5.4	0.7	2.6	0.4
Developing countries	19.2	8.9	5.9	7.7	23.9	10.8	9.6	14.8	32.0	18.2	45.6	12.8	9.3	4.3	29.4	15.0	24.4	15.6	27.6	13.1	34.7	12.3	29.5	12.5
of which: OPEC	5.2	1.9	0.3	0.6	6.7	2.3	1.7	7.3	17.7	6.9	19.7	4.5	0.7	0.5	13.9	7.1	11.5	6.1	6.3	4.8	11.3	2.2	10.8	3.9
Other developing countries	13.5	7.0	5.6	7.1	17.2	8.5	7.9	7.5	14.3	11.3	25.9	8.3	8.6	3.8	15.5	7.9	12.9	9.5	21.3	8.3	23.4	10.1	18.7	8.6
Rest of the world and unspecified	4.0	4.1	4.7	4.8	6.1	7.4	8.4	5.9	4.2	3.0	5.8	3.4	6.1	2.1	6.0	4.4	4.0	3.8	2.0	1.7	10.9	5.3	6.9	5.3
World (excl. EC)	44.5	29.3	40.0	46.2	63.7	45.7	46.3	35.9	68.2	40.9	71.7	35.2	31.1	29.2	69.8	42.6	49.3	40.1	46.6	30.9	78.2	49.0	64.8	41.2
World (incl. EC)	100	100	100	100	100	100	100	100	100	100	100	100	100	100	100	100	100	100	100	100	100	100	100	100

D: 1958: West Germany; 1991: unified Germany.

314 *European Community Economies*

Table E34 Balance of payments by main heading (1990) (Mio ECU)

Country	A – Goods and services			B – Unrequited transfers			C. current balance (A + B)	D. Long-term capital			E. Basic balance (C + D)	Short-term capital	Re-serves	Errors and omissions
	Goods (fob)	Services	Total	Private	Official	Total		Direct investment	Portfolio investment	Other long-term capital				
EUR 12	-3 091	23 326	20 235	-2 061	-25 419	-27 500	-7 265	-12 415	9 013	19 855	9 188	19 461	-35 341	6 691
Belg./Lux.	124	4 402	4 526	-296	-1 217	-1 513	3 013	1 224	-1 059	306	3 484	-6 891	-392	3 799
Denmark	3 580	-2 354	1 226	-36	-12	-48	1 178	-239	2 215	2 747	5 901	-1 251	-2 752	-1 897
Germany	55 426	-266	55 160	-5 393	-11 971	-17 364	37 796	-16 392	-3 404	-13 610	4 390	-12 685	-5 344	13 639
Greece	-7 963	1 466	-6 497	1 414	2 239	3 653	-2 844	785	0	1 577	-482	623	14	-155
Spain	-23 257	6 639	-16 618	2 394	947	3 341	-13 277	8 546	2 884	3 212	1 365	7 205	-5 365	-3 205
France	-10 664	10 491	-173	-3 152	-7 592	-10 744	-10 917	-14 215	22 621	-263	-2 774	6 947	-8 358	4 365
Ireland	2 363	-3 281	-918	63	1 978	2 041	1 123	78	-93	-188	920	958	-484	-1 394
Italy	346	-9 877	-9 531	705	-2 580	-1 875	-11 406	-592	-177	18 637	6 462	12 846	-9 216	-10 093
Netherlands	8 138	2 371	10 509	-881	-1 500	-2 381	8 128	-3 218	-3 866	1 699	2 743	643	-259	-3 127
Portugal	-5 157	737	-4 420	3 521	780	4 301	-119	1 564	590	5	2 040	-669	-2 888	1 516
United Kingdom	-26 027	12 998	-13 029	-420	-6 491	-6 911	-19 940	1 044	-10 698	5 733	-14 861	11 735	-117	3 243
USA	-85 022	29 827	-55 195	-1 511	-15 809	-17 320	-72 515	3 597	-4 864	18 871	-54 911	6 601	-1 856	50 165
Japan	49 784	-17 072	32 712	-791	-3 491	-4 282	28 430	-36 655	-12 078	5 737	-14 566	24 839	5 723	-15 997

Table E35 Exchange rates (Annual average, national currency units per ECU)

	B/L	DK	WD	GR	E	F	IRL	I	NL	P	UK	USA	Japan
1961	52.810	7.2954	4.4361	31.69	63.37	5.2145	0.37722	660.1	4.0136	30.37	0.37722	1.0562	380.23
1965	53.490	7.3893	4.2792	32.09	64.14	5.2817	0.38207	668.6	3.8727	30.76	0.38207	1.0698	385.13
1970	51.112	7.6668	3.7414	30.67	71.36	5.6777	0.42593	638.9	3.7005	29.38	0.42593	1.0222	368.00
1971	50.866	7.7526	3.6457	31.43	72.57	5.7721	0.42858	647.4	3.6575	29.64	0.42858	1.0478	363.83
1972	49.361	7.7891	3.5768	33.65	72.00	5.6572	0.44894	654.3	3.5999	30.48	0.44894	1.1218	339.72
1973	47.801	7.4160	3.2764	36.95	71.81	5.4678	0.50232	716.5	3.4285	30.27	0.50232	1.2317	333.17
1974	45.912	7.1932	3.0867	35.78	68.84	5.6745	0.51350	791.7	3.1714	29.93	0.51350	1.2021	339.68
1975	45.569	7.1227	3.0494	39.99	70.27	5.3192	0.55981	809.5	3.1349	31.44	0.56003	1.2048	360.73
1976	43.166	6.7618	2.8155	40.88	74.74	5.3449	0.62192	930.2	2.9552	33.62	0.62158	1.1180	331.21
1977	40.883	6.8557	2.6483	42.16	86.82	5.6061	0.65370	1 006.8	2.8001	43.62	0.65370	1.1411	305.81
1978	40.061	7.0195	2.5561	46.80	97.42	5.7398	0.66389	1 080.2	2.7541	55.87	0.66391	1.2741	267.08
1979	40.165	7.2079	2.5110	50.76	91.97	5.8298	0.66945	1 138.4	2.7488	67.01	0.64630	1.3705	300.46
1980	40.598	7.8274	2.5242	59.42	99.70	5.8690	0.67600	1 189.2	2.7603	69.55	0.59849	1.3923	315.04
1981	41.295	7.9226	2.5139	61.62	102.68	6.0399	0.69102	1 263.2	2.7751	68.49	0.55311	1.1164	245.38
1982	44.712	8.1569	2.3760	65.34	107.56	6.4312	0.68961	1 323.8	2.6139	78.01	0.56046	0.9797	243.55
1983	45.438	8.1319	2.2705	78.09	127.50	6.7708	0.71496	1 349.9	2.5372	98.69	0.58701	0.8902	211.35
1984	45.442	8.1465	2.2381	88.42	126.57	6.8717	0.72594	1 381.4	2.5234	115.68	0.59063	0.7890	187.09
1985	44.914	8.0188	2.2263	105.74	129.13	6.7950	0.71517	1 448.0	2.5110	130.25	0.58898	0.7631	180.56
1986	43.798	7.9357	2.1282	137.42	137.46	6.7998	0.73353	1 461.9	2.4009	147.09	0.67154	0.9842	165.00
1987	43.041	7.8847	2.0715	156.27	142.16	6.9291	0.77545	1 494.9	2.3342	162.62	0.70457	1.1544	166.60
1988	43.429	7.9515	2.0744	167.58	137.60	7.0364	0.77567	1 537.3	2.3348	170.06	0.66443	1.1825	151.46
1989	43.381	8.0493	2.0702	178.84	130.41	7.0239	0.77682	1 510.5	2.3353	173.41	0.67330	1.1017	151.94
1990	42.426	7.8565	2.0521	201.41	129.41	6.9141	0.76777	1 522.0	2.3121	181.11	0.71385	1.2734	183.66
1991	42.223	7.9086	2.0508	225.22	128.47	6.9733	0.76781	1 533.2	2.3110	178.61	0.70101	1.2392	166.49
1992	41.593	7.8093	2.0203	247.03	132.53	6.8484	0.76072	1 595.5	2.2748	174.71	0.73765	1.2981	164.22

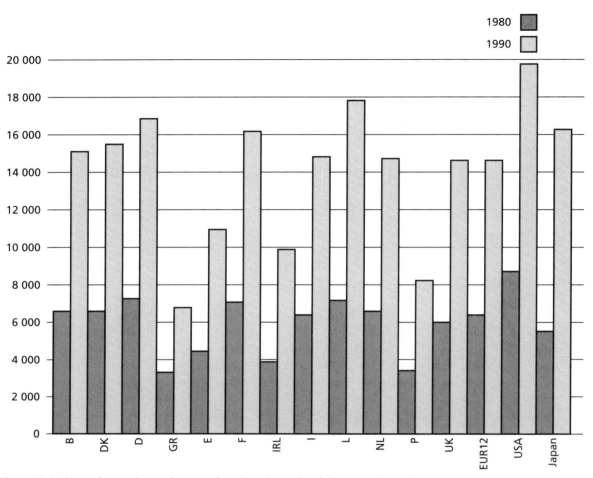

Figure E.1 Gross domestic product per head, volume (PPS) (1980 and 1990).

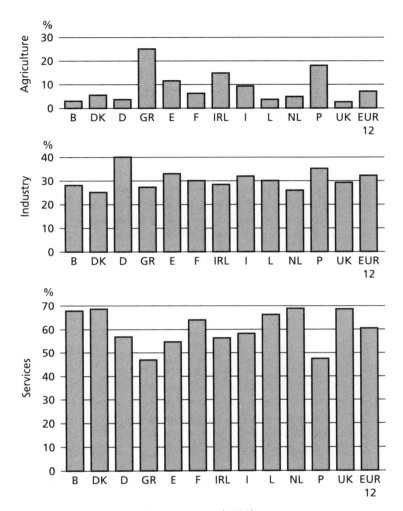

Figure E.2 Civilian employment according to sector (1990).

GLOSSARY OF ABBREVIATIONS AND
FOREIGN TERMS

Germany

AG (Aktiengesellschaft)	Joint stock company
Aufsichtsrat	Board of a company
Berufsgenossenschaften	Insurance scheme covering occupational health risks (all firms are compulsory members)
Beschäftigungs-gesellschaften	Companies offering job and training opportunities in the new states
Betriebsräte	Councils of elected representatives of employees in firms
Betriebsverfassungsgesetz	Law granting employees and their elected representatives comprehensive rights of information and consultation
BDA (Bundesvereinigung der Deutschen Arbeitgeberverbände) BDI (Bundesverband der Deutschen Industrie)	} Umbrella organisations of German employers' associations (having their headquarters in Cologne)
BMWI (Bundesministerium für Wirtschaft)	Federal Department of Commerce
Bundeskartelamt	Cartel authority (in Berlin)
Bundesländer	German states
Bundesaufsichtsamt für das Kreditwesen	Regulatory authority with respect to banking activities
Bundesregierung	Central government
Bundesstaat	Federal state
Deutsche Bundesbank	Central bank in Germany
Deutsche Bundespost	Former German PTT (now split up into three separate activities: Telecommunication, Postal Services, Banking)
DGB (Deutsche Gewerkschaftsbund) DIHT (Deutsche Industrie und Handlestag)	} Umbrella organisations for the German labour unions
Deutsche Handwerkskammertag	Regional chambers of commerce
Erblastenfonds	Treuhandanstalt debt transferred to federal government
Finanzmarktförderungsgesetz	Law to foster financial market activities
Gemeinden	Local authorities
Gesundheitsstrukturgesetz	Law relating to cost control in health care system (1992)

Gewerbekapitalsteuer	Local trade on business capital
GG (Grundgesetz)	German constitution (of 1949)
Gesetz über die Deutsche Bundesbank	Law regulating the position, tasks and instruments of the German central bank (1957)
GmbH (Gesellschaft mit beschränkter Haftung)	Limited liability company
Günstigkeitsprinzip	Principle stating that individual labour contracts may only deviate from collective agreements if such a deviation is to the advantage of the employee
GWB (Gesetz gegen Wettbewerbsbeschränkungen)	Competition law
Handwerksordnung	Craft codes
Industrie und Handelskammer Handwerkskammer	} Regional chambers of commerce
Kombinate	State enterprises in the former GDR
Landwirtschaftliche Produktionsgenossenschaften (LPG)	Agricultural co-operatives in the former GDR
Langzeitarbeitslose	Long-term unemployed (over one year)
Marktbeherrschende Unternehmen	Market dominating companies
Meisterprüfung	Formal qualification for craftsmen (second degree)
Mitbestimmungsgesetz	Law granting substantial rights of consultation, information and co-determination to employees of corporations with more than 2,000 employees
Monopolkommission	Federal commission reviewing concentration processes and providing expertise in merger cases
Personalkostenzuschuss-Programm	Programme providing subsidy for employment of R&D personnel
Pflegeuersicherung	Possible insurance scheme for the nursing of the old
Solidaritätszuschlag	A surcharge in taxation to meet costs of unification
Soziale Marktwirtschaft	Social market economy
Sozialleistungsquote	Social security expenditure as a proportion of GDP
Sozialplan	Social plan to be negotiated between management and employees in cases of mass lay-offs (of more than 10% of a firm's employees)
Statistisches Bundesamt	Central Statistics Agency

Subsidiaritätsprinzip	Principle of subsidiarity: principle whereby decision-making is delegated to the lowest possible authority
Tarifverträge	Collective labour agreements
Treuhandanstalt	Public agency concerned with the privatisation of East German state enterprises
Umbau	Restructuring (*perestrojika*)
Wellblechkonjunktur	Continuous expansion with only minor fluctuations in growth rates
Zinsabschlagsteuer	Tax on capital income

Spain

ALP	The Spanish abbreviation for liquid assets
Banco de Bilbao (nowadays, Banco Bilbao-Vizcaya)	Bank of Bilbao (one of the major Spanish banks)
Banco de España	Bank of Spain (the central bank of Spain)
Bolsa de Valores	Stock exchange market
Cajas de Ahorros	Savings banks (owned by local authorities, which have evolved from their original savings-bank financial activity to their present fully banking business)
Comisión Nacional de Valores	National Assets Commission (the institution with the task of surveying the solvency and fair play in the stock exchange market)
Comunidades Autónomas	Autonomous communities (the official name of Spanish regions)
Consejo General de la Formación Profesional	General Council of Occupational Training (a body composed of representatives of workers, employers and the administration, responsible for designing general objectives in the area of occupational training)
Cooperativas de Crédito	Credit co-operatives (private financial institutions, operating locally, and originally created to aid regional development and presently operating as banks)
Corporación Bancaria	Banking Corporation (a banking institution created in the 1980s jointly owned by the private banks and the Banco de España, which took control over some failing banks in order to sell them after re-establishing their profitability)

Dirección General de Aduanas	General Customs Direction
Disponibilidades Liquidas	The Spanish name to designate M3, a measure of the Spanish money supply
Estatuto de los Trabajadores	Workers' Statute (the legal document which sets out the workers' rights recognised by the Constitution)
Impuesto de Compensación de Gravámenes Interiores (ICGI)	Tax to compensate for home taxation (theoretically introduced in Spain in the 1960s to tax imported products as home products, but in practice meant a protection level of two or three per cent)
Instituto de Crédito Oficial (ICO)	Official Credit Institute (which comprises several (state-owned) banking institutions, each one specialising in financial transactions for specific economic activities such as industry, shipbuilding, agriculture etc.)
Instituto Español de Emigración	Spanish Institute for Emigration (the public institution responsible for emigration issues)
Mercado Continuo	Continuous market (meaning that trade of all assets in the stock exchange market can take place at any time between 09.00 and 20.00)
Mercado de Titulos de Deuda Pública Anotados en Cuenta	Treasury bill market (where there are no 'physical' transfers of titles but accounting records on books of the institutions involved)
Pagarès and Letras del Tesoro	Short-term treasury bills
Sociedades Mediadoras en el Mercado de Dinero	Monetary market intermediary firms (non-banking monetary institutions which operate between banks and other agents selling and buying different short-term assets)
Zonas de Urgente Reindustrialización (ZUR)	Areas of urgent reindustrialisation (areas set up in the late 1980s in an attempt to counteract the effects of the industrial restructuring process)

France

ANPE (Agence Nationale pour l'Emploi	Employment Office
Banque de France	Central bank
CAC (Cotation Assistée en Continu)	Stock exchange quotation system
CCI (Chambre de Commerce et d'Industrie)	Chamber of Commerce
CFDT (Confédération Française Démocratique du Travail)	Trade union (left-wing)

CGT (Confédération Générale du Travail)	Trade union (communist)
COFACE (Compagnie Française d'Assurance pour le Commerce Extérieur)	Foreign trade insurance company
CNPF (Confédération Nationale du Patronat Français)	Employers' federation
DATAR (Délégation à l'Aménagement du Territoire)	Industrial Development Board
EDF (Electricité de France)	National electricity company
FO (Force Ouvrière)	Trade union (socialist)
GEN (Grandes Entreprises Nationales)	Nationalised enterprises
Grande Ecole	Specialised university level educational establishments
INSEE (Institut National des Statistiques et des Etudes Economiques)	National Statistical Office
MATIF (Marché à Terme d'Instruments Financiers)	Finanical futures market
OPA (Offre Public d'Achat)	Take-over bid
PME (Petites et Moyennes Entreprises)	Small and medium businesses
RMI (Revenu Minimum d'Insertion)	Basic social security income
SA (Société Anonyme)	Public limited company
SARL (Société à Responsabilité Limitée)	Private limited company
SICAV (Société d'Investisement à Capital Variable)	Unit trusts
SME (Système Monétaire Europeen)	European monetary system
SMIC (Salaire Minimum Interprofessionnel de Croissance)	Minimum salary
TGV (Train à Grande Vitesse)	High speed train
TVA (Taxe sur la Valeur Ajoutée)	Value added tax
VRP (Voyageurs, Représentant Placier)	Salaried commercial salesmen

Italy

Autorità garaute della concurrenta e del mercato	Institution with general responsibility for ensuring market competition
Cassa depositi e prestiti	State institution for financing local administrations using deposits collected by the Italian Post Office
CGIL (Confederazione Generale Italiana del Lavoro)	Left-wing workers' trade union
CISL (Confederazione Italiana Sindacati Lavoratori)	Trade union whose members are, generally, supporters of the centre
Confindustria	The most relevant organisation of the Italian entrepreneurs

EFIM (Ente partecipazione e Finanziamento Industrie Manifatturiere)	State-owned industrial group
ENI (Ente Nazionale Idrocarburi)	State-owned industrial group, basically involved in chemical and oil sectors
INAIL (Istituto Nazionale di Assicurazione per gli Infortuni sul Lavoro)	State insurance institution for workers in case of accidents
INPS (Istituto Nazionale per la Previdenza Sociale)	State insurance institution for paying pensions to the workers
IRI (Istituto per la Ricostruzione Industriale)	The most relevant state-owned industrial group
ISCO (Istituto per lo Studio della Congiuntura)	Institution for studying economic cycles
Istituti speciali di credito	Finance institutions for medium and long-term loans
ISTAT (Istituto Centrale di Statistica)	State central statistical office
Montedison	The most relevant chemical group in Italy
NEC	Regions of the North-East-Centre
RAI (Radiotelevisione Italiana)	State-owned group for radio and television
SCI	Regions of the South-Centre
SME (Società Meridionale Elettrica)	State-owned industrial group of the power supply sector
SVLMEZ (associazione per lo sviluppo dell'industria nel Mezzogiorno)	Institution for the sudy of the industrialisation of the south of the country
TRI	Regions of the industrial 'triangle' (Milano–Torino–Genova)
UIL (Unione Italiana del Lavoro)	Trade union of centre-left-wing workers
USL (Unità Sanitarie Locali)	Local centres of the national health service

United Kingdom

'Chunnel'	Channel Tunnel
'Big Bang'	Deregulation of the Stock Exchange (1986)
EFTA	European Free Trade Association
G7	The seven largest western industrialised economies (USA, Japan, Germany, France, Italy, United Kingdom, Canada)
GDFCF	Gross Domestic Fixed Capital Formation
RPI	Retail price Index
MTFS	Medium-Term Financial Strategy
PSBR	Public Sector Borrowing Requirement
DA	Development Area

MMC	Mergers and Monopolies Commission
OFI	Other Financial Institutions
SE	International (formerly London) Stock Exchange
IPD	Interest, profit and dividend payments (in relation to balance of payments)

General

CAP	Common Agricultural Policy
GATT	General Agreements on Tariffs and Trade
NIC	Newly Industrialised Countries
OECD	Organisation for Economic Co-operation and Development
OPEC	Organisation of Petroleum Exporting Countries
R&D	Research and Development
USA	United States of America
VAT	Value Added Tax

The Netherlands

ABN AMRO ING RABO	} Three largest banks
Benelux	Customs union of the Netherlands, Belgium and Luxembourg
DNB (De Nederlandsche Bank)	Central bank of the Netherlands
NEPP	National Environmental Policy Plan. Introduced in 1989 (National Milieubeleidsplan, NMP)

Belgium/Luxembourg

Bank Nationale de Belgique	Central bank of Belgium (50% state-owned)
BLEU	Belgium and Luxembourg Economic Union
Generale Bank	Largest bank in Belgium
GIMV	Flemish Investment Company, assists business with investment
IMEC	Inter-University Micro-Electronics Centre (Flemish)
SRIW	Walloon Regional Investment Company

Denmark

CO Industri	Industrial trade union cartel
Dansk Industri	Employers' organisation
Nationalbank	Central bank of Denmark

Portugal

Acordo economico e social	Non-statutory prices and incomes policy
PEDIP	Specific Programme for Industrial Development in Portugal

INDEX